Programming Logic and Design

Tenth Edition

Joyce Farrell

Australia • Brazil • Canada • Mexico • Singapore • United Kingdom • United States

Programming Logic and Design,
Tenth Edition
Joyce Farrell

SVP, Higher Education Product Management: Erin Joyner

VP, Product Management and Marketing, Learning Experiences: Thais Alencar

Portfolio Product Director: Mark Santee

Portfolio Product Manager: Tran Pham

Product Assistant: Ethan Wheel

Learning Designer: Mary Convertino

Senior Content Manager: Isabelle Berthet

Senior Content Manager: Michelle Ruelos Cannistraci

Content Manager: Katherine Russillo

Associate Digital Project Manager: John Smigielski

Technical Editor: Danielle Shaw

Developmental Editor: Dan Seiter

VP, Product Marketing: Jason Sakos

Director, Product Marketing: April Danaë

Portfolio Marketing Manager: Mackenzie Paine

Senior Subject Matter Assurance Engineer: Troy Dundas

IP Analyst: Ann Hoffman

IP Project Manager: Lumina Datamatics

Production Service: Straive

Senior Designer: Erin Griffin

Cover Image Source: Armagadon/Shutterstock.com

Library of Congress Control Number: 2022922035

ISBN: 978-0-357-88087-6

Cengage
200 Pier 4 Boulevard
Boston, MA 02210
USA

Cengage is a leading provider of customized learning solutions with employees residing in nearly 40 different countries and sales in more than 125 countries around the world. Find your local representative at **www.cengage.com**.

To learn more about Cengage platforms and services, register or access your online learning solution, or purchase materials for your course, visit **www.cengage.com**.

Printed at CLDPC, USA, 08-24

Brief Contents

About the Author ix
Preface for the Instructor x

Chapter 1 An Overview of Computers and Programming 1

Chapter 2 Elements of High-Quality Programs 29

Chapter 3 Understanding Structure 65

Chapter 4 Making Decisions 93

Chapter 5 Looping 135

Chapter 6 Arrays 173

Chapter 7 File Handling and Applications 205

Chapter 8 Advanced Data Handling Concepts 239

Chapter 9 Advanced Modularization Techniques 273

Chapter 10 Object-Oriented Programming 309

Chapter 11 More Object-Oriented Programming Concepts 341

Chapter 12 Event-Driven GUI Programming, Multithreading, and Animation 373

Appendix A Understanding Numbering Systems and Computer Codes 399

Appendix B Solving Difficult Structuring Problems 405

Glossary 413
Index 427

Contents

About the Author ix

Preface for the Instructor x

Chapter 1

An Overview of Computers and Programming 1

1.1 Understanding Computer Systems 1

1.2 Understanding Simple Program Logic 4

1.3 Understanding the Program Development Cycle 6

Understanding the Problem 7

Planning the Logic 8

Coding the Program 8

Using Software to Translate the Program into Machine Language 9

Testing the Program 10

Putting the Program into Production 11

Maintaining the Program 11

1.4 Using Pseudocode Statements and Flowchart Symbols 12

Writing Pseudocode 12

Drawing Flowcharts 13

Repeating Instructions 15

1.5 Using a Sentinel Value to End a Program 16

1.6 Understanding Programming and User Environments 18

Understanding Programming Environments 18

Understanding User Environments 20

1.7 Understanding the Evolution of Programming Models 21

Chapter 2

Elements of High-Quality Programs 29

2.1 Declaring and Using Variables and Constants 29

Understanding Data Types 29

Understanding Unnamed, Literal Constants 30

Working with Variables 30

Understanding a Variable's Data Type 31

Understanding a Variable's Identifier 31

Assigning Values to Variables 33

Initializing a Variable 34

Where to Declare Variables 35

Declaring Named Constants 35

2.2 Performing Arithmetic Operations 36

Mixing Data Types 38

2.3 Understanding the Advantages of Modularization 39

Modularization Provides Abstraction 39

Modularization Helps Multiple Programmers to Work on a Problem 40

Modularization Allows You to Reuse Work 40

2.4 Modularizing a Program 41

Declaring Variables and Constants within Modules 44

Understanding the Most Common Configuration for Mainline Logic 46

Creating Hierarchy Charts 48

2.5 Features of Good Program Design 50

Using Program Comments 50

Choosing Identifiers 52
Designing Clear Statements 54
Avoiding Confusing Line Breaks 54
Using Temporary Variables to Clarify Long Statements 54
Writing Clear Prompts and Echoing Input 55
Maintaining Good Programming Habits 57

Chapter 3

Understanding Structure **65**

3.1 The Disadvantages of Unstructured Spaghetti Code **65**
3.2 Understanding the Three Basic Structures **67**
The Sequence Structure 67
The Selection Structure 67
The Loop Structure 69
Combining Structures 70
3.3 Using a Priming Input to Structure a Program **74**
3.4 Understanding the Reasons for Using Structured Techniques **79**
3.5 Recognizing Structure **80**
3.6 Structuring and Modularizing Unstructured Logic **83**

Chapter 4

Making Decisions **93**

4.1 The Selection Structure **93**
4.2 Using Relational Comparison Operators **97**
Avoiding a Common Error with Relational Operators 100
4.3 Understanding AND Logic **100**
Nesting AND Decisions for Efficiency 103
Using the AND Operator 104
Avoiding Common Errors in an AND Selection 106
Make Sure Decisions that Should Be Nested Are Nested 106
Make Sure that Boolean Expressions Are Complete 107
Make Sure that Expressions Are Not Inadvertently Trivial 107
4.4 Understanding OR Logic **108**
Writing OR Selections for Efficiency 108
Using the OR Operator 110
Avoiding Common Errors in an OR Selection 112
Make Sure that Boolean Expressions Are Complete 112
Make Sure that Selections Are Structured 112
Make Sure that You Use OR Selections When They Are Required 112
Make Sure that Expressions Are Not Inadvertently Trivial 113
4.5 Understanding NOT Logic **115**
Avoiding a Common Error in a NOT Expression 116
4.6 Making Selections Within Ranges **117**
Avoiding Common Errors When Using Range Checks 119
Eliminate Dead Paths 119
Avoid Testing the Same Range Limit Multiple Times 119
4.7 Understanding Precedence When Combining AND and OR Operators **122**
4.8 Understanding the case Structure **125**

Chapter 5

Looping 135

5.1 Creating Loop Logic 135

5.2 Using a Loop Control Variable 137

Using a Definite Loop with a Counter 137

Using an Indefinite Loop with a Sentinel Value 139

Understanding the Loop in a Program's Mainline Logic 140

5.3 Nested Loops 140

5.4 Avoiding Common Loop Mistakes 145

Mistake: Failing to Initialize the Loop Control Variable 145

Mistake: Neglecting to Alter the Loop Control Variable 145

Mistake: Using the Wrong Type of Comparison When Testing the Loop Control Variable 147

Mistake: Including Statements Inside the Loop Body that Belong Outside the Loop 148

5.5 Using a `for` Loop 152

5.6 Using a Posttest Loop 154

5.7 Recognizing the Characteristics Shared by Structured Loops 156

5.8 Common Loop Applications 157

Using a Loop to Accumulate Totals 157

Using a Loop to Validate Data 160

Limiting a Reprompting Loop 160

Validating a Data Type 163

Validating Reasonableness and Consistency of Data 163

5.9 Comparing Selections and Loops 164

Chapter 6

Arrays 173

6.1 Storing Data in Arrays 173

How Arrays Occupy Computer Memory 174

6.2 How an Array Can Replace Nested Decisions 176

6.3 Using Constants with Arrays 181

Using a Constant as the Size of an Array 181

Using Constants as Array Element Values 182

Using a Constant as an Array Subscript 182

6.4 Searching an Array for an Exact Match 183

6.5 Using Parallel Arrays 185

Improving Search Efficiency 189

6.6 Searching an Array for a Range Match 190

6.7 Remaining within Array Bounds 193

Understanding Array Size 194

Understanding Subscript Bounds 194

6.8 Using a `for` Loop to Process an Array 196

Chapter 7

File Handling and Applications 205

7.1 Understanding Computer Files 205

Organizing Files 206

7.2 Understanding the Data Hierarchy 207

7.3 Performing File Operations 209

Declaring a File Identifier 209

Opening a File 209

Reading Data from a File and Processing It 210

Writing Data to a File 212

Closing a File 212

A Program that Performs File Operations 213

7.4 Understanding Control Break Logic 214

7.5 Merging Sequential Files 218

7.6 Updating Primary Files with Transaction Records 225

7.7 Random Access Files 231

Chapter 8

Advanced Data Handling Concepts 239

8.1 Understanding the Need for Sorting Data 239

8.2 Using the Bubble Sort Algorithm 241

Understanding Swapping Values 241

Understanding the Bubble Sort 242

Sorting a List of Variable Size 248

Refining the Bubble Sort to Reduce Unnecessary Comparisons 250

Refining the Bubble Sort to Eliminate Unnecessary Passes 252

8.3 Sorting Records on Multiple Fields 253

Sorting Data Stored in Parallel Arrays 254

Sorting Records as a Whole 255

8.4 Other Sorting Algorithms 255

8.5 Using Multidimensional Arrays 257

8.6 Using Indexed Files and Linked Lists 262

Using Indexed Files 263

Using Linked Lists 264

Chapter 9

Advanced Modularization Techniques 273

9.1 The Parts of a Method 273

9.2 Using Methods with No Parameters 275

9.3 Creating Methods that Require Parameters 276

Creating Methods that Require Multiple Parameters 279

9.4 Creating Methods that Return a Value 282

Using an IPO Chart 285

9.5 Passing an Array to a Method 287

9.6 Overloading Methods 291

Avoiding Ambiguous Methods 293

9.7 Using Predefined Methods 295

9.8 Method Design Issues: Implementation Hiding, Cohesion, and Coupling 296

Understanding Implementation Hiding 296

Increasing Cohesion 297

Reducing Coupling 297

9.9 Understanding Recursion 298

Chapter 10

Object-Oriented Programming 309

10.1 Principles of Object-Oriented Programming 309

Classes and Objects 310

Polymorphism 312

Inheritance 313

Encapsulation 313

10.2 Creating Classes and Class Diagrams 314

Creating Class Diagrams 316

The Set Methods 318

The Get Methods 320

Work Methods 320

10.3 Using Public and Private Access 321

10.4 Organizing Classes 324

10.5 Using Instance Methods 325

10.6 Using Static Methods 328

10.7 Using Objects 330

Passing an Object to a Method 330

Returning an Object from a Method 331

Using Arrays of Objects 331

Chapter 11

More Object-Oriented Programming Concepts 341

11.1 Creating Constructors 341
Default Constructors 342
Nondefault Constructors 344
Overloading Instance Methods and Constructors 345

11.2 Understanding Destructors 347

11.3 Understanding Composition 349

11.4 Understanding Inheritance 350
Understanding Inheritance Terminology 352
Accessing Private Fields and Methods of a Parent Class 354
Overriding Parent Class Methods in a Child Class 357
Using Inheritance to Achieve Good Software Design 358

11.5 An Example of Using Predefined Classes: Creating GUI Objects 359

11.6 Understanding Exception Handling 360
Drawbacks to Traditional Error-Handling Techniques 360
The Object-Oriented Exception-Handling Model 361
Using Built-in Exceptions and Creating Your Own Exceptions 363

11.7 Reviewing the Advantages of Object-Oriented Programming 365

Chapter 12

Event-Driven GUI Programming, Multithreading, and Animation 373

12.1 Principles of Event-Driven Programming 373

12.2 User-Initiated Actions and GUI Components 376

12.3 Designing Graphical User Interfaces 379
The Interface Should Be Natural and Predictable 379
The Interface Should Be Attractive, Easy to Read, and Nondistracting 380
To Some Extent, It's Helpful If the User Can Customize Your Applications 380
The Program Should Be Forgiving 380
The GUI Is Only a Means to an End 381

12.4 Developing an Event-Driven Application 381
Creating Wireframes 382
Creating Storyboards 382
Defining the Storyboard Objects in an Object Dictionary 383
Defining Connections Between the User Screens 384
Planning the Logic 384

12.5 Understanding Threads and Multithreading 388

12.6 Creating Animation 390

Appendix A

Understanding Numbering Systems and Computer Codes 399

Appendix B

Solving Difficult Structuring Problems 405

Glossary 413

Index 427

About the Author

Joyce Farrell has taught computer programming at McHenry County College, Crystal Lake, Illinois; the University of Wisconsin, Stevens Point, Wisconsin; and Harper College, Palatine, Illinois. Besides *Programming Logic and Design*, she has written books on Java, C#, and C++ for Cengage.

Preface for the Instructor

Programming Logic and Design, Tenth Edition provides the beginning programmer with a guide to developing structured program logic. This textbook assumes no programming language experience. The writing is non-technical and emphasizes good programming practices. The examples are business examples; they do not assume mathematical background beyond high school business math.

Additionally, the examples illustrate one or two major points; they do not contain so many features that students become lost following irrelevant and extraneous details. The examples in this book have been created to provide students with a sound background in logic, no matter what programming languages they eventually use to write programs. This book can be used in a stand-alone logic course that students take as a prerequisite to a programming course or as a companion book to an introductory text using any programming language.

New to This Edition

Multiple improvements have been added to this edition of *Programming Logic and Design*. These include the following:

- The chapter objectives have been modified where necessary to use Bloom's taxonomy.
- The objectives, major section headings, and end-of-chapter exercises have been numbered to show how they correspond.
- Colors have been modified to make diagrams more accessible.
- The text has been modified to ensure clarity, currency, and inclusiveness.
- Code samples and figures have been edited to create consistency in spacing.
- Care has been taken to use the more generic term *modules* for program segments until object-oriented programming is discussed. After that, the term *methods* is used because that is the commonly used name for modules in object-oriented languages.
- The discussion of constructors has been expanded and uses the `new` operator, which is common in object-oriented languages. The `new` operator is also used for constructing `Exception` objects.

Inclusivity and Diversity

Cengage is committed to providing educational content that is inclusive and welcoming to all learners. Research demonstrates that students who experience a sense of belonging in class more successfully make meaning out of, and find relevance in, what they encounter in learning content. To improve both the learning process and outcomes, our materials seek to affirm the fullness of human diversity with respect to ability, language, culture, gender, age, socioeconomics, and other forms of human difference that students may bring to the classroom.

Across the computing industry, standard language such as *master* and *slave* is being retired in favor of language that is more inclusive, such as *primary/replica* or *leader/follower*. Different software development and web media companies are adopting their own replacement language, and currently there is no shared standard.

In addition, the terms *master* and *slave* remain deeply embedded in legacy code, and understanding this terminology remains necessary for new programmers. When required for understanding, Cengage will introduce the noninclusive term in the first instance but will then provide an appropriate replacement term for the remainder of the discussion or example. We appreciate your feedback as we work to make our products more inclusive for all.

For more information about Cengage's commitment to inclusivity and diversity, please visit *www.cengage.com/inclusion-diversity/*.

Organization of the Text

Programming Logic and Design, Tenth Edition introduces students to programming concepts and enforces good style and logical thinking. General programming concepts are introduced in Chapter 1.

Chapter 2 discusses using data and introduces two important concepts: modularization and creating high-quality programs. It is important to emphasize these topics early so students start thinking in a modular way and concentrate on making their programs efficient, robust, easy to read, and easy to maintain.

Chapter 3 covers the key concepts of structure, including what structure is, how to recognize it, and most importantly, the advantages to writing structured programs. This chapter's content is unique among programming texts. The early overview of structure presented here provides students a solid foundation for thinking in a structured way.

Chapters 4, 5, and 6 explore the intricacies of decision making, looping, and array manipulation. Chapter 7 provides details of file handling so that students can create programs that process a significant amount of data.

In Chapters 8 and 9, students learn more advanced techniques in array manipulation and modularization. Chapters 10 and 11 provide a thorough, yet accessible, introduction to concepts and terminology used in object-oriented programming. Students learn about classes, objects, instance and static class members, constructors, destructors, inheritance, and the advantages of object-oriented thinking. Chapter 12 explores some additional object-oriented programming issues: event-driven GUI programming, multithreading, and animation.

Two appendices instruct students on working with numbering systems and providing structure for large programs.

Programming Logic and Design, Tenth Edition combines text explanation with flowcharts and pseudocode examples to provide students with alternative means of expressing structured logic. Numerous detailed, full-program exercises at the end of each chapter illustrate the concepts explained within the chapter and reinforce understanding and retention of the material presented.

Programming Logic and Design, Tenth Edition distinguishes itself from other programming logic books in the following ways:

- It is written and designed to be non-language specific. The logic used in this book can be applied to any programming language.
- The examples are everyday business examples: no special knowledge of mathematics, accounting, or other disciplines is assumed.
- The concept of structure is covered earlier than in many other texts. Students are exposed to structure naturally, so that they will automatically create properly designed programs.
- Text explanation is interspersed with flowcharts and pseudocode so that students can become comfortable with these logic development tools and understand their interrelationship. Screenshots of running programs also are included, providing students with a clear and concrete image of the programs' execution.
- Complex programs are built through the use of complete business examples. Students see how an application is constructed from start to finish instead of studying only segments of a program.

Features of the Text

This text focuses on helping students become better programmers as well as helping them understand the big picture in program development through a variety of features. Each chapter begins with objectives and ends with a list of key terms and a summary; these useful features will help students prepare for and organize their learning experience. Review Questions, Programming Exercises, Performing Maintenance, and Game Zone exercises are aligned with the objectives listed at the beginning of each chapter. This alignment is clearly indicated in parentheses at the end of each question. Debugging Exercises, while internally aligned with the chapter objectives, do not display this alignment so as not to reveal the error in the program sample.

Note | These notes provide additional information—for example, a common error to watch out for or background information on a topic.

Two Truths & a Lie

These quizzes appear after each chapter section, with answers provided. Each quiz contains three statements based on the preceding section of text—two statements are true and one is false.

Answers give immediate feedback without "giving away" answers to the multiple-choice questions and programming problems later in the chapter. Students also have the option to take these quizzes in MindTap.

Don't Do It

These icons illustrate how *not* to do something—for example, having a dead code path in a program. They provide a visual jolt to the student, emphasizing that particular practices are *not* to be emulated and making students more careful to recognize problems in existing code.

Assessment

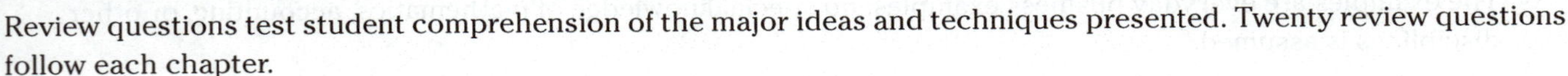

Review Questions

Review questions test student comprehension of the major ideas and techniques presented. Twenty review questions follow each chapter.

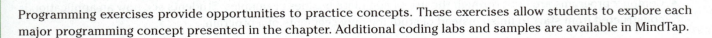

Programming Exercises

Programming exercises provide opportunities to practice concepts. These exercises allow students to explore each major programming concept presented in the chapter. Additional coding labs and samples are available in MindTap.

Performing Maintenance

These exercises ask students to modify working logic based on new requested specifications. This activity mirrors real-world tasks that students are likely to encounter in their first programming jobs.

Debugging Exercises

Debugging exercises are included with each chapter because examining programs critically and closely is a crucial programming skill. Students and instructors can download these exercises at *www.cengage.com*.

Game Zone Exercises

These exercises are included at the end of each chapter. Students can create the logic for games as an additional entertaining way to understand key programming concepts.

Additional Features of the Text

This edition of the text includes many features to help students become better programmers and understand the big picture in program development.

- **Emphasis on modularity.** Students are encouraged to write code in concise, easily manageable, and reusable modules. Instructors have found that modularization should be encouraged early to instill good habits and a clearer understanding of structure.
- **Emphasis on structure.** More than its competitors, this book emphasizes structure. Chapter 3 provides an early picture of the major concepts of structured programming.
- **Flowcharts, figures, and illustrations.** These graphics provide the reader with a visual learning experience.
- **Clear explanations.** The language and explanations in this book have been refined over nine previous editions, providing the clearest possible explanations of difficult concepts.
- **Objectives.** Each chapter begins with a list of objectives so that the student knows the topics that will be presented in the chapter. In addition to providing a quick reference to topics covered, this feature provides a useful study aid.
- **Summaries.** Following each chapter is a summary that recaps the concepts and techniques covered in the chapter.
- **Key terms.** Each chapter identifies key terms and provides a list of the terms at the end of the chapter. A glossary at the end of the book lists all the key terms in alphabetical order, along with their working definitions.

Course Solutions

Online Learning Platform: MindTap

Today's leading online learning platform, MindTap for *Programming Logic and Design, Tenth Edition* gives you complete control of your course to craft a personalized, engaging learning experience that challenges students, builds confidence, and elevates performance.

MindTap introduces students to core concepts from the beginning of your course using a simplified learning path that progresses from understanding to application and delivers access to eBooks, study tools, interactive media, auto-graded assessments, and performance analytics.

Use MindTap for *Programming Logic and Design, Tenth Edition* as is, or personalize it to meet your specific course needs. You can also easily integrate MindTap into your Learning Management System (LMS).

The MindTap course for *Programming Logic and Design, Tenth Edition* includes coding labs in C++, Java, and Python, study tools, videos, and interactive quizzing, all integrated into an eReader that includes the full content of the printed text. In addition to the readings, the *Programming Logic and Design, Tenth Edition* MindTap course includes the following:

- **Coding labs.** These supplemental assignments provide real-world application and encourage students to practice new programming logic and design concepts in a complete online IDE in any one of three programming languages: Java, Python, or C++. New and improved Guided Feedback provides personalized and immediate feedback to students as they proceed through their coding assignments so that they can understand and correct errors in their code.
- **Gradeable assessments and activities.** All assessments and activities from the readings will be available as gradeable assignments within MindTap, including Review Questions, Performing Maintenance, Debugging Exercises, Game Zone, and Two Truths & a Lie.
- **Programming and Learning Guides.** Supplemental Programming and Learning Guides (PAL Guides) are provided as downloads in the learning path for those interested in applying the programming learning and design concepts to any of the three major programming languages: Java, Python, and C++. The guides have been carefully developed to extend learning from conceptual understanding to application through exercises and labs. The guides follow along chapter by chapter with the core narrative of the textbook.
- **Interactive study aids.** Flashcards and PowerPoint lectures help users review main concepts from the units.

Ancillary Package

Additional instructor resources for this product are available online. Instructor assets include an Instructor Manual, Educator's Guide, PowerPoint® slides, and a test bank powered by Cognero®. Sign up or sign in at *www.cengage.com* to search for and access this product and its online resources.

- **Instructor Manual.** The Instructor Manual follows the text chapter by chapter to assist in planning and organizing an effective, engaging course. The manual includes learning objectives, chapter overviews, lecture notes, ideas for classroom activities, and additional resources.
- **PowerPoint presentations.** This text provides PowerPoint slides to accompany each chapter. Slides are included to guide classroom presentations and can be made available to students for chapter review or to print as classroom handouts.
- **Solution and Answer Guide (SAG).** Solutions and rationales to review questions and exercises are provided to assist with grading and student understanding.
- **Solutions.** Solutions to all programming exercises are available. If an input file is needed to understand a programming exercise, it is included with the solution file.
- **Data files.** Data files necessary to complete some of the steps and projects in the course are available. The Data Files folder also includes Java, Python, and C++ files for every program that appears in the Programming and Learning (PAL) Guide.
- **Educator's Guide.** The Educator's Guide contains a detailed outline of the corresponding MindTap course.
- **Transition Guide.** The Transition Guide outlines information on what has changed from the Ninth Edition.

- **Test Bank®.** Cengage Learning Testing Powered by Cognero is a flexible, online system that allows you to:
  - Author, edit, and manage test bank content from multiple Cengage Learning solutions.
  - Create multiple test versions in an instant.
  - Deliver tests from your LMS, your classroom, or anywhere you want.

Acknowledgments

I would like to thank all of the people who helped to make this book a reality, especially Tran Pham, Isabelle Berthet, Katherine Russillo, Michelle Ruelos Cannistraci, Troy Dundas, Mary Convertino, and all the other professionals at Cengage who made this book possible. Thank you to Technical Editor Danielle Shaw, who ensures that all technical content in the narrative and accompanying data files is accurate and error free. Thank you to my Development Editor, Dan Seiter, who is the most thorough, competent editor I have ever met, and who made this a better book. Thank you to Keith Morneau of ECPI University and Dwight Watt of Georgia Northwestern Technical College for their reviews of the manuscript. Thanks, too, to my husband, Geoff, and our daughters, Andrea and Audrey, for their support. This book, as were all its previous editions, is dedicated to them.

Chapter 1

An Overview of Computers and Programming

Learning Objectives

When you complete this chapter, you will be able to:

1.1 Describe the components of computer systems

1.2 Develop simple program logic

1.3 List the steps involved in the program development cycle

1.4 Write pseudocode statements and draw flowchart symbols

1.5 Use a sentinel value to end a program

1.6 Describe programming and user environments

1.7 Describe the evolution of programming models

1.1 Understanding Computer Systems

A **computer system** is a combination of all the components required to process and store data using a computer. Every computer system is composed of multiple pieces of hardware and software.

- **Hardware** is the equipment, or the physical devices, associated with a computer. For example, keyboards, mice, speakers, and printers are all hardware. The devices are manufactured differently for computers of varying sizes—for example, large mainframes, laptops, and very small devices embedded into products such as phones, cars, and thermostats. The types of operations performed by different-sized computers, however, are very similar. Computer hardware needs instructions that control its operations, including how and when data items are input, how they are processed, and the form in which they are output or stored.

- **Software** is computer instructions that tell the hardware what to do. Software is programs. A **program** is a set of computer instructions written by a programmer. You can buy prewritten programs that are stored on a CD or DVD or that you download from the Web. For example, businesses use word-processing and accounting programs, and casual computer users enjoy programs that play music and games. Alternatively, you can write your own programs. When you write software instructions, you are **programming**. This course focuses on developing program logic. The **logic** of a computer program is the complete sequence of tasks that lead to a problem's solution. A program's logic is similar to a story's plot—it is a series of steps that lead to a conclusion.

  Software can be classified into two broad types:

- **Application software** comprises all the programs you apply to a task, such as word-processing programs, spreadsheets, payroll and inventory programs, and games. When you hear people say they have "downloaded an **app**," they are simply using an abbreviation of *application software*.
- **System software** comprises the programs that you use to manage your computer, including operating systems. An **operating system** is the software that supports a computer's basic functions, including controlling devices such as keyboards and mice and scheduling tasks. Some operating systems you might know include Windows, Linux, or UNIX for larger computers and Google Android and Apple iOS for smartphones.

This course focuses on the logic used to write application software programs rather than system software programs, but many of the concepts apply to both types of software.

Together, computer hardware and software accomplish three major operations in most programs:

- **Input**: **Data items** include all the text, numbers, and other raw material that are entered into and processed by a computer. Data items enter the computer system and are placed in memory, where they can be processed. Hardware devices that perform input operations include keyboards and mice. In business, many of the data items used are facts and figures about such entities as products, customers, and personnel. Data, however, also can include items such as images, sounds, and a user's mouse or finger-swiping movements.
- **Processing**: Processing data items means working with them—for example, organizing or sorting them, checking them for accuracy, or performing calculations with them. The hardware component that performs these types of tasks is the **central processing unit (CPU)**. Some devices, such as tablets and smartphones, usually contain multiple processors, including those that specialize in processing graphics; efficiently using several CPUs requires special programming techniques.
- **Output**: Programming professionals often use the term *data* for input items, but they use the term **information** for data items that have been processed and output. After data items have been processed, the resulting information usually is sent to a printer, monitor, or some other output device so people can view, interpret, and use the results. Sometimes you place output on a **storage device**, such as your hard drive, flash media, or a cloud-based device. (The **cloud** refers to devices at remote locations accessed through the Internet.) People cannot read or interpret data directly from these storage devices, but the devices hold information for later retrieval. When you send output to a storage device, sometimes it is used later as input for another program.

You write computer instructions in a computer **programming language** such as Visual Basic, C#, C++, or Java. Just as some people speak English and others speak Japanese, programmers write programs in different languages. Some programmers work exclusively in one language, whereas others know several and use the one that is best suited to the task at hand.

The set of instructions you write using a programming language is called **program code**; when you write instructions, you are **coding the program**.

Every programming language has rules governing its word usage and punctuation. These rules are called the language's **syntax**. Mistakes in a language's usage are **syntax errors**. If you ask, "How the geet too store do I?" in English, most people can figure out what you probably mean, even though you have not used proper English syntax—you have mixed up the word order, misspelled a word, and used an incorrect word. However, computers are not nearly as smart as most people; in this case, you might as well have asked the computer, "Xpu mxv ort dod nmcad bf B?" Unless the syntax is perfect, the computer cannot interpret the programming language instruction at all.

Table 1-1 shows how you can use several common programming languages to write a statement that displays the word *Hello* on a single line on a computer monitor. Notice that the syntax of some languages requires that a statement start with an uppercase letter, while the syntax of others does not. Notice that some languages end statements with a semicolon, some with a period, and some with no ending punctuation at all. Also notice that different verbs are used to mean *display*, and that some are spelled like their English word counterparts, while others like *cout* and *System.out.println* are not regular English words. The different formats you see are just a hint of the various syntaxes used by languages.

Table 1-1 Displaying the word *Hello* in some common programming languages

Language	Statement that displays Hello on a single line
Java	`System.out.println("Hello");`
C++	`cout << "Hello" << endl;`
Visual Basic	`Console.WriteLine("Hello");`
Python	`print "Hello"`
COBOL	`DISPLAY "Hello".`

Note After you learn French, you automatically know, or can easily figure out, many Spanish words. Similarly, after you learn one programming language, it is much easier to understand other languages.

When you write a program, you usually type its instructions using a keyboard. When you type program instructions, they are stored in **computer memory**, which is a computer's temporary, internal storage. **Random access memory (RAM)** is a form of internal, volatile memory. Programs that are running and data items that are being used are stored in RAM for quick access. Internal storage is **volatile**—its contents are lost when the computer is turned off or loses power. Usually, you want to be able to retrieve and perhaps modify the stored instructions later, so you also store them on a permanent storage device, such as a disk. Permanent storage devices are **nonvolatile**—that is, their contents are persistent and are retained even when power is lost. If you have had a power loss while working on a computer but were able to recover your work when power was restored, it's not because the work was still in RAM; it's because your system was configured to automatically save your work at regular intervals on a nonvolatile storage device—often your hard drive or a remote drive on the Web.

After a computer program is typed using programming language statements and stored in memory, it must be translated to **machine language** that represents the millions of on/off circuits within the computer. Your programming language statements are called **source code**, and the translated machine language statements are **object code**.

Each programming language uses a piece of software, called a **compiler** or an **interpreter**, to translate your source code into machine language. Machine language is also called **binary language** and is represented as a series of 0s and 1s. The compiler or interpreter that translates your code tells you if any programming language component has been used incorrectly. Syntax errors are relatively easy to locate and correct because your compiler or interpreter highlights them. If you write a computer program using a language such as C++, but spell one of its words incorrectly or reverse the proper order of two words, the software lets you know that it found a mistake by displaying an error message as soon as you try to translate the program.

Note Although there are differences in how compilers and interpreters work, their basic function is the same—to translate your programming statements into code the computer can use. When you use a compiler, an entire program is translated before it can execute; when you use an interpreter, each instruction is translated just prior to execution. Usually, you do not choose which type of translation to use—it depends on the programming language. However, some languages can use both compilers and interpreters.

After a program's source code is translated successfully to machine language, the computer can carry out the program instructions. When instructions are carried out, a program **runs**, or **executes**. In a typical program, some input will be accepted, some processing will occur, and results will be output.

> **Note** Besides the popular, comprehensive programming languages such as Java and C++, many programmers use a **scripting language** (also called a *scripting programming language* or *script language*) such as Python, Lua, Perl, or PHP. Scripts written in a scripting language usually can be typed directly from a keyboard and be stored as text rather than as binary executable files. Scripting language programs are interpreted line by line each time the program executes, instead of being stored in a compiled (binary) form. Still, with all programming languages, each instruction must be translated to machine language before it can execute.

Two Truths & a Lie | Understanding Computer Systems

In each Two Truths & a Lie section, two of the numbered statements are true and one is false. Identify the false statement and explain why it is false.

1. Hardware is the equipment, or the devices, associated with a computer, and software is computer instructions.
2. The grammar rules of a computer programming language are its syntax.
3. You write programs using machine language, and translation software converts the statements to a programming language.

The false statement is #3. You write programs using a programming language such as Visual Basic or Java, and a translation program (called a compiler or an interpreter) converts the statements to machine language, which is 0s and 1s.

1.2 Understanding Simple Program Logic

For a program to work properly, you must develop correct logic; that is, you must write program instructions in a specific sequence, you must not leave out any instructions, and you must not add extraneous instructions. A program with syntax errors cannot be translated fully and cannot execute. A program with no syntax errors is translatable and can execute, but it still might contain **logical errors** and produce incorrect output as a result.

Suppose you instruct someone to make a cake as follows:

```
Get a bowl
Stir
Add two eggs
Add a gallon of gasoline
Bake at 350 degrees for 45 minutes
Add three cups of flour
```

Don't Do It
Don't bake a cake like this!

> **Note** The dangerous cake-baking instructions are shown with a Don't Do It icon. You will see this icon when the sample instructions contain an example of what *not* to do.

Even though the cake-baking instructions use English language syntax correctly, the instructions are out of sequence, some are missing, and some instructions belong to procedures other than baking a cake. If you follow these instructions, you will not make an edible cake, and you may end up with a disaster. Many logical errors are more difficult to locate than syntax errors—it is easier for you to determine whether *eggs* is spelled incorrectly in a recipe than it is for you to tell if there are too many eggs or if they are added too soon.

Most simple computer programs include steps that perform input, processing, and output. Suppose you want to write a computer program to double any number you provide. You can write the program in a programming language such as Visual Basic or Java, but if you were to write it using English-like statements, it would look like this:

```
input myNumber
myAnswer = myNumber * 2
output myAnswer
```

The number-doubling process includes three instructions:

- The instruction to `input myNumber` is an example of an input operation. When the computer interprets this instruction, it knows to look to an input device to obtain a number. When you work in a specific programming language, you write instructions that tell the computer which device to access for input. For example, when a user enters a number as data for a program, the user might click on the number with a mouse, type it from a keyboard, or speak it into a microphone. Logically, however, it doesn't matter which hardware device is used, as long as the computer knows to accept a number. When the number is retrieved from an input device, it is placed in the computer's memory in a variable named `myNumber`. A **variable** is a named memory location whose value can vary—that is, hold different values at different points in time. For example, the value of `myNumber` might be 3 when the program is used for the first time and 45 when it is used the next time. In this course (as well as in almost all programming languages), variable names will not contain embedded spaces; for example, a variable name might be `myNumber` instead of `my Number`.

Note From a logical perspective, when you input, process, or output a value, the hardware device is irrelevant. The same is true in your daily life. If you follow the instruction "Get eggs for the cake," it does not really matter if you purchase them from a store or harvest them from your own chickens—you get the eggs either way. There might be different practical considerations to getting the eggs, just as there are for getting data from a large database as opposed to getting data from an inexperienced user working at home on a laptop computer. This course is concerned only with the logic of operations, not the minor details.

Note A college classroom is similar to a named variable in that its name (for example, *204 Adams Building*) can hold different contents at different times. For example, your Logic class might meet there on Monday night, and a math class might meet there on Tuesday morning.

- The instruction `myAnswer = myNumber * 2` is an example of a processing operation. In most programming languages, an asterisk is used to indicate multiplication, so this instruction means "Change the value of the memory location `myAnswer` to equal the value at the memory location `myNumber` times two." Mathematical operations are not the only kind of processing operations, but they are very typical. As with input operations, the type of hardware used for processing is irrelevant—after you write a program, it can be used on computers of different brand names, sizes, and speeds.

- In the number-doubling program, the `output myAnswer` instruction is an example of an output operation. Within a particular program, this statement could cause the output to appear on the monitor (which might be a flat-panel plasma screen or a smartphone display), the output could go to a printer (which could be laser or ink-jet), the output could be written to a disk or DVD, or the output could be spoken words sent to headphones. The logic of the output process is the same no matter what hardware device you use. When this instruction executes, the value stored in memory at the location named `myAnswer` is sent to an output device. (The output value also remains in computer memory until something else is stored at the same memory location or power is lost.)

Note Computer memory consists of millions of numbered locations where data can be stored. The memory location of `myNumber` has a specific numeric address each time you run the program that contains it, but when you write programs, you seldom need to be concerned with the value of the memory address; instead, you use the easy-to-remember name you created. Computer programmers often refer to memory addresses using hexadecimal notation, or base 16. Using this system, they might use a value like 42FF01A to refer to a memory address. Despite the use of letters, such an address is still a number. Appendix A contains information about the hexadecimal numbering system.

Two Truths & a Lie | Understanding Simple Program Logic

1. A program with syntax errors can execute but might produce incorrect results.
2. Although the syntax of programming languages differs, the same program logic can be expressed in different languages.
3. Most simple computer programs include steps that perform input, processing, and output.

The false statement is #1. A program with syntax errors cannot execute; a program with no syntax errors can execute, but might produce incorrect results.

1.3 Understanding the Program Development Cycle

A programmer's job involves writing instructions (such as those in the doubling program in the preceding section), but a professional programmer usually does not just sit down at a computer keyboard and start typing. **Figure 1-1** illustrates the **program development cycle**, which can be broken down into at least seven steps:

1. Understand the problem.
2. Plan the logic.
3. Code the program.
4. Use software (a compiler or an interpreter) to translate the program into machine language.
5. Test the program.
6. Put the program into production.
7. Maintain the program.

Figure 1-1 The program development cycle

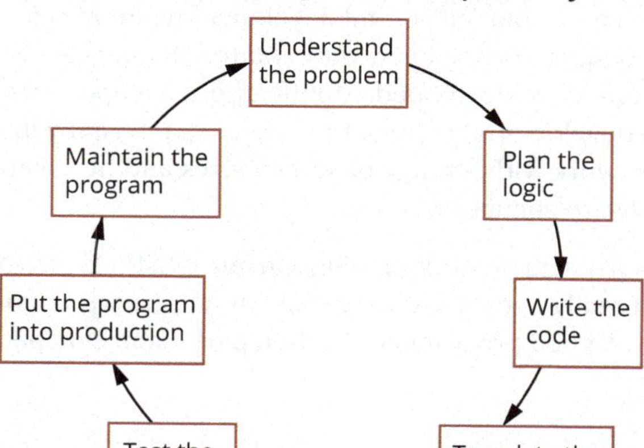

Understanding the Problem

Professional computer programmers write programs to satisfy the needs of others, called users or end users. Examples of end users include a Human Resources department that needs a printed list of all employees, a Billing department that wants a list of clients who are 30 or more days overdue on their payments, and an Order department that needs a website to provide buyers with an online shopping cart. Because programmers are providing a service to these users, programmers must first understand what the users want. When a program runs, you usually think of the logic as a cycle of input-processing-output operations, but when you plan a program, you think of the output first. After you understand what the desired result is, you can plan the input and processing steps to achieve it.

Suppose the director of Human Resources says to a programmer, "Our department needs a list of all employees who have been here over five years, because we want to invite them to a special thank-you dinner." On the surface, this seems like a simple request. An experienced programmer, however, will know that the request is incomplete. For example, you might not know the answers to the following questions about which employees to include:

- Does the director want a list of full-time employees only, or a list of full- and part-time employees together?
- Does the director want to include people who have worked for the company on a month-to-month contractual basis over the past five years, or only regular, permanent employees?
- Do the listed employees need to have worked for the organization for five years as of today, as of the date of the dinner, or as of some other cutoff date?
- What about an employee who worked three years, took a two-year leave of absence, and has been back for three years?

The programmer cannot make any of these decisions; the user (in this case, the Human Resources director) must address these questions.

More decisions still might be required. For example:

- What data should be included for each listed employee? Should the list contain both first and last names? Social Security numbers? Phone numbers? Addresses?
- Should the list be in alphabetical order? Employee ID number order? Length-of-service order? Some other order?
- Should the employees be grouped by any criteria, such as department number or years of service?

Several pieces of documentation often are provided to help the programmer understand the problem. Documentation consists of all the supporting paperwork for a program; it might include items such as original requests for the program from users, sample output, and descriptions of the data items available for input.

Understanding the problem might be even more difficult if you are writing an app that you hope to market for mobile devices. Business developers usually are approached by a user with a need, but successful developers of mobile apps often try to identify needs that users aren't even aware of yet. For example, no one knew they wanted to play specific online games or post photos to social media before such applications were developed. Mobile app developers also must consider a wider variety of user skills than programmers who develop applications that are used internally in a corporation. Mobile app developers must make sure their programs work with a range of screen sizes and hardware specifications because software competition is intense and the hardware changes quickly.

Fully understanding the problem may be one of the most difficult aspects of programming. On any job, the description of what the user needs may be vague—worse yet, users may not really know what they want, and users who think they know frequently change their minds after seeing sample output. A good programmer is often part counselor, part detective!

Planning the Logic

The heart of the programming process lies in planning the program's logic. During this phase of the process, the programmer plans the steps of the program, deciding what steps to include and how to order them. You can plan the solution to a problem in many ways. Two common planning tools are flowcharts and pseudocode. You will learn more about these tools later in this chapter and you will work with many examples of flowcharts and pseudocode throughout this course. Both tools involve writing the steps of the program in English, much as you would plan a trip on paper before getting into the car or plan a party theme before shopping for food and favors.

You may hear programmers refer to planning a program as "developing an algorithm." An **algorithm** is the sequence of steps or rules you follow to solve a problem.

The programmer shouldn't worry about the syntax of any particular language during the planning stage, but should focus on figuring out what sequence of events will lead from the available input to the desired output. Planning a program's logic includes thinking carefully about all the possible data values a program might encounter and how you want the program to handle each scenario. The process of walking through a program's logic on paper before you actually write the program is called **desk-checking**. You will learn more about planning the logic throughout this course; in fact, the course focuses on this crucial step almost exclusively.

Coding the Program

The programmer can write the source code for a program only after the logic is developed. Hundreds of programming languages are available. Programmers choose particular languages because some have built-in capabilities that make them more efficient than others at handling certain types of operations. Despite their differences, programming languages are quite alike in their basic capabilities—each can handle input operations, arithmetic processing, output operations, and other standard functions. The logic developed to solve a programming problem can be executed using any number of languages. Only after choosing a language must the programmer be concerned with proper punctuation and the correct spelling of commands—in other words, using the correct *syntax*.

Some experienced programmers can successfully combine logic planning and program coding in one step. This may work for planning and writing a very simple program, just as you can plan and write a postcard to a friend using one step. A good term paper or a Hollywood screenplay, however, needs planning before writing—and so do most programs.

Which step is harder: planning the logic or coding the program? Right now, it may seem to you that writing in a programming language is a very difficult task, considering all the spelling and syntax rules you must learn. However, the planning step is actually more difficult. Which is more difficult: thinking up the twists and turns to the plot of a best-selling mystery novel, or writing a translation of an existing novel from English to Spanish? And who do you think gets paid more, the writer who creates the plot or the translator? (Try asking friends to name any famous translator!)

Note In some organizations, systems analysts, programmers, and coders have slightly different jobs. An analyst might talk with users to determine their needs, a programmer might design the logical steps in a program, and a coder might then write the designed instructions in a programming language. However, there is overlap in these jobs, and one employee might fill all three roles in some organizations.

Using Software to Translate the Program into Machine Language

Even though there are many programming languages, each computer works internally with only one language—its machine language, which consists of 1s and 0s. Computers understand machine language because they are made up of thousands of tiny electrical switches, each of which can be set in either the on state or the off state, which are represented by a 1 or 0, respectively.

Languages such as Java or Visual Basic are available for programmers because someone has written a translator program (a compiler or an interpreter) that changes the programmer's English-like **high-level programming language** into machine language that the computer understands. (Machine language is an example of a **low-level programming language**; some other languages not far removed from machine language are also referred to as low-level languages.) When you learn the syntax of a programming language, the commands work on any machine on which the language software has been installed. Your commands, however, then are translated to machine language, which differs in various computer makes and models.

If you write a programming statement incorrectly (for example, by misspelling a word, using a word that doesn't exist in the language, or using "illegal" grammar), the translator program doesn't know how to proceed and issues an error message identifying a syntax error. Although making errors is never desirable, syntax errors are not a programmer's deepest concern, because the compiler or interpreter catches every syntax error and displays a message about the problem. The computer will not execute a program that contains even one syntax error.

Typically, a programmer develops logic, writes the code, and compiles the program, receiving a list of syntax errors. The programmer then corrects the syntax errors and compiles the program again. Correcting the first set of errors frequently reveals new errors that originally were not apparent to the compiler. For example, if you could use an English compiler and submit the sentence *The dg chase the cat*, the compiler at first might point out only one syntax error. The second word, *dg*, is illegal because it is not part of the English language. Only after you corrected the word to *dog* would the compiler find another syntax error on the third word, *chase*, because it is the wrong verb form for the subject *dog*. This doesn't mean *chase* is necessarily the wrong word. Maybe *dog* is wrong; perhaps the subject should be *dogs*, in which case *chase* is right. Compilers don't always know exactly what you mean, nor do they know what the proper correction should be, but they do know when something is wrong with your syntax.

Programmers often compile their code one section at a time. It is far less overwhelming and easier to understand errors that are discovered in 20 lines of code at a time than to try to correct mistakes after 2,000 lines of code have been written. When writing a program, a programmer might need to recompile the code several times. An executable program is created only when the code is free of syntax errors. After a program has been translated into machine language, the machine language program is saved and can be run any number of times without repeating the translation step. You need to retranslate your code only if you make changes to your source code statements. **Figure 1-2** shows a diagram of this entire process.

Figure 1-2 Creating an executable program

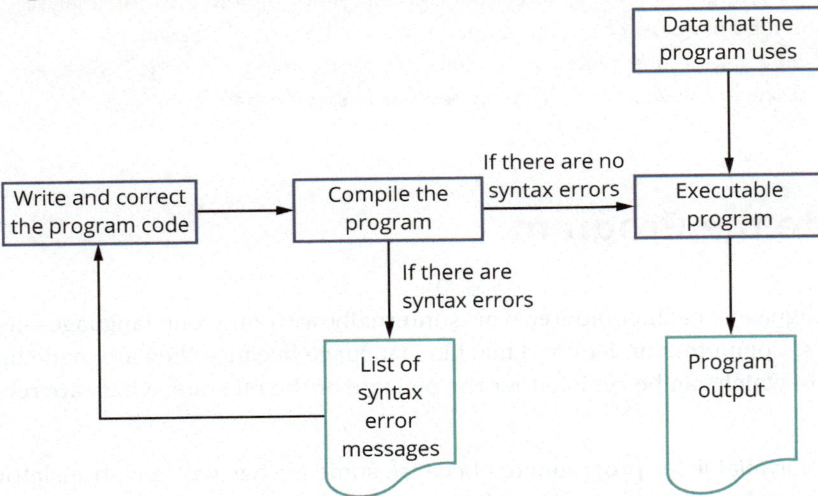

Testing the Program

A program that is free of syntax errors is not necessarily free of logical errors. A logical error results when you use a syntactically correct statement but use the wrong one for the current context. For example, the English sentence *The dog chases the cat*, although syntactically perfect, is not logically correct if the dog chases a ball or the cat is the aggressor.

After a program is free of syntax errors, the programmer can test it—that is, execute it with some sample data to see whether the results are logically correct. Recall the number-doubling program:

```
input myNumber
myAnswer = myNumber * 2
output myAnswer
```

If you execute the program, provide the value 2 as input to the program, and the answer 4 is displayed, you have executed one successful test run of the program. However, if the answer 40 is displayed, maybe the program contains a logical error. Maybe the second line of code was mistyped with an extra zero, so that the program reads:

```
input myNumber
myAnswer = myNumber * 20
output myAnswer
```

Don't Do It

The programmer typed 20 instead of 2.

Placing 20 instead of 2 in the multiplication statement caused a logical error. Notice that nothing is syntactically wrong with this second program—it is just as reasonable to multiply a number by 20 as by 2—but if the programmer intends only to double `myNumber`, then a logical error has occurred.

The process of finding and correcting program errors is called **debugging**. You debug a program by testing it using many sets of data. For example, if you write the program to double a number, then enter 2 and get an output value of 4, that doesn't necessarily mean you have a correct program. Perhaps you have typed this program by mistake:

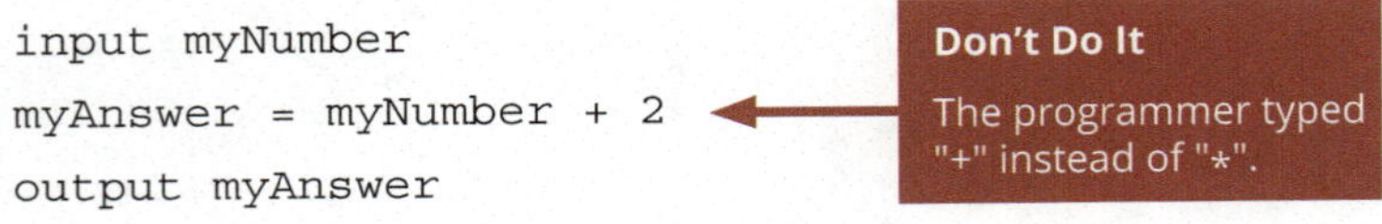

An input of 2 results in an answer of 4, but that doesn't mean your program doubles numbers—it actually only adds 2 to them. If you test your program with additional data and get the wrong answer—for example, if you enter 7 and get an answer of 9—you know there is a problem with your code.

Selecting test data is somewhat of an art in itself, and it should be done carefully. If the Human Resources department wants a list of the names of five-year employees, it would be a mistake to test the program with a small sample file of only long-term employees. If no newer employees are part of the data being used for testing, you do not really know if the program would have eliminated them from the five-year list. Many companies do not know that their software has a problem until an unusual circumstance occurs—for example, the first time an employee has more than nine dependents, the first time a customer orders more than 999 items at a time, or when the Internet runs out of allocated IP addresses, a problem known as *IPV4 exhaustion*.

Putting the Program into Production

After the program is thoroughly tested and debugged, it is ready for the organization to use. Putting the program into production might mean simply running the program once if it was written to satisfy a user's request for a special list. However, the process might take months if the program will be run on a regular basis, or if it is one of a large system of programs being developed. Perhaps data-entry people must be trained to prepare the input for the new program, users must be trained to understand the output, or existing data in the company must be changed to an entirely new format to accommodate this program. **Conversion**, the entire set of actions an organization must take to switch over to using a new program or set of programs, can sometimes take months or years to accomplish.

Maintaining the Program

After programs are put into production, making necessary changes is called **maintenance**. Maintenance can be required for many reasons: As examples, new tax rates are legislated, the format of an input file is altered, or the end user requires additional information not included in the original output specifications. Frequently, your first programming job will require maintaining previously written programs. When you maintain the programs others have written, you will appreciate the effort the original programmer put into writing clear code, using reasonable variable names, and documenting his or her work. When you make changes to existing programs, you repeat the development cycle. That is, you must understand the changes, then plan, code, translate, and test them before putting them into production. If a substantial number of program changes are required, the original program might be retired, and the program development cycle might be started for a new program.

Two Truths & a Lie | Understanding the Program Development Cycle

1. Understanding the problem that must be solved can be one of the most difficult aspects of programming.
2. The two most commonly used logic-planning tools are flowcharts and pseudocode.
3. Developing program logic is a very different process when you use different programming languages to implement the logic.

The false statement is #3. Despite their differences, programming languages are quite alike in their basic capabilities—each can handle input operations, arithmetic processing, output operations, and other standard functions. The logic developed to solve a programming problem can be executed using any number of languages.

1.4 Using Pseudocode Statements and Flowchart Symbols

When programmers plan the logic for a solution to a programming problem, they often use one of two tools: pseudocode (pronounced *sue-doe-code*) or flowcharts.

- **Pseudocode** is an English-like representation of the logical steps it takes to solve a problem. *Pseudo* is a prefix that means *false*, and to *code* a program means to put it in a programming language; therefore, *pseudocode* simply means *false code*, or sentences that are similar to those written in a computer programming language but do not necessarily follow all the syntax rules of any specific language.
- A **flowchart** is a pictorial representation of the same logical steps.

Writing Pseudocode

You already have seen examples of statements that represent pseudocode earlier in this chapter, and there is nothing mysterious about them. The following five statements constitute a pseudocode representation of a number-doubling problem:

```
start
    input myNumber
    myAnswer = myNumber * 2
    output myAnswer
stop
```

Using pseudocode involves writing down all the steps you will use in a program. Usually, programmers preface their pseudocode with a beginning statement like `start` and end it with a terminating statement like `stop`. The statements between `start` and `stop` look like English and are indented slightly so that `start` and `stop` stand out. Most programmers do not bother with punctuation such as periods at the end of pseudocode statements, although it would not be wrong to use them if you prefer that style. Similarly, there is no need to capitalize the first word in a statement, although you might choose to do so.

Pseudocode is fairly flexible because it is a planning tool and not the final product. Therefore, for example, you might prefer any of the following:

- Instead of `start` and `stop`, some pseudocode developers would use other terms such as `begin` and `end`.
- Instead of writing `input myNumber`, some developers would write `get myNumber` or `read myNumber`.
- Instead of writing `myAnswer = myNumber * 2`, some developers would write `calculate myAnswer = myNumber times 2` or `myAnswer is assigned myNumber doubled`.
- Instead of writing `output myAnswer`, many pseudocode developers would write `display myAnswer`, `print myAnswer`, or `write myAnswer`.

The point is, the pseudocode statements are instructions to retrieve an original number from an input device and store it in memory where it can be used in a calculation, and then to get the calculated answer from memory and send it to an output device so a person can see it. When you eventually convert your pseudocode to a specific programming language, you do not have such flexibility because specific syntax will be required. For example, if you use the C# programming language and write the statement to output the answer to the monitor, you can code the following:

```
Console.Write(myAnswer);
```

The exact use of words, capitalization, and punctuation are important in the C# statement, but not in the pseudocode statement. Pseudocode standards might be slightly different in an organization where you work. Following is a list of the standards used in this course:

- Programs begin with `start` and end with `stop`; these two words are always aligned.
- Program statements are indented a few spaces.
- Each program statement appears on a single line if possible. When this is not possible, continuation lines are indented.
- Program statements begin with lowercase letters.
- No punctuation is used to end a statement.
- Each program statement performs one action—for example, input, processing, or output.

Shortly, you will learn about program modules. Two additional standards will apply to modules:

- Whenever a module name is used, it is followed by a set of parentheses.
- Modules begin with the module name and end with `return`; these are always aligned.

> **Note** As you learn to create pseudocode and flowchart statements, you will develop a sense for how much detail to include. The statements represent the main steps that must be accomplished without including minute points. The concept is similar to writing an essay outline in which each statement of the outline represents a paragraph.

Drawing Flowcharts

Some professional programmers prefer writing pseudocode to drawing flowcharts, because using pseudocode is more similar to writing the final statements in the programming language. Others prefer drawing flowcharts to represent the logical flow, because flowcharts allow programmers to visualize more easily how the program statements will connect. Especially for beginning programmers, a flowchart is an excellent tool that helps them to visualize how the statements in a program are interrelated.

You can draw a flowchart by hand or use software, such as Microsoft Word and Microsoft PowerPoint, that contains flowcharting tools. You can use several other software programs, such as Lucidchart, Flowgorithm, Visio, and Visual Logic, to create flowcharts. When you create a flowchart, you draw geometric shapes that contain the individual statements and that are connected with arrows.

In a flowchart, you use a parallelogram to represent an input symbol, which indicates an input operation. You write an input statement in English inside the parallelogram, as shown in **Figure 1-3**.

Figure 1-3 Input symbol

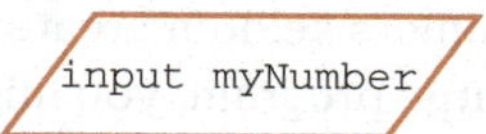

Arithmetic operation statements are examples of processing. In a flowchart, you use a rectangle as the processing symbol that contains a processing statement, as shown in **Figure 1-4**.

Figure 1-4 Processing symbol

```
myAnswer =
myNumber * 2
```

To represent an output statement, you use the same symbol as for input statements—the output symbol is a parallelogram, as shown in **Figure 1-5**. Because the parallelogram is used for both input and output, it is often called the input/output symbol or I/O symbol.

Figure 1-5 Output symbol

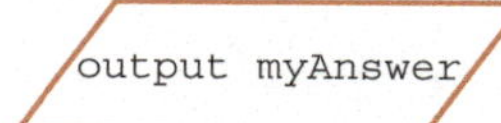

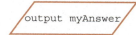

> **Note** Some software programs that use flowcharts (such as Visual Logic) use a right-slanting parallelogram to represent input and a left-slanting parallelogram to represent output. As long as the flowchart creator and the flowchart reader are communicating, the actual shape used is irrelevant. This course will follow the most standard convention of using the right-slanting parallelogram for both input and output.

To show the correct sequence of statements, you use arrows, or **flowlines**, to connect the steps. Whenever possible, most of a flowchart should read from top to bottom or from left to right on a page. That's the way we read English, so when flowcharts follow this convention, they are easier for us to understand.

To be complete, a flowchart should include two more elements: **terminal symbols**, or start/stop symbols, at each end. Often, you place a word like `start` or `begin` in the first terminal symbol and a word like `end` or `stop` in the other. The standard terminal symbol is shaped like a racetrack; many programmers refer to this shape as a *lozenge*, because it resembles the shape of the medication you might use to soothe a sore throat. **Figure 1-6** shows a complete flowchart for the program that doubles a number, and the pseudocode for the same problem. You can see from the figure that the flowchart and pseudocode statements are the same—only the presentation format differs.

Figure 1-6 Flowchart and pseudocode for program that doubles a number

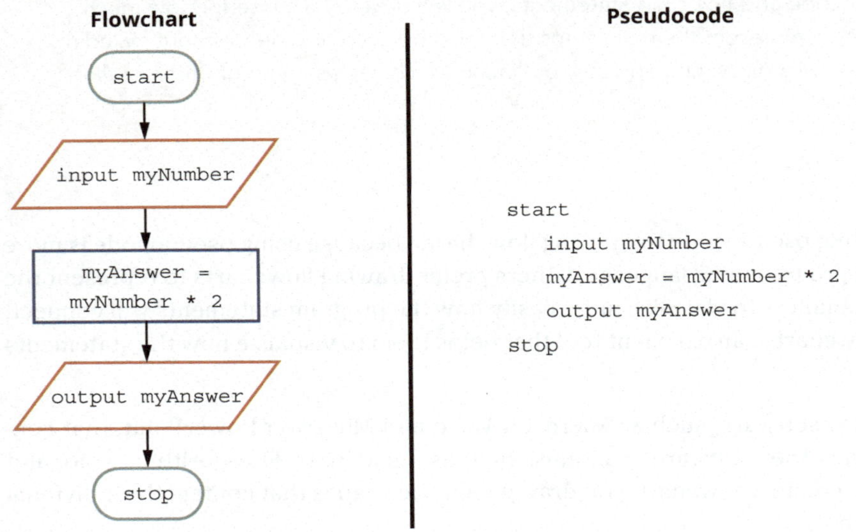
Flowchart
start
input myNumber
myAnswer =
myNumber * 2
output myAnswer
stop
Pseudocode
start
input myNumber
myAnswer = myNumber * 2
output myAnswer
stop

Programmers seldom create both pseudocode and a flowchart for the same problem; you usually use one or the other. In a large program, you might even prefer to write pseudocode for some parts and to draw a flowchart for others. When you tell a friend how to get to your house, you might write a series of instructions or you might draw a map. Pseudocode is similar to written, step-by-step instructions; a flowchart, like a map, is a visual representation of the same thing. **Figure 1-7** summarizes the flowchart symbols used in this course.

Figure 1-7 Flowchart symbols

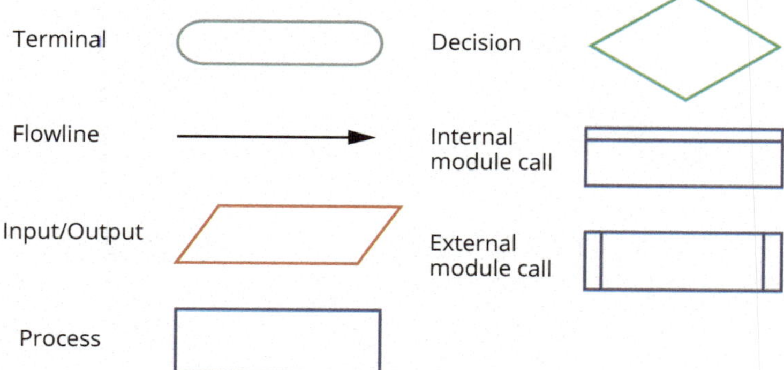

Repeating Instructions

After the flowchart or pseudocode has been developed, the programmer needs only to: (1) buy a computer, (2) buy a language compiler, (3) learn a programming language, (4) code the program, (5) attempt to compile it, (6) fix the syntax errors, (7) compile it again, (8) test it with several sets of data, and (9) put it into production.

"Whoa!" you are probably saying to yourself. "This is simply not worth it! All that work to create a flowchart or pseudocode, and *then* all those other steps? For five dollars, I can buy a pocket calculator that will double any number for me instantly!" You are absolutely right. If this were a real computer program, and all it did was double the value of a number, it would not be worth the effort. Writing a computer program would be worthwhile only if you had many numbers (let's say 10,000) to double in a limited amount of time—let's say the next two minutes.

Unfortunately, the program represented in Figure 1-6 does not double 10,000 numbers; it doubles only one. You could execute the program 10,000 times, of course, but that would require you to sit at the computer and run the program over and over again. You would be better off with a program that could process 10,000 numbers, one after the other.

One solution is to write the program shown in **Figure 1-8** and execute the same steps 10,000 times. Of course, writing this program would be very time consuming; you might as well buy the calculator.

Figure 1-8 Inefficient pseudocode for program that doubles 10,000 numbers

```
start
   input myNumber
   myAnswer = myNumber * 2
   output myAnswer
   input myNumber
   myAnswer = myNumber * 2
   output myAnswer
   input myNumber
   myAnswer = myNumber * 2
   output myAnswer
   ...and so on for 9,997 more times
```

Don't Do It
You would never want to write such a repetitious list of instructions.

A better solution is to have the computer execute the same set of three instructions repeatedly, as shown in **Figure 1-9**. The repetition of a series of steps is called a **loop**. With this approach, the computer gets a number, doubles it, displays the answer, and then starts again with the first instruction. The same spot in memory, called `myNumber`, is reused for the second number and for any subsequent numbers. The spot in memory named `myAnswer` is reused each time to store the result of the multiplication operation. However, the logic illustrated in the flowchart in Figure 1-9 contains a major problem—the sequence of instructions never ends. This programming situation is known as an **infinite loop**—a repeating flow of logic with no end. You will learn one way to handle this problem later in this chapter; you will learn a superior way later.

Figure 1-9 Flowchart of infinite number-doubling program

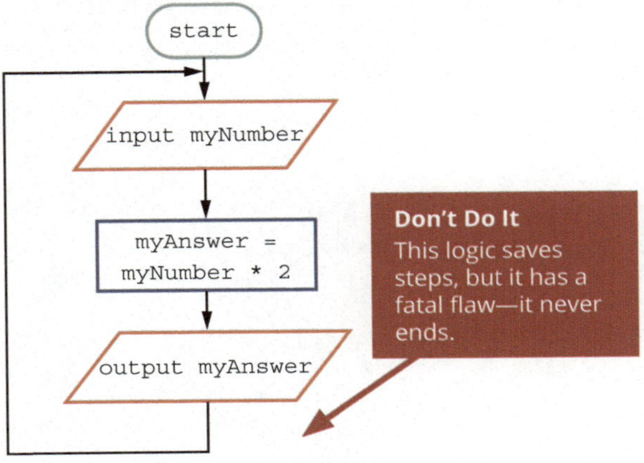
start
input myNumber
myAnswer =
myNumber * 2
output myAnswer
Don't Do It
This logic saves steps, but it has a fatal flaw—it never ends.

Two Truths & a Lie | Using Pseudocode Statements and Flowchart Symbols

1. When you draw a flowchart, you use a parallelogram to represent an input operation.
2. When you draw a flowchart, you use a parallelogram to represent a processing operation.
3. When you draw a flowchart, you use a parallelogram to represent an output operation.

The false statement is #2. When you draw a flowchart, you use a rectangle to represent a processing operation.

1.5 Using a Sentinel Value to End a Program

The logic in the flowchart for doubling numbers, shown in Figure 1-9, has a major flaw—the program contains an infinite loop. If, for example, the input numbers are being entered at the keyboard, the program will keep accepting numbers and outputting their doubled values forever. Of course, the user could refuse to type any more numbers. But the program cannot progress any further while it is waiting for input; meanwhile, the program is occupying computer memory and tying up operating system resources. Refusing to enter any more numbers is not a practical solution. Another way to end the program is simply to turn off the computer. But again, that's neither the best solution nor an elegant way for the program to end.

A better way to end the program is to set a predetermined value for `myNumber` that means *Stop the program!* For example, the programmer and the user could agree that the user will never need to know the double of 0 (zero), so the user could enter a 0 to stop. The program then could test any incoming value contained in `myNumber` and, if it is a 0, stop the program.

In a flowchart, you represent testing a value or evaluating an expression by drawing a **decision symbol**, which is shaped like a diamond. The diamond usually contains a question or evaluation, the answer to which is one of two mutually exclusive options. All good computer questions have only two mutually exclusive answers, such as `yes` and `no` or `true` and `false`. For example, "What day of the year is your birthday?" is not a good computer question because there are 366 possible answers. However, "Is your birthday June 24?" is a good computer question because the answer is always either *yes* or *no*.

The question to stop the doubling program should be, "Is the value of myNumber just entered equal to 0?" or "myNumber = 0?" for short. The complete flowchart will now look like the one shown in **Figure 1-10**.

Figure 1-10 Flowchart of number-doubling program with sentinel value 0

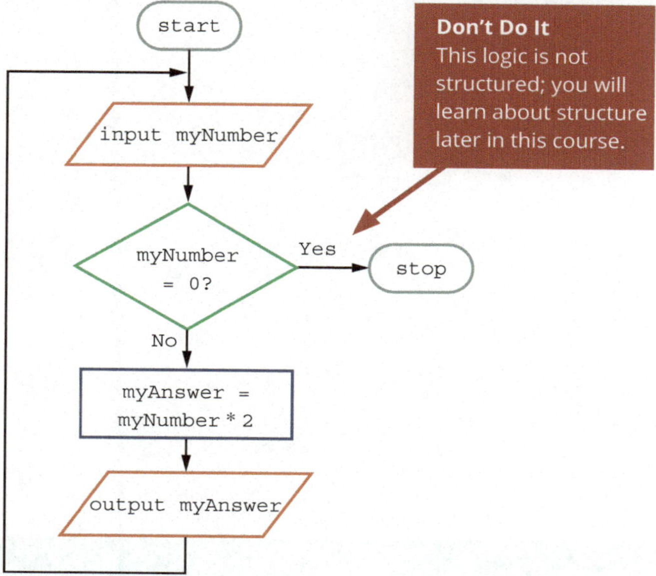
start
input myNumber
myNumber = 0?
Yes
stop
No
myAnswer = myNumber * 2
output myAnswer
Don't Do It
This logic is not structured; you will learn about structure later in this course.

Note Programmers use different notations when they want to express a negative question in pseudocode or a flowchart. For example, if a programmer wanted to ask whether myNumber was not 0, the programmer might write myNumber not = 0? Other programmers would use an equal sign with a slash through it, as in myNumber ≠ 0? Probably the most common approach is to use a less-than sign followed by a greater-than sign, as in myNumber <> 0? Programming languages use different notations, but pseudocode and flowcharts are more flexible as long as your meaning is clear.

One drawback to using 0 to stop a program, of course, is that it won't work if the user does need to find the double of 0. In that case, some other data-entry value that the user never will need, such as 999 or –1, could be selected to signal that the program should end. A preselected value that stops the execution of a program is often called a **dummy value** because it does not represent real data, but just a signal to stop. Sometimes, such a value is called a **sentinel value** because it represents an entry or exit point, like a sentinel who guards a fortress.

Not all programs rely on user data entry from a keyboard; many read data from an input device, such as a disk. When organizations store data on a disk or other storage device, they do not commonly use a dummy value to signal the end of the file. For one thing, an input record might have hundreds of fields, and if you store a dummy record in every file, you are wasting a large quantity of storage on "nondata." Additionally, it is often difficult to choose sentinel values for fields in a company's data files. Any balanceDue, even a zero or a negative number, can be a legitimate value, and any customerName, even *ZZ*, could be someone's name. Fortunately, programming languages can recognize the end of data in a file automatically, through a code that is stored at the end of the data. Many programming languages use the term **eof** (for *end of file*) to refer to this marker that automatically acts as a sentinel. This course, therefore, uses eof to indicate the end of data whenever using a dummy value is impractical or inconvenient. **Figure 1-11** contains a flowchart that shows the eof evaluation in the decision symbol.

Figure 1-11 Flowchart using `eof`

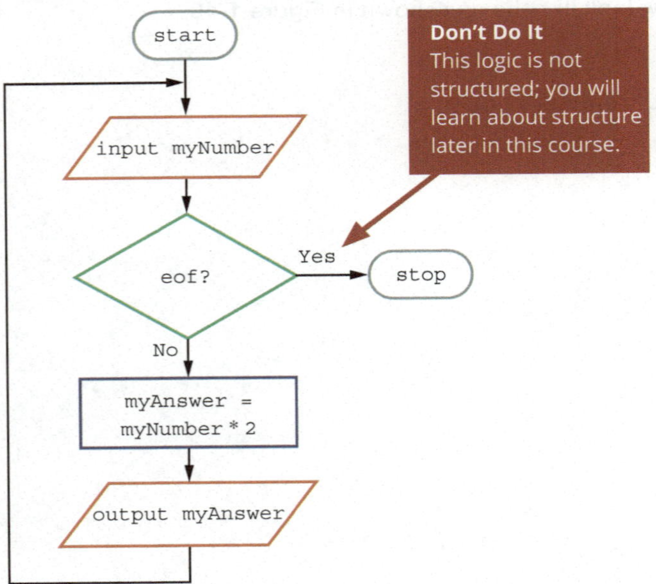
start
input myNumber
eof?
Yes
stop
No
myAnswer =
myNumber * 2
output myAnswer
Don't Do It
This logic is not structured; you will learn about structure later in this course.

Two Truths & a Lie | Using a Sentinel Value to End a Program

1. A program that contains an infinite loop is one that never ends.
2. A preselected value that stops the execution of a program is often called a dummy value or a sentinel value.
3. Many programming languages use the term `fe` (for *file end*) to refer to a marker that automatically acts as a sentinel.

The false statement is #3. The term `eof` (for *end of file*) is the common term for a file sentinel.

1.6 Understanding Programming and User Environments

Many approaches can be used to write and execute a computer program. When you plan a program's logic, you can use a flowchart, pseudocode, or a combination of the two. When you code the program, you can type statements into a variety of text editors. When your program executes, it might accept input from a keyboard, mouse, microphone, or any other input device, and when you provide a program's output, you might use text, images, or sound. This section describes the most common environments you will encounter as a new programmer.

Understanding Programming Environments

When you plan the logic for a computer program, you can use paper and pencil to create a flowchart, or you might use software that allows you to manipulate flowchart shapes. If you choose to write pseudocode, you can do so by hand or by using a word-processing program.

To enter the program into a computer so you can translate and execute it, you usually use a keyboard to type program statements into an editor. You can type a program into one of the following:

- A plain text editor
- A text editor that is part of an integrated development environment.

A **text editor** is a program that you use to create simple text files. It is similar to a word processor, but without as many features. You can use a text editor such as Notepad that is included with Microsoft Windows. **Figure 1-12** shows a C# program in Notepad that accepts a number and doubles it. An advantage to using a simple text editor to type and save a program is that the completed program does not require much disk space for storage. For example, the file shown in Figure 1-12 occupies only 314 bytes of storage.

Figure 1-12 A C# number-doubling program in Notepad

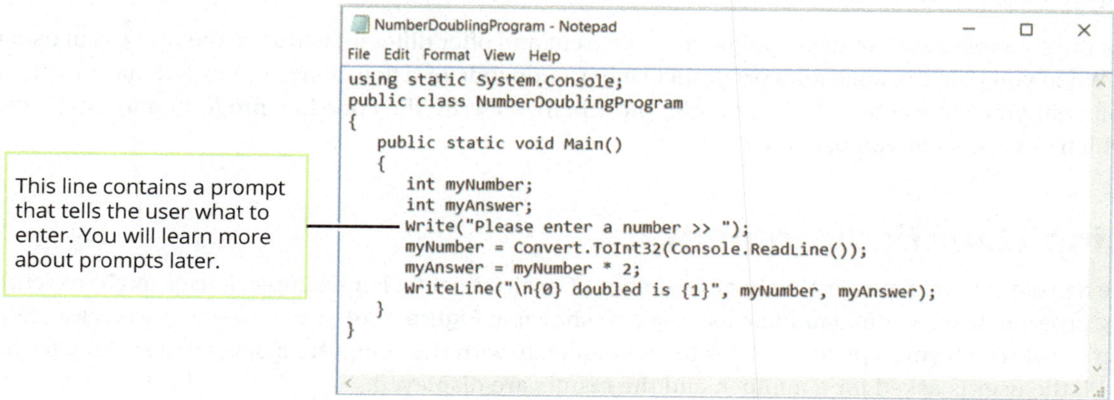

You can use the editor of an **integrated development environment (IDE)** to enter your program. An IDE is a software package that provides an editor, compiler, and other programming tools. For example, **Figure 1-13** shows a C# program in the Microsoft Visual Studio IDE, an environment that contains tools useful for creating programs in Visual Basic, C++, and C#.

Figure 1-13 A C# number-doubling program in Visual Studio

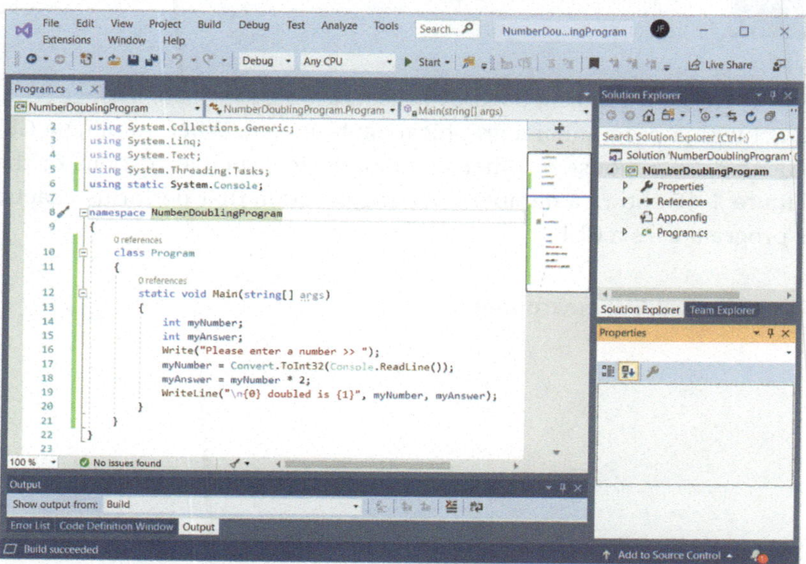

Using an IDE is helpful to programmers because usually it provides features similar to those you find in many word processors. In particular, an IDE's editor commonly includes such features as the following:

- It uses different colors to display various language components, making elements like data types easier to identify.
- It highlights syntax errors visually for you.
- It employs automatic statement completion; when you start to type a statement, the IDE suggests a likely completion, which you can accept with a keystroke.
- It provides tools that allow you to step through a program's execution one statement at a time so you can more easily follow the program's logic and determine the source of any errors.

When you use the IDE to create and save a program, you occupy much more disk space than when using a plain text editor. For example, the program in Figure 1-13 occupies more than 49,000 bytes of disk space.

Although various programming environments might look different and offer different features, the process of using them is very similar. When you plan the logic for a program using pseudocode or a flowchart, it does not matter which programming environment you will use to write your code, and when you write the code in a programming language, it does not matter which environment you use to write it.

Understanding User Environments

A user might execute a program you have written in any number of environments. For example, a user might execute the number-doubling program from a command line like the one shown in **Figure 1-14**. A command line is a location on your computer screen at which you type text entries to communicate with the computer's operating system. In the program in Figure 1-14, the user is asked for a number, and the results are displayed.

Figure 1-14 Executing a number-doubling program in a command-line environment

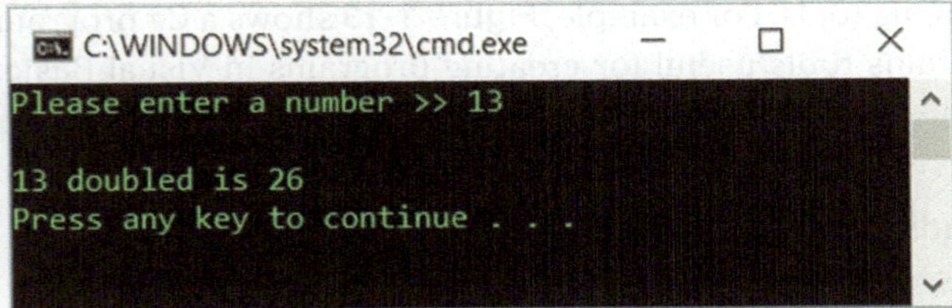

Many programs are not run at the command line in a text environment but are run using a graphical user interface (GUI, pronounced *gooey*), which allows users to interact with a program in a graphical environment. When running a GUI program, the user might type input into a text box or use a mouse or other pointing device, such as a stylus or the user's finger, to select options on the screen. **Figure 1-15** shows a number-doubling program that performs exactly the same task as the one in Figure 1-14, but this program uses a GUI.

Figure 1-15 Executing a number-doubling program in a GUI environment

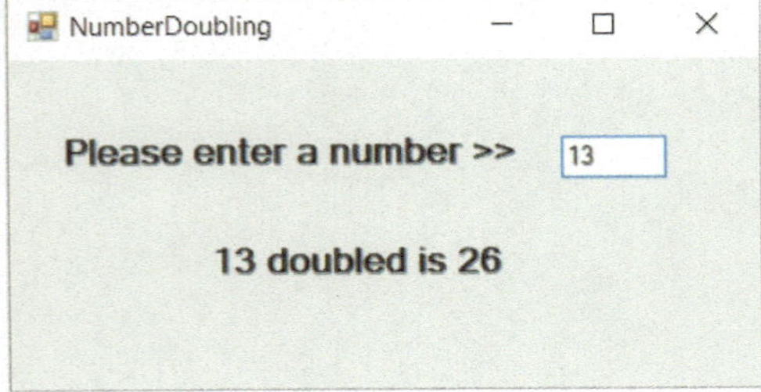

A command-line program and a GUI program might be written in the same programming language. (For example, the programs shown in Figures 1-14 and 1-15 were both written using C#.) However, no matter which environment is used to write or execute a program, the logical process is the same. The two programs both accept input, perform multiplication, and perform output. In this course, you will not concentrate on which environment is used to type a program's statements, nor will you care about the type of environment the user will see. Instead, you will be concerned with the logic that applies to all programming situations.

Two Truths & a Lie | Understanding Programming and User Environments

1. You can type a program into an editor that is part of an integrated development environment, but using a plain text editor provides you with more programming help.
2. When a program runs from the command line, a user types text to provide input.
3. Although GUI and command-line environments look different, the logic of input, processing, and output applies to both program types.

The false statement is #1. An integrated development environment provides more programming help than a plain text editor.

1.7 Understanding the Evolution of Programming Models

People have been writing modern computer programs since the 1940s. The oldest programming languages required programmers to work with memory addresses and to memorize awkward codes associated with machine languages. Newer programming languages look much more like natural language and are easier to use, partly because they allow programmers to name variables instead of using unwieldy memory addresses. Also, newer programming languages allow programmers to create self-contained modules or program segments that can be pieced together in a variety of ways.

The oldest computer programs were written in one piece, from start to finish, but modern programs are rarely written that way—they are created by teams of programmers, each developing reusable and connectable program procedures. Writing several small modules is easier than writing one large program, and most large tasks are easier when you break the work into units and get other workers to help with some of the units.

Note | Ada Byron Lovelace predicted the development of software in 1843; she is often regarded as the first programmer. The basis for most modern software was proposed by Alan Turing in 1935.

Currently, programmers use two major models or paradigms to develop programs and their procedures:

- **Procedural programming** focuses on the procedures that programmers create. That is, procedural programmers focus on the actions that are carried out—for example, getting input data for an employee and writing the calculations needed to produce a paycheck from the data. Procedural programmers would approach the job of producing a paycheck by breaking down the process into manageable subtasks.
- **Object-oriented programming (OOP)** focuses on objects, or "things," and describes their features (also called attributes) and behaviors. For example, object-oriented programmers might design a payroll application by thinking about employees and paychecks and by describing their attributes. Employees have names and Social Security numbers, and paychecks have names and check amounts. Then the programmers would think about the behaviors of employees and paychecks, such as employees getting raises and adding dependents and paychecks being calculated and output. Object-oriented programmers then would build applications from these entities.

With either approach, procedural or object oriented, you can produce a correct paycheck, and both models employ reusable program modules. The major difference lies in the focus the programmer takes during the earliest planning stages of a project. For now, this course focuses on procedural programming techniques. The skills you gain in programming procedurally—declaring variables, accepting input, making decisions, producing output, and so on—will serve you well whether you eventually write programs using a procedural approach, an object-oriented approach, or both. The programming language in which you write your source code might determine your approach. You can write a procedural program in any language that supports object orientation, but the opposite is not always true.

Two Truths & a Lie | Understanding the Evolution of Programming Models

1. The oldest computer programs were written in many separate modules.
2. Procedural programmers focus on actions that are carried out by a program.
3. Object-oriented programmers focus on a program's objects and their attributes and behaviors.

The false statement is #1. The oldest programs were written in a single piece; newer programs are divided into modules.

Summary

- Together, computer hardware (physical devices) and software (instructions) accomplish three major operations: input, processing, and output. You write computer instructions in a computer programming language that requires specific syntax; the instructions are translated into machine language by a compiler or an interpreter. When both the syntax and logic of a program are correct, you can run, or execute, the program to produce the desired results.
- For a program to work properly, you must develop correct logic. Logical errors are much more difficult to locate than syntax errors.
- A programmer's job involves understanding the problem, planning the logic, coding the program, translating the program into machine language, testing the program, putting the program into production, and maintaining it.
- When programmers plan the logic for a solution to a programming problem, they often use flowcharts or pseudocode. When you draw a flowchart, you use parallelograms to represent input and output operations, and rectangles to represent processing. Programmers also use decisions to control repetition of instruction sets.
- To avoid creating an infinite loop when you repeat instructions, you can test for a sentinel value. You represent a decision in a flowchart by drawing a diamond-shaped symbol that contains a true-false or yes-no evaluation.
- You can type a program into a plain text editor or one that is part of an integrated development environment. When a program's data values are entered from a keyboard, they can be entered at the command line in a text environment or in a GUI. Either way, the logic is similar.
- Procedural and object-oriented programmers approach problems differently. Procedural programmers concentrate on the actions performed with data. Object-oriented programmers focus on objects and their behaviors and attributes.

Key Terms

algorithm
app
application software
binary language
central processing unit (CPU)
cloud
coding the program
command line
compiler
computer memory
computer system
conversion
data items
debugging
decision symbol
desk-checking
documentation
dummy value
end users
`eof`
executes
flowchart
flowlines
graphical user interface (GUI)
hardware
high-level programming language
infinite loop
information
input
input symbol
input/output symbol or I/O symbol
integrated development environment (IDE)
interpreter
logic
logical errors
loop
low-level programming language
machine language
maintenance
nonvolatile
object code
object-oriented programming (OOP)
operating system
output
output symbol
procedural programming
processing
processing symbol
program
program code
program development cycle
programming
programming language
pseudocode
random access memory (RAM)
runs
scripting language
sentinel value
software
source code
storage device
syntax
syntax errors
system software
terminal symbols
text editor
users
variable
volatile

Review Questions

1. Computer programs also are known as ________________. (1.1)
   a. data
   b. hardware
   c. software
   d. information
2. The major operations performed by all sizes of computers include ________________. (1.1)
   a. input, processing, and output
   b. hardware and software
   c. sequence and looping
   d. spreadsheets and word processing
3. Visual Basic, C++, and Java are all examples of computer ________________. (1.1–1.3)
   a. operating systems
   b. programming languages
   c. hardware
   d. machine languages

4. A programming language's rules are its ______________. (1.1)
   a. syntax
   b. logic
   c. format
   d. options

5. The most important task of a compiler or an interpreter is to ______________. (1.1)
   a. create the rules for a programming language
   b. translate English statements into a language such as Java
   c. translate programming language statements into machine language
   d. execute machine language programs to perform useful tasks

6. Which of the following is temporary, internal storage? (1.1)
   a. CPU
   b. hard disk
   c. keyboard
   d. memory

7. Which of the following pairs of steps in the programming process is in the correct order? (1.3)
   a. code the program, plan the logic
   b. test the program, translate it into machine language
   c. put the program into production, understand the problem
   d. code the program, translate it into machine language

8. A programmer's most important task before planning the logic of a program is to ______________. (1.3)
   a. decide which programming language to use
   b. code the problem
   c. train the users of the program
   d. understand the problem

9. The two most commonly used tools for planning a program's logic are ______________. (1.3)
   a. ASCII and EBCDIC
   b. Java and Visual Basic
   c. flowcharts and pseudocode
   d. word processors and spreadsheets

10. Writing a program in a language such as C++ or Java is known as ______________ the program. (1.3)
    a. translating
    b. coding
    c. interpreting
    d. compiling

11. An English-like programming language such as Java or Visual Basic is a ______________ programming language. (1.3)
    a. machine-level
    b. low-level
    c. high-level
    d. binary-level

12. Which of the following is an example of a syntax error? (1.3)
    a. producing output before accepting input
    b. subtracting when you meant to add
    c. misspelling a programming language word
    d. using a high-level programming language when a low-level language would have been more appropriate

13. Which of the following is an example of a logical error? (1.3)
    a. ending a statement with a period in a language that requires a semicolon
    b. using the word `start` when a language requires `begin`
    c. dividing by 3 when you meant to divide by 30
    d. starting a statement with an uppercase letter in a language that requires all lowercase

14. The parallelogram is the flowchart symbol representing ______________. (1.4)
    a. input
    b. output
    c. either input or output
    d. neither input nor output

15. In a flowchart, a rectangle represents ______________. (1.4)

    a. input
    b. a sentinel
    c. a question
    d. processing

16. In flowcharts, the decision symbol is a ______________. (1.4)

    a. parallelogram
    b. rectangle
    c. lozenge
    d. diamond

17. The term `eof` represents ______________. (1.5)

    a. a standard input device
    b. a generic sentinel value
    c. a condition in which no more memory is available for storage
    d. the logical flow in a program

18. When you use an IDE instead of a simple text editor to develop a program, ______________. (1.6)

    a. the logic is more complicated
    b. the logic is simpler
    c. the syntax is different
    d. some help is provided

19. When you write a program that will run in a GUI environment as opposed to a command-line environment, ______________. (1.6)

    a. the logic is very different
    b. some syntax is different
    c. you do not need to plan the logic
    d. users are more confused

20. As compared to procedural programming, with object-oriented programming, ______________. (1.7)

    a. the programmer's focus differs
    b. you cannot use some languages such as Java
    c. you do not accept input
    d. you do not code calculations; they are created automatically

Programming Exercises

1. Match the definition with the appropriate term. (1.1)

    1. Computer system devices
    2. Another word for *program*
    3. Language rules
    4. Order of instructions
    5. Language translator

    a. compiler
    b. syntax
    c. logic
    d. hardware
    e. software

2. In your own words, describe the steps to writing a computer program. (1.3)

3. Draw a flowchart or write pseudocode to represent the logic of a program that allows the user to enter a value. The program multiplies the value by 10 and outputs the result. (1.4)

4. Draw a flowchart or write pseudocode to represent the logic of a program that allows the user to enter a value for one edge of a cube. The program calculates the surface area of one side of the cube, the surface area of the cube, and its volume. The program outputs all the results. (1.4)

5. Draw a flowchart or write pseudocode to represent the logic of a program that allows the user to enter a value for hours worked in a day. The program calculates the hours worked in a five-day week and the hours worked in a 252-day work year. The program outputs all the results. (1.4)

6. Draw a flowchart or write pseudocode to represent the logic of a program that allows the user to enter two values. The program outputs the sum of and the difference between the two values. (1.4)

7. Draw a flowchart or write pseudocode to represent the logic of a program that allows the user to enter values for the current year and the user's birth year. The program outputs the age of the user this year. (1.4)

8. a. Draw a flowchart or write pseudocode to represent the logic of a program that allows the user to enter an hourly pay rate and hours worked. The program outputs the user's gross pay.

   b. Modify the program that computes gross pay to allow the user to enter the withholding tax rate. The program outputs the net pay after taxes have been withheld. (1.4)

9. Research current rates of monetary exchange. Draw a flowchart or write pseudocode to represent the logic of a program that allows the user to enter a number of dollars and convert it to Euros and Japanese yen. (1.4)

10. A mobile phone app allows a user to press a button that starts a timer that counts seconds. When the user presses the button again, the timer stops. Draw a flowchart or write pseudocode that accepts the elapsed time in seconds and displays the value in minutes and seconds. For example, if the elapsed time was 130 seconds, the output would be 2 minutes and 10 seconds. (1.4)

Performing Maintenance

1. You have learned that some of the tasks assigned to new programmers frequently involve maintenance—making changes to existing programs because of new requirements. The Chapter01 folder of your downloadable student files contains a file named *MAINTENANCE01-01.txt*. Assume that this program is a working program in your organization and that it needs modifications as described in the comments (lines that begin with two slashes) at the beginning of the file. Your job is to alter the program to meet the new specifications. (1.4)

Debugging Exercises

Since the early days of computer programming, program errors have been called bugs. The term is often said to have originated from an actual moth that was discovered trapped in the circuitry of a computer at Harvard University in 1945. However, the term *bug* was in use prior to 1945 to mean trouble with any electrical apparatus; even during Thomas Edison's life, it meant an industrial defect. The term *debugging*, however, is more closely associated with correcting program syntax and logic errors than with any other type of trouble.

1. The Chapter01 folder of your downloadable files includes *DEBUG01-01.txt*, *DEBUG01-02.txt*, *DEBUG01-03.txt*, and *DEBUG01-04.jpg*. Each file contains pseudocode or a flowchart that has mistakes. Find and correct all the bugs.

Game Zone

1. In 1952, A. S. Douglas wrote his University of Cambridge Ph.D. dissertation on human-computer interaction and created the first graphical computer game—a version of Tic-Tac-Toe. The game was programmed on an EDSAC vacuum-tube mainframe computer. The first computer game is generally assumed to be *Spacewar!*, developed in 1962 at MIT; the first commercially available video game was *Pong*, introduced by Atari in 1972. In 1980, Atari's *Asteroids* and *Lunar Lander* became the first video games to be registered with the U.S. Copyright Office. Throughout the 1980s, players spent hours with games that now seem very simple and unglamorous. Today, commercial computer games are much more complex; they require many programmers, graphic artists, and testers to develop them, and large management and marketing staffs are needed to promote them. A game might cost many millions of dollars to develop and market, but a successful game might earn hundreds of millions of dollars. Obviously, with the brief introduction to programming you have had so far, you cannot create a very sophisticated game. However, you can get started.

   Mad Libs is a children's game in which players provide a few words that are then incorporated into a silly story. The game helps children understand different parts of speech because they are asked to provide specific types of words. For example, you might ask a child for a noun, another noun, an adjective, and a past-tense verb. The child might reply with such answers as *table*, *book*, *silly*, and *studied*.

   The newly created Mad Lib might be:

   Mary had a little *table*.

   Its *book* was *silly* as snow,

   And everywhere that Mary *studied*

   The *table* was sure to go.

   Create the logic for a Mad Lib program that accepts four words from input, then creates and displays a short story or nursery rhyme that uses them. (1.4)

Chapter 2

Elements of High-Quality Programs

Learning Objectives

When you complete this chapter, you will be able to:

2.1 Declare and use variables and constants

2.2 Perform arithmetic operations

2.3 Describe the advantages of modularization

2.4 Modularize a program

2.5 Describe the features of good program design

2.1 Declaring and Using Variables and Constants

Data items include all the text, numbers, and other material processed by a computer. When you input data items to be used by a program, they are stored in memory where they can be processed and converted to information that is output.

When you write programs, you work with data of two different types: numeric and string. You also work with data in three different forms: literals (or unnamed constants), variables, and named constants.

Understanding Data Types

A data item's **data type** is a classification that describes the following:

- What values can be held by the item
- How the item is stored in computer memory
- What operations can be performed on the item

All programming languages support two broad data types:

- **Numeric** describes data that consists of numbers, possibly with a decimal point or a sign; numeric data can be used in arithmetic operations.
- **String** describes data items that are nonnumeric; string data cannot be used in arithmetic operations.

Most programming languages support several additional data types. Languages such as C++, C#, Visual Basic, and Java distinguish between variables that hold **integer values** (whole number values) and **floating-point values**, which contain a decimal point. (Floating-point numbers are also called **real numbers**.) Thus, in some languages, the values 4 and 4.3 would be stored in different types of numeric variables. Additionally, many languages allow you to distinguish between very small and very large values that occupy different numbers of bytes in memory. You will learn more about these specialized data types when you study a programming language, but this course uses only the two broadest types: numeric and string.

Understanding Unnamed, Literal Constants

When you use a specific value in a computer program, it is one of two types of constants:

- A **numeric constant** (or **literal numeric constant**) is a number that does not change—for example, 43. When you store a numeric value in computer memory, additional characters such as dollar signs and commas typically are not input or stored. Those characters might be added to output for readability, but they are not part of the number.
- A **string constant** (or **literal string constant**) appears within quotation marks in computer programs. String values are also called **alphanumeric values** because they can contain alphabetic characters as well as numbers and other characters. For example, `"Amanda"`, `"43"`, and `"$3,215.99 U.S."` all are strings because they are enclosed in quotation marks. Although strings can contain numbers, numeric values cannot contain alphabetic characters.

The numeric constant 43 is an **unnamed constant** (or more specifically, an **unnamed numeric constant**); it does not have an identifier like a variable does. Similarly, the string constant `"Amanda"` is an **unnamed string constant**.

Working with Variables

Variables are named memory locations whose contents can vary or differ over time. For example, in the number-doubling program in **Figure 2-1**, `myNumber` and `myAnswer` are variables. At any moment in time, a variable holds just one value. Sometimes, `myNumber` holds 2 and `myAnswer` holds 4; at other times, `myNumber` holds 6 and `myAnswer` holds 12.

Figure 2-1 Flowchart and pseudocode for the number-doubling program

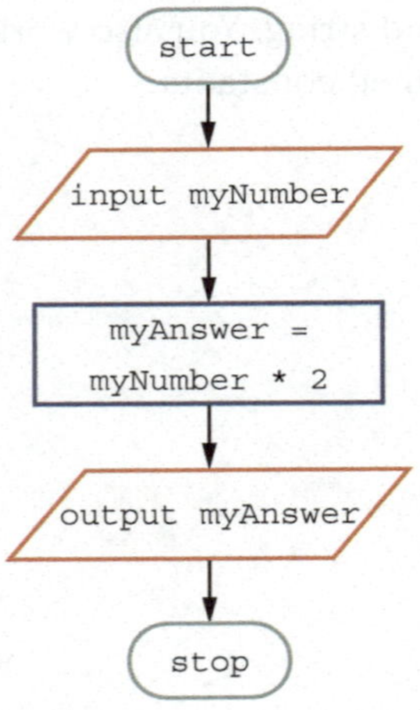

start
input myNumber
myAnswer = myNumber * 2
output myAnswer
stop

```
start
   input myNumber
   myAnswer = myNumber * 2
   output myAnswer
stop
```

The ability of variables to change in value is what makes computers and programming worthwhile. Because one memory location can be used repeatedly with different values, you can write program instructions once and then use them for thousands of separate calculations. *One* set of payroll instructions at your company produces each employee paycheck, and *one* set of instructions at your electric company produces each household's bill.

In most programming languages, before you can use any variable, you must include a declaration for it. A **declaration** is a statement that provides these things for a variable:

- A data type
- An identifier
- Optionally, an initial value

Understanding a Variable's Data Type

Every programming language requires that you specify the correct type for each variable, and that you use each type appropriately.

- A **numeric variable** is one that can hold digits and have mathematical operations performed on it. In the statement `myAnswer = myNumber * 2`, both `myAnswer` and `myNumber` are numeric variables; that is, their intended contents are numeric values, such as 6 and 3, 14.8 and 7.4, or 58 and 29. This course will use `num` as the name of the data type that can hold a numeric value.
- A **string variable** can hold text, such as letters of the alphabet, and other special characters, such as punctuation marks. If a working program contains the statement `lastName = "Lincoln"`, then `lastName` is a string variable. Programmers frequently use strings to hold digits when they will never be used in arithmetic statements—for example, an account number or a zip code. This course will use `string` as the name of the data type that can hold text.

Type-safety is the feature of some programming languages that prevents assigning values of an incorrect data type. In those languages, you can assign a data item to a variable only if the data item is the correct type. (Such languages are called *strongly typed*.) If you declare `taxRate` as a numeric variable and `inventoryItem` as a string, then the following statements are valid:

```
taxRate = 2.5
inventoryItem = "monitor"
```

The following are invalid because the type of data being assigned does not match the variable type:

```
taxRate = "2.5"
inventoryItem = 2.5
taxRate = inventoryItem
inventoryItem = taxRate
```

Don't Do It
If `taxRate` is numeric and `inventoryItem` is a string, then these assignments are invalid.

Understanding a Variable's Identifier

An **identifier** is a program component's name; it is chosen by the programmer. The number-doubling example in Figure 2-1 requires two variable identifiers: `myNumber` and `myAnswer`. Alternatively, these variables could be named `userEntry` and `programSolution`, or `inputValue` and `twiceTheValue`. As a programmer, you choose reasonable and descriptive names for your variables. The language translator (interpreter or compiler) then associates the names you choose with specific memory addresses.

Every computer programming language has its own set of rules for creating identifiers. Most languages allow letters and digits within identifiers. Some languages allow hyphens in variable names, such as `hourly-wage`, and some allow underscores, as in `hourly_wage`. Some languages allow dollar signs or other special characters in variable names (for example, `hourly$`); others allow foreign-alphabet characters, such as π or Ω. Each programming language has a few (perhaps 100 to 200) reserved **keywords** that are not allowed as variable names because they are part of the language's syntax. For example, the data type names in a language, such as `num` and `string`, would not be allowed as variable names. When you learn a programming language, you will learn its list of keywords.

Different languages put different limits on the length of variable names, although in general, the length of identifiers in newer languages is virtually unlimited. In the oldest computer languages, all variable names were written using all uppercase letters because the keypunch machines used at that time created only uppercase letters. In most modern languages, identifiers are case sensitive, so `HoUrLyWaGe`, `hourlywage`, and `hourlyWage` are three separate variable names. Programmers use multiple conventions for naming variables, often depending on the programming language or standards adopted by their employers. **Table 2-1** describes commonly used variable naming conventions. Adopting a naming convention for variables and using it consistently will help make your programs easier to read and understand.

Table 2-1 Variable naming conventions

Convention for naming variables	Examples	Languages in which commonly used
Camel casing is the convention in which the variable starts with a lowercase letter and any subsequent word begins with an uppercase letter. It is sometimes called **lower camel casing** to emphasize the difference from Pascal casing.	`hourlyWage` `lastName`	Java, C#
Pascal casing is a convention in which the first letter of a variable name is uppercase. It is sometimes called **upper camel casing** to distinguish it from lower camel casing.	`HourlyWage` `LastName`	Visual Basic
Hungarian notation is a form of camel casing in which a variable's data type is part of the identifier.	`numHourlyWage` `stringLastName`	C for Windows API programming
Snake casing is a convention in which parts of a variable name are separated by underscores.	`hourly_wage` `last_name`	C, C++, Python, Ruby
Mixed case with underscores is a variable naming convention similar to snake casing, but new words start with an uppercase letter.	`Hourly_Wage` `Last_Name`	Ada
Kebob case is sometimes used as the name for the style that uses dashes to separate parts of a variable name. The name derives from the fact that the words look like pieces of food on a skewer.	`hourly-wage` `last-name`	Lisp (with lowercase letters), COBOL (with uppercase letters)

Even though every language has its own rules for naming variables, you should not concern yourself with the specific syntax of any particular computer language when designing the logic of a program. The logic, after all, works with any language. The variable names used throughout this course follow only three rules:

1. *Variable names must be one word.* The name can contain letters, digits, hyphens, or underscores. No language allows embedded spaces in variable names, and most do not allow punctuation such as periods, commas, or colons. This course uses only alphabetic letters, digits, and underscores in variable names. Therefore, `r` is a legal variable name, as are `rate` and `interestRate`. The variable name `interest rate` is not allowed because of the space.

> **Note** When you write a program using an editor that is packaged with a compiler in an IDE, the compiler may display variable names in a different color from other program components. This visual aid helps your variable names stand out from words that are part of the programming language.

2. *Variable names must start with a letter.* Some programming languages allow variable names to start with a nonalphabetic character such as an underscore. Almost all programming languages prohibit variable names that start with a digit. This course follows the most common convention of starting variable names with a letter.
3. *Variable names should have some appropriate meaning.* This is not a formal rule of any programming language. When computing an interest rate in a program, the computer does not care if you call the variable `g`, `u84`, or `fred`. As long as the correct numeric result is placed in the variable, its actual name doesn't matter. However, it's much easier to follow the logic of a statement like `interestEarned = initialInvestment * interestRate` than a statement like `f = i * r` or `someBanana = j89 * myDogSpot`. When a program requires changes, which could be months or years after you write the original version, you and your fellow programmers will appreciate clear, descriptive variable names in place of cryptic identifiers. Later in this chapter, you will learn more about selecting good identifiers.

The flowchart and pseudocode in **Figure 2-2** each declare two variables; both variables have the data type `num`. Notice that the flowchart in Figure 2-2 follows the rules for naming variables: Both variable names, `myNumber` and `myAnswer`, are single words without embedded spaces, and they have appropriate meanings. Some programmers name variables after friends or create puns with them, but computer professionals consider such behavior unprofessional and amateurish.

Figure 2-2 Flowchart and pseudocode of number-doubling program with variable declarations

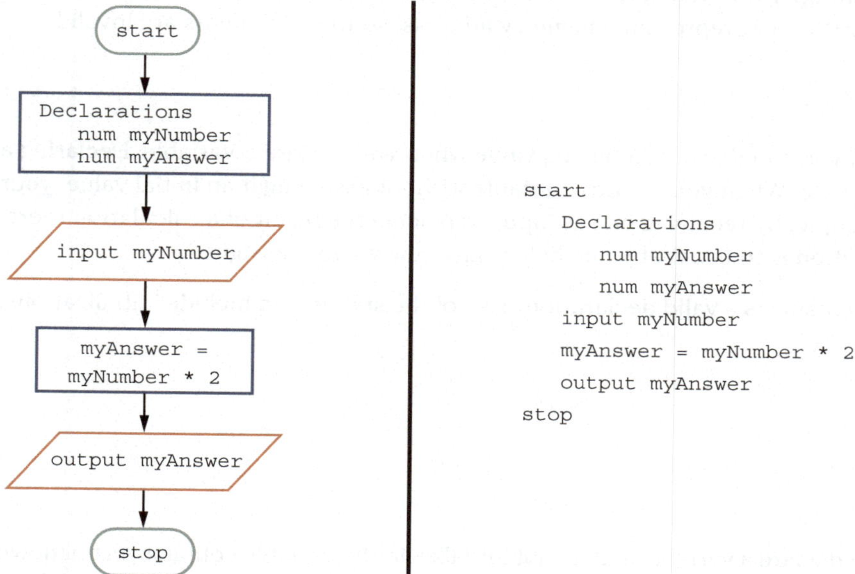
start
Declarations
num myNumber
num myAnswer
input myNumber
myAnswer =
myNumber * 2
output myAnswer
stop

```
start
   Declarations
      num myNumber
      num myAnswer
   input myNumber
   myAnswer = myNumber * 2
   output myAnswer
stop
```

Assigning Values to Variables

When you create a flowchart or pseudocode for a program that doubles numbers, you can include a statement such as the following:

```
myAnswer = myNumber * 2
```

Such a statement is an **assignment statement**. It contains an **assignment operator (=)**. This statement incorporates two actions. First, the computer calculates the arithmetic value of `myNumber * 2`. Second, the computed value is stored in the `myAnswer` memory location.

The assignment operator is an example of a **binary operator**, meaning it requires two operands—one on each side. (An **operand** is simply a value used by an operator.) The assignment operator always operates from right to left, which means that it has **right-associativity** or **right-to-left associativity**. This means that the value of the expression to the right of the assignment operator is evaluated first, and then the result is assigned to the operand on the left. The operand to the right of an assignment operator must be a value—for example, a named or unnamed constant or an arithmetic expression. The operand to the left of an assignment operator must be a name that represents a memory address—the name of the location where the result will be stored. The assignment operator is used with both numeric and string data.

For example, if you have declared two numeric variables named `someNumber` and `someOtherNumber`, then each of the following is a valid assignment statement:

```
someNumber = 2
someNumber = 3 + 7
someOtherNumber = someNumber
someOtherNumber = someNumber * 5
```

In each case, the expression to the right of the assignment operator is evaluated and stored at the location referenced on the left side. The result to the left of an assignment operator is called an **lvalue**. The *l* is for left. Lvalues are always memory address identifiers.

The following statements, however, are *not* valid:

```
2 + 4 = someNumber
someOtherNumber * 10 = someNumber
someNumber + someOtherNumber = 10
```

Don't Do It
The operand to the left of an assignment operator must represent a memory address.

The operand to the left of an assignment operator must represent a memory address. In each of these cases, the value to the left of the assignment operator does not represent a memory address, so the statements are invalid.

Initializing a Variable

Besides using a data type and an identifier, you can declare a starting value when you declare a variable. Declaring a starting value is known as **initializing a variable**. When you create a variable without assigning it an initial value, your intention is to assign a value later—for example, by receiving one as input or placing the result of a calculation there. When you assign an initial value, your intention is to use that value before any new value is assigned.

For example, each of the following statements is a valid declaration. Two of the statements include initializations, and two do not:

```
num myPayRate
num yourPayRate = 24.55
string myName
string yourName = "Juanita"
```

In many programming languages, if you declare a variable and do not initialize it, the variable contains an unknown value until it is assigned a value. A variable's unknown value commonly is called **garbage**. Although some languages use a default value for some variables (such as assigning 0 to any unassigned numeric variable), this course will assume that an unassigned variable holds garbage. In many languages it is illegal to use a garbage-holding variable in an arithmetic or output statement. Even if you work with a language that allows you to display garbage, it serves no purpose to do so and constitutes a logical error.

Where to Declare Variables

Variables must be declared before they are used for the first time in a program. Some languages require all variables to be declared at the beginning of the program, others allow variables to be declared at the beginning of each module, and others allow variables to be declared anywhere at all as long as they are declared before their first use. As in Figure 2-2, this course will follow the convention of declaring all variables together.

Declaring Named Constants

Besides variables, most programming languages allow you to create named constants. A **named constant** is similar to a variable, except it can be assigned a value only once. You use a named constant when you want to assign a useful name for a value that will never be changed during a program's execution. Using named constants makes your programs easier to understand by eliminating magic numbers. A **magic number** is an unnamed constant, like 0.06, whose purpose is not immediately apparent.

For example, if a program uses a sales tax rate of 6 percent, you might want to declare a named constant as follows:

```
num SALES_TAX_RATE = 0.06
```

After `SALES_TAX_RATE` is declared, the following statements have identical meaning:

```
taxAmount = price * 0.06
taxAmount = price * SALES_TAX_RATE
```

The way in which named constants are declared differs among programming languages. This course follows the convention of using all uppercase letters in constant identifiers and using underscores to separate words for readability. Using these conventions makes named constants easier to recognize. In many languages, a constant must be assigned its value when it is declared, but in some languages, a constant can be assigned its value later. In both cases, however, a constant's value cannot be changed after the first assignment. This course follows the convention of initializing all constants when they are declared.

When you declare a named constant, program maintenance becomes easier. For example, if the value of the sales tax rate changes from 0.06 to 0.07 in the future, and you have declared a named constant `SALES_TAX_RATE`, you only need to change the value assigned to the named constant at the beginning of the program, then retranslate the program into machine language, and all references to `SALES_TAX_RATE` are automatically updated. If you used the unnamed literal 0.06 instead, you would have to search for every instance of the value and replace it with the new one. Additionally, if the literal 0.06 was used in other calculations within the program (for example, as a discount rate or price), you would have to carefully select which instances of the value to alter, and you would be likely to make a mistake.

Note Sometimes, using unnamed literal constants is appropriate in a program, especially if their meaning is clear to most readers. For example, in a program that calculates half of a value by dividing by two, you might choose to use the unnamed literal 2 instead of incurring the extra time and memory costs of creating a named constant `HALF` and assigning 2 to it. Extra costs that result from adding variables or instructions to a program are known as **overhead**.

Two Truths & a Lie | Declaring and Using Variables and Constants

1. A variable's data type describes the kind of values the variable can hold and the types of operations that can be performed with it.
2. If `name` is a string variable, then the assignment statement `name = "Ed"` is valid.
3. The operand to the right of an assignment operator must be a name that represents a memory address.

The false statement is #3. The operand to the left of an assignment operator must be a name that represents a memory address—the name of the location where the result will be stored. The value to the right of an assignment operator might be a constant, arithmetic expression, or other value.

2.2 Performing Arithmetic Operations

Most programming languages use the following standard arithmetic operators:

+ (plus sign)—addition
- (minus sign)—subtraction
* (asterisk)—multiplication
/ (slash)—division

Many languages also support additional operators that calculate the remainder after division, raise a number to a power, manipulate individual bits stored within a value, and perform other operations.

Like the assignment operator, each of the standard arithmetic operators is a binary operator; that is, each requires an expression on both sides. For example, the following statement adds two test scores and assigns the sum to a variable named `totalScore`:

```
totalScore = test1 + test2
```

The following adds 10 to `totalScore` and stores the result in `totalScore`:

```
totalScore = totalScore + 10
```

In other words, this example increases the value of `totalScore`. This last example looks odd in algebra because it might appear that the programmer is indicating that the value of `totalScore` and `totalScore` plus 10 are equivalent. You must remember that the equal sign is the assignment operator, and that the statement is actually taking the original value of `totalScore`, adding 10 to it, and assigning the result to the memory address on the left of the operator, which is `totalScore`. In other words, the operation changes the value in `totalScore`.

In programming languages, you can combine arithmetic statements. When you do, every operator follows **rules of precedence** (also called the **order of operations**) that dictate the order in which operations in the same statement are carried out. The rules of precedence for the basic arithmetic statements are as follows:

- Expressions within parentheses are evaluated first. If there are multiple sets of parentheses, the expression within the innermost parentheses is evaluated first.
- Multiplication and division are evaluated next, from left to right.
- Addition and subtraction are evaluated next, from left to right.

The assignment operator has a very low precedence. Therefore, in a statement such as `d = e * f + g`, the operations on the right of the assignment operator (in this case, multiplication and addition) are always performed before the final assignment to the variable on the left.

> **Note** When you learn a specific programming language, you will learn about all the operators that are used in that language. Reference documentation for various programming languages often contains tables that specify the relative precedence of every operator used in the language.

For example, consider the following two arithmetic statements:

```
firstAnswer = 2 + 3 * 4
secondAnswer = (2 + 3) * 4
```

After these statements execute, the value of `firstAnswer` is 14. According to the rules of precedence, multiplication is carried out before addition, so:

- 3 is multiplied by 4, giving 12.
- Then 2 and 12 are added, and 14 is assigned to `firstAnswer`.

The value of `secondAnswer`, however, is 20, because the parentheses force the contained addition operation to be performed first, as follows:

- 2 and 3 are added, producing 5.
- Then 5 is multiplied by 4, and 20 is assigned to `secondAnswer`.

Forgetting about the rules of arithmetic precedence, or forgetting to add parentheses when you need them, can cause logical errors that are difficult to find in programs. For example, the following statement might appear to average two test scores:

```
average = score1 + score2 / 2
```

However, it does not. Because division has a higher precedence than addition, the preceding statement takes half of `score2`, adds it to `score1`, and stores the result in `average`. The correct statement is:

```
average = (score1 + score2) / 2
```

You are free to add parentheses even when you don't need them to force a different order of operations; sometimes you use them just to make your intentions clearer. For example, the following statements operate identically:

```
totalPriceWithTax = price + price * TAX_RATE
totalPriceWithTax = price + (price * TAX_RATE)
```

In both cases, `price` is multiplied by `TAX_RATE` first, then it is added to `price`, and finally the result is stored in `totalPriceWithTax`. Because multiplication occurs before addition on the right side of the assignment operator, both statements are the same. However, if you feel that the statement with the parentheses makes your intentions clearer to someone reading your program, then you should use them.

All the arithmetic operators have **left-to-right associativity**. This means that operations with the same precedence take place from left to right. Consider the following statement:

```
answer = a + b + c * d / e - f
```

Multiplication and division have higher precedence than addition or subtraction, so the multiplication and division are carried out from left to right as follows: `c` is multiplied by `d`, and the result is divided by `e`, giving a new result. Therefore, the statement becomes:

```
answer = a + b + (temporary result just calculated) - f
```

Then, addition and subtraction are carried out from left to right as follows: a and b are added, the temporary result is added, and then f is subtracted. The final result is then assigned to answer.

Another way to say this is that the following two statements are equivalent:

```
answer = a + b + c * d / e - f
answer = a + b + ((c * d) / e) - f
```

Table 2-2 summarizes the precedence and associativity of the five most frequently used operators.

Table 2-2 Precedence and associativity of five common operators

Operator symbol	Operator name	Precedence (compared to other operators in this table)	Associativity
=	Assignment	Lowest	Right-to-left
+	Addition	Medium	Left-to-right
–	Subtraction	Medium	Left-to-right
*	Multiplication	Highest	Left-to-right
/	Division	Highest	Left-to-right

Mixing Data Types

As mentioned earlier in this chapter, many modern programming languages allow programmers to make fine distinctions between numeric data types. In particular, many languages treat integer numeric values (whole numbers) and floating-point numeric values (numbers with decimal places) differently. In these languages, you can always assign an integer, such as 3, to a floating-point variable or named constant, and it will be converted to 3.0. However, you cannot assign a floating-point value (such as 3.0) directly to an integer variable, because the decimal position values will be lost, even when they are 0.

When you work with a language that makes distinctions between integer and floating-point values, you can combine the different types in arithmetic expressions. When you do, addition, subtraction, and multiplication work as expected. For example, the result of 2.3 + 5 is 7.3, and the result of 4.2 * 2 is 8.4. When you mix types, division works as expected as well. For example, the result of 9.3 / 3 is 3.1.

However, in many languages, dividing an integer by another integer is a special case. In languages such as Java, C++, and C#, dividing two integers results in an integer, and any fractional part of the result is lost. For example, in these languages, the result of 7 / 2 is 3, not 3.5 as you might expect. Programmers say that the decimal portion of the result is cut off, or *truncated*.

Note When programming in a language that truncates the results of integer division, you must be particularly careful with numbers lower than 1. For example, if you write a program that halves a recipe, you might use an expression such as `1 / 2 * cupsSugar`. No matter what the value of `cupsSugar` is, the result will always be 0 because 1 is divided by 2 first and 2 goes into 1 zero whole times, so the expression results in 0 multiplied by `cupsSugar`.

Many programming languages also support a **remainder operator**, which is sometimes called the *modulo operator* or the *modulus operator*. When used with two integer operands, the remainder operator is the value that remains after division. For example, 24 Mod 10 is 4 because when 24 is divided by 10, 4 is the remainder. In Visual Basic, the remainder operator is the keyword Mod. In Java, C++, and C#, the operator is the percent sign (%).

The remainder operator can be useful in a variety of situations. For example, you can determine whether a number is even or odd by finding the remainder when the number is divided by 2. Any number that has a remainder of 0 when divided by 2 is even, and any number with a remainder of 1 is odd.

Because the remainder operator differs among programming languages, and because the operation itself is handled differently when used with negative operands, the remainder operator will not be used in the rest of this language-independent course. Similarly, this course uses one data type, `num`, for all numeric values, and it is assumed that both integer and floating-point values can be stored in `num` variables and named constants.

Two Truths & a Lie | Performing Arithmetic Operations

1. Parentheses have higher precedence than any of the common arithmetic operators.
2. Operations in arithmetic statements occur from left to right in the order in which they appear.
3. The following adds 5 to a variable named `points`: `points = points + 5`

The false statement is #2. Operations of equal precedence in an arithmetic statement are carried out from left to right, but operations within parentheses are carried out first, multiplication and division are carried out next, and addition and subtraction take place last.

2.3 Understanding the Advantages of Modularization

Programmers seldom write programs as one long series of steps. Instead, they break down their programming problems into smaller units and tackle one cohesive task at a time. Each of these smaller units is a **module**. Programmers also refer to a module as a **subroutine**, **procedure**, **function**, or **method**; the name usually reflects the programming language being used. For example, Visual Basic programmers use *procedure* (or *subprocedure*). C and C++ programmers call their modules *functions*, whereas C#, Java, and other object-oriented language programmers are more likely to use *method*. Programmers in COBOL, RPG, and BASIC (all older languages) are most likely to use *subroutine*.

A program or module executes another module by calling it. To **call a module** is to use its name to invoke the module, causing it to execute. When the module's tasks are complete, control returns to the spot from which the module was called. When you access a module, the action is similar to pausing a video. You abandon your primary action (watching a video), take care of some other task (for example, making a sandwich), and then return to the main task exactly where you left off.

The process of breaking down a large program into modules is **modularization**; computer scientists also call it **functional decomposition**. You are never required to modularize a large program to make it run on a computer, but there are at least three reasons for doing so:

- Modularization provides abstraction.
- Modularization helps multiple programmers to work on a problem.
- Modularization allows you to reuse work more easily.

Modularization Provides Abstraction

One reason that modularized programs are easier to understand is that they enable a programmer to see the "big picture." **Abstraction** is the process of paying attention to important properties while ignoring nonessential details. Abstraction is selective ignorance. Life would be tedious without abstraction. For example, you can create a list of things to accomplish today:

```
Do laundry
Call Aunt Nan
Start term paper
```

Without abstraction, the list of chores would begin:

```
Pick up laundry basket
Put laundry basket in car
Drive to Laundromat
Get out of car with basket
Walk into Laundromat
Set basket down
Find quarters for washing machine
… and so on.
```

You might list a dozen more steps before you finish the laundry and move on to the second chore on your original list. If you had to consider every small, low-level detail of every task in your day, you probably would never make it out of bed in the morning. Using a higher-level, more abstract list makes your day manageable. Abstraction makes complex tasks look simple.

Note Abstract artists create paintings in which they see only the big picture—color and form—and ignore the details. Abstraction has a similar meaning among programmers.

Likewise, some level of abstraction occurs in every computer program. Sixty years ago, a programmer had to understand the low-level circuitry instructions the computer used. But now, newer high-level programming languages allow you to use English-like vocabulary in which one broad statement corresponds to dozens of machine instructions. No matter which high-level programming language you use, if you display a message on the monitor, you are never required to understand how a monitor works to create each pixel on the screen. You write an instruction like `output message` and the details of the hardware operations are handled for you by the operating system.

Modules provide another way to achieve abstraction. For example, a payroll program can call a module named `computeFederalWithholdingTax()`. When you call this module from your program, you use one statement; the module itself might contain dozens of statements. You can write the mathematical details of the module later, someone else can write them, or you can purchase them from an outside source. When you plan your main payroll program, your only concern is that a federal withholding tax will have to be calculated; you save the details for later.

Modularization Helps Multiple Programmers to Work on a Problem

When you divide any large task into modules, you gain the ability to more easily divide the task among various people. Rarely does a single programmer write a commercial program that you buy. Consider any word-processing, spreadsheet, or database program you have used. Each program has so many options and responds to user selections in so many possible ways, that it would take years for a single programmer to write all the instructions. Professional software developers can write new programs in weeks or months, instead of years, by dividing large programs into modules and assigning each module to an individual programmer or team.

Modularization Allows You to Reuse Work

If a module is useful and well written, you may want to use it more than once within a program or in other programs. For example, a routine that verifies the validity of dates is useful in many programs written for a business. (For example, a month value is valid if it is not lower than 1 or higher than 12, a day value is valid if it is not lower than 1 or higher than 31 if the month is 1, and so on.) If a computerized personnel file contains each employee's birth date, hire date, last promotion date, and termination date, the date-validation module can be used four times with each employee record. Other programs in an organization also can use the module; these programs might ship customer orders, plan employees' birthday parties, or calculate when loan payments should be made. If you write the date-checking instructions so they are entangled with other statements in a program, they are difficult to isolate and reuse. On the other hand, if you place the instructions in a separate module, the unit is easy to use and portable to other applications. The feature of modular programs that allows individual modules to be used in a variety of applications is **reusability**.

You can find many real-world examples of reusability. When you build a house, you don't invent plumbing and heating systems; you incorporate systems with proven designs. This certainly reduces the time and effort it takes to build a house. The systems you choose are in service in other houses, so they have been tested under a variety of circumstances, increasing their reliability. **Reliability** is the feature of programs that assures you a module has been proven to function correctly. Reliable software saves time and money. If you create the functional components of your programs as stand-alone modules and test them in your current programs, much of the work already will be done when you use the modules in future applications.

Two Truths & a Lie | Understanding the Advantages of Modularization

1. Modularization eliminates abstraction, a feature that makes programs more confusing.
2. Modularization makes it easier for multiple programmers to work on a problem.
3. Modularization allows you to reuse work more easily.

The false statement is #1. Modularization enables abstraction, which allows you to see the big picture.

2.4 Modularizing a Program

Most programs consist of a **main program**, which contains the basic steps, or the **mainline logic**, of the program. The main program then accesses modules that provide more refined details. When you create a module, you include the following:

- A header—The **module header** includes the module identifier and possibly other necessary identifying information.
- A body—The **module body** contains all the statements in the module. (When developing a program, programmers sometimes include a module with an *empty body* that contains no statements, but that is just temporary for testing purposes.)
- A `return` statement—The **module `return` statement** marks the end of the module and identifies the point at which control returns to the program or module that called the module. In most programming languages, if you do not include a `return` statement at the end of a module, the logic will still return. However, this course follows the convention of explicitly including a `return` statement with every module.

Naming a module is similar to naming a variable. The rules and conventions for naming modules are slightly different in every programming language, but in this text, module names follow the same general rules used for variable identifiers:

- Module names must start with a letter and cannot contain spaces.
- Module names should have meaning.

> **Note** Although it is not a requirement of any programming language, it frequently makes sense to use a verb as all or part of a module's name, because modules perform some action. Typical module names begin with action words such as `get`, `calculate`, and `display`. When you program in visual languages that use screen components such as buttons and text boxes, the module names frequently contain verbs representing user actions, such as `click` or `drag`.

Additionally, in this text, module names are followed by a set of parentheses. This will help you distinguish module names from variable names. This style corresponds to the way modules are named in many programming languages, such as Java, C++, and C#.

> **Note** As you learn more about modules in specific programming languages, you will find that you sometimes place variable names within the parentheses that follow module names. Any variables enclosed in the parentheses contain information you want to send to the module. For now, the parentheses at the end of module names will be empty in this course.

When a main program wants to use a module, it calls the module, or invokes it. A module can call another module, and the called module can call another. The number of chained calls is limited only by the amount of memory available on your computer. In this course, the flowchart symbol used to call a module is a rectangle with a bar across the top. You place the name of the module you are calling inside the rectangle.

> **Note** Some programmers use a rectangle with stripes down each side to represent a module in a flowchart, and this course uses that convention if a module is external to a program. For example, prewritten, built-in modules that generate random numbers, compute standard trigonometric functions, and sort values often are external to your programs. However, if the module is being created as part of the program, this course uses a rectangle with a single stripe across the top.

In a flowchart, you draw each module separately with its own sentinel symbols. The beginning sentinel contains the name of the module. This name must be identical to the name used in the calling program or module. The ending sentinel contains `return`, which indicates that when the module ends, the logical progression of statements will exit the module and return to the calling program or module. Similarly, in pseudocode, you start each module with its name and end with a `return` statement; the module name and `return` statements are vertically aligned and all the module statements are indented between them. **Encapsulation** is the technique of grouping program elements within a module.

For example, consider the program in **Figure 2-3**, which does not contain any modules. It accepts a customer's name and balance due as input and produces a bill. At the top of the bill, the company's name and address are displayed on three lines, which are followed by the customer's name and balance due. To display the company name and address, you can simply include three `output` statements in the mainline logic of a program, as shown in Figure 2-3, or you can modularize the program by creating both the mainline logic and a `displayAddressInfo()` module, as shown in **Figure 2-4**.

Figure 2-3 Program that produces a bill using only main program

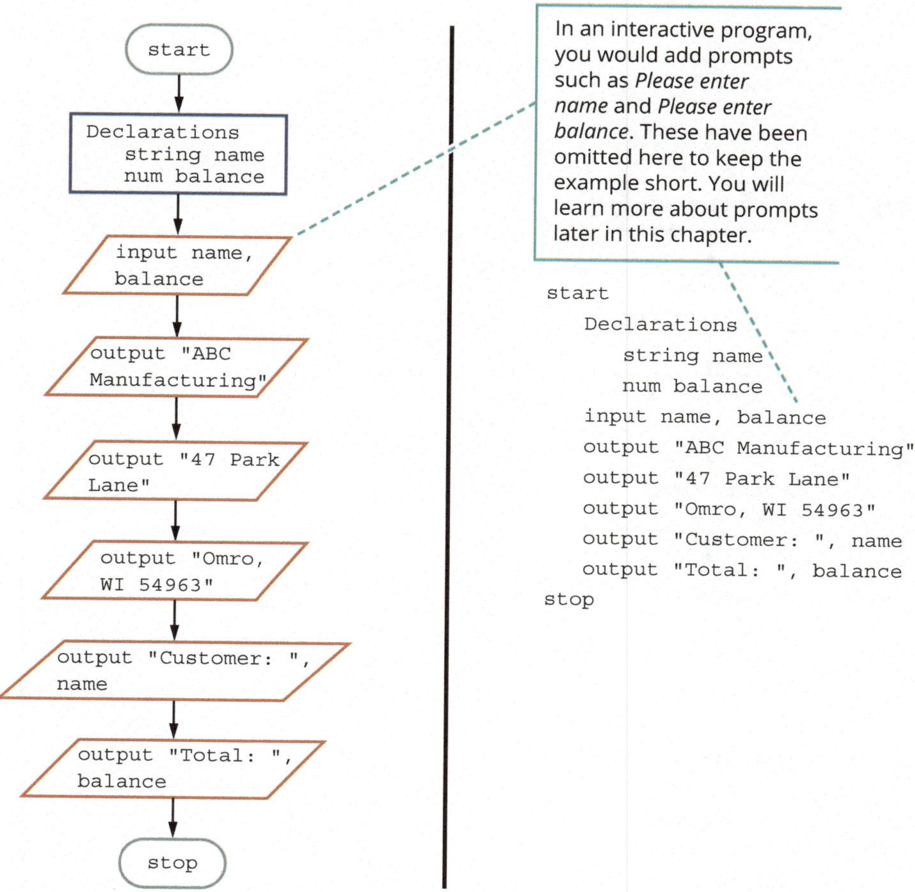
start
Declarations
string name
num balance
input name, balance
output "ABC Manufacturing"
output "47 Park Lane"
output "Omro, WI 54963"
output "Customer: ", name
output "Total: ", balance
stop
In an interactive program, you would add prompts such as *Please enter name* and *Please enter balance*. These have been omitted here to keep the example short. You will learn more about prompts later in this chapter.

```
start
   Declarations
      string name
      num balance
   input name, balance
   output "ABC Manufacturing"
   output "47 Park Lane"
   output "Omro, WI 54963"
   output "Customer: ", name
   output "Total: ", balance
stop
```

When the `displayAddressInfo()` module is called in Figure 2-4, logic transfers from the main program to the `displayAddressInfo()` module, as shown by the large red arrow in both the flowchart and the pseudocode. There, each module statement executes in turn before logical control is transferred back to the main program, where it continues with the statement that follows the module call, as shown by the large blue arrow.

Neither of the programs in Figures 2-3 and 2-4 is superior to the other in terms of functionality; both perform exactly the same tasks in the same order. However, you may prefer the modularized version of the program for at least two reasons:

- First, the main program remains short and easy to follow because it contains just one statement to call the module, rather than three separate `output` statements to perform the work of the module.
- Second, a module is easy to reuse. After you create the address information module, you can use it in any application that needs the company's name and address. In other words, you do the work once, and then you can use the module many times.

Note A drawback to creating modules and moving between them is the overhead incurred. The computer keeps track of the correct memory address to which it should return after executing a module by recording the memory address in a location known as the **stack**. This process requires a small amount of computer time and resources. In most cases, the advantage to creating modules far outweighs the small amount of overhead required.

Figure 2-4 Program that produces a bill using main program that calls `displayAddressInfo()` module

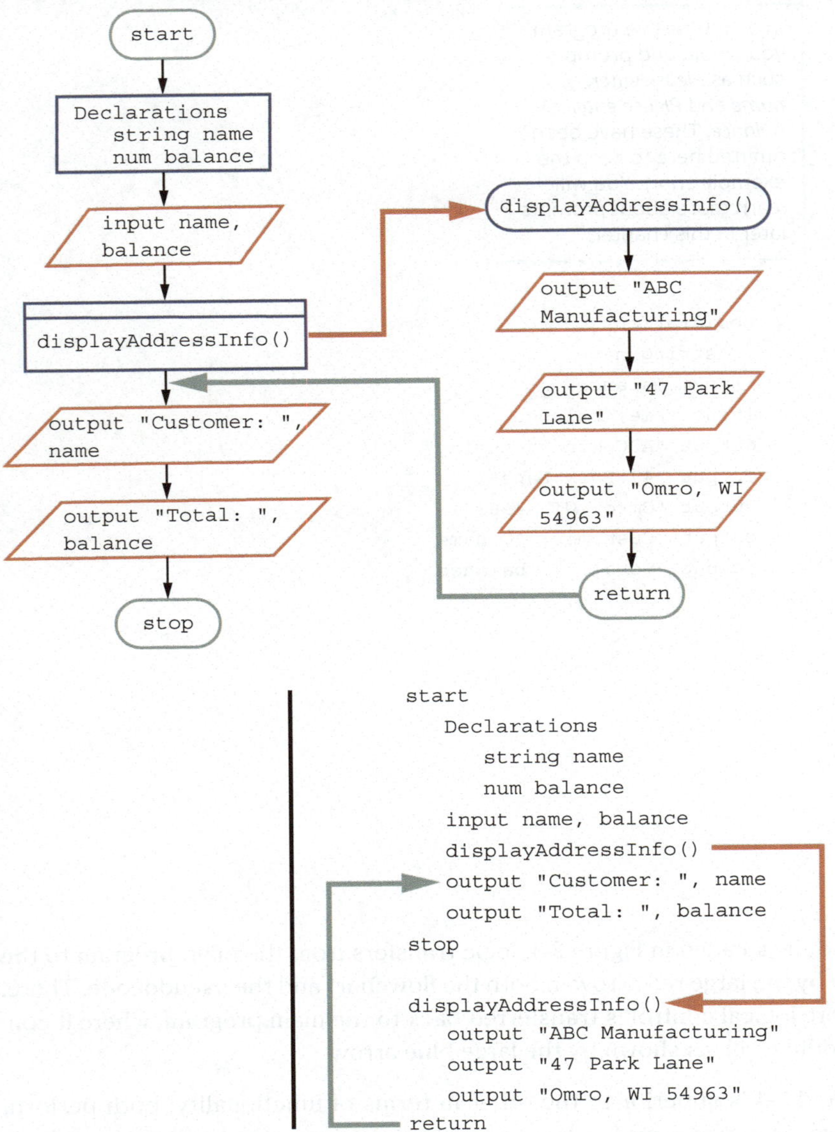
start
Declarations
string name
num balance
input name, balance
displayAddressInfo()
output "Customer: ", name
output "Total: ", balance
stop
displayAddressInfo()
output "ABC Manufacturing"
output "47 Park Lane"
output "Omro, WI 54963"
return
start
Declarations
string name
num balance
input name, balance
displayAddressInfo()
output "Customer: ", name
output "Total: ", balance
stop
displayAddressInfo()
output "ABC Manufacturing"
output "47 Park Lane"
output "Omro, WI 54963"
return

Determining when to modularize a program does not depend on a fixed set of rules; it requires experience and insight. Programmers do follow some guidelines when deciding how far to break down modules or how much to put in each of them. Some companies may have arbitrary rules, such as "a module's instructions should never take more than a page," or "a module should never have more than 30 statements," or "never have a module with only one statement." Rather than use such arbitrary rules, a better policy is to place together statements that contribute to one specific task. The more the statements contribute to the same job, the greater the **functional cohesion** of the module. A module that checks the validity of a date's value, or one that displays warranty information for a product, is considered cohesive. A module that checks date validity, deducts insurance premiums, and computes federal withholding tax for an employee would be less cohesive.

Declaring Variables and Constants within Modules

You can place any statements within modules, including input, processing, and output statements. You also can include variable and constant declarations within modules. For example, you might decide to modify the billing program in Figure 2-4 so it looks like the one in **Figure 2-5**. In this version of the program, three named constants that hold the three lines of company data are declared within the `displayAddressInfo()` module.

Figure 2-5 The billing program with constants declared within the module

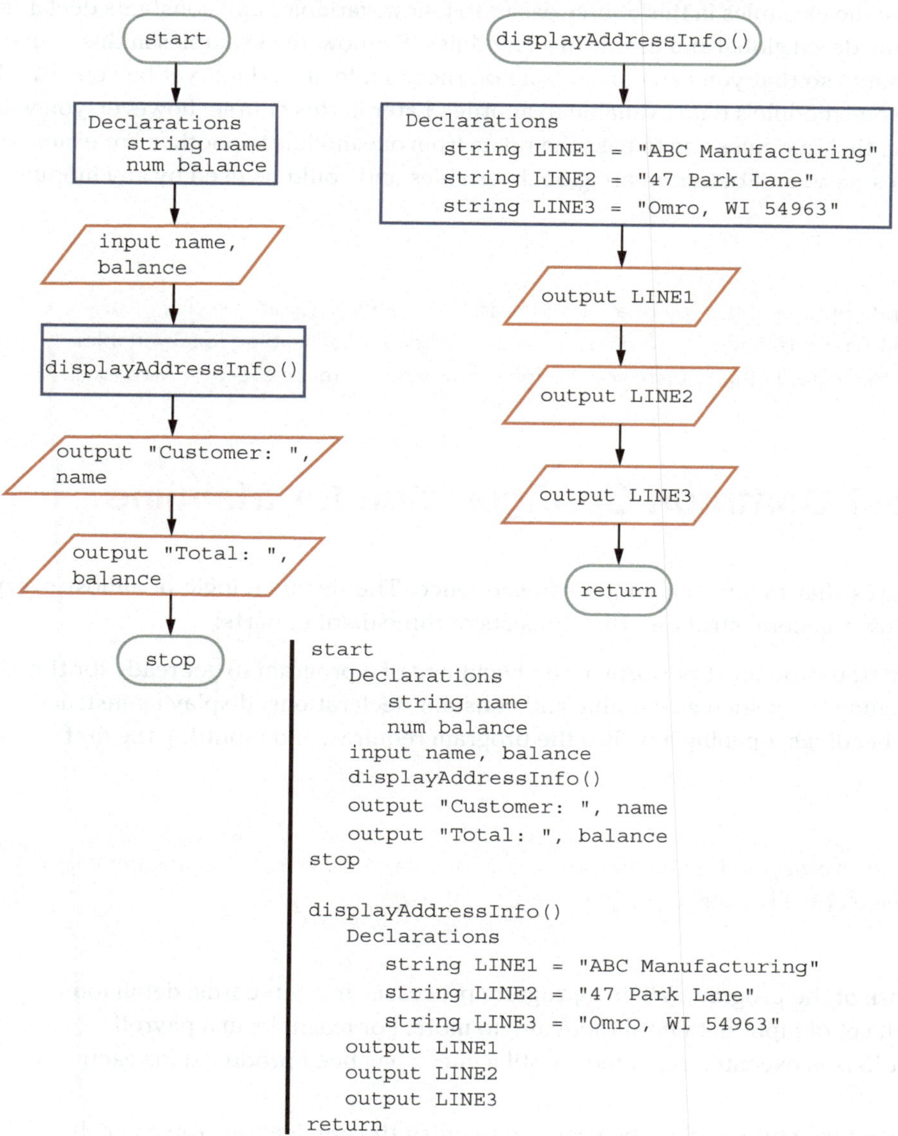
start
Declarations
string name
num balance
input name, balance
displayAddressInfo()
output "Customer: ", name
output "Total: ", balance
stop
displayAddressInfo()
Declarations
string LINE1 = "ABC Manufacturing"
string LINE2 = "47 Park Lane"
string LINE3 = "Omro, WI 54963"
output LINE1
output LINE2
output LINE3
return
start
Declarations
string name
num balance
input name, balance
displayAddressInfo()
output "Customer: ", name
output "Total: ", balance
stop
displayAddressInfo()
Declarations
string LINE1 = "ABC Manufacturing"
string LINE2 = "47 Park Lane"
string LINE3 = "Omro, WI 54963"
output LINE1
output LINE2
output LINE3
return

Variables and constants are usable only in the module in which they are declared. Programmers say the data items are **visible** or **in scope** only within the module in which they are declared. That means the program only recognizes them there. Programmers also say that variables and constants are **local** to the module in which they are declared. In other words, when the strings `LINE1`, `LINE2`, and `LINE3` are declared in the `displayAddressInfo()` module in Figure 2-5, they are not recognized and cannot be used by the main module.

One of the motivations for creating modules is that separate modules are easily reusable in multiple programs. If the `displayAddressInfo()` module will be used by several programs within the organization, it makes sense that the definitions for its variables and constants must come with it. This makes the modules more **portable**; that is, they are self-contained units that are transported easily.

Besides local variables and constants, you can create global variables and constants. **Global** variables and constants are known to the entire program; they are said to be declared at the *program level*. That means they are visible to and usable in all the modules called by the program. The opposite is not true—variables and constants declared within a module are not usable elsewhere; they are visible only to that module.

In many modern programming languages, the main program itself is a module, so variables and constants declared there cannot be used elsewhere. To make the examples in this course easier to follow, variables and constants declared at the start of a main program will be considered global and usable in all modules. For now, the examples in this course will use only global variables and constants so that you can concentrate on the main logic and not yet be concerned with the techniques necessary to make one module's data available to another. Later in this course, however, you will learn how to make most variables local to their modules and to pass their data from one module to another. For example, in Figure 2-5, the main program variables `name` and `balance` are global variables and could be used by any module.

Note | Many programmers do not approve of using global variables and constants. They are used here so you can more easily understand modularization before you learn the techniques of sending local variables from one module to another. Later in this course, you will learn how you can make every variable local.

Understanding the Most Common Configuration for Mainline Logic

Procedural programs contain procedures that follow one another in sequence. The mainline logic of almost every procedural computer program can follow a general structure that consists of three distinct parts:

1. **Housekeeping tasks** include any steps you must perform at the beginning of a program to get ready for the rest of the program. They can include tasks such as variable and constant declarations, displaying instructions to users, displaying report headings, opening any files the program requires, and inputting the first piece of data.

Note | Inputting the first data item is always part of the housekeeping module. You will learn the theory behind this practice when you learn about structured programming.

2. **Detail loop tasks** do the core work of the program. When a program processes many records, detail loop tasks execute repeatedly for each set of input data until there are no more. For example, in a payroll program, the same set of calculations is executed repeatedly until a check has been produced for each employee.
3. **End-of-job tasks** are the steps you take at the end of the program to finish the application. You can call these *finish-up tasks* or *clean-up tasks*. They might include displaying totals or other final messages and closing any open files.

Figure 2-6 shows the relationship of these three typical program parts. Notice how the `housekeeping()` and `endOfJob()` tasks are executed just once, but the `detailLoop()` tasks repeat as long as the `eof` condition has not been met. The flowchart uses a flowline to show how the `detailLoop()` module repeats; the pseudocode uses the words `while` and `endwhile` to contain statements that execute in a loop. You will learn more about the `while` and `endwhile` terms in subsequent chapters; for now, understand that they are a way of expressing repeated actions.

Note | Notice the loop-ending question in Figure 2-6 is `not eof?` rather than just `eof?` Asking the question in the negative makes the language of describing the logic more natural. A program would say, "While it is not the end of file, continue to execute the `detailLoop()` module."

Figure 2-6 Flowchart and pseudocode of mainline logic for a typical procedural program

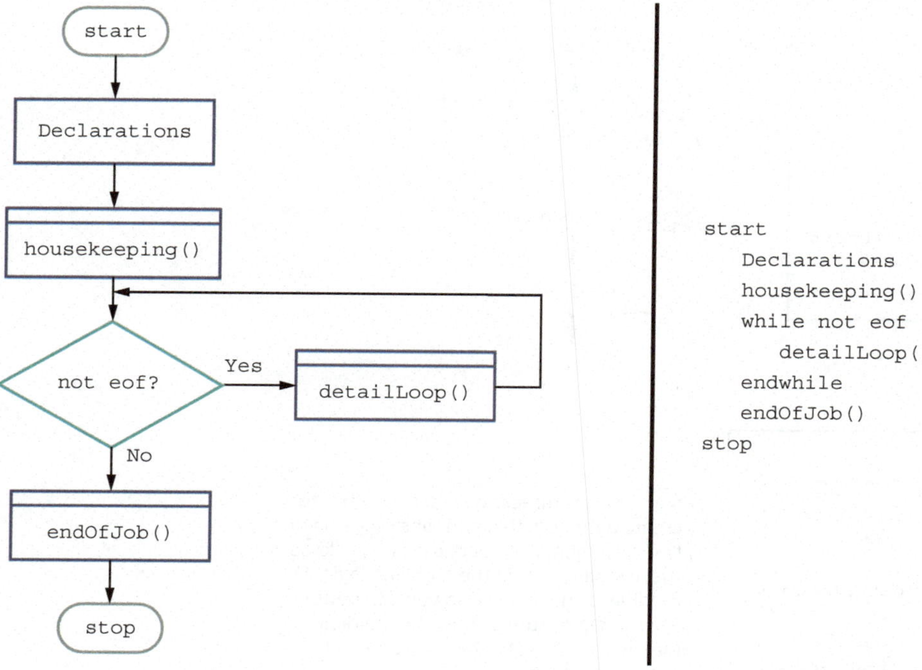


```
start
    Declarations
    housekeeping()
    while not eof
        detailLoop()
    endwhile
    endOfJob()
stop
```

Many everyday tasks follow the three-module format just described. For example, a candy factory opens in the morning, and the machines are started and filled with ingredients. These housekeeping tasks occur just once at the start of the day. Then, repeatedly during the day, candy is manufactured. This process might take many steps, each of which occurs many times. These are the steps in the detail loop. Then, at the end of the day, the machines are cleaned and shut down. These are the end-of-job tasks.

Not all programs take the format of the logic shown in Figure 2-6, but many do. Keep this general configuration in mind as you think about how you might organize many programs. For example, **Figure 2-7** shows a sample payroll report for a small company. A user enters employee names until there are no more to enter, at which point the user enters *XXX*. As long as the entered name is not *XXX*, the user enters the employee's weekly gross pay. Deductions are computed as a flat 25 percent of the gross pay, and the statistics for each employee are output. The user enters another name, and as long as it is not *XXX*, the process continues. Examine the logic in **Figure 2-8** to identify the components in the housekeeping, detail loop, and end-of-job tasks. A typical payroll program might contain many more calculations, but for now, concentrate on the big picture of how a typical application works.

Figure 2-7 Sample payroll report

Payroll Report

Name	Gross	Deductions	Net
Ali	1000.00	250.00	750.00
Brown	1400.00	350.00	1050.00
Carter	1275.00	318.75	956.25
Young	1100.00	275.00	825.00

***End of report

Figure 2-8 Logic for payroll report

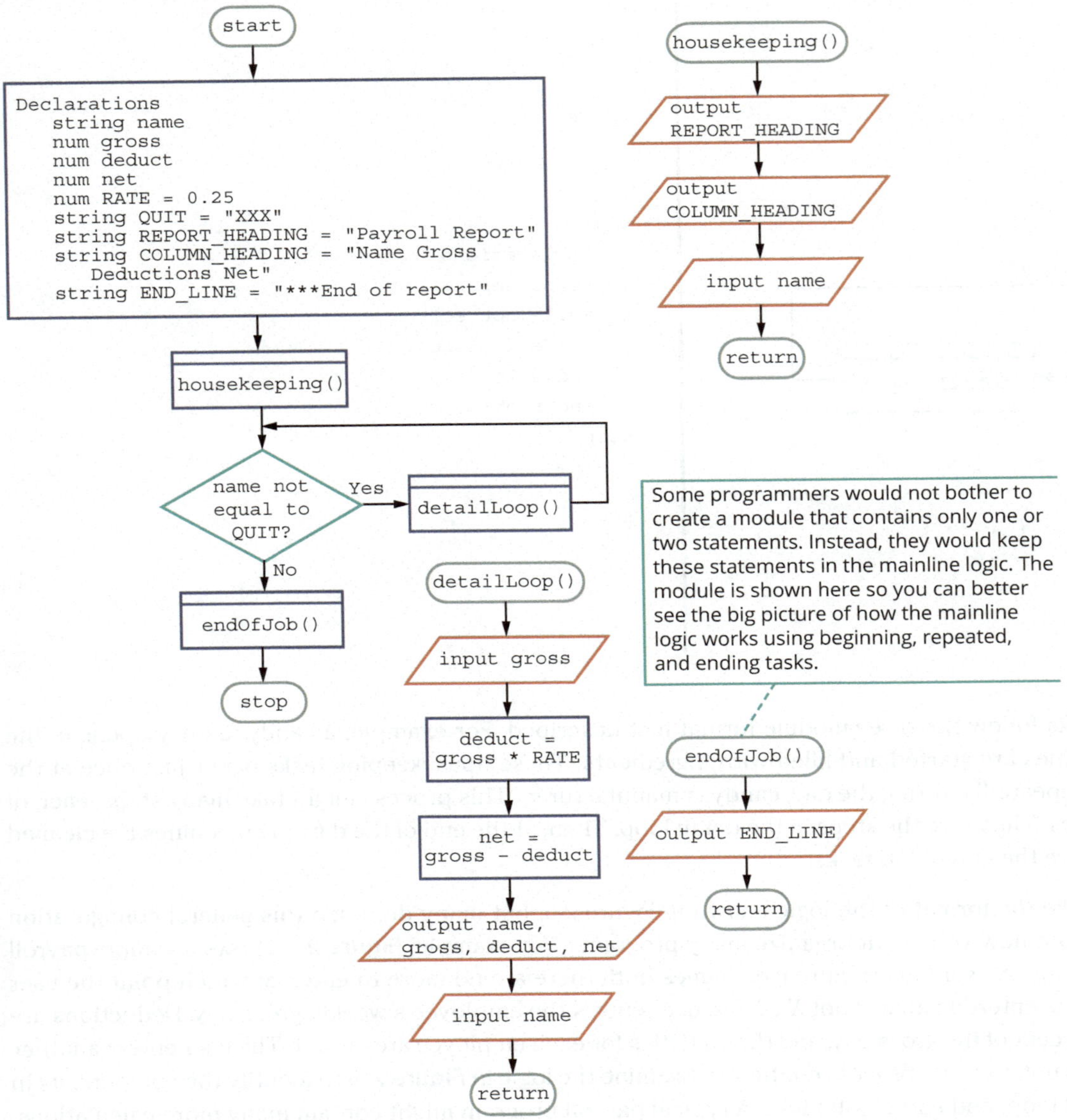

start
Declarations
string name
num gross
num deduct
num net
num RATE = 0.25
string QUIT = "XXX"
string REPORT_HEADING = "Payroll Report"
string COLUMN_HEADING = "Name Gross Deductions Net"
string END_LINE = "***End of report"
housekeeping()
name not equal to QUIT?
Yes
No
detailLoop()
endOfJob()
stop
housekeeping()
output REPORT_HEADING
output COLUMN_HEADING
input name
return
Some programmers would not bother to create a module that contains only one or two statements. Instead, they would keep these statements in the mainline logic. The module is shown here so you can better see the big picture of how the mainline logic works using beginning, repeated, and ending tasks.
detailLoop()
input gross
deduct = gross * RATE
net = gross - deduct
output name, gross, deduct, net
input name
return
endOfJob()
output END_LINE
return

Creating Hierarchy Charts

You may have seen organizational hierarchy charts, such as the one in **Figure 2-9**. The chart shows who reports to whom in a company, not when or how often they report or the details of what their reports contain.

Figure 2-9 An organizational hierarchy chart

CEO
VP of Marketing
VP of Information
Eastern Sales Manager
Western Sales Manager
Operations Manager
Programming Manager
Sales Rep
Sales Rep
Sales Rep
Sales Rep
Sales Rep
Evening Operator
Programmer
Programmer

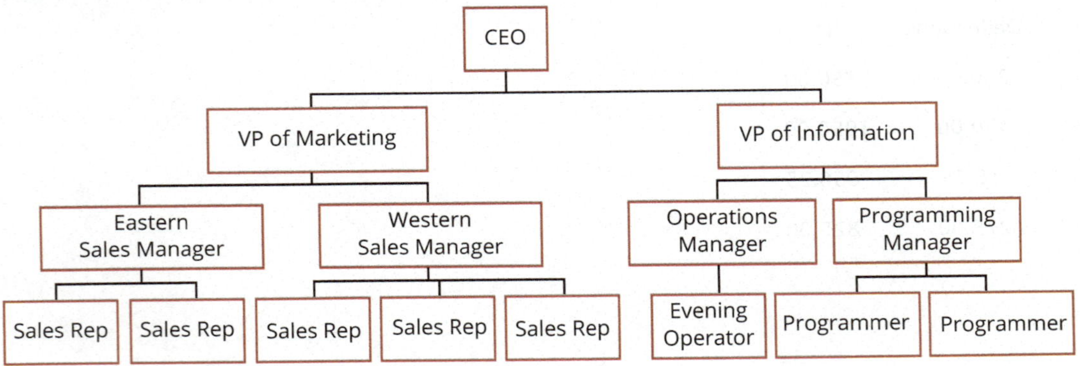

When a program has several modules calling other modules, programmers often use a program hierarchy chart (sometimes called a *structure chart*) that operates in a similar manner to show the overall picture of how modules are related to one another. A hierarchy chart does not tell you what tasks are to be performed *within* a module, *when* the modules are called, *how* a module executes, or *why* they are called—that information is in the flowchart or pseudocode. A hierarchy chart tells you only *which* modules exist within a program and *which* modules call others. The hierarchy chart for the payroll program in Figure 2-8 looks like **Figure 2-10**. It shows that the main module calls three others—`housekeeping()`, `detailLoop()`, and `endOfJob()`.

Figure 2-10 Hierarchy chart of payroll program in Figure 2-8

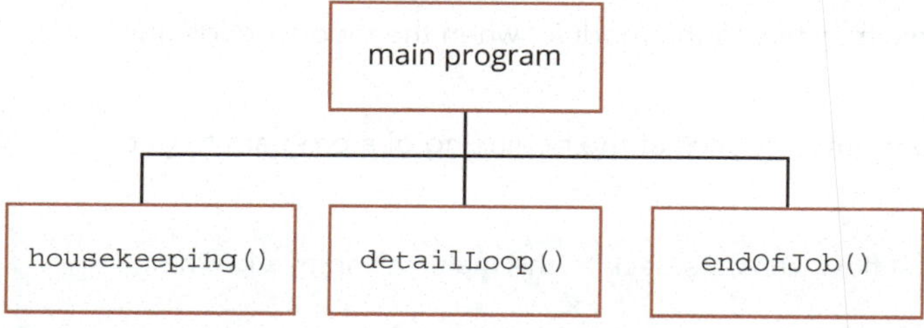

Figure 2-11 shows an example of a hierarchy chart for the billing program of a mail-order company. The hierarchy chart is for a more complicated program, but like the payroll report chart in Figure 2-10, it supplies module names and a general overview of the tasks to be performed, without specifying any details.

Figure 2-11 Billing program hierarchy chart

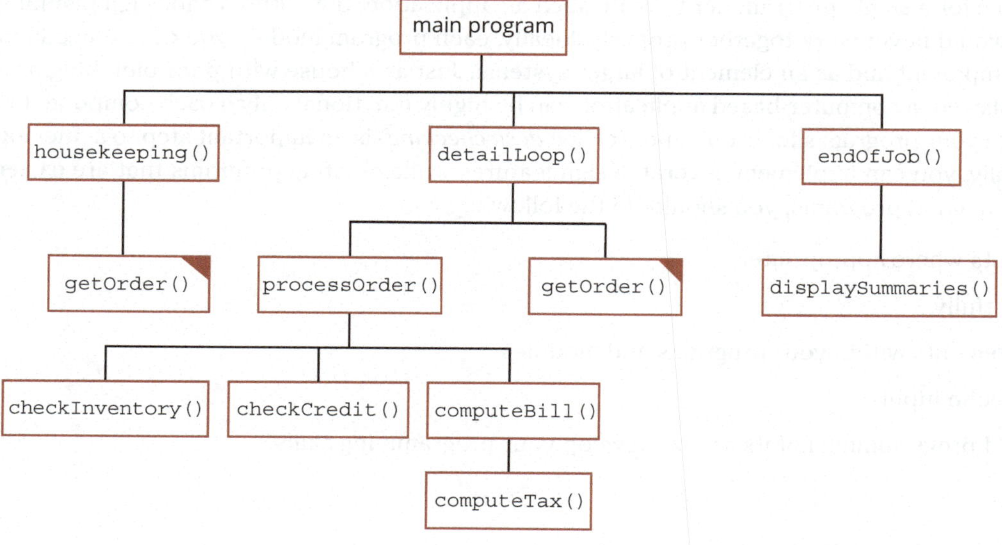

Because program modules are reusable, a specific module can be called from several locations within a program. For example, in the billing program hierarchy chart in Figure 2-11, you can see that the `getOrder()` module is used twice. By convention, you blacken a corner of each box that represents a module used more than once. This action alerts readers that any change to this module could have consequences in multiple locations.

A hierarchy chart can be both a planning tool for developing the overall relationship of program modules before you write them and a documentation tool to help others see how modules are related after a program is written. For example, if a tax law changes, a programmer might be asked to rewrite the `computeTax()` module in the billing program diagrammed in Figure 2-11. As the programmer changes the `computeTax()` module, the hierarchy chart shows other dependent modules that might be affected. A hierarchy chart is useful for getting the big picture in a complex program.

Note Hierarchy charts are used in procedural programming, but other types of diagrams frequently are used in object-oriented environments. For example, the Unified Modeling Language (UML) uses a set of diagrams to describe a system.

Two Truths & a Lie | Modularizing a Program

1. A calling program calls a module's name when it wants to use the module.
2. Whenever a main program calls a module, the logic transfers to the module; when the module ends, the program ends.
3. Housekeeping tasks include any steps you must perform just once at the beginning of a program to get ready for the rest of the program.

The false statement is #2. When a module ends, the logical flow transfers back to the main calling module and resumes where it left off.

2.5 Features of Good Program Design

As your programs become larger and more complicated, the need for good planning and design increases. Think of an application you use, such as a word processor or a spreadsheet. The number and variety of user options are staggering. Not only would it be impossible for a single programmer to write such an application, but without thorough planning and design, the components would never work together properly. Ideally, each program module you design needs to work well as a stand-alone component and as an element of larger systems. Just as a house with poor plumbing or a car with bad brakes is fatally flawed, a computer-based application can be highly functional only if each component is designed well. Walking through your program's logic on paper (called *desk-checking*) is an important step to achieving superior programs. Additionally, you can implement several design features while creating programs that are easier to write and maintain. To create good programs, you should do the following:

- Provide program comments where appropriate.
- Choose identifiers thoughtfully.
- Strive to design clear statements within your programs and modules.
- Write clear prompts and echo input.
- Continue to maintain good programming habits as you develop your programming skills.

Using Program Comments

When you write programs, you often might want to insert program comments. **Program comments** are written explanations that are not part of the program logic but that serve as documentation for readers of the program. In other words, they are nonexecuting statements that help readers understand programming statements. Readers might include users who help you test the program and other programmers who might have to modify your programs in the future. Even you, as the program's author, will appreciate comments when you make future modifications and forget why you constructed a statement in a certain way.

The syntax used to create program comments differs among programming languages. This course starts comments in pseudocode with two forward slashes. For example, **Figure 2-12** contains comments that explain the origins and purposes of variables in a real estate program.

Note Program comments are a type of **internal documentation**. This term distinguishes them from supporting documents outside the program, which are called **external documentation**.

Figure 2-12 Pseudocode that declares variables and includes comments

```
Declarations
   num sqFeet
      // sqFeet is an estimate provided by the seller of the property
   num pricePerFoot
      // pricePerFoot is determined by current market conditions
   num lotPremium
      // lotPremium depends on amenities such as whether lot is waterfront
```

In a flowchart, you can use an annotation symbol to hold information that expands on what is stored within another flowchart symbol. An **annotation symbol** is most often represented by a three-sided box that is connected to the step it references by a dashed line. Annotation symbols are used to hold comments or sometimes statements that are too long to fit neatly into a flowchart symbol. For example, **Figure 2-13** shows how a programmer might use some annotation symbols in a flowchart for a payroll program.

Figure 2-13 Flowchart that includes annotation symbols

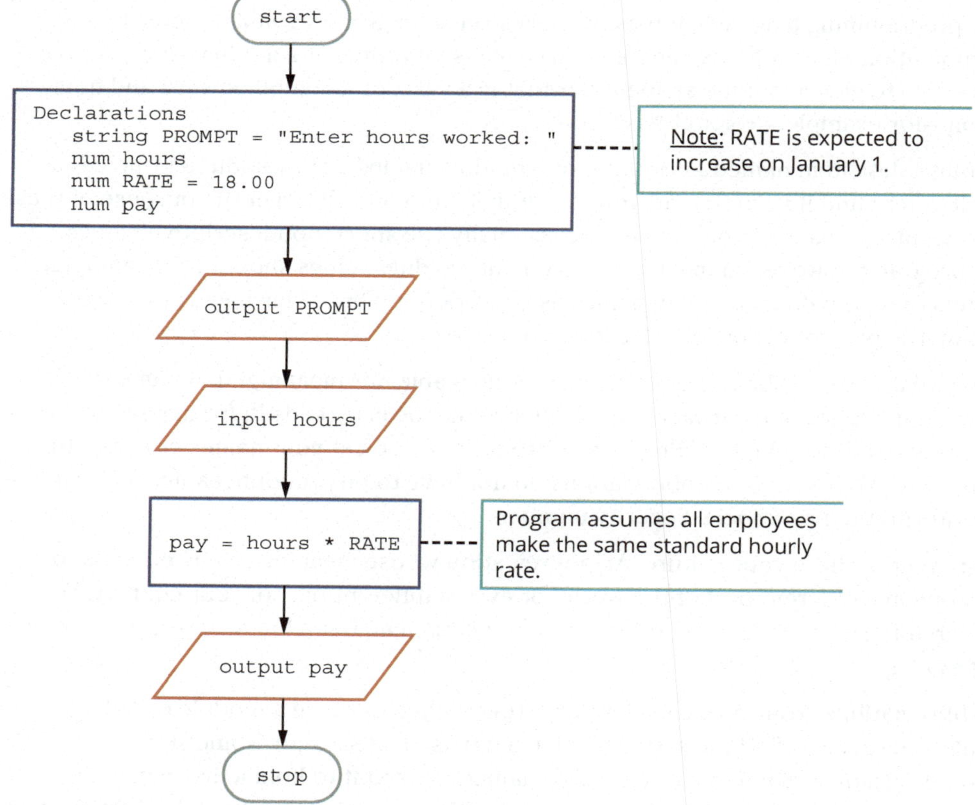

Note You probably will use comments in your coded programs more frequently than you use them in pseudocode or flowcharts. For one thing, flowcharts and pseudocode are more English-like than the code in some languages, so your statements might be less cryptic. Also, your comments will remain in the program as part of the program documentation, but your planning tools are likely to be discarded when the program goes into production.

Including program comments is not necessary to create a working program, but comments can help you to remember the purpose of variables or to explain complicated calculations, especially when you come back to a program months or years after writing it. Some students do not like to include comments in their programs because it takes time to type them and they aren't part of the "real" program, but the programs you write in the future probably will require some comments. When you acquire your first programming job and modify a program written by another programmer, you will appreciate well-placed comments that explain complicated sections of the code.

> **Note** | An additional responsibility regarding comments is that they must be kept current as a program is modified. Outdated comments can provide misleading information about a program's status.

Choosing Identifiers

The selection of good identifiers is an often-overlooked element in program design. When you write programs, you choose identifiers for variables, constants, and modules. You learned the rules for naming variables and modules earlier in this chapter: Each must be a single word with no embedded spaces and must start with a letter. Those simple rules provide a lot of leeway in naming program elements, but not all identifiers are equally good. Choosing good identifiers simplifies your programming job and makes it easier for others to understand your work. Some general guidelines include the following:

- Although not required in any programming language, it usually makes sense to give a variable or constant a name that is a noun (or a combination of an adjective and a noun) because it represents a thing—for example, `payRate`. Similarly, it makes sense to give a module an identifier that is a verb, or a combined verb and noun, because a module takes action—for example, `computePayRate()`.
- Use meaningful names. Creating a data item named `someData` or a module named `firstModule()` makes a program cryptic. Not only will others find it hard to read your programs, but you will forget the purpose of these identifiers even within your own programs. All programmers occasionally use short, nondescriptive names such as `x` or `temp` in a quick program; however, in most cases, data and module names should be meaningful. Programmers refer to programs that contain meaningful names as **self-documenting**. This means that even without further documentation, the program code explains itself to readers.
- Use pronounceable names. A variable name like `pzf` is neither pronounceable nor meaningful. A name that looks meaningful when you write it might not be as meaningful when someone else reads it; for instance, `preparead()` might mean "Prepare ad" to you, but "Prep a read" to others. Look at your names critically to make sure they can be pronounced. Very standard abbreviations do not have to be pronounceable. For example, most businesspeople would interpret *ssn* as a Social Security number.
- Don't forget that not all programmers share your culture. An abbreviation whose meaning seems obvious to you might be cryptic to someone in a different part of the world, or even a different part of your country. For example, you might name a variable `roi` to hold a value for *return on investment*, but a French-speaking person might interpret the meaning as *king*.
- Be judicious in your use of abbreviations. You can save a few keystrokes when creating a module called `getStat()`, but is the module's purpose to find the state in which a city is located, input some statistics, or determine the status of some variables? Similarly, is a variable named `fn` meant to hold a first name, file number, or something else? Abbreviations can also confuse people in different lines of work: AKA might suggest a sorority (Alpha Kappa Alpha) to a college administrator, a registry (American Kennel Association) to a dog breeder, or an alias (*also known as*) to a police detective.

Note To save typing time when you develop a program, you can use a short name like `efn`. After the program operates correctly, you can use a text editor's Search and Replace feature to replace your coded name with a more meaningful name, such as `employeeFirstName`. When working in an integrated development environment, you can use the technique known as *refactoring* to rename every instance of an identifier.

Note Many IDEs support an automatic statement-completion feature that saves typing time. After the first time you use a name like `employeeFirstName`, you need to type only the first few letters before the compiler editor offers a list of available names from which to choose. The list is constructed from all the names you have used that begin with the same characters.

- Usually, avoid digits in a name. A zero can be confused with the letter *O*, and the lowercase letter *l* is misread as the numeral 1. Of course, use your judgment: The zero in the name `budgetFor2026` probably will not be misinterpreted.
- Use the rules your language allows to separate words in long, multiword variable names. For example, if the programming language you use allows hyphens or underscores, then use a module name like `initialize-data()` or `initialize_data()`, which is easier to read than `initializedata()`. Another option is to use camel casing to create an identifier such as `initializeData()`. If you use a language that is case sensitive, it is legal but confusing to use variable names that differ only in case. For example, if a single program contains `empName`, `EmpName`, and `Empname`, confusion is sure to follow.
- Consider including a form of the verb *to be*, such as *is* or *are*, in names for variables that are intended to hold a status. For example, use `isFinished` as a string variable that holds a *Y* or *N* to indicate whether a file is exhausted. The shorter name `finished` is more likely to be confused with a module that executes when a program is done. (Many languages support a Boolean data type, which you assign to variables meant to hold only true or false. Using a form of *to be* in identifiers for Boolean variables is appropriate.)
- Many programmers follow the convention of naming constants using all uppercase letters, inserting underscores between words for readability. In this chapter you saw examples such as `SALES_TAX_RATE`.
- Organizations sometimes enforce different rules for programmers to follow when naming program components. It is your responsibility to find out the conventions used in your organization and to adhere to them.

Note Programmers sometimes create a **data dictionary**, which is a list of every variable name used in a program, along with its type, size, and description. When a data dictionary is created, it becomes part of the program documentation.

When you begin to write programs, the process of determining what variables, constants, and modules you need and what to name them all might seem overwhelming. The design process, however, is crucial. When you acquire your first professional programming assignment, the design process might very well be completed already. Most likely, your first assignment will be to write or modify one small member module of a much larger application. The more the original programmers adhered to naming guidelines, the better the original design was, and the easier your job of modification will be.

Designing Clear Statements

In addition to using program comments and selecting good identifiers, you can use the following tactics to contribute to the clarity of the statements within your programs:

- Avoid confusing line breaks.
- Use temporary variables to clarify long statements.

Avoiding Confusing Line Breaks

Some older programming languages require that program statements be placed in specific columns. Most modern programming languages are free-form; you can arrange your lines of code any way you see fit. As in real life, with freedom comes responsibility; when you have flexibility in arranging your lines of code, you must take care to make sure your meaning is clear. With free-form code, programmers are allowed to place two or three statements on a line, or, conversely, to spread a single statement across multiple lines. Both make programs harder to read. All the pseudocode examples in this course use appropriate, clear spacing and line breaks.

Using Temporary Variables to Clarify Long Statements

When you need several mathematical operations to determine a result, consider using a series of temporary variables to hold intermediate results. A **temporary variable** (or **work variable**) is not used for input or output, but instead is just a working variable that you use during a program's execution. For example, **Figure 2-14** shows two ways to calculate a value for a real estate `salespersonCommission` variable. Each example achieves the same result—the salesperson's commission is based on the square feet multiplied by the price per square foot, plus any premium for a lot with special features, such as a wooded or waterfront lot. However, the second example uses two temporary variables: `basePropertyPrice` and `totalSalePrice`. When the computation is broken down into less complicated, individual steps, it is easier to see how the total price is calculated. In calculations with even more computation steps, performing the arithmetic in stages would become increasingly helpful.

Figure 2-14 Two ways of achieving the same `salespersonCommission` result

```
//Using a single statement to compute commission
salespersonCommission = (sqFeet * pricePerFoot + lotPremium) * commissionRate

// Using multiple statements to compute commission
basePropertyPrice = sqFeet * pricePerFoot
totalSalePrice = basePropertyPrice + lotPremium
salespersonCommission = totalSalePrice * commissionRate
```

> **Note** Programmers might say using temporary variables, like the second example in Figure 2-14, is *cheap*. When executing a lengthy arithmetic statement, even if you don't explicitly name temporary variables, the programming language compiler creates them behind the scenes (although without descriptive names), so declaring them yourself does not cost much in terms of program execution time.

Writing Clear Prompts and Echoing Input

When program input should be retrieved from a user, you almost always want to provide a prompt for the user. A **prompt** is a message that is displayed on a screen to ask the user for a response and perhaps explain how that response should be formatted. Prompts are used both in command-line and GUI interactive programs.

For example, suppose a program asks a user to enter a catalog number for an item the user is ordering. The following prompt is not very helpful:

```
Please enter a number.
```

The following prompt is more helpful:

```
Please enter a five-digit catalog item number.
```

The following prompt is even more helpful:

```
The five-digit catalog item number appears to the right of the item's picture in
the catalog. Please enter it now without any embedded spaces.
```

When program input comes from a stored file instead of a user, prompts are not needed. When a program expects a user response, however, prompts are valuable. For example, **Figure 2-15** shows the flowchart and pseudocode for the beginning of the bill-producing program shown earlier in this chapter. If the input was coming from a data file, no prompt would be required, and the logic might look like the logic in Figure 2-15.

Figure 2-15 Beginning of a program that accepts a name and a balance as input

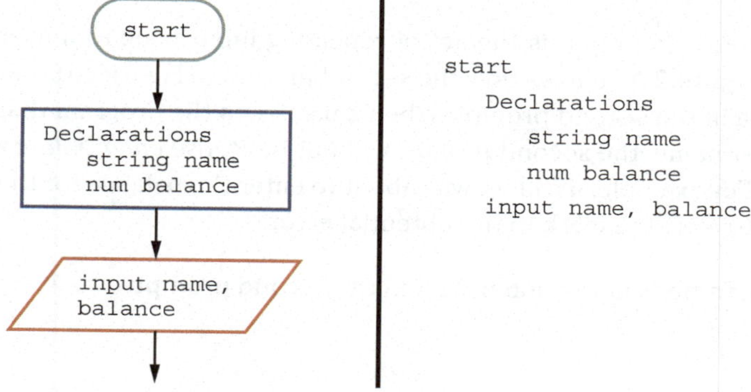
start
Declarations
string name
num balance
input name,
balance

```
start
   Declarations
      string name
      num balance
   input name, balance
```

However, if the input was coming from a user, including prompts would be helpful. You could supply a single prompt, such as *Please enter a customer's name and balance due*, but inserting more requests into a prompt generally makes it less likely that the user can remember to enter all the parts or enter them in the correct order. It is almost always best to include a separate prompt for each item to be entered. **Figure 2-16** shows an example.

Figure 2-16 Beginning of a program that accepts a name and a balance as input and uses a separate prompt for each item

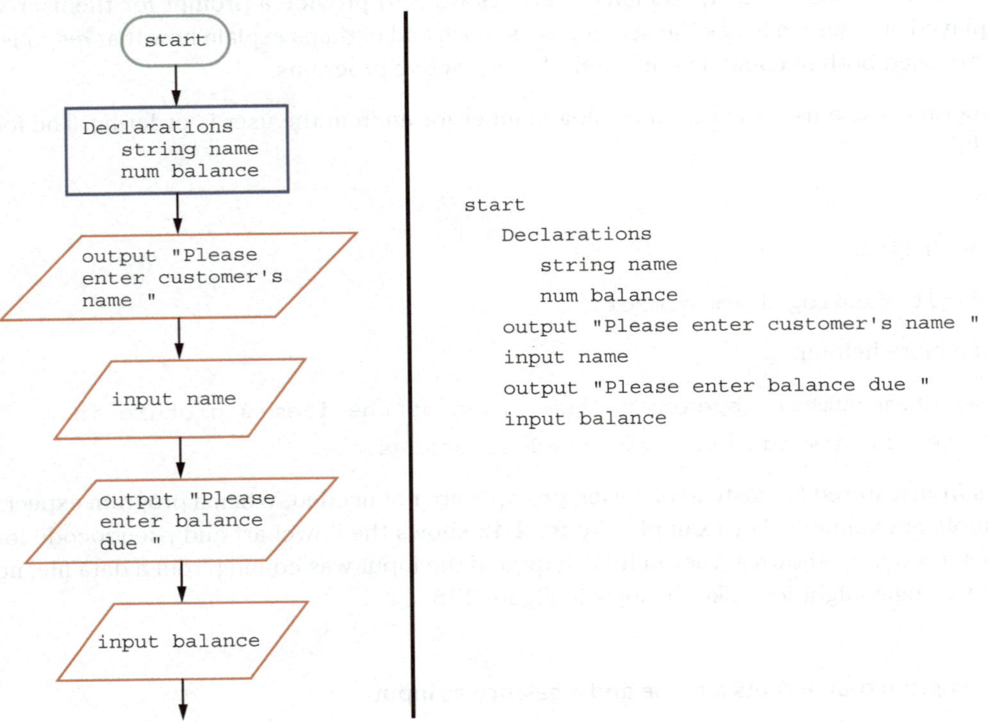


```
start
   Declarations
      string name
      num balance
   output "Please enter customer's name "
   input name
   output "Please enter balance due "
   input balance
```

Users also find it helpful when you echo their input. **Echoing input** is the act of repeating input back to a user either in a subsequent prompt or in output. For example, **Figure 2-17** shows how the second prompt in Figure 2-16 can be improved by echoing the user's first piece of input data in the second prompt. When a user runs the program that is started in Figure 2-17 and enters *Garcia* for the customer name, the second prompt will not be *Please enter balance due*. Instead, it will be *Please enter balance due for Garcia*. For example, if a clerk was about to enter the balance for the wrong customer, the mention of *Garcia* might be enough to alert the clerk to the potential error.

Figure 2-17 Beginning of a program that accepts a customer's name and uses it in the second prompt

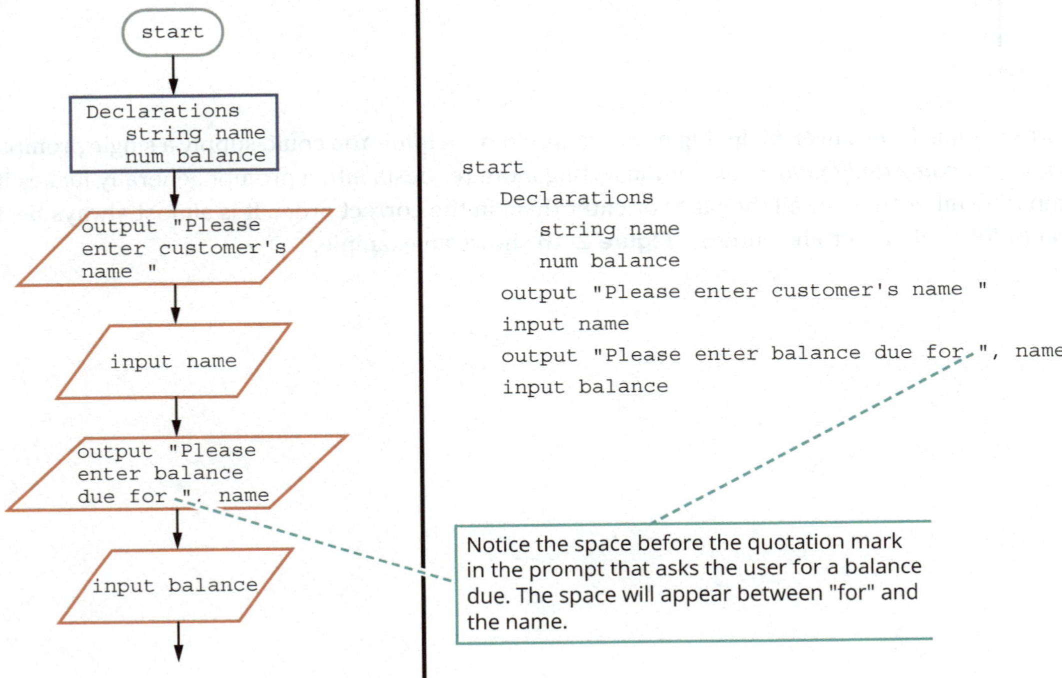


```
start
   Declarations
      string name
      num balance
   output "Please enter customer's name "
   input name
   output "Please enter balance due for ", name
   input balance
```

Maintaining Good Programming Habits

When you learn a programming language and begin to write lines of program code, it is easy to forget the principles you have learned in this text. Having some programming knowledge and a keyboard at your fingertips can lure you into typing lines of code before you think things through. But every program you write will be better if you plan before you code. Maintaining the habits of first drawing flowcharts or writing pseudocode, as you have learned here, will make your future programming projects go more smoothly. If you desk-check your program logic on paper before coding statements in a programming language, your programs will run correctly sooner. If you think carefully about the variable and module names you choose, and design program statements to be easy to read and use, your programs will be easier to develop and maintain.

Two Truths & a Lie | Features of Good Program Design

1. A program comment is a message that is displayed on a screen to ask the user for a response and perhaps explain how that response should be formatted.
2. It usually makes sense to give each variable a name that contains a noun and to give each module a name that contains a verb.
3. Echoing input can help a user to confirm that a data item was entered correctly.

The false statement is #1. A program comment is a written explanation that is not part of the program logic but that serves as documentation for those reading the program. A prompt is a message that is displayed on a screen to ask the user for a response and perhaps explain how that response should be formatted.

Summary

- Programs contain data in three different forms: literals (or unnamed constants), variables, and named constants. Each of these types of data can be numeric or string. Variables are named memory locations, the contents of which can vary. A variable declaration includes a data type and an identifier; optionally, it can include an initialization. Every computer programming language has its own set of rules for naming variables; however, all variable names must be written as one word without embedded spaces and should have appropriate meaning. A named constant is similar to a variable, except it can be assigned a value only once.
- Most programming languages use +, −, *, and / as the four standard arithmetic operators. Every operator follows rules of precedence that dictate the order in which operations in the same statement are carried out; multiplication and division always take precedence over addition and subtraction. The rules of precedence can be overridden using parentheses.
- Programmers break down programming problems into smaller, cohesive units called *modules*, *subroutines*, *procedures*, *functions*, or *methods*. To execute a module, you call it from another program or module. Any program can contain an unlimited number of modules, and each module can be called an unlimited number of times. Modularization provides abstraction, allows multiple programmers to work on a problem, and makes it easier for you to reuse work.
- When you create a module, you include a header, a body, and a `return` statement. A program or module calls a module's name to execute it. You can place any statements within modules, including declarations, which are local to the module. Global variables and constants are those that are known to the entire program. The mainline logic

of almost every procedural computer program can follow a general structure that consists of three distinct parts: housekeeping tasks, detail loop tasks, and end-of-job tasks.

- A hierarchy chart illustrates modules and their relationships; it indicates which modules exist within a program and which modules call others.
- As programs become larger and more complicated, the need for good planning and design increases. You should use program comments where appropriate. Choose identifiers wisely, strive to design clear statements within your programs and modules, write clear prompts and echo input, and continue to maintain good programming habits as you develop your programming skills.

Key Terms

abstraction
alphanumeric values
annotation symbol
assignment operator (=)
assignment statement
binary operator
call a module
camel casing
data dictionary
data type
declaration
detail loop tasks
echoing input
encapsulation
end-of-job tasks
external documentation
floating-point values
function
functional cohesion
functional decomposition
garbage
global
housekeeping tasks
Hungarian notation
identifier
in scope
initializing a variable
integer values
internal documentation
kebob case
keywords
left-to-right associativity
literal numeric constant
literal string constant
local
lower camel casing
lvalue
magic number
main program
mainline logic
method
mixed case with underscores
modularization
module
module body
module header
module `return` statement
named constant
numeric
numeric constant
numeric variable
operand
order of operations
overhead
Pascal casing
portable
procedure
program comments
program hierarchy chart
prompt
real numbers
reliability
remainder operator
reusability
right-associativity
right-to-left associativity
rules of precedence
self-documenting
snake casing
stack
string
string constant
string variable
subroutine
temporary variable
type-safety
unnamed constant
unnamed numeric constant
unnamed string constant
upper camel casing
visible
work variable

Review Questions

1. What does a declaration always provide for a variable? (2.1)
   a. a name
   b. a data type
   c. a name and a data type
   d. a name, a data type, and a value
2. A variable's data type describes all of the following *except* ______________. (2.1)
   a. what values the variable can hold
   b. the scope of the variable
   c. how the variable is stored in memory
   d. what operations can be performed with the variable
3. The value stored in an uninitialized variable is ______________. (2.1)
   a. null
   b. garbage
   c. compost
   d. its identifier
4. The value 3 is a ______________. (2.1)
   a. numeric variable
   b. string variable
   c. numeric constant
   d. string constant
5. The assignment operator ______________. (2.1)
   a. is a binary operator
   b. has left-to-right associativity
   c. is most often represented by a colon
   d. is used with string data but not numeric data
6. Multiplication has a lower precedence than ______________. (2.2)
   a. division
   b. subtraction
   c. assignment
   d. parentheses
7. Which of the following is not a term used as a synonym for *module*? (2.3)
   a. method
   b. object
   c. procedure
   d. subroutine
8. Modularization ______________. (2.3)
   a. eliminates abstraction
   b. reduces overhead
   c. facilitates reusability
   d. increases the need for correct syntax
9. What is the name for the process of paying attention to important properties while ignoring nonessential details? (2.3)
   a. abstraction
   b. extraction
   c. extinction
   d. modularization
10. Every module has all of the following *except* ______________. (2.4)
    a. a header
    b. local variables
    c. a body
    d. a `return` statement
11. Programmers say that one module can ______________ another, meaning that the first module causes the second module to execute. (2.3)
    a. declare
    b. define
    c. enact
    d. call

12. The more that a module's statements contribute to the same job, the greater the ________________ of the module. (2.3)
    - a. functional cohesion
    - b. structure
    - c. modularity
    - d. size
13. In most modern programming languages, a variable or constant that is declared in a module is ________________ in that module. (2.4)
    - a. global
    - b. invisible
    - c. in scope
    - d. undefined
14. Which of the following is *not* a typical housekeeping task? (2.4)
    - a. displaying instructions
    - b. printing summaries
    - c. opening files
    - d. displaying report headings
15. Which module in a typical program will execute the most times? (2.4)
    - a. the housekeeping module
    - b. the detail loop
    - c. the end-of-job module
    - d. It is different in every program.
16. A hierarchy chart tells you ________________. (2.4)
    - a. which modules call other modules
    - b. what tasks are to be performed within each program module
    - c. when a module executes
    - d. the number of statements in a program
17. What are nonexecuting statements that programmers place within code to explain program statements in English? (2.5)
    - a. pseudocode
    - b. trivia
    - c. user documentation
    - d. comments
18. Program comments are ________________. (2.5)
    - a. required to create a runnable program
    - b. a form of external documentation
    - c. required to create both a runnable program and a form of external documentation
    - d. neither required in a program nor a form of external documentation
19. Which of the following is valid advice for naming variables? (2.5)
    - a. To save typing, make most variable names one or two letters.
    - b. To avoid conflict with names that others are using, use unusual or unpronounceable names.
    - c. To make names easier to read, separate long names by using underscores or capitalization for each new word.
    - d. To maintain your independence, shun the conventions of your organization.
20. A message that asks a user for input is a(n) ________________. (2.5)
    - a. prompt
    - b. comment
    - c. echo
    - d. declaration

Programming Exercises

1. Explain why each of the following names does or does not seem like a good variable name to represent a state sales tax rate. (2.1, 2.5)

   a. `stateTaxRate`
   b. `txRt`
   c. `t`
   d. `stateSalesTaxRateValue`
   e. `state tax rate`
   f. `taxRate`
   g. `1TaxRate`
   h. `moneyCharged`

2. If `productCost` and `productPrice` are numeric variables, and `productName` is a string variable, which of the following statements are valid assignments? If a statement is not valid, explain why not. (2.1)

   a. `productCost = 100`
   b. `productPrice = productCost`
   c. `productPrice = productName`
   d. `productPrice = "24.95"`
   e. `15.67 = productCost`
   f. `productCost = $1,345.52`
   g. `productCost = productPrice - 10`
   h. `productName = "mouse pad"`
   i. `productCost + 20 = productPrice`
   j. `productName = 3-inch nails`
   k. `productName = 43`
   l. `productName = "44"`
   m. `"99" = productName`
   n. `productName = brush`
   o. `battery = productName`
   p. `productPrice = productPrice`
   q. `productName = productCost`

3. Assume that `speed = 10` and `miles = 5`. What is the value of each of the following expressions? (2.2)

   a. `speed + 12 - miles * 2`
   b. `speed + miles * 3`
   c. `(speed + miles) * 3`
   d. `speed + speed * miles + miles`
   e. `(10 - speed) + miles / miles`

4. Draw a typical hierarchy chart for a program that produces a monthly bill for a cell phone customer. Try to think of at least 10 separate modules that might be included. For example, one module might calculate the charge for daytime phone minutes used. (2.4)

5. a. Draw the hierarchy chart and then plan the logic for a program needed by Hometown Bank. The program determines a monthly checking account fee. Input includes an account balance and the number of times the account was overdrawn. The output is the fee, which is 1 percent of the balance minus 5 dollars for each time the account was overdrawn. Use three modules. The main program declares global variables and calls housekeeping, detail, and end-of-job modules. The housekeeping module prompts for and accepts a balance. The detail module prompts for and accepts the number of overdrafts, computes the fee, and displays the result. The end-of-job module displays the message *Thanks for using this program.*

   b. Revise the banking program so that it runs continually for any number of accounts. The detail loop executes continually while the balance entered is not negative; in addition to calculating the fee, it prompts the user for and gets the balance for the next account. The end-of-job module executes after a number less than 0 is entered for the account balance. (2.1, 2.2, 2.4)

6. a. Draw the hierarchy chart and then plan the logic for a program that calculates a person's body mass index (BMI). BMI is a statistical measure that compares a person's weight and height. The program uses three modules. The first prompts a user for and accepts the user's height in inches. The second module accepts the user's weight in pounds and converts the user's height to meters and weight to kilograms. Then, it calculates BMI as weight in kilograms divided by height in meters squared and displays the results. There are 2.54 centimeters in an inch, 100 centimeters in a meter, 453.59 grams in a pound, and 1,000 grams in

a kilogram. Use named constants whenever you think they are appropriate. The last module displays the message *End of job*.

   b. Revise the BMI-determining program to execute continually until the user enters 0 for the height in inches. (2.1, 2.2, 2.4)

7. Draw the hierarchy chart and design the logic for a program that calculates service charges for Hazel's Housecleaning service. The program contains housekeeping, detail loop, and end-of-job modules. The main program declares any needed global variables and constants and calls the other modules. The housekeeping module displays a prompt for and accepts a customer's last name. While the user does not enter *ZZZZ* for the name, the detail loop accepts the number of bathrooms and the number of other rooms to be cleaned. The service charge is computed as $40 plus $15 for each bathroom and $10 for each of the other rooms. The detail loop also displays the service charge and then prompts the user for the next customer's name. The end-of-job module, which executes after the user enters the sentinel value for the name, displays a message that indicates the program is complete. (2.1, 2.2, 2.4)

8. Draw the hierarchy chart and design the logic for a program that calculates the projected cost of a remodeling project. Assume that the labor cost is $30 per hour. Design a program that prompts the user for a number of hours projected for the job and the wholesale cost of materials. The program computes and displays the cost of the job, which is the number of hours multiplied by the hourly rate plus 120 percent of the wholesale cost of materials. The program accepts data continually until 0 is entered for the number of hours. Use appropriate modules, including one that displays *End of program* when the program is finished. (2.1, 2.2, 2.4)

9. a. Draw the hierarchy chart and design the logic for a program needed by the manager of the Stengel County softball team, who wants to compute slugging percentages for his players. A slugging percentage is the total bases earned with base hits divided by the player's number of at-bats. Design a program that prompts the user for a player jersey number, the number of bases earned, and the number of at-bats, and then displays all the data, including the calculated slugging average. The program accepts players continually until 0 is entered for the jersey number. Use appropriate modules, including one that displays *End of job* after the sentinel is entered for the jersey number.

   b. Modify the slugging percentage program to also calculate a player's on-base percentage. An on-base percentage is calculated by adding a player's hits and walks, and then dividing by the sum of at-bats, walks, and sacrifice flies. Prompt the user for all the additional data needed and display all the data for each player.

   c. Modify the softball program so that it also computes a gross production average (GPA) for each player. A GPA is calculated by multiplying a player's on-base percentage by 1.8, then adding the player's slugging percentage, and then dividing by four. (2.1, 2.2, 2.4)

10. Draw the hierarchy chart and design the logic for a program for Wong's Appliances. Design a program that prompts the user for a refrigerator model name and the interior height, width, and depth in inches. Calculate the refrigerator capacity in cubic feet by first multiplying the height, width, and depth to get cubic inches, and then dividing by 1728 (the number of cubic inches in a cubic foot). The program accepts model names continually until *XXX* is entered. Use named constants where appropriate. Also use modules, including one that displays *End of job* after the sentinel is entered for the model name. (2.1, 2.2, 2.4)

Performing Maintenance

1. A file named *MAINTENANCE02-01.txt* is included in the Chapter02 folder of your downloadable student files. Assume that this program is a working program in your organization and that it needs modifications as described in the comments (lines that begin with two slashes) at the beginning of the file. Your job is to alter the program to meet the new specifications. (2.1, 2.4)

Debugging Exercises

1. Your downloadable files for Chapter 2 include *DEBUG02-01.txt*, *DEBUG02-02.txt*, *DEBUG02-03.txt*, and *DEBUG02-04.jpg*. Each file starts with some comments that describe the problem. Comments are lines that begin with two slashes (//). Each file contains pseudocode or a flowchart that has mistakes. Find and correct all the bugs.

Game Zone

1. For games to hold your interest, they almost always include some random, unpredictable behavior. For example, a game in which you shoot asteroids loses some of its fun if the asteroids follow the same, predictable path each time you play. Therefore, generating random values is a key component in creating most interesting computer games. Many programming languages come with a built-in module you can use to generate random numbers. The syntax varies in each language, but it is usually something like the following:

```
myRandomNumber = random(10)
```

In this statement, `myRandomNumber` is a numeric variable you have declared and the expression `random(10)` means "call a previously written, external module that generates and returns a random number between 1 and 10." By convention, in a flowchart, you would place a statement that calls an external module in a processing symbol with two vertical stripes at the edges, as shown in **Figure 2-18**.

Figure 2-18 Flowchart symbol that represents calling an external module

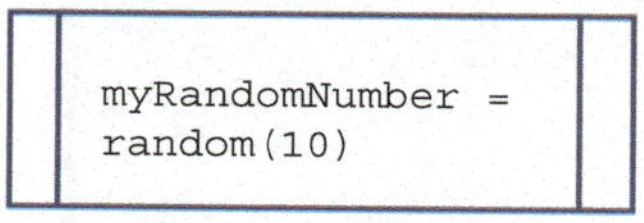

```
myRandomNumber =
random(10)
```

Create a flowchart or pseudocode that shows the logic for a program that generates a random number, then asks the user to think of a number between 1 and 10. Then display the randomly generated number so the user can see whether the guess was accurate. (In future chapters, you will improve this game so that the user can enter a guess and the program can determine whether the user was correct.) (2.4)

Chapter 3

Understanding Structure

Learning Objectives

When you complete this chapter, you will be able to:

3.1 Describe the disadvantages of unstructured spaghetti code

3.2 Describe the three basic structures—sequence, selection, and loop

3.3 Use a priming input to structure a program

3.4 Describe the reasons for using structured techniques

3.5 Recognize structure

3.6 Structure and modularize unstructured logic

3.1 The Disadvantages of Unstructured Spaghetti Code

Professional business applications usually get far more complicated than the examples you have seen so far in this course. Imagine the number of instructions in the computer programs that guide an airplane's flight or audit an income tax return. Even the program that produces your paycheck at work contains many, many instructions. Designing the logic for such a program can be a time-consuming task. When you add hundreds or thousands of instructions to a program, it is easy to create a complicated mess.

The descriptive name for logically snarled program statements is **spaghetti code**, because the logic is as hard to follow as one noodle through a plate of spaghetti. Not only is spaghetti code confusing, but also the programs that contain it are prone to error, difficult to reuse, and hard to use as building blocks for larger applications. Programs that use spaghetti code logic are **unstructured programs**; that is, they do not follow the rules of structured logic that you will learn in this chapter. **Structured programs** *do* follow those rules, and eliminate the problems caused by spaghetti code.

For example, suppose that you start a job as a dog washer and that you receive the instructions shown in **Figure 3-1**. This flowchart is an example of unstructured spaghetti code. A computer program that is organized similarly might "work"—that is, it might produce correct results—but it would be difficult to read and maintain, and its logic would be hard to follow.

Figure 3-1 Spaghetti code logic for washing a dog

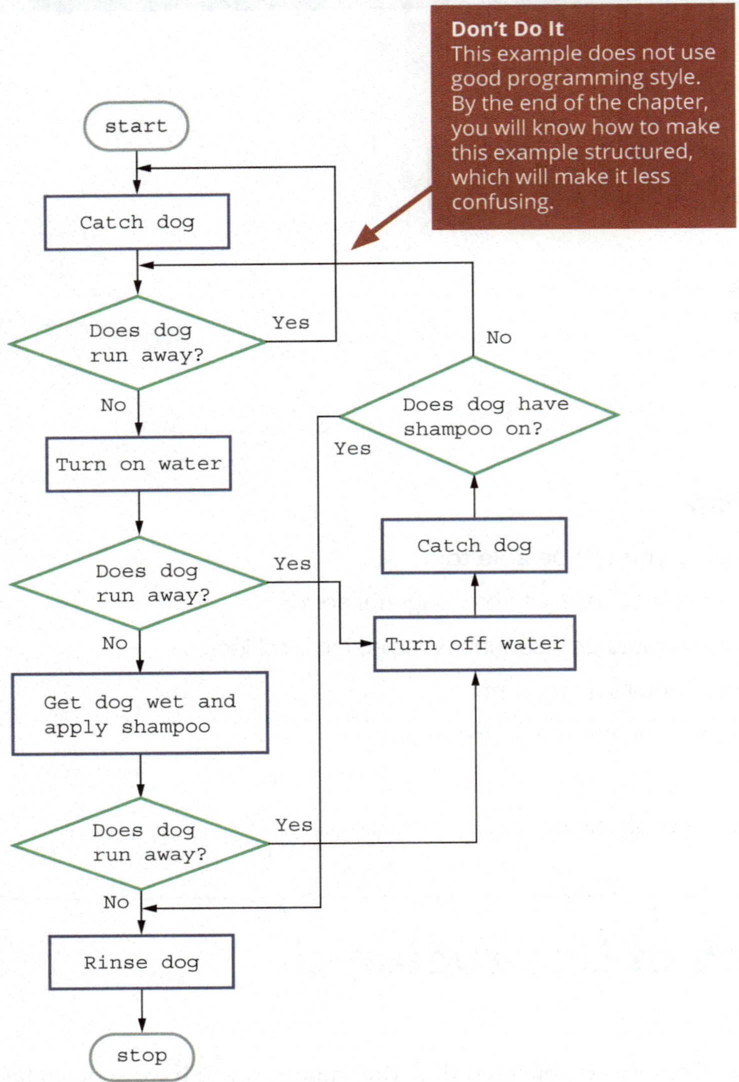

You might be able to follow the logic of the dog-washing process in Figure 3-1 for two reasons:

- You might already know how to wash a dog.
- The flowchart contains a limited number of steps.

Imagine, however, that you were not familiar with dog washing, or that the process was far more complicated. (For example, imagine you must wash 100 dogs concurrently while applying flea and tick medication, giving them haircuts, and researching their genealogy.)

Depicting more complicated logic in an unstructured way would be cumbersome. By the end of this chapter, you will understand how to make the unstructured process in Figure 3-1 clearer and less error-prone.

Note Software developers say that a program that contains spaghetti code has a shorter life than one with structured code. This means that programs developed using spaghetti code exist as production programs in an organization for less time. Such programs are so difficult to alter that when improvements are required, developers often find it easier to abandon the existing program and start from scratch. This takes extra time and costs more money.

Two Truths & a Lie | The Disadvantages of Unstructured Spaghetti Code

1. Spaghetti code is the descriptive name for logically snarled programs.
2. Programs written using spaghetti code cannot produce correct results.
3. Programs written using spaghetti code are more difficult to maintain than other programs.

The false statement is #2. Programs written using spaghetti code can produce correct results, but they are more difficult to understand and maintain than programs that use structured techniques.

3.2 Understanding the Three Basic Structures

In the mid-1960s, mathematicians proved that any program, no matter how complicated, can be constructed using one or more of only three structures. A **structure** is a basic unit of programming logic; each structure is one of the following:

- sequence
- selection
- loop

With these three structures alone, you can diagram any task, from doubling a number to performing brain surgery. You can diagram each structure with a specific configuration of flowchart symbols.

The Sequence Structure

The **sequence structure** is shown in **Figure 3-2**. It performs actions or tasks in order, one after the other. A sequence can contain any number of tasks, but there is no option to branch off and skip any of the tasks. Once you start a series of actions in a sequence, you must continue step by step until the sequence ends.

Figure 3-2 Sequence structure

As an example, driving directions often are listed as a sequence. To tell a friend how to get to your house from school, you might provide the following sequence, in which one step follows the other and no steps can be skipped:

```
go north on First Avenue for 3 miles
turn left on Washington Boulevard
go west on Washington for 2 miles
stop at 634 Washington
```

The Selection Structure

The **selection structure**, or **decision structure**, is shown in **Figure 3-3**. With this structure, one of two courses of action is taken based on the result of testing a condition, or in other words, evaluating a Boolean expression. A **Boolean expression** is one whose value can be only one of two opposing values, usually expressed as *true* and *false* or *yes* and *no*. True/false evaluation is natural from a computer's standpoint, because computer circuitry consists of two-state on-off switches, often represented by 1 or 0. Every computer decision yields a true-or-false, yes-or-no, 1-or-0 result. A Boolean expression is used to control every selection structure.

Figure 3-3 Selection structure

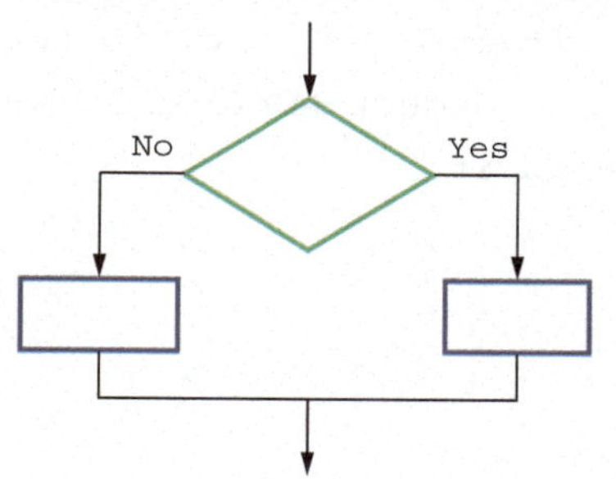

> **Note** Mathematician George Boole (1815–1864) approached logic more simply than his predecessors did, by expressing logical selections with common algebraic symbols. He is considered the founder of mathematical logic, and Boolean (true/false) expressions are named for him.

A flowchart that describes a selection structure begins with a decision symbol that contains a Boolean expression, and the branches of the decision must join at the bottom of the structure. Pseudocode that describes a selection structure starts with `if`. Pseudocode uses the **end-structure statement** `endif` to clearly show where the structure ends.

Some people call the selection structure an `if-then-else` because it fits the following statement:

```
if someCondition is true then
    do oneProcess
else
    do theOtherProcess
endif
```

For example, you might provide part of the directions to your house as follows:

```
if traffic is backed up on Washington Boulevard then
    continue for 1 block on First Avenue and turn left on Adams Lane
else
    turn left on Washington Boulevard
endif
```

Similarly, a payroll program might include a statement such as:

```
if hoursWorked is more than 40 then
    calculate regularPay and overtimePay
else
    calculate regularPay
    overtimePay = 0
endif
```

Each of these `if-else` examples can also be called a **dual-alternative `if`** (or **dual-alternative selection**) because each contains two alternatives—the action taken when the tested condition is true and the action taken when it is false. Note that it is perfectly correct for one branch of the selection to be a "do nothing" branch. In each of the following examples, an action is taken only when the tested condition is true:

```
if it is raining then
    take an umbrella
endif
if employee participates in the dental plan then
    deduct $40 from employee gross pay
endif
```

Each of the previous examples without `else` clauses is a **single-alternative `if`** (or **single-alternative selection**); a diagram of a single-alternative `if` structure is shown in **Figure 3-4**. In these cases, you do not take any special action if it is not raining or if the employee does not belong to the dental plan. The structure is also called an **`if-then`** because it takes the following form:

Figure 3-4 Single-alternative selection structure

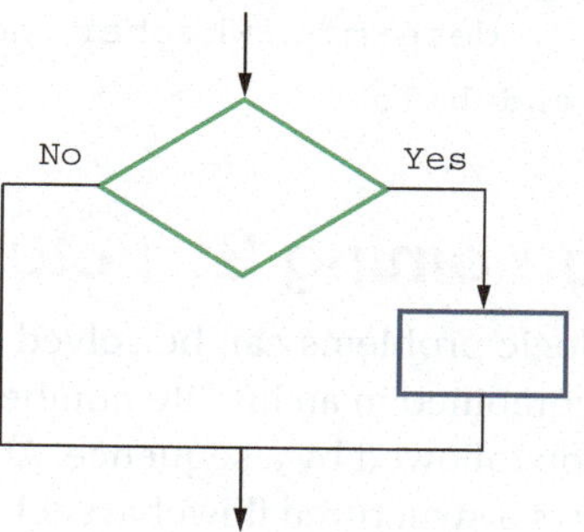


```
if someCondition is true then
    do aProcess
endif
```

The case when the loop-controlling condition is false and in which no action is taken is called the **null case**.

The Loop Structure

Figure 3-5 Loop structure

Yes
No

The **loop structure** is shown in **Figure 3-5**. A loop continues to repeat actions while a tested condition remains true. The action or actions that occur within the loop are the **loop body**. In the most common type of loop, a condition is evaluated; if the answer is true, you execute the loop body and evaluate the condition again. If the condition is still true, you execute the loop body again and then reevaluate the condition. This continues while the condition remains true, or in other words, until the condition becomes false—then you exit the loop structure. Programmers call this structure a **`while` loop**; pseudocode that describes this type of loop starts with `while` and ends with the end-structure statement `endwhile`. A flowchart that describes the `while` loop structure always begins with a decision symbol that contains a Boolean expression and that has a branch that returns to the evaluation. You might hear programmers refer to looping as **repetition** or **iteration**.

> **Note** The `while` loop tests a condition before executing the loop body even once. Another type of structured loop tests a condition after the first loop body execution. You will learn more about this alternate type of loop later in this course. For the rest of this chapter, assume that all loops are `while` loops that test the controlling condition before the loop body ever executes. All logical problems can be solved using only the three structures—sequence, selection, and `while` loop.

Some programmers call a `while` loop a **`while...do` loop** because it fits the following statement:

```
while testCondition continues to be true
    do someProcess
endwhile
```

When you provide directions to your house, which is at street address 634, part of the directions might be:

```
while the address of the house you are passing remains below 634
    travel forward to the next house
    look at the address on the house
endwhile
```

You encounter examples of looping every day, as in each of the following:

```
while you continue to be hungry
    take another bite of food
    determine whether you still feel hungry
endwhile
```

```
while unread pages remain in the reading assignment
    read another unread page
    determine whether there are more pages to read
endwhile
```

Combining Structures

All logic problems can be solved using only three structures—sequence, selection, and loop—but the structures can be combined in an infinite number of ways. For example, you can have a sequence of tasks followed by a selection, or a loop followed by a sequence. Attaching structures end to end is called stacking structures. For example, **Figure 3-6** shows a structured flowchart achieved by stacking structures and shows pseudocode that follows the flowchart logic.

Figure 3-6 Structured flowchart and pseudocode with three stacked structures

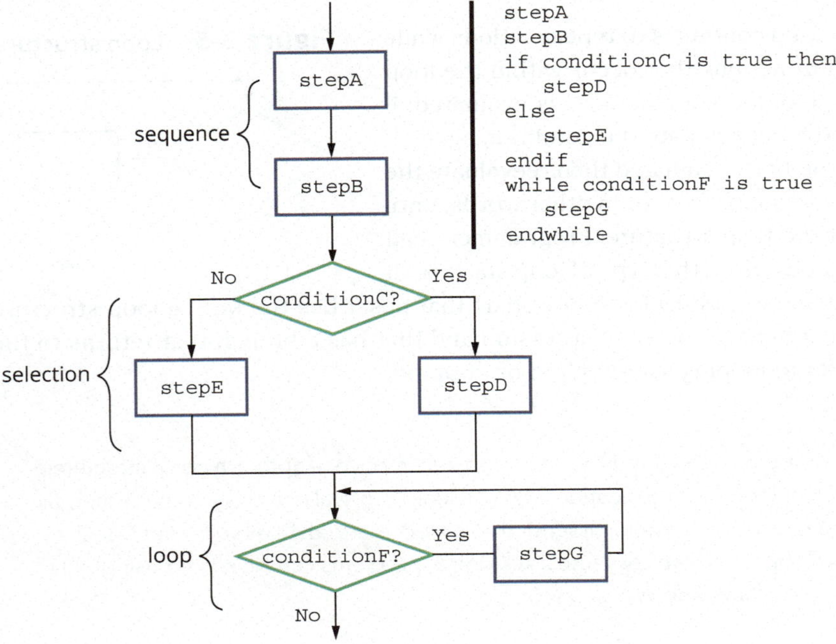


```
stepA
stepB
if conditionC is true then
    stepD
else
    stepE
endif
while conditionF is true
    stepG
endwhile
```

> **Note** Whether you are drawing a flowchart or writing pseudocode, you can use any opposite, mutually exclusive words to represent decision outcomes—for example, *Yes* and *No* or *true* and *false*. This course follows the convention of using *Yes* and *No* in flowchart diagrams and *true* and *false* in pseudocode.

The pseudocode in Figure 3-6 shows a sequence, followed by a selection, followed by a loop. The logic proceeds as follows:

- First `stepA` and `stepB` execute in sequence.
- Then a selection structure starts with the test of `conditionC`, which represents a Boolean expression.
- The instruction that follows the `if` clause `(stepD)` executes when its tested condition `(conditionC)` is true, the instruction that follows `else (stepE)` executes when the tested condition is false, and any instructions that follow `endif` execute in either case. In other words, statements beyond the `endif` statement are "outside" the selection structure.
- Similarly, the `endwhile` statement shows where the loop structure ends. In Figure 3-6, while `conditionF` continues to be true, `stepG` continues to execute. If any statements followed the `endwhile` statement, they would be outside of, and not a part of, the loop.

Besides stacking structures, you can replace any individual steps in a structured flowchart diagram or pseudocode with additional structures. This means that any sequence, selection, or loop can contain other sequence, selection, or loop structures. For example, you can have a sequence of three tasks on one branch of a selection, as shown in **Figure 3-7**. Placing a structure within another structure is called **nesting structures**.

Figure 3-7 Flowchart and pseudocode showing nested structures—a sequence nested within a selection

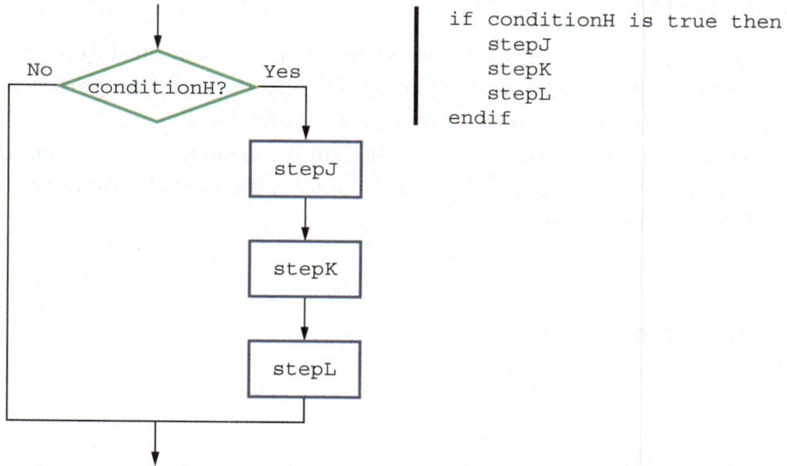


```
if conditionH is true then
   stepJ
   stepK
   stepL
endif
```

In the pseudocode for the logic shown in Figure 3-7, the indentation shows that all three statements (`stepJ`, `stepK`, and `stepL`) must execute if `conditionH` is true. These three statements constitute a **block**, or a group of statements that executes as a single unit.

In place of one of the steps in the sequence in Figure 3-7, you can insert another structure. In **Figure 3-8**, the process named `stepK` has been replaced with a loop structure that begins with a test of the condition named `conditionM`.

Figure 3-8 Flowchart and pseudocode showing nested structures—a loop nested within a sequence, nested within a selection

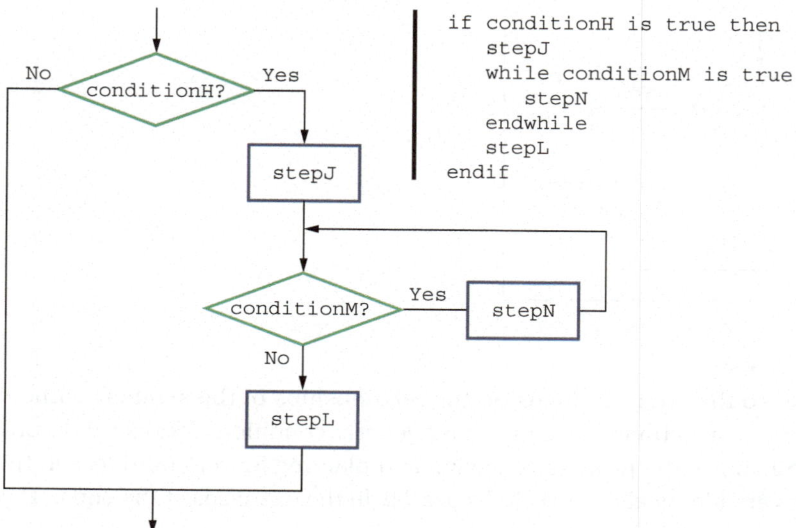


```
if conditionH is true then
   stepJ
   while conditionM is true
      stepN
   endwhile
   stepL
endif
```

In the pseudocode shown in Figure 3-8, notice that `if` and `endif` are vertically aligned. This shows that they are "on the same level." Similarly, `stepJ`, `while`, `endwhile`, and `stepL` are aligned, and they are evenly indented. In the flowchart in Figure 3-8, you could draw a vertical line through the symbols containing `stepJ`, the entry and exit points of the `while` loop, and `stepL`. The flowchart and the pseudocode represent exactly the same logic.

When you nest structures, the statements that start and end a structure are always on the same level and are always in pairs. Structures cannot overlap. For example, if you have an `if` structure that contains a `while` structure, then the `endwhile` statement will come before the `endif`. On the other hand, if you have a `while` that contains an `if`, then the `endif` statement will come before the `endwhile`.

There is no limit to the number of levels you can create when you nest and stack structures. For example, **Figure 3-9** shows logic that has been made more complicated by replacing `stepN` with a selection. The structure that performs `stepP` or `stepQ` based on the outcome of `conditionO` is nested within the loop that is controlled by `conditionM`. In the pseudocode in Figure 3-9, notice how the `if`, `else`, and `endif` that describe the condition selection are aligned with each other and within the `while` structure that is controlled by `conditionM`. As before, the indentation used in the pseudocode reflects the logic laid out graphically in the flowchart.

Figure 3-9 Flowchart and pseudocode for a selection within a loop within a sequence within a selection

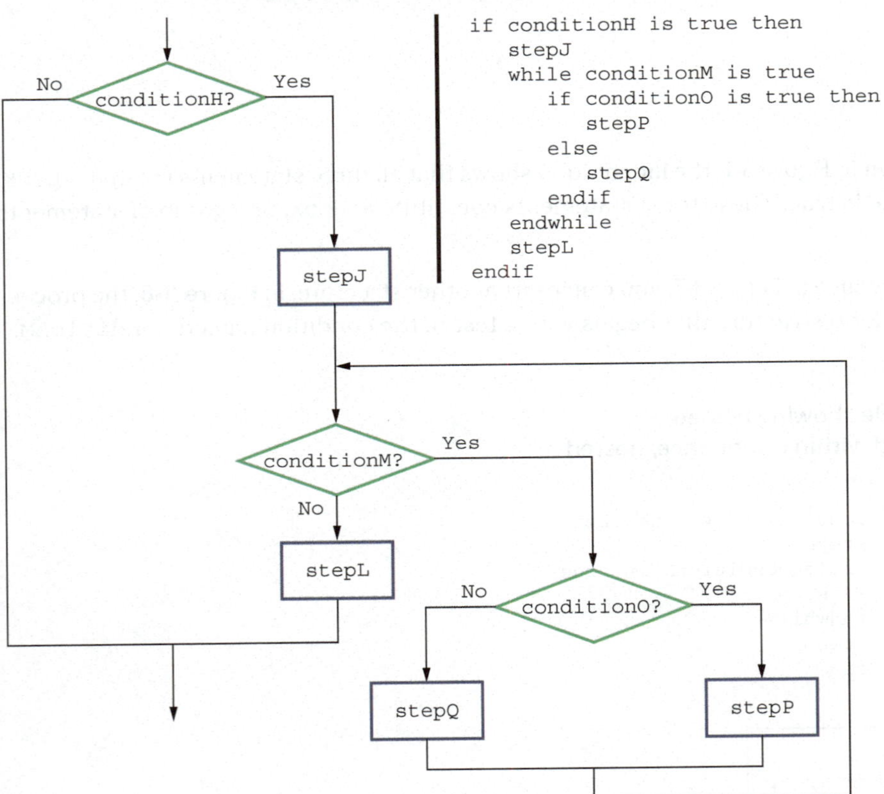


```
if conditionH is true then
   stepJ
   while conditionM is true
      if conditionO is true then
         stepP
      else
         stepQ
      endif
   endwhile
   stepL
endif
```

Many of the preceding examples are generic so that you can focus on the relationships of the symbols without worrying what they do. Keep in mind that generic instructions like `stepA` and generic conditions like `conditionC` can stand for anything. For example, **Figure 3-10** shows the process of buying and planting flowers outdoors in the spring. The flowchart and pseudocode structures are identical to those in Figure 3-9. In the exercises at the end of this chapter, you will be asked to develop more scenarios that fit the same pattern.

Figure 3-10 The process of buying and planting flowers in the spring

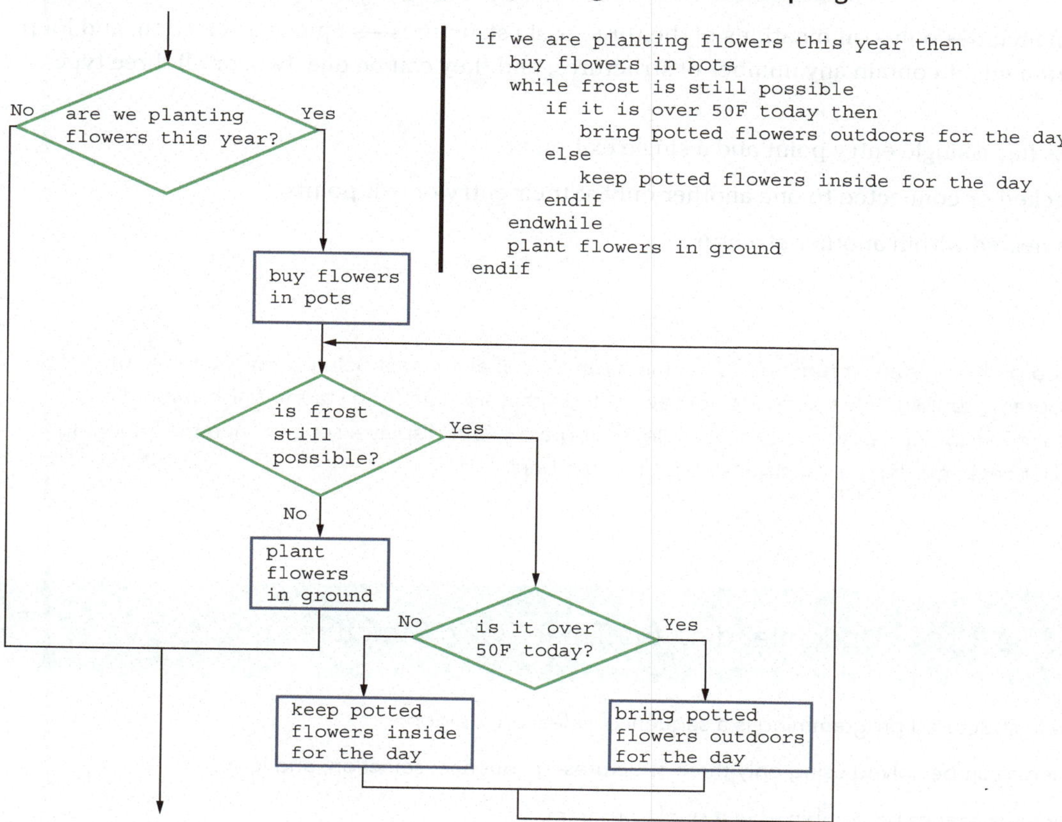


```
if we are planting flowers this year then
   buy flowers in pots
   while frost is still possible
      if it is over 50F today then
         bring potted flowers outdoors for the day
      else
         keep potted flowers inside for the day
      endif
   endwhile
   plant flowers in ground
endif
```

The possible combinations of logical structures are endless, but each segment of a structured program is a sequence, a selection, or a loop. The three structures are summarized in **Figure 3-11**. Notice that each structure has one entry point and one exit point. One structure can attach to another only at one of these points.

Figure 3-11 The three structures

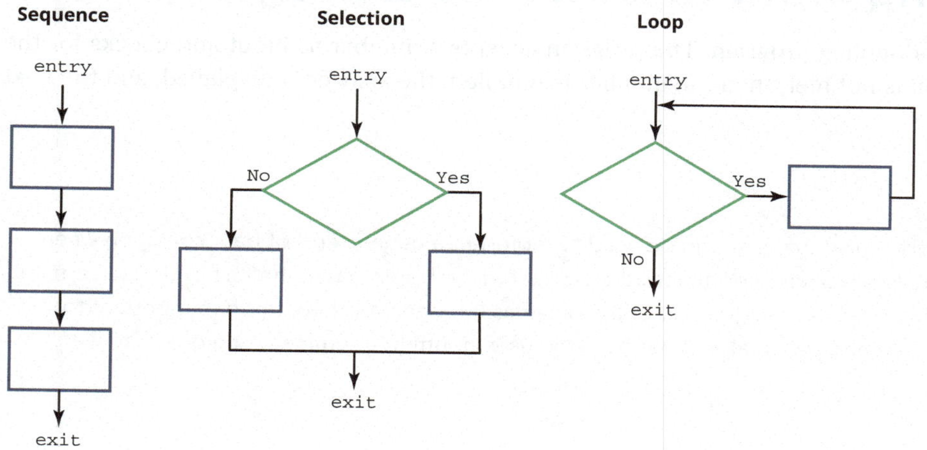

> **Note** Try to imagine physically picking up any of the three structures using the entry and exit "handles." These are the spots at which you could connect one structure to another. Similarly, any complete structure, from its entry point to its exit point, can be inserted within the process symbol of any other structure, forming nested structures.

In summary, a structured program has the following characteristics:

- A structured program includes only combinations of the three basic structures—sequence, selection, and loop. Any structured program might contain any number of structures, and they can be one, two, or all three types of structures.
- Each of the structures has a single entry point and a single exit point.
- Structures can be stacked or connected to one another only at their entry or exit points.
- Any structure can be nested within another structure.

> **Note** A structured program is never required to contain examples of all three structures. For example, many simple programs contain only a sequence of several tasks that execute from start to finish without any needed selections or loops. As another example, a program might display a series of numbers, looping to do so, but never making any decisions about the numbers.

Two Truths & a Lie | Understanding the Three Basic Structures

1. Each structure in structured programming is a sequence, selection, or loop.
2. All logic problems can be solved using only three structures—sequence, selection, and loop.
3. The three structures cannot be combined in a single program.

The false statement is #3. The three structures can be stacked or nested in an infinite number of ways.

3.3 Using a Priming Input to Structure a Program

Figure 3-12 shows a simple number-doubling program. The program accepts a number as input and checks for the end-of-data condition. If the condition is not met, then the number is doubled, the answer is displayed, and the next number is input.

> **Note** Recall from earlier in this course that `eof` can be used to represent a generic end-of-data condition when the exact tested parameters are not important to the discussion. In this example, the test is for `not eof` because processing will continue while the end of the data has not been reached. It is not important to the discussion whether the end eventually comes from the user inputting a sentinel value or a data file reaching its endpoint.

Is the program represented by Figure 3-12 structured? The three allowed structures were illustrated in Figure 3-11, and the flowchart in Figure 3-12 does not look exactly like any of those three shapes. However, because you can stack and nest structures while retaining overall structure, at first glance it might be difficult to determine whether a flowchart as a whole is structured. It is easiest to analyze the flowchart in Figure 3-12 one step at a time.

Figure 3-12 Unstructured flowchart of a number-doubling program

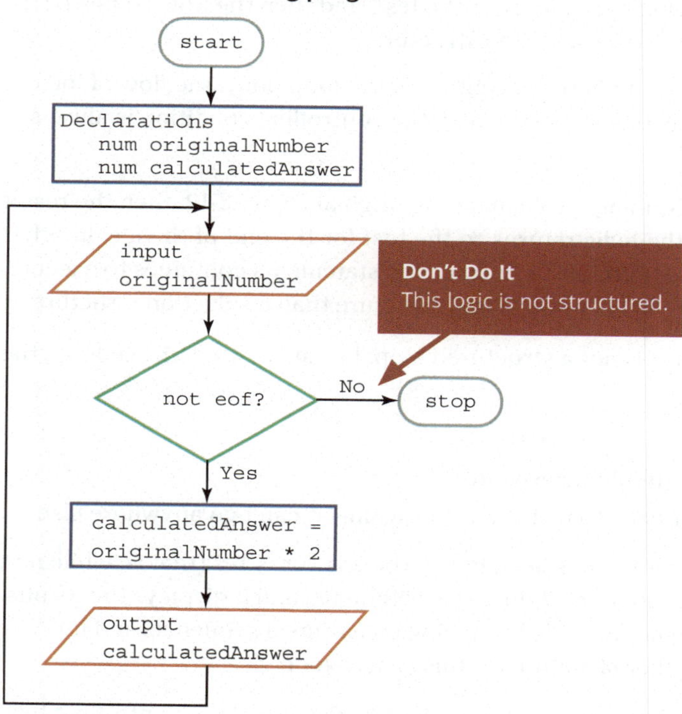

The beginning of the flowchart in Figure 3-12 looks like **Figure 3-13**. Is this portion of the flowchart structured? Yes, it is a sequence of two tasks—making declarations and inputting a value.

Adding the next piece of the original flowchart looks like **Figure 3-14**. After a value is input for `originalNumber`, the `not eof?` condition is tested. The sequence is finished; either a selection or a loop is starting. You might not know which one, but you do know that with a sequence, each task or step must follow without any opportunity to branch off. So, which type of structure starts with the test in Figure 3-14? Is it a selection or a loop?

Figure 3-13 Beginning of a number-doubling flowchart

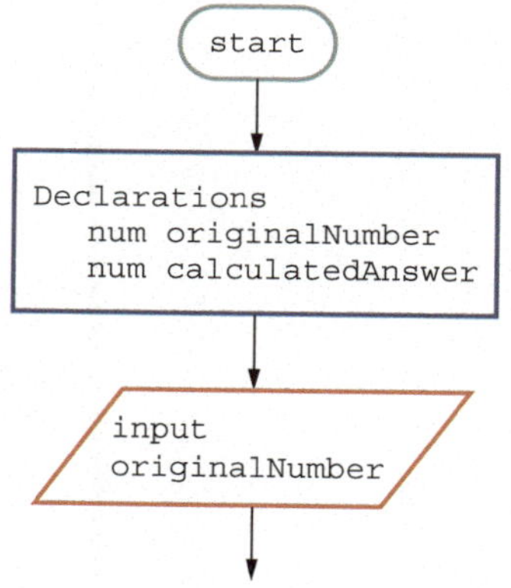

Figure 3-14 Number-doubling flowchart continued

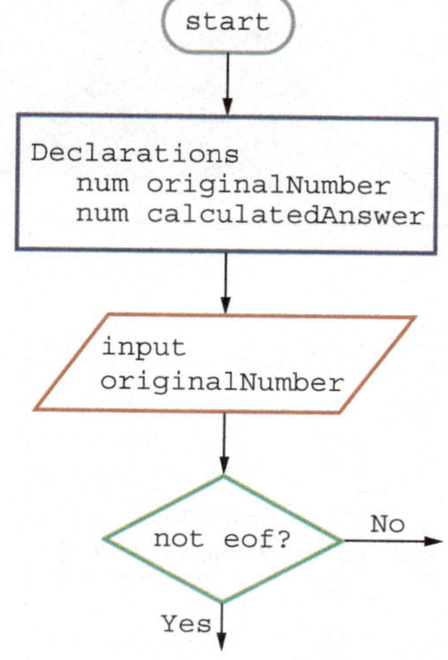

Selection and loop structures both start by testing a condition, but they differ as follows:

- In a selection structure, the logic branches in one of two directions after the test, and then the flow comes back together; the condition is not tested a second time within the selection structure.
- In a loop, each time the result of the conditional test results in the execution of the loop body, the flow of logic returns to the test that started the loop. When the body of a loop executes, the controlling condition is always tested again.

If the end-of-data condition is not met in the number-doubling problem in the original Figure 3-12, then the result is calculated and output, a new number is obtained, and the logic returns to the test for the end of the file. In other words, while the answer to the `not eof?` question continues to be *Yes*, a body of two statements continues to execute. Therefore, the `not eof?` test starts a structure that is more likely to be a loop structure than a selection structure.

The number-doubling process *does* contain a loop, but it is not a structured loop. In a structured `while` loop, the rules are:

1. A condition is tested.
2. If the value of the condition indicates the loop body should be executed, then it is.
3. After the loop body executes, the logic must go right back to test the value again—it can't go anywhere else!

The flowchart in Figure 3-12 tests whether the `eof` condition has been met. If the answer is *Yes* (that is, while `not eof?` is true), then the program performs two tasks in the loop body: It does the arithmetic, and it displays the results. Performing two tasks is acceptable because two tasks with no possible branching constitute a sequence, and it is fine to nest one structure (in this case, a sequence) within another structure (in this case, a loop).

However, in Figure 3-12, when the sequence ends, the logic does not flow right back to the loop-controlling test. Instead, it goes *above* the test to get another number. For the loop in Figure 3-12 to be a structured loop, the logic must return to the `not eof?` evaluation when the embedded sequence ends.

The flowchart in **Figure 3-15** shows the program with the flow of logic returning to the `not eof?` test immediately after the nested two-step sequence. Figure 3-15 shows a structured flowchart, but it has one major flaw—the flowchart does not do the job of continually doubling different numbers.

Figure 3-15 Structured, but nonfunctional, flowchart of number-doubling problem

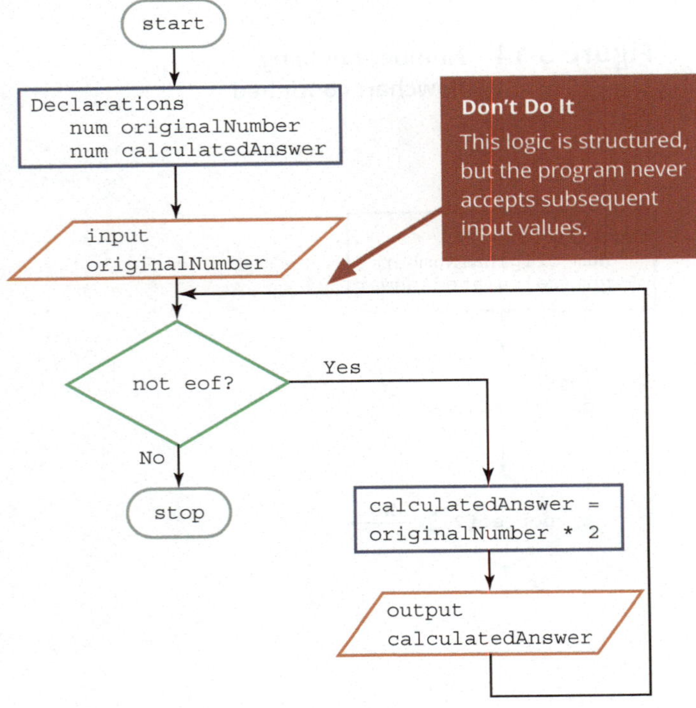

Follow the flowchart in Figure 3-15 through a typical program run, assuming the eof condition is an input value of 0.

- Suppose that when the program starts, the user enters *9* for the value of originalNumber. That is not eof, so the number is multiplied by 2, and 18 is displayed as the value of calculatedAnswer.
- Then the not eof? value is tested again. The not eof? condition still must be true because a new value representing the sentinel (ending) value has not been entered and cannot be entered. The logic never returns to the input originalNumber task, so the value of originalNumber never changes. Therefore, 9 doubles again and the answer 18 is displayed again.
- The not eof? result still is true, so the same steps are repeated.
- This goes on *forever*, with the answer 18 being calculated and output repeatedly.

The program logic shown in Figure 3-15 is structured, but it does not work as intended.

Conversely, the program in **Figure 3-16** works, but it is not structured because after the tasks execute within a structured loop, the flow of logic must return directly to the loop-controlling test. In Figure 3-16, the logic does not return to this test; instead, it goes "too high" outside the loop to repeat the input originalNumber task.

Figure 3-16 Functional but unstructured flowchart

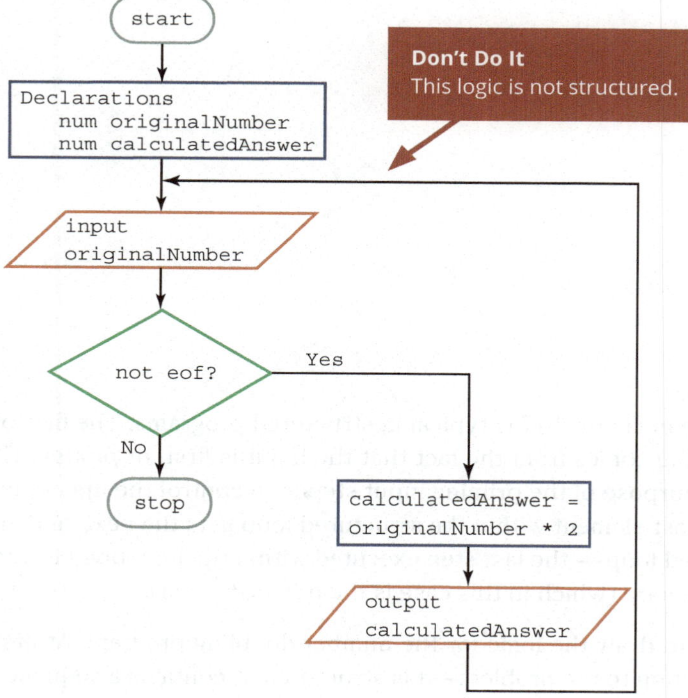

How can the number-doubling problem be both structured and work as intended? Often, for a program to be structured, you must add something extra. In this case, it is a priming input step. A **priming input** or **priming read** is an added statement that gets the first input value in a program. For example, if a program will receive 100 data values as input, you input the first value in a statement that is separate from the other 99. You must do this to keep the program structured.

Consider the solution in **Figure 3-17**; it is structured, *and* it does what it is supposed to do. It contains an additional `input originalNumber` statement. The program logic contains a sequence and a loop. The loop contains another sequence.

Figure 3-17 Functional, structured flowchart for the number-doubling program

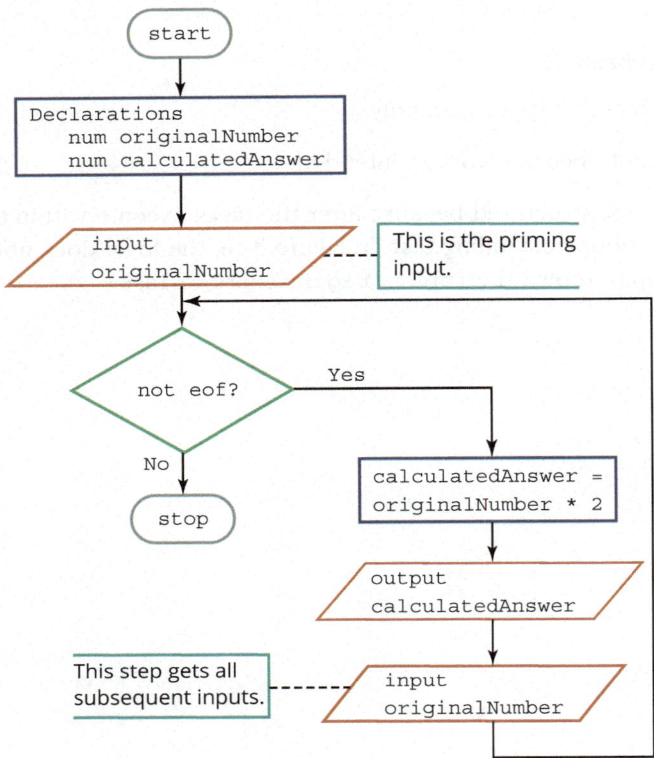

The additional `input originalNumber` step shown in Figure 3-17 is typical in structured programs. The first of the two input steps is the priming input. The term *priming* comes from the fact that the input is first, or *primary* (it gets the process going, as in "priming the pump"). The purpose of the priming input step is to control the upcoming loop that begins with the `not eof?` condition test. The last element within the structured loop gets the next, and all subsequent, input values. This is also typical in structured loops—the last step executed within the loop body is one that can alter the value of the condition that controls the loop (which in this case is the `not eof?` test).

Figure 3-18 shows another way you might attempt to draw the logic for the number-doubling program. At first glance, the figure might seem to show an acceptable solution to the problem—it is structured, it contains a sequence followed by a single loop with a sequence of three steps nested within it, and it appears to eliminate the need for the priming input statement. When the program starts, the declarations are made and the `not eof?` condition is tested. If it is not the end of input data, then the program gets a number, doubles it, and displays it. Then, if the `not eof?` condition remains true, the program gets another number, doubles it, and displays it. The program might continue while many numbers are input. At some point, the input number will represent the `eof` condition; for example, the program might have been written to recognize the value 0 as the program-terminating value. After the `eof` value is entered, its condition is not immediately tested. Instead, a result is calculated and displayed one last time before the loop-controlling test is made again. If the program was written to recognize `eof` when `originalNumber` is 0, then an extraneous answer of 0 will be displayed before the program ends. Depending on the language you are using and on the type of input being used, the results might be worse: The program might terminate by displaying an error message or the value output might be indecipherable garbage. In any case, this last output is superfluous—no value should be doubled and output after the `eof` condition is encountered.

Figure 3-18 Structured but incorrect solution to the number-doubling program

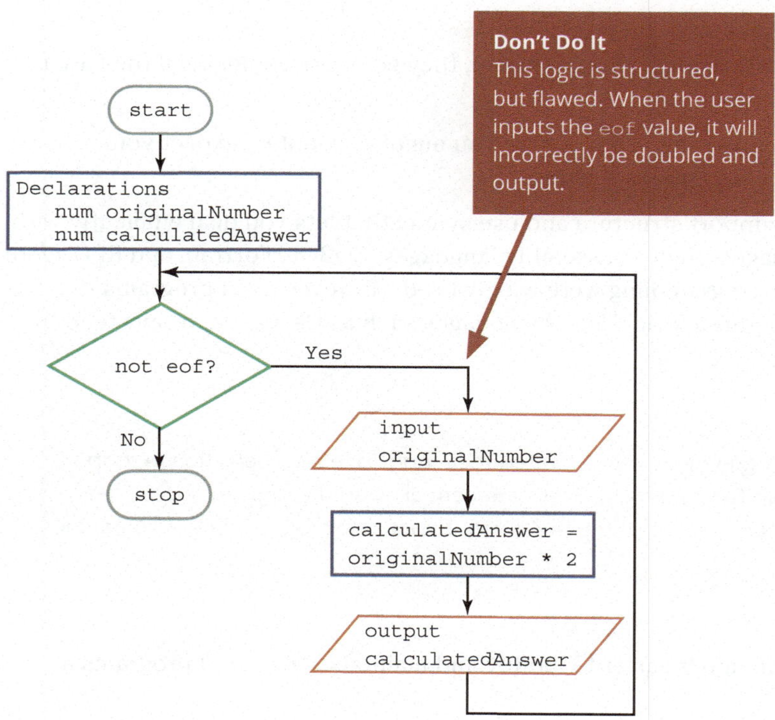

As a general rule, a program-ending test should always come immediately after an input statement because that's the earliest point at which it can be evaluated. Therefore, the best solution to the number-doubling problem remains the one shown in Figure 3-17—the structured solution containing the priming input statement.

Two Truths & a Lie | Using a Priming Input to Structure a Program

1. A priming input is the statement that repeatedly gets all the data that is input in a program.
2. A structured program might contain more instructions than an unstructured one.
3. A program can be structured yet still be incorrect.

The false statement is #1. A priming input gets the first input.

3.4 Understanding the Reasons for Using Structured Techniques

At this point, you might very well be saying, "I liked the original number-doubling program back in Figure 3-12 just fine. I could follow it. Also, the first program had one less step in it, so it was less work. Who cares if a program is structured?"

Until you have some programming experience, it is difficult to appreciate the reasons for using only the three structures—sequence, selection, and loop. However, staying with these three structures is better for the following reasons:

- *Clarity*—The number-doubling program is small. As programs get bigger, they get more confusing if they are not structured.
- *Professionalism*—All other programmers (and programming teachers you might encounter) expect your programs to be structured. It is the way things are done professionally.
- *Efficiency*—Most newer computer languages support structure and use syntax that lets you deal efficiently with sequence, selection, and looping. Older languages, such as assembly languages, COBOL, Fortran, and RPG, were developed before the principles of structured programming were widely used. However, even programs that use those older languages can be written in a structured form. Newer languages such as C#, C++, and Java tend to enforce structure by their syntax.

Note In the early days of programming, programmers often created their logic to leave a selection or loop before it was complete by using a "go to" statement. The statement allowed the logic to "go to" any other part of the program breaking out of a structure prematurely. Structured programming is sometimes called **goto-less programming**.

- *Maintenance*—You and other programmers will find it easier to modify and maintain structured programs as changes are required in the future.
- *Modularity*—Structured programs can be broken down easily into modules that can be assigned to any number of programmers. The routines then are pieced back together like modular furniture at each routine's single entry or exit point. Additionally, a module often can be used in multiple programs, saving development time in the new project.

Two Truths & a Lie | Understanding the Reasons for Using Structured Techniques

1. Structured programs are clearer than unstructured programs.
2. You and other programmers will find it easier to modify and maintain structured programs as changes are required in the future.
3. Structured programs are not easily divided into parts, making them less prone to error.

The false statement is #3. Structured programs can be broken down easily into modules that can be assigned to any number of programmers.

3.5 Recognizing Structure

When you are beginning to learn about structured program design, it is difficult to detect whether a flowchart of a program's logic is structured. For example, is the flowchart segment in **Figure 3-19** structured?

Yes, it is. It has a sequence and a selection structure.

Is the flowchart segment in **Figure 3-20** structured?

Yes, it is. It has a loop and a selection within the loop.

Is the flowchart segment in the upper-left corner of **Figure 3-21** structured?

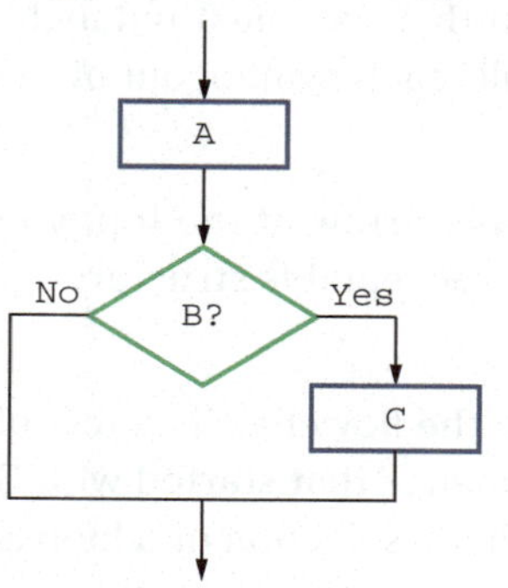

Figure 3-19 Example 1

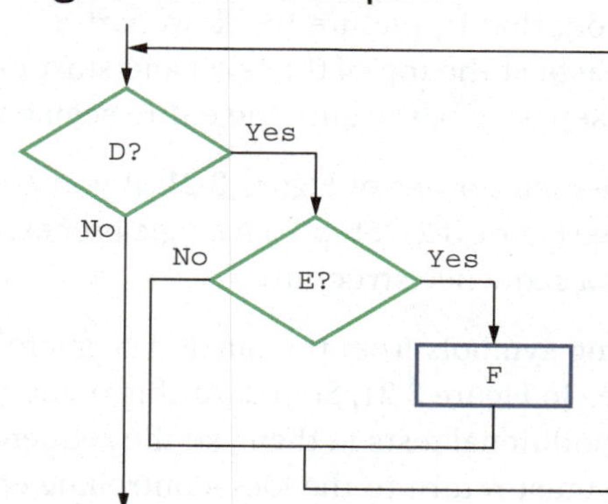

Figure 3-20 Example 2

Figure 3-21 Example 3 and process to structure it

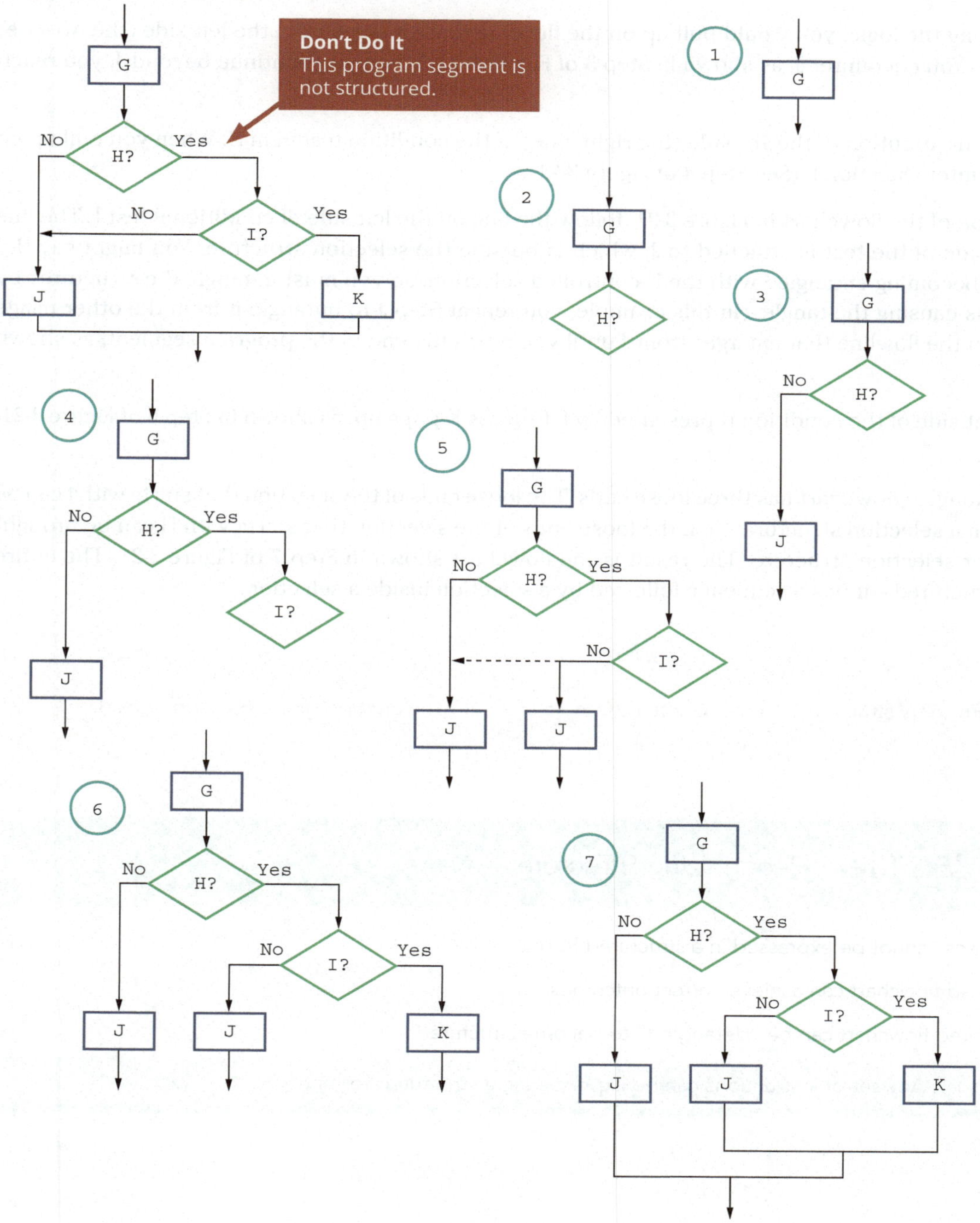

Don't Do It
This program segment is not structured.

No, it is not built from the three basic structures. One way to straighten out an unstructured flowchart segment is to use the "spaghetti bowl" method; that is, picture the flowchart as a bowl of spaghetti that you must untangle. Imagine you can grab one piece of pasta at the top of the bowl and start pulling. As you "pull" each symbol out of the tangled mess, you can untangle the separate paths until the entire segment is structured.

Look at the diagram in the upper-left corner of Figure 3-21. If you could start pulling the arrow at the top, you would encounter a box labeled G. (See Figure 3-21, Step 1.) A single process like G is part of an acceptable structure—it constitutes at least the beginning of a sequence structure.

Imagine that you continue pulling symbols from the tangled segment. The next item in the flowchart is a test of a condition labeled H, as you can see in Figure 3-21, Step 2. At this point, you know the sequence that started with G has ended. Sequences never have conditional tests in them, so the sequence is finished; either a selection or a loop is beginning with the test of H. A loop must return to the loop-controlling conditional test at some later point. You can see from the original logic that whether the value of H is *Yes* or *No*, the logic never returns to H. Therefore, H begins a selection structure, not a loop structure.

To continue detangling the logic, you would pull up on the flowline that emerges from the left side (the *No* side) of the conditional test H. You encounter J, as shown in Step 3 of Figure 3-21. When you continue beyond J, you reach the end of the flowchart.

Now you can turn your attention to the *Yes* side (the right side) of the condition tested in H. When you pull up on the right side, you encounter Question I. (See Step 4 of Figure 3-21.)

In the original version of the flowchart in Figure 3-21, follow the line on the left side of conditional test I. The line emerging from the left side of the test is attached to J, which is outside the selection structure. You might say the I-controlled selection is becoming entangled with the H-controlled selection, so you must untangle the structures by repeating the step that is causing the tangle. (In this example, you repeat Step J to untangle it from the other usage of J.) Continue pulling on the flowline that emerges from J until you reach the end of the program segment, as shown in Step 5 of Figure 3-21.

Now pull on the right side of the condition represented by I. Process K pops up, as shown in Step 6 of Figure 3-21; then you reach the end.

At this point, the untangled flowchart has three loose ends. The loose ends of the selection that starts with I can be brought together to form a selection structure; then the loose ends of the selection that starts with H can be brought together to form another selection structure. The result is the flowchart shown in Step 7 of Figure 3-21. The entire flowchart segment is structured—it has a sequence followed by a selection inside a selection.

Note | If you want to try structuring a more difficult example of an unstructured program, see Appendix B.

Two Truths & a Lie | Recognizing Structure

1. Some processes cannot be expressed in a structured format.
2. An unstructured flowchart can achieve correct outcomes.
3. Any unstructured flowchart can be "detangled" to become structured.

The false statement is #1. Any set of instructions can be expressed in a structured format.

3.6 Structuring and Modularizing Unstructured Logic

Recall the dog-washing process illustrated in Figure 3-1 at the beginning of this chapter. When you look at it now, you should recognize it as an unstructured process. Can this process be reconfigured to perform precisely the same tasks in a structured way? Of course!

Figure 3-22 demonstrates how you might approach structuring the dog-washing logic. Part 1 of the figure shows the beginning of the process. The first step, *Catch dog*, is a simple sequence. This step is followed by testing whether the dog runs away. When a conditional test is encountered, the sequence is over, and either a loop or a selection structure starts. In this case, after the dog runs away, you must catch the dog and determine whether he runs away again, so a loop begins. To create a structured loop like the ones you have seen earlier in this chapter, you can repeat the *Catch dog* process and return immediately to the *Does dog run away?* test.

Figure 3-22 Steps to structure the dog-washing program

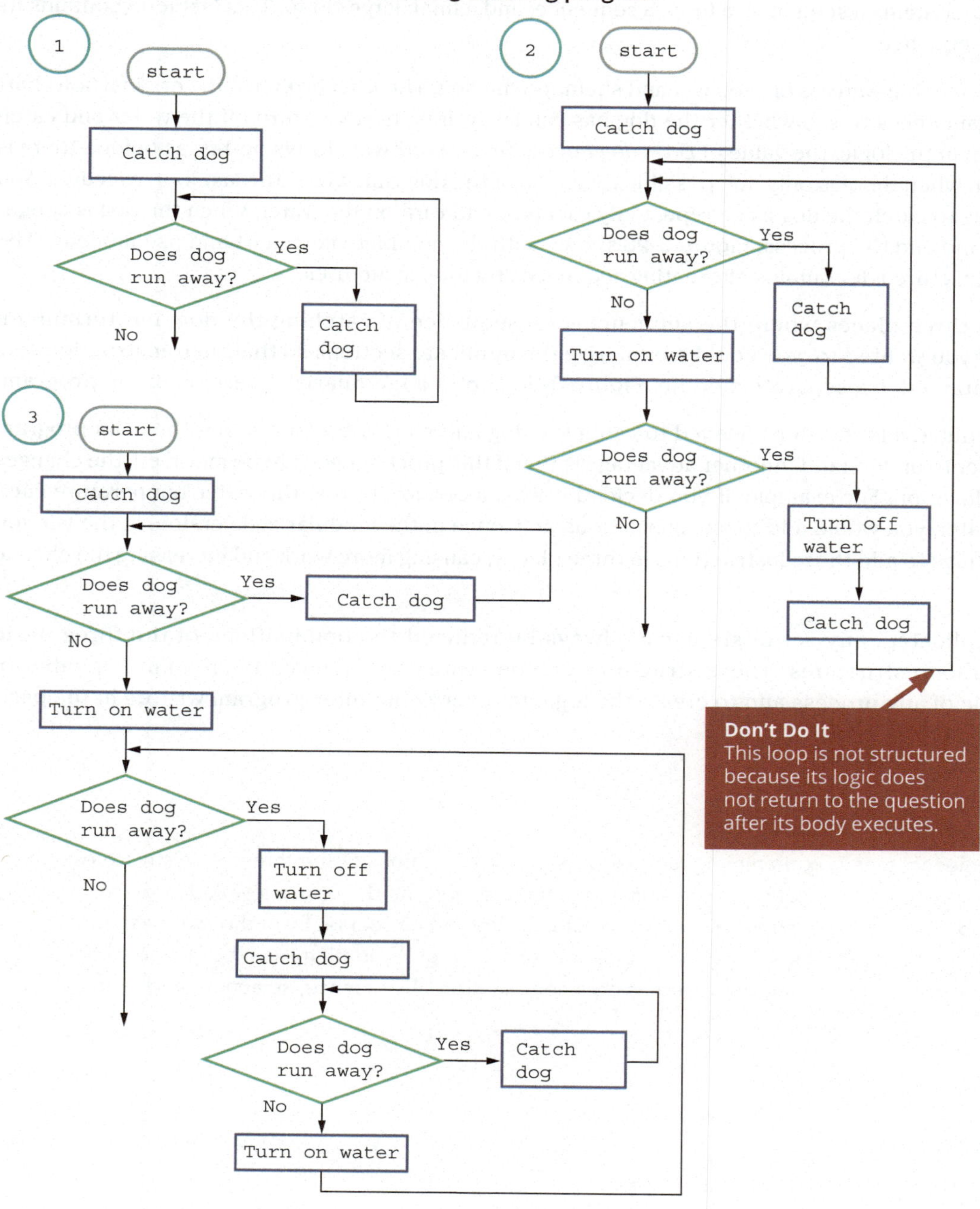

In the original flowchart in Figure 3-1, you turn on the water when the dog does not run away. This step is a simple sequence, so it can correctly be added after the loop. When the water is turned on, the original logic checks whether the dog runs away after this new development. This starts a loop. In the original flowchart, the lines cross, creating a tangle, so you repeat as many steps as necessary to detangle the lines. After you turn off the water and catch the dog, you encounter the question that tests the condition *Does dog have shampoo on?* Because the logic has not yet reached the shampooing step, there is no need to make this test—the answer at this point always will be *No*. When one of the logical paths emerging from a conditional test can never be traveled, you can eliminate the test. Part 2 of Figure 3-22 shows that if the dog runs away after you turn on the water, but before you've gotten the dog wet and shampooed him, you must turn off the water, catch the dog, and return to testing whether the dog runs away.

The logic in Part 2 of Figure 3-22 is not structured because the second loop that begins with *Does dog run away?* does not immediately return to the loop-controlling test after its body executes. So, to make the loop structured, you can repeat the actions that occur before returning to the loop-controlling test. The flowchart segment in Part 3 of Figure 3-22 is structured; it contains a sequence, a loop, a sequence, and a final, larger loop. This last loop contains its own sequence, loop, and sequence.

After the dog is caught and the water is on, you wet and shampoo the dog. Then, according to the original flowchart in Figure 3-1, you once again check to see whether the dog has run away. If he has, you turn off the water and catch the dog. From this location in the logic, the value of *Does dog have shampoo on?* will always be *Yes*; as before, there is no need to test a condition when there is only one possible result. So, if the dog runs away, the last loop executes. You turn off the water, continue to catch the dog as he repeatedly escapes, and turn on the water. When the dog is caught at last, you rinse the dog and end the process. **Figure 3-23** shows both the complete flowchart and pseudocode. The logic is complete and is structured. It contains alternating sequence and loop structures.

Figure 3-23 includes three places where the sequence-loop-sequence of catching the dog and turning on the water are repeated. If you wanted to, you could modularize the duplicate sections so that their instruction sets are written once and contained in a separate module. **Figure 3-24** shows a modularized version of the program.

One advantage to modularizing the steps needed to catch the dog and start the water is that the main program becomes shorter and easier to understand. Another advantage is that if this process needs to be modified, the changes can be made in just one location. For example, if you decided it was necessary to test the water temperature each time you turned on the water, you would add those instructions only once in the modularized version. In the version in Figure 3-23, you would have to add those instructions in three places, causing more work and increasing the chance for errors.

No matter how complicated, any set of steps can always be reduced to combinations of the three basic sequence, selection, and loop structures. These structures can be nested and stacked in an infinite number of ways to describe the logic of any process and to create the logic for every computer program written in the past, present, or future.

Note

For convenience, many programming languages allow two variations of the three basic structures. The `case` structure is a variation of the selection structure, and the `do` loop is a variation of the `while` loop. You can learn about these two structures later in this course. Even though these extra structures can be used in most programming languages, all logical problems can be solved without them. All logical problems can be solved using a combination of sequence, selection, and loop structures.

Figure 3-23 Structured dog-washing flowchart and pseudocode

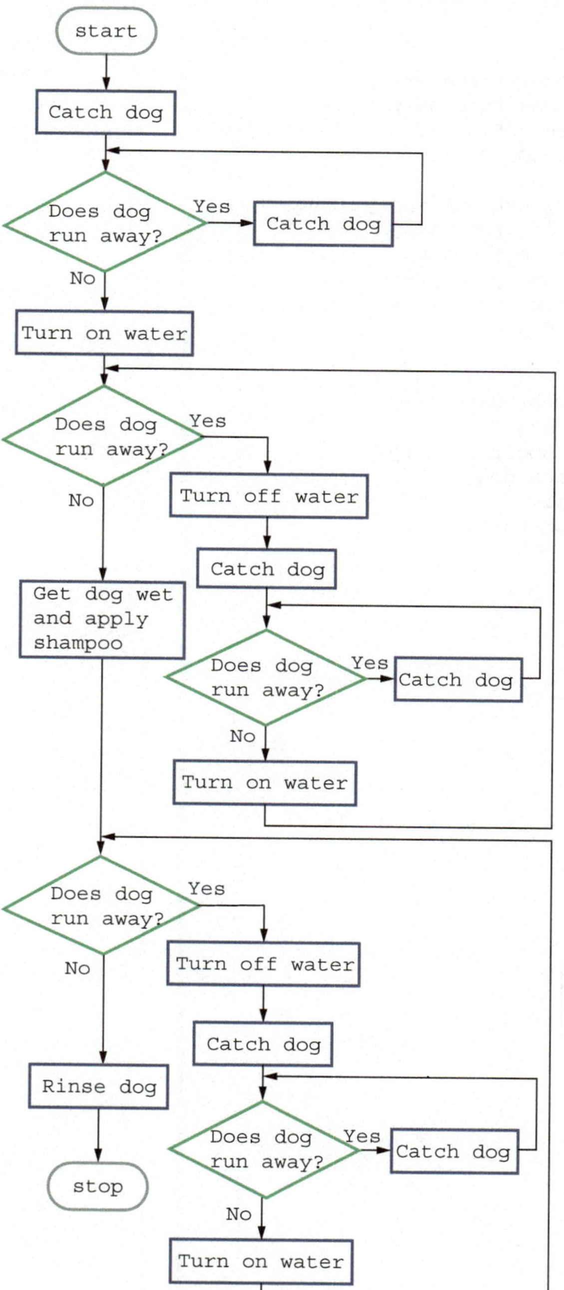


```
start
   Catch dog
   while dog runs away
      Catch dog
   endwhile
   Turn on water
   while dog runs away
      Turn off water
      Catch dog
      while dog runs away
         Catch dog
      endwhile
      Turn on water
   endwhile
   Get dog wet and apply shampoo
   while dog runs away
      Turn off water
      Catch dog
      while dog runs away
         Catch dog
      endwhile
      Turn on water
   endwhile
   Rinse dog
stop
```

Figure 3-24 Modularized version of the dog-washing program

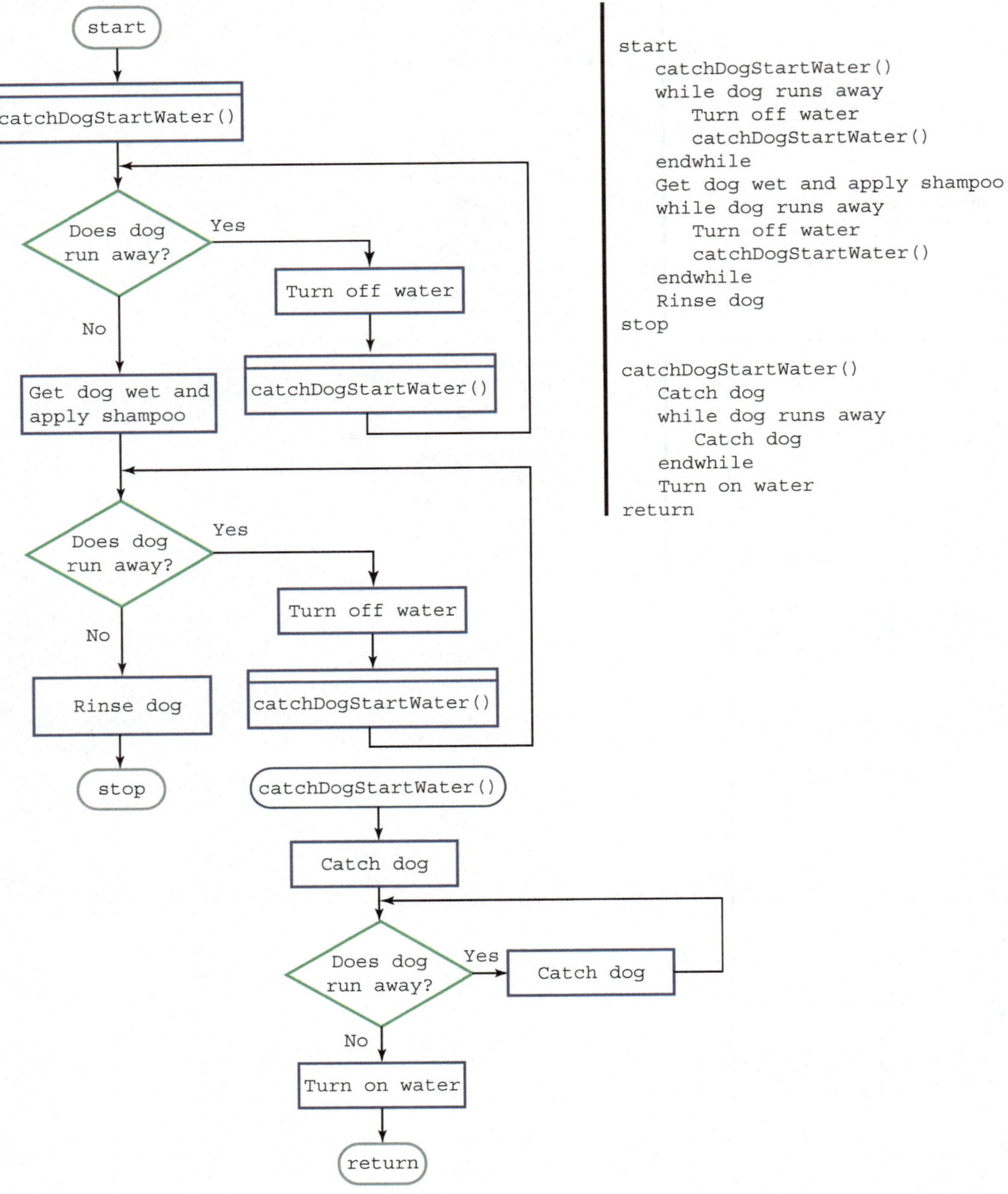
start
catchDogStartWater()
Does dog run away?
Yes
No
Turn off water
catchDogStartWater()
Get dog wet and apply shampoo
Does dog run away?
Yes
No
Turn off water
catchDogStartWater()
Rinse dog
stop
catchDogStartWater()
Catch dog
Does dog run away?
Yes
Catch dog
No
Turn on water
return
start
catchDogStartWater()
while dog runs away
Turn off water
catchDogStartWater()
endwhile
Get dog wet and apply shampoo
while dog runs away
Turn off water
catchDogStartWater()
endwhile
Rinse dog
stop
catchDogStartWater()
Catch dog
while dog runs away
Catch dog
endwhile
Turn on water
return

Two Truths & a Lie | Structuring and Modularizing Unstructured Logic

1. When you encounter a conditional test in a logical diagram, a sequence should be ending.
2. In a structured loop, the logic returns to the loop-controlling conditional test after the loop body executes.
3. If a flowchart or pseudocode contains a conditional test for which the result never varies, you can eliminate the test.

The false statement is #1. When you encounter a conditional test in a logical diagram, either a selection or a loop should start. Any type of structure might end, however, before the test is encountered.

Summary

- Spaghetti code is the descriptive name for unstructured program statements that do not follow the rules of structured logic.
- Clearer programs can be constructed using only three basic structures: sequence, selection, and loop. These three structures can be combined in an infinite number of ways by stacking and nesting them. Each structure has a single entry point and a single exit point; one structure can attach to another only at one of these points.
- A priming input is the statement that gets the first input value prior to starting a structured loop. Usually, the last step within the loop body gets the next and all subsequent input values.
- Programmers use structured techniques to promote clarity, professionalism, efficiency, and modularity.
- One way to order an unstructured flowchart segment is to imagine it as a bowl of spaghetti that you must untangle.
- Any set of logical steps can be rewritten to conform to the three structures: sequence, selection, and loop.

Key Terms

block
Boolean expression
decision structure
dual-alternative `if`
dual-alternative selection
end-structure statement
goto-less programming
`if-then`
`if-then-else`
iteration
loop body
loop structure
nesting structures
null case
priming input
priming read
repetition
selection structure
sequence structure
single-alternative `if`
single-alternative selection
spaghetti code
stacking structures
structure
structured programs
unstructured programs
`while` loop
`while...do` loop

Review Questions

1. Snarled program logic is called ______________ code. (3.1)
   a. snake
   b. spaghetti
   c. linguini
   d. gnarly
2. The three structures of structured programming are ______________. (3.2)
   a. sequence, selection, and loop
   b. decision, loop, and iteration
   c. sequence, order, and process
   d. loop, iteration, and refraction

3. A sequence structure can contain ________________. (3.2)
   a. only one task
   b. exactly three tasks
   c. no more than three tasks
   d. any number of tasks
4. Which of the following is *not* another term for a selection structure? (3.2)
   a. loop structure
   b. decision structure
   c. dual-alternative `if` structure
   d. `if-then-else` structure
5. A ________________ expression has one of two values, often expressed as true or false. (3.2)
   a. Georgian
   b. Boolean
   c. Selection
   d. Caesarian
6. Placing a structure within another structure is called ________________ structures. (3.2)
   a. untangling
   b. nesting
   c. building
   d. stacking
7. Attaching structures end to end is called ________________. (3.2)
   a. nesting
   b. untangling
   c. building
   d. stacking
8. When an action is required if a condition is true, but no action is needed if it is false, you use a ________________. (3.2)
   a. sequence
   b. stack
   c. dual-alternative selection
   d. single-alternative selection
9. To take action repeatedly as long as a condition remains true, you use a ________________. (3.2)
   a. sequence
   b. loop
   c. stack
   d. selection
10. When you must perform one action when a condition is true and a different one when it is false, and then the program continues, you use a ________________. (3.2)
    a. sequence
    b. loop
    c. dual-alternative selection
    d. single-alternative selection
11. Which of the following attributes do all three basic structures share? (3.2)
    a. Their flowcharts all contain exactly three processing symbols.
    b. They all begin with a process.
    c. They all have one entry and one exit point.
    d. They all contain a conditional test.
12. Which is true of stacking structures? (3.2)
    a. Each structure has only one point where it can be stacked on top of another.
    b. Two incidences of the same structure cannot be stacked adjacently.
    c. When you stack structures, you cannot nest them in the same program.
    d. When you stack structures, the top structure must be a sequence.
13. When you input data in a loop within a program, the input statement that precedes the loop ________________. (3.3)
    a. is the only part of the program allowed to be unstructured
    b. cannot result in `eof`
    c. is called a priming input
    d. executes hundreds or even thousands of times in most business programs

14. A group of statements that executes as a unit is a ______________. (3.2)

   a. block
   b. family
   c. chunk
   d. cohort

15. Placing a decision within a loop is ______________. (3.2)

   a. an out-of-date technique
   b. a practice allowed only with newer programming languages
   c. an acceptable structured programming technique
   d. more correct than placing a loop within a decision

16. In a selection structure, the structure-controlling condition is ______________. (3.2)

   a. tested once at the beginning of the structure
   b. tested once at the end of the structure
   c. tested repeatedly until it is false
   d. tested repeatedly until it is true

17. When a loop executes, the structure-controlling condition is ______________. (3.2)

   a. tested exactly once
   b. never tested more than once
   c. tested either before or after the loop body executes
   d. tested only if it is true, and not asked if it is false

18. Which of the following is *not* a reason for enforcing structure rules in computer programs? (3.4)

   a. Structured programs are clearer to understand than unstructured ones.
   b. Other professional programmers will expect programs to be structured.
   c. Structured programs usually are shorter than unstructured ones.
   d. Structured programs can be broken down into modules easily.

19. Which of the following is *not* a benefit of modularizing programs? (3.4)

   a. Modular programs are easier to read and understand than nonmodular ones.
   b. If you use modules, you can ignore the rules of structure.
   c. Modular components are reusable in other programs.
   d. Multiple programmers can work on different modules at the same time.

20. Which of the following is true of structured logic? (3.6)

   a. You can use structured logic with newer programming languages, such as Java and C#, but not with older ones.
   b. Any task can be described using some combination of the three structures: sequence, selection, and loop.
   c. Structured programs require that you break the code into easy-to-handle modules that each contain no more than five actions.
   d. Structured logic works in flowcharts, but not pseudocode.

Programming Exercises

1. In Figure 3-10, the process of buying and planting flowers in the spring was shown using the same structures as the generic example in Figure 3-9. Use the same logical structure as in Figure 3-9 to create a flowchart or pseudocode that describes some other process you know. (3.2)

2. Each of the flowchart segments in **Figure 3-25** is unstructured. Redraw each segment so that it performs the same processes under the same conditions but is structured. (3.1, 3.2, 3.5, 3.6)

Figure 3-25 Flowcharts for Exercise 2

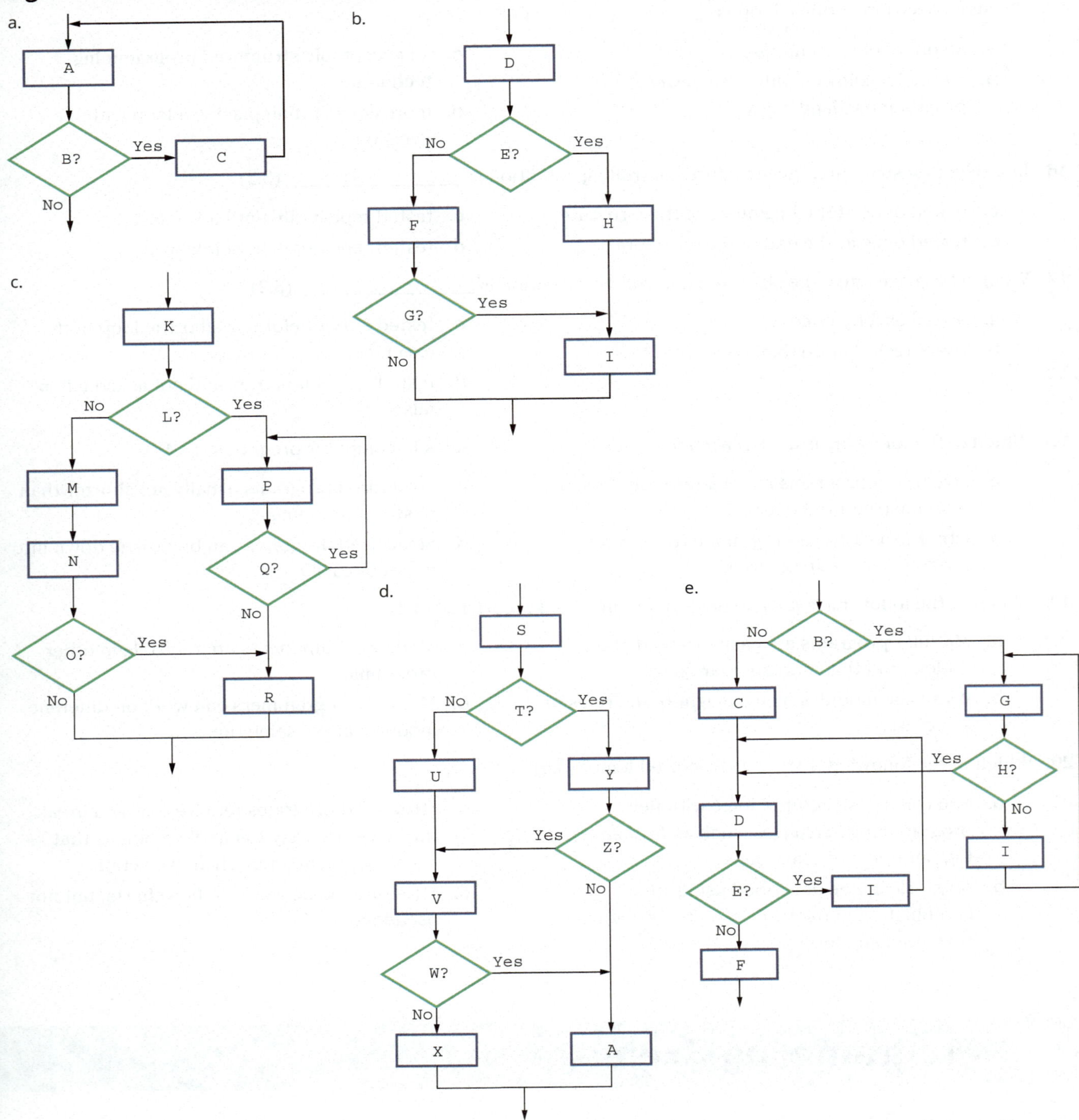

3. Write pseudocode for each example (a through e) in Exercise 2, making sure your pseudocode is structured and accomplishes the same tasks as the flowchart segment. (3.1, 3.2, 3.3, 3.5, 3.6)

4. Assume that you have created a mechanical arm that can hold a pen and that you have a piece of paper. The arm can perform the following tasks:

   - Lower the pen to the piece of paper. The first time the pen is lowered, it is facing right and ready to move to the right.
   - Raise the pen from the paper.
   - Move the pen 1 inch along a straight line. The line is drawn in the direction the pen is facing. (If the pen is lowered, this action draws a 1-inch line; if the pen is raised, this action just repositions the pen 1 inch.)
   - Turn 90 degrees to the right.
   - Draw a circle that is 1 inch in diameter. The circle is drawn clockwise from the starting point.
   - Additionally, assume the arm knows the answer to any question such as, "Is the pen facing right?"

   Draw a structured flowchart or write structured pseudocode describing the logic that would cause the arm to draw or write the following. Have a fellow student act as the mechanical arm and carry out your instructions. Don't reveal the desired outcome to your partner until the exercise is complete.

   a. 1-inch square
   b. 2-inch by 1-inch rectangle
   c. string of three beads
   d. short word that can be constructed from lines and circles (for example, *bit*)
   e. four-digit number (3.6)

5. Assume that you have created a mechanical robot that can perform the following tasks:

   - Stand up.
   - Sit down.
   - Turn left 90 degrees.
   - Turn right 90 degrees.
   - Take a step.

   Additionally, the robot can determine the answer to one test condition:

   - Am I touching something?

   a. Place two chairs 20 feet apart, directly facing each other. Draw a structured flowchart or write pseudocode describing the logic that would allow the robot to start from a sitting position in one chair, cross the room, and end up sitting in the other chair. Have a fellow student act as the robot and carry out your instructions.

   b. Draw a structured flowchart or write pseudocode describing the logic that would allow the robot to start from a sitting position in one chair, stand up and circle the chair, cross the room, circle the other chair, return to the first chair, and sit. Have a fellow student act as the robot and carry out your instructions. (3.2, 3.5, 3.6)

6. Draw a structured flowchart or write pseudocode that describes the process of guessing a number between 1 and 100. After each guess, the player is told that the guess is too high or too low. The process continues until the player guesses the correct number. Pick a number and have a fellow student try to guess it by following your instructions. (3.2, 3.5)

7. Looking up a word in a dictionary can be a complicated process. For example, assume that you want to look up *logic*. You might open the dictionary to a random page and see *juice*. You know this word comes alphabetically before *logic*, so you flip forward and see *lamb*. That is still not far enough, so you flip forward and see *monkey*. You have gone too far, so you flip back, and so on. Draw a structured flowchart or write pseudocode that describes the process of looking up a word in a dictionary. Pick a word at random and have a fellow student attempt to carry out your instructions. (3.2, 3.5)

8. Draw a structured flowchart or write structured pseudocode describing how to get from your home to your school. Include at least two decisions and two loops. (3.2, 3.5)

9. Draw a structured flowchart or write structured pseudocode describing how to decide what college to attend. Include at least two decisions and two loops. (3.2, 3.5)

10. Draw a structured flowchart or write structured pseudocode describing how to buy a new shirt. Include at least two decisions and two loops. (3.2, 3.5)

Performing Maintenance

1. A file named *MAINTENANCE03-01.jpg* is included in the Chapter03 folder of your downloadable student files. Assume that this program is a working program in your organization and that it needs modifications as described in the comments (lines that begin with two slashes) at the beginning of the file. Your job is to alter the program to meet the new specifications. (3.2, 3.5, 3.6)

Debugging Exercises

1. Your downloadable files for Chapter 3 include *DEBUG03-01.txt, DEBUG03-02.txt, DEBUG03-03.txt*, and *DEBUG03-04.jpg*. Each file starts with some comments that describe the problem. Comments are lines that begin with two slashes (//). Each file contains pseudocode or a flowchart that has mistakes. Find and correct all the bugs.

Game Zone

1. Choose a simple children's game and describe its logic, using a structured flowchart or pseudocode. For example, you might try to explain Rock, Paper, Scissors; Musical Chairs; Duck, Duck, Goose; the card game War; or the elimination game Eenie, Meenie, Minie, Moe. (3.2)

2. Choose a television game show such as *Wheel of Fortune* or *Jeopardy*! and describe its rules using a structured flowchart or pseudocode. (3.2)

3. Choose a sport such as baseball or football and describe the actions in one limited play period (such as an at-bat in baseball or a possession in football) using structured pseudocode. (3.2)

Chapter 4

Making Decisions

Learning Objectives

When you complete this chapter, you will be able to:

- **4.1** Describe the selection structure
- **4.2** List the relational comparison operators
- **4.3** Use `AND` logic
- **4.4** Use `OR` logic
- **4.5** Use `NOT` logic
- **4.6** Make selections within ranges
- **4.7** Describe precedence when combining `AND` and `OR` operators
- **4.8** Use the `case` structure

4.1 The Selection Structure

The reason people frequently think computers are smart lies in the ability of computer programs to make decisions. A medical diagnosis program that can decide if your symptoms fit various disease profiles seems quite intelligent, as does a program that can offer different potential driving routes based on your destination. You have learned that the selection structure is one of the three basic structures; it starts with the evaluation of a Boolean expression and takes one of two paths based on the outcome. The two forms of the selection structure appear in **Figure 4-1**.

Figure 4-1 The dual-alternative and single-alternative selection structures

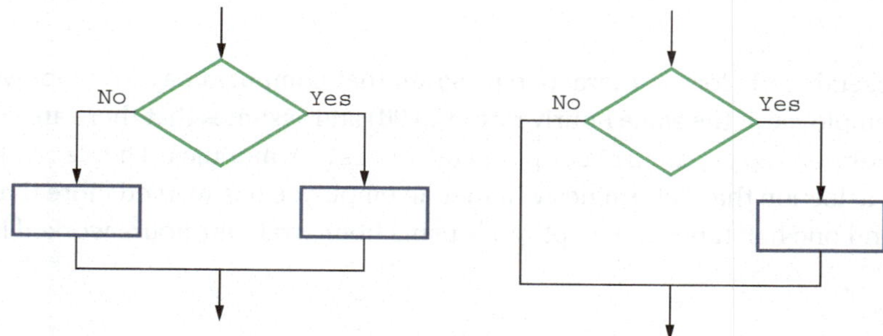

The structure on the left side of Figure 4-1 is a dual-alternative selection because an action is associated with each of two possible outcomes: Depending on the evaluation of the Boolean expression in the decision symbol, the logical flow proceeds either to the left branch of the structure or to the right. The choices are mutually exclusive; that is, the logic can flow to only one of the two alternatives, never to both. This form of the selection structure is an `if-then-else` selection.

The flowchart segment on the right side of Figure 4-1 represents a single-alternative selection in which action is required for only one outcome of the question. This form of the selection structure is called an `if-then` selection, because no alternative or `else` action is necessary.

> **Note** This course follows the convention that the two logical paths emerging from a selection are drawn to the right and left of a diamond in a flowchart. Some programmers draw one of the flowlines emerging from the bottom of the diamond. The exact format of the diagram is not as important as the idea that one logical path flows into a selection, and two possible outcomes emerge. Your flowcharts will be easier for readers to follow if you are consistent when you draw selections. For example, if the *Yes* branch flows to the right for one selection, it should flow to the right for all subsequent selections in the same flowchart.

Figure 4-2 shows the pseudocode standards used to construct `if` statements in this course.

Figure 4-2 `if` statement pseudocode standards

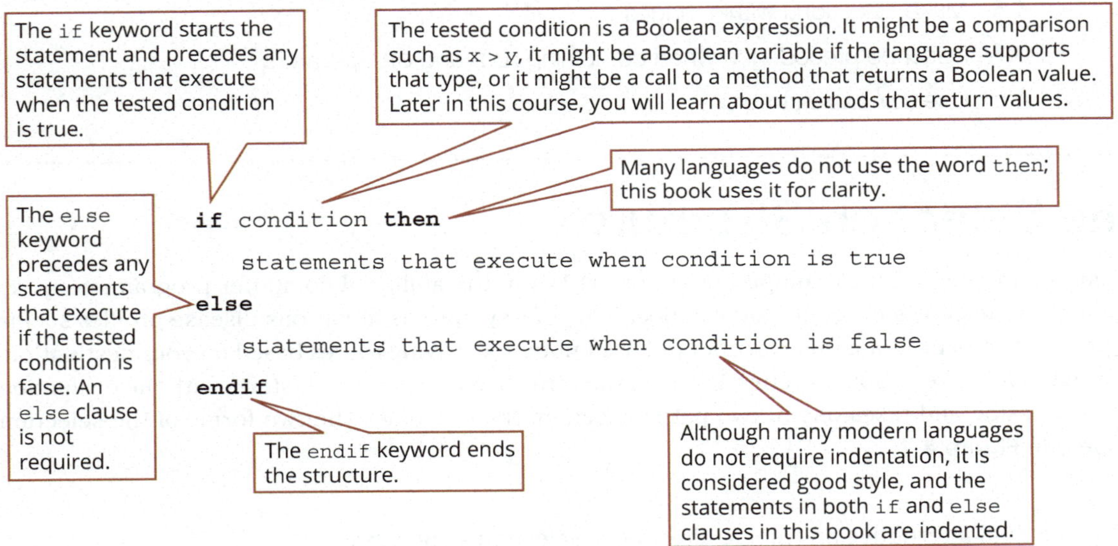

The if keyword starts the statement and precedes any statements that execute when the tested condition is true.
The tested condition is a Boolean expression. It might be a comparison such as x > y, it might be a Boolean variable if the language supports that type, or it might be a call to a method that returns a Boolean value. Later in this course, you will learn about methods that return values.
Many languages do not use the word then; this book uses it for clarity.
The else keyword precedes any statements that execute if the tested condition is false. An else clause is not required.
if condition then
statements that execute when condition is true
else
statements that execute when condition is false
endif
The endif keyword ends the structure.
Although many modern languages do not require indentation, it is considered good style, and the statements in both if and else clauses in this book are indented.

Figure 4-3 shows the flowchart and pseudocode for an interactive program that computes pay for employees. The program displays the weekly pay for each employee at the same hourly rate ($20.00) and assumes that there are no payroll deductions. The mainline logic calls `housekeeping()`, `detailLoop()`, and `finish()` modules. The `detailLoop()` module contains a typical dual-alternative selection that determines whether an employee has worked more than a standard workweek (40 hours) and pays one and one-half times the employee's usual hourly rate for hours worked in excess of 40 per week.

> **Note** Throughout this course, many examples are presented in both flowchart and pseudocode form. When you analyze a solution, you might find it easier to concentrate on just one of the two design tools at first. When you understand how the program works using one design tool (for example, the flowchart), you can confirm that the solution is identical using the other tool.

Figure 4-3 Flowchart and pseudocode for overtime payroll program

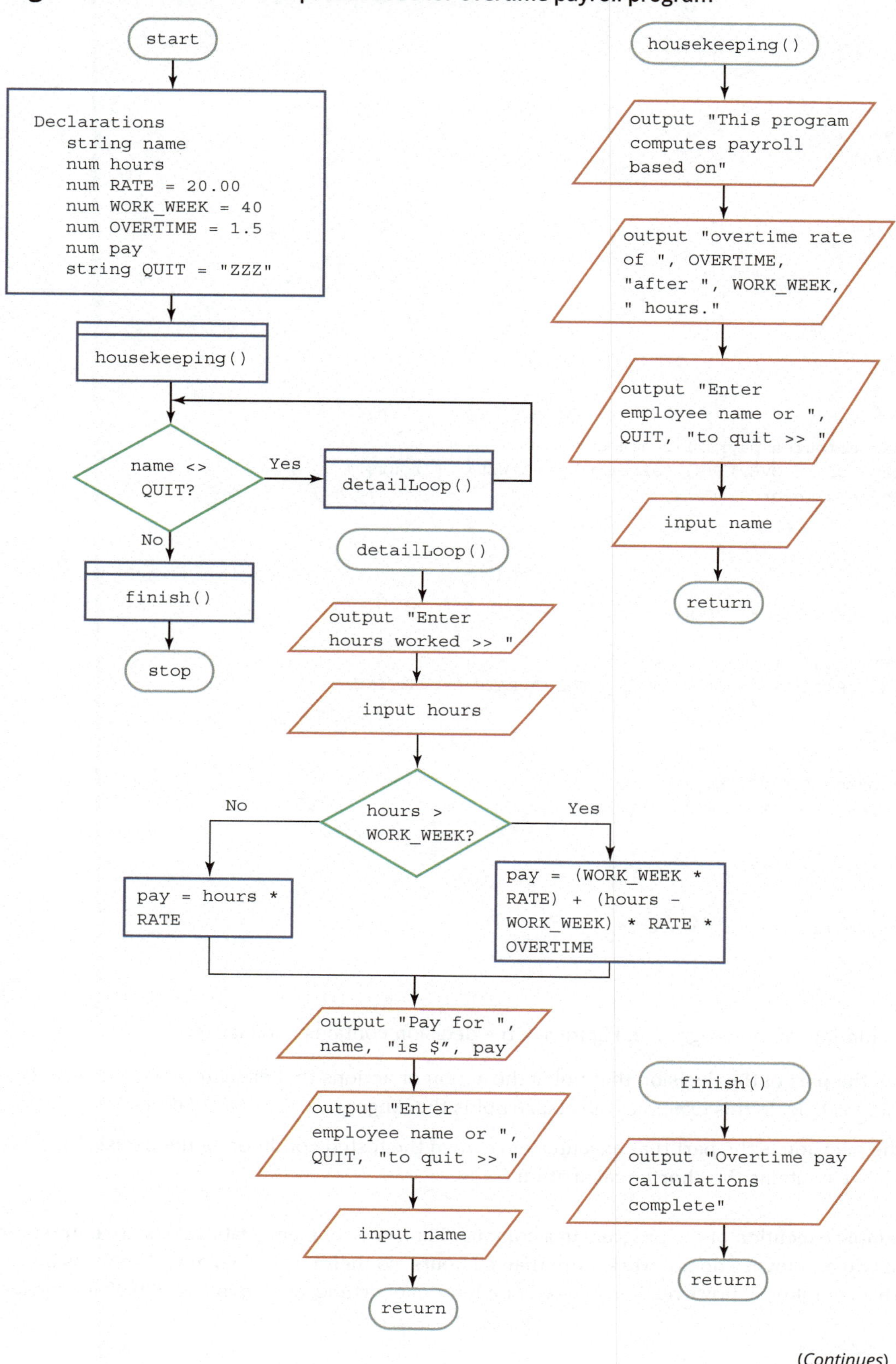

(*Continues*)

Figure 4-3 *(Continued)*

```
start
   Declarations
      string name
      num hours
      num RATE = 20.00
      num WORK_WEEK = 40
      num OVERTIME = 1.5
      num pay
      string QUIT = "ZZZ"
   housekeeping()
   while name <> QUIT
      detailLoop()
   endwhile
   finish()
stop

housekeeping()
   output "This program computes payroll based on"
   output "overtime rate of ", OVERTIME, "after ", WORK_WEEK, " hours."
   output "Enter employee name or ", QUIT, "to quit >> "
   input name
return

detailLoop()
   output "Enter hours worked >> "
   input hours
   if hours > WORK_WEEK then
      pay = (WORK_WEEK * RATE) + (hours - WORK_WEEK) * RATE * OVERTIME
   else
      pay = hours * RATE
   endif
   output "Pay for ", name, "is $", pay
   output "Enter employee name or ", QUIT, "to quit >> "
   input name
return

finish()
   output "Overtime pay calculations complete"
return
```

In the `detailLoop()` module of the program in Figure 4-3, the decision contains two clauses:

- The **`if-then` clause** is the part of the decision that holds the action or actions that execute when the tested condition in the decision is true. In this example, the clause holds the longer overtime calculation.
- The **`else` clause** of the decision is the part that executes only when the tested condition in the decision is false. In this example, the clause contains the shorter calculation.

Figure 4-4 shows a sample execution of the program in a command-line environment. Data values are entered for three employees. The first two employees do not work more than 40 hours, so their pay is displayed simply as `hours` multiplied by 20.00. The third employee, however, has worked one hour of overtime, and so makes $30.00 for the last hour instead of $20.00.

Figure 4-4 Sample execution of the overtime payroll program in Figure 4-3

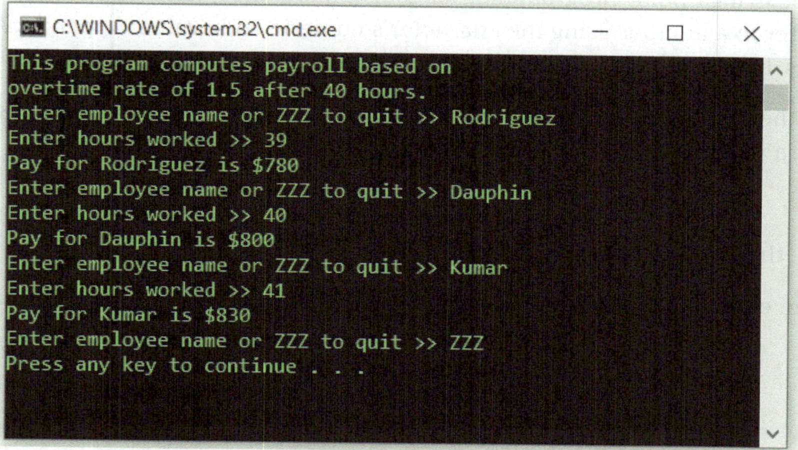

C:\WINDOWS\system32\cmd.exe
This program computes payroll based on
overtime rate of 1.5 after 40 hours.
Enter employee name or ZZZ to quit >> Rodriguez
Enter hours worked >> 39
Pay for Rodriguez is $780
Enter employee name or ZZZ to quit >> Dauphin
Enter hours worked >> 40
Pay for Dauphin is $800
Enter employee name or ZZZ to quit >> Kumar
Enter hours worked >> 41
Pay for Kumar is $830
Enter employee name or ZZZ to quit >> ZZZ
Press any key to continue . . .

Two Truths & a Lie | The Selection Structure

1. The `if-then` clause is the part of a decision that executes when a tested condition in a decision is true.
2. The `else` clause is the part of a decision that executes when a tested condition in a decision is true.
3. A Boolean expression is one whose value is true or false.

The false statement is #2. The `else` clause is the part of a decision that executes when a tested condition in a decision is false.

4.2 Using Relational Comparison Operators

Table 4-1 describes the six **relational comparison operators** supported by all modern programming languages. Each of these operators is binary—that is, like the arithmetic operators such as + and *, each relational comparison operator in Table 4-1 requires two operands, one on each side. Each expression that uses one of these operators evaluates to true or false. Notice that some operators are formed using two characters with no space between them.

Table 4-1 Relational comparison operators

Operator	Name	Discussion
=	Equivalency operator	Evaluates as true when its operands are equivalent.
>	Greater-than operator	Evaluates as true when the left operand is greater than the right operand.
<	Less-than operator	Evaluates as true when the left operand is less than the right operand.
>=	Greater-than-or-equal-to operator	Evaluates as true when the left operand is greater than or equivalent to the right operand.
<=	Less-than-or-equal-to operator	Evaluates as true when the left operand is less than or equivalent to the right operand.
<>	Not-equal-to operator	Evaluates as true when its operands are not equivalent.

Both operands in a comparison expression must be the same data type; that is, you can compare numeric values to other numeric values, and text strings to other strings. Some programming languages allow exceptions; for example, some languages allow you to compare a character to a number using the character's numeric code value. Appendix A contains more information about coding systems. In this course, only operands of the same data type will be compared.

In any comparison, the two values can be either variables or constants. For example, the following Boolean expression uses the equivalency operator to compare a variable, `currentTotal`, to an unnamed numeric constant, 100:

```
currentTotal = 100
```

Depending on the value of `currentTotal`, the expression is true or false.

The following Boolean expression uses the equivalency operator to compare a variable, `currentTotal`, to a named numeric constant, `MAX`:

```
currentTotal = MAX
```

Note An expression that uses the equivalency operator (=) looks like an assignment statement. For that reason, some languages use a different symbol—for example, two equal signs (= =)—to represent equivalency. This course will use the single equal sign. You can determine whether an expression is a comparison or an assignment by its context. If a statement containing an equal sign appears in a diamond in a flowchart or in an `if` statement in pseudocode, then it is a comparison operator.

As another example, both values in the following expression are variables, and the result is also true or false depending on the values stored in each of the two variables:

```
currentTotal = previousTotal
```

Although it's legal, you would never use expressions in which you compare two literal constants—for example, `20 = 20` or `30 = 40`. Such expressions are **trivial expressions** because each will always evaluate to the same result: true for `20 = 20` and false for `30 = 40`.

Some languages require special operations to compare strings, but this course will assume that the standard comparison operators work correctly with strings based on their alphabetic values. For example, the comparison `"black" < "blue"` would be evaluated as true because `"black"` precedes `"blue"` alphabetically. Usually, string variables are not considered to be equal unless they are identical, including the spacing and whether they appear in uppercase or lowercase. For example, `"black pen"` is not equal to `"blackpen"`, `"BLACK PEN"`, or `"Black Pen"`.

Any decision can be made using combinations of just three types of comparisons: equal, greater than, and less than. You never need the three additional comparisons (greater than or equal, less than or equal, or not equal), but using them often makes decisions more convenient. For example, assume that you need to issue a 10 percent discount to any customer whose age is 65 or greater, and charge full price to other customers. **Figure 4-5** shows how you can use either the greater-than-or-equal-to symbol or the less-than symbol to express the same logic that sets a discount when `customerAge` is at least 65.

Figure 4-5 Identical logic expressed using >= and <

`if customerAge >= 65 then`
`   discount = 0.10`
`else`
`   discount = 0`
`endif`
	`if customerAge < 65 then`
	`   discount = 0`
	`else`
	`   discount = 0.10`
	`endif`

Action taken when `customerAge >= 65` is true

In any decision for which `a >= b` is true, then `a < b` is false. Conversely, if `a >= b` is false, then `a < b` is true. By rephrasing the question and swapping the actions taken based on the outcome, you can make the same decision in multiple ways. The clearest route is often to ask a question so the positive or true outcome results in the action that was your motivation for making the test. When your company policy is to "provide a discount for those who are 65 and older," the phrase *greater than or equal to 65* comes to mind, so it is the most natural to use. Conversely, if your policy is to "provide no discount for those under 65," then it is more natural to use the *less than 65* syntax. Either way, the same people receive a discount.

Comparing two amounts to decide if they are *not* equal to each other is the most confusing of all the comparisons. Using *not equal to* in decisions involves thinking in double negatives, which can make you prone to introducing logical errors into your programs. For example, consider the flowchart segment in **Figure 4-6**.

Figure 4-6 Using a negative comparison

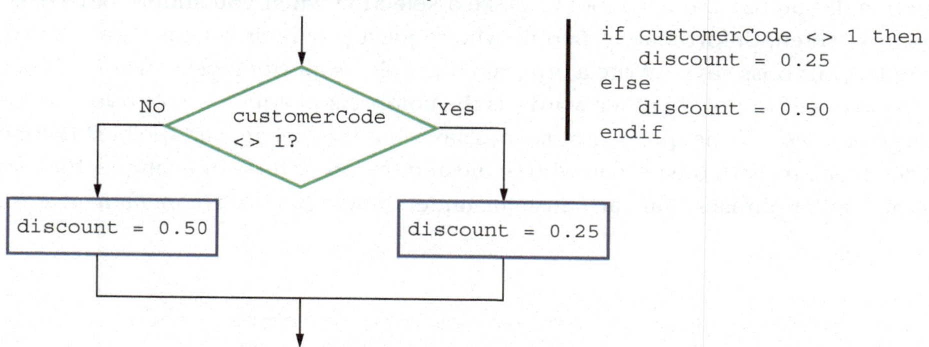


```
if customerCode <> 1 then
   discount = 0.25
else
   discount = 0.50
endif
```

> **Note** Instead of <>, some languages use an exclamation point followed by an equal sign (!=) as the not-equal-to operator. In a flowchart or pseudocode, you might prefer to use the algebraic not-equal-to symbol (≠) or to spell out the words *not equal to*.

In Figure 4-6, if the value of `customerCode` *is* equal to 1, the logical flow follows the false branch of the selection. If `customerCode <> 1` is true, the discount is 0.25; if `customerCode <> 1` is not true, it means the `customerCode` *is* 1, and the `discount` is 0.50. Even reading the phrase "if `customerCode` is not equal to 1 is not true" is awkward.

Figure 4-7 shows the same decision, this time asked using positive logic. Making the decision based on what `customerCode` *is* is clearer than trying to determine what `customerCode` is *not*.

Figure 4-7 Using the positive equivalent of the negative comparison in **Figure 4-6**

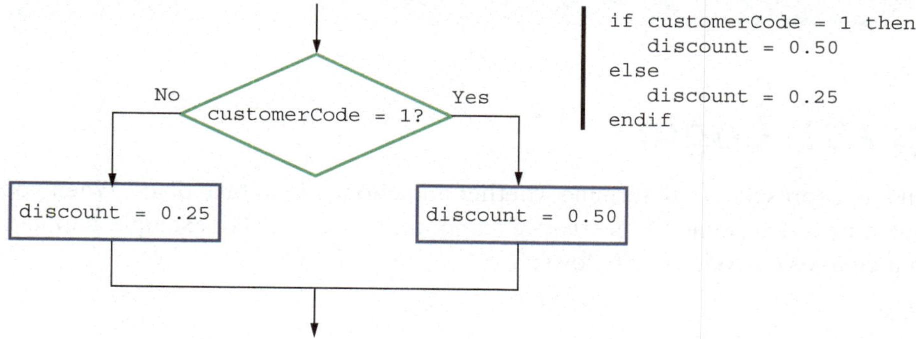


```
if customerCode = 1 then
   discount = 0.50
else
   discount = 0.25
endif
```

> **Note** Although negative comparisons can be awkward to use, your meaning is sometimes clearest when using them. Frequently, this occurs when you use an `if` without an `else`, taking action only when some comparison is false. An example would be:

```
if customerZipCode <> LOCAL_ZIP_CODE then
   total = total + deliveryCharge
endif
```

Avoiding a Common Error with Relational Operators

A common error that occurs when programming with relational operators is using the wrong one and missing the boundary or limit required for a selection. If you use the > symbol to make a selection when you should have used >=, all the cases that are equal will go unselected. Unfortunately, people who request programs do not always speak as precisely as a computer. If, for example, your boss says, "Write a program that selects all employees over 65," does your boss mean to include employees who are 65 or not? In other words, is the comparison `age > 65` or `age >= 65`? Although the phrase *over 65* indicates *greater than 65*, people do not always say what they mean, and the best course of action is to double-check the intended meaning with the person who requested the program—for example, the end user, your supervisor, or your instructor. Similar phrases that can cause misunderstandings are *no more than*, *at least*, and *not under*.

> **Note** Many modern programming languages support Boolean data types. Instead of holding numbers or words, each Boolean variable can hold only one of two values—true or false. In other words, if `hasWorkedOvertime` is a Boolean variable, then the result of evaluating `hours > 40` can be assigned to it.

Two Truths & a Lie | Using Relational Comparison Operators

1. Usually, you can compare only values that are of the same data type.
2. A Boolean expression is defined as one that decides whether two values are equal.
3. In any logical comparison expression, the two values compared can be either variables or constants.

The false statement is #2. Although deciding whether two values are equal is a Boolean expression, so is deciding whether one is greater than or less than another. A Boolean expression is one that results in a true or false value.

4.3 Understanding AND Logic

Often, you need to evaluate more than one expression to determine whether an action should take place. When you make multiple evaluations before an outcome is determined, you create a **compound condition**. For example, suppose you work for a cell phone company that charges customers as follows:

- The basic monthly service bill is $30.
- An additional $20 is billed to customers who make more than 100 calls that last for a total of more than 500 minutes.

The logic needed for this billing program includes an **AND decision**—an expression that tests a condition with two parts that must both evaluate to true for an action to take place. In this case, both a minimum number of calls must be made *and* a minimum number of minutes must be used before the customer is charged the premium amount. A decision that uses an AND expression can be constructed using a **nested decision**, or a **nested `if`**—that is, a decision within the `if-then` or `else` clause of another decision. A series of nested `if` statements is also called a **cascading `if` statement**. The flowchart and pseudocode for the program that determines the charges for cell phone customers is shown in **Figure 4-8**.

Figure 4-8 Flowchart and pseudocode for cell phone billing program

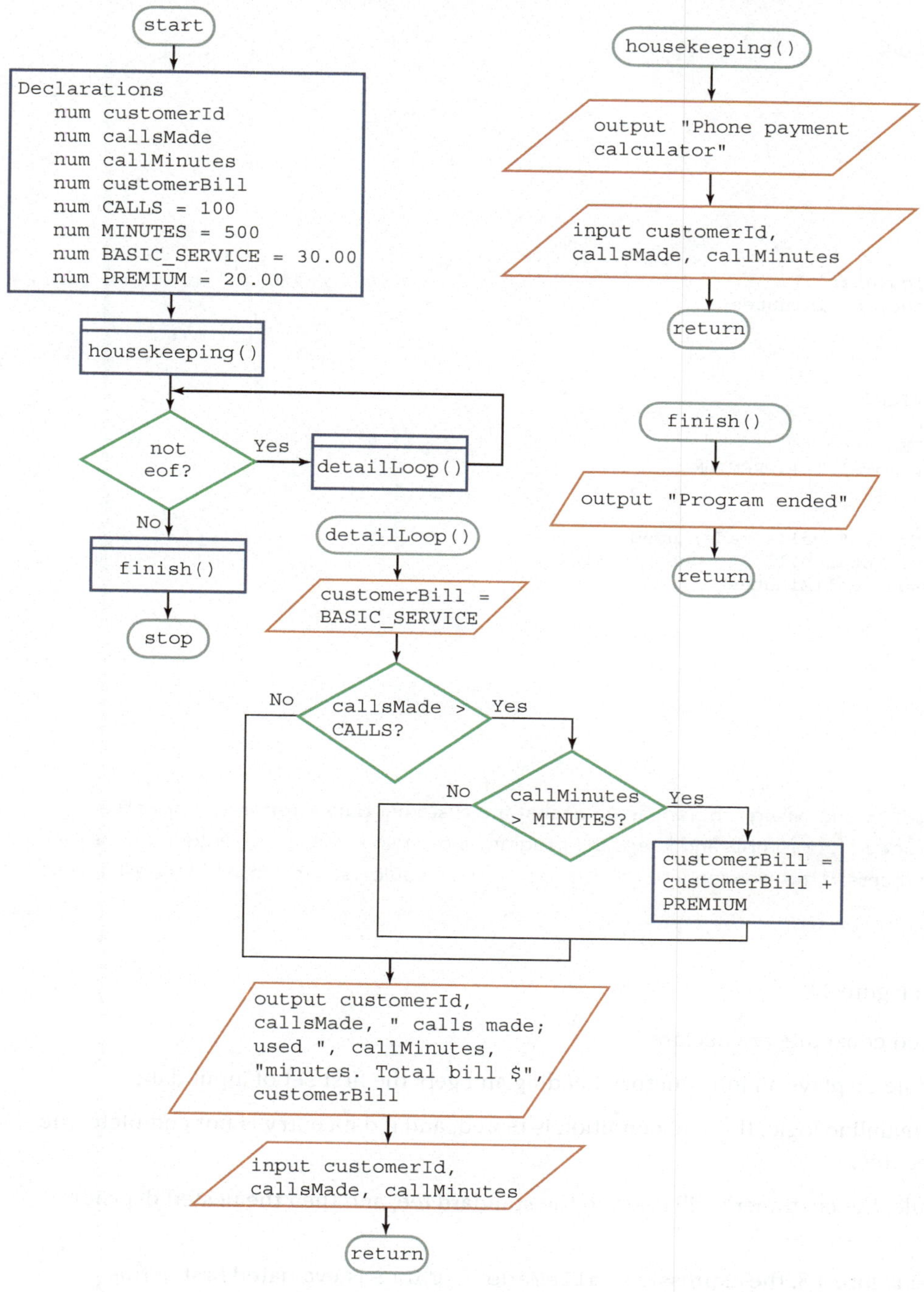

(Continues)

Figure 4-8 *(Continued)*

```
start
   Declarations
      num customerId
      num callsMade
      num callMinutes
      num customerBill
      num CALLS = 100
      num MINUTES = 500
      num BASIC_SERVICE = 30.00
      num PREMIUM = 20.00
   housekeeping()
   while not eof
      detailLoop()
   endwhile
   finish()
stop

housekeeping()
   output "Phone payment calculator"
   input customerId, callsMade, callMinutes
return

detailLoop()
   customerBill = BASIC_SERVICE
   if callsMade > CALLS then
      if callMinutes > MINUTES then
         customerBill = customerBill + PREMIUM
      endif
   endif
   output customerId, callsMade, " calls made; used ",
      callMinutes, " minutes. Total bill $", customerBill
   input customerId, callsMade, callMinutes
return

finish()
   output "Program ended"
return
```

Note The logic for the cell phone billing program assumes that the customer data is retrieved from a file. This eliminates the need for prompts and keeps the program shorter so you can concentrate on the decision-making process. If this were an interactive program, you would use a prompt before each input statement.

The following steps occur in Figure 4-8:

- The appropriate variables and constants are declared.
- The `housekeeping()` module displays an introductory heading and gets the first set of input data.
- After control returns to the mainline logic, the `eof` condition is tested, and if data entry is not complete, the `detailLoop()` module executes.
- In the `detailLoop()` module, the customer's bill is set to the standard fee, and then the nested decision executes.
- In the nested `if` structure in Figure 4-8, the expression `callsMade > CALLS` is evaluated first. If this expression is true, only then is the second Boolean expression (`callMinutes > MINUTES`) evaluated. If that expression is also true, then the $20 premium is added to the customer's bill.
- If either of the tested conditions is false, the customer's bill value is never altered, retaining the initially assigned `BASIC_SERVICE` value of $30.

Nesting AND Decisions for Efficiency

When you nest two decisions, you must choose which of the decisions to make first. Logically, either expression in an AND decision can be evaluated first. You often can improve your program's performance, however, by correctly choosing which of two selections to make first.

For example, **Figure 4-9** shows two ways to design the nested decision structure that assigns a premium to customers' bills if they make more than 100 cell phone calls and use more than 500 minutes in a billing period. The program can take two approaches:

- The program can ask about calls made first, eliminate customers who have not made more than the minimum, and then ask about the minutes used only for customers who pass (that is, are evaluated as true on) the minimum calls test.
- Or, the program could ask about the minutes first, eliminate those who do not qualify, and then ask about the number of calls only for customers who pass the minutes test.

Figure 4-9 Two ways to produce cell phone bills using identical criteria

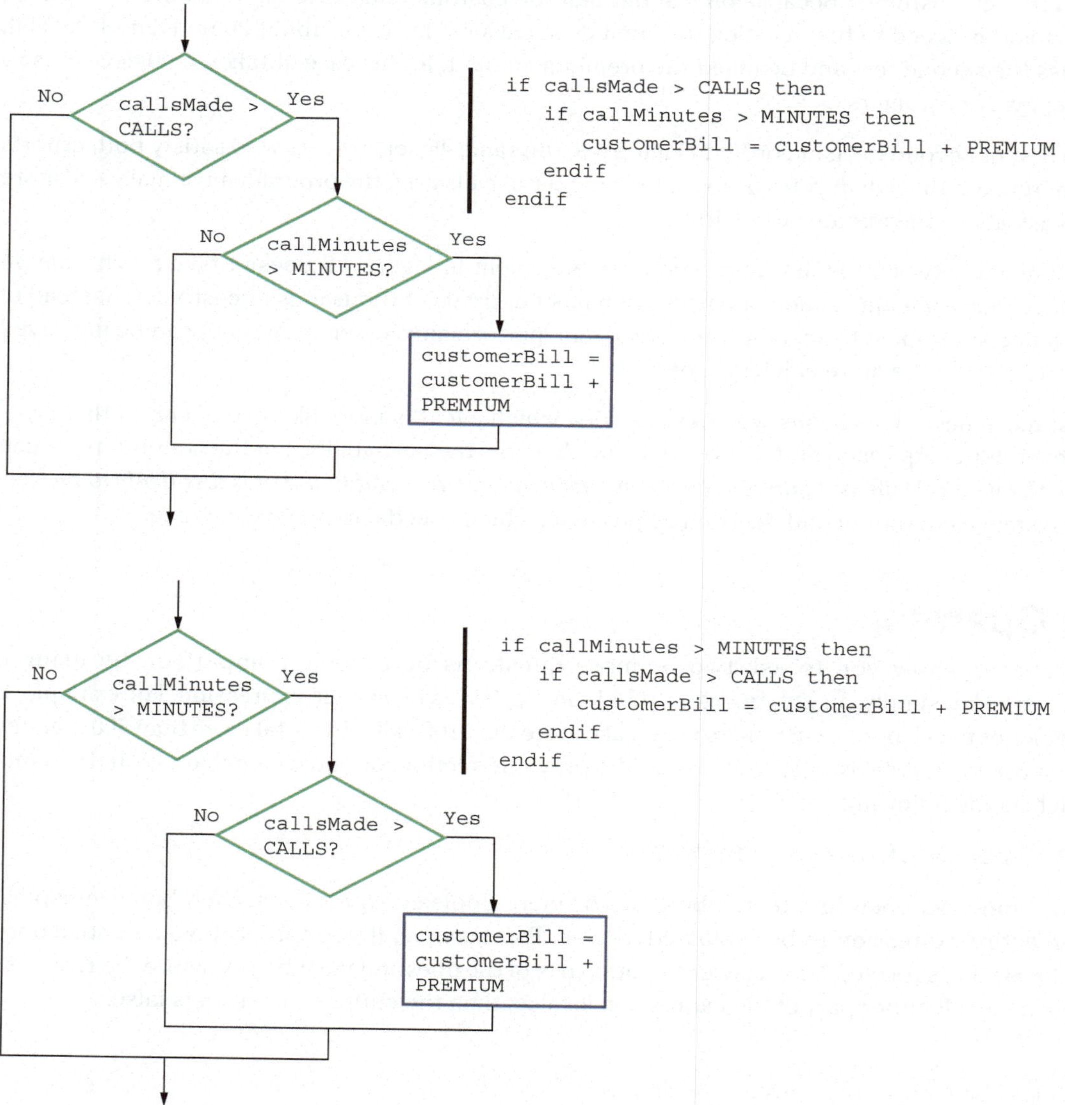
No
callsMade > CALLS?
Yes
No
callMinutes > MINUTES?
Yes
customerBill = customerBill + PREMIUM
if callsMade > CALLS then
if callMinutes > MINUTES then
customerBill = customerBill + PREMIUM
endif
endif
No
callMinutes > MINUTES?
Yes
No
callsMade > CALLS?
Yes
customerBill = customerBill + PREMIUM
if callMinutes > MINUTES then
if callsMade > CALLS then
customerBill = customerBill + PREMIUM
endif
endif

Either way, only customers who exceed both limits must pay the premium. Does it make a difference which question is asked first? As far as the result goes, no. Either way, the same customers pay the premium—those who qualify on the basis of both criteria. As far as program efficiency goes, however, it *might* make a difference which question is asked first.

Assume that you know the following statistics:

- Out of 1000 cell phone customers, about 90 percent, or 900, make more than 100 calls in a billing period.
- Only about half the 1000 customers, or 500, use more than 500 minutes of call time.

If you use the logic shown first in Figure 4-9, and you need to produce 1000 phone bills, the first question, `callsMade > CALLS`, will execute 1000 times. For approximately 90 percent of the customers, or 900 of them, the answer is true, so 100 customers are eliminated from the premium assignment, and 900 proceed to the next question about the minutes used. Only about half the customers use more than 500 minutes, so 450 of the 900 pay the premium, and it takes 1900 decisions to identify them.

Using the alternate logic shown second in Figure 4-9, the first question, `callMinutes > MINUTES`, also will be asked 1000 times—once for each customer. Because only about half the customers use the high number of minutes, only 500 will pass this test and proceed to the question for number of calls made. Then, about 90 percent of the 500, or 450 customers, will pass the second test and be billed the premium amount. In this case, it takes 1500 decisions to identify the 450 premium-paying customers.

Whether you use the first or second decision order in Figure 4-9, the same 450 customers who satisfy both criteria pay the premium. The difference is that when you ask about the number of calls first, the program must make 400 more decisions than when you ask about the minutes used first.

The 400-decision difference between the first and second arrangement in Figure 4-9 doesn't take much time on most computers. But it does take *some* time, and if a corporation has hundreds of thousands of customers instead of only 1000, or if many such decisions must be made within a program, performance (execution time) can be improved significantly by making decisions in the more efficient order.

Often when you must make nested decisions, you have no idea which event is more likely to occur; in that case, you can legitimately make either comparison first. However, if you do know the probabilities of the conditions, or can make a reasonable guess, the general rule is: *In an AND decision, first evaluate the condition that is less likely to be true.* This eliminates as many instances of the second decision as possible, which speeds up processing time.

Using the AND Operator

Most programming languages allow you to ask two or more questions in a single comparison by using a **conditional AND operator**, or more simply, an **AND operator** that joins decisions in a single expression. For example, if you want to bill an extra amount to cell phone customers who make more than 100 calls that total more than 500 minutes in a billing period, you can use nested decisions, as shown in the previous section, or you can include both decisions in a single expression such as the following:

```
callsMade > CALLS AND callMinutes > MINUTES
```

When you use one or more AND operators to combine two or more Boolean expressions, each Boolean expression must be true for the entire expression to be evaluated as true. For example, if you ask, "Are you a native-born U.S. citizen and are you at least 35 years old?," the answer to both parts of the question must be *yes* before the response can be a single, summarizing *yes*. If either part of the expression is false, then the entire expression is false.

Note | The conditional AND operator in Java, C++, and C# consists of two ampersands, with no spaces between them (&&). In Visual Basic, you use the keyword `And`. This course uses AND.

One tool that can help you understand the AND operator is a truth table. A **truth table** is a diagram used in mathematics and logic to help describe the truth of an entire expression based on the truth of its parts. **Table 4-2** contains a truth table that lists all the possibilities with an AND operator. As the table shows, for any two expressions x and y, the expression x AND y is true only if both x and y are individually true. If either x or y alone is false, or if both are false, then the expression x AND y is false.

Table 4-2 Truth table for the AND operator

x?	y?	x AND y?
True	True	True
True	False	False
False	True	False
False	False	False

If the programming language you use allows an AND operator, you must realize that the Boolean expression you place first (to the left of the AND operator) is the one that will be evaluated first, and cases that are eliminated based on the first evaluation will not proceed to the second one. In other words, each part of an expression that uses an AND operator is evaluated only as far as necessary to determine whether the entire expression is true or false. This feature is called **short-circuit evaluation**. A computer can make only one decision at a time, so even when your logic uses an AND operator and looks like the first example in **Figure 4-10**, the computer will execute the logic as two separate decisions,

Figure 4-10 Using an AND operator and the logic behind it

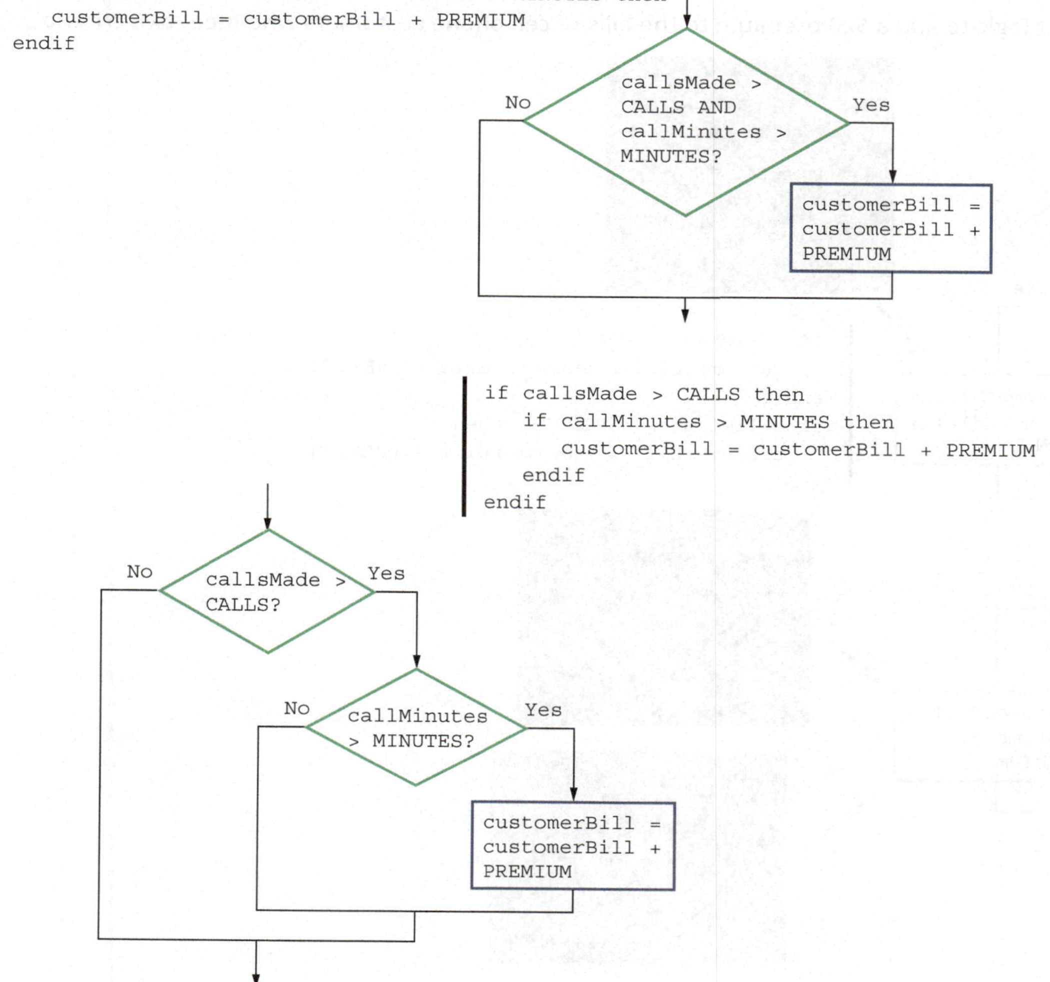
if callsMade > CALLS AND callMinutes > MINUTES then
customerBill = customerBill + PREMIUM
endif
No
callsMade > CALLS AND callMinutes > MINUTES?
Yes
customerBill = customerBill + PREMIUM
if callsMade > CALLS then
if callMinutes > MINUTES then
customerBill = customerBill + PREMIUM
endif
endif
No
callsMade > CALLS?
Yes
No
callMinutes > MINUTES?
Yes
customerBill = customerBill + PREMIUM

as shown in the second example in the figure. Even when you use an AND operator, a computer evaluates expressions one at a time, and in order from left to right. As you can see in the truth table, if the first half of an AND expression is false, then the entire expression is false. In that case, there is no point in evaluating the second half. In other words, evaluating an AND expression is interrupted as soon as either part of it is determined to be false.

When two conditions must be true for an action to take place, you are never required to use the AND operator because using nested `if` statements can always achieve the same result. However, using the AND operator often makes your code more concise, less error-prone, and easier to understand.

Note There can be confusion between the terms *conditional operator* and *logical operator*. *Conditional operator* most often is used when short-circuit evaluation is in effect, but you sometimes will hear programmers use the two terms interchangeably. To complicate matters, some programmers call the operators *conditional logical operators*.

Avoiding Common Errors in an AND Selection

Make Sure Decisions that Should Be Nested Are Nested

When you need to satisfy two or more criteria to initiate an event in a program, you must make sure that the second decision is made entirely within the first decision. For example, if a program's objective is to add a $20 premium to the bill of cell phone customers who exceed 100 calls and 500 minutes in a billing period, then the program segment shown in **Figure 4-11** contains three different types of logic errors.

Figure 4-11 Incorrect logic to add a $20 premium to the bills of cell phone customers who meet two criteria

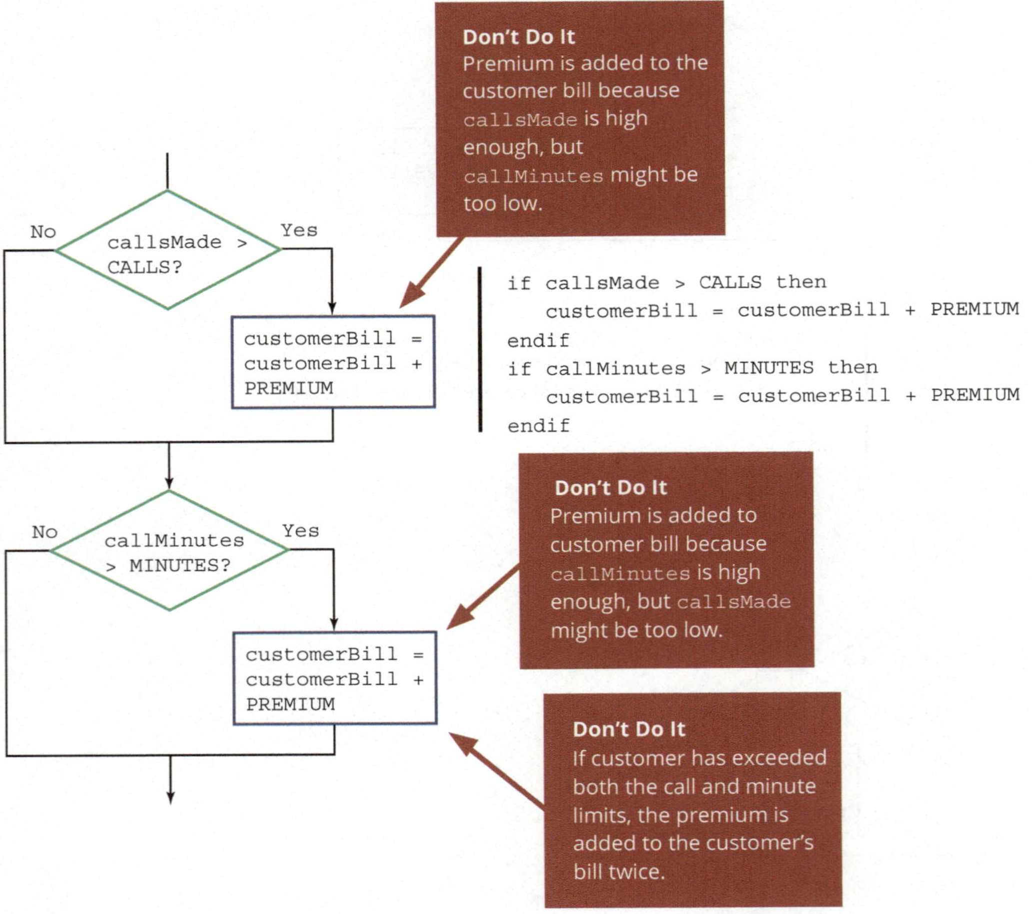

The logic in Figure 4-11 shows that if a customer makes too many calls, $20 is added to the bill. This customer should not necessarily be billed extra because the customer's minutes might be low. In addition, in Figure 4-11, a customer who has made few calls is not eliminated from the second decision. Instead, all customers are subjected to the minutes evaluation, and some are assigned the premium even though they might have made only a few calls. Additionally, any customer who passes both tests because calls and minutes are both high has the premium added to the bill twice. The decisions in Figure 4-11 are stacked when they should be nested, so the logic they represent is *not* correct for this problem.

Make Sure that Boolean Expressions Are Complete

When you use the AND operator in most languages, you must provide a complete Boolean expression on each side of the operator. In other words, the following expression would be valid to use to find `callMinutes` between 100 and 200:

```
callMinutes > 100 AND callMinutes < 200
```

However, `callMinutes > 100 AND < 200` would not be valid because the less-than sign and 200 that follow the AND operator do not constitute a complete Boolean expression.

For clarity, you can enclose each Boolean expression in a compound expression in its own set of parentheses. This makes it easier for you to see that each of the AND operator's operands is a complete Boolean expression. Use this format if it is clearer to you. For example, you might write the following:

```
if (callMinutes > MINUTES) AND (callsMade > CALLS) then
   customerBill = customerBill + PREMIUM
endif
```

Make Sure that Expressions Are Not Inadvertently Trivial

When you use the AND operator, it is easy to inadvertently create trivial expressions that are always true or always false. For example, suppose that you want to display a message if any cell phone customer makes a very low or high number of calls—say, fewer than 5 or more than 2000. You might be tempted to write the following expression, but it would be incorrect:

```
if callsMade < 5 AND callsMade > 2000 then
   output "Irregular usage"
endif
```

Don't Do It
This AND expression is always false.

This `if` statement never results in a displayed message because both parts of the AND expression can never be true at the same time. For example, if the value of `callsMade` is greater than 2000, its value is not less than 5, and if `callsMade` is less than 5, it is not greater than 2000. The programmer intended to use the following code:

```
if callsMade < 5 then
   output "Irregular usage"
else
   if callsMade > 2000 then
      output "Irregular usage"
   endif
endif
```

Alternately, the programmer might use an OR operator, as you will see in the next section.

Two Truths & a Lie | Understanding AND Logic

1. When you nest selection structures because the resulting action requires that two conditions be true, either decision logically can be made first and the results will be the same.
2. When two selections are required for an action to take place, you often can improve your program's performance by appropriately choosing which selection to make first.
3. To improve efficiency in a nested selection in which two conditions must be true for some action to occur, you should first evaluate the condition that is more likely to be true.

The false statement is #3. For efficiency in a nested selection, you should first evaluate the condition that is less likely to be true.

4.4 Understanding OR Logic

Sometimes you want to take action when one *or* the other of two conditions is true. This is called an **OR decision** because either one condition *or* some other condition must be met in order for some action to take place. If someone asks, "Are you free for dinner Friday or Saturday?" only one of the two conditions has to be true for the answer to the whole question to be *yes*; only if the answers to both halves of the question are false is the value of the entire expression false. For example, suppose the cell phone company has established a new fee schedule as follows:

- The basic monthly service bill is $30.
- An additional $20 is billed to customers who make more than 100 calls or send more than 200 text messages.

Figure 4-12 shows the `detailLoop()` module of the billing program that accomplishes this objective. Assume that declarations have been made for the `textsSent` variable and a `TEXTS` constant that has been assigned the value 200.

The `detailLoop()` in the program in Figure 4-12 tests the expression `callsMade > CALLS`, and if the result is true, the premium amount is added to the customer's bill. Because making many calls is enough for the customer to incur the premium, there is no need for further questioning. If the customer has not made more than 100 calls, only then does the program need to ask whether `textsSent > TEXTS` is true. If the customer did not make more than 100 calls, but did send more than 200 text messages, then the premium amount is added to the customer's bill.

Writing OR Selections for Efficiency

As with an AND condition, when you use an OR condition, you can choose to ask either question first. For example, you can add an extra $20 to the bills of customers who meet one or the other of two criteria using the logic in either part of **Figure 4-13**.

You might have guessed that one of these solutions is superior to the other when you have some background information about the relative likelihood of each tested condition. For example, let's say you know these statistics:

- Out of 1000 cell phone customers, about 90 percent, or 900, make more than 100 calls in a billing period.
- Only about half of the 1000 customers, or 500, send more than 200 text messages.

When you use the logic shown in the first half of Figure 4-13, you first evaluate calls made. For 900 customers, the value of `callsMade` is greater than `CALLS`, so you add the premium to their bills. Only about 100 sets of customer data continue to the next decision regarding the text messages, where about 50 percent of the 100, or 50, are billed the extra amount. In the end, you have made 1100 decisions to correctly add premium amounts for 950 customers.

Figure 4-12 Flowchart and pseudocode for cell phone billing program in which a customer must meet at least one of two criteria to be billed a premium

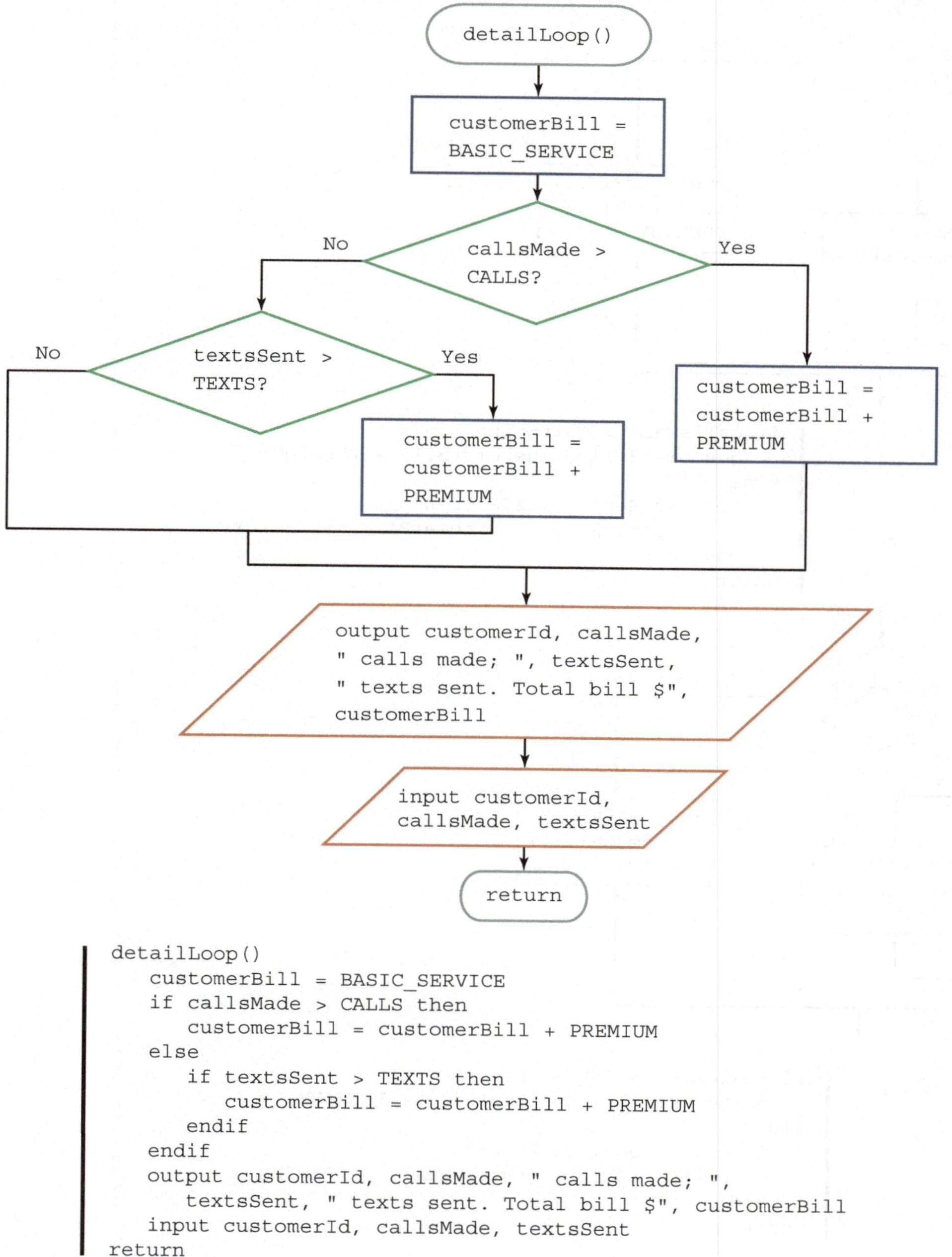


```
detailLoop()
   customerBill = BASIC_SERVICE
   if callsMade > CALLS then
      customerBill = customerBill + PREMIUM
   else
      if textsSent > TEXTS then
         customerBill = customerBill + PREMIUM
      endif
   endif
   output customerId, callsMade, " calls made; ",
      textsSent, " texts sent. Total bill $", customerBill
   input customerId, callsMade, textsSent
return
```

If you use the OR logic in the second half of Figure 4-13, you ask about text messages first—1000 times, once each for 1000 customers. The result is true for 50 percent, or 500 customers, whose bill is increased. For the other 500 customers, you ask about the number of calls made. For 90 percent of the 500, the result is true, so premiums are added for 450 additional people. In the end, the same 950 customers are billed an extra $20—but this approach requires executing 1500 decisions, 400 more decisions than when using the first decision logic.

The general rule is: *In an* OR *decision, first evaluate the condition that is more likely to be true.* This approach eliminates as many executions of the second decision as possible, and the time it takes to process all the data is decreased. As with the AND situation, in an OR situation, it is more efficient to eliminate as many extra decisions as possible.

Figure 4-13 Two ways to assign a premium to bills of customers who meet one of two criteria

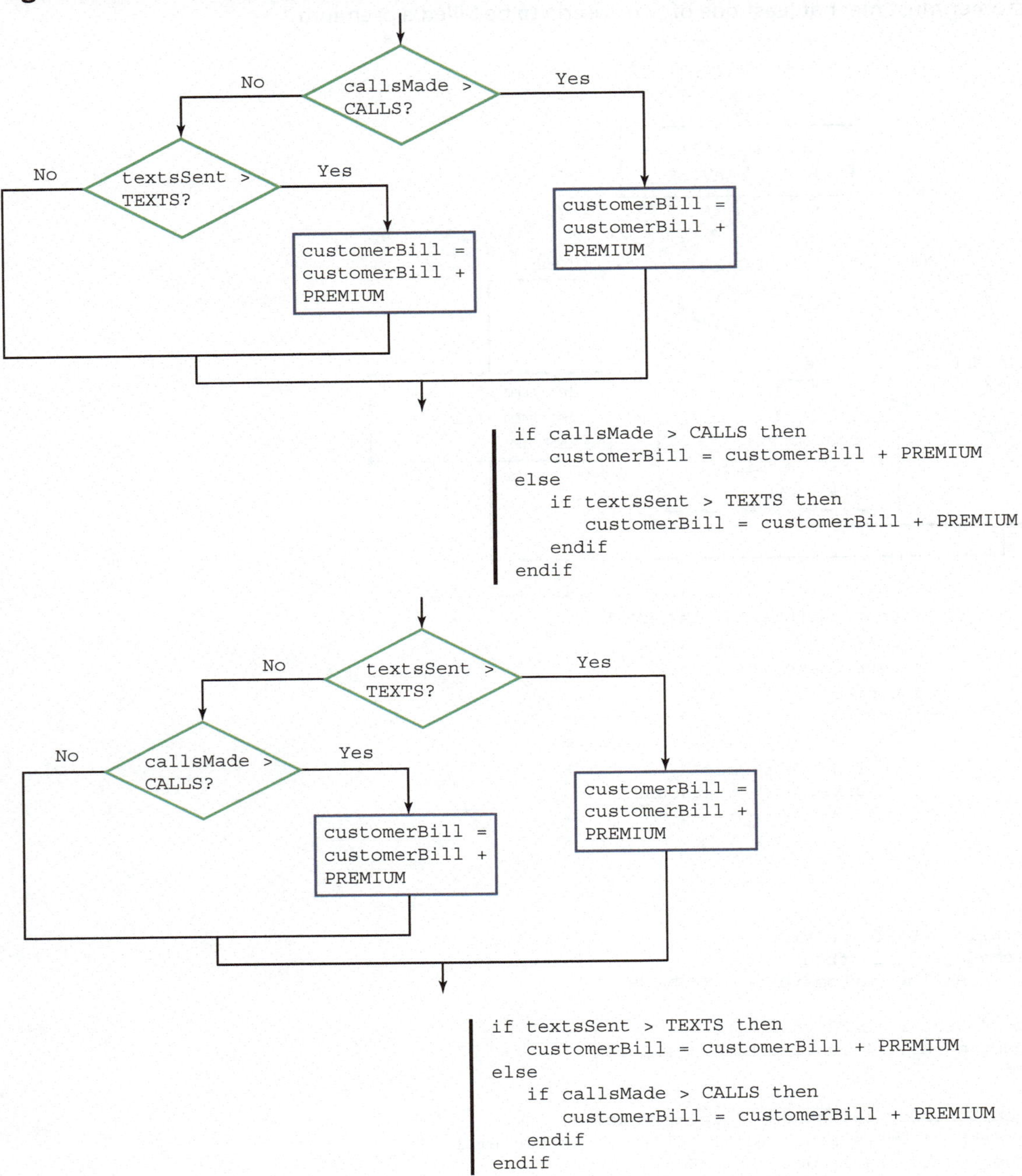
No
callsMade > CALLS?
Yes
No
textsSent > TEXTS?
Yes
customerBill = customerBill + PREMIUM
customerBill = customerBill + PREMIUM
if callsMade > CALLS then
   customerBill = customerBill + PREMIUM
else
   if textsSent > TEXTS then
      customerBill = customerBill + PREMIUM
   endif
endif
No
textsSent > TEXTS?
Yes
No
callsMade > CALLS?
Yes
customerBill = customerBill + PREMIUM
customerBill = customerBill + PREMIUM
if textsSent > TEXTS then
   customerBill = customerBill + PREMIUM
else
   if callsMade > CALLS then
      customerBill = customerBill + PREMIUM
   endif
endif

Using the OR Operator

If you need to take action when either one or the other of two conditions is met, you can use two separate, nested selection structures, as in the previous examples. Most programming languages, however, allow you to make two or more decisions in a single comparison by using a **conditional OR operator** (or simply the **OR operator**). For example, you can make the following evaluation:

```
callsMade > CALLS OR textsSent > TEXTS
```

When you use the logical OR operator, only one of the listed conditions must be met for the resulting action to take place. **Table 4-3** contains the truth table for the OR operator. As you can see in the table, the entire expression `x OR y` is false only when `x` and `y` each are false individually.

Table 4-3 Truth table for the OR operator

x?	y?	x OR y?
True	True	True
True	False	True
False	True	True
False	False	False

If the programming language you use supports an OR operator, you still must realize that the comparison you place first is the expression that will be evaluated first, and cases that pass the test of the first comparison will not proceed to the second comparison. As with the AND operator, this feature is called *short-circuiting*. The computer can make only one decision at a time; even when you write code as shown at the top of **Figure 4-14**, the computer will execute the logic shown at the bottom.

> **Note** | C#, C++, C, and Java use two pipe symbols (||) as the logical OR operator. In Visual Basic, the keyword used for the operator is Or. This course uses OR.

Figure 4-14 Using an OR operator and the logic behind it

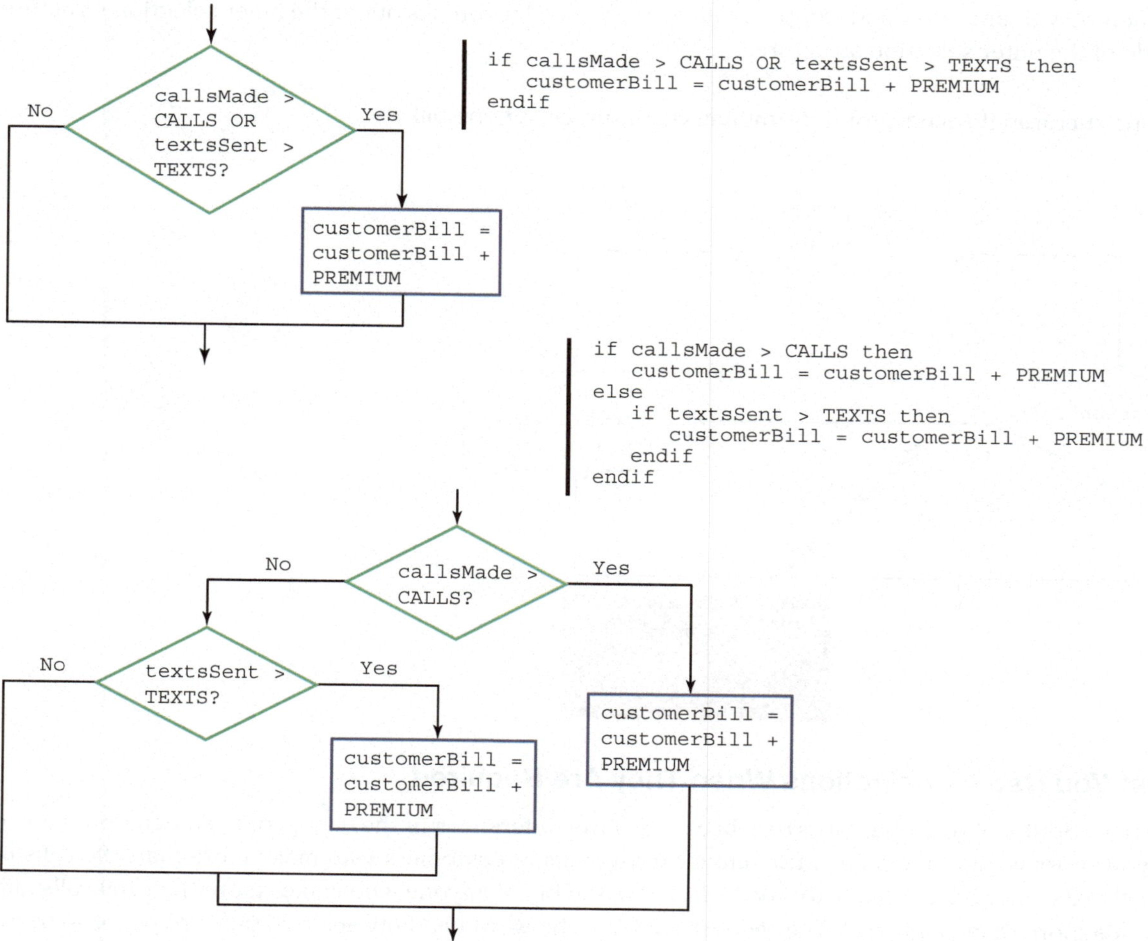

No
callsMade > CALLS OR textsSent > TEXTS?
Yes
customerBill = customerBill + PREMIUM
if callsMade > CALLS OR textsSent > TEXTS then
customerBill = customerBill + PREMIUM
endif
if callsMade > CALLS then
customerBill = customerBill + PREMIUM
else
if textsSent > TEXTS then
customerBill = customerBill + PREMIUM
endif
endif
No
callsMade > CALLS?
Yes
No
textsSent > TEXTS?
Yes
customerBill = customerBill + PREMIUM
customerBill = customerBill + PREMIUM

Avoiding Common Errors in an OR Selection

Make Sure that Boolean Expressions Are Complete

As with the AND operator, most programming languages require a complete Boolean expression on each side of the OR operator. For example, if you wanted to display a message when customers make either no calls or more than 2000 calls, the expression `callsMade = 0 OR callsMade > 2000` is appropriate but `callsMade = 0 OR > 2000` is not, because the expression to the right of the OR operator is not a complete Boolean expression.

Also, as with the AND operator, you can enclose each simple comparison within parentheses for clarity if you want, as in the following statement:

```
if (callsMade = 0) OR (callsMade > 2000) then
   output "Irregular usage"
endif
```

Make Sure that Selections Are Structured

You might have noticed that the assignment statement `customerBill = customerBill + PREMIUM` appears twice in the decision-making processes in Figures 4-13 and 4-14. When you create a flowchart, the temptation is to draw the logic to look like **Figure 4-15**. Logically, you might argue that the flowchart in Figure 4-15 is correct because the correct customers are billed the extra $20. This flowchart, however, is not structured. The second question is not a self-contained structure with one entry and exit point; instead, the flowline breaks out of the inner selection structure to join the Yes side of the outer selection structure.

Figure 4-15 Unstructured flowchart for determining customer cell phone bill

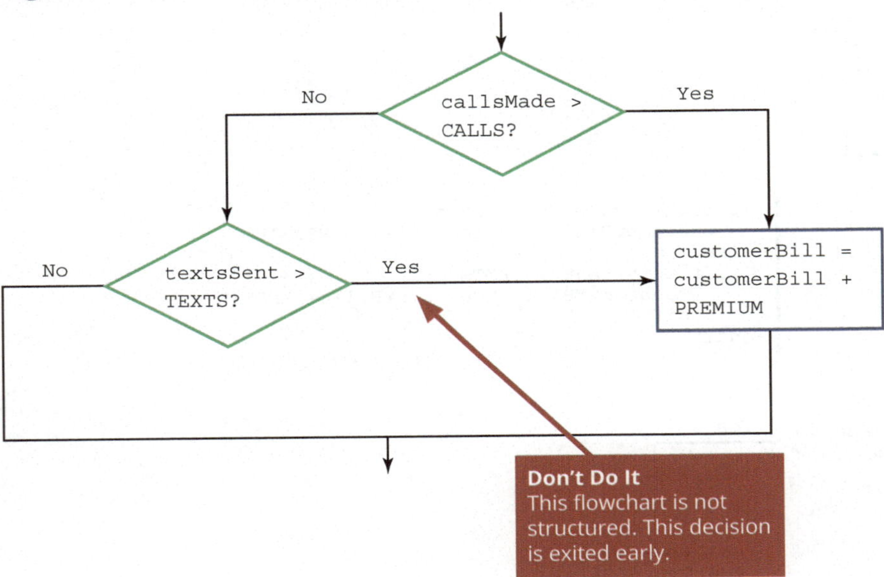
No
callsMade >
CALLS?
Yes
No
textsSent >
TEXTS?
Yes
customerBill =
customerBill +
PREMIUM
Don't Do It
This flowchart is not structured. This decision is exited early.

Make Sure that You Use OR Selections When They Are Required

The OR selection has additional potential for errors because of the differences in the way people and computers use language. When your boss wants to add an extra amount to the bills of customers who make more than 100 calls *or* send more than 200 texts, your boss is likely to say, "Add $20 to the bill of anyone who makes more than 100 calls and to anyone who sends more than 200 texts." The request contains the word *and* between two types of people—those who made many calls and those who sent many texts—placing the emphasis on the people.

However, each decision you make is about the added $20 for a single customer who has met one criterion *or* the other *or* both. In other words, the OR condition is between each customer's attributes, and not between different customers. Instead of the previous statement, it would be clearer if your boss said, "Add $20 to the bill of anyone who has made more than 100 calls or has sent more than 200 texts," but you can't count on people to speak like computers. As a programmer, you have the job of clarifying what really is being requested. Often, a casual request for A *and* B logically means a request for A *or* B.

Make Sure that Expressions Are Not Inadvertently Trivial

The way we use English can cause another type of error when you are required to find whether a value falls between two other values. For example, a movie theater manager might say, "Provide a discount to patrons who are under 13 years old and to those who are over 64 years old; otherwise, charge the full price." Because the manager has used the word *and* in the request, you might be tempted to create the decision shown in **Figure 4-16**; however, this logic will not provide a discounted price for any movie patron. You must remember that every time the decision is made in Figure 4-16, it is made for a single movie patron. If `patronAge` contains a value lower than 13, then it cannot possibly contain a value over 64. Similarly, if `patronAge` contains a value over 64, there is no way it can contain a lesser value. Therefore, no value could be stored in `patronAge` for which both parts of the AND condition could be true—and the price will never be set to the discounted price for any patron. In other words, the decision made in Figure 4-16 is trivial. **Figure 4-17** shows the correct logic.

Figure 4-16 Incorrect logic that attempts to provide a discount for young and old movie patrons

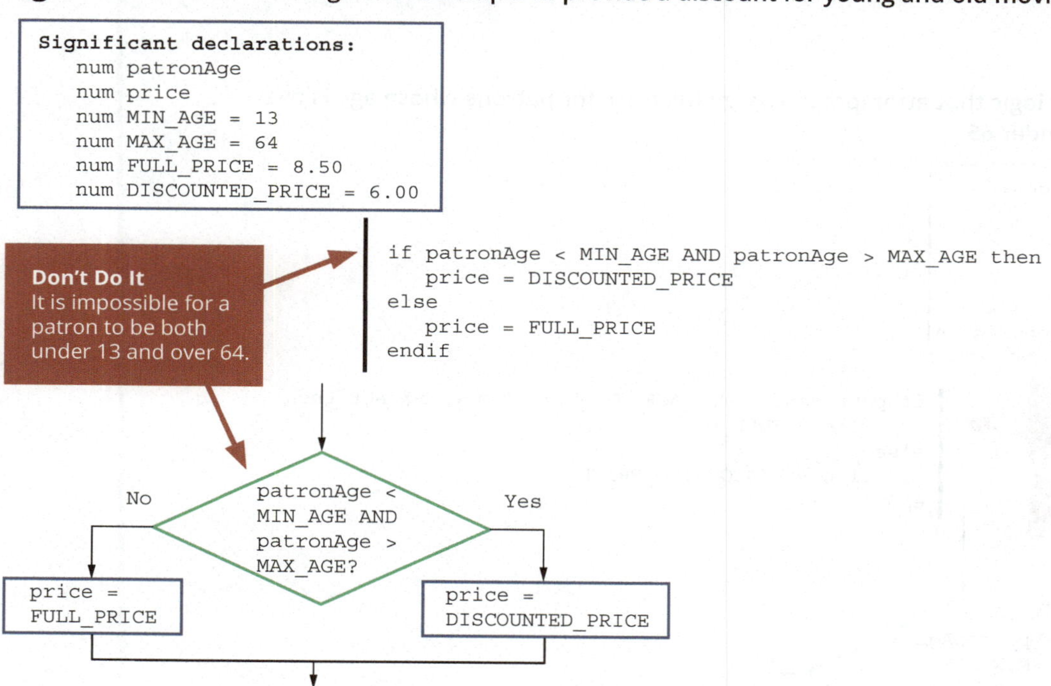
Significant declarations:
num patronAge
num price
num MIN_AGE = 13
num MAX_AGE = 64
num FULL_PRICE = 8.50
num DISCOUNTED_PRICE = 6.00
if patronAge < MIN_AGE AND patronAge > MAX_AGE then
price = DISCOUNTED_PRICE
else
price = FULL_PRICE
endif
Don't Do It
It is impossible for a patron to be both under 13 and over 64.
No
patronAge < MIN_AGE AND patronAge > MAX_AGE?
Yes
price = FULL_PRICE
price = DISCOUNTED_PRICE

A similar error can occur in your logic if the theater manager says something like, "Don't give a discount—that is, do charge full price—if a patron is over 12 or under 65." Because the word *or* appears in the request, you might plan your logic to resemble **Figure 4-18**. No patron ever receives a discount because every patron is either over 12 or under 65. Remember, in an OR decision, only one of the conditions needs to be true for the entire expression to be evaluated as true. So, for example, because a patron who is 10 is under 65, the full price is charged, and because a patron who is 70 is over 12, the full price also is charged. **Figure 4-19** shows the correct logic for this decision.

Figure 4-17 Correct logic that provides a discount for young and old movie patrons

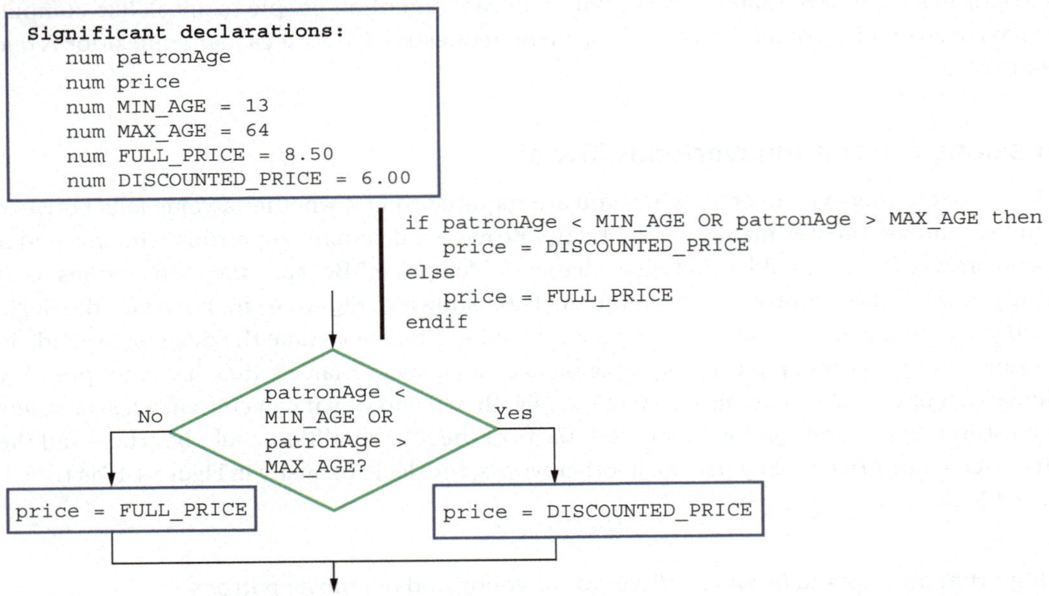
Significant declarations:
num patronAge
num price
num MIN_AGE = 13
num MAX_AGE = 64
num FULL_PRICE = 8.50
num DISCOUNTED_PRICE = 6.00
if patronAge < MIN_AGE OR patronAge > MAX_AGE then
price = DISCOUNTED_PRICE
else
price = FULL_PRICE
endif
No
patronAge < MIN_AGE OR patronAge > MAX_AGE?
Yes
price = FULL_PRICE
price = DISCOUNTED_PRICE

Figure 4-18 Incorrect logic that attempts to charge full price for patrons whose age is over 12 and under 65

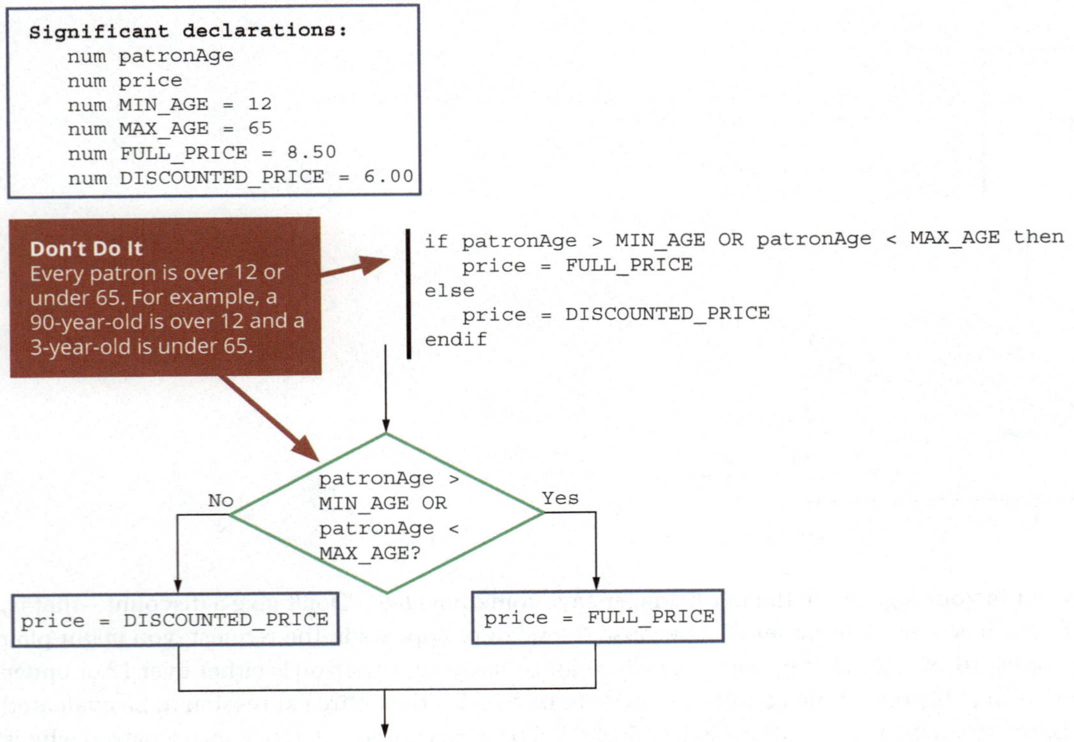
Significant declarations:
num patronAge
num price
num MIN_AGE = 12
num MAX_AGE = 65
num FULL_PRICE = 8.50
num DISCOUNTED_PRICE = 6.00
Don't Do It
Every patron is over 12 or under 65. For example, a 90-year-old is over 12 and a 3-year-old is under 65.
if patronAge > MIN_AGE OR patronAge < MAX_AGE then
price = FULL_PRICE
else
price = DISCOUNTED_PRICE
endif
No
patronAge > MIN_AGE OR patronAge < MAX_AGE?
Yes
price = DISCOUNTED_PRICE
price = FULL_PRICE

Figure 4-19 Correct logic that charges full price for patrons whose age is over 12 and under 65

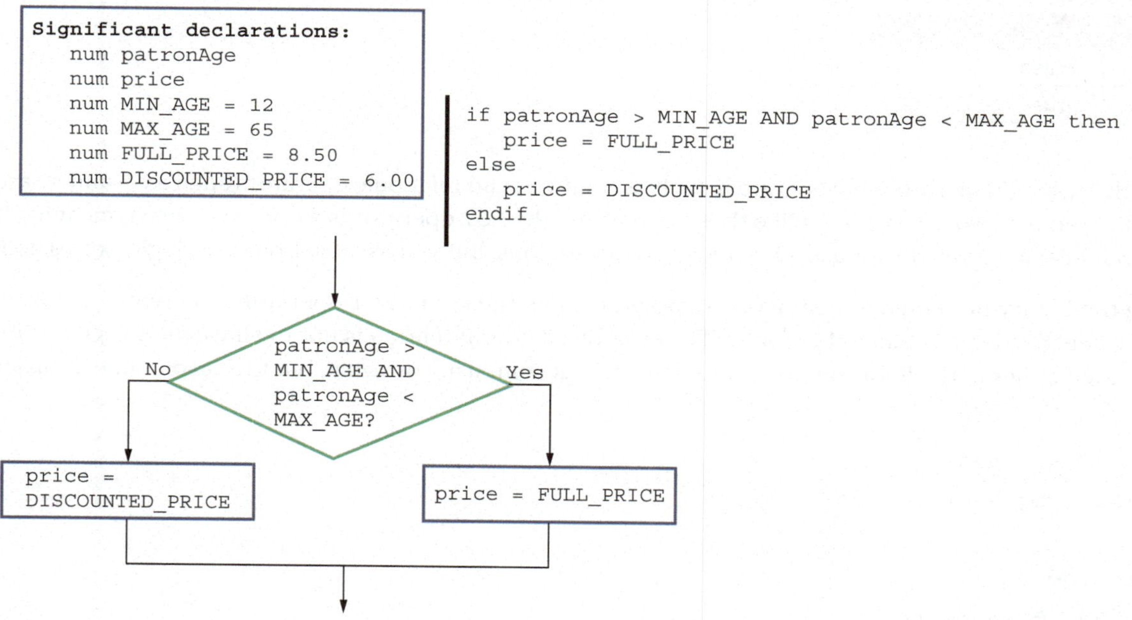
Significant declarations:
num patronAge
num price
num MIN_AGE = 12
num MAX_AGE = 65
num FULL_PRICE = 8.50
num DISCOUNTED_PRICE = 6.00
if patronAge > MIN_AGE AND patronAge < MAX_AGE then
price = FULL_PRICE
else
price = DISCOUNTED_PRICE
endif
patronAge > MIN_AGE AND patronAge < MAX_AGE?
No
Yes
price = DISCOUNTED_PRICE
price = FULL_PRICE

Two Truths & a Lie | Understanding OR Logic

1. In an OR selection, two or more conditions must be met in order for an event to take place.
2. When you use an OR selection with two conditions, you can choose to evaluate either condition first and still achieve a usable program.
3. The general rule is: In an OR decision, first evaluate the condition that is more likely to be true.

The false statement is #1. In an OR selection, only one of two conditions must be met in order for an event to take place.

4.5 Understanding NOT Logic

Besides AND and OR operators, most languages support a NOT operator. You use the **NOT operator** to reverse the meaning of a Boolean expression. For example, the following statement outputs *Can register to vote* when age is greater than or equal to 18:

```
if NOT (age < 18) then
   output "Can register to vote"
endif
```

This example uses parentheses around the expression `age < 18` to show that the NOT operator applies to the entire Boolean expression `age < 18`. Without the parentheses, some languages might try to evaluate the expression `NOT age` before testing the less-than comparison. Depending on the programming language, the result would either be incorrect or the statement would not execute at all.

Table 4-4 contains the truth table for the NOT operator. As you can see, any expression that would be true without the operator becomes false with it, and any expression that would be false without the operator becomes true with it.

Table 4-4 Truth table for the `NOT` operator

x?	NOT x?
True	False
False	True

You have already learned that arithmetic operators such as + and −, and relational operators such as > and <, are binary operators that require two operands. Unlike those operators, the NOT operator is a **unary operator**, meaning it takes only one operand—that is, you do not use it between two expressions, but you use it in front of a single expression.

As when using the binary not-equal-to comparison operator, using the unary NOT operator can create confusing statements because negative logic is difficult to follow. For example, if your intention is not to allow voter registration for those under 18, then either of the following two statements will accomplish your goal, but the second one is easier to understand:

```
if NOT (age < 18) then
   output "Can register to vote"
endif
if age >= 18 then
   output "Can register to vote"
endif
```

Avoiding a Common Error in a NOT Expression

Because thinking with negatives is hard, you need to be careful not to create trivial expressions when using NOT logic. For example, suppose your boss tells you to display a message for all employees *except* those in Departments 1 and 2. You might write the following incorrect code:

```
if NOT (employeeDept = 1) OR NOT (employeeDept = 2) then
   output "Employee is not in Department 1 or 2"
endif
```

Don't Do It
This logic does not eliminate employees in Departments 1 and 2.

Suppose that an employee is in Department 2, and therefore no message should be displayed. For that employee, the following expression is false:

```
employeeDept = 1
```

Therefore, this expression is true:

```
NOT (employeeDept = 1)
```

Because the OR operator's left operand is true, the entire Boolean expression is true, and the message is inappropriately displayed.

Suppose that an employee is in Department 1, and therefore no message should be displayed. For that employee, the following expression is true:

```
employeeDept = 1
```

Therefore, this expression is false:

```
NOT (employeeDept = 1)
```

However, then the second part of the compound condition is evaluated, and this expression is true:

```
NOT (employeeDept = 2)
```

Because the OR operator's right operand is true, the entire Boolean expression is true, and again the message is inappropriately displayed.

The correct decision follows:

```
if NOT (employeeDept = 1 OR employeeDept = 2) then
   output "Employee is not in Department 1 or 2"
endif
```

Note In C++, Java, and C#, the exclamation point is the symbol used for the NOT operator. In those languages, the exclamation point can be used in front of an expression or combined with other comparison operators. For example, the expression *a not equal to b* can be written as `!(a = b)` or as `a != b`. In Visual Basic, the operator is the keyword `Not`. This course uses `NOT`.

Two Truths & a Lie | Understanding NOT Logic

1. The value of `x <> 0` is the same as the value of `NOT (x = 0)`.
2. The value of `x > y` is the same as the value of `NOT (x < y)`.
3. The value of `x = y OR x > 5` is the same as the value of `x = y OR NOT (x <= 5)`.

The false statement is #2. The value of `x > y` is not the value of `NOT (x < y)` because the first expression is false and the second one is true when `x` and `y` are equal. The value of `x > y` is the same as the value of `NOT (x <= y)`.

4.6 Making Selections Within Ranges

You often need to take action when a variable falls within a range of values. For example, suppose your company provides various customer discounts based on the number of items ordered, as follows:

- 10 or fewer items—no discount
- 11 to 24 items—10% discount
- 25 to 50 items—15% discount
- 51 or more items—20% discount

When you write the program that determines a discount rate based on the number of items, you could make hundreds of decisions, evaluating `itemQuantity = 1`, `itemQuantity = 2`, and so on. However, it is more convenient to find the correct discount rate by using a range check.

When you use a **range check**, you compare a variable to a series of values that mark the limiting ends of ranges. To perform a range check, make comparisons using either the lowest or highest value in each range of values. For example, to successfully find each discount rate listed above, you can make comparisons using either the low end of each range or the high end of each range.

If you want to use the low ends of the ranges (11, 25, and 51), either of these techniques works:

- You can ask: Is `itemQuantity` less than 11? If not, is it less than 25? If not, is it less than 51?
- You can ask: Is `itemQuantity` greater than or equal to 51? If not, is it greater than or equal to 25? If not, is it greater than or equal to 11?

If you want to use the high ends of the ranges (10, 24, and 50), either of these techniques works:

- You can ask: Is `itemQuantity` greater than 50? If not, is it greater than 24? If not, is it greater than 10?
- You can ask: Is `itemQuantity` less than or equal to 10? If not, is it less than or equal to 24? If not, is it less than or equal to 50?

Figure 4-20 shows the flowchart and pseudocode that represent the logic for a program that determines the correct discount for each order quantity using the high ends of the ranges. The logic proceeds as follows:

- First, `itemsOrdered` is compared to the high end of the lowest-range group (`RANGE1`). If `itemsOrdered` is less than or equal to that value (10), then you know the correct discount, `DISCOUNT1`; if not, you continue checking.
- If `itemsOrdered` is less than or equal to the high end of the next range (`RANGE2`), then the customer's discount is `DISCOUNT2`; if not, you continue checking.
- The customer's discount eventually is set to `DISCOUNT3` or `DISCOUNT4`.

In the pseudocode in Figure 4-20, notice how each associated `if`, `else`, and `endif` aligns vertically.

Figure 4-20 Flowchart and pseudocode of logic that selects correct discount based on items ordered

```
Significant declarations:
   num itemsOrdered
   num customerDiscount
   num RANGE1 = 10
   num RANGE2 = 24
   num RANGE3 = 50
   num DISCOUNT1 = 0
   num DISCOUNT2 = 0.10
   num DISCOUNT3 = 0.15
   num DISCOUNT4 = 0.20
```

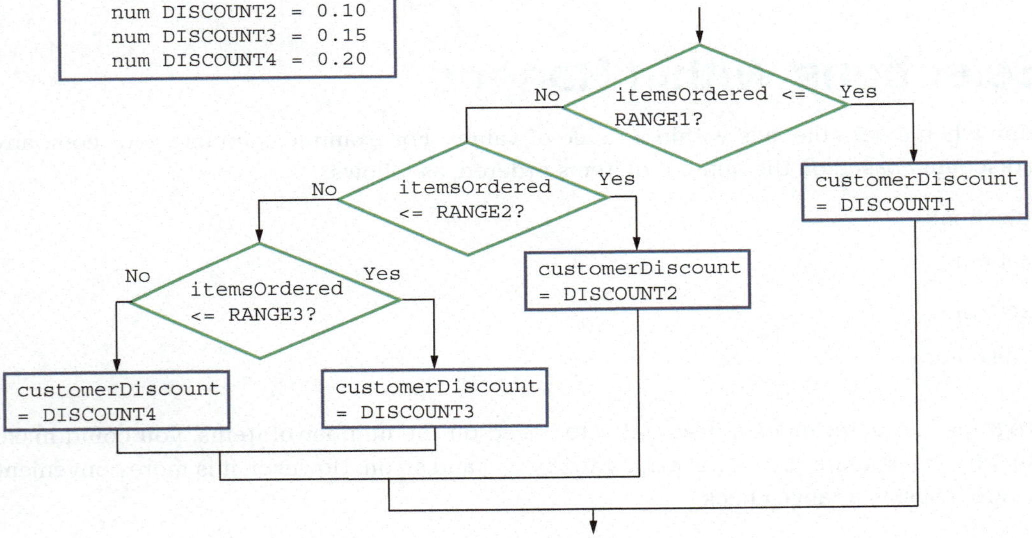

itemsOrdered <= RANGE1?
No
Yes
customerDiscount = DISCOUNT1
itemsOrdered <= RANGE2?
No
Yes
customerDiscount = DISCOUNT2
itemsOrdered <= RANGE3?
No
Yes
customerDiscount = DISCOUNT4
customerDiscount = DISCOUNT3

```
if itemsOrdered <= RANGE1 then
   customerDiscount = DISCOUNT1
else
   if itemsOrdered <= RANGE2 then
      customerDiscount = DISCOUNT2
   else
      if itemsOrdered <= RANGE3 then
         customerDiscount = DISCOUNT3
      else
         customerDiscount = DISCOUNT4
      endif
   endif
endif
```

> **Note** In computer memory, a percent sign (%) is not stored with a numeric value that represents a percentage. Instead, the mathematical equivalent is stored. For example, 15% is stored as 0.15. You can store a percent value as a string, as in `"15%"`, but then you cannot perform arithmetic with it.

For example, consider an order for 30 items. The expression `itemsOrdered <= RANGE1` evaluates as false, so the `else` clause of the decision executes. There, `itemsOrdered <= RANGE2` also evaluates to false, so its `else` clause executes. The expression `itemsOrdered <= RANGE3` is true, so `customerDiscount` becomes `DISCOUNT3`, which is 0.15. Walk through the logic with other values for `itemsOrdered` and verify for yourself that the correct discount is applied each time.

Avoiding Common Errors When Using Range Checks

To create well-written programs that include range checks, you should be careful to eliminate dead paths and to avoid testing the same range limit multiple times.

Eliminate Dead Paths

When new programmers perform range checks, they are prone to including logic that has too many decisions, entailing more work than is necessary.

Figure 4-21 shows a program segment that contains a range check in which the programmer has asked one question too many. If you know that `itemsOrdered` is not less than or equal to `RANGE1`, not less than or equal to `RANGE2`, and not less than or equal to `RANGE3`, then `itemsOrdered` must be greater than `RANGE3`. The comparison to `RANGE3` is trivial, so asking whether `itemsOrdered` is greater than `RANGE3` is a waste of time; no customer order can ever travel the logical path on the far left of the flowchart. You might say such a path is a **dead path** or **unreachable path**, and that the statements written there constitute dead or unreachable code. Although a program that contains such logic will execute and assign the correct discount to customers who order more than 50 items, providing such a path is inefficient.

> **Note** With people, sometimes there are good reasons to ask questions for which you already know the answers. For example, a good trial lawyer seldom asks a question in court if the answer will be a surprise. With computer logic, however, such questions are an inefficient waste of time.

Avoid Testing the Same Range Limit Multiple Times

Another error that programmers make when writing the logic to perform a range check also involves asking unnecessary questions. **Figure 4-22** shows an inefficient range selection that asks two unneeded questions. In the figure, if `itemsOrdered` is less than or equal to `RANGE1`, `customerDiscount` is set to `DISCOUNT1`. If `itemsOrdered` is not less than or equal to `RANGE1`, then it must be greater than `RANGE1`, so the first half of the next decision is unnecessary. The computer logic will never get to the spot where it makes the second decision unless `itemsOrdered` is already greater than `RANGE1`—that is, unless the logic follows the false branch of the first selection.

If you use the logic in Figure 4-22, you are wasting computer time with a trivial decision that tests a range limit that has already been tested. The same logic applies to the third decision in Figure 4-22. Beginning programmers sometimes justify their use of unnecessary questions as "just making really sure." Such caution is unnecessary when writing computer logic.

Figure 4-21 Inefficient range selection including unreachable path

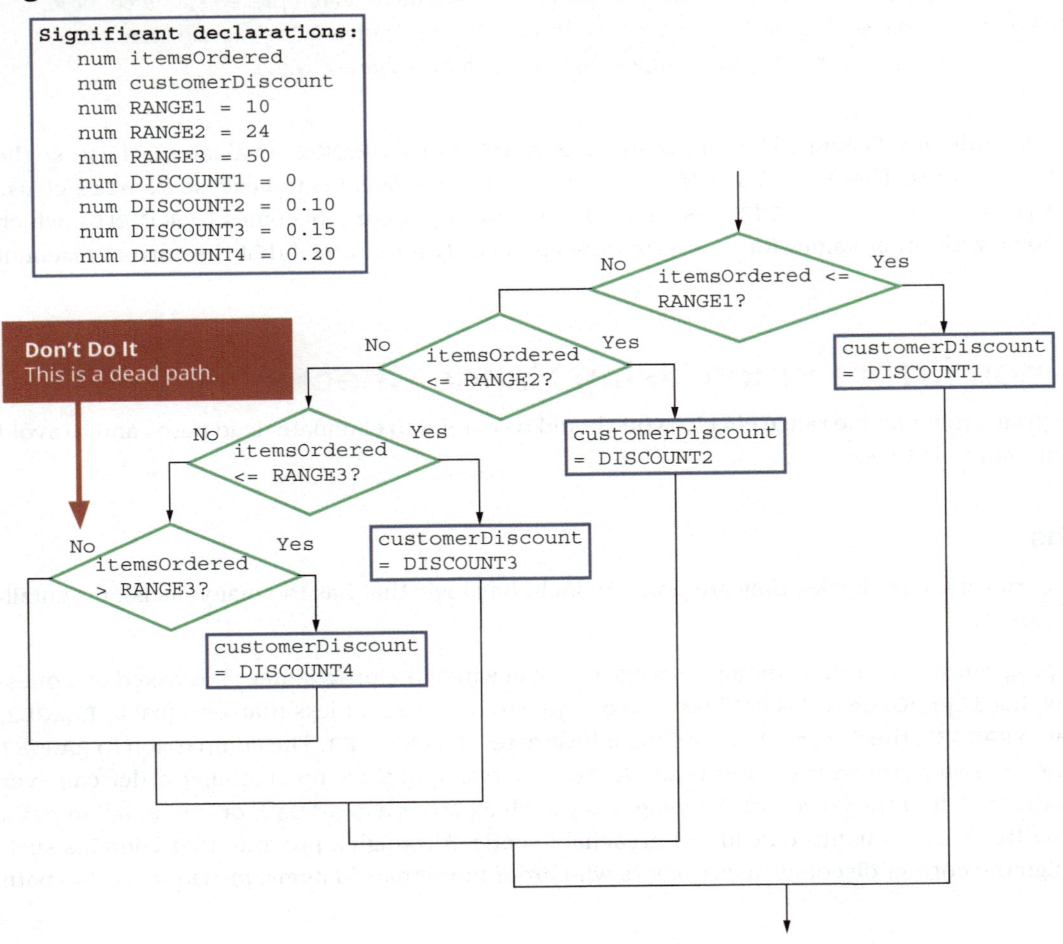
Significant declarations:
num itemsOrdered
num customerDiscount
num RANGE1 = 10
num RANGE2 = 24
num RANGE3 = 50
num DISCOUNT1 = 0
num DISCOUNT2 = 0.10
num DISCOUNT3 = 0.15
num DISCOUNT4 = 0.20
Don't Do It
This is a dead path.
No
itemsOrdered <= RANGE1?
Yes
customerDiscount = DISCOUNT1
No
itemsOrdered <= RANGE2?
Yes
customerDiscount = DISCOUNT2
No
itemsOrdered <= RANGE3?
Yes
customerDiscount = DISCOUNT3
No
itemsOrdered > RANGE3?
Yes
customerDiscount = DISCOUNT4

```
if itemsOrdered <= RANGE1 then
   customerDiscount = DISCOUNT1
else
   if itemsOrdered <= RANGE2 then
      customerDiscount = DISCOUNT2
   else
      if itemsOrdered <= RANGE3 then
         customerDiscount = DISCOUNT3
      else
         if itemsOrdered > RANGE3 then
            customerDiscount = DISCOUNT4
         endif
      endif
   endif
endif
```

Don't Do It
This decision can never be false.

Figure 4-22 Inefficient range selection including unnecessary questions

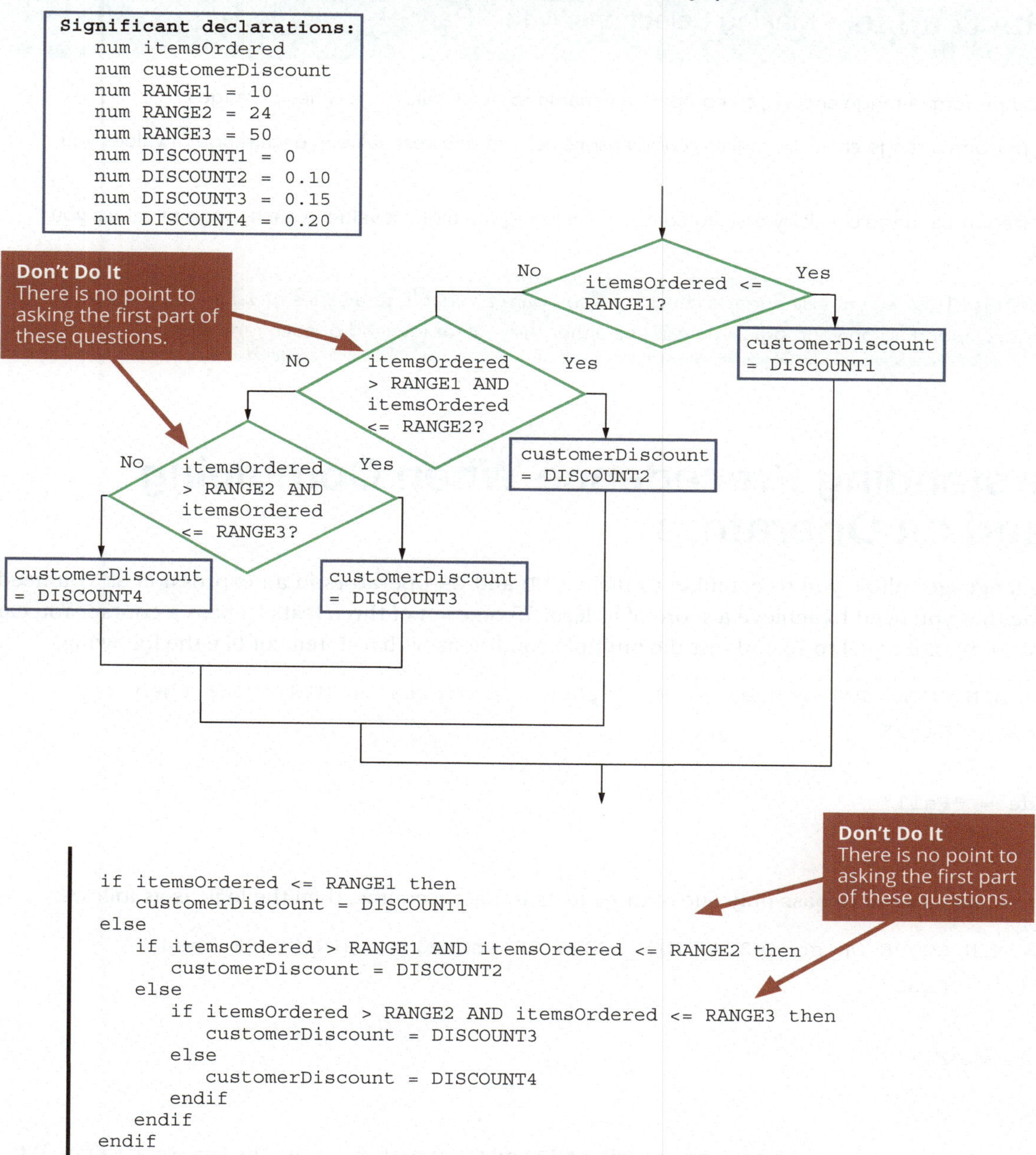
Significant declarations:
num itemsOrdered
num customerDiscount
num RANGE1 = 10
num RANGE2 = 24
num RANGE3 = 50
num DISCOUNT1 = 0
num DISCOUNT2 = 0.10
num DISCOUNT3 = 0.15
num DISCOUNT4 = 0.20
Don't Do It
There is no point to asking the first part of these questions.
No
itemsOrdered <= RANGE1?
Yes
customerDiscount = DISCOUNT1
No
itemsOrdered > RANGE1 AND itemsOrdered <= RANGE2?
Yes
customerDiscount = DISCOUNT2
No
itemsOrdered > RANGE2 AND itemsOrdered <= RANGE3?
Yes
customerDiscount = DISCOUNT4
customerDiscount = DISCOUNT3
Don't Do It
There is no point to asking the first part of these questions.

```
if itemsOrdered <= RANGE1 then
   customerDiscount = DISCOUNT1
else
   if itemsOrdered > RANGE1 AND itemsOrdered <= RANGE2 then
      customerDiscount = DISCOUNT2
   else
      if itemsOrdered > RANGE2 AND itemsOrdered <= RANGE3 then
         customerDiscount = DISCOUNT3
      else
         customerDiscount = DISCOUNT4
      endif
   endif
endif
```

Two Truths & a Lie | Making Selections Within Ranges

1. When you perform a range check, you compare a variable to every value in a series of ranges.
2. You can perform a range check by making comparisons using the lowest value in each range of values you are using.
3. You can perform a range check by making comparisons using the highest value in each range of values you are using.

The false statement is #1. When you use a range check, you compare a variable to a series of values that represent the ends of ranges. Depending on your logic, you can use either the high or low end of each range.

4.7 Understanding Precedence When Combining AND and OR Operators

Most programming languages allow you to combine as many AND and OR operators in an expression as you need. For example, assume that you need to achieve a score of at least 75 on each of three tests to pass a course. You can declare a constant MIN_SCORE equal to 75 and test the multiple conditions with a statement like the following:

```
if score1 >= MIN_SCORE AND score2 >= MIN_SCORE AND score3 >= MIN_SCORE then
   classGrade = "Pass"
else
   classGrade = "Fail"
endif
```

On the other hand, if you need to pass only one of three tests to pass a course, then the logic is as follows:

```
if score1 >= MIN_SCORE OR score2 >= MIN_SCORE OR score3 >= MIN_SCORE then
   classGrade = "Pass"
else
   classGrade = "Fail"
endif
```

The logic becomes more complicated when you combine AND and OR operators within the same statement. When you do, the AND operators take precedence, meaning the Boolean values of the AND expressions are evaluated first.

Note | You have already learned that in arithmetic statements, multiplication and division have precedence over addition and subtraction. You also have learned that precedence is sometimes referred to as *order of operations*.

For example, consider a program that determines whether a movie theater patron can purchase a discounted ticket. Assume that discounts are allowed for children and senior citizens who attend G-rated movies. The following code looks reasonable, but it produces incorrect results because the expression that contains the AND operator evaluates before the one that contains the OR operator.

```
if age <= 12 OR age >= 65 AND rating = "G" then
   output "Discount applies"
endif
```

Don't Do It

The AND expression evaluates first, which is not the intention.

For example, assume that a movie patron is 10 years old, and the movie rating is R. The patron should not receive a discount (or be allowed to see the movie!). However, within the `if` statement, the part of the expression that contains the AND operator, `age >= 65 AND rating = "G"`, is evaluated first. For a 10-year-old and an R-rated movie, the question is false (on both counts), so the entire `if` statement becomes the equivalent of the following:

```
if age <= 12 OR aFalseExpression then
   output "Discount applies"
endif
```

Because the patron is 10, `age <= 12` is true, so the original `if` statement becomes the equivalent of:

```
if aTrueExpression OR aFalseExpression then
   output "Discount applies"
endif
```

The combination of true OR false evaluates as true. Therefore, the string `"Discount applies"` is output when it should not be.

Many programming languages allow you to use parentheses to correct the logic and force the OR expression to be evaluated first, as shown in the following pseudocode:

```
if (age <= 12 OR age >= 65) AND rating = "G" then
   output "Discount applies"
endif
```

With the added parentheses, if the patron's `age` is 12 or under OR the `age` is 65 or over, the expression is evaluated as:

```
if aTrueExpression AND rating = "G" then
   output "Discount applies"
endif
```

In this statement, when the age value qualifies a patron for a discount, then the rating value also must be acceptable before the discount applies. This was the original intention.

You can use the following techniques to avoid confusion when mixing AND and OR operators:

- You can use parentheses to override the default order of operations.
- You can use parentheses for clarity even though they do not change what the order of operations would be without them. For example, if a customer should be between 12 and 19 or have a school ID to receive a high school discount, you can use the expression `(age > 12 AND age < 19) OR validId = "Yes"`, even though the evaluation would be the same without the parentheses.
- You can use nested `if` statements instead of using AND and OR operators. With the flowchart and pseudocode shown in **Figure 4-23**, it is clear which movie patrons receive the discount. In the flowchart, you can see that the OR is nested entirely within the *Yes* branch of the `rating = "G"` decision. Similarly, in the pseudocode in Figure 4-23, you can see by the alignment that if the rating is not *G*, the logic proceeds directly to the last `endif` statement, bypassing any checking of age at all.

Figure 4-23 Nested decisions that determine movie patron discount

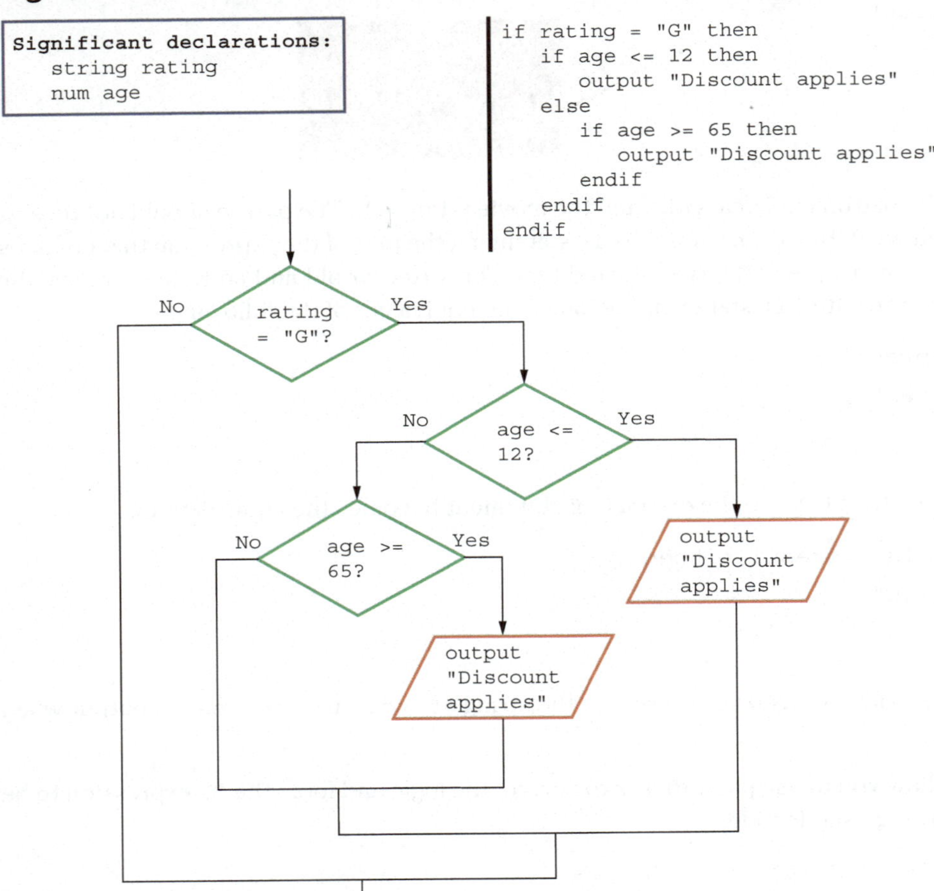
Significant declarations:
string rating
num age
if rating = "G" then
if age <= 12 then
output "Discount applies"
else
if age >= 65 then
output "Discount applies"
endif
endif
endif
No
rating = "G"?
Yes
No
age <= 12?
Yes
No
age >= 65?
Yes
output "Discount applies"
output "Discount applies"

Two Truths & a Lie — Understanding Precedence When Combining AND and OR Operators

1. Most programming languages allow you to combine as many AND and OR operators in an expression as you need.
2. When you combine AND and OR operators, the OR operators take precedence, meaning their Boolean values are evaluated first.
3. You always can avoid the confusion of mixing AND and OR decisions by nesting `if` statements instead of using AND and OR operators.

The false statement is #2. When you combine AND and OR operators, the AND operators take precedence, meaning the Boolean values of their expressions are evaluated first.

4.8 Understanding the case Structure

Most programming languages allow a specialized selection structure called the **case structure** when there are several distinct possible values for a single variable and each value requires a different subsequent action.

Suppose that you work at a school at which tuition varies per credit hour, depending on whether a student is a freshman, sophomore, junior, or senior. The structured flowchart and pseudocode in **Figure 4-24** show a series of decisions that assigns different `tuition` values depending on the value of `year`.

Figure 4-24 Flowchart and pseudocode of tuition decisions

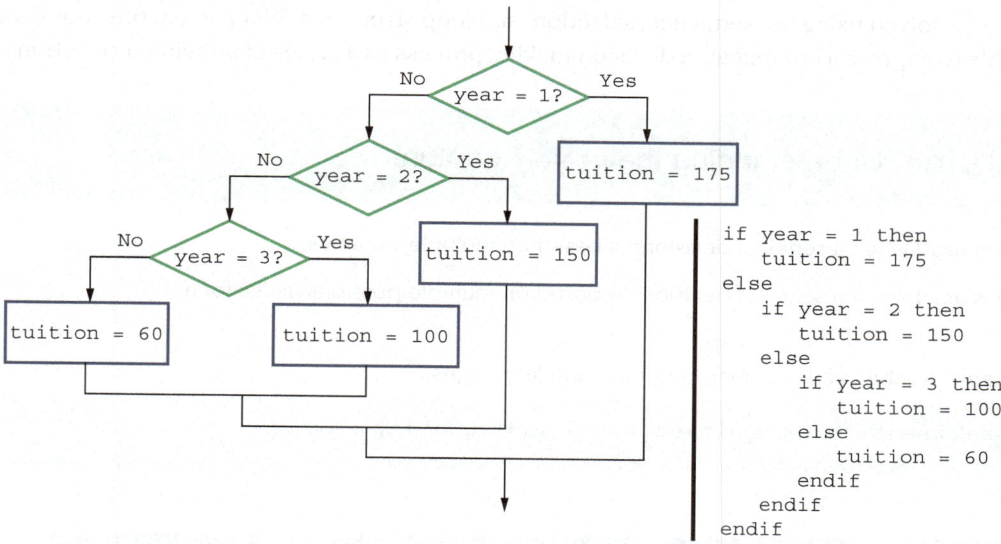


```
if year = 1 then
   tuition = 175
else
   if year = 2 then
      tuition = 150
   else
      if year = 3 then
         tuition = 100
      else
         tuition = 60
      endif
   endif
endif
```

The logic shown in Figure 4-24 is correct and completely structured. The `year = 3?` selection structure is contained within the `year = 2?` structure, which is contained within the `year = 1?` structure. (This example assumes that if `year` is not 1, 2, or 3, the student receives the senior tuition rate.)

Even though the program segments in Figure 4-24 are correct and structured, many programming languages permit using a `case` structure, as shown in **Figure 4-25**. When using the `case` structure, you test a variable against a series of values, taking appropriate action based on the variable's value. Many people believe programs that contain the `case` structure are easier to read than a program with a long series of decisions, and the `case` structure is allowed because the same results *could* be achieved with a series of structured selections (thus making the program structured). That is, if the first program is structured and the second one reflects the first one point by point, then the second one must be structured as well.

Figure 4-25 Flowchart and pseudocode of case structure that determines tuition

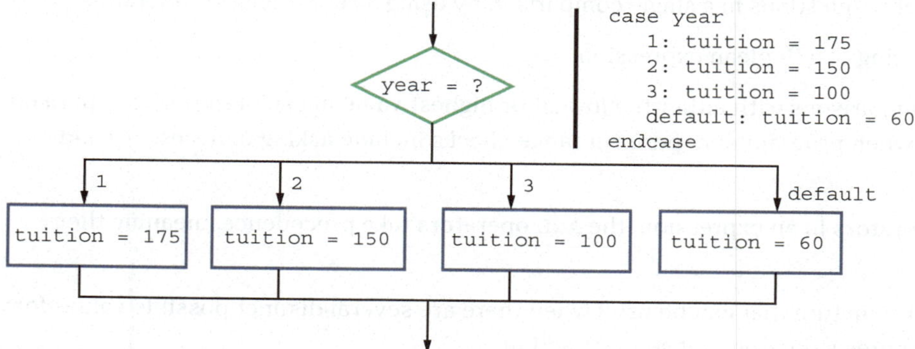


```
case year
   1: tuition = 175
   2: tuition = 150
   3: tuition = 100
   default: tuition = 60
endcase
```

Note | The term *default* in Figure 4-25 means *if none of the other cases is true*. Various programming languages use different syntaxes for the default case.

In many programming languages, you can use the `case` structure only when a series of decisions is based on a single expression. If multiple expressions are tested, then you must use a series of decisions. Besides being easier to read and possibly less prone to error, the `case` structure often executes more quickly in many languages than the series of decisions it represents. The speed of execution depends on a number of technical factors, including how the language compiler was written and how many clauses appear in the `case` statement.

The syntax used in the `case` structure varies widely among languages. Remember that logically, the `case` structure is "extra." All logical problems can be solved using the sequence, selection, and loop structures. When you write your own programs, it is always acceptable to express a complicated decision-making process as a series of individual selections.

Two Truths & a Lie | Understanding the `case` Structure

1. The `case` structure is used when a series of decisions is based on multiple variables.
2. The `case` structure is used when a series of decisions is based on multiple possible values for a single variable.
3. The syntax of the `case` structure varies among programming languages.

The false statement is #1. The `case` structure is used to test a single variable for multiple values.

Summary

- Computer program decisions are made by evaluating Boolean expressions. You can use `if-then-else` or `if-then` structures to choose between two possible outcomes.
- You can use relational comparison operators to compare two operands of the same data type. The standard relational comparison operators are =, >, <, >=, <=, and <>.
- In an AND decision, two conditions must be true for a resulting action to take place. An AND decision requires a nested decision or the use of an AND operator. In an AND decision, the most efficient approach is to start by evaluating the expression that is less likely to be true.
- In an OR decision, at least one of two conditions must be true for a resulting action to take place. In an OR decision, the most efficient approach is to start by evaluating the expression that is more likely to be true. Most programming languages allow you to ask two or more questions in a single comparison by using a conditional OR operator.
- The NOT operator reverses the meaning of a Boolean expression.
- To perform a range check, make comparisons with either the lowest or highest value in each range of comparison values. Common errors that occur when programmers perform range checks include asking unnecessary and previously answered questions.
- When you combine AND and OR operators in an expression, the AND operators take precedence, meaning their Boolean values are evaluated first.
- The `case` structure is a specialized structure that can be used when there are several distinct possible values for a single variable and each value requires a different subsequent action.

Key Terms

AND decision
AND operator
cascading `if` statement
`case` structure
compound condition
conditional AND operator
conditional OR operator
dead path
`else` clause
`if-then` clause
nested decision
nested `if`
NOT operator
OR decision
OR operator
range check
relational comparison operators
short-circuit evaluation
trivial expressions
truth table
unary operator
unreachable path

Review Questions

1. A ______________ expression has one of two values: true or false. (4.1)
   a. Georgian
   b. Boolean
   c. Barbarian
   d. Selective
2. In a selection, the statements in an `else` clause execute ______________. (4.1)
   a. only after the statements in the `if` clause execute
   b. when the tested condition is true
   c. when the tested condition is false
   d. always
3. An expression that uses a greater-than operator evaluates as true when ______________. (4.2)
   a. the right operand is greater than the left operand
   b. the left operand is greater than the right operand
   c. the right operand is equal to the left operand
   d. either operand is greater than the other
4. A trivial Boolean expression is one that ______________. (4.2)
   a. always has the same value
   b. uses only two operands
   c. is always true
   d. is always false
5. If `x <= y` is true, then ______________. (4.2)
   a. `x = y` is true
   b. `y <= x` is true
   c. `x > y` is false
   d. `x >= y` is false
6. If `j <> k` is true, then ______________. (4.2)
   a. `j = k` is true
   b. `j > k` is true
   c. `j < k` might be true
   d. both `j > k` and `k > j` are true
7. In an AND condition, the most efficient technique is to first ask the question that ______________. (4.3)
   a. uses a named constant
   b. is most likely to be true
   c. contains the most operands
   d. is least likely to be true

8. If `a` is true and `b` is false, then ______________. (4.3, 4.4)

a. `a AND b` is true

b. `a AND b` is false

c. `a OR b` is false

d. `a OR b` cannot be determined

9. If `p` is true and `q` is false, then ______________. (4.3, 4.4)

a. `p OR q` is true

b. `p OR q` is false

c. `p AND q` is true

d. `q` is greater than `p`

10. Which of the lettered choices is equivalent to the following decision? (4.3, 4.4)

```
if x > 10 then
   if y > 10 then
      output "X"
   endif
endif
```

a. `if x > 10 OR y > 10 then output "X" endif`

b. `if x > 10 AND x > y then output "X" endif`

c. `if y > x then output "X" endif`

d. `if x > 10 AND y > 10 then output "X" endif`

11. If `conditionA` is 30 percent likely to be true and `conditionB` is 10 percent likely to be true, then it is most efficient to test `conditionA` first ______________. (4.3, 4.4)

a. in an `OR` decision

b. in an `AND` decision

c. in any decision

d. never

12. Which of the following is a poorly written, trivial Boolean expression? (4.3, 4.4)

a. `a > b AND b > c`

b. `a = 100 OR b > 200`

c. `a < b AND c < 100 AND d <> 5`

d. `a < 10 AND a > 40`

13. Which of the following must always be false? (4.3, 4.4)

a. `e > 12 AND e < 15`

b. `e = 10 OR e = 20`

c. `e > 12 OR f > 12`

d. `e > 10 AND e < 7`

14. Which of the following must always be true? (4.3, 4.4)

a. `g < 12 AND g < 18`

b. `g = 12 OR h = 17`

c. `g <> 12 OR g <> 15`

d. `g > 12 AND g < 21`

15. In the following pseudocode, what percentage raise will an employee in Department 8 receive? (4.6)

```
if department < 5 then
   raise = SMALL_RAISE
else
   if department < 14 then
      raise = MEDIUM_RAISE
   else
      if department < 9 then
         raise = BIG_RAISE
      endif
   endif
endif
```

a. `SMALL_RAISE`
b. `MEDIUM_RAISE`
c. `BIG_RAISE`
d. It is impossible to tell.

16. In the following pseudocode, what percentage raise will an employee in Department 10 receive? (4.6)

```
if department < 2 then
   raise = SMALL_RAISE
else
   if department < 6 then
      raise = MEDIUM_RAISE
   else
      if department < 10 then
         raise = BIG_RAISE
      endif
   endif
endif
```

a. `SMALL_RAISE`
b. `MEDIUM_RAISE`
c. `BIG_RAISE`
d. It is impossible to tell.

17. When you use a range check, you always compare a variable to ____________ value in the range. (4.6)

a. the lowest
b. the highest
c. either the lowest or highest
d. the average

18. If `sales = 100`, `rate = 0.10`, and `expenses = 50`, which of the following expressions is true? (4.3, 4.4)

a. `sales >= expenses AND rate < 1`
b. `sales < 100 OR expenses < 50`
c. `expenses = rate OR sales = rate`
d. `rate < 1 AND expenses > sales`

19. If `a` is true, `b` is true, and `c` is false, which of the following expressions is true? (4.3, 4.4, 4.7)

a. `a OR b AND c`
b. `a AND b AND c`
c. `c AND b OR c`
d. `c AND b OR c AND a`

20. If `d` is true, `e` is false, and `f` is false, which of the following expressions is true? (4.3, 4.4, 4.7)

a. `e OR f AND d`
b. `f AND d OR e`
c. `d OR e AND f`
d. `d AND e AND f`

Programming Exercises

1. Assume that the following variables contain the values shown:

```
numberBig = 100
numberMedium = 10
numberSmall = 1
wordBig = "Constitution"
wordMedium = "Dance"
wordSmall = "Toy"
```

For each of the following Boolean expressions, decide whether the statement is true or false. (4.1–4.4)

a. `numberBig > numberSmall`

b. `numberBig < numberMedium`

c. `numberMedium = numberSmall`

d. `numberBig = wordBig`

e. `numberBig = "Big"`

f. `wordMedium > wordSmall`

g. `wordSmall = "TOY"`

h. `numberBig <= 5 * numberMedium + 50`

i. `numberBig >= 2000`

j. `numberBig > numberMedium + numberSmall`

k. `numberBig > numberMedium AND numberBig < numberSmall`

l. `numberBig = 100 OR numberBig > numberSmall`

m. `numberBig < 10 OR numberSmall > 10`

n. `numberBig = 300 AND numberMedium = 10 OR numberSmall = 1`

o. `wordSmall > wordBig`

p. `wordSmall > wordMedium`

2. Design a flowchart or pseudocode for a program that accepts two numbers from a user and displays one of the following messages: *First is larger, Second is larger, Numbers are equal.* (4.1–4.4)

3. Design a flowchart or pseudocode for a program that accepts three numbers from a user and displays a message if the sum of any two numbers equals the third. (4.1, 4.2, 4.4)

4. Cecilia's Boutique wants several lists of salesperson data. Design a flowchart or pseudocode for the following:

- **a.** A program that accepts one salesperson's ID number, number of items sold in the last month, and total value of the items and displays a data message only if the salesperson is a high performer—defined as a person who sells more than 200 items in the month.
- **b.** A program that accepts the salesperson's data and displays a message only if the salesperson is a high performer—defined as a person who sells more than 200 items worth at least $1,000 in the month.
- **c.** A program that accepts salesperson data continually until a sentinel value is entered and displays a list of the ID numbers of those who sell more than 100 items in the month.
- **d.** A program that accepts salesperson data continually until a sentinel value is entered and displays a list of salespeople who sold between 50 and 100 items in the month. (4.1–4.4)

5. ShoppingBay is an online auction service that requires several reports. Data for each auctioned item includes an ID number, item description, length of auction in days, and minimum required bid. Design a flowchart or pseudocode for the following:

- **a.** A program that accepts data for one auctioned item. Display data for an auction only if the minimum required bid is more than $250.00.
- **b.** A program that continually accepts auction item data until a sentinel value is entered and displays all data for auctions in which the minimum required bid is more than $300.00.
- **c.** A program that continually accepts auction item data and displays data for every auction in which there are no bids yet (in other words, the minimum bid is $0.00) and the length of the auction is seven days or less.
- **d.** A program that continually accepts auction data and displays data for every auction in which the length is between 14 and 28 days inclusive.
- **e.** A program that prompts the user for a maximum required bid, and then continually accepts auction data and displays data for every auction in which the minimum bid is less than or equal to the amount entered by the user. (4.1–4.4)

6. The Dash Cell Phone Company charges customers a basic rate of $5 per month to send text messages. Additional rates are as follows:

- The first 100 messages per month, regardless of message length, are included in the basic bill.
- An additional three cents are charged for each text message after the 100th message, up to and including 300 messages.

- An additional two cents are charged for each text message after the 300th message.
- Federal, state, and local taxes add a total of 14 percent to each bill.

Design a flowchart or pseudocode for the following:

a. A program that accepts the following data about one customer's messages: area code (three digits), phone number (seven digits), and number of text messages sent. Display all the data, including the month-end bill both before and after taxes are added.

b. A program that continually accepts data about text messages until a sentinel value is entered and displays all the details.

c. A program that continually accepts data about text messages until a sentinel value is entered and displays details only about customers who send more than 100 text messages.

d. A program that continually accepts data about text messages until a sentinel value is entered and displays details only about customers whose total bill with taxes is over $10.

e. A program that prompts the user for a three-digit area code from which to select bills. Then the program continually accepts text message data until a sentinel value is entered and displays data only for messages sent from the specified area code. (4.1–4.4)

7. The Drive-Rite Insurance Company provides automobile insurance policies for drivers. Design a flowchart or pseudocode for the following:

a. A program that accepts insurance policy data, including a policy number, customer last name, customer first name, age, premium due date (month, day, and year), and number of driver accidents in the last three years. If an entered policy number is not between 1000 and 9999 inclusive, set the policy number to 0. If the month is not between 1 and 12 inclusive, or the day is not correct for the month (for example, not between 1 and 31 for January or 1 and 29 for February), set the month, day, and year to 0. Display the policy data after any revisions have been made.

b. A program that continually accepts policy holders' data until a sentinel value has been entered and displays the data for any policy holder over 40 years old.

c. A program that continually accepts policy holders' data until a sentinel value has been entered and displays the data for any policy holder who is at least 18 years old.

d. A program that continually accepts policy holders' data and displays the data for any policy holder no more than 60 years old.

e. A program that continually accepts policy holders' data and displays the data for any policy holder whose premium is due no later than April 30 any year.

f. A program that continually accepts policy holders' data and displays the data for any policy holder whose premium is due up to and including January 1, 2025.

g. A program that continually accepts policy holders' data and displays the data for any policy holder whose premium is due by June 1, 2025.

h. A program that continually accepts policy holders' data and displays the data for anyone who has a policy number between 1000 and 4000 inclusive, whose policy comes due in September or October of any year, and who has had three or fewer accidents. (4.1–4.4)

8. The Barking Lot is a dog day care center. Design a flowchart or pseudocode for the following:

a. A program that accepts data for an ID number of a dog's owner, and the name, breed, age, and weight of the dog. Display a bill containing all the input data as well as the weekly day care fee, which is $55 for dogs weighing less than 15 pounds, $75 for dogs from 15 to 30 pounds inclusive, $105 for dogs from 31 to 80 pounds inclusive, and $125 for dogs weighing more than 80 pounds.

b. A program that continually accepts dogs' data until a sentinel value is entered and displays billing data for each dog.

c. A program that continually accepts dogs' data until a sentinel value is entered and displays billing data for dog owners who owe more than $100.

d. A program that continually accepts dogs' data until a sentinel value is entered and displays billing data for dogs that weigh less than 20 pounds or more than 100 pounds. (4.1–4.4)

9. Ajax Drakos is a carpenter who creates personalized house signs. Ajax wants an application to compute the price of any sign a customer orders, based on the following factors:

- The minimum charge for all signs is $30.
- If the sign is made of oak, add $15. No charge is added for pine.
- The first six letters or numbers are included in the minimum charge; there is a $3 charge for each additional character.
- Black or white characters are included in the minimum charge; there is an additional $12 charge for gold-leaf lettering.

Design a flowchart or pseudocode for the following:

a. A program that accepts data for an order number, customer name, wood type, number of characters, and color of characters. Display all the entered data and the final price for the sign.

b. A program that continually accepts sign order data and displays all the relevant information for oak signs with five white letters.

c. A program that continually accepts sign order data and displays all the relevant information for pine signs with gold-leaf lettering and more than 10 characters. (4.2–4.4)

10. Black Dot Printing is attempting to organize carpools to save energy. Each input record contains an employee's name and town of residence. Ten percent of the company's employees live in Wonder Lake; 30 percent live in the adjacent town of Woodstock. Black Dot wants to encourage employees who live in either town to drive to work together. Design a flowchart or pseudocode for the following:

a. A program that accepts an employee's data and displays it with a message that indicates whether the employee is a candidate for the carpool (because he lives in one of the two cities).

b. A program that continually accepts employee data until a sentinel value is entered and displays a list of all employees who are carpool candidates. Make sure the decision-making process is as efficient as possible.

c. A program that continually accepts employee data until a sentinel value is entered and displays a list of all employees who are ineligible to carpool because they do not live in either Wonder Lake or Woodstock. Make sure the decision-making process is as efficient as possible. (4.2–4.4)

Performing Maintenance

1. A file named *MAINTENANCE04-01.jpg* is included in the Chapter04 folder of your downloadable student files. Assume that this program is a working program in your organization and that it needs modifications as described in the comments (lines that begin with two slashes) at the beginning of the file. Your job is to alter the program to meet the new specifications. (4.1–4.4)

Debugging Exercises

1. Your downloadable files for Chapter 4 include *DEBUG04-01.txt, DEBUG04-02.txt, DEBUG04-03.txt,* and *DEBUG04-04.jpg*. Each file starts with some comments that describe the problem. Comments are lines that begin with two slashes (//). Each file contains pseudocode or a flowchart that has mistakes. Find and correct all the bugs.

Game Zone

1. You can generate a random number between 1 and a limiting value named `limit` by using a statement similar to `randomNumber = random(limit)`. Create the logic for a guessing game in which the application generates a random number between 1 and 100 and the player tries to guess it. Display a message indicating whether the player's guess was correct, too high, or too low. (4.1–4.3)

2. Create the pseudocode for a lottery game application. Generate three random numbers, each between 0 and 9. Allow the user to guess three numbers. Compare each of the user's guesses to the three random numbers and display a message that includes the user's guess, the randomly determined three digits, and the amount of money the user has won, as shown in **Figure 4-26**.

Figure 4-26 Determining lottery awards

Matching numbers	Award ($)
No matches	0
Any one matching	10
Any two matching	100
Three matching, not in order	1000
Three matching in exact order	1,000,000

Make certain that your application accommodates repeating digits. For example, if a user guesses 1, 2, and 3, and the randomly generated digits are 1, 1, and 1, do not give the user credit for three correct guesses—just one. (4.1–4.3, 4.6)

Chapter 5

Looping

Learning Objectives

When you complete this chapter, you will be able to:

5.1 Create loop logic
5.2 Use a loop control variable
5.3 Create nested loops
5.4 Avoid common loop mistakes
5.5 Use a `for` loop
5.6 Use a posttest loop
5.7 Recognize the characteristics shared by all structured loops
5.8 Describe common loop applications
5.9 Compare selections and loops

5.1 Creating Loop Logic

Although making decisions is what makes computers seem intelligent, looping makes computer programming both efficient and worthwhile. When you use a loop, one set of instructions can operate on multiple, separate sets of data. Using fewer instructions results in less time required for design and coding, fewer errors, and shorter compile times.

Recall that the loop structure looks like **Figure 5-1**. As long as a Boolean expression remains true, the body of a `while` loop executes.

Figure 5-1 The loop structure

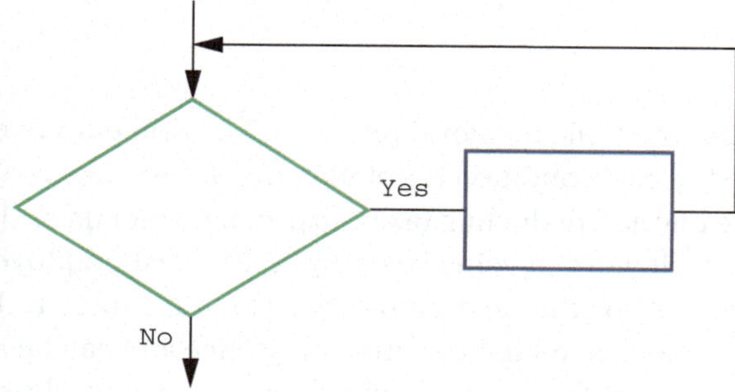

Pseudocode for a `while` statement looks like the following:

```
while condition
   statements that execute when condition is true
endwhile
```

In the pseudocode, notice that:

- The word `while` starts the statement.
- The condition that follows `while` is a Boolean expression. Often it is an expression like `x > y`, but if the programming language supports the Boolean data type, it might be a Boolean variable or a call to a module that returns a Boolean value. (You will learn about modules that return values later.)
- By convention, the statement or statements that appear within the `while` statement are indented for readability.
- The word `endwhile` ends the structure. After `endwhile`, the condition at the start of the `while` statement is tested again.

You already have learned that many programs use a loop to control repetitive tasks. For example, **Figure 5-2** shows the basic structure of many business programs. After some housekeeping tasks are completed, the detail loop repeats once for every data record that must be processed.

Figure 5-2 The mainline logic common to many business programs

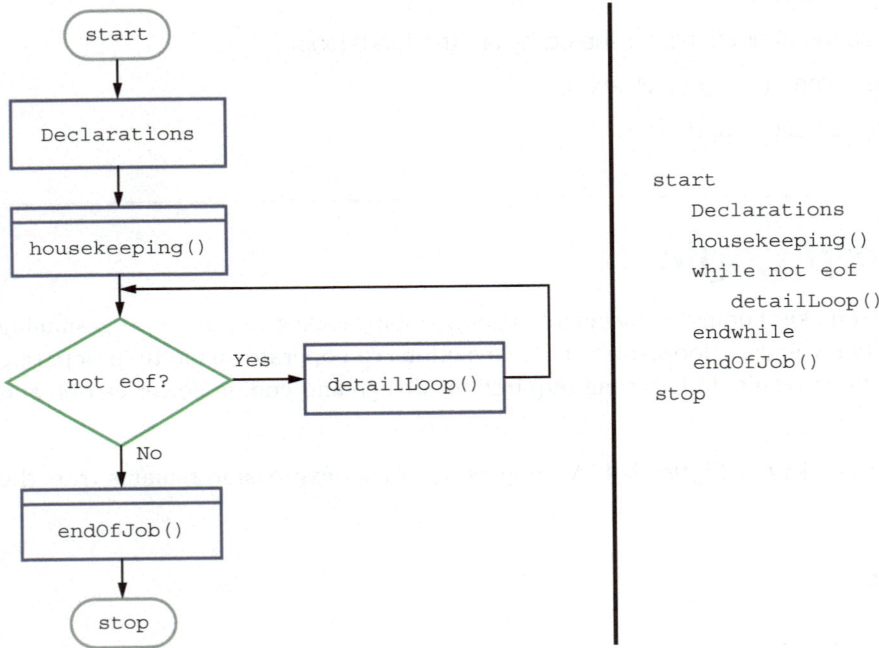


```
start
   Declarations
   housekeeping()
   while not eof
      detailLoop()
   endwhile
   endOfJob()
stop
```

For example, Figure 5-2 might represent the mainline logic of a typical payroll program. The first employee's data would be entered in the `housekeeping()` module, and while the `eof` condition is not met, the `detailLoop()` module would perform such tasks as determining regular and overtime pay and deducting taxes, insurance premiums, charitable contributions, union dues, and other items. Then, after the employee's paycheck is output, the next employee's data would be entered, and the `detailLoop()` module would repeat for the next employee. The advantage to having a computer produce payroll checks is that the calculation instructions need to be written only once and can be repeated indefinitely. At some point, when the program attempts to retrieve data for a new employee, the `eof` condition would be met, and the loop that contains the `detailLoop()` would be exited. Then the `endOfJob()` module would execute; it might contain tasks such as making sure data files are closed or displaying payroll totals.

Two Truths & a Lie | Creating Loop Logic

1. When you use a loop, you can write one set of instructions that operates on multiple, separate sets of data.
2. A major advantage of having a computer perform complicated tasks is the ability to repeat them.
3. A loop is a structure that branches in two logical paths before continuing.

The false statement is #3. A loop is a structure that repeats actions while some condition continues.

5.2 Using a Loop Control Variable

You can use a `while` loop to execute a body of statements continually as long as some condition continues to be true. The body of a loop might contain any number of statements, including input and output statements, arithmetic calculations, module calls, selection structures, and other loops. To make a `while` loop end correctly, you can declare a **loop control variable** to manage the number of repetitions a loop performs. Three separate actions should occur using a loop control variable:

- The loop control variable is initialized before entering the loop.
- The loop control variable's value is tested, and if the result is true, the loop body is entered. Recall that the loop body is the set of statements within a loop.
- The loop control variable is altered within the body of the loop so that the tested condition that starts the loop eventually is false.

If you omit any of these actions—initialize, test, alter—or perform them incorrectly, you run the risk of creating an infinite loop. Once your logic enters the body of a structured loop, the entire loop body must execute. Program logic can leave a structured loop only at the evaluation of the loop control variable. Commonly, you can control a loop's repetitions in one of two ways:

- Use a counter to create a definite, counter-controlled loop.
- Use a sentinel value to create an indefinite loop.

Using a Definite Loop with a Counter

Figure 5-3 shows a loop that displays *Hello* four times. The variable `count` is the loop control variable. This loop is a **definite loop** because it executes a definite, predetermined number of times—in this case, four. The loop is a **counted loop**, or **counter-controlled loop**, because the program keeps track of the number of loop repetitions by counting them.

The loop in Figure 5-3 executes as follows:

- The loop control variable, `count`, is initialized to 0.
- The `while` expression compares `count` to 4.
- The value of `count` is less than 4, so the loop body executes. The loop body shown in Figure 5-3 consists of two statements that, in sequence, display *Hello* and add 1 to `count`.
- The next time the condition `count < 4` is evaluated, the value of `count` is 1, which is still less than 4, so the loop body executes again. *Hello* is displayed a second time and `count` is incremented to 2.
- *Hello* is displayed a third time and `count` becomes 3, then *Hello* is displayed a fourth time and `count` becomes 4.
- Now when the expression `count < 4?` evaluates, it is `false`, so the loop ends.

Figure 5-3 A counted `while` loop that outputs *Hello* four times

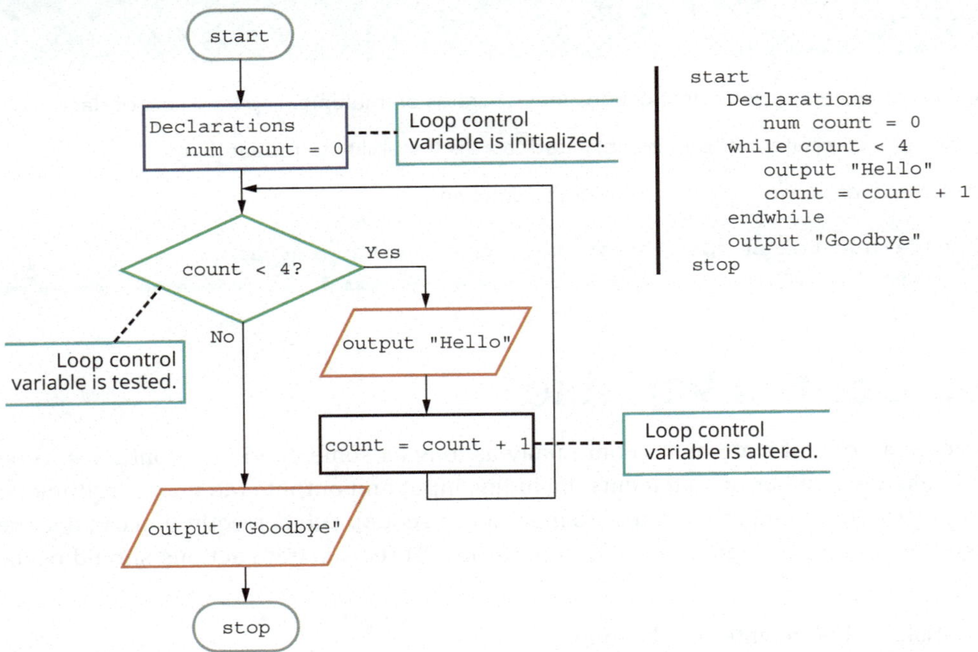
start
Declarations
num count = 0
Loop control
variable is initialized.
count < 4?
Yes
No
Loop control
variable is tested.
output "Hello"
count = count + 1
Loop control
variable is altered.
output "Goodbye"
stop
start
Declarations
num count = 0
while count < 4
output "Hello"
count = count + 1
endwhile
output "Goodbye"
stop

Within a loop's body, you can change the value of the loop control variable in multiple ways. For example:

- You might simply assign a new value to the loop control variable.
- You might retrieve a new value from an input device.
- You might **increment**, or increase, the loop control variable, as in the logic in Figure 5-3.
- You might reduce, or **decrement**, the loop control variable. For example, the loop in Figure 5-3 could be rewritten so that `count` is initialized to 4 and reduced by 1 on each pass through the loop. The loop would then continue while `count` remains greater than 0.

The terms *increment* and *decrement* usually refer to small changes; often the value used to increase or decrease the loop control variable is 1. However, loops also are controlled by adding or subtracting values other than 1. For example, to display company profits at five-year intervals for the next 50 years, you would want to add 5 to a loop control variable during each iteration.

> **Note** Because you frequently need to increment a variable, many programming languages contain a shortcut operator for incrementing. For example, in C++, C#, and Java, the expression `++value` is a shortcut for the expression `value = value + 1`. You will learn about these shortcut operators when you study a programming language that uses them.

The looping logic shown in Figure 5-3 uses a counter. A **counter** is any numeric variable that counts the number of times an event has occurred. In everyday life, people usually count things starting with 1. Many programmers prefer starting their counted loops with a variable containing 0 for two reasons:

- In many computer applications, numbering starts with 0 because of the 0-and-1 nature of computer circuitry.
- When you learn about arrays later in this course, you will discover that array manipulation naturally lends itself to 0-based loops.
- If you initialize a loop control variable to 0 and add one after each loop body execution, the variable always contains the number of times the loop has executed, and you might want to use this number for future comparisons or to display.

Using an Indefinite Loop with a Sentinel Value

Often, the value of a loop control variable is not altered by arithmetic, but instead is altered by user input. For example, perhaps you want to keep performing some task while the user indicates a desire to continue. In that case, you do not know when you write the program whether the loop will be executed two times, 200 times, or at all. This type of loop is an **indefinite loop**.

Consider an interactive program that displays *Hello* repeatedly as long as the user wants to continue. The loop is indefinite because each time the program executes, the loop might be performed a different number of times. The program appears in **Figure 5-4**.

Figure 5-4 An indefinite `while` loop that displays *Hello* as long as the user wants to continue

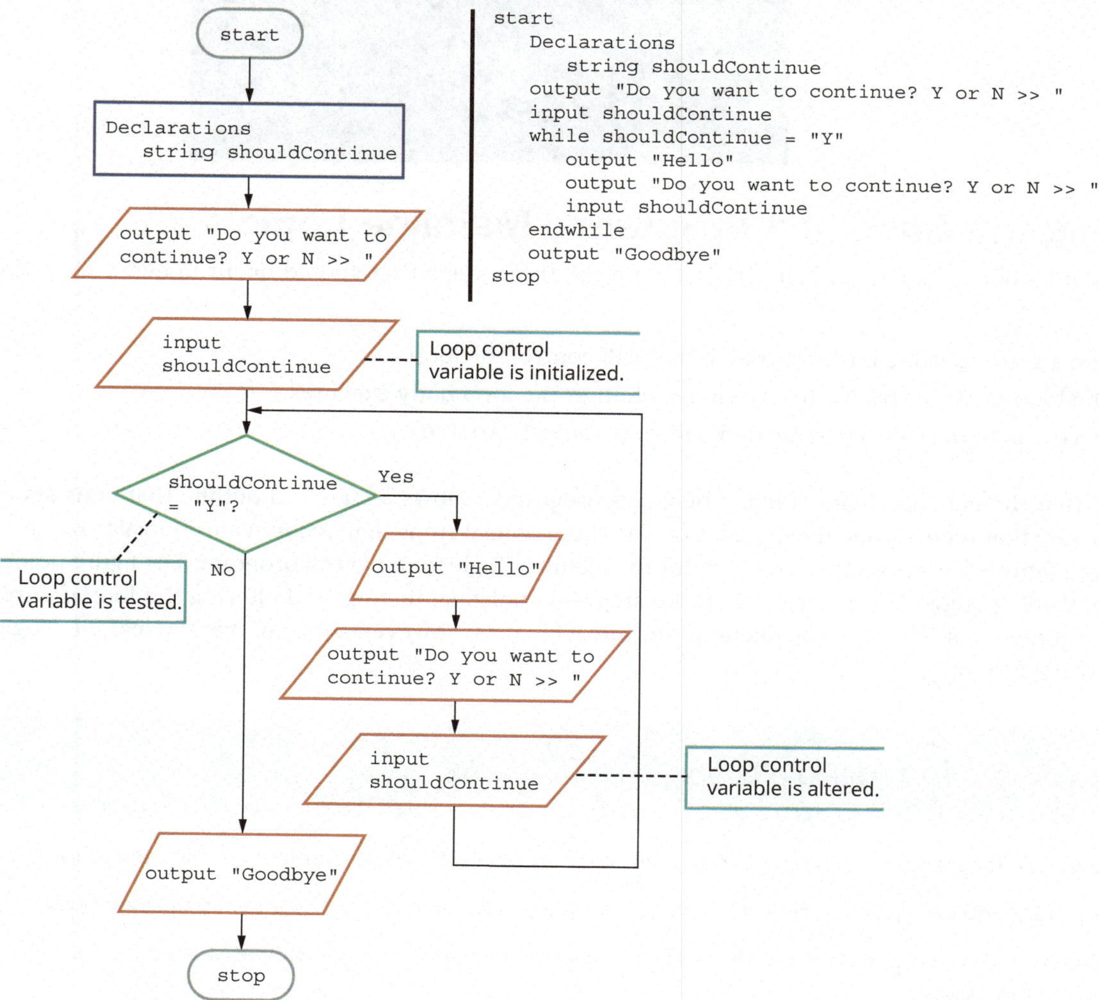


```
start
   Declarations
      string shouldContinue
   output "Do you want to continue? Y or N >> "
   input shouldContinue
   while shouldContinue = "Y"
      output "Hello"
      output "Do you want to continue? Y or N >> "
      input shouldContinue
   endwhile
   output "Goodbye"
stop
```

In the program in Figure 5-4, the loop control variable is `shouldContinue`. The program executes as follows:

- The first `input shouldContinue` statement in the application in Figure 5-4 is a priming input statement. In this statement, the loop control variable is initialized by the user's first response.
- The `while` expression compares the loop control variable to the sentinel value *Y*. (Recall that a sentinel value is compared to a loop control value to determine when a loop's repetitions end.)
- If the user has entered *Y*, then *Hello* is output, and the user is asked whether the program should continue. In this step, the value of `shouldContinue` might change.
- At any point, if the user enters any value other than *Y*, the loop ends. In most programming languages, simple comparisons are case sensitive, so any entry other than *Y*, including *y*, will end the loop.

Figure 5-5 shows how the program might look when it is executed at the command line and in a GUI environment. The screens in Figure 5-5 show programs that perform exactly the same tasks using different environments. In each environment, the user can continue choosing to see *Hello* messages, or can choose to quit the program and display *Goodbye*.

Figure 5-5 Typical executions of the program in Figure 5-4 in two environments

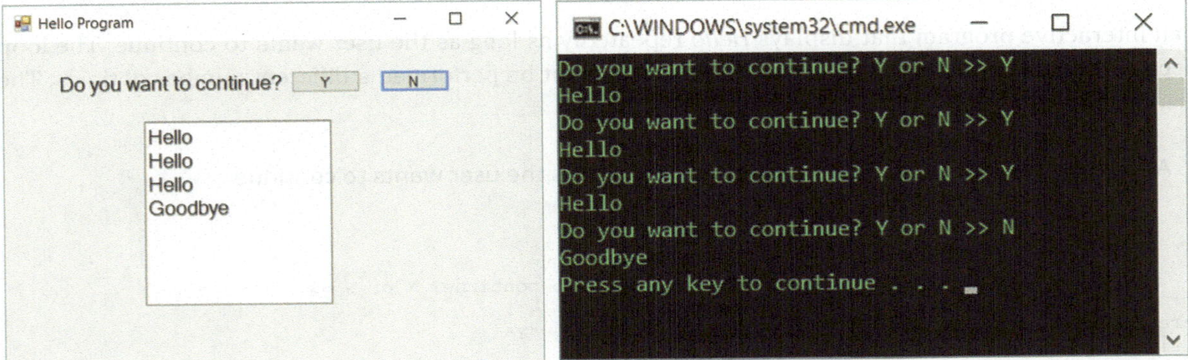

Understanding the Loop in a Program's Mainline Logic

The flowchart and pseudocode segments in Figure 5-4 contain the three steps that should occur in every properly functioning loop:

1. You must provide a starting value for the variable that will control the loop.
2. You must test the loop control variable to determine whether the loop body executes.
3. Within the loop, you must provide a way to alter the loop control variable.

You have learned that the mainline logic of many business programs follows a standard outline that consists of housekeeping tasks, a loop that repeats, and finishing tasks. The three crucial steps that occur in any loop also occur in standard mainline logic. **Figure 5-6** shows the flowchart for the mainline logic for a payroll program. The figure points out the three loop-controlling steps. In this case, the three steps—initializing, testing, and altering the loop control variable—are in different modules. The steps all occur in the correct places, however, showing that the mainline logic uses a standard and correct loop.

Two Truths & a Lie | Using a Loop Control Variable

1. To make a `while` loop execute correctly, a loop control variable must be set to 0 before entering the loop.
2. To make a `while` loop execute correctly, a loop control variable should be tested before entering the loop body.
3. To make a `while` loop execute correctly, the body of the loop must take some action that alters the value of the loop control variable.

The false statement is #1. A loop control variable must be initialized, but not necessarily to 0.

5.3 Nested Loops

Program logic gets more complicated when you must use loops within loops, or **nested loops**. When loops are nested, the loop that contains the other loop is called the **outer loop**, and the loop that is contained is called the **inner loop**. You need to create nested loops when the values of two or more variables repeat to produce every combination of values. Usually, when you create nested loops, each loop has its own loop control variable.

Figure 5-6 A payroll program showing how the loop control variable is used

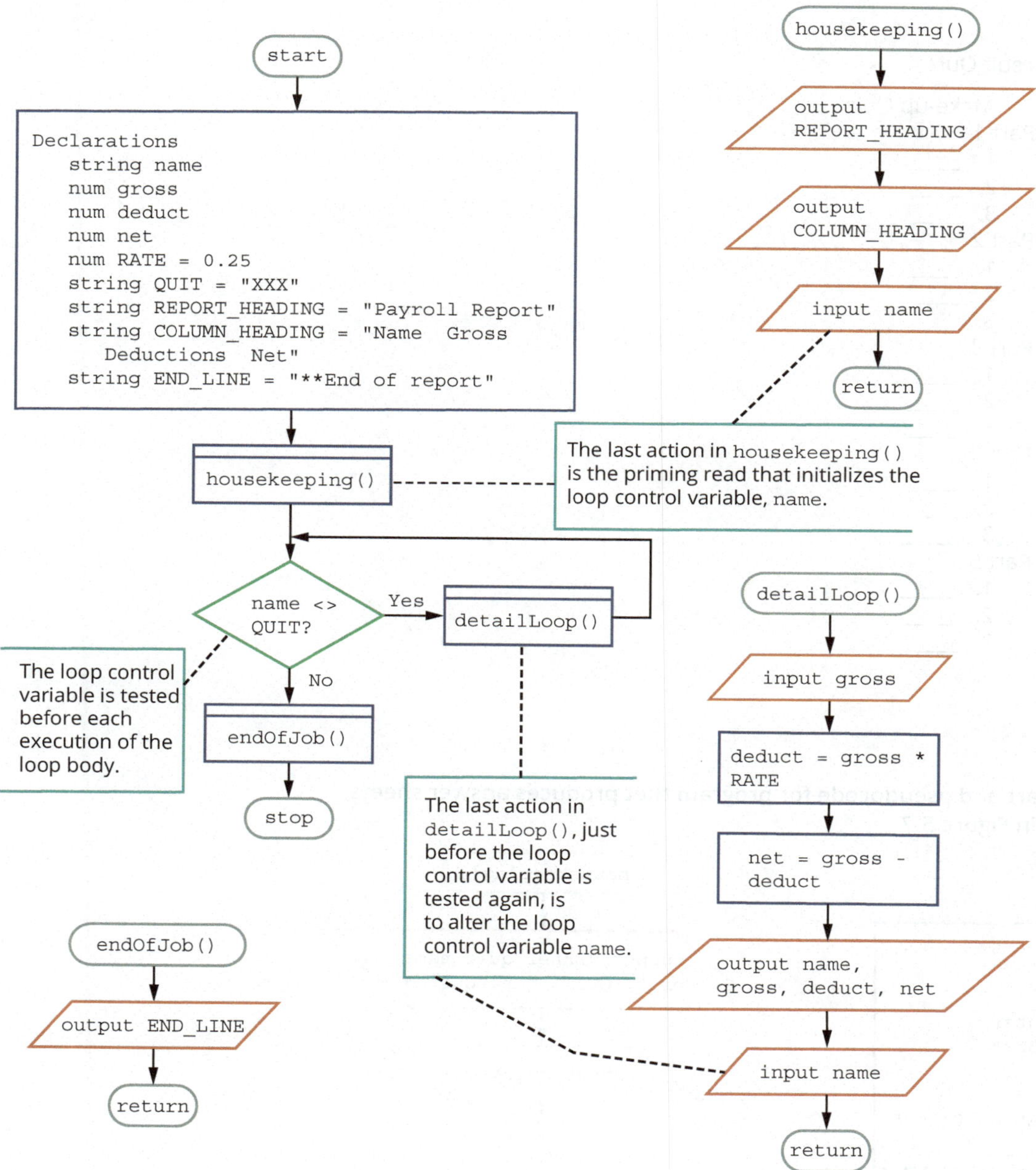

For example, suppose you want to write a program that produces quiz answer sheets like the ones shown in **Figure 5-7**. Each answer sheet has a unique heading followed by five parts with three questions in each part, and you want a fill-in-the-blank line for each question. You could write a program that uses 63 separate output statements to produce three sheets (each sheet contains 21 printed lines), but it is more efficient to use nested loops.

Figure 5-8 shows the logic for the program that produces answer sheets. Three loop control variables are declared for the program:

- `quizName` controls the `detailLoop()` module that is called from the mainline logic.
- `partCounter` controls the outer loop within the `detailLoop()` module; it keeps track of the answer sheet parts.
- `questionCounter` controls the inner loop in the `detailLoop()` module; it keeps track of the questions and answer lines within each part section on each answer sheet.

Figure 5-7 Quiz answer sheets

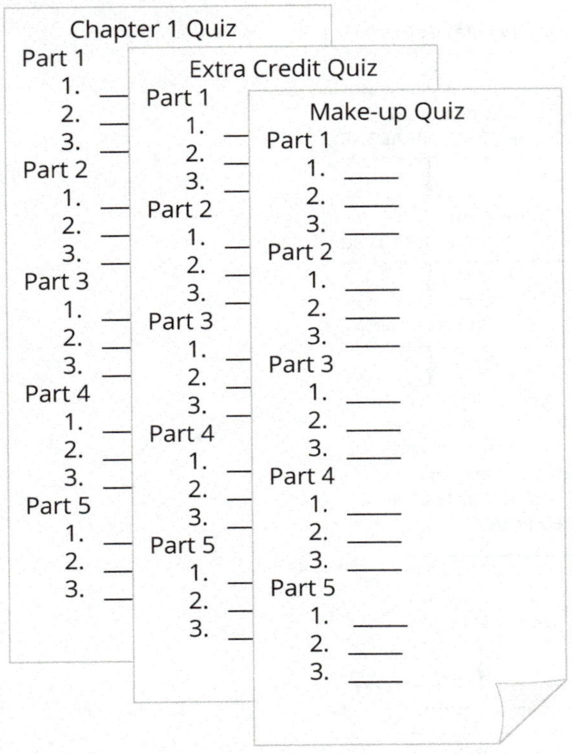

Figure 5-8 Flowchart and pseudocode for program that produces answer sheets shown in Figure 5-7

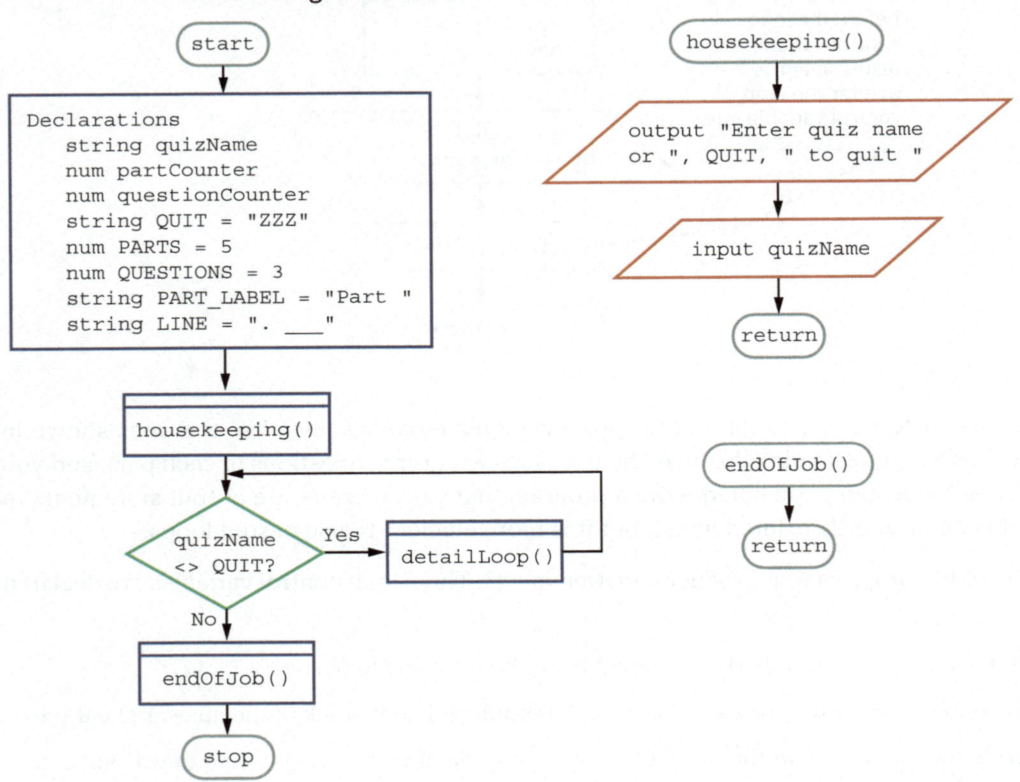

(*Continues*)

Figure 5-8 *(Continued)*

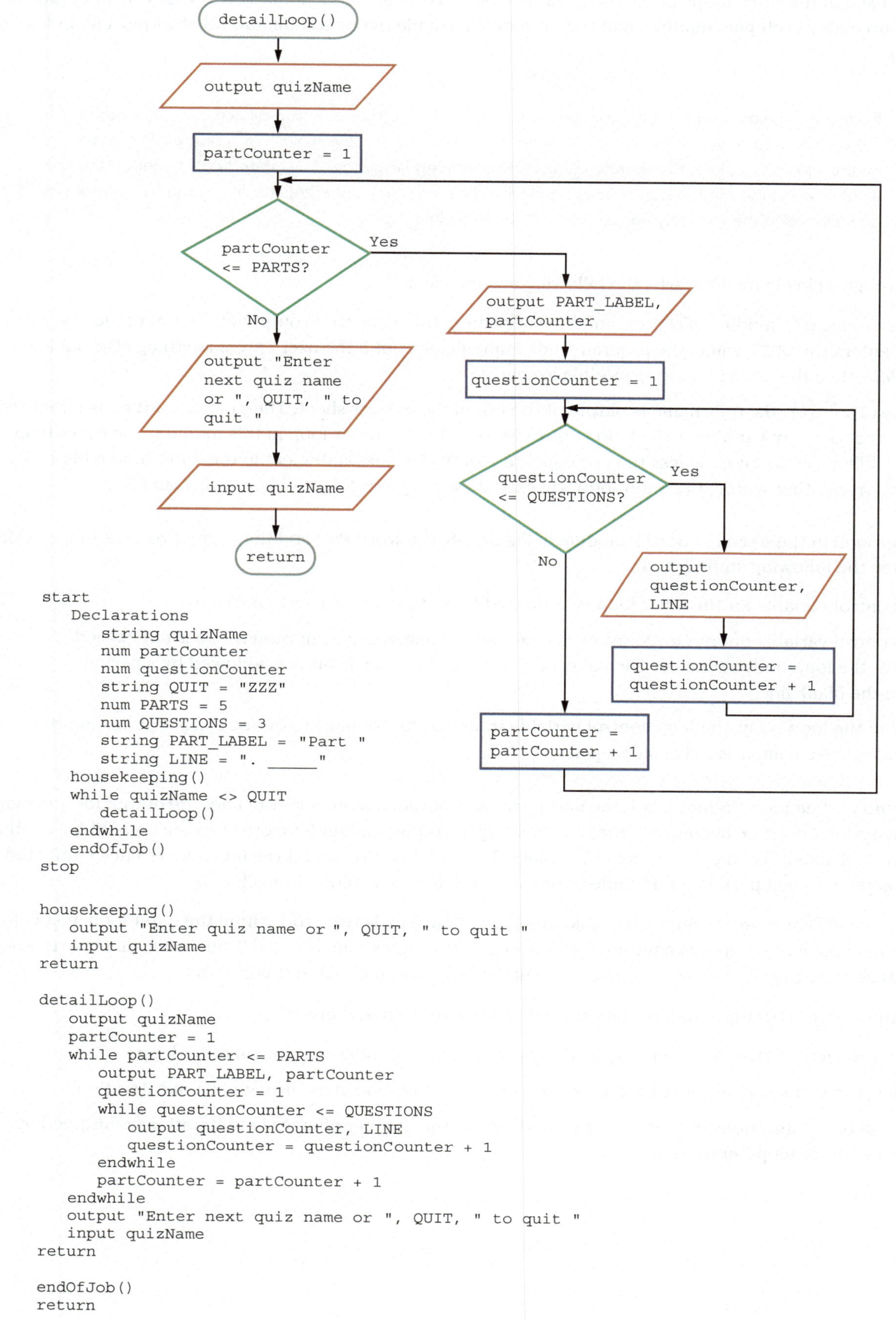


```
start
   Declarations
      string quizName
      num partCounter
      num questionCounter
      string QUIT = "ZZZ"
      num PARTS = 5
      num QUESTIONS = 3
      string PART_LABEL = "Part "
      string LINE = ". ______"
   housekeeping()
   while quizName <> QUIT
      detailLoop()
   endwhile
   endOfJob()
stop

housekeeping()
   output "Enter quiz name or ", QUIT, " to quit "
   input quizName
return

detailLoop()
   output quizName
   partCounter = 1
   while partCounter <= PARTS
      output PART_LABEL, partCounter
      questionCounter = 1
      while questionCounter <= QUESTIONS
         output questionCounter, LINE
         questionCounter = questionCounter + 1
      endwhile
      partCounter = partCounter + 1
   endwhile
   output "Enter next quiz name or ", QUIT, " to quit "
   input quizName
return

endOfJob()
return
```

Five named constants are also declared. Three of these constants (`QUIT`, `PARTS`, and `QUESTIONS`) hold the sentinel values for each of the three loops in the program. The other two constants hold the text that will be output (the word *Part* that precedes each part number, and the period-space-underscore combination that forms a fill-in line for each question).

Note In Figure 5-8, some output (the user prompt) would be sent to one output device, such as a monitor. Other output (the quiz sheet) would be sent to another output device, such as a printer. The statements needed to send output to separate devices differ among languages. The statements to set up the printer would be included in the `housekeeping()` module, and the statements to disengage the printer would be included in the currently empty `endOfJob()` module.

When the program in Figure 5-8 starts, the following events occur:

- The `housekeeping()` module executes, and the user enters the name to be output at the top of the first quiz. If the user enters the `QUIT` value, the program ends immediately, but if the user enters anything else, such as *Make-up Quiz*, then the `detailLoop()` module executes.
- In the `detailLoop()`, the quiz name is output at the top of the answer sheet. Then `partCounter` is initialized to 1. The `partCounter` variable is the loop control variable for the outer loop in this module. The outer loop continues while `partCounter` is less than or equal to `PARTS`. The last statement in the outer loop adds 1 to `partCounter`. In other words, the outer loop will execute when `partCounter` is 1, 2, 3, 4, and 5.

In the outer loop in the `detailLoop()` module in Figure 5-8, the word *Part* and the current `partCounter` value are output. Then the following steps execute:

- The loop control variable for the inner loop is initialized by setting `questionCounter` to 1.
- The loop control variable `questionCounter` is evaluated. While `questionCounter` does not exceed `QUESTIONS`, the loop body executes: The value of `questionCounter` is output, followed by a period and a fill-in-the-blank line.
- At the end of the loop body, the loop control variable is altered by adding 1 to `questionCounter`, and the `questionCounter` comparison is made again.

In other words, when `partCounter` is 1, the part heading is output and underscore lines are output for questions 1, 2, and 3. Then `partCounter` becomes 2, the part heading is output, and underscore lines are created for another set of questions 1, 2, and 3. Then `partCounter` becomes 3, 4, and 5 in turn, and three underscore lines numbered 1, 2, and 3 are created for each part. In all, 15 underscore answer lines are created for each quiz.

In the program in Figure 5-8, it is important that `questionCounter` is reset to 1 within the outer loop, just before entering the inner loop. If this step was omitted, Part 1 would contain questions 1, 2, and 3, but subsequent parts would be empty because `questionCounter` would never again be less than or equal to `QUESTIONS`.

Studying the answer sheet program reveals several facts about nested loops:

- Nested loops never overlap. An inner loop is always completely contained within an outer loop.
- An inner loop goes through all of its iterations each time its outer loop goes through just one iteration.
- The total number of iterations executed by a nested loop is the number of inner loop iterations multiplied by the number of outer loop iterations.

Two Truths & a Lie | Nested Loops

1. When one loop is nested inside another, the loop that contains the other loop is called the outer loop.
2. You need to create nested loops when the values of two or more variables repeat to produce every combination of values.
3. The number of times a loop executes always depends on a constant.

The false statement is #3. The number of times a loop executes might depend on a constant, but it might also depend on a value that varies.

5.4 Avoiding Common Loop Mistakes

Programmers make the following common mistakes with loops:

- Failing to initialize the loop control variable
- Neglecting to alter the loop control variable
- Using the wrong type of comparison when testing the loop control variable
- Including statements inside the loop body that belong outside the loop

The following sections explain these common mistakes in more detail.

Mistake: Failing to Initialize the Loop Control Variable

Failing to initialize a loop's control variable is a mistake. For example, consider the program in **Figure 5-9**. It prompts the user for a name, and while the value of `name` continues not to be the sentinel value *ZZZ*, the program outputs a greeting that uses the name and asks for the next name. This program works correctly.

Figure 5-10 shows an incorrect program in which the loop control variable is not assigned a starting value. If the `name` variable is not set to a starting value, then when the `eof` condition is tested, there is no way to predict whether it will be true. If the user does not enter a value for `name`, the garbage value originally held by that variable might or might not be *ZZZ*. So, one of two scenarios follows:

- Most likely, the uninitialized value of `name` is not *ZZZ*, so the first greeting output will include garbage—for example, *Hello 12BGr5*.
- By a remote chance, the uninitialized value of `name` is *ZZZ*, so the program ends immediately before the user can enter any names.

Mistake: Neglecting to Alter the Loop Control Variable

Different sorts of errors will occur if you fail to provide a way to alter a loop control variable within a loop. For example, in the program in Figure 5-9 that accepts and displays names, you create such an error if you don't accept names within the loop. **Figure 5-11** shows the resulting incorrect logic.

If you remove the `input name` instruction from the end of the loop in the program in Figure 5-11, no name is ever entered after the first one. For example, assume that when the program starts, the user enters *Diego*. *Diego* is not the `eof` value, and the loop will be entered. After a greeting is output for Diego, no new name is entered, so when the logic returns to the loop-controlling evaluation, the `name` will still not be *ZZZ*, and greetings for Diego will continue to be output infinitely. Under normal conditions, you never want to create a loop that cannot terminate.

Figure 5-9 Correct logic for greeting program

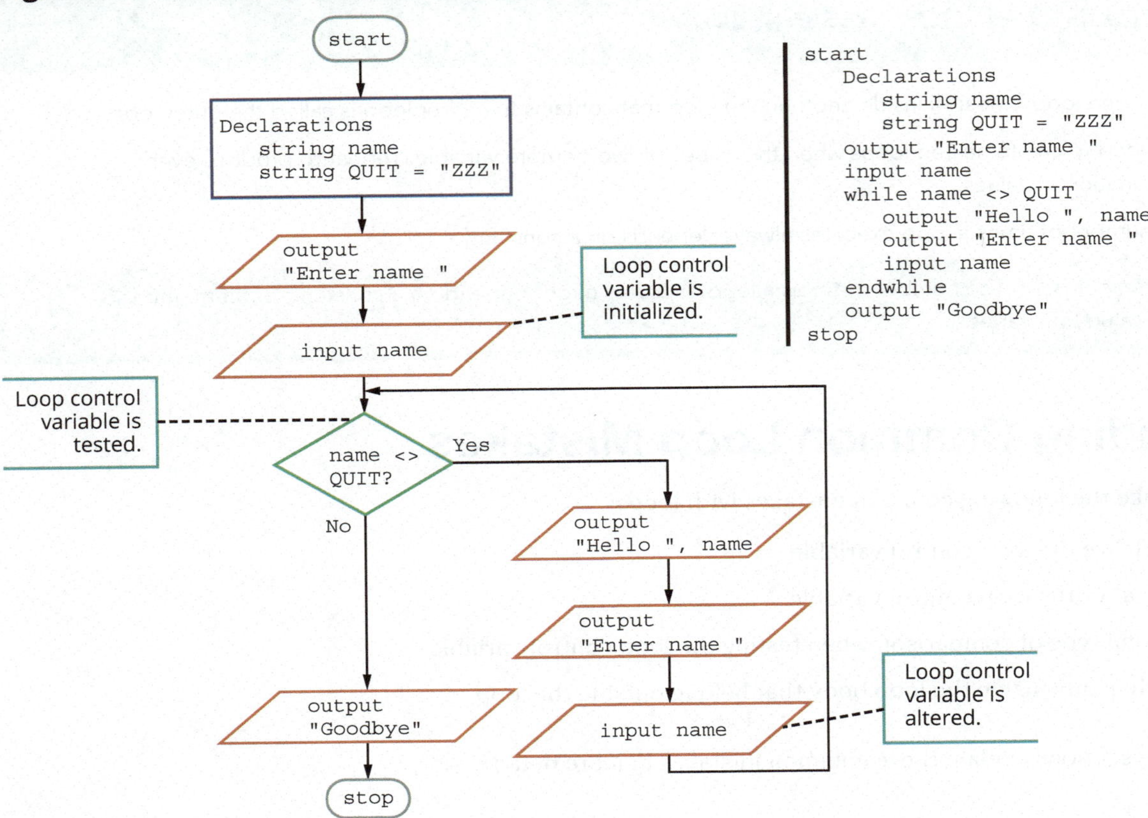


```
start
   Declarations
      string name
      string QUIT = "ZZZ"
   output "Enter name "
   input name
   while name <> QUIT
      output "Hello ", name
      output "Enter name "
      input name
   endwhile
   output "Goodbye"
stop
```

Figure 5-10 Incorrect logic for greeting program because the loop control variable initialization is missing

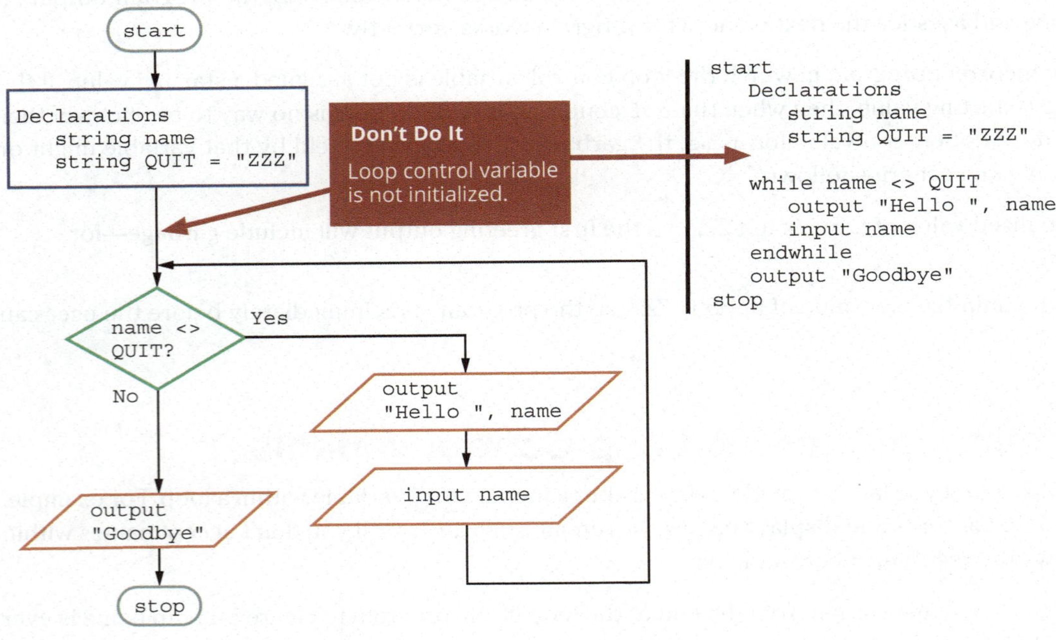


```
start
   Declarations
      string name
      string QUIT = "ZZZ"

   while name <> QUIT
      output "Hello ", name
      input name
   endwhile
   output "Goodbye"
stop
```

Figure 5-11 Incorrect logic for greeting program because the loop control variable is not altered

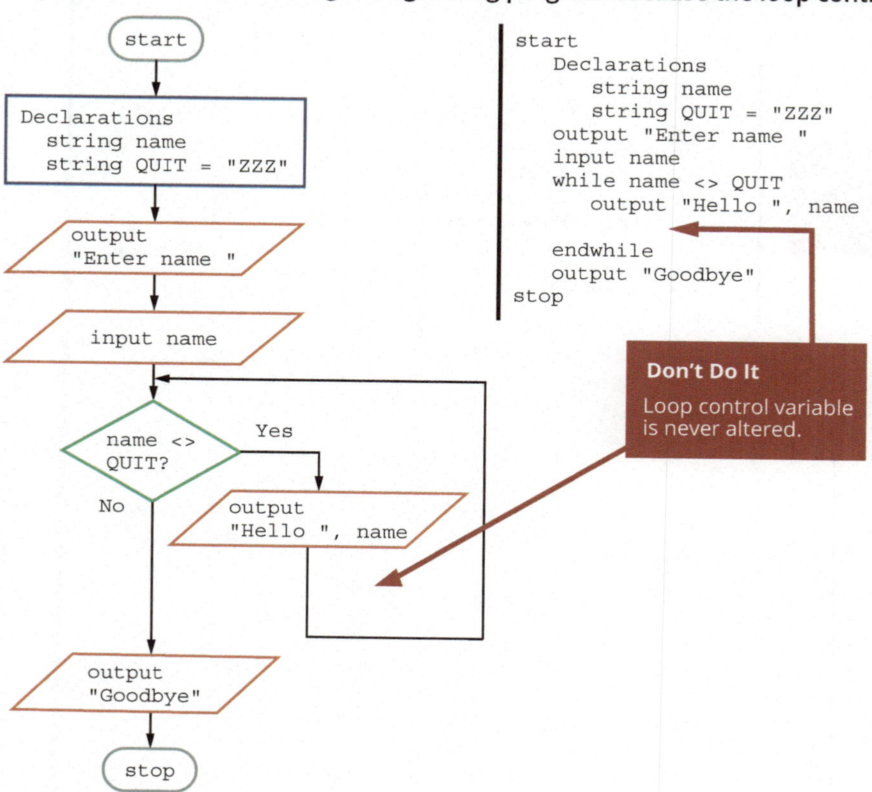
start
Declarations
string name
string QUIT = "ZZZ"
output "Enter name "
input name
name <> QUIT?
Yes
No
output "Hello ", name
output "Goodbye"
stop
start
Declarations
string name
string QUIT = "ZZZ"
output "Enter name "
input name
while name <> QUIT
output "Hello ", name
endwhile
output "Goodbye"
stop
Don't Do It
Loop control variable is never altered.

Mistake: Using the Wrong Type of Comparison When Testing the Loop Control Variable

Programmers must be careful to use the correct type of comparison in the evaluation that controls a loop. A comparison is correct only when the appropriate operands and operator are used. For example, although only one keystroke differs between the original greeting program in Figure 5-9 and the one in **Figure 5-12**, the original program correctly produces named greetings and the second one does not.

In Figure 5-12, a greater-than comparison (>) is made instead of a not-equal-to (<>) comparison. Suppose that when the program executes, the user enters *Diego* as the first name. In most programming languages, when the comparison between *Diego* and *ZZZ* is made, the values are compared alphabetically. *Diego* is not greater than *ZZZ*, so the loop is never entered, and the program ends.

Using the wrong type of comparison in a loop can have serious effects. For example, in a counted loop, if you use <= instead of < to compare a counter to a sentinel value, the program will perform one loop execution too many. If the loop's purpose is only to display greetings, the error might not be critical, but if such an error occurred in a loan company application, each customer might be charged a month's additional interest. If the error occurred in an airline's application, it might overbook a flight. If the error occurred in a pharmacy's drug-dispensing application, each patient might receive one extra (and possibly harmful) unit of medication.

Figure 5-12 Incorrect logic for greeting program because the wrong test is made with the loop control variable

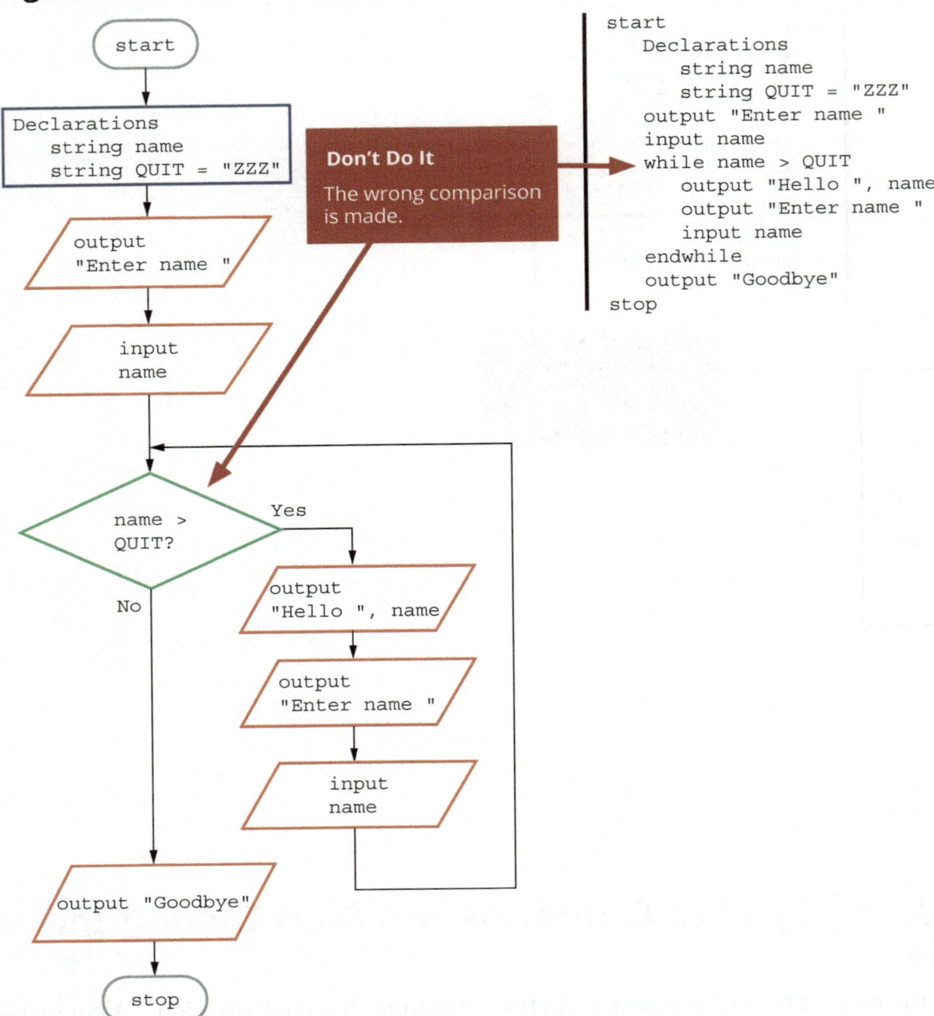
start
Declarations
string name
string QUIT = "ZZZ"
output "Enter name "
input name
name > QUIT?
Yes
No
output "Hello ", name
output "Enter name "
input name
output "Goodbye"
stop
Don't Do It
The wrong comparison is made.
start
Declarations
string name
string QUIT = "ZZZ"
output "Enter name "
input name
while name > QUIT
output "Hello ", name
output "Enter name "
input name
endwhile
output "Goodbye"
stop

Mistake: Including Statements Inside the Loop Body that Belong Outside the Loop

Suppose that you write a program for a store manager who wants to discount every item sold by 30 percent. The manager wants 100 new price label stickers for each item. The user enters a price, the new discounted price is calculated, 100 stickers are printed, and the next price is entered. **Figure 5-13** shows a program that performs the job inefficiently because the same value, `newPrice`, is calculated 100 separate times for each `price` that is entered.

Figure 5-13 Inefficient way to produce 100 discount price stickers for differently priced items

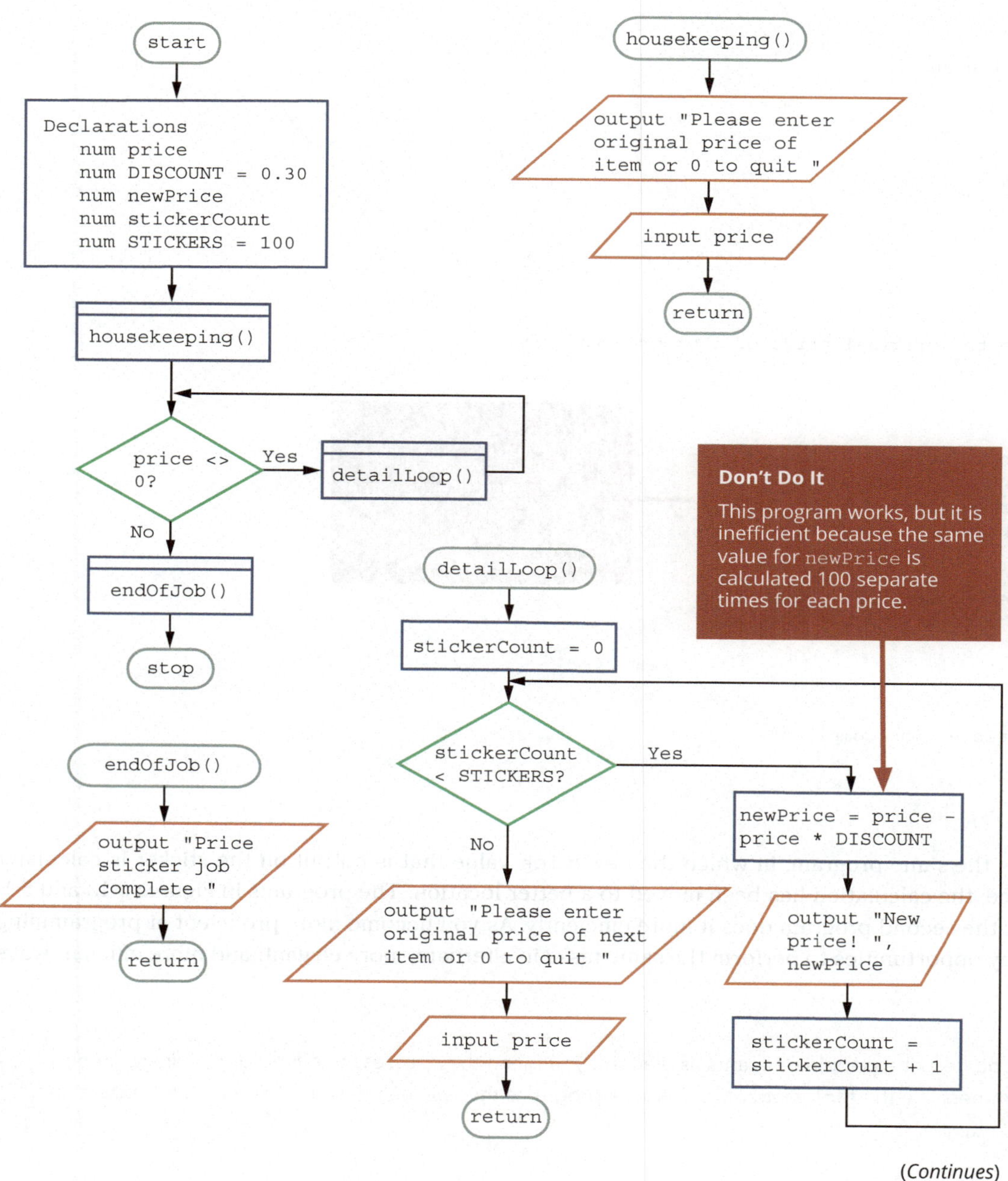

(*Continues*)

Figure 5-13 *(Continued)*

```
start
   Declarations
      num price
      num DISCOUNT = 0.30
      num newPrice
      num stickerCount
      num STICKERS = 100
   housekeeping()
   while price <> 0
      detailLoop()
   endwhile
   endOfJob()
stop

housekeeping()
   output "Please enter original price of item or 0 to quit "
   input price
return

detailLoop()
   stickerCount = 0
   while stickerCount < STICKERS
      newPrice = price - price * DISCOUNT
      output "New price! ", newPrice
      stickerCount = stickerCount + 1
   endwhile
   output "Please enter original price of
      next item or 0 to quit "
   input price
return

endOfJob()
   output "Price sticker job complete"
return
```

Don't Do It

This program works, but it is inefficient because the same value for `newPrice` is calculated 100 separate times for each price.

Figure 5-14 shows the same program, in which the `newPrice` value that is output on the sticker is calculated only once per new price; the calculation has been moved to a better location. The programs in Figures 5-13 and 5-14 do the same thing, but the second program does it more efficiently. As you become more proficient at programming, you will recognize many opportunities to perform the same tasks in alternate, more elegant, and more efficient ways.

Note When you describe people or events as elegant, you mean they possess a refined gracefulness. Similarly, programmers use the term *elegant* to describe programs that are well designed and easy to understand and maintain.

Two Truths & a Lie | Avoiding Common Loop Mistakes

1. In a loop, neglecting to initialize the loop control variable is a mistake.
2. In a loop, neglecting to alter the loop control variable is a mistake.
3. In a loop, comparing the loop control variable using >= or <= is a mistake.

The false statement is #3. Many loops are created correctly using <= or >=.

Figure 5-14 Improved discount sticker-making program

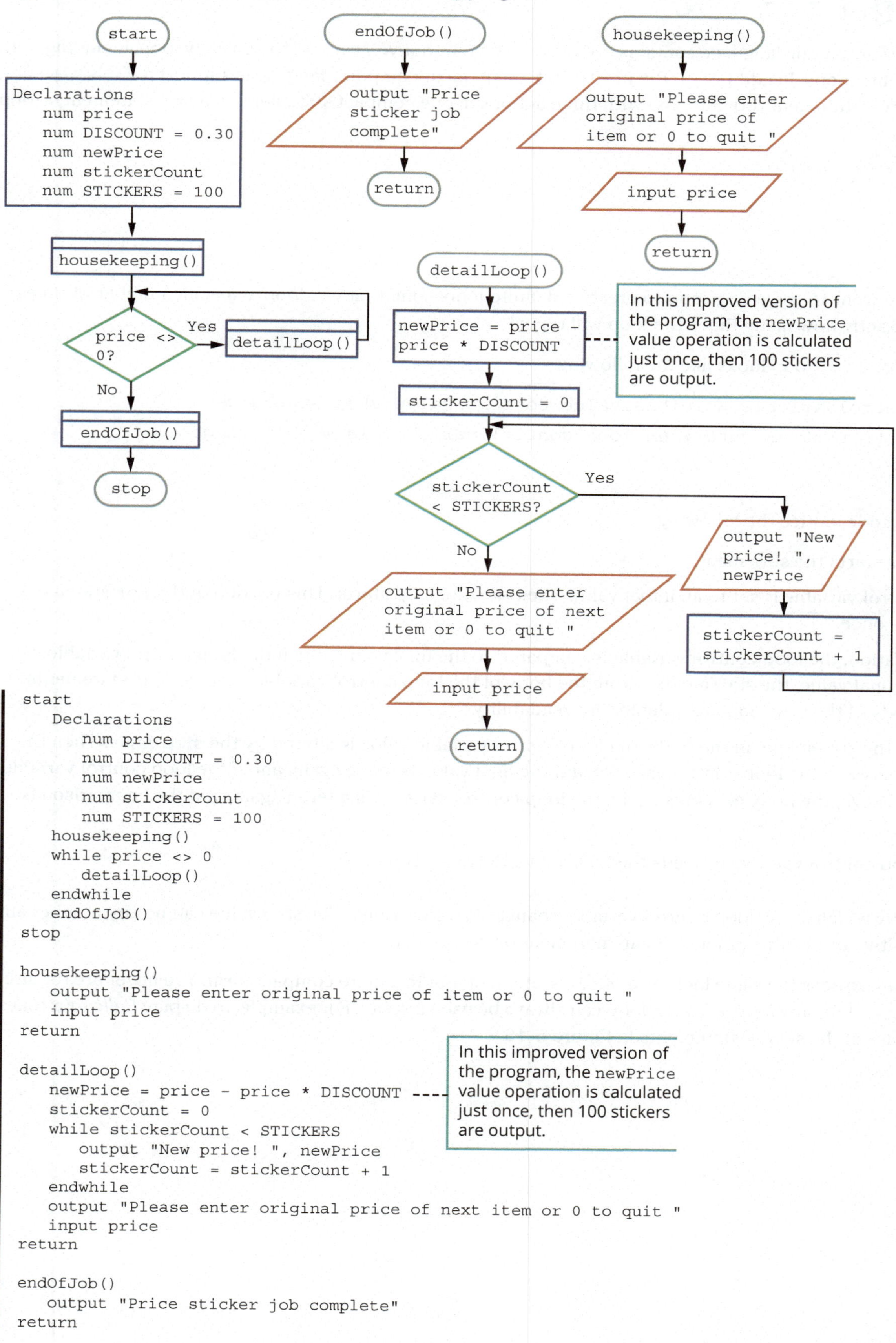


```
start
   Declarations
      num price
      num DISCOUNT = 0.30
      num newPrice
      num stickerCount
      num STICKERS = 100
   housekeeping()
   while price <> 0
      detailLoop()
   endwhile
   endOfJob()
stop

housekeeping()
   output "Please enter original price of item or 0 to quit "
   input price
return

detailLoop()
   newPrice = price - price * DISCOUNT
   stickerCount = 0
   while stickerCount < STICKERS
      output "New price! ", newPrice
      stickerCount = stickerCount + 1
   endwhile
   output "Please enter original price of next item or 0 to quit "
   input price
return

endOfJob()
   output "Price sticker job complete"
return
```

In this improved version of the program, the newPrice value operation is calculated just once, then 100 stickers are output.

5.5 Using a `for` Loop

Every high-level programming language contains a `while` statement that you can use to code any loop, including both indefinite and definite loops. In addition to the `while` statement, most computer languages support a **`for` statement**, or **`for` loop**. The `for` statement provides you with three actions in one compact statement. In a `for` statement, a loop control variable is:

- Initialized
- Tested
- Altered

You frequently want to use a `for` loop to create a definite loop—one that will loop a specific number of times—when you know exactly how many times the loop will repeat.

Pseudocode for a `for` loop looks like the following:

```
for loopControlVariable = initialValue to finalValue step stepValue
   statements that execute when loop control variable is within range
endfor
```

In the pseudocode, notice the following:

- The word `for` starts the statement.
- The loop control variable is set to an initial value when the `for` loop starts. This portion of the `for` statement executes only once.
- On every iteration, the loop control variable is compared to the final value. When the loop control variable is less than the final value, the statements within the body of the loop control variable execute. The statements within the body of the `for` loop are indented for readability.
- At the end of the statements in the body, the loop control variable value is altered by the **step value**. Then the comparison between the loop control variable and the final value is made again, and if the loop control variable is still within range, the body executes again, the loop control variable is altered again, and the comparison is made again.
- When the loop control variable exceeds the final value, the loop stops.

The amount by which a `for` loop control variable changes is a step value. The step value can be any number and can be either positive or negative; that is, it can increment or decrement.

A `for` loop can express the same logic as a `while` statement, but in a more compact form. You never are required to use a `for` statement for any loop; a `while` loop can always be used instead. For example, to display *Hello* four times, you can write either of the sets of statements in **Figure 5-15**.

Figure 5-15 Comparable `while` and `for` statements that each output *Hello* four times

```
count = 0
while count <= 3
   output "Hello"
   count = count + 1
endwhile
```

```
for count = 0 to 3 step 1
   output "Hello"
endfor
```

The code segments in Figure 5-15 each accomplish the same tasks:

- The variable `count` is initialized to 0.
- The `count` variable is compared to the limit value 3; while `count` is less than or equal to 3, the loop body executes.
- As the last statement in the loop execution, the value of `count` increases by 1. After the increase, the comparison to the limit value is made again.

A `while` loop can always be used instead of a `for` loop, but when a loop's execution is based on a loop control variable progressing from a known starting value to a known ending value in equal steps, the `for` loop provides a convenient shorthand. It is easy for others to read, and because the loop control variable's initialization, testing, and alteration are all performed in one location, you are less likely to leave out one of these crucial elements.

Although `for` loops are commonly used to control execution of a block of statements a fixed number of times, the programmer doesn't need to know the starting, final, or step value for the loop control variable when the program is written. For example, any of the values might be entered by the user or might be the result of a calculation.

Note

In Java, C++, and C#, a `for` loop that displays 21 values (0 through 20) might look similar to the following:

```
for(count = 0; count <= 20; count++)
{
   output count;
}
```

The three actions (initializing, evaluating, and altering the loop control variable) are separated by semicolons within a set of parentheses that follow the keyword `for`. The expression `count++` increases `count` by 1. In each of the three languages, the block of statements that depends on the loop sits between a pair of curly braces, so the `endfor` keyword is not used. None of the three languages uses the keyword `output`, but all of them end output statements with a semicolon.

In Visual Basic, the `for` loop takes the following format:

```
for counter = 0 to 20
   output count
next counter
```

Both the `while` loop and the `for` loop are examples of pretest loops. In a **pretest loop**, the loop control variable is tested before each iteration. That means the loop body might never execute because the evaluation controlling the loop might be false the first time it is made.

Note Some books and flowchart programs use a symbol that looks like a hexagon to represent a `for` loop in a flowchart. However, no special symbols are needed to express a `for` loop's logic. A `for` loop is simply a code shortcut, so this course uses standard flowchart symbols to represent initializing the loop control variable, testing it, and altering it.

Two Truths & a Lie | Using a `for` Loop

1. The `for` statement provides you with three actions in one compact statement: initializing, testing, and altering a loop control variable.
2. A `for` statement body always executes at least one time.
3. In most programming languages, you can provide a `for` loop with any step value.

The false statement is #2. A `for` statement body might not execute depending on the initial value of the loop control variable.

5.6 Using a Posttest Loop

Most languages allow you to use a variation of the pretest looping structure that tests the loop control variable after each iteration rather than before. In a **posttest loop**, the loop body executes at least one time because the loop control variable is not tested until after the first iteration.

Recall that a structured loop (often called a `while` loop) looks like **Figure 5-16**. A posttest loop, sometimes called a `do-while` loop, looks like **Figure 5-17**.

Figure 5-16 Structure of a `while` loop, which is a pretest loop

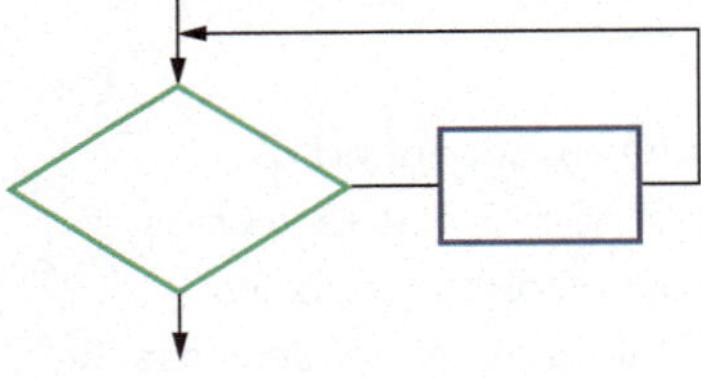

Figure 5-17 Structure of a `do-while` loop, which is a posttest loop

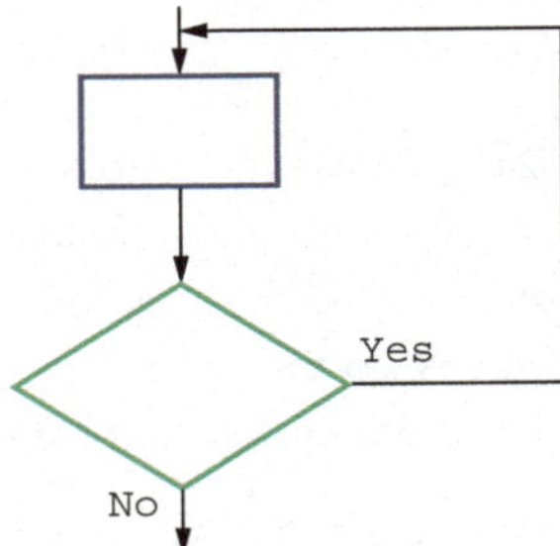

An important difference exists between the structures in Figures 5-16 and 5-17. In a `while` loop, you evaluate a condition and, depending on the result, you might or might not enter the loop to execute the loop's body. In other words, the condition that controls the loop is tested at the top of the loop.

Conversely, in a **`do-while` loop**, you ensure that the procedure executes at least once; then, depending on the result of the loop-controlling evaluation, the loop body may or may not execute additional times. In other words, you test the loop-controlling condition at the bottom of the loop.

Notice that the word *do* begins the name of the `do-while` loop. This should remind you that the action you "do" precedes testing the condition.

You encounter examples of do-while looping every day. For example:

```
do
   pay a bill
while more bills remain to be paid
```

As another example:

```
do
   wash a dish
while more dishes remain to be washed
```

In these examples, the activity (paying a bill or washing a dish) must occur at least one time. With a do-while loop, you evaluate the condition that determines whether you continue only after the activity has been executed at least once. You never are required to use a posttest loop; you can duplicate the same series of actions by creating a sequence followed by a standard, pretest while loop. Consider the flowcharts and pseudocode in **Figure 5-18**.

Figure 5-18 Flowchart and pseudocode for do-while loop and sequence with while loop that do the same thing

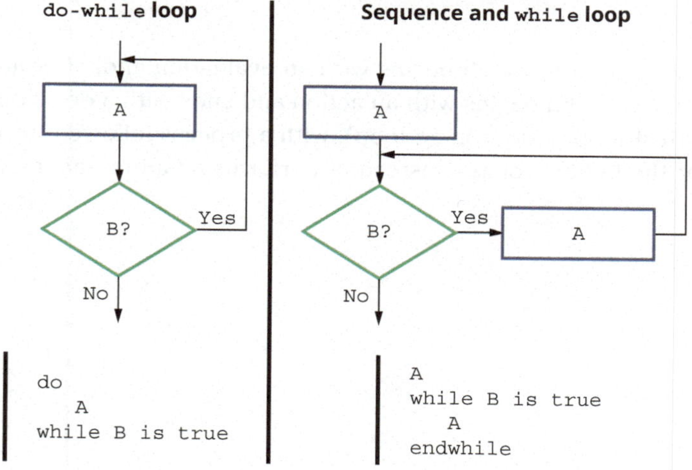

The logic in Figure 5-18 operates as follows:

- On the left side of Figure 5-18, A executes, and then B is tested. If B is true, then A executes and B is tested again.
- On the right side of the figure, A executes, and then B is tested. If B is true, then A executes and B is tested again.

In other words, both sets of flowchart and pseudocode segments in Figure 5-18 do exactly the same thing.

Because programmers understand that any posttest loop (do-while) can be expressed with a sequence followed by a while loop, most languages allow at least one version of the posttest loop for convenience.

Two Truths & a Lie | Using a Posttest Loop

1. In a while loop, the loop body might not execute.
2. In a do-while loop, the loop body might not execute.
3. The logic expressed by a do-while loop can always be expressed using a sequence and a while loop.

The false statement is #2. In a do-while loop, the loop body executes at least once.

5.7 Recognizing the Characteristics Shared by Structured Loops

As you examine Figures 5-16 and 5-17, notice that in the `while` loop, the loop-controlling evaluation is placed at the beginning of the steps that repeat, and in the `do-while` loop, the loop-controlling evaluation is placed at the end of the sequence of steps that repeat.

All structured loops, both pretest and posttest, share these two characteristics:

- The loop-controlling evaluation must provide either the entry to or exit from the structure.
- The loop-controlling evaluation provides the *only* entry to or exit from the structure.

In other words, there is exactly one loop-controlling evaluation, and it provides either the only entrance to or the only exit from the loop.

> **Note** | Some languages support a **`do-until` loop**, which is a posttest loop that iterates until the loop-controlling evaluation is false. The `do-until` loop also follows structured loop rules.

Figure 5-19 shows an unstructured loop. It is not a `while` loop, which begins with an evaluation and, after an action, returns to the decision. It is also not a `do-while` loop, which begins with an action and ends with a decision that might repeat the action. Instead, it begins like a posttest loop (a `do-while` loop), with a process followed by a decision, but one branch of the decision does not repeat the initial process. Instead, it performs an additional new action before repeating the initial process.

Figure 5-19 Unstructured loop

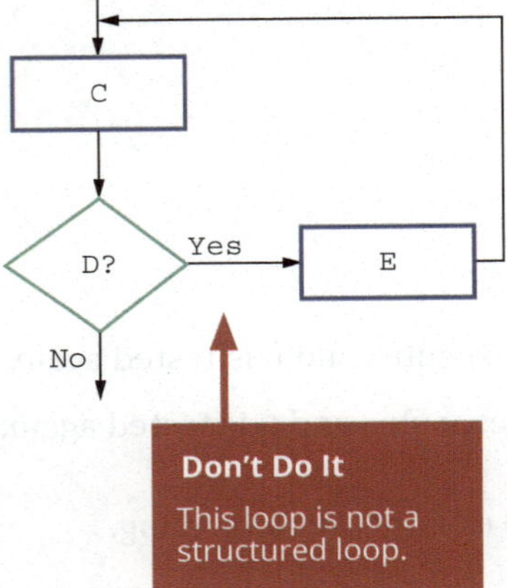
C
D?
Yes
E
No
Don't Do It
This loop is not a structured loop.

If you need to use the logic shown in Figure 5-19—performing a task, evaluating a condition, and performing an additional task before looping back to the first process—then the way to make the logic structured is to repeat the initial process within the loop at the end of the loop. **Figure 5-20** shows the same logic as Figure 5-19, but now it is structured logic, with a sequence of two actions occurring within the loop.

> **Note** | Especially when you are first mastering structured logic, you might prefer to use only the three basic structures—sequence, selection, and `while` loop. Every logical problem can be solved using only these three structures, and you can understand all of the examples in this course using only these three structures.

Figure 5-20 Sequence and structured loop that accomplish the same tasks as Figure 5-19

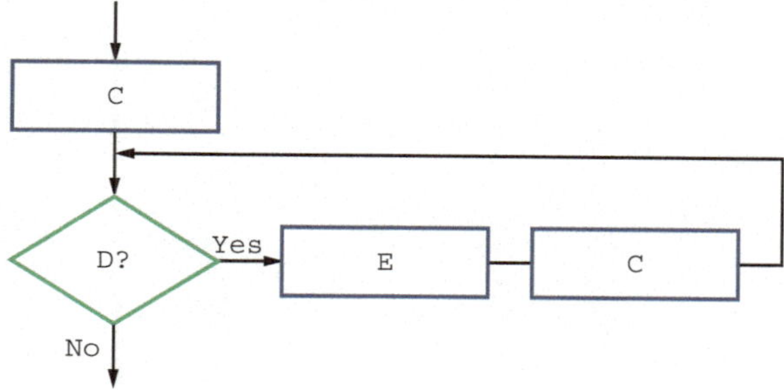

Two Truths & a Lie Recognizing the Characteristics Shared by Structured Loops

1. In a structured loop, the loop-controlling evaluation must provide either the entry to or exit from the repeating structure.
2. In a structured loop, the loop-controlling evaluation provides the *only* entry to or exit from the structure.
3. If you need to perform a task, evaluate a condition, and perform an additional task, you cannot use a structured loop.

The false statement is #3. All looping tasks can be made to be structured.

5.8 Common Loop Applications

Although every computer program is different, many techniques are common to a variety of applications. Loops, for example, are frequently used to accumulate totals and to validate data.

Using a Loop to Accumulate Totals

Business reports often include totals. The supervisor who requests a list of employees in the company dental plan is often as interested in the number of participating employees as in who they are. When you receive your credit card bill each month, you usually check the total as well as charges for the individual purchases.

Assume that a real estate broker wants to see a list of all properties sold in the last month as well as the total value for all the properties. A program might accept sales data that includes the street address of each property sold and its selling price. The data records might be entered by a clerk as each sale is made and then stored in a file until the end of the month; then they can be used in a monthly report. **Figure 5-21** shows an example of such a report.

To create the sales report, you must output the address and price for each property sold and add its value to an accumulator. An **accumulator** is a variable that you use to gather or accumulate values, and is very similar to a counter that you use to count loop iterations. Usually, however, you add just one to a counter, whereas you add some other value to an accumulator. If the real estate broker wants to know how many listings the company holds, you *count* them. When the broker wants to know the total real estate value, you *accumulate* it.

To accumulate total real estate prices, you declare a numeric variable such as `accumPrice` and initialize it to 0. As you get data for each real estate transaction, you output it and add its value to the accumulator `accumPrice`, as shown in **Figure 5-22**.

Figure 5-21 Month-end real estate sales report

```
MONTH-END SALES REPORT

Address             Price

287 Acorn St      150,000
12 Maple Ave      310,000
8723 Marie Ln      65,500
222 Acorn St      127,000
29 Bahama Way     450,000

Total           1,102,500
```

Figure 5-22 Flowchart and pseudocode for real estate sales report program

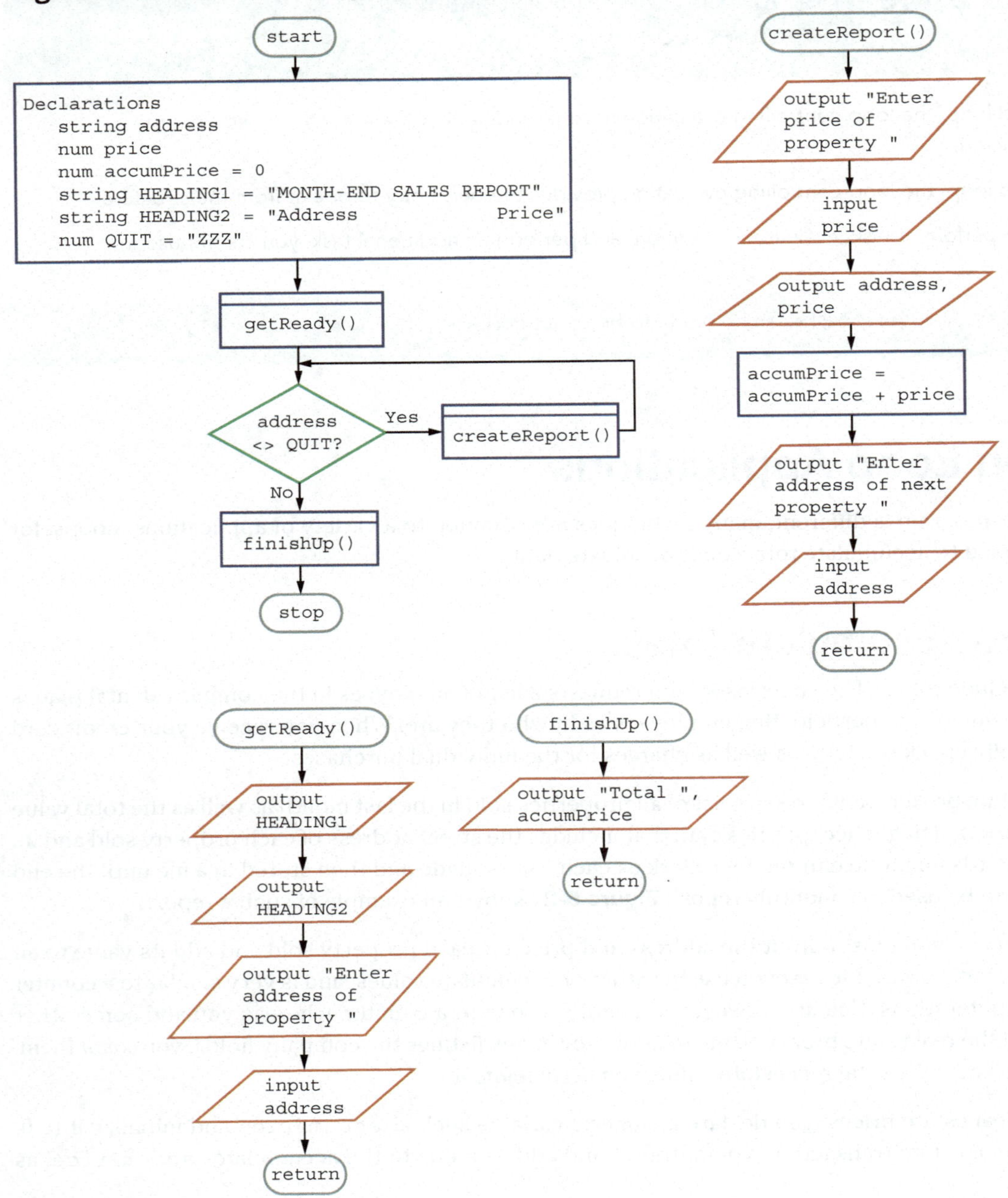

(Continues)

Figure 5-22 *(Continued)*

```
start
   Declarations
      string address
      num price
      num accumPrice = 0
      string HEADING1 = "MONTH-END SALES REPORT"
      string HEADING2 = "Address                     Price"
      num QUIT = "ZZZ"
   getReady()
   while address <> QUIT
      createReport()
   endwhile
   finishUp()
stop

getReady()
   output HEADING1
   output HEADING2
   output "Enter address of property "
   input address
return

createReport()
   output "Enter price of property "
   input price
   output address, price
   accumPrice = accumPrice + price
   output "Enter address of next property "
   input address
return

finishUp()
   output "Total ", accumPrice
return
```

Note Some programming languages assign 0 to a variable you fail to initialize explicitly, but many do not. When you try to add a value to an uninitialized variable, most languages will issue an error message; worse, some languages, such as C and C++, will let you incorrectly start with an accumulator that holds garbage. All the examples in this course assign the value 0 to each accumulator before using it.

Note In earlier program examples in this chapter, the modules were named `housekeeping()`, `detailLoop()`, and `endOfJob()`. In the program in Figure 5-22, they are named `getReady()`, `createReport()`, and `finishUp()`. You can assign modules any names that make sense to you, as long as you are consistent with the names within a program.

After the program in Figure 5-22 gets and displays the last real estate transaction, the user enters the sentinel value and loop execution ends. At that point, the accumulator will hold the grand total of all the real estate values. The program displays the word *Total* and the accumulated value `accumPrice`. Then the program ends. Figure 5-22 includes the three actions you usually must take with accumulators:

- Accumulators are initialized to 0.
- Accumulators are altered, usually once for every data set processed, and most often are altered through addition.
- At the end of processing, accumulators are output.

After outputting the value of `accumPrice`, new programmers often want to reset it to 0. Their argument is that they are "cleaning up after themselves." Although you can take this step without harming the execution of the program, it serves no useful purpose. You cannot set `accumPrice` to 0 in anticipation of having it ready for the next program, or even for the next time you execute the same program. Variables exist only during an execution of the program, and even if a future application happens to contain a variable named `accumPrice`, the variable will not necessarily occupy the same memory location as this one. Even if you run the same application a second time, the variables might occupy physical memory locations different from those during the first run. At the beginning of any module, it is the programmer's responsibility to initialize all variables that must start with a specific value. There is no benefit to changing a variable's value when it will never be used again during the current execution.

A business report might be a **summary report** that contains only totals with no data for individual records. In the sample report in Figure 5-21, suppose that the broker did not care about details of individual sales, but only about the total for all transactions. You could create a summary report by using the logic in Figure 5-22 but omitting the step that outputs `address` and `price` from the `createReport()` module. Then you could simply output `accumPrice` at the end of the program.

Using a Loop to Validate Data

When you ask a user to enter data into a computer program, you have no assurance that the data will be accurate. Incorrect user entries are by far the most common source of computer errors. The programs you write will be improved if you employ **defensive programming**, which means trying to prepare for all possible errors before they occur. Loops are frequently used to **validate data**—that is, to make sure it is meaningful and useful. For example, validation might ensure that a value is the correct data type or that it falls within an acceptable range.

Suppose that part of a program you are writing asks users to enter a number that represents their birth month. If a user types a number lower than 1 or greater than 12, you must take some sort of action. For example:

- You could display an error message and stop the program.
- You could choose to assign a default value for the month (for example, 1) before proceeding.
- You could reprompt the user for valid input.

If you choose this last course of action, you then could take at least two approaches. You could use a selection structure, and if the month is invalid, you could ask the user to reenter a number, as shown in **Figure 5-23**.

The problem with the logic in Figure 5-23 is that the comparisons of `month` to `LOW_MONTH` and `HIGH_MONTH` are made only once, and the user still might not enter valid data on the second attempt. Of course, you could add a third decision, but you still couldn't control what the user enters.

The superior solution is to use a loop to continually prompt a user for a month until the user enters it correctly. **Figure 5-24** shows this approach.

Of course, data validation doesn't prevent all errors; just because a data item is valid does not mean that it is correct. For example, a program can determine that 5 is a valid birth month, but not that your birthday actually falls in month 5. Programmers employ the acronym **GIGO** for *garbage in, garbage out*. It means that if your input is incorrect, your output is worthless.

Limiting a Reprompting Loop

Reprompting a user is a good way to try to ensure valid data, but it can be frustrating to a user if the requests continue indefinitely. For example, suppose the user must enter a valid birth month from 1 through 12, but has used another application in which January was month 0. The user might keep entering 0 for the month no matter how many times you repeat the prompt. One helpful addition to the program would be to use the limiting values as part of the prompt.

Figure 5-23 Reprompting a user once after an invalid month is entered

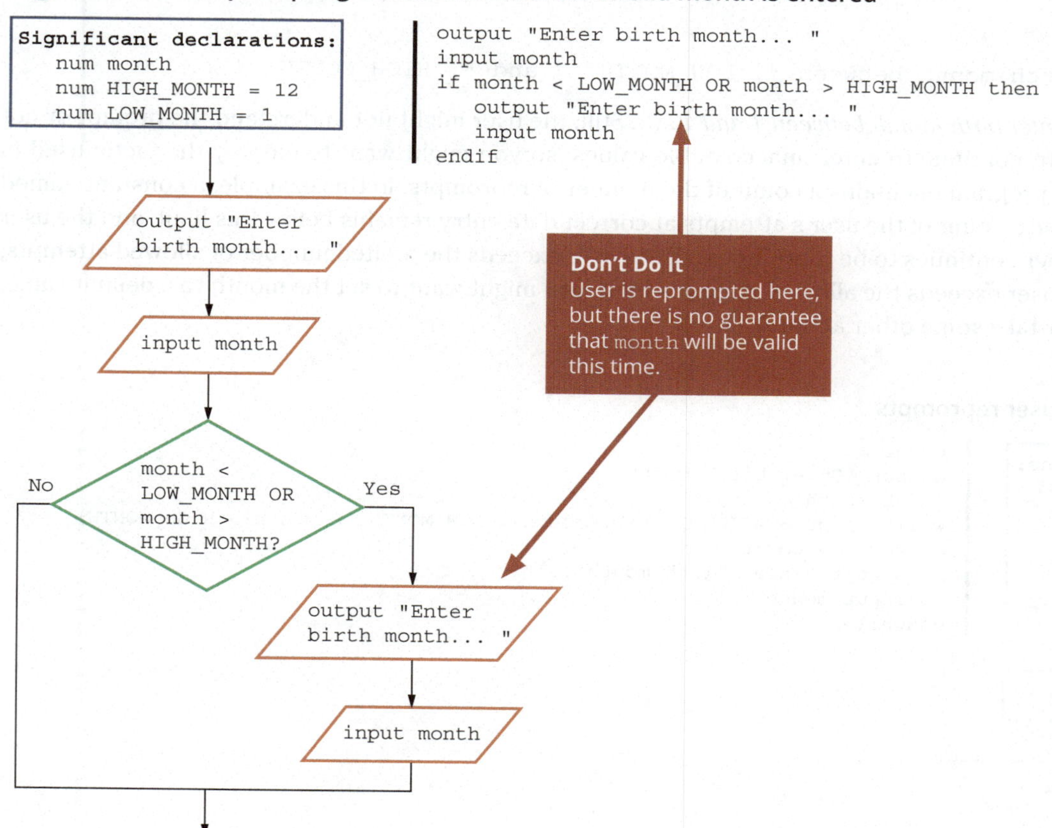
Significant declarations:
num month
num HIGH_MONTH = 12
num LOW_MONTH = 1
output "Enter birth month... "
input month
if month < LOW_MONTH OR month > HIGH_MONTH then
output "Enter birth month... "
input month
endif
output "Enter birth month... "
input month
month < LOW_MONTH OR month > HIGH_MONTH?
No
Yes
output "Enter birth month... "
input month
Don't Do It
User is reprompted here, but there is no guarantee that month will be valid this time.

Figure 5-24 Reprompting a user continually after an invalid month is entered

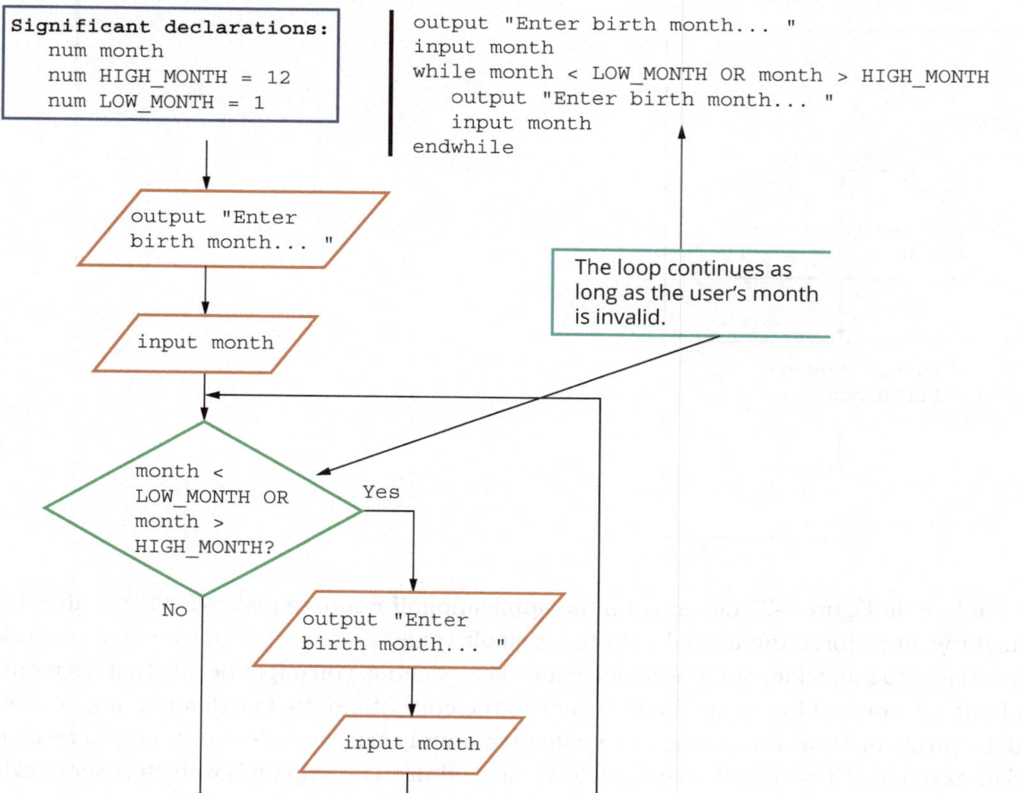
Significant declarations:
num month
num HIGH_MONTH = 12
num LOW_MONTH = 1
output "Enter birth month... "
input month
while month < LOW_MONTH OR month > HIGH_MONTH
output "Enter birth month... "
input month
endwhile
output "Enter birth month... "
input month
The loop continues as long as the user's month is invalid.
month < LOW_MONTH OR month > HIGH_MONTH?
Yes
No
output "Enter birth month... "
input month

In other words, instead of the statement `output "Enter birth month ... "`, the following statement might be more useful:

```
output "Enter birth month between ", LOW_MONTH, " and ", HIGH_MONTH, " ... "
```

The user would see *Enter birth month between 1 and 12 ....* Still, the user might not understand the prompt or not read it carefully, and might continue to enter unacceptable values, so you might want to employ the tactic used in **Figure 5-25**, in which the program maintains a count of the number of reprompts. In this example, a constant named `ATTEMPTS` is set to 3. While a count of the user's attempts at correct data entry remains below this limit, and the user enters invalid data, the user continues to be reprompted. If the user exceeds the limited number of allowed attempts, the loop ends. (After the user exceeds the allowed attempts limit, you might want to set the month to a default value, terminate the program, or take some other action.)

Figure 5-25 Limiting user reprompts

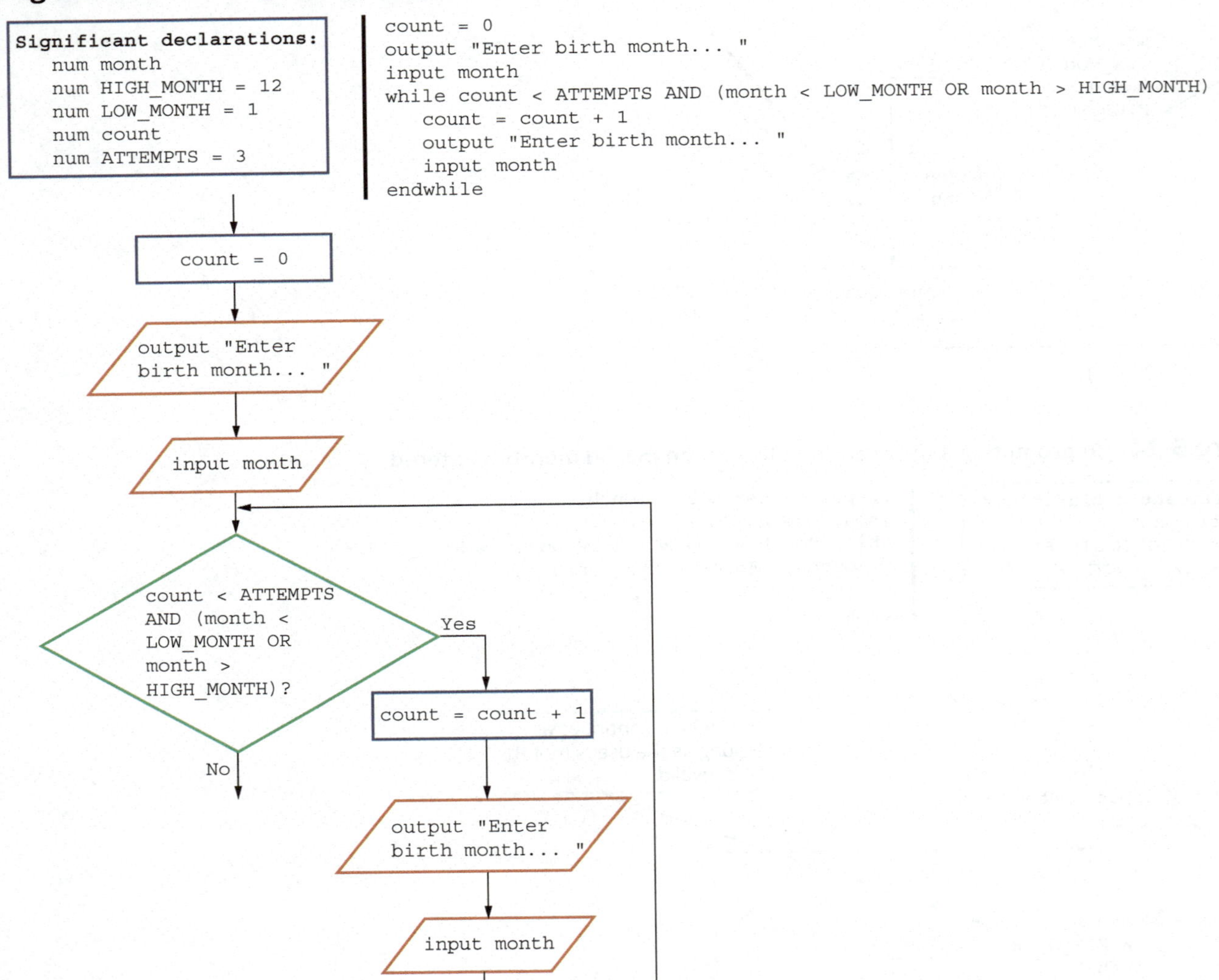
Significant declarations:
num month
num HIGH_MONTH = 12
num LOW_MONTH = 1
num count
num ATTEMPTS = 3
count = 0
output "Enter birth month... "
input month
while count < ATTEMPTS AND (month < LOW_MONTH OR month > HIGH_MONTH)
count = count + 1
output "Enter birth month... "
input month
endwhile
count = 0
output "Enter birth month... "
input month
count < ATTEMPTS AND (month < LOW_MONTH OR month > HIGH_MONTH)?
Yes
No
count = count + 1
output "Enter birth month... "
input month

The action that follows the loop in Figure 5-25 depends on the application. If `count` equals `ATTEMPTS` after the data-entry loop ends, you might want to force the invalid data to a default value. **Forcing data** means you override incorrect data by setting the variable to a specific, predetermined value. For example, you might decide that if a month value does not fall between 1 and 12, you will force the month to 0 or to the current month. In a different application, you might just choose to end the program. However, ending a program prematurely can frustrate users and can result in lost revenue for a company. For example, if it is difficult to complete a transaction on a company's website, users might give up and not do business with the organization. In an interactive, Web-based program, if a user has trouble providing valid data, you might choose to have a customer service representative start a chat session with the user to offer help.

Validating a Data Type

The data you use within computer programs is varied. It stands to reason that validating data requires a variety of methods. For example, some programming languages allow you to check data items to make sure they are the correct data type. Although this technique varies from language to language, you often can make a statement like the one shown in **Figure 5-26**. In this program segment, `isNumeric()` represents a call to a module; it is used to check whether the entered employee `salary` falls within the category of numeric data. You check to ensure that a value is numeric for many reasons—an important one is that only numeric values can be used correctly in arithmetic statements. A module such as `isNumeric()` most often is provided with the language translator you use to write your programs. Such a module operates as a black box; in other words, you can use the module's results without understanding its internal statements.

Figure 5-26 Checking data for correct type

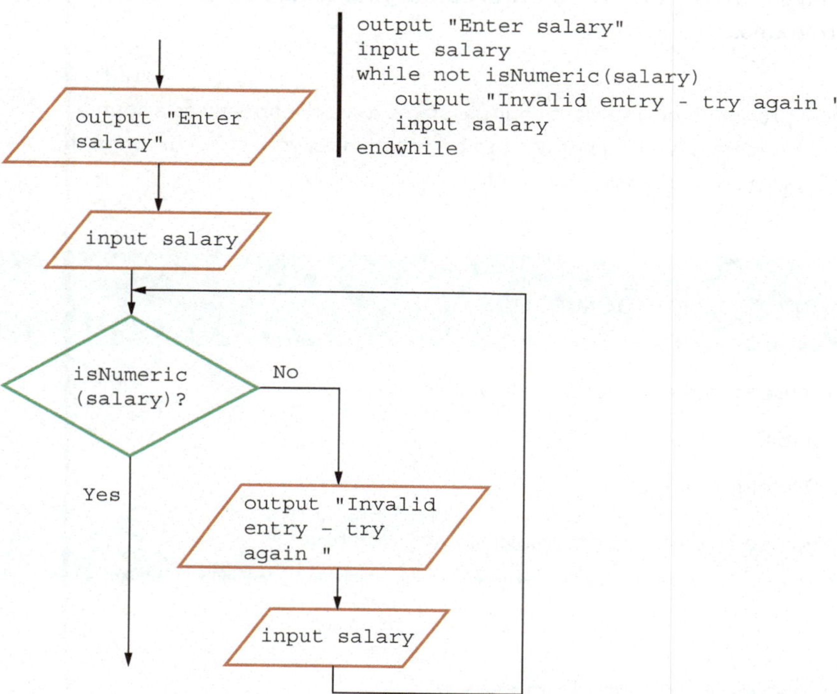
output "Enter salary"
input salary
while not isNumeric(salary)
output "Invalid entry - try again "
input salary
endwhile
output "Enter salary"
input salary
isNumeric (salary)?
No
Yes
output "Invalid entry - try again "
input salary

Besides allowing you to check whether a value is numeric, some languages contain modules such as `isChar()`, which checks whether a value is a character data type; `isWhitespace()`, which checks whether a value is a nonprinting (whitespace) character, such as a space or tab; and `isUpper()`, which checks whether a value is a capital letter.

In many languages, you accept all user data as a string of characters, and then use built-in modules to attempt to convert the characters to the correct data type for your application. When the conversion modules succeed, you have useful data. When the conversion modules fail because the user has entered the wrong data type, you can take appropriate action, such as issuing an error message, reprompting the user, or forcing the data to a default value.

Validating Reasonableness and Consistency of Data

Data items can be the correct type and within range, but still be incorrect. You have experienced this problem yourself if anyone has ever misspelled your name or overbilled you. The data might have been the correct type—for example, alphabetic letters were used in your name—but the name itself was incorrect. Many data items cannot be checked for reasonableness; for example, the names *Catherine*, *Katherine*, and *Kathryn* are equally reasonable, but only one spelling is correct for a particular person.

However, many data items can be checked for reasonableness. For example:

- If you make a purchase on October 3, 2026, then the payment cannot possibly be due prior to that date.
- Perhaps within your organization, you cannot make more than $20 per hour if you work in Department 12.
- If your zip code is 90201, your state of residence cannot be New York.
- If your store's cash on hand was $3,000 when it closed on Tuesday, the amount should not be different when the store opens on Wednesday.

Each of these examples involves comparing two data items for reasonableness or consistency. You should consider making as many such comparisons as possible when writing your own programs.

Frequently, testing for reasonableness and consistency involves using additional data files. For example, to check that a user has entered a valid county of residence for a state, you might use a file that contains every county name within every state in the United States to check the user's county against those contained in the file. Good defensive programs try to foresee all possible inconsistencies and errors. The more accurate your data, the more useful information you will produce as output from your programs.

Note When you become a professional programmer, you want your programs to work correctly as a source of professional pride. On a more basic level, you do not want to be called in to work at 3 a.m. when the overnight run of your program fails because of errors you created.

Two Truths & a Lie | Common Loop Applications

1. An accumulator is a variable that you use to gather or accumulate values.
2. An accumulator typically is initialized to 0.
3. An accumulator is typically reset to 0 after it is output.

The false statement is #3. There is typically no need to reset an accumulator after it is output.

5.9 Comparing Selections and Loops

New programmers sometimes struggle when determining whether to use a selection or a loop to solve some programming problems. Much of the confusion occurs because selections and loops both start by testing conditions and continue by taking action based on the outcome of the test.

An important difference between a selection and a loop, however, is that in the selection structure, the two logical paths that emerge from testing the condition join following their actions. In the loop structure, the paths that emerge from the test do not join. Instead, with a loop, one of the logical branches that emerges from the structure-controlling decision eventually returns to the same test. **Figure 5-27** compares flowcharts for a selection structure and a loop structure.

When a client describes a programming need, you can listen for certain words to help you decide whether to use a selection or a loop structure. For example, when program requirements contain words like *if*, *else*, *unless*, and *otherwise*, the necessary logic might be a selection structure. On the other hand, when program requirements contain words like *while*, *until*, *as long as*, *during*, *for each*, *repeat*, and *continue*, the necessary logic might include a loop. As you have learned with AND and OR logic, clients do not always use language as precisely as computers, so listening for such keywords is only a guideline.

Figure 5-27 Comparing a selection and a loop

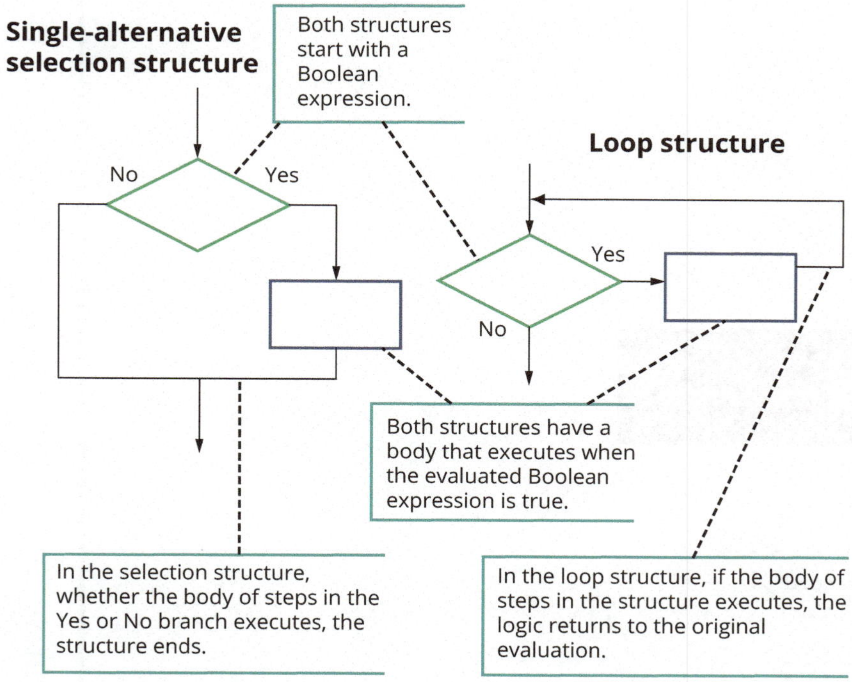

When you find yourself repeating selection structures that are very similar, you should consider using a loop. For example, suppose your supervisor says, "If you don't reach the end of the file when you are reading an employee record, display the record and read another one. Keep doing this until you run out of records." Because the supervisor used the word *if* to start the request, your first inclination might be to create logic that looks like **Figure 5-28**.

The logic in Figure 5-28 works—each time an employee record is input and the `eof` condition is not met, the data is displayed and another record is input. However, the logic in Figure 5-28 is flawed. First, if you do not know how many input records there are, the logic might never end. After each record is input, it is always necessary to check again for the `eof` condition. Second, even if you do know the number of input records, the logic becomes very unwieldy after three or four records. When you examine Figure 5-28, you see that the same set of steps is repeated. Actions that are repeated are best handled in a loop. **Figure 5-29** shows a better solution to the problem. In Figure 5-29, the first employee record is input, and as long as the `eof` condition is not met, the program continually displays and reads additional records.

Two Truths & a Lie | Comparing Selections and Loops

1. Selection and loop structures differ in that selection structures only take action when a test condition is true.
2. Selection and loop structures are similar in that the tested condition that begins either structure always has two possible outcomes.
3. One difference between selection and loop structures is that the structure-controlling evaluation is repeated in a loop structure.

The false statement is #1. Selection structures can take different actions when a test condition is true and when it is false.

Figure 5-28 Inefficient logic for reading and displaying employee records

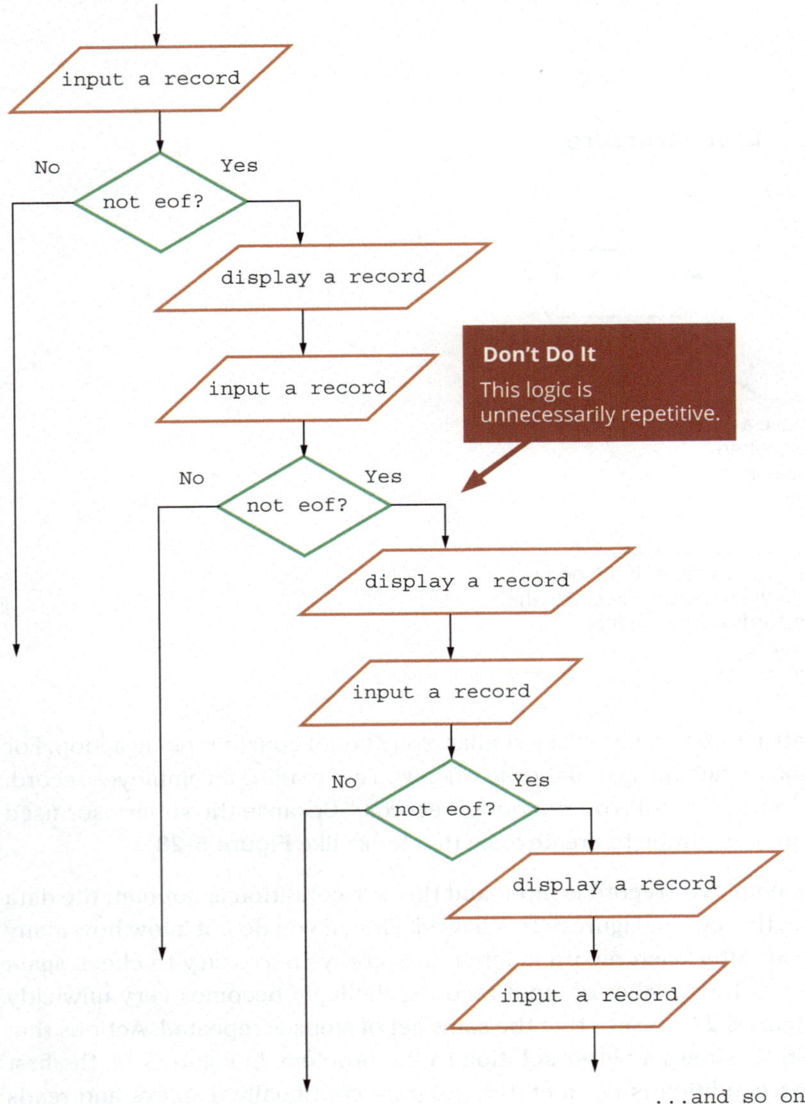

Figure 5-29 Efficient and structured logic for reading and displaying employee records

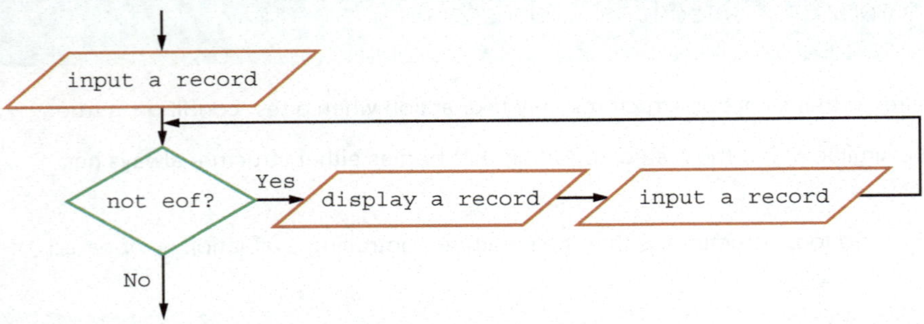

Summary

- A loop contains one set of instructions that operates on multiple, separate sets of data.
- Three actions are taken with a loop control variable in every `while` loop: You must initialize a loop control variable, compare the variable to some value that controls whether the loop continues or stops, and alter the variable that controls the loop.
- Nested loops are loops that execute within the confines of other loops. When nesting loops, you maintain two separate loop control variables and alter each at the appropriate time.
- Common mistakes that programmers make when writing loops include failing to initialize the loop control variable, neglecting to alter the loop control variable, using the wrong comparison expression with the loop control variable, and including statements inside the loop that belong outside the loop.
- Most computer languages support a `for` statement or `for` loop that you can use with definite loops when you know how many times a loop will repeat. The `for` statement uses a loop control variable that it automatically initializes, tests, and alters.
- In a posttest loop, the loop body executes at least one time because the loop control variable is not tested until after the first iteration.
- In all structured loops, there is exactly one loop-controlling value, and it provides either the only entrance to or the only exit from the loop.
- Loops are used in many applications—for example, to accumulate totals in business reports. Loops also are used to ensure that user data entries are valid by repeatedly reprompting the user.
- In the selection structure, the two logical paths that emerge from a test join following their actions. In the loop structure, the paths that emerge from the test do not join; instead, one of the paths eventually returns to the same test.

Key Terms

accumulator
counted loop
counter
counter-controlled loop
decrement
defensive programming
definite loop
`do-until` loop
`do-while` loop
`for` loop
`for` statement
forcing data
GIGO
increment
indefinite loop
inner loop
loop control variable
nested loops
outer loop
posttest loop
pretest loop
step value
summary report
validate data

Review Questions

1. The structure that allows you to write one set of instructions that operates on multiple, separate sets of data is the ______________. (5.1)
   - a. sequence
   - b. loop
   - c. selection
   - d. case
2. The loop that frequently appears in a program's mainline logic ______________. (5.1)
   - a. always depends on whether a variable equals 0
   - b. is an example of an infinite loop
   - c. is an unstructured loop
   - d. works correctly based on the same logic as other loops
3. Which of the following is *not* a step that must occur with every correctly working loop? (5.1, 5.2)
   - a. Initialize a loop control variable before the loop starts.
   - b. Compare the loop control value to a sentinel during each iteration.
   - c. Set the loop control value equal to a sentinel during each iteration.
   - d. Allow the loop control variable to be altered during each iteration.
4. The statements executed within a loop are known collectively as the ______________. (5.2)
   - a. loop body
   - b. loop controls
   - c. sequences
   - d. sentinels
5. A counter keeps track of ______________. (5.2)
   - a. the number of times an event has occurred
   - b. the number of machine cycles required by a segment of a program
   - c. the number of loop structures within a program
   - d. the number of times software has been revised
6. Adding 1 to a variable is also called ______________ it. (5.2)
   - a. digesting
   - b. resetting
   - c. decrementing
   - d. incrementing
7. Which of the following is a definite loop? (5.2)
   - a. a loop that executes as long as a user continues to enter valid data
   - b. a loop that executes 1,000 times
   - c. any loop except an infinite loop
   - d. an infinite loop
8. Which of the following is an indefinite loop? (5.2)
   - a. a loop that executes exactly 10 times
   - b. a loop that follows a prompt that asks a user how many repetitions to make and uses the value to control the loop
   - c. an infinite loop
   - d. a loop that asks the user whether to continue during each iteration
9. When two loops are nested, the loop that is contained by the other is the ______________ loop. (5.3)
   - a. captive
   - b. unstructured
   - c. inner
   - d. outer

10. When loops are nested, ______________. (5.3)

    a. they typically share a loop control variable
    b. one must end before the other begins
    c. both must be the same type—definite or indefinite
    d. the inner loop ends before the outer loop

11. Most programmers use a `for` loop ______________. (5.5)

    a. for every loop they write
    b. when they know the exact number of times a loop will repeat
    c. when a loop must repeat many times
    d. when a loop will not repeat

12. A report that lists only totals, with no details about individual records, is a(n) ______________ report. (5.8)

    a. accumulator
    b. final
    c. group
    d. summary

13. Typically, the value added to a counter variable is ______________. (5.2)

    a. 0
    b. 1
    c. 2
    d. different in each iteration

14. Typically, the value added to an accumulator variable is ______________. (5.8)

    a. 0
    b. 1
    c. the same for each iteration
    d. different in each iteration

15. After an accumulator or counter variable is displayed at the end of a program, it is best to ______________. (5.8)

    a. delete the variable from the program
    b. reset the variable to 0
    c. subtract 1 from the variable
    d. do nothing to the variable's value

16. When you ______________, you make sure data items are the correct type and fall within the correct range. (5.8)

    a. validate data
    b. employ offensive programming
    c. use object orientation
    d. count loop iterations

17. Overriding a user's entered value by setting it to a predetermined value is known as ______________. (5.8)

    a. forcing
    b. accumulating
    c. validating
    d. pushing

18. To ensure that a user's entry is the correct data type, frequently you ______________. (5.8)

    a. prompt the user to verify that the type is correct
    b. use a module built into the programming language
    c. include a statement at the beginning of the program that lists the data types allowed
    d. force all data to strings

19. A variable cannot hold an incorrect value when it is ______________. (5.8)

    a. the correct data type
    b. within a required range
    c. a constant coded by the programmer
    d. A variable might always hold an incorrect value.

20. A `do-while` loop ______________. (5.6)

    a. has a body that might never execute
    b. is a type of pretest loop
    c. can be replaced by a sequence and a `while` loop
    d. is not structured, and is therefore obsolete

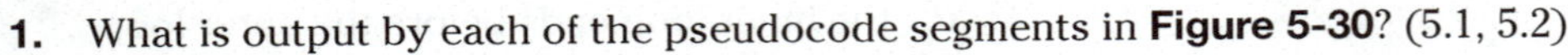

Programming Exercises

1. What is output by each of the pseudocode segments in **Figure 5-30**? (5.1, 5.2)

Figure 5-30 Pseudocode segments for Exercise 1

a.
```
a = 1
b = 2
c = 5
while a < c
   a = a + 1
   b = b + c
endwhile
output a, b, c
```

b.
```
d = 4
e = 6
f = 7
while d > f
   d = d + 1
   e = e - 1
endwhile
output d, e, f
```

c.
```
g = 4
h = 6
while g < h
   g = g + 1
endwhile
output g, h
```

d.
```
j = 2
k = 5
n = 9
while j < k
   m = 6
   while m < n
      output "Goodbye"
      m = m + 1
   endwhile
   j = j + 1
endwhile
```

e.
```
j = 2
k = 5
m = 6
n = 9
while j < k
   while m < n
      output "Hello"
      m = m + 1
   endwhile
   j = j + 1
endwhile
```

f.
```
p = 2
q = 4
while p < q
   output "Adios"
   r = 1
   while r < q
      output "Adios"
      r = r + 1
   endwhile
   p = p + 1
endwhile
```

2. Design the logic for a program that outputs every number from 1 through 15. (5.1, 5.2)
3. Design the logic for a program that outputs every number from 1 through 15 along with its value multiplied by 10 and by 100. (5.1, 5.2)
4. Design the logic for a program that outputs every even number from 2 through 200. (5.1, 5.2)
5. Design the logic for a program that outputs numbers in reverse order from 10 down to 0. (5.1, 5.2)
6. Design the logic for a program that allows a user to enter a number. Display the sum of every number from 1 through the entered number. (5.1, 5.2)
7. Design the logic for a program that allows a user to continually enter numbers until the user enters *0*. Display the sum of the numbers entered. (5.2)
8. Design a program that allows a user to enter any quantity of numbers until a negative number is entered. Then display the highest number and the lowest number. (5.2)
9. **a.** Design an application for Step Up E-Z Loans. The application accepts a client's loan amount and monthly payment amount. Output the customer's loan balance each month until the loan is paid off.

   b. Modify the Step Up E-Z Loans application so that after the payment is made each month, a finance charge of 1 percent is added to the balance. (5.2)

10. a. Design a program for Hunterville College. The current tuition is $20,000 per year, and tuition is expected to increase by 3 percent each year. Display the tuition each year for the next 10 years.

    b. Modify the Hunterville College program so that the user enters the rate of tuition increase instead of having it fixed at 3 percent.

    c. Modify the Hunterville College program so that the user enters the rate of tuition increase for the first year. The rate then increases by 0.5 percent each subsequent year. (5.1, 5.2)

11. Design a retirement planning calculator for Skulling Financial Services. Allow a user to enter a value that represents the number of working years remaining in the user's career and another value for the annual amount of money the user can save. Assume that the user earns 3 percent simple interest on savings annually. Program output is a schedule that lists each year number in retirement starting with year 0 and the user's savings at the start of that year. Assume that the user spends $60,000 per year in retirement and then earns 3 percent interest on the remaining balance. End the list after 30 years or when the user's balance is 0 or less, whichever comes first. (5.2)

12. a. Design a program for the Hollywood Movie Rating Guide, which can be installed in a kiosk in theaters. Each theater patron enters a value from 0 to 4 indicating the number of stars that the patron awards to the Rating Guide's featured movie of the week. If a user enters a star value that does not fall in the correct range, reprompt the user continually until a correct value is entered. The program executes continually until the theater manager enters a negative number to quit. At the end of the program, display the average star rating for the movie.

    b. Modify the movie-rating program so that a user gets three tries to enter a valid rating. After three incorrect entries, the program issues an appropriate message and continues with a new user. (5.8)

13. Design a program for the Café Noir Coffee Shop to provide some customer market research data. When a customer places an order, a clerk asks for the customer's zip code and age. The clerk enters that data as well as the number of items the customer orders. The program operates continually until the clerk enters a 0 for zip code at the end of the day. When the clerk enters an invalid zip code (more than 5 digits) or an invalid age (defined as less than 10 or more than 110), the program reprompts the clerk continually. When the clerk enters fewer than 1 or more than 10 items ordered, the program reprompts the clerk two more times. If the clerk enters a high value on the third attempt, the program accepts the high value, but if the clerk enters a negative value on the third attempt, an error message is displayed and the order is not counted. At the end of the program, display a count of the number of items ordered by customers from the same zip code as the coffee shop (54984), and a count from other zip codes. Also display the average customer age as well as counts of the number of items ordered by customers under 45 and by customers 45 and older. (5.8)

Performing Maintenance

1. A file named *MAINTENANCE05-01.txt* is included in the Chapter05 folder of your downloadable student files. Assume that this program is a working program in your organization and that it needs modifications as described in the comments (lines that begin with two slashes) at the beginning of the file. Your job is to alter the program to meet the new specifications. (5.1, 5.2)

Debugging Exercises

1. Your downloadable files for Chapter 5 include *DEBUG05-01.txt*, *DEBUG05-02.txt*, *DEBUG05-03.txt*, and *DEBUG05-04.jpg*. Each file starts with some comments that describe the problem. Comments are lines that begin with two slashes (//). Following the comments, each file contains pseudocode or a flowchart that has mistakes. Find and correct all the bugs.

Game Zone

1. You have learned that in many programming languages you can generate a random number between 1 and a limiting value named `LIMIT` by using a statement similar to `randomNumber = random(LIMIT)`. Create the logic for a guessing game in which a random number from 1 to 100 is generated and a user tries to guess its value. After each guess, display a message indicating whether the player's guess was correct, too high, or too low. When the player eventually guesses the correct number, display a count of the number of guesses that were required. (5.1, 5.2)

2. Create the logic for a game that simulates rolling two dice by generating two random numbers between 1 and 6 inclusive. The player chooses a number between 2 and 12 (the lowest and highest totals possible for two dice). The player then "rolls" two dice up to three times. If the number chosen by the user comes up, the user wins and the game ends. If the number does not come up within three rolls, the computer wins. (5.1, 5.2)

3. Create the logic for the dice game Pig, in which a player can compete with the computer. The object of the game is to be the first to score 100 points. The user and computer take turns "rolling" a pair of dice following these rules:
   - On a turn, each player rolls two dice. If no 1 appears, the dice values are added to a running total for the turn, and the player can choose whether to roll again or pass the turn to the other player. When a player passes, the accumulated turn total is added to the player's game total.
   - If a 1 appears on one of the dice, the player's turn total becomes 0; in other words, nothing more is added to the player's game total for that turn, and it becomes the other player's turn.
   - If a 1 appears on both of the dice, not only is the player's turn over, but the player's entire accumulated total is reset to 0.
   - When the computer does not roll a 1 and can choose whether to roll again, generate a random value from 1 to 2. The computer then will decide to continue when the value is 1 and decide to quit and pass the turn to the player when the value is not 1. (5.1, 5.2)

Chapter 6

Arrays

Learning Objectives

When you complete this chapter, you will be able to:

6.1 Store data in arrays

6.2 Describe how an array can replace nested decisions

6.3 Use constants with arrays

6.4 Search an array for an exact match

6.5 Use parallel arrays

6.6 Search an array for a range match

6.7 Remain within array bounds

6.8 Use a `for` loop to process an array

6.1 Storing Data in Arrays

An **array** is a series or list of values in computer memory. All the values must be the same data type. Usually, all the values in an array have something in common; for example, they might represent a list of employee ID numbers or prices for items sold in a store.

Whenever you require multiple storage locations for objects, you can use a real-life counterpart of a programming array. If you store important papers in a series of file folders and label each folder with a consecutive letter of the alphabet, then you are using the equivalent of an array. If you keep receipts in a stack of shoe boxes and label each box with a month, you are also using the equivalent of an array. Similarly, when you plan courses for the next semester at your school by looking down a list of course offerings, you are using an array.

> **Note** | The arrays discussed in this chapter are single-dimensional arrays, which are similar to lists. Arrays with multiple dimensions are covered later in this course.

Each of these real-life arrays helps you organize objects or information. You *could* store all your papers or receipts in one huge cardboard box or find courses if they were printed randomly in one large book. However, using an organized storage and display system makes your life easier in each case. Similarly, an array provides an organized storage and display system for a program's data.

How Arrays Occupy Computer Memory

When you declare an array, you declare a structure that contains multiple data items; each data item is one **element** of the array. Each element has the same data type, and each element occupies an area in memory next to, or contiguous to, the others. You can indicate the number of elements an array will hold—the **size of the array**—when you declare the array along with your other variables and constants. For example, you might declare an uninitialized, three-element numeric array named `prices` and an uninitialized string array of 10 employee names as follows:

```
num prices[3]
string employeeNames[10]
```

When naming arrays, programmers follow the same rules as when naming variables. That is, array names must start with a letter and contain no embedded spaces. Additionally, many programmers observe one of the following conventions when naming arrays to make it more obvious that the name represents a group of items:

- Arrays are often named using a plural noun such as `prices` or `employeeNames`.
- Arrays are often named by adding a final word that implies a group, such as `priceList`, `priceTable`, or `priceArray`.

Each array element is differentiated from the others with a unique **subscript**, also called an **index**, which is a number that indicates the position of a particular item within an array. All array elements have the same group name, but each individual element also has a unique subscript indicating how far away it is from the first element. For example, a five-element array uses subscripts 0 through 4, and a ten-element array uses subscripts 0 through 9. In all languages, subscript values must be sequential integers (whole numbers). In most modern languages, such as Visual Basic, Java, C++, and C#, the first array element is accessed using subscript 0, and this course follows that convention.

To use an array element, you place its subscript within square brackets or parentheses (depending on the programming language) after the group name. This course will use square brackets to hold array subscripts so that you don't mistake array names for module names. Many programming languages such as C++, Java, and C# also use the square bracket notation.

After you declare an array, you can assign values to some or all of the elements individually. Providing array values sometimes is called **populating the array**. The following code shows a three-element array declaration, followed by three separate statements that populate the array:

```
Declarations
    num prices[3]
prices[0] = 25.00
prices[1] = 36.50
prices[2] = 47.99
```

Figure 6-1 shows an array named `prices` that contains three elements, so the elements are `prices[0]`, `prices[1]`, and `prices[2]`. The array elements have been assigned the values 25.00, 36.50, and 47.99, respectively. The element `prices[0]` is zero numbers away from the beginning of the array. The element `prices[1]` is one number away from the beginning of the array, and `prices[2]` is two numbers away.

> **Note** | When programmers refer to array element `prices[0]`, they say "`prices` sub 0" or simply "`prices` zero." Similarly, the last element in the array is "`prices` sub 2" or "`prices` two."

Figure 6-1 Appearance of a three-element array in computer memory

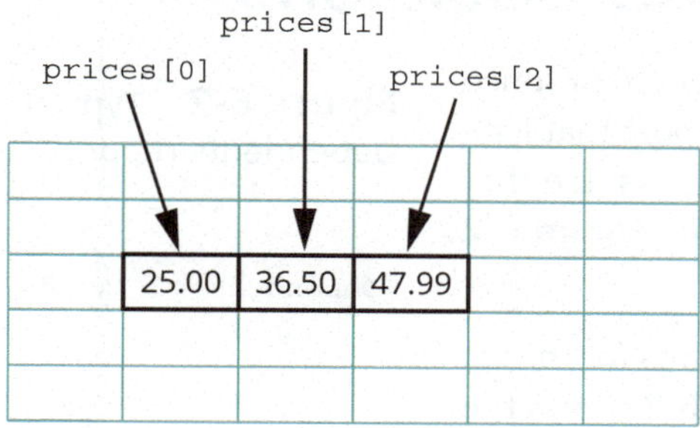

If appropriate, you can declare and initialize array elements in one statement. Most programming languages use a statement similar to the following to declare a three-element array and assign a list of values to it:

```
num prices[3] = 25.00, 36.50, 47.99
```

The series of values assigned to the array elements when it is declared is an **initialization list**. Some programming languages allow you to avoid explicitly declaring the size of an array if you provide an initialization list, as in the following example:

```
num prices[] = 25.00, 36.50, 47.99
```

When you use a list of values to initialize an array, the first value you list is assigned to the first array element (element 0), and the subsequent values are assigned to the remaining elements in order. Many programming languages allow you to initialize an array with fewer starting values than there are array elements declared, but no language allows you to initialize an array using more starting values than positions available. When starting values are supplied for an array in this course, each element will be provided with a value.

After an array has been declared and appropriate values have been assigned to specific elements, you can use an individual element in the same way you would use any other data item of the same type. For example, you can assign new values to array elements, you can output the values, and, if the elements are numeric, you can perform arithmetic with them.

In summary:

- An array is a list of data items in contiguous memory locations.
- Each data item in an array is an *element*.
- Each array element is the same data type; by default, this means that each element is the same size.
- Each element is differentiated from the others by a subscript, which is a whole number.
- Usable subscripts for an array range from 0 to one less than the number of elements in an array.
- Each array element can be used in the same way as a single item of the same data type.

Two Truths & a Lie | Storing Data in Arrays

1. In an array, each element has the same data type.
2. Each array element is accessed using a subscript, which can be a number or a string.
3. Array elements always occupy adjacent memory locations.

The false statement is #2. An array subscript must be a whole number. It can be a named constant, an unnamed constant, or a variable.

6.2 How an Array Can Replace Nested Decisions

Consider an application requested by a company's human resources department to produce statistics about employees' claimed dependents. The department wants a report that lists the number of employees who have claimed 0, 1, 2, 3, 4, or 5 dependents. (Assume that you know that no employees have more than five dependents.) For example, **Figure 6-2** shows a typical report.

Figure 6-2 Typical Dependents report

Dependents	Count
0	43
1	35
2	24
3	11
4	5
5	7

Without using an array, you could write the application that produces counts for the six categories of dependents (0 through 5) by using a series of decisions. **Figure 6-3** shows the pseudocode and flowchart for the decision-making part of such an application. Although this logic works, its length and complexity are unnecessary once you understand how to use an array.

Figure 6-3 Flowchart and pseudocode of decision-making process using a series of decisions—the hard way

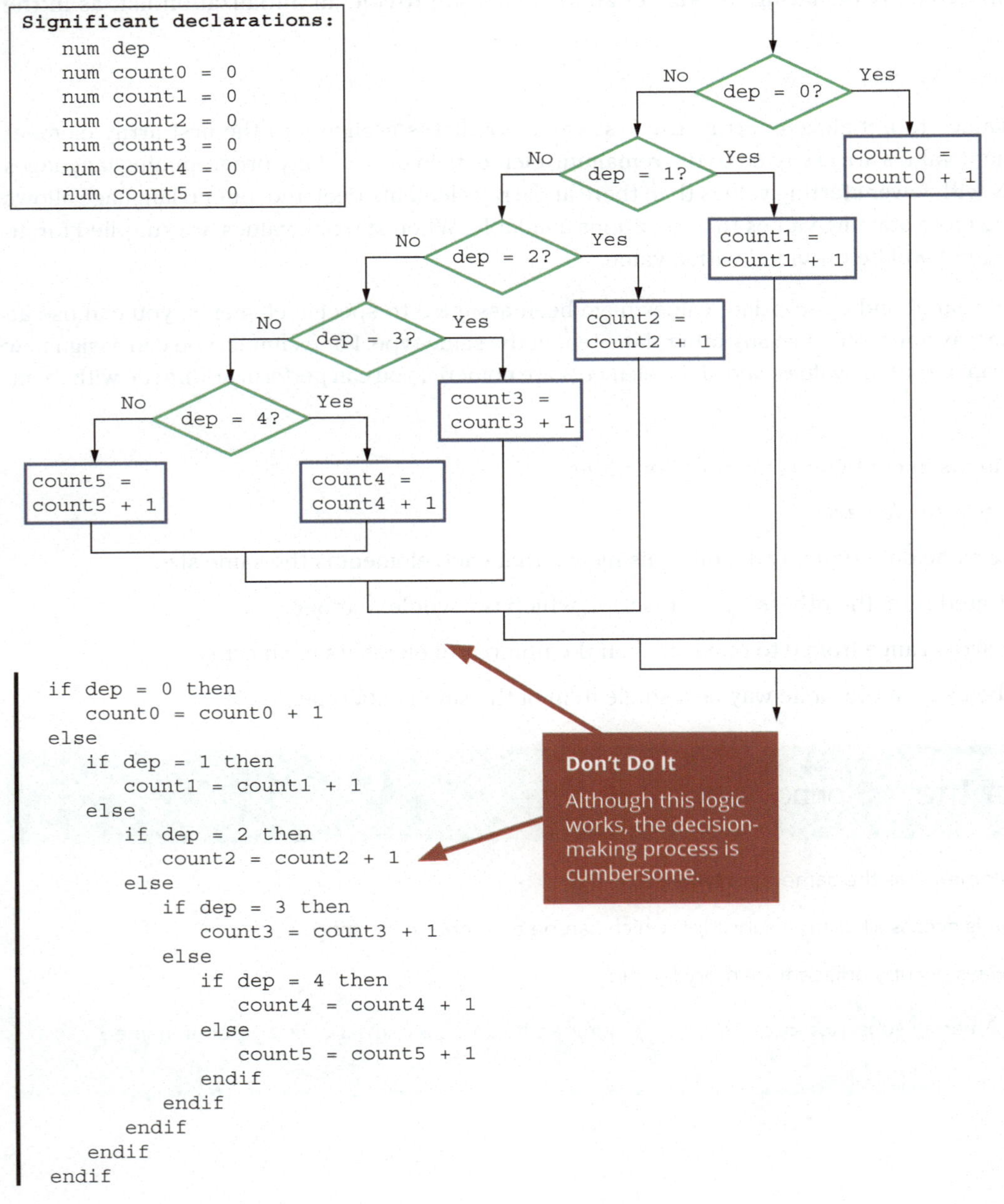
Significant declarations:
num dep
num count0 = 0
num count1 = 0
num count2 = 0
num count3 = 0
num count4 = 0
num count5 = 0
dep = 0?
No
Yes
count0 = count0 + 1
dep = 1?
No
Yes
count1 = count1 + 1
dep = 2?
No
Yes
count2 = count2 + 1
dep = 3?
No
Yes
count3 = count3 + 1
dep = 4?
No
Yes
count4 = count4 + 1
count5 = count5 + 1
Don't Do It
Although this logic works, the decision-making process is cumbersome.

```
if dep = 0 then
   count0 = count0 + 1
else
   if dep = 1 then
      count1 = count1 + 1
   else
      if dep = 2 then
         count2 = count2 + 1
      else
         if dep = 3 then
            count3 = count3 + 1
         else
            if dep = 4 then
               count4 = count4 + 1
            else
               count5 = count5 + 1
            endif
         endif
      endif
   endif
endif
```

Note The decision-making process in Figure 6-3 accomplishes its purpose, and the logic is correct, but the process is cumbersome and certainly not recommended. Follow the logic here so that you understand how the application works. In the next pages, you will see how to make the application more elegant.

In Figure 6-3, the variable `dep` is compared to 0. If it is 0, 1 is added to `count0`. If it is not 0, then `dep` is compared to 1. Based on the evaluation, 1 is added to `count1` or `dep` is compared to 2, and so on. Each time the application executes this decision-making process, 1 ultimately is added to one of the six variables that acts as a counter. The dependent-counting logic in Figure 6-3 works, but even with only six categories of dependents, the decision-making process is unwieldy. What if the number of dependents might be any value from 0 to 10, or 0 to 20? With either of these scenarios, the basic logic of the program would remain the same; however, you would need to declare many additional variables to hold the counts, and you would need many additional decisions.

Using an array provides an alternate approach to this programming problem and greatly reduces the number of statements you need. When you declare an array, you provide a group name for a number of associated variables in memory. For example, the six dependent count accumulators can be redefined as a single array named `counts`. The individual elements become `counts[0]`, `counts[1]`, `counts[2]`, `counts[3]`, `counts[4]`, and `counts[5]`, as shown in the revised decision-making process in **Figure 6-4**.

Figure 6-4 Flowchart and pseudocode of decision-making process—but still the hard way

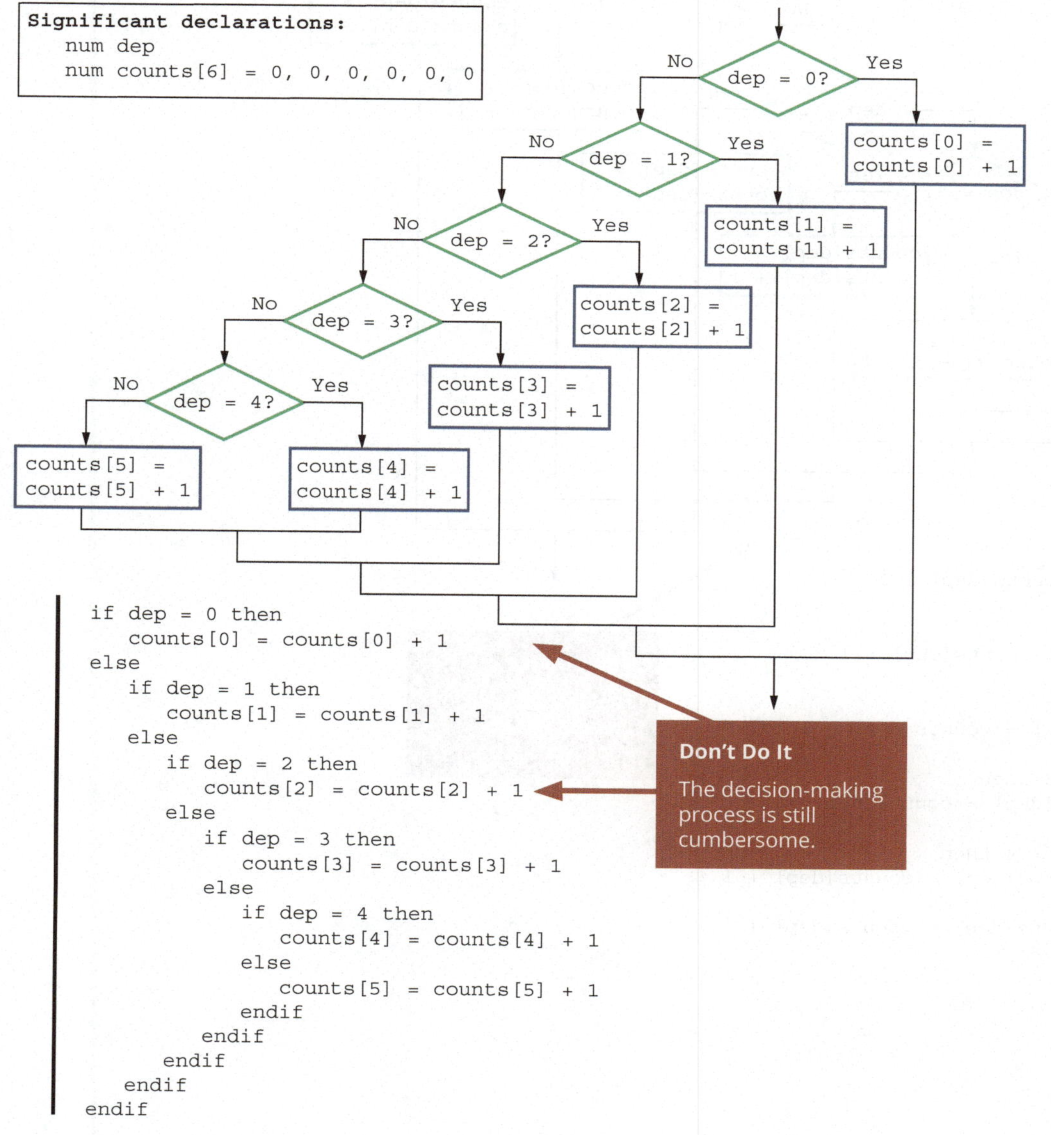
Significant declarations:
num dep
num counts[6] = 0, 0, 0, 0, 0, 0
dep = 0?
No
Yes
counts[0] = counts[0] + 1
dep = 1?
counts[1] = counts[1] + 1
dep = 2?
counts[2] = counts[2] + 1
dep = 3?
counts[3] = counts[3] + 1
dep = 4?
counts[4] = counts[4] + 1
counts[5] = counts[5] + 1
if dep = 0 then
counts[0] = counts[0] + 1
else
if dep = 1 then
counts[1] = counts[1] + 1
else
if dep = 2 then
counts[2] = counts[2] + 1
else
if dep = 3 then
counts[3] = counts[3] + 1
else
if dep = 4 then
counts[4] = counts[4] + 1
else
counts[5] = counts[5] + 1
endif
endif
endif
endif
endif
Don't Do It
The decision-making process is still cumbersome.

Figure 6-4 shows that when dep is 0, 1 is added to counts[0]. If dep is not 0, but it is 1, 1 is added to counts[1]; when dep is 2, 1 is added to counts[2], and so on. When the dep value is 5, this means it was not 1, 2, 3, or 4, so 1 is added to counts[5]. In other words, 1 is added to one of the elements of the counts array instead of to an individual variable named count0, count1, count2, count3, count4, or count5. Is this version a big improvement over the original in Figure 6-3? Of course it isn't. You still have not taken advantage of the benefits of using the array in this application.

The true benefit of using an array lies in your ability to use a variable as a subscript to the array, instead of using a literal constant such as 0 or 5. Notice in the logic in Figure 6-4 that within each decision, the value compared to dep and the constant that is the subscript in the resulting *Yes* process are always identical. That is, when dep is 0, the subscript used to add 1 to the counts array is 0; when dep is 1, the subscript used for the counts array is 1, and so on. Therefore, you can just use dep as a subscript to the array. You can rewrite the decision-making process as shown in **Figure 6-5**.

Figure 6-5 Flowchart and pseudocode of decision-making process using an array—but still a hard way

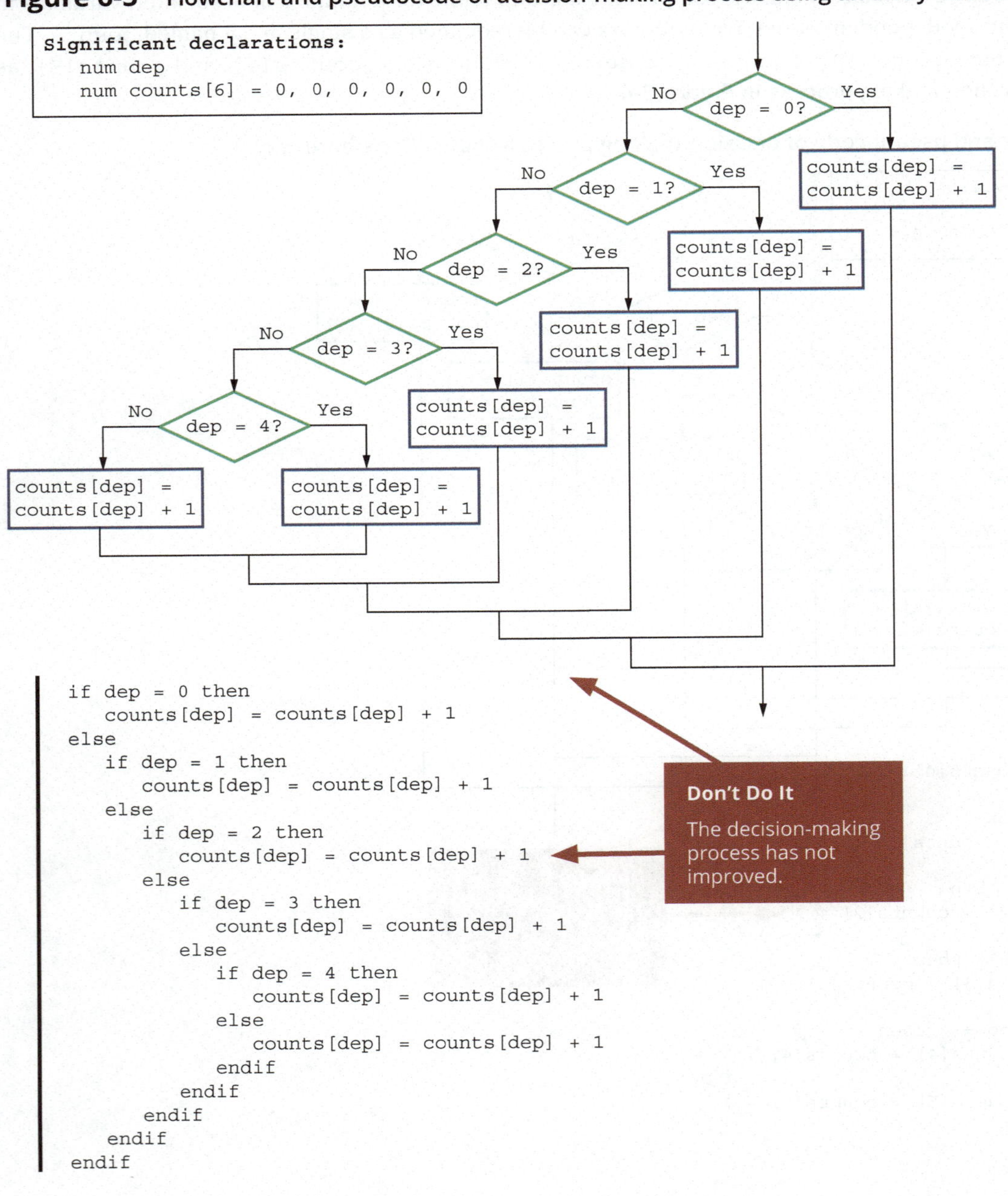
Significant declarations:
num dep
num counts[6] = 0, 0, 0, 0, 0, 0
dep = 0?
dep = 1?
dep = 2?
dep = 3?
dep = 4?
No
Yes
counts[dep] =
counts[dep] + 1
Don't Do It
The decision-making process has not improved.

```
if dep = 0 then
   counts[dep] = counts[dep] + 1
else
   if dep = 1 then
      counts[dep] = counts[dep] + 1
   else
      if dep = 2 then
         counts[dep] = counts[dep] + 1
      else
         if dep = 3 then
            counts[dep] = counts[dep] + 1
         else
            if dep = 4 then
               counts[dep] = counts[dep] + 1
            else
               counts[dep] = counts[dep] + 1
            endif
         endif
      endif
   endif
endif
```

The code segment in Figure 6-5 looks no more efficient than the one in Figure 6-4. However, notice in Figure 6-5 that the process that occurs after each decision is exactly the same. In each case, no matter what the value of `dep` is, you always add 1 to `counts[dep]`. If you always will take the same action no matter what the answer to a question is, there is no need to ask the question. Instead, you can rewrite the decision-making process as shown in **Figure 6-6**.

Figure 6-6 Flowchart and pseudocode of efficient decision-making process using an array

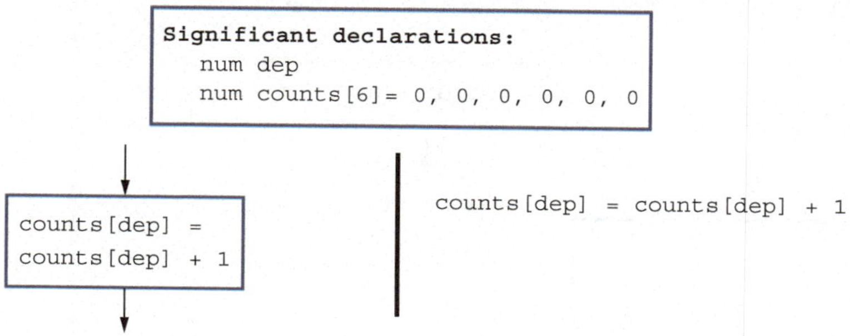

The single statement in Figure 6-6 eliminates the *entire* decision-making process in Figure 6-5! When `dep` is 2, 1 is added to `counts[2]`; when `dep` is 4, 1 is added to `counts[4]`, and so on. *Now* you have significantly improved the original logic. What's more, this process does not change whether there are 20, 30, or any other number of possible categories. To use more than five accumulators, you would declare additional `counts` elements in the array, but the categorizing logic would remain the same as it is in Figure 6-6.

Figure 6-7 shows an entire program that takes advantage of the array to produce the report that shows counts for dependent categories. Variables and constants are declared and, in the `getReady()` module, a first value for `dep` is entered into the program. In the `countDependents()` module, 1 is added to the appropriate element of the count array and the next value is input.

The loop in the mainline logic in Figure 6-7 is an indefinite loop; it continues as long as the user does not enter the sentinel value. When data entry is complete, the `finishUp()` module displays the report. First, the heading is output, then `dep` is reset to 0, and then each `dep` and `counts[dep]` are output in a loop. The first output statement contains 0 (as the number of dependents) and the value stored in `counts[0]`. Then, 1 is added to `dep` and the same set of instructions is used again to display the counts for each number of dependents. The loop in the `finishUp()` module is a definite loop; it executes precisely six times.

Note The program in Figure 6-7 could be improved by making sure that the value of the subscript dep is within range before adding 1 to `counts[dep]`. Later in this chapter, you learn more about ensuring that a subscript falls within the valid range for an array.

The dependent-counting program would have *worked* if it contained a long series of decisions and output statements, but the program is easier to write when you use an array and access its values using the number of dependents as a subscript. Additionally, the new program is more efficient, easier for other programmers to understand, and easier to maintain. Arrays are never mandatory, but often they can drastically cut down on your programming time and make your logic easier to understand.

Learning to use arrays properly can make many programming tasks far more efficient and professional. When you understand how to use arrays, you will be able to provide elegant solutions to problems that otherwise would require tedious programming steps.

Figure 6-7 Flowchart and pseudocode for Dependents report program

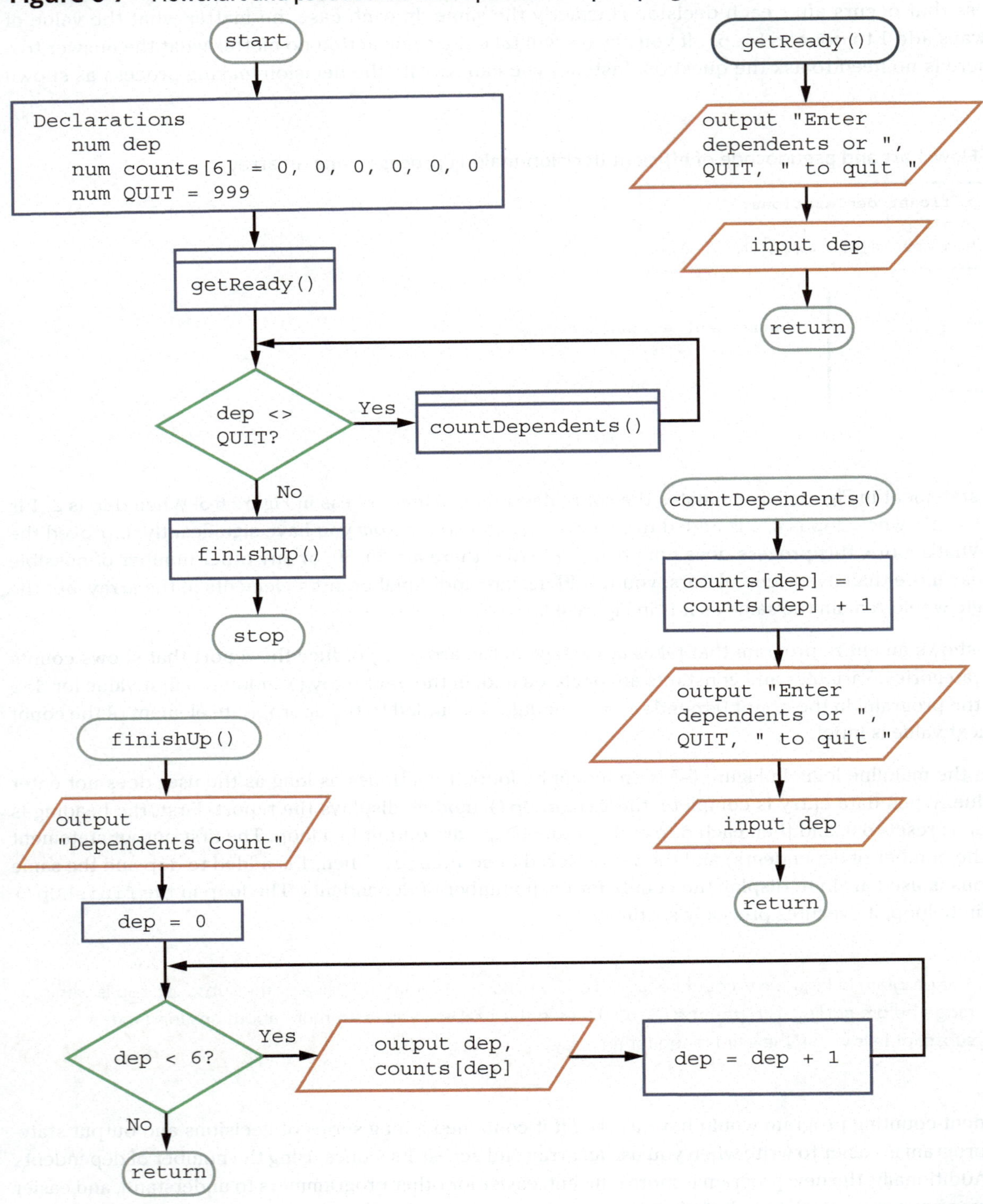

(Continues)

Figure 6-7 *(Continued)*

```
start
   Declarations
      num dep
      num counts[6] = 0, 0, 0, 0, 0, 0
      num QUIT = 999
   getReady()
   while dep <> QUIT
      countDependents()
   endwhile
   finishUp()
stop

getReady()
   output "Enter dependents or ", QUIT, " to quit "
   input dep
return

countDependents()
   counts[dep] = counts[dep] + 1
   output "Enter dependents or ", QUIT, " to quit "
   input dep
return

finishUp()
   output "Dependents Count"
   dep = 0
   while dep < 6
      output dep, counts[dep]
      dep = dep + 1
   endwhile
return
```

Two Truths & a Lie | How an Array Can Replace Nested Decisions

1. Frequently, you can use an array to replace a long series of decisions.
2. You experience a major benefit of arrays when you use an unnamed numeric constant as a subscript as opposed to using a variable.
3. The process of displaying every element in a 10-element array is basically no different from displaying every element in a 100-element array.

The false statement is #2. You experience a major benefit of arrays when you use a variable as a subscript as opposed to using a constant.

6.3 Using Constants with Arrays

Named constants hold values that do not change during a program's execution. When working with arrays, you can use constants in several ways:

- To hold the size of an array
- As the array values
- As subscripts

Using a Constant as the Size of an Array

The program in Figure 6-7 still contains one minor flaw. Throughout this course, you have learned to avoid *magic numbers*—that is, unnamed constants. As the totals are output in the loop at the end of the program in Figure 6-7, the array subscript is compared to the constant 6. The program can be improved if you use a named constant instead.

Using a named constant makes your code easier to modify and understand. In most programming languages, you can take one of two approaches:

- You can declare a named numeric constant such as `ARRAY_SIZE = 6`. Then you can use this constant in a comparison every time you access the array, always making sure any subscript you use remains less than the constant value.
- In many languages, a value that represents the array size is automatically provided for each array you create. For example, in Java, after you declare an array named `counts`, its size is stored in a field named `counts.length`. In both C# and Visual Basic, the array size is `counts.Length`, with an uppercase *L*. No automatically created value exists in C or C++.

Using Constants as Array Element Values

Sometimes the values stored in arrays should be constants because they are not changed during program execution. For example, suppose that you create an array that holds names for the months of the year. When declaring an array of named constants, programmers conventionally use all uppercase letters with underscores separating words. Don't confuse the array identifier with its contents—the convention in this course is to use all uppercase letters in constant identifiers, but not necessarily in array values. An array named `MONTHS` that holds constant values might be declared as follows:

```
string MONTHS[12] = "January", "February", "March",
   "April", "May", "June", "July", "August", "September",
   "October", "November", "December"
```

Using a Constant as an Array Subscript

Occasionally you will want to use an unnamed numeric constant as a subscript to an array. For example, to display the first value in an array named `salesArray`, you might write a statement that uses an unnamed literal constant as a subscript, as follows:

```
output salesArray[0]
```

You also might have occasion to use a named constant as a subscript. For example, if `salesArray` holds sales values for each of 20 states covered by your company, and Indiana is state 5, you could output the value for Indiana using an unnamed constant as follows:

```
output salesArray[5]
```

However, if you declare a named constant as `num INDIANA = 5`, then you can display the same value using this statement:

```
output salesArray[INDIANA]
```

An advantage to using a named constant in this case is that the statement becomes self-documenting—anyone who reads your statement more easily understands that your intention is to display the sales value for Indiana.

Two Truths & a Lie | Using Constants with Arrays

1. If you create a named constant equal to an array size, you can use it as a subscript to the array.
2. If you create a named constant equal to an array size, you can use it as a limit against which to compare subscript values.
3. When you declare an array in Java, C#, or Visual Basic, a constant that represents the array size is automatically provided.

The false statement is #1. If the constant is equal to the array size, then it is larger than any valid array subscript.

6.4 Searching an Array for an Exact Match

In the dependent-counting application in this chapter, the array's subscript variable conveniently held small whole numbers—the number of dependents allowed was 0 through 5—and the `dep` variable directly accessed the array. Unfortunately, real life doesn't always happen in small integers. Sometimes you don't have a variable that conveniently holds an array position; sometimes you have to search through an array to find a value you need.

Consider a mail-order business in which customers place orders that contain a name, address, item number, and quantity ordered. Assume that the item numbers from which a customer can choose are three-digit numbers, but perhaps they are not consecutively numbered 001 through 999. For example, let's say that you offer six items: 106, 108, 307, 405, 457, and 688, as shown in the `VALID_ITEMS` array declaration in **Figure 6-8**. The array is declared as constant because the item numbers do not change during program execution. When a customer orders an item, a clerical worker can tell whether the order is valid by looking down the list and manually verifying that the ordered item number is on it. In a similar fashion, a computer program can use a loop to test the ordered item number against each `VALID_ITEMS` element, looking for an exact match. When you search through a list from one end to the other, you are performing a **linear search**.

To determine if an ordered item number is valid, you could use a series of six decisions to compare the number to each of the six allowed values. However, the superior approach shown in Figure 6-8 is to create an array that holds the list of valid item numbers and then to search through the array for an exact match to the ordered item. If you search through the entire array without finding a match for the item the customer ordered, it means the ordered item number is not valid.

The `findItem()` module in Figure 6-8 takes the following steps to verify that an item number exists:

- A flag variable named `foundIt` is set to `"N"`. A **flag** is a variable that is set to indicate whether some event has occurred. In this example, *N* indicates that the item number has not yet been found in the list. (See the first statement in the `findItem()` module in Figure 6-8.)
- A subscript, `sub`, is set to 0. This subscript will be used to access each `VALID_ITEMS` element.

Figure 6-8 Flowchart and pseudocode for program that verifies item availability

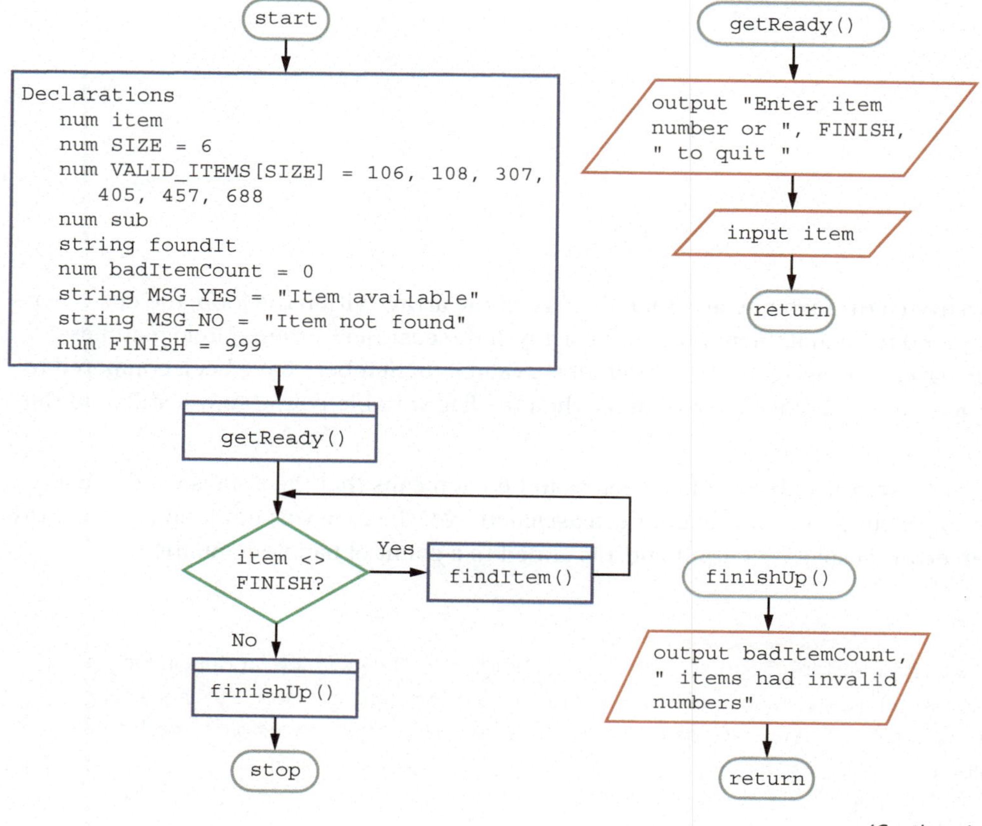

(Continues)

Figure 6-8 *(Continued)*

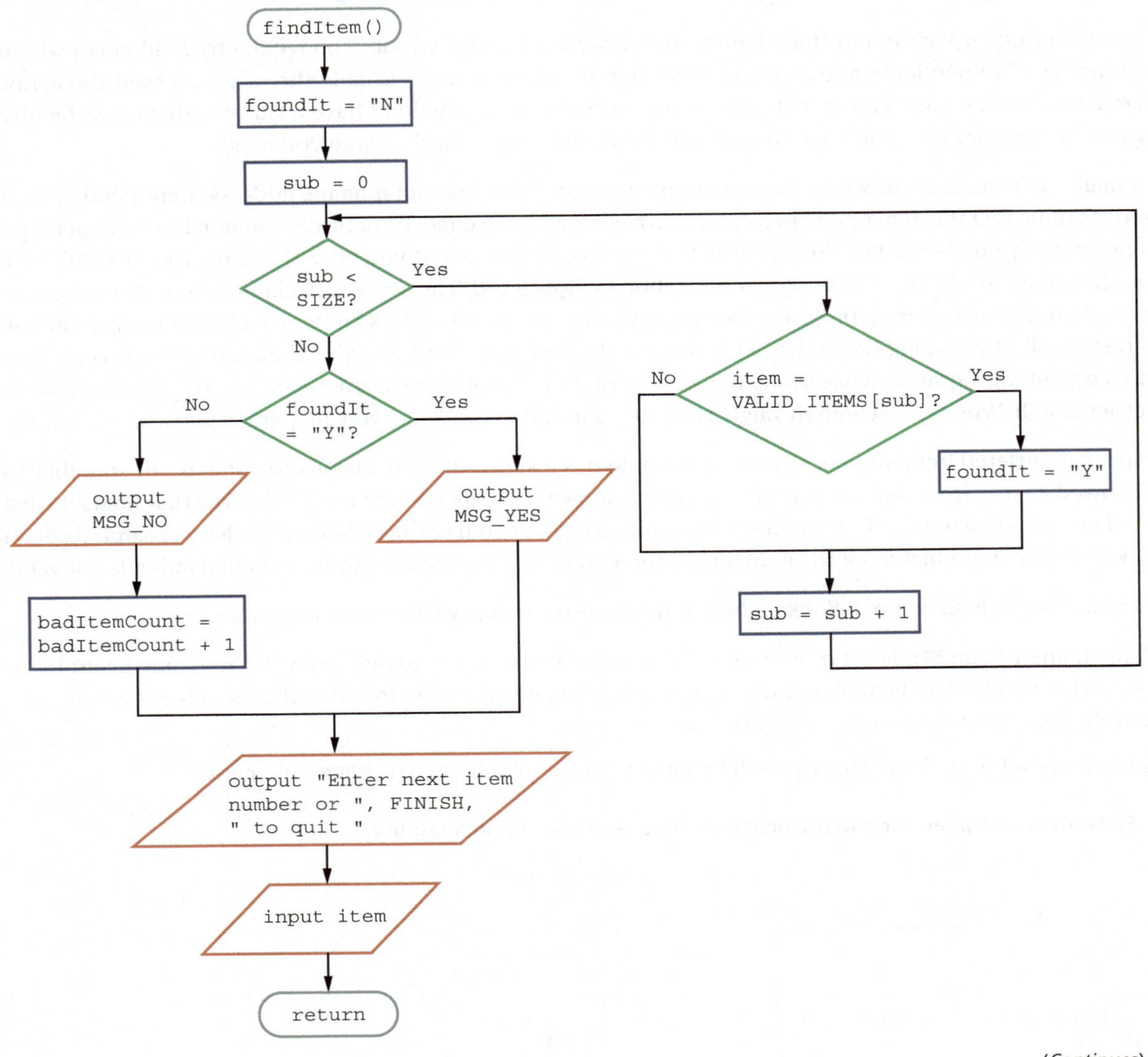

(Continues)

- A loop executes, varying `sub` from 0 through one less than the size of the array. Within the loop, the customer's ordered item number is compared to each item number in the array. If the customer-ordered item matches any item in the array, the flag variable is assigned `"Y"`. After all six valid item numbers have been compared to the ordered item, if the customer item matches none of them, then the flag variable `foundIt` will still hold the value `"N"`.
- If the flag variable's value is `"Y"` after the entire list has been searched, it means that the item is valid and an appropriate message is displayed, but if the flag has not been assigned `"Y"`, the item was not found in the array of valid items. In this case, an error message is output and 1 is added to a count of bad item numbers.

Note As an alternative to using the string `foundIt` variable that holds `"Y"` or `"N"` in the module in Figure 6-8, you might prefer to use a numeric variable that you set to 1 or 0. Most programming languages also support a Boolean data type that you can use for `foundIt`; when you declare a variable to be Boolean, you can set its value to `true` or `false`.

Figure 6-8 *(Continued)*

```
start
   Declarations
      num item
      num SIZE = 6
      num VALID_ITEMS[SIZE] = 106, 108, 307,
         405, 457, 688
      num sub
      string foundIt
      num badItemCount = 0
      string MSG_YES = "Item available"
      string MSG_NO = "Item not found"
      num FINISH = 999
   getReady()
   while item <> FINISH
      findItem()
   endwhile
   finishUp()
stop

getReady()
   output "Enter item number or ", FINISH, " to quit "
   input item
return

findItem()
   foundIt = "N"
   sub = 0
   while sub < SIZE
      if item = VALID_ITEMS[sub] then
         foundIt = "Y"
      endif
      sub = sub + 1
   endwhile
   if foundIt = "Y" then
      output MSG_YES
   else
      output MSG_NO
      badItemCount = badItemCount + 1
   endif
   output "Enter next item number or ", FINISH, " to quit "
   input item
return

finishUp()
   output badItemCount, " items had invalid numbers"
return
```

Two Truths & a Lie | Searching an Array for an Exact Match

1. Only whole numbers can be stored in arrays.
2. Only whole numbers can be used as array subscripts.
3. A flag is a variable that indicates whether some event has occurred.

The false statement is #1. Whole numbers can be stored in arrays, but so can many other objects, including strings and numbers with decimal places.

6.5 Using Parallel Arrays

When you accept an item number into a mail-order company program, you usually want to accomplish more than simply verifying the item's existence. For example, you might want to determine the name, price, or available quantity of the ordered item. Tasks like these can be completed efficiently using parallel arrays. **Parallel arrays** are two or more arrays in which each element in one array is associated with the element in the same relative position in the other array. Although any array can contain just one data type, each array in a set of parallel arrays might be a different type.

Suppose that you have a list of item numbers and their associated prices. One array named VALID_ITEMS contains six elements; each element is a valid item number. Its parallel array also has six elements. The array is named VALID_PRICES; each element is a price of an item. Each price in the VALID_PRICES array is conveniently and purposely stored in the same position as the corresponding item number in the VALID_ITEMS array. **Figure 6-9** shows how the parallel arrays might look in computer memory.

Figure 6-9 Parallel arrays in memory

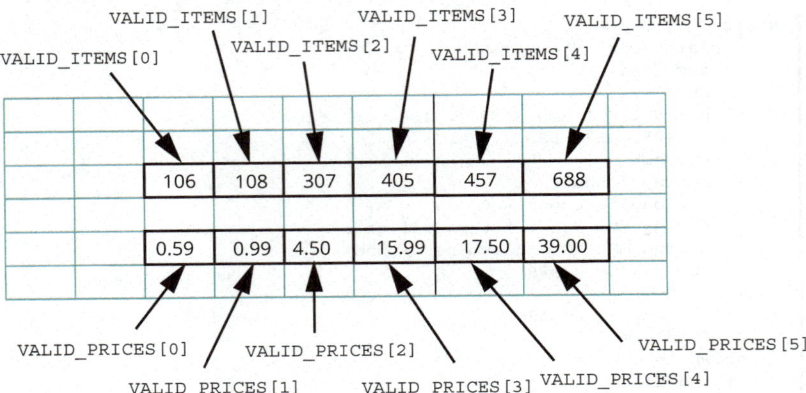

When you use parallel arrays:

- Two or more arrays contain related data.
- A subscript relates the arrays. That is, elements at the same position in each array are logically related.

Figure 6-10 shows a program that declares parallel arrays. Each element in the VALID_PRICES array corresponds to a valid item number.

Figure 6-10 Flowchart and pseudocode of program that finds item price using parallel arrays

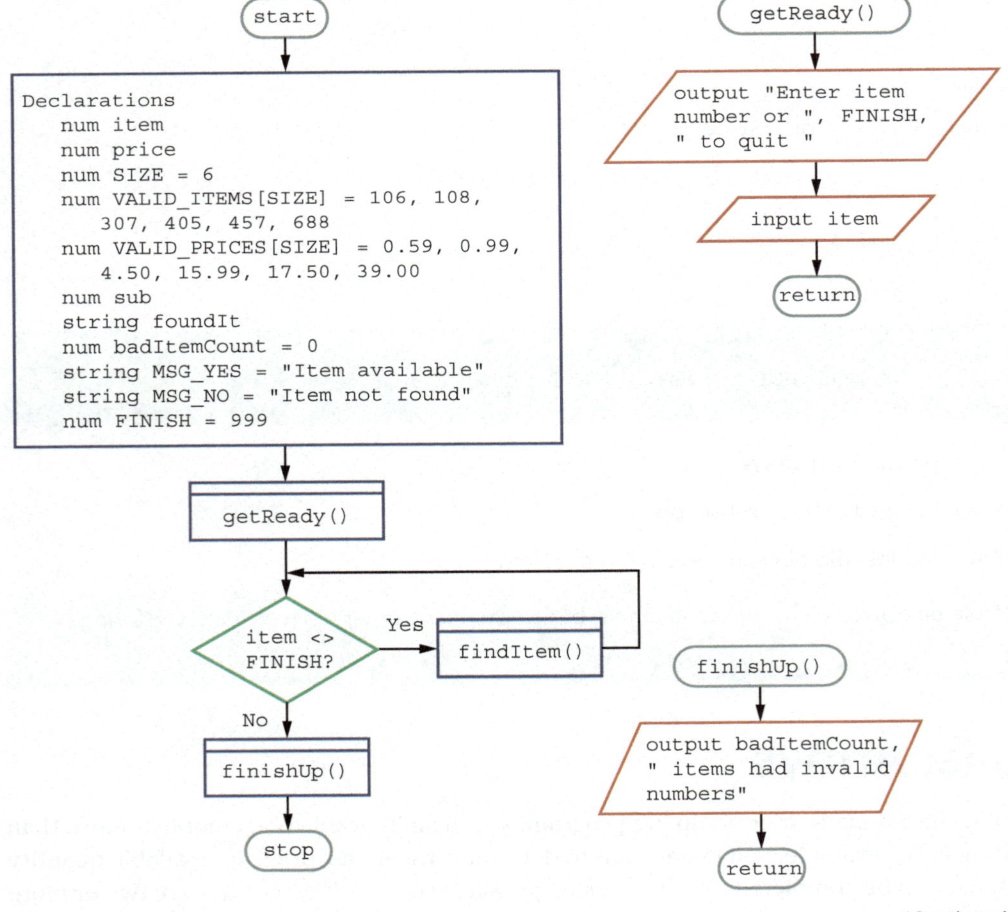

(*Continues*)

Figure 6-10 (*Continued*)

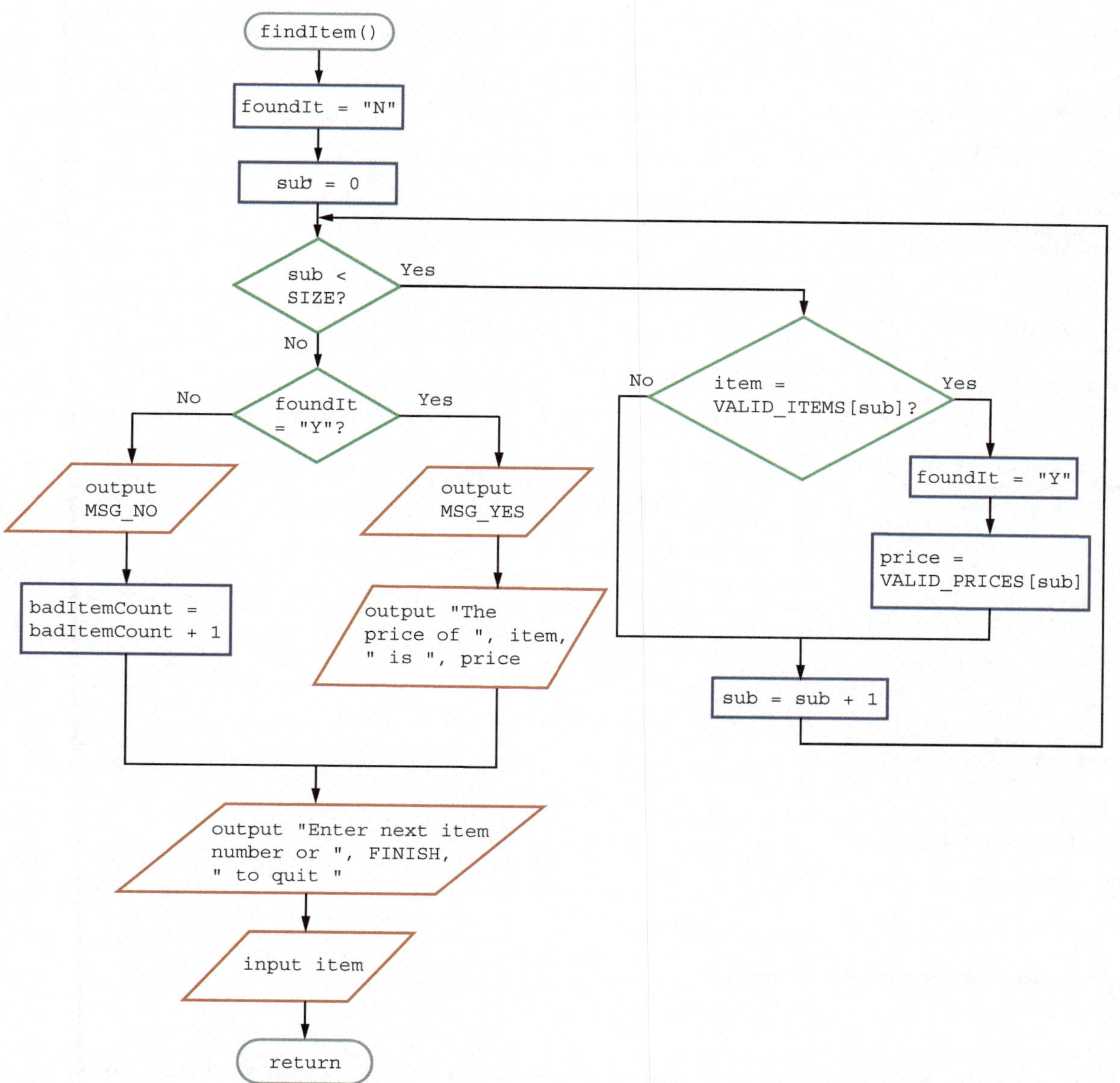

(*Continues*)

Figure 6-10 (*Continued*)

```
start
   Declarations
      num item
      num price
      num SIZE = 6
      num VALID_ITEMS[SIZE] = 106, 108, 307,
         405, 457, 688
      num VALID_PRICES[SIZE] = 0.59, 0.99,
         4.50, 15.99, 17.50, 39.00
      num sub
      string foundIt
      num badItemCount = 0
      string MSG_YES = "Item available"
      string MSG_NO = "Item not found"
      num FINISH = 999
   getReady()
   while item <> FINISH
      findItem()
   endwhile
   finishUp()
stop

getReady()
   output "Enter item number or ", FINISH, " to quit "
   input item
return

findItem()
   foundIt = "N"
   sub = 0
   while sub < SIZE
      if item = VALID_ITEMS[sub] then
         foundIt = "Y"
         price = VALID_PRICES[sub]
      endif
      sub = sub + 1
   endwhile
   if foundIt = "Y" then
      output MSG_YES
      output "The price of ", item, " is ", price
   else
      output MSG_NO
      badItemCount = badItemCount + 1
   endif
   output "Enter next item number or ", FINISH, " to quit "
   input item
return

finishUp()
   output badItemCount, " items had invalid numbers"
return
```

Note

Some programmers object to using a cryptic variable name for a subscript, such as `sub` in Figure 6-10, because such names are not descriptive. These programmers would prefer a name like `priceIndex`. Others approve of short names when the variable is used only in a limited area of a program, as it is used here, to step through an array. Programmers disagree about many style issues such as this one. As a programmer, it is your responsibility to find out what conventions are used among your peers in an organization.

As the program in Figure 6-10 receives a customer's order, it looks through each of the `VALID_ITEMS` values separately by varying the subscript `sub` from `0` to the number of items available. When a match for the item number is found, the program copies the value of the corresponding parallel price in the list of `VALID_PRICES` values and stores it in the `price` variable.

Suppose that a customer orders item 457. Using the flowchart or pseudocode in Figure 6-10, walk through the logic yourself to see if you come up with the correct price per item, $17.50. Then, suppose that a customer orders item 458. Walk through the logic and see whether the appropriate *Item not found* message is displayed. The relationship between an item's number and its price is an **indirect relationship**. That means you don't access a price directly by knowing the item number. Instead, you determine the price by knowing an item number's array position. Once you find a match for the ordered item number in the `VALID_ITEMS` array, you know that the price of the item is in the same position in the other array, `VALID_PRICES`. When `VALID_ITEMS[sub]` is the correct item, `VALID_PRICES[sub]` must be the correct price, so sub links the parallel arrays. Parallel arrays are most useful when value pairs have an indirect relationship. If values in your program have a direct relationship, you probably don't need parallel arrays. For example, if items were numbered 0, 1, 2, 3, and so on consecutively, you could use the item number itself as a subscript to the price array instead of using a parallel array to hold item numbers. Even if the items were numbered 200, 201, 202, and so on consecutively, you could subtract a constant value (200) from each and use that as a subscript instead of using a parallel array.

Improving Search Efficiency

The mail-order program in Figure 6-10 is still a little inefficient. When a customer orders item 106 or 108, a match is found on the first or second pass through the loop and continuing to search provides no further benefit. However, even after a match is made, the program in Figure 6-10 continues searching through the item array until sub reaches the value SIZE. One way to stop the search when the item has been found and foundIt is set to "Y" is to change the loop-controlling question. Instead of simply continuing the loop while the number of comparisons does not exceed the highest allowed array subscript, you should continue the loop while the searched item is not found *and* the number of comparisons has not exceeded the maximum. Leaving the loop as soon as a match is found improves the program's efficiency. The larger the array, the more beneficial it becomes to exit the searching loop as soon as you find the desired value.

Figure 6-11 shows the improved version of the findItem() module with the altered loop-controlling question.

Figure 6-11 Flowchart and pseudocode of the module that finds an item price and exits the loop as soon as it is found

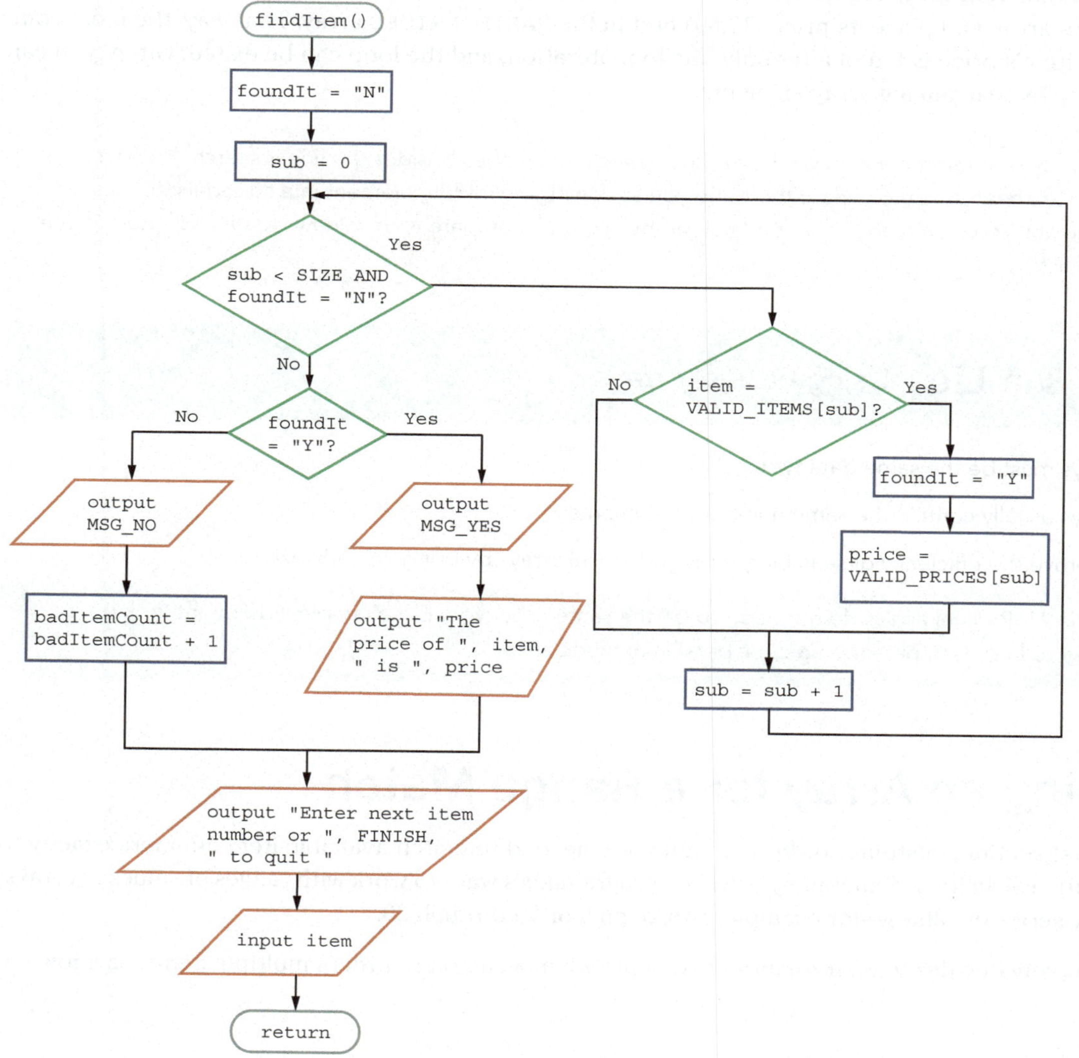

(*Continues*)

Figure 6-11 *(Continued)*

```
findItem()
   foundIt = "N"
   sub = 0
   while sub < SIZE AND foundIt = "N"
      if item = VALID_ITEMS[sub] then
         foundIt = "Y"
         price = VALID_PRICES[sub]
      endif
      sub = sub + 1
   endwhile
   if foundIt = "Y" then
      output MSG_YES
      output "The price of ", item, " is ", price
   else
      output MSG_NO
      badItemCount = badItemCount + 1
   endif
   output "Enter next item number or ", FINISH, " to quit "
   input item
return
```

Notice that the price-finding program offers the greatest efficiency when the most frequently ordered items are stored at the beginning of the array, so that only the seldom-ordered items require many loops before finding a match. For example, if you know that item 457 is ordered more frequently than any other item, you can place that item number first in the `VALID_ITEMS` array and place its price (17.50) first in the `VALID_PRICES` array. That way, the most common scenario is that an item's price is found after only one loop iteration, and the loop can be exited. Often, you can improve search efficiency by rearranging array elements.

Note As you study programming, you will learn other search techniques besides the linear search. For example, with a **binary search** you compare the value you seek with the middle element in a sorted list. If your value is lower, you eliminate the second half of the list, then compare your value to the middle item in the new half-list.

Two Truths & a Lie | Using Parallel Arrays

1. Parallel arrays must be the same data type.
2. Parallel arrays usually contain the same number of elements.
3. You can improve the efficiency of searching through parallel arrays by using an early exit.

The false statement is #1. Parallel arrays do not need to be the same data type. For example, you might look up a name in a string array to find each person's age in a parallel numeric array.

6.6 Searching an Array for a Range Match

In the example in the last section, customer order item numbers needed to match available item numbers exactly to determine the correct price of an item. Sometimes, however, programmers want to work with ranges of values in arrays. A range of values is any series of values—for example, 1 through 5 or 20 through 30.

Suppose that a company decides to offer quantity discounts when a customer orders multiple items, as shown in **Figure 6-12**.

Figure 6-12 Discounts on orders by quantity

Quantity	Discount %
0–8	0
9–12	10
13–25	15
26 or more	20

You want to be able to read in customer order data and determine a discount percentage based on the quantity ordered. For example, if a customer has ordered 20 items, you want to be able to output *Your discount is 15 percent.* One ill-advised approach might be to set up an array with as many elements as any customer might ever order, and store the appropriate discount for each possible number, as shown in **Figure 6-13**. This array is set up to contain the discount for 0 items, 1 item, 2 items, and so on.

Figure 6-13 Usable—but inefficient—discount array

```
num DISCOUNTS[76]
 = 0, 0, 0, 0, 0, 0, 0, 0, 0,
   0.10, 0.10, 0.10, 0.10,
   0.15, 0.15, 0.15, 0.15, 0.15,
   0.15, 0.15, 0.15, 0.15, 0.15,
   0.15, 0.15, 0.15,
   0.20, 0.20, 0.20, 0.20, 0.20,
   0.20, 0.20, 0.20, 0.20, 0.20,
   0.20, 0.20, 0.20, 0.20, 0.20,
   0.20, 0.20, 0.20, 0.20, 0.20,
   0.20, 0.20, 0.20, 0.20, 0.20,
   0.20, 0.20, 0.20, 0.20, 0.20,
   0.20, 0.20, 0.20, 0.20, 0.20,
   0.20, 0.20, 0.20, 0.20, 0.20,
   0.20, 0.20, 0.20, 0.20, 0.20,
   0.20, 0.20, 0.20, 0.20, 0.20
```

Don't Do It

Although this array correctly lists discounts for each quantity, it is repetitious, prone to error, and difficult to use.

Using the approach shown in Figure 6-13 has at least three drawbacks:

- It requires a very large array that uses a lot of memory.
- You must store the same value repeatedly. For example, each of the first nine elements receives the same value, 0, and each of the next four elements receives the same value, 0.10.
- How do you know you have enough array elements? Is a customer order quantity of 75 items enough? What if a customer orders 100 or 1,000 items? No matter how many elements you place in the array, there's always a chance that a customer will order more.

A better approach is to create two parallel arrays, each with four elements, as shown in **Figure 6-14**. Each discount rate is listed once in the `DISCOUNTS` array, and the low end of each quantity range is listed in the `QUAN_LIMITS` array.

Figure 6-14 Parallel arrays to use for determining discount

```
num DISCOUNTS[4] =    0, 0.10, 0.15, 0.20
num QUAN_LIMITS[4] = 0,     9,   13,   26
```

To find the correct discount for any customer's ordered quantity, you can start with the *last* quantity range limit (`QUAN_LIMITS[3]`). If the quantity ordered is at least that value, 26, the loop is never entered and the customer gets the highest discount rate (`DISCOUNTS[3]`, or 20 percent). If the quantity ordered is not at least `QUAN_LIMITS[3]`—that is, if it is less than 26—then you reduce the subscript and check to see if the quantity is at least `QUAN_LIMITS[2]`, or 13. If so, the customer receives `DISCOUNTS[2]`, or 15 percent, and so on. **Figure 6-15** shows a program that accepts a customer's quantity ordered and determines the appropriate discount rate.

An alternate approach to the one taken in Figure 6-15 is to store the high end of every range in an array. Then you start with the *lowest* element and check for values *less than or equal to* each array element value.

Figure 6-15 Program that determines discount rate

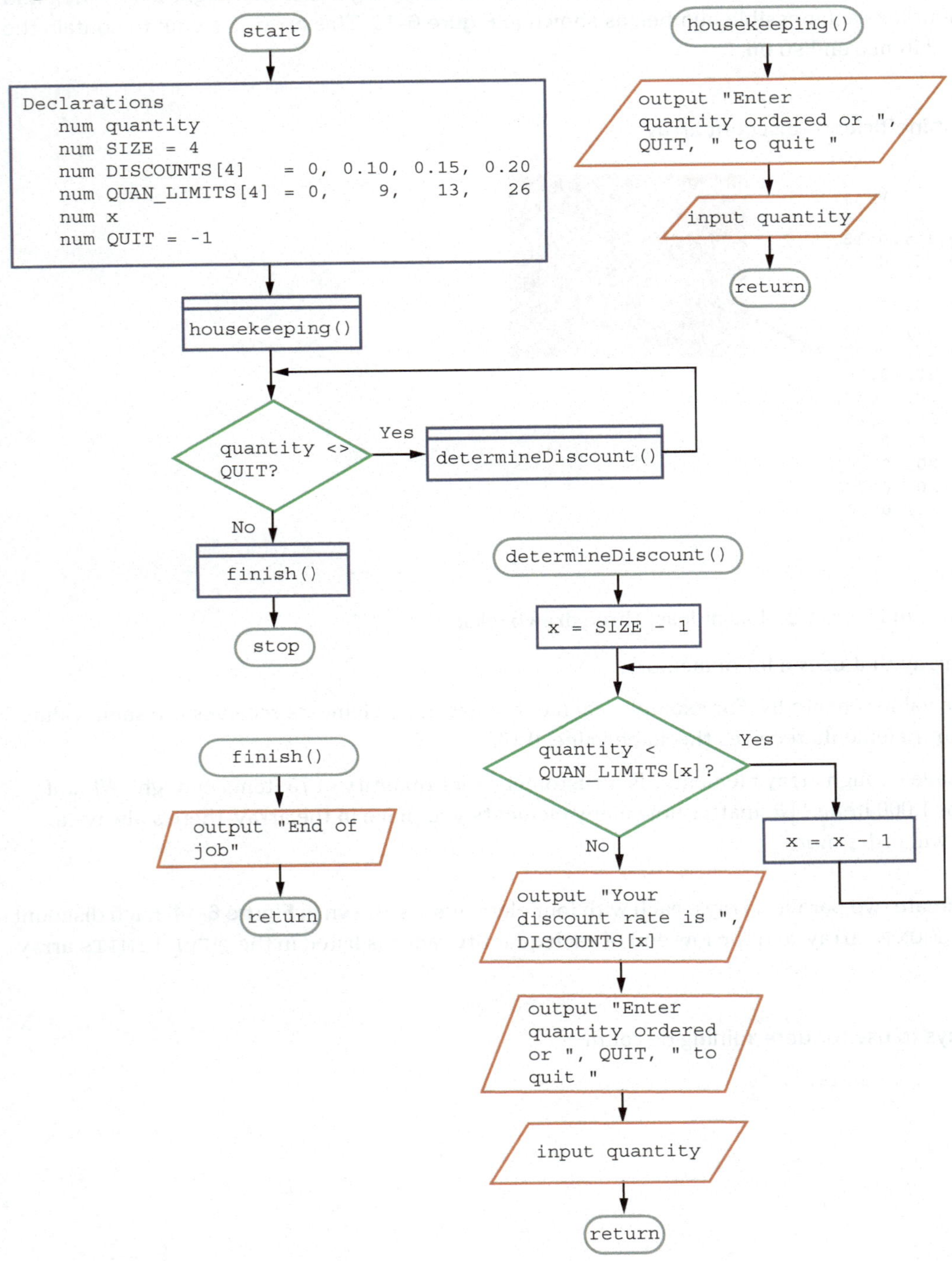

(Continues)

Figure 6-15 *(Continued)*

```
start
   Declarations
      num quantity
      num SIZE = 4
      num DISCOUNTS[4] =   0, 0.10, 0.15, 0.20
      num QUAN_LIMITS[4] = 0,    9,   13,   26
      num x
      num QUIT = -1
   housekeeping()
   while quantity <> QUIT
     determineDiscount()
   endwhile
   finish()
stop

housekeeping()
   output "Enter quantity ordered or ", QUIT, " to quit "
   input quantity
return

determineDiscount()
   x = SIZE - 1
   while quantity < QUAN_LIMITS[x]
      x = x - 1
   endwhile
   output "Your discount rate is ", DISCOUNTS[x]
   output "Enter quantity ordered or ", QUIT, " to quit "
   input quantity
return

finish()
   output "End of job"
return
```

When using an array to store range limits, you use a loop to make a series of comparisons that otherwise would require many separate decisions. The program that determines customer discount rates in Figure 6-15 requires fewer instructions than one that does not use an array, and modifications to the program will be easier to make in the future.

Two Truths & a Lie | Searching an Array for a Range Match

1. To help locate a range within which a value falls, you can store the highest value in each range in an array.
2. To help locate a range within which a value falls, you can store the lowest value in each range in an array.
3. When using an array to store range limits, you use a series of comparisons that would otherwise require many separate loop structures.

The false statement is #3. When using an array to store range limits, you use a loop to make a series of comparisons that would otherwise require many separate decisions.

6.7 Remaining within Array Bounds

To ensure that valid subscripts are used with an array, you must understand two related concepts:

- The array's size
- The bounds of usable subscripts

Understanding Array Size

Every array has a finite size. You can think of an array's size in one of two ways—either by the number of elements in the array or by the number of bytes in the array. Arrays are always composed of elements of the same data type, and elements of the same data type always occupy the same number of bytes of memory, so the number of bytes in an array is always a multiple of the number of elements in an array. For example, in Java, integers occupy 4 bytes of memory, so an array of 10 integers occupies exactly 40 bytes.

Note | For a complete discussion of bytes and how they measure computer memory, read Appendix A.

Understanding Subscript Bounds

In every programming language, when you access data stored in an array you must use a subscript containing a value that accesses memory occupied by the array. If you do, your subscript is **in bounds**; if you do not, your subscript is **out of bounds**.

A subscript accesses an array element using arithmetic. An array name is a memory address, and a subscript indicates the value that should be multiplied by the data type size to calculate the subscript's element address. For example, assume that a `prices` array is stored at memory location 4000, as shown in **Figure 6-16**, and assume that your computer stores numeric variables using four bytes each. As the figure shows, element 0 is at memory location 4000 + 0 * 4, or 4000, element 1 is at memory location 4000 + 1 * 4, or 4004, and element 2 is at memory location 4000 + 2 * 4, or 4008. If you use a subscript that is out of bounds, your program will attempt to access an address that is not part of the array's space.

Figure 6-16 An array and its associated memory addresses

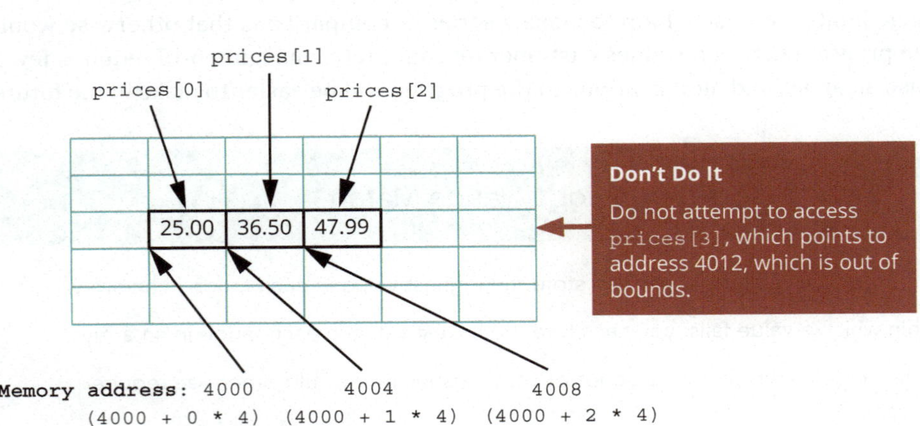

A common error made by beginning programmers is to forget that array subscripts start with 0. If you assume that an array's first subscript is 1, you will always be "off by one" in your array manipulation. For example, if you try to manipulate a 10-element array using subscripts 1 through 10, you will commit two errors: You will fail to access the first element that uses subscript 0, and you will attempt to access an extra element at position 10 when the highest usable subscript is 9.

Examine the program in **Figure 6-17**. The program accepts a numeric value for `monthNum` and displays the name associated with that month. The logic in Figure 6-17 makes a questionable assumption: that every number entered by the user is a valid month number.

Figure 6-17 Determining the month string from a user's numeric entry

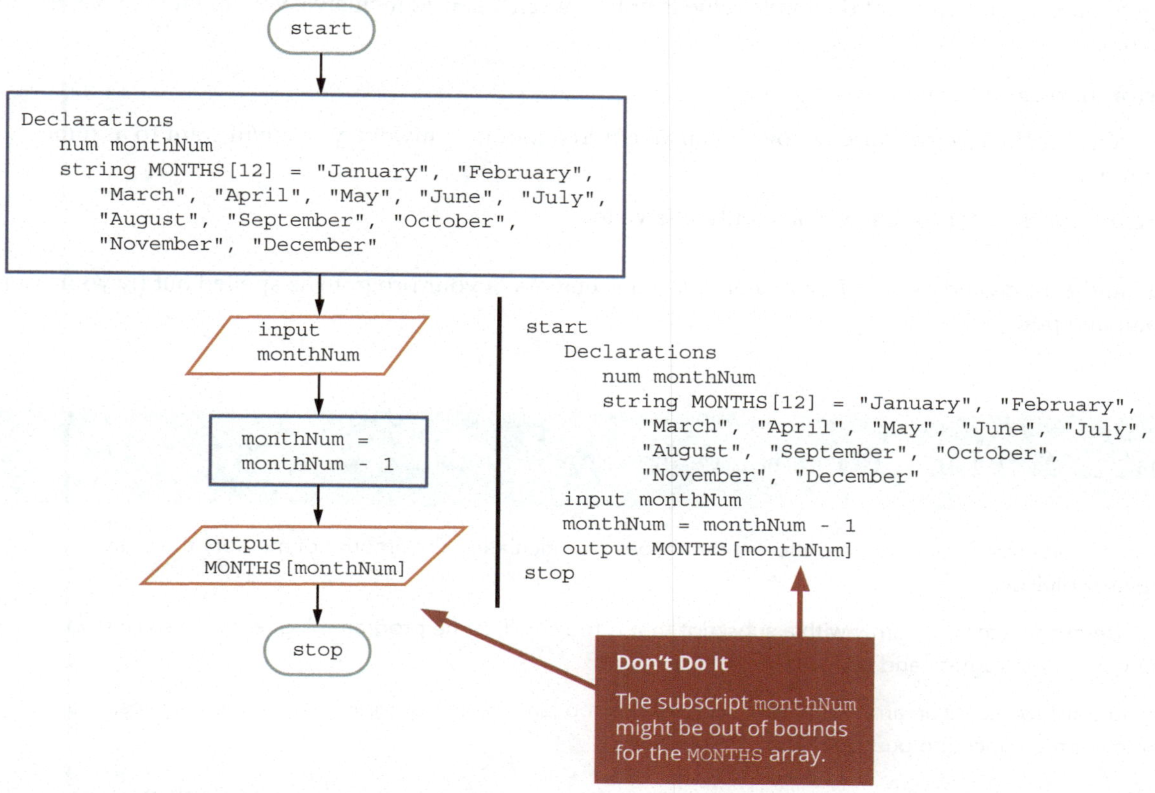

Note In the program in Figure 6-17, notice that 1 is subtracted from `monthNum` before it is used as a subscript. Although January is the first month in the year, its name occupies the location in the array with the 0 subscript. With values that seem naturally to start with 1, like month numbers, some programmers would prefer to create a 13-element array and simply never use the zero-position element. That way, each "natural" month number would be the correct value to access its data without subtracting. Other programmers dislike wasting memory by creating an extra, unused array element. Although workable programs can be created with or without the extra array element, professional programmers should follow the conventions and preferences of their colleagues and managers.

In Figure 6-17, if the user enters a number that is too small or too large, one of two things will happen depending on the programming language you use. When you use a subscript value that is negative or higher than the highest allowed subscript:

- Some programming languages will stop execution of the program and issue an error message.
- Other programming languages will not issue an error message but will access a value in a memory location that is outside the area occupied by the array. That area might contain garbage, or worse, it accidentally might contain the name of an incorrect month.

Either way, a logical error occurs. Users enter incorrect data frequently; a good program should be able to handle the mistake and not allow the subscript to be out of bounds.

Note A user might enter an invalid number or might not enter a number at all. Many languages have a built-in module with a name like `isNumeric()` that can test for such mistakes.

You can improve the program in Figure 6-17 by adding a test that ensures the subscript used to access the array is within the array bounds. If you find that the input value is not between 1 and 12 inclusive, you might take one of the following approaches:

- Display an error message and end the program.
- Use a default value for the month. For example, when an entered month is invalid, you might want to assume that it is December.
- Continually reprompt the user for a new value until it is valid.

The way you handle an invalid month depends on the requirements of your program as spelled out by your user, supervisor, or company policy.

Two Truths & a Lie | Remaining within Array Bounds

1. Elements in an array frequently are different data types, so calculating the amount of memory the array occupies is difficult.
2. If you attempt to access an array with a subscript that is too small, some programming languages will stop execution of the program and issue an error message.
3. If you attempt to access an array with a subscript that is too large, some programming languages access an incorrect memory location outside the array bounds.

The false statement is #1. Array elements are always the same data type, and elements of the same data type always occupy the same number of bytes of memory, so the number of bytes in an array is always a multiple of the number of elements in an array.

6.8 Using a `for` Loop to Process an Array

When you studied looping earlier in this course, you learned about the `for` loop—a loop that, in a single statement, initializes a loop control variable, compares it to a limit, and alters it. The `for` loop is a particularly convenient tool when working with arrays because you frequently need to process every element of an array from beginning to end. As with a `while` loop, when you use a `for` loop, you must be careful to stay within array bounds, remembering that the highest usable array subscript is one less than the size of the array. **Figure 6-18** shows a `for` loop that correctly displays all of a company's department names that are stored in an array declared as `DEPTS`. Notice that `dep` is incremented through one less than the number of departments because with a five-item array, the subscripts you can use are 0 through 4.

Figure 6-18 Pseudocode that uses a `for` loop to display an array of department names

```
start
   Declarations
      num dep
      num SIZE = 5
      string DEPTS[SIZE] = "Accounting", "Personnel",
         "Technical", "Customer Service", "Marketing"
   for dep = 0 to SIZE - 1 step 1
      output DEPTS[dep]
   endfor
stop
```

The loop in Figure 6-18 is slightly inefficient because, as it executes five times, the subtraction operation that deducts 1 from SIZE occurs each time. Five subtraction operations do not consume much computer power or time, but in a loop that processes thousands or millions of array elements, the program's efficiency would be compromised. **Figure 6-19** shows a superior solution. A new constant called ARRAY_LIMIT is calculated once, then used repeatedly in the comparison operation to determine when to stop cycling through the array.

Figure 6-19 Pseudocode that uses a more efficient for loop to output department names

```
start
   Declarations
      num dep
      num SIZE = 5
      num ARRAY_LIMIT = SIZE - 1
      string DEPTS[SIZE] = "Accounting", "Personnel",
         "Technical", "Customer Service", "Marketing"
   for dep = 0 to ARRAY_LIMIT step 1
      output DEPTS[dep]
   endfor
stop
```

Two Truths & a Lie | Using a for Loop to Process an Array

1. The for loop is a particularly convenient tool when working with arrays because initializing, testing, and altering a loop control variable are coded together.
2. You frequently need to process every element of an array from beginning to end in a linear fashion.
3. One advantage to using a for loop to process array elements is that you need not be concerned with array bounds.

The false statement is #3. As with a while loop, when you use a for loop, you must be careful to stay within array bounds.

Summary

- An array is a named series or list of values in computer memory, all of which have the same data type but are differentiated with subscripts. Each array element occupies an area in memory next to, or contiguous to, the others.
- You often can use a variable as a subscript to an array, which allows you to replace multiple nested decisions with many fewer statements.
- Constants can be used to hold an array's size, to represent its values, or as subscripts. Using named constants can make programs easier to understand and maintain.
- Searching through an array to find a value you need involves initializing a subscript, using a loop to test each array element, and setting a flag when a match is found.
- With parallel arrays, each element in one array is associated with the element in the same relative position in the other array.
- When you need to compare a value to a range of values in an array, you can store either the low- or high-end value of each range for comparison.
- When you access data stored in an array, it is important to use a subscript containing a value that accesses memory within the array bounds.
- The for loop is a particularly convenient tool when processing every element of an array sequentially.

Key Terms

array
binary search
element
flag
in bounds
index
indirect relationship
initialization list
linear search
out of bounds
parallel arrays
populating the array
size of the array
subscript

Review Questions

1. A subscript is a(n) ______________. (6.1)
   a. element in an array
   b. alternate name for an array
   c. number that represents the highest value stored within an array
   d. number that indicates the position of an array element

2. Each element in an array must have the same ______________ as the others. (6.1)
   a. data type
   b. subscript
   c. value
   d. memory location

3. Suppose that you have declared a numeric array named `values` that has 13 elements. Which of the following must be true? (6.1)
   a. `values[0]` is smaller than `values[1]`
   b. `values[2]` is stored adjacent to `values[4]`
   c. `values[13]` is out of bounds
   d. `values[12]` holds the largest value in the array

4. The subscripts of any array are always ______________. (6.1)
   a. integers
   b. fractions
   c. characters
   d. strings of characters

5. Suppose that you have declared a numeric array named `numbers`, and two of its elements are `numbers[1]` and `numbers[4]`. You know that ______________. (6.1)
   a. the two elements hold the same value
   b. the array holds exactly four elements
   c. there are exactly two elements between those two elements
   d. the two elements are at the same memory location

6. Suppose that you have declared a numeric array named `numbers`, and two of its elements are `numbers[1]` and `numbers[4]`. You know that ______________. (6.1)
   a. `numbers[4]` is larger than `numbers[1]`
   b. the array has at least five elements
   c. the array has been initialized
   d. the two elements are three bytes apart in memory

7. Suppose that you want to write a program that inputs customer data, including `name`, `zipCode`, `balance`, and `regionNum`. At the end of the program, a summary displays the number of customers in each of 12 sales regions who owe more than $1,000 each. The most likely statement during the main processing loop would be ______________. (6.2)

   a. `customerCounts[balance] = customerCounts[balance] + 1`

   b. `customerCounts[regionNum] = customerCounts[regionNum] + 1`

   c. `customerCounts[regionNum] = regionNum + 1`

   d. `customerCounts[balance] = balance + customerCounts[regionNum]`

8. A program contains a seven-element array that holds the names of the days of the week. At the start of the program, you display the day names using a subscript named `dayNum`. You display the same array values again at the end of the program, where you ______________ as a subscript to the array. (6.2)

   a. must use `dayNum`

   b. can use `dayNum`, but can also use another numeric value

   c. must not use `dayNum`

   d. must use a numeric constant instead of a variable

9. Suppose that you have declared an array as follows: `num values[4] = 0, 0, 0, 0`. Which of the following is *not* an allowed operation? (6.1, 6.3)

   a. `values[2] = 17`

   b. `input values[0]`

   c. `values[3] = values[0] + 10`

   d. `output values[4]`

10. Suppose that you have declared an array as follows: `num values[4] = 0, 0, 0, 0`. Which of the following is an allowed operation? (6.1)

    a. `values[4] = 80`

    b. `values[2] = values[4] - values[0]`

    c. `output values[3]`

    d. `values[1] = "30"`

11. Filling an array with values during a program's execution is known as ______________ the array. (6.1)

    a. executing

    b. colonizing

    c. populating

    d. declaring

12. A ______________ is a variable that can be set to indicate whether some event has occurred. (6.5)

    a. subscript

    b. banner

    c. counter

    d. flag

13. Two arrays in which each element in one array is associated with the element in the same relative position are ______________. (6.5)

    a. cohesive

    b. parallel

    c. hidden

    d. perpendicular

14. In most modern programming languages, the highest subscript you should use with a 12-element array is ______________. (6.1, 6.7)

    a. 10

    b. 11

    c. 12

    d. 13

15. The values stored in parallel arrays ______________. (6.5)

    a. frequently have an indirect relationship

    b. never have an indirect relationship

    c. must be the same data type

    d. must not be the same data type

16. Each element in a seven-element array can hold ______________ value(s). (6.1)

    a. one

    b. seven

    c. at least seven

    d. an unlimited number of

17. Suppose that an instructor assigns different letter grades based on points earned on a 10-point quiz, and that all scores have been verified to be between 0 and 10 inclusive. Also suppose that four possible letter grades can be assigned and that 9 or 10 points is an A, 7 or 8 points is a B, 6 points is a C, and 5 or fewer points is an F. To assign letter grades, the most efficient numeric array containing point values would contain ______ elements. (6.6)

    a. ten
    b. five
    c. four
    d. three

18. When you use a subscript value that is negative or higher than the number of elements in an array, ______. (6.1, 6.7)

    a. execution of the program stops, and an error message is issued
    b. a value in a memory location that is outside the area occupied by the array will be accessed
    c. a value in a memory location that is outside the area occupied by the array will be accessed, but only if the value is the correct data type
    d. the resulting action depends on the programming language used

19. In every array, a subscript is out of bounds when it is ______. (6.7)

    a. negative
    b. 0
    c. 1
    d. 999

20. You can access every element of an array using ______. (6.8)

    a. a `while` loop but not a `for` loop
    b. a `for` loop but not a `while` loop
    c. either a `while` loop or a `for` loop
    d. neither a `while` loop nor a `for` loop

Programming Exercises

1. a. Design the logic for a program that allows a user to enter 20 numbers, then displays them in the reverse order of entry.

   b. Modify the reverse-display program so that the user can enter any number of values up to 20 until a sentinel value is entered. (6.1, 6.2)

2. a. Design the logic for a program that allows a user to enter 20 numbers, then displays each number and its difference from the numeric average of the numbers entered.

   b. Modify the program in Exercise 2a so that the user can enter any number of values up to 20 until a sentinel value is entered. (6.1, 6.2)

3. a. Design the logic for a program that allows a user to enter 20 numbers, then displays all of the numbers, the largest number, and the smallest.

   b. Modify the program in Exercise 3a so that the user can enter any number of values up to 20 until a sentinel value is entered. (6.1, 6.2)

4. Trainers at Yakamura Athletic Club are encouraged to enroll new members. Write an application that allows the club manager to enter the names of the 25 trainers who work there and the number of new members each trainer has enrolled this year. Output is a count of the number of trainers who have enrolled 0 to 5 members, 6 to 12 members, 13 to 20 members, and more than 20 members. (6.1, 6.2)

5. a. The Downdog Yoga Studio offers five types of classes, as shown in **Figure 6-20**. Design a program that accepts a number representing a class and then displays the name of the class.

   b. Modify the Downdog Yoga Studio program so that numeric class requests can be entered continually until a sentinel value is entered. Then display each class number, name, and a count of the number of requests for each class. (6.1, 6.2)

Figure 6-20 Downdog Yoga Studio classes

Class number	Class name
1	Yoga 1
2	Yoga 2
3	Children's Yoga
4	Prenatal Yoga
5	Senior Yoga

6. Search the Web to discover 10 commonly used passwords and store them in an array. Design a program that prompts a user for a password, and continue to prompt until the user has not chosen one of the common passwords. (6.4)

7. The Jumpin' Jive coffee shop charges $2 for a cup of coffee and offers the add-ins shown in **Figure 6-21**. Design the logic for an application that allows a user to enter ordered add-ins continually until a sentinel value is entered. After each item, display its price or the message *Sorry, we do not carry that* as output. After all items have been entered, display the total price for the order. (6.4, 6.5)

Figure 6-21 Add-in list for Jumpin' Jive coffee shop

Product	Price ($)
Whipped cream	0.89
Cinnamon	0.25
Chocolate sauce	0.59
Amaretto	1.50
Irish whiskey	1.75

8. Design the application logic for a company that wants a report containing a breakdown of payroll by department. Input includes each employee's department number, hourly salary, and number of hours worked. The output is a list of the seven departments in the company and the total gross payroll (rate multiplied by hours) for each department. The department names are shown in **Figure 6-22**. (6.2)

Figure 6-22 Department numbers and names

Department number	Department name
1	Personnel
2	Marketing
3	Manufacturing
4	Computer Services
5	Sales
6	Accounting
7	Shipping

9. Design a program that computes pay for employees. Allow a user to continually input employees' names until an appropriate sentinel value is entered. Also input each employee's hourly wage and hours worked. Compute each employee's gross pay (hours multiplied by rate), withholding tax percentage (based on **Figure 6-23**), withholding tax amount, and net pay (gross pay minus withholding tax). Display all the results for each employee. After the last employee has been entered, display the sum of all the hours worked, the total gross payroll, the total withholding for all employees, and the total net payroll. (6.5, 6.6)

Figure 6-23 Withholding percentage based on gross pay

Weekly gross pay ($)	Withholding percentage (%)
0.00–300.00	10
300.01–550.00	13
550.01–800.00	16
800.01 and up	20

10. a. *Daily Life Magazine* wants an analysis of the demographic characteristics of its readers. The marketing department has collected reader survey records containing the age, gender, marital status, and annual income of readers. Design an application that reads the stored records and produces a count of readers by age groups as follows: younger than 20, 20–29, 30–39, 40–49, and 50 and older.

    b. Modify the *Daily Life Magazine* program so that it produces a count of readers by gender within each age group—that is, under-20 females, under-20 males, and so on.

    c. Modify the *Daily Life Magazine* program so that it produces a count of readers by income groups as follows: under $30,000, $30,000–$49,999, $50,000–$69,999, and $70,000 and up. (6.5, 6.6)

11. Glen Ross Vacation Property Sales employs seven salespeople, as shown in **Figure 6-24**. When a salesperson makes a sale, a record is created, including the salesperson's ID number and the month, day, and dollar amount of the sale. All fields are numeric, and the sale amount is expressed in whole dollars. Salespeople earn a commission that differs for each sale, based on the rate schedule in **Figure 6-25**.

    Design an application that produces each of the following:

    a. A list of each salesperson number, name, total sales, and total commissions

    b. A list of each month of the year as both a number and a word (for example, *01 January*), and the total sales for the month for all salespeople. (6.4–6.6)

Figure 6-24 Glen Ross salespeople

ID number	Salesperson name
103	Darwin
104	Kratz
201	Patel
319	Fortune
367	Wickert
388	Rodriguez
435	Kumar

Figure 6-25 Glen Ross commission schedule

Sale amount ($)	Commission rate (%)
0–50,999	4
51,000–125,999	5
126,000–200,999	6
201,000 and up	7

12. a. Design an application in which the number of days for each month in the year is stored in an array. (For example, January has 31 days, February has 28, and so on. Assume that the year is not a leap year.) Display 12 sentences in the same format for each month; for example, the sentence displayed for January is *Month 1 has 31 days.*

    b. Modify the months and days program to contain a parallel array that stores month names. Display 12 sentences in the same format; for example, the first sentence is *January has 31 days.*

    c. Modify the months and days program to prompt the user for a month number and display the corresponding sentence—for example, *January has 31 days.*

    d. Prompt a user to enter a birth month and day and continue to prompt until the day entered is in range for the month. Compute the day's numeric position in the year. (For example, February 2 is day 33.) Then, using parallel arrays, find and display the traditional Zodiac sign for the date. For example, the sign for February 2 is Aquarius. (6.4, 6.5)

Performing Maintenance

1. A file named *MAINTENANCE06-01.txt* is included with your downloadable student files. Assume that this program is a working program in your organization and that it needs modifications as described in the comments (lines that begin with two slashes) at the beginning of the file. Your job is to alter the program to meet the new specifications. (6.2–6.5)

Debugging Exercises

1. Your downloadable files for Chapter 6 include *DEBUG06-01.txt, DEBUG06-02.txt, DEBUG06-03.txt*, and *DEBUG06-04.jpg*. Each file starts with some comments that describe the problem. Comments are lines that begin with two slashes (//). Following the comments, each file contains pseudocode or a flowchart that has mistakes. Find and correct all the bugs.

Game Zone

1. Create the logic for a Magic 8 Ball game in which the user enters a question such as *What does my future hold?* The program randomly selects one of eight possible vague answers, such as *It remains to be seen*. (6.1–6.3)

2. Create the logic for an application that contains an array of five multiple-choice questions related to your favorite hobby. Each question contains three answer choices. Also create a parallel array that holds the correct answer to each question—*A*, *B*, or *C*. Display each question and verify that the user enters only *A*, *B*, or *C* as the answer—if not, keep prompting the user until a valid response is entered. If the user responds to a question correctly, display *Correct!*; otherwise, display *The correct answer is* and the letter of the correct answer. After the user answers all the questions, display the number of correct and incorrect answers. (6.1, 6.2, 6.3, 6.5)

3. **a.** Create the logic for a dice game. The application randomly "throws" five dice for the computer and five dice for the player. After each random throw, store the results in an array. The application displays all the values, which can be from 1 to 6 inclusive for each die. Decide the winner based on the following hierarchy of die values. Any higher combination beats a lower one; for example, five of a kind beats four of a kind.

   - Five of a kind
   - Four of a kind
   - Three of a kind
   - A pair

   For this game, the numeric dice values do not count. For example, if both players have three of a kind, it's a tie, no matter what the values of the three dice are. Additionally, the game does not recognize a full house (three of a kind plus two of a kind). **Figure 6-26** shows how the game might be played in a command-line environment.

   b. Improve the dice game so that when both players have the same number of matching dice, the higher value wins. For example, two 6s beats two 5s. (6.1, 6.2)

Figure 6-26 Typical execution of the dice game

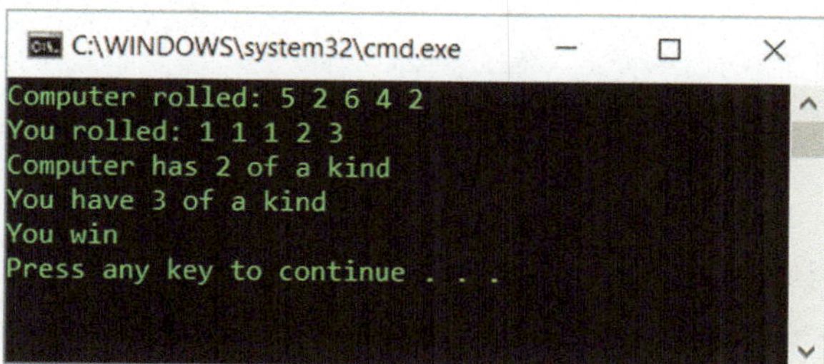

4. Design the logic for the game Hangman, in which the user guesses letters in a hidden word. Store the letters of a word in an array of characters. Display a dash for each missing letter. Allow the user to continually guess a letter until all the letters in the word are guessed correctly. As the user enters each guess, display the word again, filling in the guessed letter if it was correct. For example, if the hidden word is *computer*, first display a series of eight dashes: --------. After the user guesses *p*, the display becomes ---*p*----. Make sure that when a user makes a correct guess, all the matching letters are filled in. For example, if the word is *banana* and the user guesses *a*, all three *a* characters should be filled in. (6.1, 6.3, 6.5)

5. Create two parallel arrays that represent a standard deck of 52 playing cards. One array is numeric and holds the values 1 through 13 (representing *Ace*, *2* through *10*, *Jack*, *Queen*, and *King*). The other array is a string array that holds suits (*Clubs*, *Diamonds*, *Hearts*, and *Spades*). Create the arrays so that all 52 cards are represented. Then, create a War card game that randomly selects two cards (one for the player and one for the computer) and declares a winner or a tie based on the numeric value of the two cards. The game should last for 26 rounds and use a full deck with no repeated cards. For this game, assume that the lowest card is the Ace. Display the values of the player's and computer's cards, compare their values, and determine the winner. When all the cards in the deck are exhausted, display a count of the number of times the player wins, the number of times the computer wins, and the number of ties. Here are some hints:
    - Start by creating an array of all 52 playing cards.
    - Select a random number for the deck position of the player's first card and assign the card at that array position to the player.
    - Move every higher-positioned card in the deck "down" one to fill in the gap. In other words, if the player's first random number is 49, select the card at position 49 (both the numeric value and the string), move the card that was in position 50 to position 49, and move the card that was in position 51 to position 50. Only 51 cards remain in the deck after the player's first card is dealt, so the available-card array is smaller by one.
    - In the same way, randomly select a card for the computer and "remove" the card from the deck. (6.1, 6.3, 6.6)

Chapter 7

File Handling and Applications

Learning Objectives

When you complete this chapter, you will be able to:

- **7.1** Describe computer files
- **7.2** Describe the data hierarchy
- **7.3** Perform file operations
- **7.4** Perform control break logic
- **7.5** Merge files
- **7.6** Update primary files with transaction records
- **7.7** Work with random access files

7.1 Understanding Computer Files

You have learned that computer memory, or random access memory (RAM), is volatile, temporary storage. When you write a program that stores a value in a variable, you are using temporary storage; the value you store is lost when the program ends or the computer loses power.

Permanent, nonvolatile storage, on the other hand, is not lost when a computer loses power. Permanent storage is *durable* in the sense that after data items are saved to durable storage, they are available for future use. When you write a program and save it to a disk, you are using a **permanent storage device**. Permanent storage can be a hard drive on your computer or a hard drive on the cloud that you access remotely through the Internet. Permanent storage can also be on a solid-state drive (SSD), which acts like a hard disk but uses electronic circuits, eliminating a traditional hard drive's moving parts and making data access faster. Other examples of permanent storage include such media as DVDs, USB drives that you insert and remove from your computer, and tape libraries and optical jukeboxes that are accessed by robotic arms.

> **Note** When discussing computer storage, *temporary* and *permanent* refer to volatility, not length of time. For example, a temporary variable might exist for several hours in a very large program or one that runs in an infinite loop, but a permanent piece of data might be saved and then deleted by a user within a few seconds. Because you can erase data from files, some programmers prefer the term *persistent storage* to permanent storage. In other words, you can remove data from a file stored on a device such as a disk drive, so it is not technically permanent. However, the data remains in the file even when the computer loses power, so, unlike in RAM, the data persists.

A **computer file** is a collection of data stored on a nonvolatile device in a computer system. Two broad categories of computer files are text files and binary files.

- A **text file** contains data that can be read in a text editor because the data has been encoded using a scheme such as ASCII or Unicode. (Appendix A describes ASCII and Unicode in detail.) A text file might include facts and figures used by a business program, such as a payroll file that contains employee numbers, names, and salaries. The programs in this chapter will use text files.
- A **binary file** contains data that has not been encoded as text. Examples include images and music. Executable files also are binary files. Executable files are runnable programs that have been translated from the programmer's code.

Although their contents vary, files have many common characteristics, such as:

- Each has a **filename** that identifies the computer file and frequently describes its contents—for example, *JanuaryPayroll* or *PreviousMonthSales*. The name often includes a dot and a **filename extension**, which is a group of characters added to the end of a filename that describes the type of the file. For example, the full name of a file might be *JanuaryPayroll.txt*, in which *.txt* is the filename extension. The extension *.txt* indicates a plain text file, *.dat* is a common extension for a data file, and *.jpg* is used as an extension on image files in Joint Photographic Experts Group format. A filename's extension frequently designates the software that will be used to open a file; for example, a file that uses the extension *.docx* will usually be opened by Microsoft Word by default.
- Each file has specific times associated with it—for example, its creation time and the time it was last modified.
- Each file occupies space on a section of a storage device; that is, each file has a size. Sizes are measured in bytes. A **byte** is a small unit of storage; for example, in a simple text file, a byte holds only one character. Because a byte is so small, file sizes usually are expressed in **kilobytes** (thousands of bytes), **megabytes** (millions of bytes), **gigabytes** (billions of bytes), or even larger groupings.

Appendix A contains more information about bytes and how file sizes are expressed. **Figure 7-1** shows how some files look when you view them in Microsoft Windows.

Organizing Files

Computer files on a storage device are the electronic equivalent of paper files stored in file cabinets. With a paper file, the easiest way to store a document is to toss it into a file cabinet drawer without a folder. However, for better organization, most office clerks place paper documents in folders—and most computer users organize their files into folders or directories. **Directories** and **folders** are organization units on storage devices; each can contain multiple files as well as additional directories. The combination of the disk drive plus the complete hierarchy of directories in which a file resides is the **file's path**. For example, in the Windows operating system, the following line would be the complete path for a file named *PayrollData.dat* on the C drive in a folder named *SampleFiles* within a folder named *Logic*:

```
C:\Logic\SampleFiles\PayrollData.dat
```

Figure 7-1 Four stored files showing their names, dates, types, and sizes

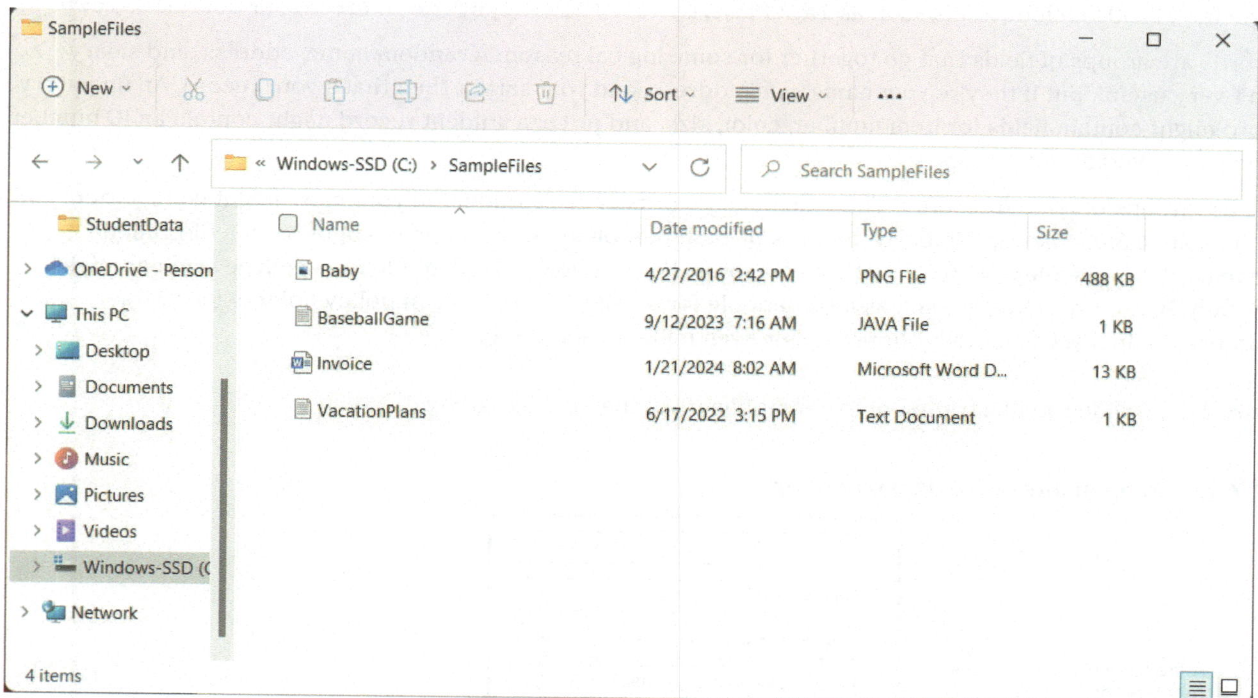

Note The terms *directory* and *folder* are used synonymously to mean an entity that organizes files. *Directory* is the more general term; the term *folder* came into use in graphical systems. For example, Microsoft began calling directories folders with the introduction of Windows 95.

Two Truths & a Lie | Understanding Computer Files

1. Temporary storage is volatile.
2. Computer files exist on permanent storage devices, such as RAM.
3. A file's path is the hierarchy of folders in which the file is stored.

The false statement is #2. Computer files exist on permanent storage devices, such as hard disks, SSDs, DVDs, USB drives, and reels of magnetic tape.

7.2 Understanding the Data Hierarchy

When businesses store data items on computer systems, they often are stored in a framework called the **data hierarchy** that describes the relationships among data components. The data hierarchy consists of the following:

- **Characters** are letters, numbers, and special symbols, such as *A*, 7, and *$*. Anything you can type from the keyboard in one keystroke is a character, including seemingly "empty" characters such as spaces and tabs. Computers also recognize characters you cannot enter from a standard keyboard, such as foreign-alphabet characters such as Ω or Π. Characters are made up of smaller elements called bits, but just as most human beings can use a pencil without caring whether atoms are flying around inside it, most computer users store characters without thinking about these bits.

- **Fields** are data items that each represent a single attribute of a record; fields are composed of one or more characters. Fields include items such as `lastName`, `middleInitial`, `streetAddress`, or `annualSalary`.
- **Records** are groups of fields that go together for some logical reason. A random name, address, and salary aren't very useful, but if they're *your* name, *your* address, and *your* salary, then that's your record. An inventory record might contain fields for item number, color, size, and price; a student record might contain an ID number, grade point average, and major.
- **Files** are groups of related records. The individual records of each student in your class might go together in a file called *Students.dat*. Similarly, records of each person at your company might be in a file called *Personnel.dat*. Some files can have just a few records. For example, a student file for a college seminar might have only 10 records. Others, such as a student file for a university or a file of policy holders for a large insurance company, can contain thousands or even millions of records.

Figure 7-2 provides an illustration of the components of the data hierarchy.

Figure 7-2 Components of the data hierarchy

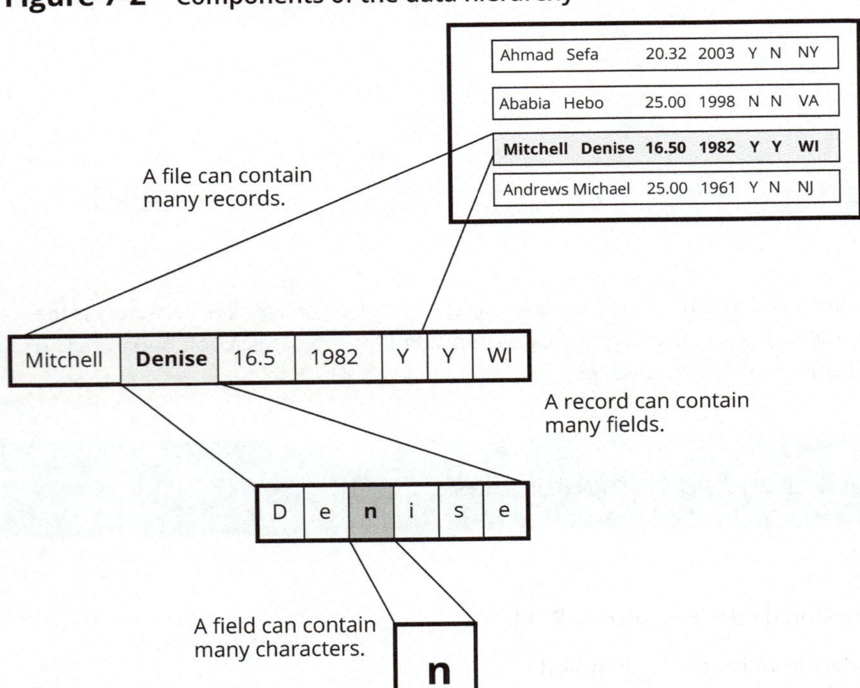

> **Note** A **database** holds related file data in tables. Database software establishes and maintains relationships between fields in these tables, so that users can pull related data items together in a format that allows businesspeople to make managerial decisions efficiently.

Two Truths & a Lie | Understanding the Data Hierarchy

1. In the data hierarchy, a field is a single data item, such as `lastName`, `streetAddress`, or `annualSalary`.
2. In the data hierarchy, fields are grouped together to form a record; records are groups of fields that go together for some logical reason.
3. In the data hierarchy, related records are grouped together to form a field.

The false statement is #3. Related records form a file.

7.3 Performing File Operations

To use data files in your programs, you need to understand several file operations:

- Declaring a file identifier
- Opening a file
- Reading from a file and processing the data
- Writing to a file
- Closing a file

Declaring a File Identifier

Most languages support several types of files, but one way of categorizing files is by whether they can be used for input or for output. Just as variables and constants have data types such as `num` and `string`, each file has a data type that is defined in the language you are using. For example, a file's type might be `InputFile`. Just like variables and constants, files are declared by giving each a data type and an identifier. As examples, you might declare two files as follows:

```
InputFile employeeData
OutputFile updatedData
```

The `InputFile` and `OutputFile` types are capitalized in this course because their equivalents are capitalized in most programming languages. This approach helps to distinguish these complex types from simple types such as `num` and `string`. The identifiers given to files, such as `employeeData` and `updatedData`, are internal to the program, just as variable names are. To make a program read a file's data from a storage device, you also need to associate the program's internal filename with the operating system's name for the file. Often, this association is accomplished when you open the file.

Opening a File

In most programming languages, before an application can use a data file, it must open the file. **Opening a file** locates it on a storage device and associates a variable name within your program with the file. For example, if the identifier `employeeData` has been declared as type `InputFile`, then you might make a statement like the following:

```
open employeeData "EmployeeData.dat"
```

This statement associates the file named *EmployeeData.dat* on the storage device with the program's internal name `employeeData`. If the data file is not stored in the same directory as the program, you usually specify a more complete path, as in the following:

```
open employeeData "C:\CompanyFiles\CurrentYear\EmployeeData.dat"
```

Reading Data from a File and Processing It

You never use the data values that are stored on a storage device directly. Instead, you use a copy that is transferred into memory. When you copy data from a file on a storage device into RAM, you are **reading from a file**.

> **Note** When data items are stored on a disk, their location might not be clear to you—data just seems to be "in the computer." To a casual computer user, the lines between permanent storage and temporary memory are often blurred because many programs automatically save data for you periodically without asking your permission. However, at any moment in time, the version of a file in memory might differ from the version that was last saved to a storage device.

Once the program's identifier `employeeData` has been associated with the stored file, you can write separate programming statements to input each field, as in the following example:

```
input name from employeeData
input address from employeeData
input payRate from employeeData
```

Most languages also allow you to write a single statement in the following format:

```
input name, address, payRate from employeeData
```

As a further simplification, many programming languages allow you to declare a group item when you declare other variables, as in the following example:

```
EmployeeRecord
    string name
    string address
    num payRate
```

In this example, `EmployeeRecord` is a group name for the values stored in the three fields `name`, `address`, and `payRate`. After the group is defined, you can input all the data items in a record with a single instruction, such as the following:

```
input EmployeeRecord from employeeData
```

You usually do not want to input several items in a single statement when you read data from a keyboard, because you want to prompt the user for each item separately as you input it. However, when you retrieve data from a file, prompts are not needed. Instead, each item is retrieved in sequence and stored in memory at the appropriate named location.

Programming languages have different ways of determining how much data to input when a command is issued to read a variable's value from a file. In many languages, a **delimiter** such as a comma, semicolon, or tab character is stored between data fields. Sometimes, data items are stored in a compact form so that they are not decipherable when the file is opened in a text editor, but sometimes data items are stored in a readable format. For example, **Figure 7-3** shows what a readable comma-delimited data file of employee names, addresses, and pay rates might look like in a text reader. The amount of data retrieved depends on the data types of the variables in the input statement. For example, reading a numeric value might imply that four bytes will be read. When you learn to program in a specific language, you will learn how data items are stored and retrieved in that language.

Figure 7-3 How employee data in a readable comma-delimited file might appear in a text reader

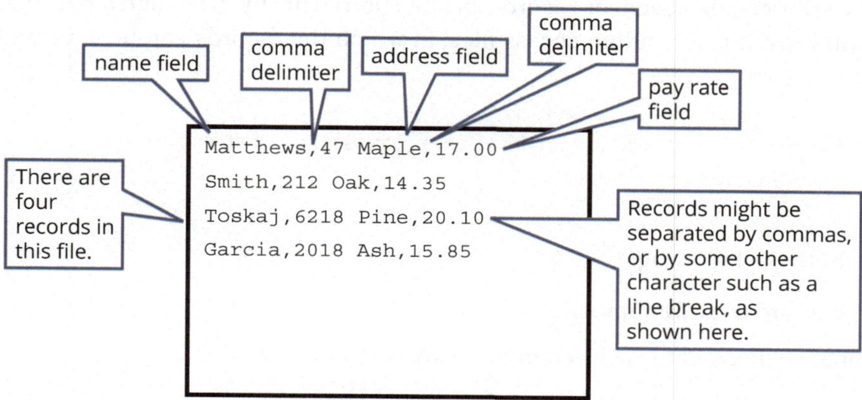

Figure 7-4 shows an example of how a statement gets data from a file. When the input statement executes, each field stored in the file is copied and placed in the appropriate variable in computer memory. Nothing on the disk indicates a field name associated with any of the data; the variable names exist within the program only. For example, although this program uses the variable names `name`, `address`, and `payRate`, another program could use the same file as input and call the fields `surname`, `street`, and `salary`.

Figure 7-4 Reading three data items from a storage device into memory

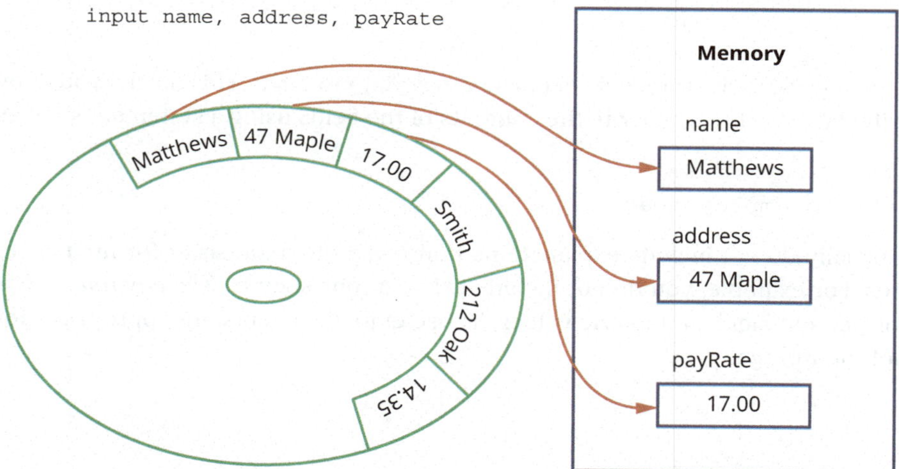

> **Note** | Variable names are not included in a data file, but when you create or use a database, you almost always include multiple files, and a field name is associated with each data value.

When you read data from a file, you usually must read all the fields that are stored even though you might not want to use all of them. For example, suppose that you want to read an employee data file that contains names, addresses, and pay rates for each employee, and you want to output a list of names. Even though you are not concerned with the address or pay rate fields for each employee, you typically read them into your program before you can get to the name for the next employee.

A computer program can read records from a file sequentially or randomly. When programs use **sequential files**, they read all the records in the files from beginning to end, processing them one at a time. Frequently, although not always, records in a sequential file have been sorted based on the contents of one or more fields. **Sorting** is the process of placing records in order by the value in a specific field or fields. **Ascending order** describes records sorted in order from lowest to highest values; **descending order** describes records in order from highest to lowest values. Records in a file can be sorted manually before they are entered and saved, or records can be entered in any order and a program can sort them. Later in this chapter, you will learn about random access files, in which the records can be accessed in any order.

> **Note** | You can learn about sorting techniques later in this course. In this chapter, it is assumed that if a file needs to be sorted, the sorting process has already been completed.

Examples of sorted, sequential files include the following:

- A file of employees whose data is stored in order by ID number
- A file of parts for a manufacturing company whose data is stored in order by part number
- A file of customers for a business whose data is stored in alphabetical order by name

After data fields have been read into memory, you can process them. Depending on the application, examples of processing the data might include performing arithmetic with some of the numeric fields or altering some of the string fields by adding or removing characters. Changes made to the fields in memory do not affect the original data stored on the input device. Typically, after the data field contents are processed, you want to output them. If the processed information needs to be visible only to people, you might display it on a screen. If the information will be used by another program, however, then you would want to write the processed information to a file.

Writing Data to a File

When you store data in a computer file on a persistent storage device, you are **writing to a file**. This means you copy data from RAM to the file. When you write data to a file, you write the contents of the fields using a statement such as the following:

```
output name, address, payRate to employeeData
```

When you write data to a file, you usually do not include explanations that make the data easier for humans to interpret; you just write facts and figures. For example, you do not include explanations such as *The pay rate is*, nor do you include commas, dollar signs, or percent signs in numeric values. Those embellishments are appropriate for output on a monitor or on paper, but not for storage.

Closing a File

When you finish using a file, the program should close the file. **Closing a file** makes it no longer available to your application. Failing to close an input file (a file from which you are reading data) usually does not present serious consequences; the data still exists in the file. However, if you fail to close an output file (a file to which you are writing data), the data might not be saved correctly and might become inaccessible. You should always close every file you open, and you should close the file as soon as you no longer need it. When you leave a file open for no reason, you use computer resources, and your computer's performance suffers. Also, within a network, another program might be waiting to use the file.

> **Note** | Although you open and close files on storage devices such as disks, most programming languages allow you to read data from a keyboard or write it to the display monitor without having to issue open or close commands because the keyboard and monitor are the **default input and output devices**, respectively.

A Program that Performs File Operations

Figure 7-5 contains a program that opens two files—an input file and an output file. The program reads each employee record from the input file, alters the employee's pay rate, and writes the updated record to an output file. After all the records have been processed, the program closes the files. When creating flowcharts, some programmers place file open and close statements in a process box (rectangle), but the convention in this course is to place file open and close statements in parallelograms, because they are operations closely related to input and output.

In the program in Figure 7-5, after each employee's pay rate is read into memory, it is increased by $2.00. The value of the pay rate on the input storage device is not altered. When processing is complete, the input file retains the original data for each employee, and the output file contains the revised data. Many organizations would keep the original file as a backup file. A **backup file** is a copy that is kept in case values need to be restored to their original state. The backup copy is called a **parent file** and the newly revised copy is a **child file**.

Figure 7-5 Flowchart and pseudocode for program that uses files

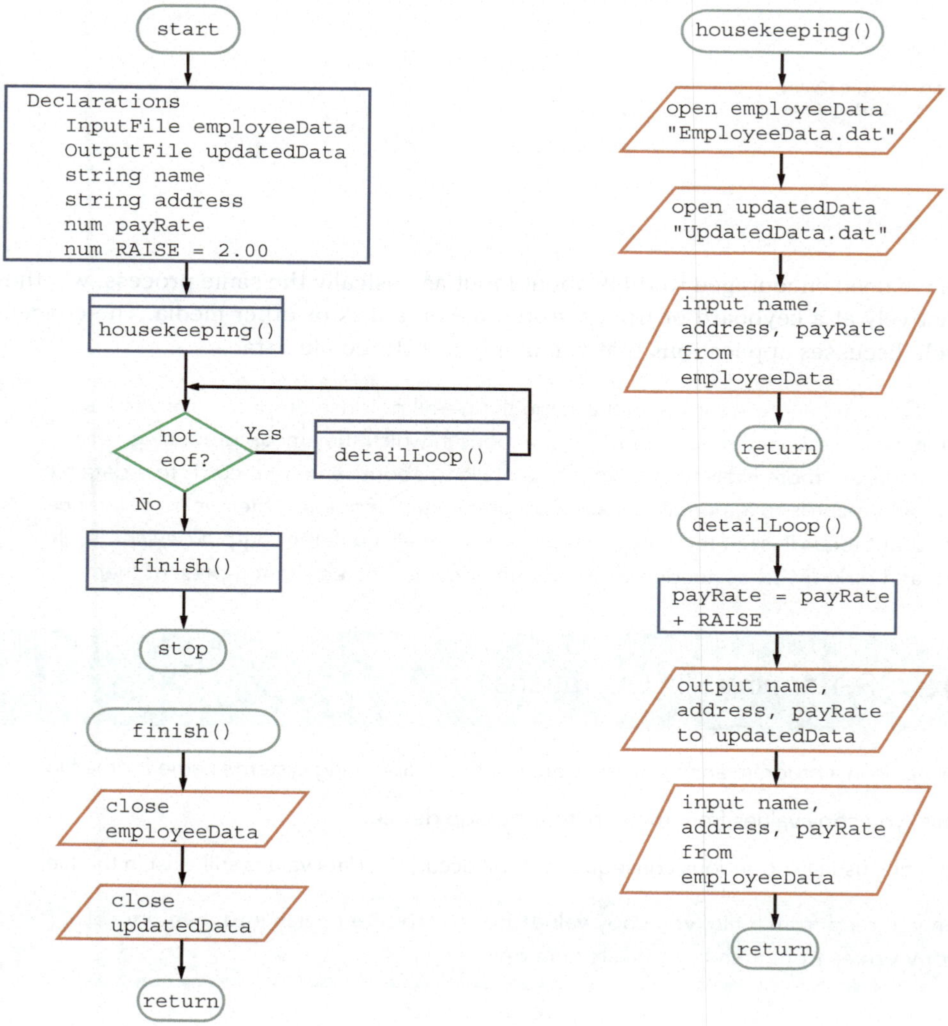

(Continues)

Figure 7-5 *(Continued)*

```
start
   Declarations
      InputFile employeeData
      OutputFile updatedData
      string name
      string address
      num payRate
      num RAISE = 2.00
   housekeeping()
   while not eof
      detailLoop()
   endwhile
   finish()
stop

housekeeping()
   open employeeData "EmployeeData.dat"
   open updatedData "UpdatedData.dat"
   input name, address, payRate from employeeData
return

detailLoop()
   payRate = payRate + RAISE
   output name, address, payRate to updatedData
   input name, address, payRate from employeeData
return

finish()
    close employeeData
    close updatedData
return
```

Throughout this course, you have been encouraged to think about input as basically the same process, whether it comes from a user typing interactively at a keyboard or from a stored file on a disk or other media. The concept remains valid for this chapter, which discusses applications that commonly use stored file data.

Note Logically, the verbs *print*, *write*, and *display* mean the same thing—all produce output. In conversation, however, programmers often reserve the word *print* for situations in which they mean producing hard copy output. Programmers are more likely to use *write* when talking about sending records to a data file and *display* when sending records to a monitor. In some programming languages, there is no difference in the verb used for output regardless of the hardware; you simply assign different output devices (such as printers, monitors, and disk drives) as needed to programmer-named objects that represent them.

Two Truths & a Lie | Performing File Operations

1. You give a file an internal name in a program and then associate it with the operating system's name for the file.
2. When you read from a file, you copy values from memory to a storage device.
3. If you fail to close an input file, usually no serious consequences will occur; the data values still exist in the file.

The false statement is #2. When you read from a file, you copy values from a storage device into memory. When you write to a file, you copy values from memory to a storage device.

7.4 Understanding Control Break Logic

A **control break** is a temporary detour in the logic of a program. Programmers use a **control break program** to do the following:

- Read in records from a sorted sequential file so that all records that belong to specific groups are stored together in sequence.

- Process each record, checking to determine if it still belongs to the same group as the previous record.
- Pause for special processing whenever a new group of records is encountered.

For example, a control break program might be used to generate a report that lists all company clients in order by state of residence, with a count of clients after each state's client list. See **Figure 7-6** for an example of a **control break report** that breaks after each change in state.

Figure 7-6 A control break report with totals after each state

Company Clients by State of Residence

Name	City	State	
Albertson	Birmingham	Alabama	
Minh	Birmingham	Alabama	
Lawrence	Montgomery	Alabama	
		Count for Alabama	3
Smith	Anchorage	Alaska	
Young	Anchorage	Alaska	
Davis	Fairbanks	Alaska	
Yamamoto	Juneau	Alaska	
Zimmer	Juneau	Alaska	
		Count for Alaska	5
Edwards	Phoenix	Arizona	
		Count for Arizona	1

Other examples of control break reports produced by control break programs could include:

- All employees listed in order by department number, with a new page started for each department
- All books for sale in a bookstore listed in order by category (such as reference or self-help), with a count following each category of book
- All items sold in order by date of sale, with a different ink color for each new month

Each of these reports shares two traits:

- The records used in a report are listed in order by a specific variable: state, department, category, or date.
- When the value of that variable changes in a new record, the program takes special action: It starts a new page, prints a count or total, or switches ink color.

To generate a control break report, the input records must be organized in sequential order based on the field that will cause the breaks. In other words, to write a program that produces a report of customers by state, such as the one in Figure 7-6, the records must be grouped by state before you begin processing.

Note With some languages, such as SQL (Structured Query Language, which is used with database processing), the details of control break processing are handled automatically. Still, understanding how control break programs work improves your competence as a programmer.

Suppose that you have an input file that contains client names, cities, and states, and you want to produce a report like the one in Figure 7-6. The basic logic of the program works like this:

- Each time you read a client's record from the input file, you determine whether the client resides in the same state as the previous client.
- If so, you simply output the client's data, add 1 to a counter, and read another record, without any special processing. If there are 20 clients in a state, these steps are repeated 20 times in a row—read a client's data, count it, and output it.

- Eventually you will read a record for a client who is not in the same state. At that point, before you output the data for the first client in the new state, you must output the count for the previous state. You also must reset the counter to 0 so it is ready to start counting customers in the next state. Then you can proceed to handle client records for the new state, and you continue to do so until the next time you encounter a client from a different state.

This type of program contains a **single-level control break**, a break in the logic of the program (in this case, pausing or detouring to output a count) that is based on the value of a single variable (in this case, the state). The technique you must use to "remember" the old state so you can compare it with each new client's state is to create a special variable, called a **control break field**, to hold the previous state. As you read each new record, comparing the new and old state values determines when it is time to output the count for the previous state.

Figure 7-7 shows the mainline logic and `getReady()` module for a program that produces the report in Figure 7-6. In the mainline logic, the control break variable `oldState` is declared.

Figure 7-7 Mainline logic and `getReady()` module for the program that produces a list of clients by state

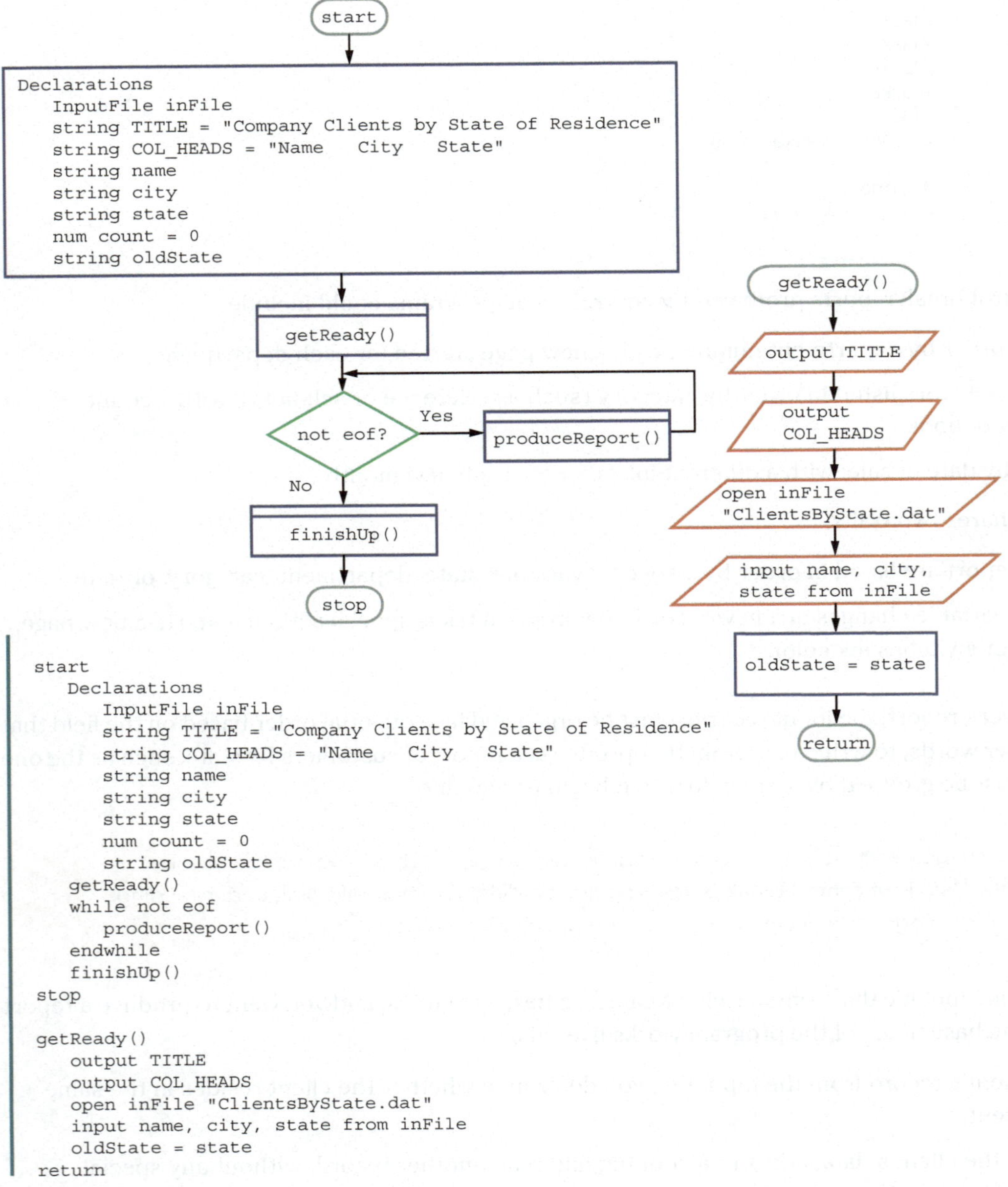


```
start
   Declarations
      InputFile inFile
      string TITLE = "Company Clients by State of Residence"
      string COL_HEADS = "Name    City    State"
      string name
      string city
      string state
      num count = 0
      string oldState
   getReady()
   while not eof
      produceReport()
   endwhile
   finishUp()
stop

getReady()
   output TITLE
   output COL_HEADS
   open inFile "ClientsByState.dat"
   input name, city, state from inFile
   oldState = state
return
```

In the `getReady()` module, the report headings are output, the file is opened, and the first record is read into memory. Then, the state value in the first record is copied to the `oldState` variable. Note that it would be incorrect to initialize `oldState` when it is declared. When you declare the variables at the beginning of the main program, you have not yet read the first input record; therefore, you don't know what the value of the first state will be. You might assume that it is *Alabama* because that is the first state alphabetically, and you might be right, but perhaps this data set contains no records for *Alabama* and the first state is *Alaska* or even *Wyoming*. You are assured of storing the correct first state value if you copy it from the first input record.

Figure 7-8 shows the `produceReport()` and `controlBreak()` modules for the program. Within the `produceReport()` module, the first task is to check whether `state` holds the same value as `oldState`. For the first record, on the first pass through this module, the values are equal (because you set them to be equal right after getting the first input record in the `getReady()` module). Therefore, you proceed by outputting the first client's data, adding 1 to `count`, and inputting the next record.

Figure 7-8 The `produceReport()` and `controlBreak()` modules for the program that produces a list of clients by state

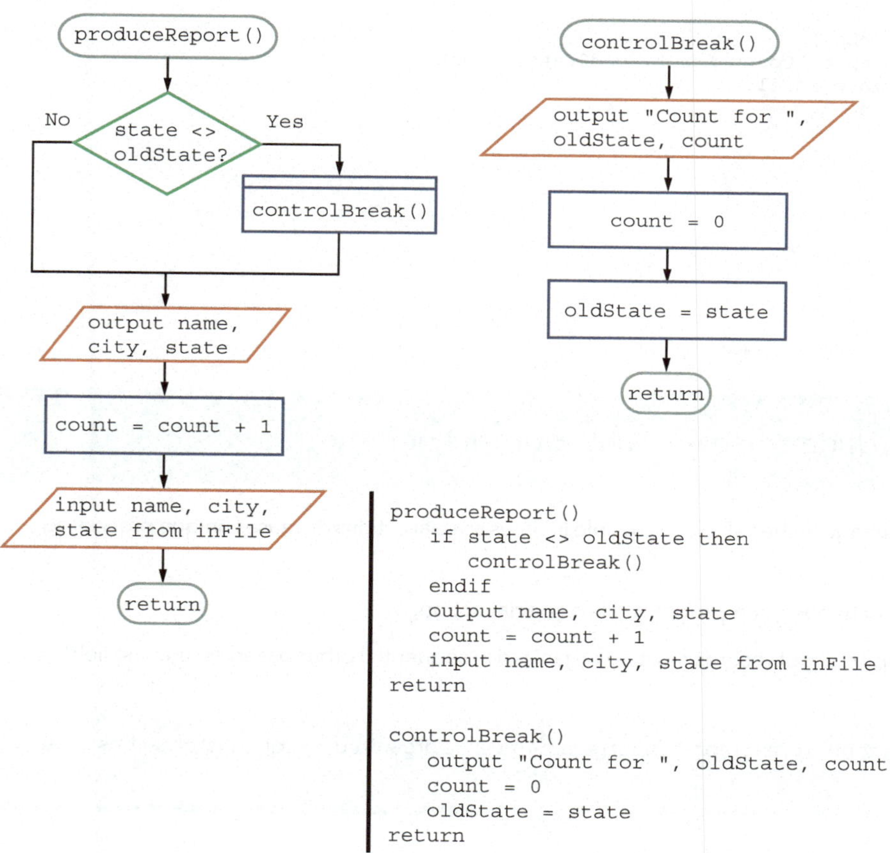


```
produceReport()
   if state <> oldState then
      controlBreak()
   endif
   output name, city, state
   count = count + 1
   input name, city, state from inFile
return

controlBreak()
   output "Count for ", oldState, count
   count = 0
   oldState = state
return
```

As long as each new record holds the same `state` value, you continue outputting, counting, and inputting, never pausing to output the count. Eventually, you will read in a client whose state is different from the previous one. That's when the control break occurs and the `controlBreak()` module executes.

Whenever a new state differs from the old one, three tasks must be performed:

- The count for the previous state must be output.
- The count must be reset to 0 so it can start counting records for the new state.
- The control break field must be updated to hold the new state.

When the `produceReport()` module receives a client record for which `state` is not the same as `oldState`, you force a break in the normal flow of the program. The new client record must "wait" while the count for the just-finished state is output and `count` and the control break field `oldState` acquire new values.

The `produceReport()` module continues to output client names, cities, and states until the end of the file is reached; then the `finishUp()` module executes. As shown in **Figure 7-9**, the module that executes after processing the last record in a control break program must complete any required processing for the last group that was handled. In this case, the `finishUp()` module must display the count for the last state that was processed. After the input file is closed, the logic can return to the main program, where the program ends.

Figure 7-9 The `finishUp()` module for the program that produces a list of clients by state

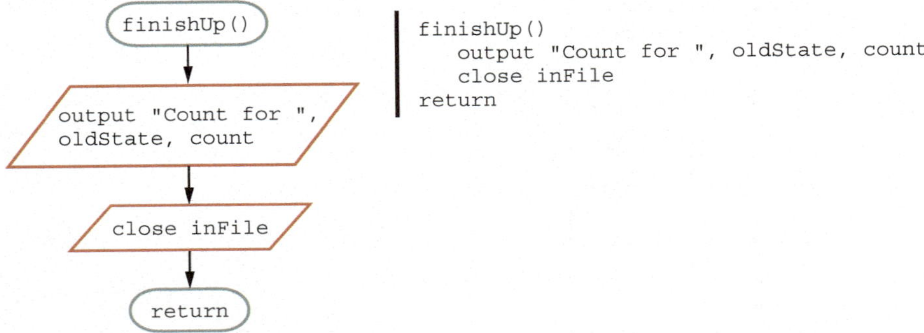


```
finishUp()
   output "Count for ", oldState, count
   close inFile
return
```

Two Truths & a Lie | Understanding Control Break Logic

1. In a control break program, a change in the value of a variable initiates special actions or causes unique processing to occur.
2. When a control break variable changes, the program takes special action.
3. To generate a control break report, input records must be organized in sequential order based on the first field in the record.

The false statement is #3. To generate a control break report, input records must be organized in sequential order based on the field that will trigger the break.

7.5 Merging Sequential Files

Businesses often need to merge two or more sequential files. **Merging files** involves combining two or more files while maintaining the sequential order of the records. For example:

- Suppose that you have a file of current employees in ID number order and a file of newly hired employees, also in ID number order. You need to merge these two files into one combined file in ID number order before running this week's payroll program.

- Suppose that you have a file of parts manufactured in the Northside factory in part-number order and a file of parts manufactured in the Southside factory, also in part-number order. You want to merge these two files into one combined file, creating a combined list of available parts in order by part number.
- Suppose that you have a file that lists last year's customers in alphabetical order and another file that lists this year's customers in alphabetical order. You want to create a mailing list of all customers in order by last name.

Before you can easily merge files, two conditions must be met:

- Each file must contain the same record layout.
- Each file used in the merge must be sorted in the same order based on the same field.

For example, suppose that your business has two locations, one on the East Coast and one on the West Coast, and each location maintains a customer file in alphabetical order by customer name. Each file contains fields for name and customer balance. You can call the fields in the East Coast file `eastName` and `eastBalance`, and the fields in the West Coast file `westName` and `westBalance`. You want to merge the two files, creating one combined file containing records for all customers. **Figure 7-10** shows some sample data for the files; you want to create a merged file like the one shown in **Figure 7-11**.

Figure 7-10 Sample data contained in two customer files

East Coast File		West Coast File	
`eastName`	`eastBalance`	`westName`	`westBalance`
Able	100.00	Chen	200.00
Bishara	50.00	Edgar	125.00
Dougherty	25.00	Fu	75.00
Hanson	300.00	Grand	100.00
Ingram	400.00		
Johnson	30.00		

Figure 7-11 Merged customer file

Merged File	
`mergedName`	`mergedBalance`
Able	100.00
Bishara	50.00
Chen	200.00
Dougherty	25.00
Edgar	125.00
Fu	75.00
Grand	100.00
Hanson	300.00
Ingram	400.00
Johnson	30.00

The mainline logic for a program that merges two files is like the main logic you've used before in other programs: It contains preliminary, housekeeping tasks; a detail module that repeats until the end of the program; and some clean-up, end-of-job tasks. Most programs you have studied, however, processed records until an `eof` condition was met, either because an input data file reached its end or because a user entered a sentinel value in an interactive program. In a program that merges two input files, checking for `eof` in only one of them is insufficient. Instead, the program can't end until both input files are exhausted.

One way to end a file-merging program is to create a string flag variable with a name such as `areBothAtEnd`. You might initialize `areBothAtEnd` to `"N"` but change its value to `"Y"` after you have encountered `eof` in both input files. (If the language you use supports a Boolean data type, you can use the values `true` and `false` instead of strings.) **Figure 7-12** shows the mainline logic for a program that merges the files shown in Figure 7-10. After the `getReady()` module executes, the question that sends the logic to the `finishUp()` module tests the `areBothAtEnd` variable. When it holds `"Y"`, the program ends.

Figure 7-12 Mainline logic of a program that merges files

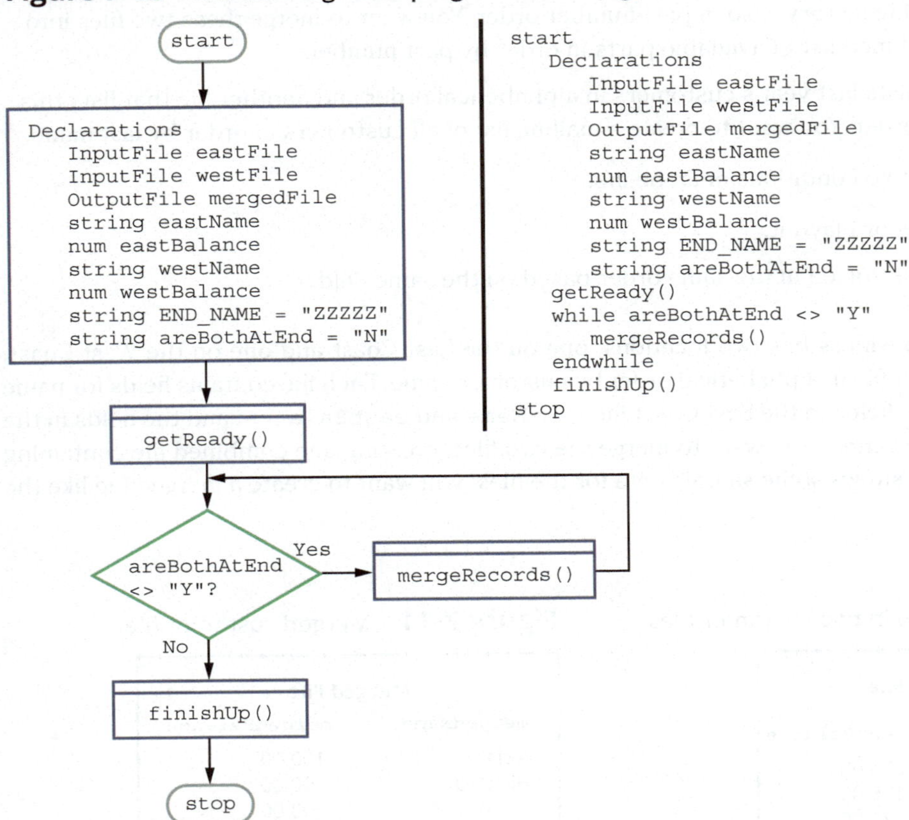

```
start
   Declarations
      InputFile eastFile
      InputFile westFile
      OutputFile mergedFile
      string eastName
      num eastBalance
      string westName
      num westBalance
      string END_NAME = "ZZZZZ"
      string areBothAtEnd = "N"
   getReady()
   while areBothAtEnd <> "Y"
      mergeRecords()
   endwhile
   finishUp()
stop
```

The `getReady()` module for the file-merging program is shown in **Figure 7-13**. It opens three files—the input files for the east and west customers and an output file in which to place the merged records. The program then reads one record from each input file. If either file has reached its end, the `END_NAME` constant is assigned to the variable that holds the file's customer name. The `getReady()` module then checks to see whether both files are finished (admittedly, a rare occurrence in the `getReady()` portion of the program's execution) and sets the `areBothAtEnd` flag variable to `"Y"` if they are. Assuming that at least one record is available, the logic then would enter the `mergeRecords()` module.

When you begin the `mergeRecords()` module in the program using the files shown in Figure 7-10, two records—one from `eastFile` and one from `westFile`—are sitting in the memory of the computer. One of these records needs to be written to the new output file first. Which one? Because the two input files contain records stored in alphabetical order, and you want the new file to store records in alphabetical order, you first output the input record that has the lower alphabetical value in the name field. Therefore, the process begins as shown in **Figure 7-14**.

Using the sample data from Figure 7-10, you can see that the *Able* record from the East Coast file should be written to the output file, while Chen's record from the West Coast file waits in memory. The `eastName` value *Able* is alphabetically lower than the `westName` value *Chen*.

After you write Able's record, should Chen's record be written to the output file next? Not necessarily. It depends on the next `eastName` following Able's record in `eastFile`. When data records are read into memory from a file, a program typically does not "look ahead" to determine the values stored in the next record. Instead, a program usually reads the record into memory before making decisions about its contents. In this program, you need to read the next `eastFile` record into memory and compare it to *Chen*. Because in this case the next record in `eastFile` contains the name *Bishara*, another `eastFile` record is written; no `westFile` records are written yet.

Figure 7-13 The `getReady()`, `readEast()`, `readWest()`, and `checkEnd()` modules for a program that merges files

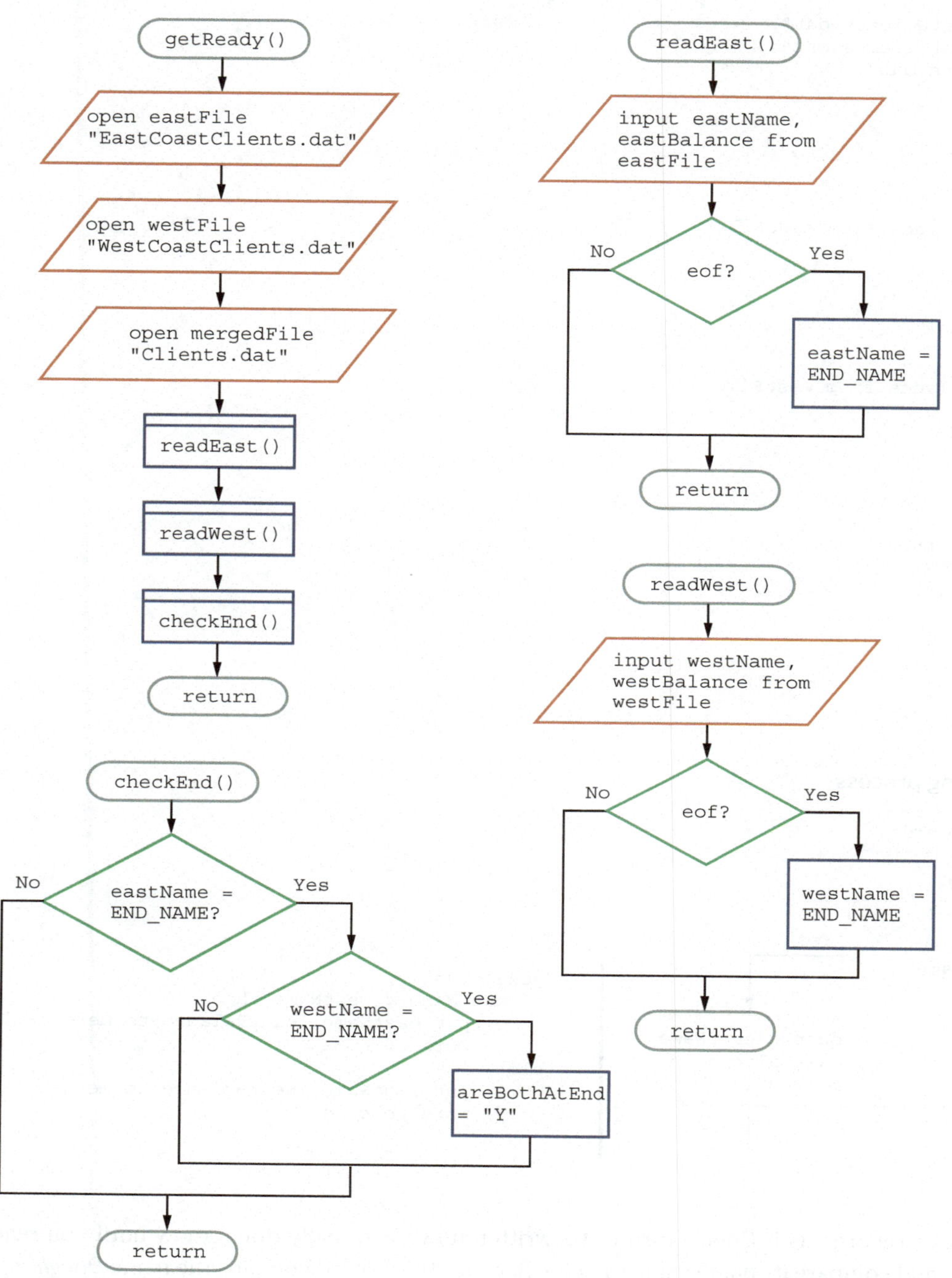

(Continues)

Figure 7-13 *(Continued)*

```
getReady()
   open eastFile "EastCoastClients.dat"
   open westFile "WestCoastClients.dat"
   open mergedFile "Clients.dat"
   readEast()
   readWest()
   checkEnd()
return

readEast()
   input eastName, eastBalance from eastFile
   if eof then
      eastName = END_NAME
   endif
return

readWest()
   input westName, westBalance from westFile
   if eof then
      westName = END_NAME
   endif
return

checkEnd()
   if eastName = END_NAME then
      if westName = END_NAME then
         areBothAtEnd = "Y"
      endif
   endif
return
```

Figure 7-14 Start of merging process

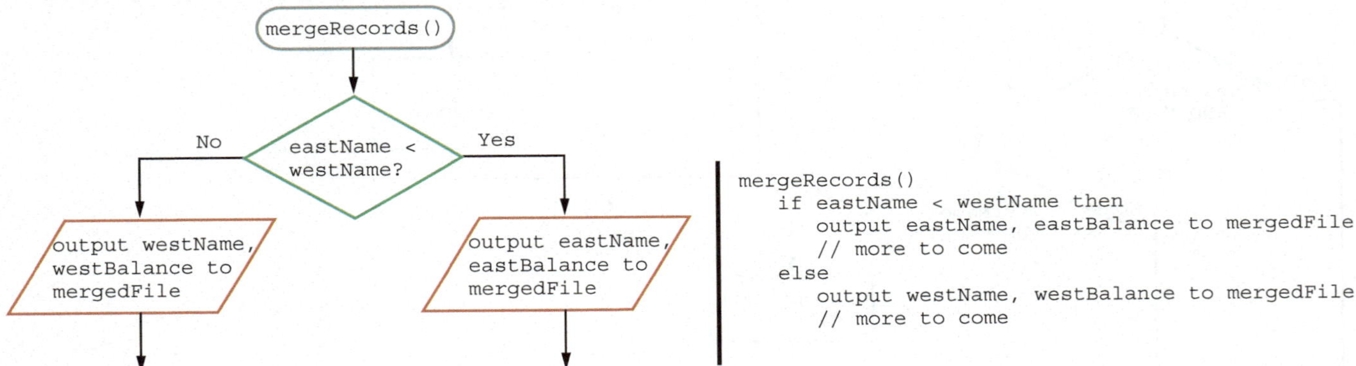

After the first two `eastFile` records, is it Chen's turn to be written now? You really don't know until you read another record from `eastFile` and compare its name value to *Chen*. Because this record contains the name *Dougherty*, it is indeed time to write Chen's record. After Chen's record is written, should you now write Dougherty's record? Until you read the next record from `westFile`, you don't know whether that record should be placed before or after Dougherty's record.

Therefore, the merging module proceeds like this: Compare two records, write the record with the lower alphabetical name, and read another record from the *same* input file. See **Figure 7-15**.

Recall the names from the two original files in Figure 7-10 and walk through the processing steps.

1. Compare *Able* and *Chen*. Write Able's record. Read Bishara's record from `eastFile`.
2. Compare *Bishara* and *Chen*. Write Bishara's record. Read Dougherty's record from `eastFile`.

Figure 7-15 Continuation of merging process

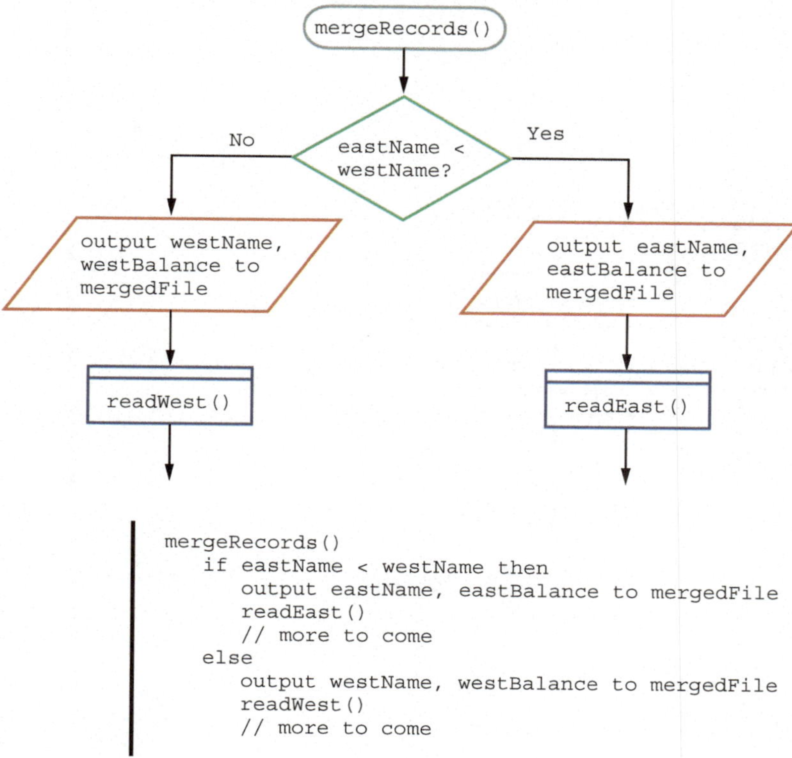


```
mergeRecords()
   if eastName < westName then
      output eastName, eastBalance to mergedFile
      readEast()
      // more to come
   else
      output westName, westBalance to mergedFile
      readWest()
      // more to come
```

3. Compare *Dougherty* and *Chen*. Write Chen's record. Read Edgar's record from `westFile`.
4. Compare *Dougherty* and *Edgar*. Write Dougherty's record. Read Hanson's record from `eastFile`.
5. Compare *Hanson* and *Edgar*. Write Edgar's record. Read Fu's record from `westFile`.
6. Compare *Hanson* and *Fu*. Write Fu's record. Read Grand's record from `westFile`.
7. Compare *Hanson* and *Grand*. Write Grand's record. Read from `westFile`, encountering `eof`. This causes `westName` to be set to `END_NAME`.

What happens when you reach the end of the West Coast file? Is the program over? It shouldn't be because records for *Hanson*, *Ingram*, and *Johnson* all need to be included in the new output file, and none of them is written yet. Because the `westName` field is set to `END_NAME`, and `END_NAME` has a very high alphabetic value (*ZZZZZ*), each subsequent `eastName` will be lower than the value of `westName`, and the rest of the `eastFile` records will be processed. With a different set of data, the `eastFile` might have ended first. In that case, `eastName` would be set to `END_NAME`, and each subsequent `westFile` record would be processed. **Figure 7-16** shows the complete `mergeRecords()` module and the `finishUp()` module.

> **Note** As the value for `END_NAME`, you should make sure that the high value you choose is actually higher than any legitimate value. For example, you might choose to use 10 or 20 *Z*s instead of only five, although it is unlikely that a person will have the last name ZZZZZ.

After Grand's record is processed, `westFile` is read and `eof` is encountered, so `westName` gets set to `END_NAME`. Now, when you enter the loop again, `eastName` and `westName` are compared, and `eastName` is still *Hanson*. The `eastName` value (*Hanson*) is lower than the `westName` value (*ZZZZZ*), so the data for `eastName`'s record is written to the output file, and another `eastFile` record (*Ingram*) is read.

Figure 7-16 The `mergeRecords()` and `finishUp()` modules for the file-merging program

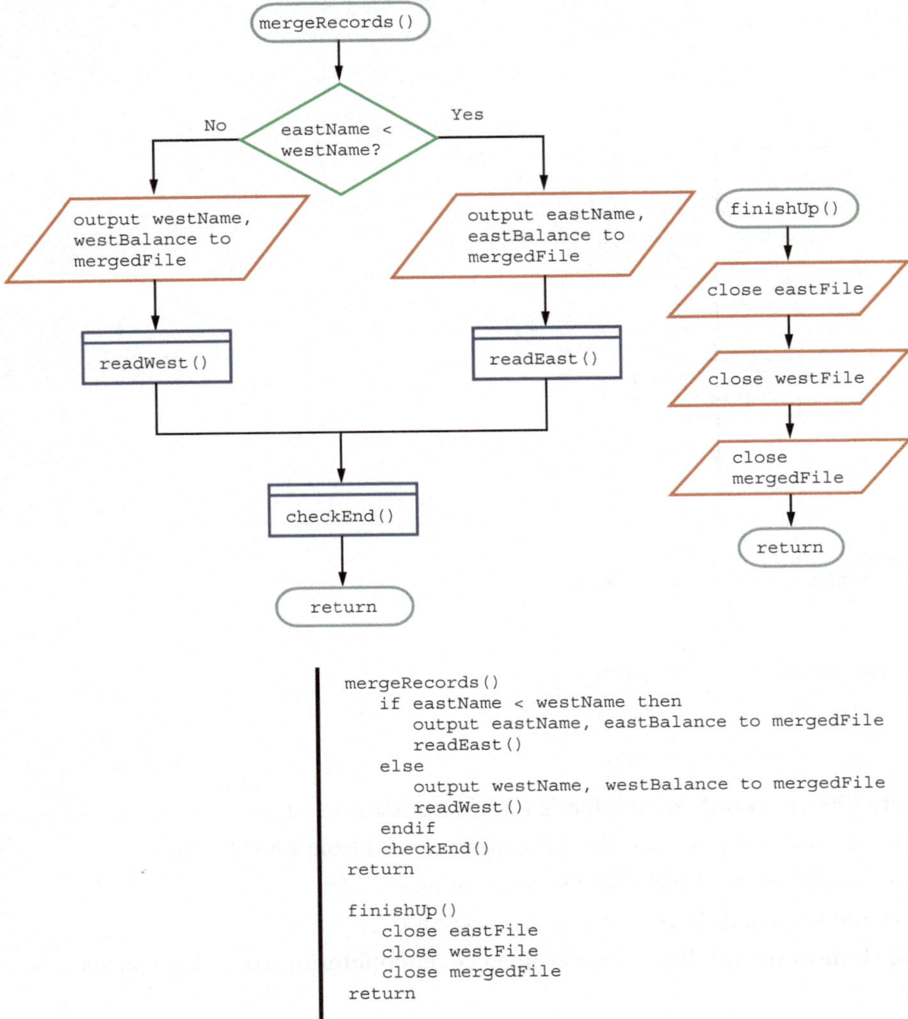


```
mergeRecords()
   if eastName < westName then
      output eastName, eastBalance to mergedFile
      readEast()
   else
      output westName, westBalance to mergedFile
      readWest()
   endif
   checkEnd()
return

finishUp()
   close eastFile
   close westFile
   close mergedFile
return
```

The complete run of the file-merging program has now executed the first six of the seven steps listed previously, and then proceeds as shown in Figure 7-16 and as follows, starting with a modified Step 7:

7. Compare *Hanson* and *Grand*. Write Grand's record. Read from `westFile`, encountering `eof` and setting `westName` to *ZZZZZ*.
8. Compare *Hanson* and *ZZZZZ*. Write Hanson's record. Read Ingram's record.
9. Compare *Ingram* and *ZZZZZ*. Write Ingram's record. Read Johnson's record.
10. Compare *Johnson* and *ZZZZZ*. Write Johnson's record. Read from `eastFile`, encountering `eof` and setting `eastName` to *ZZZZZ*.
11. Now that both names are *ZZZZZ*, set the flag `areBothAtEnd` equal to `"Y"`.

When the `areBothAtEnd` flag variable equals `"Y"`, the loop is finished, the files are closed, and the program ends.

Note

If two names are equal during the merge process—for example, when there is a Hanson record in each file—then both Hanson records will be included in the final file. When `eastName` and `westName` match, `eastName` is not lower than `westName`, so you write the `westFile` Hanson record. After you read the next `westFile` record, `eastName` will be lower than the next `westName`, and the `eastFile` Hanson record will be output. A more complicated merge program could check another field, such as first name, when last-name values match.

You can merge any number of files. To merge more than two files, the logic is only slightly more complicated; you must compare the key fields from all the files before deciding which file is the next candidate for output.

Two Truths & a Lie | Merging Sequential Files

1. A sequential file is a file in which records are stored one after another in some order. Most frequently, the records are stored based on the contents of one or more fields within each record.
2. Merging files involves combining two or more files while maintaining the sequential order of the records.
3. Before you can easily merge files, each file must contain the same number of records.

The false statement is #3. Before you can easily merge files, each file must contain the same record layout and each file used in the merge must be sorted in the same order based on the same field.

7.6 Updating Primary Files with Transaction Records

In the last section, you learned how to merge related sequential files in which each record in each file contained the same fields. Some related sequential files, however, do not contain the same fields. Instead, some related files have a primary file–transaction file relationship.

- A **primary file** holds complete and relatively permanent data. For example, a primary customer file might hold records that each contain a customer's name, address, phone number, and balance. In the past, primary files were sometimes called *master files*.
- A **transaction file** holds more temporary data. For example, a customer transaction file might contain data that describes each customer's most recent purchase.

Commonly, you gather transactions for a period of time, store them in a file, and then use them one by one to update matching records in a primary file. You **update a primary file** by making appropriate changes to the values in its fields based on the recent transactions. For example, a file containing transaction purchase data for a customer might be used to update each balance due field in a customer record primary file.

Here are a few other examples of files that have a primary–transaction relationship:

- A library maintains a primary file of all patrons and a transaction file with information about each book or other items checked out.
- A college maintains a primary file of all students and a transaction file for each course registration.
- A phone company maintains a primary file for every phone number and a transaction file with information about every call.

When you update a primary file, you can take two approaches:

- You can actually change the information in the primary file. When you use this approach, the information that existed in the primary file prior to the transaction processing is lost.
- You can create a copy of the primary file, making the changes in the new version. Then, you can store the previous, parent version of the primary file for a period, in case there are questions or discrepancies regarding the update process. The updated, child version of the file becomes the new primary file used in subsequent processing. This approach is used in a program later in this chapter.

> **Note** When a child file is updated, it becomes a parent, and its parent becomes a grandparent. Organizations create policies concerning the number of generations of backup files they will save before discarding them. The terms *parent* and *child* refer to file backup generations, but they are used for a different purpose in object-oriented programming. You will learn more about object-oriented programming later in this course.

The logic you use to perform a match between primary and transaction file records is similar to the logic you use to perform a merge. As with a merge, you must begin with both files sorted in the same order on the same field. **Figure 7-17** shows the mainline logic for a program that matches files. The primary file contains a customer number, a name, and a field that holds the total dollar amount of all purchases the customer has made previously. The transaction file holds data for sales, including a transaction number, the number of the customer who made the transaction, and the amount of the transaction.

Figure 7-17 Mainline logic for a program that applies transactions to a primary file

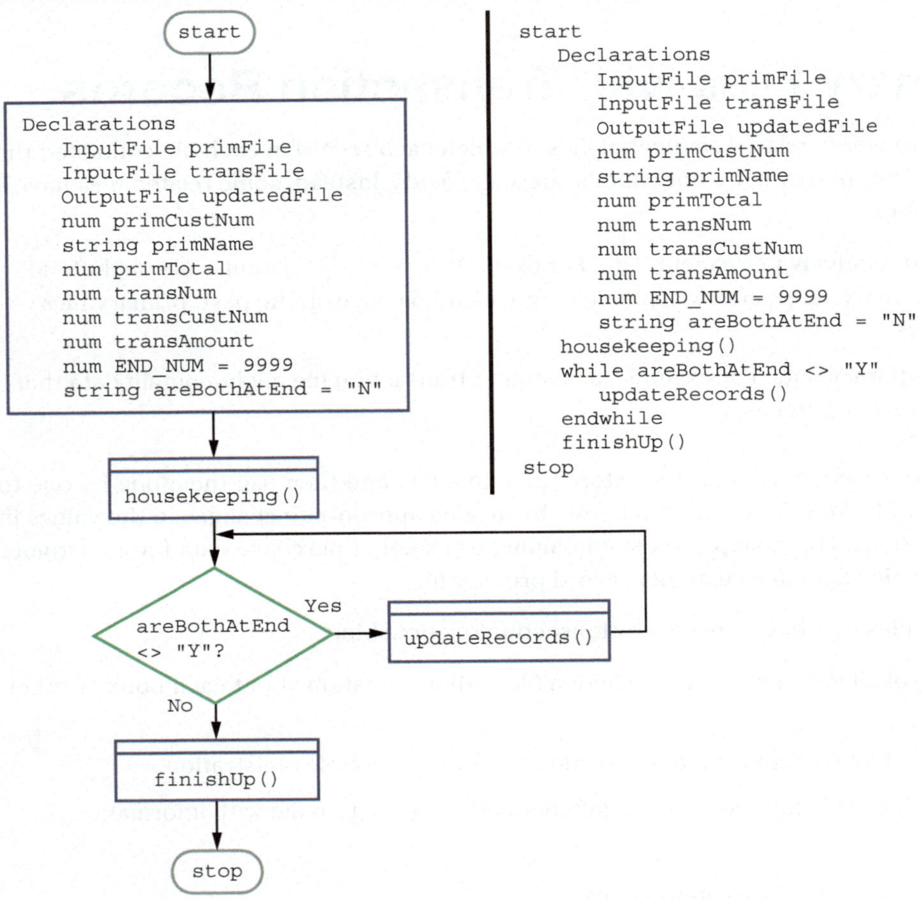

```
start
   Declarations
      InputFile primFile
      InputFile transFile
      OutputFile updatedFile
      num primCustNum
      string primName
      num primTotal
      num transNum
      num transCustNum
      num transAmount
      num END_NUM = 9999
      string areBothAtEnd = "N"
   housekeeping()
   while areBothAtEnd <> "Y"
      updateRecords()
   endwhile
   finishUp()
stop
```

Figure 7-18 contains the `housekeeping()` module for the program and the modules it calls. These modules resemble their counterparts in the file-merging program earlier in the chapter. When the program begins, one record is read from each file. When any file ends, the field used for matching is set to a high numeric value, 9999, and when both files end, a flag variable is set so the mainline logic can test for the end of processing. The assumption is that 9999 is higher than any valid customer number.

Figure 7-18 The `housekeeping()`, `readPrim()`, `readTrans()`, and `checkEnd()` modules for a program that applies transactions to a primary file

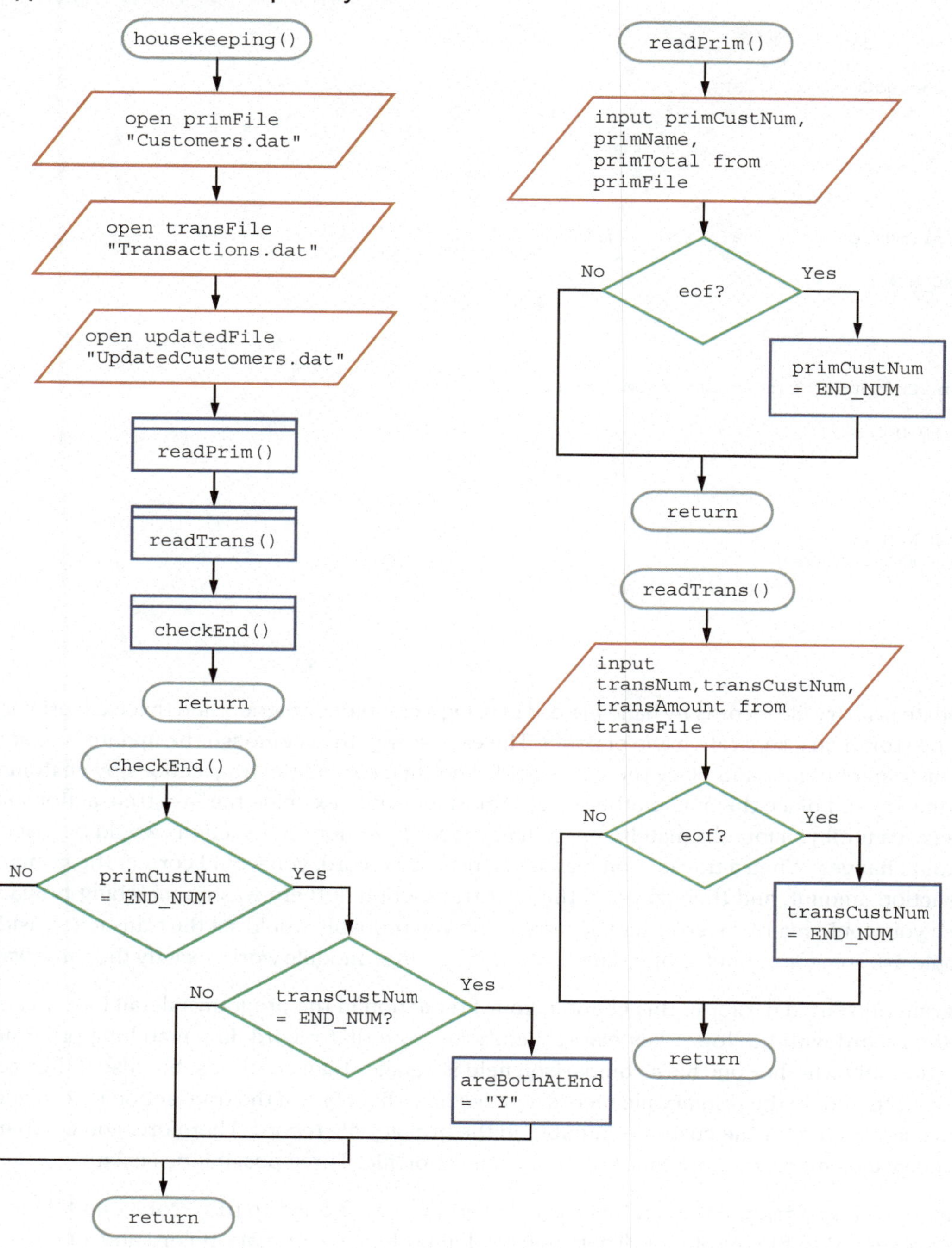

(*Continues*)

Figure 7-18 *(Continued)*

```
housekeeping()
   open primFile "Customers.dat"
   open transFile "Transactions.dat"
   open updatedFile "UpdatedCustomers.dat"
   readPrim()
   readTrans()
   checkEnd()
return

readPrim()
   input primCustNum, primName, primTotal from primFile
   if eof then
      primCustNum = END_NUM
   endif
return

readTrans()
   input transNum, transCustNum, transAmount from transFile
   if eof then
      transCustNum = END_NUM
   endif
return

checkEnd()
   if primCustNum = END_NUM then
      if transCustNum = END_NUM then
         areBothAtEnd = "Y"
      endif
   endif
return
```

Imagine that you will update primary file records by hand instead of using a computer program, and that each primary and transaction record will be stored on a separate piece of paper. The easiest way to accomplish the update is to sort all the primary records by customer number and place them in a stack, and then sort all the transactions by customer number (not transaction number) and place them in another stack. You then would examine the first transaction and look through the primary records until you found a match. Any primary records without transactions would be placed in a "completed" stack without changes. When a transaction matched a primary record, you would correct the primary record using the new transaction amount, and then go on to the next transaction. If there was no matching primary record for a transaction, then you would realize an error had occurred, and you probably would set the transaction aside before continuing so you could ask someone about it later. The `updateRecords()` module works exactly the same way.

In the file-merging program presented earlier in this chapter, your first action in the program's detail loop was to determine which file held the record with the lower key value; then, you wrote that record. In a matching program, you are trying to determine not only whether one file's comparison field is smaller than another's, but also if they are *equal*. In this example, you want to update the primary file record's `primTotal` field only if the transaction record field `transCustNum` contains an exact match for the customer number in the primary file record. Therefore, you compare `primCustNum` from the primary file and `transCustNum` from the transaction file. Three possibilities exist:

- The `transCustNum` value equals `primCustNum`. In this case, you add `transAmount` to `primTotal` and then write the updated primary record to the output file. Then, you read in both a new primary record and a new transaction record.
- The `transCustNum` value is higher than `primCustNum`. This means a sale was not recorded for that customer. That's all right; not every customer makes a transaction every period, so you simply write the original customer record with exactly the same information it contained when input. Then, you get the next customer record to see if this customer made the transaction currently under examination.
- The `transCustNum` value is lower than `primCustNum`. This means you are trying to apply a transaction for which no primary record exists, so there must be an error, because a transaction should always have a primary record. You could handle this error in a variety of ways; here, you will write an error message to an output device before reading the next transaction record. A human operator can then read the message and take appropriate action.

Note | The logic used here assumes that there can be only one transaction per customer. In the exercises at the end of this chapter, you will develop the logic for a program in which the customer can have multiple transactions.

Whether `transCustNum` was higher than, lower than, or equal to `primCustNum`, after reading the next transaction or primary record (or both), you check whether both `primCustNum` and `transCustNum` have been set to *9999*, indicating that the end of the file has been reached. When both are 9999, you set the `areBothAtEnd` flag to `"Y"`.

Figure 7-19 shows the `updateRecords()` module that carries out the logic of the file-matching process. **Figure 7-20** shows some sample data you can use to walk through the logic for this program.

Figure 7-19 The `updateRecords()` module for a program that applies transactions to a primary file

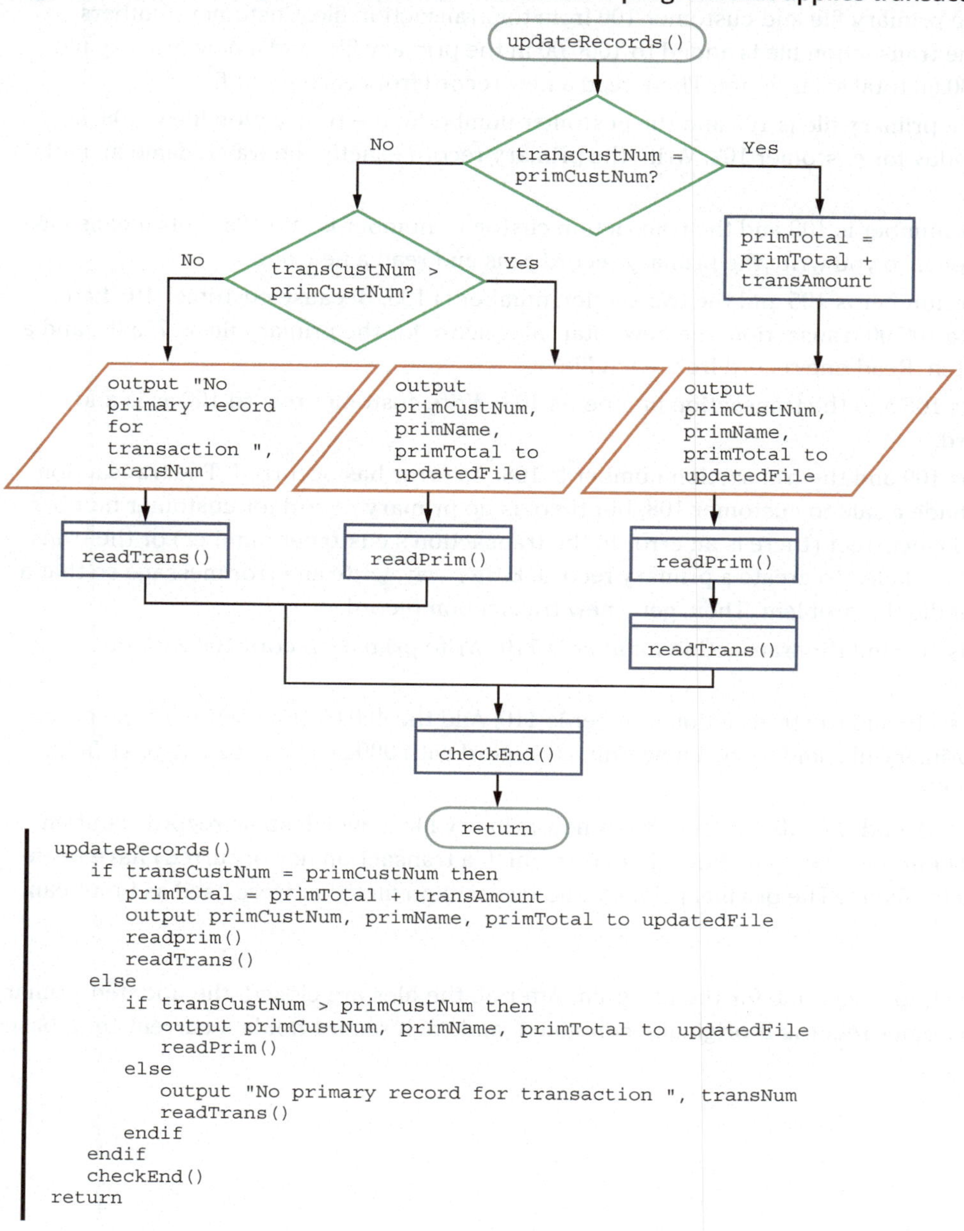


```
updateRecords()
   if transCustNum = primCustNum then
      primTotal = primTotal + transAmount
      output primCustNum, primName, primTotal to updatedFile
      readprim()
      readTrans()
   else
      if transCustNum > primCustNum then
         output primCustNum, primName, primTotal to updatedFile
         readPrim()
      else
         output "No primary record for transaction ", transNum
         readTrans()
      endif
   endif
   checkEnd()
return
```

Figure 7-20 Sample data for a program that applies transactions to a primary file

Primary File		Transaction File	
`primCustNum`	`primTotal`	`transCustNum`	`transAmount`
100	1000.00	100	400.00
102	50.00	105	700.00
103	500.00	108	100.00
105	75.00	110	400.00
106	5000.00		
109	4000.00		
110	500.00		

The program proceeds as follows:

1. Read customer 100 from the primary file and customer 100 from the transaction file. Customer numbers are equal, so 400.00 from the transaction file is added to 1000.00 in the primary file, and a new primary file record is written with a 1400.00 total sales figure. Then, read a new record from each input file.
2. The customer number in the primary file is 102 and the customer number in the transaction file is 105, so there are no transactions today for customer 102. Write the primary record exactly the way it came in, and read a new primary record.
3. Now, the primary customer number is 103 and the transaction customer number is still 105. This means customer 103 has no transactions, so you write the primary record as is and read a new one.
4. Now, the primary customer number is 105 and the transaction number is 105. Because customer 105 had a 75.00 balance and now has a 700.00 transaction, the new total sales figure for the primary file is 775.00, and a new primary record is written. Read one record from each file.
5. Now, the primary number is 106 and the transaction number is 108. Write customer record 106 as is and read another primary record.
6. Now, the primary number is 109 and the transaction number is 108. An error has occurred. The transaction record indicates that you made a sale to customer 108, but there is no primary record for customer number 108. Either the transaction is incorrect (there is an error in the transaction's customer number) or the transaction is correct, but you have failed to create a primary record. Either way, write an error message so that a clerk is notified and can handle the problem. Then, get a new transaction record.
7. Now, the primary number is 109 and the transaction number is 110. Write primary record 109 with no changes and read a new one.
8. Now, the primary number is 110 and the transaction number is 110. Add the 400.00 transaction to the previous 500.00 balance in the primary file, and write a new primary record with 900.00 in the `primTotal` field. Read one record from each file.
9. Because both files are finished, end the job. The result is a new primary file in which some records contain exactly the same data they contained going in, but others (for which a transaction has occurred) have been updated with a new total sales figure. The original primary and transaction files that were used as input can be saved as backups.

Figure 7-21 shows the `finishUp()` module for the program. After all the files are closed, the updated primary customer file contains all the customer records it originally contained, and each record holds a current total based on the recent group of transactions.

Figure 7-21 The `finishUp()` module for a program that applies transactions to a primary file


```
finishUp()
   close primFile
   close transFile
   close updatedFile
return
```

Two Truths & a Lie | Updating Primary Files with Transaction Records

1. A primary file typically holds temporary data related to transaction file records.
2. A transaction file typically holds data that is used to update a primary file.
3. The original version of a primary file is the parent file; the updated version is the child file.

The false statement is #1. A primary file holds relatively permanent data.

7.7 Random Access Files

The files used as examples so far in this chapter are sequential access files, which means that the records are accessed in order from beginning to end. Businesses store data in sequential order when they use the records for **batch processing**, or processing that involves performing the same tasks with many records, one after the other. For example, when a company produces paychecks, the records for the pay period are gathered in a batch and the checks are calculated and printed in sequence. It really doesn't matter whose check is produced first because no checks are distributed to employees until all have been processed. Batch processing usually implies some delay in processing from the time events occur. For example, most companies produce paychecks for time that employees have already worked. Likewise, a customer might order an item but not receive the bill for a month.

> **Note** | Besides indicating a system that works with many records, the term *batch processing* also can mean a system in which many programs can run in sequence without human intervention. Batch processing is an old computing technique, but it is still crucial for such common business tasks as updating records and generating reports.

For many applications, sequential access is inefficient. These applications, known as **real-time applications**, require that a record be accessed immediately while a client is waiting. A program in which the user makes direct requests is an **interactive program**. For example, if a customer calls a department store with a question about a monthly bill, the customer service representative does not need or want to access every customer account in sequence (perhaps tens of thousands) to find the caller's account. Instead, customer service representatives require **random access files**, files in which records can physically be located in any order. Files in which records must be accessed immediately also are called **instant access files**. Because they enable clients to locate a particular record directly (without reading all of the preceding records), random access files are also called **direct access files**. In many programming languages, you can declare a random access file with a statement similar to the following:

```
RandomFile customerFile
```

This statement associates the identifier `customerFile` with a stored file that can be accessed randomly. You can use read, write, and close operations with a random access file just as you can with a sequential file. With random access files, however, you have the additional capability to find a record directly. For example, you might be able to use a statement like the following to find customer number 712 in a random access file:

```
seek record 712
```

This feature is particularly useful in real-time, interactive programs. Consider a business with 20,000 customer accounts. When a service representative wants to find the balance for the customer who has the 14,607th record in the file, it is convenient for the representative to be able to access the 14,607th record directly instead of first reading in data for the 14,606 records that precede the requested one. **Figure 7-22** illustrates this concept.

The precise techniques for working with random access files vary among programming languages. You will learn more about this concept when you study a programming language.

Figure 7-22 Accessing a record in a sequential file and in a random access file

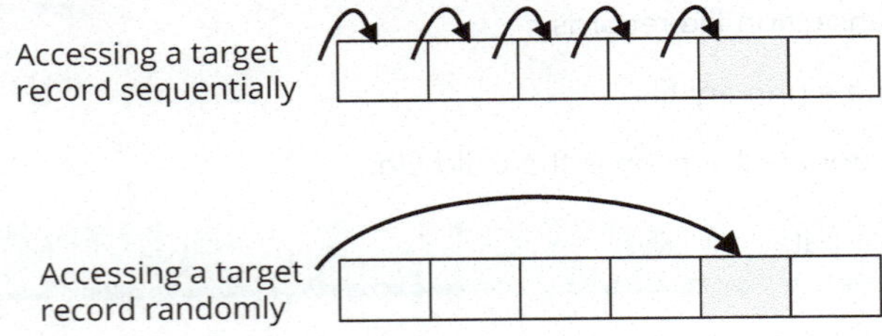

Two Truths & a Lie | Random Access Files

1. A batch program typically uses instant access files.
2. In a real-time application, a record is accessed immediately while a client is waiting.
3. An interactive program usually uses random access files.

The false statement is #1. A batch program typically uses sequential files; interactive programs use random, instant access files.

Summary

- A computer file is a collection of data stored on a nonvolatile device in a computer system. Although the contents of files differ, each file occupies space on a section of a storage device, and each has a name and specific set of times associated with it. Computer files are organized in directories or folders. A file's complete list of directories is its path.
- Data items in a file usually are stored in a hierarchy. Characters are letters, numbers, and special symbols, such as *A*, *7*, and *$*. Fields are data items that each represent a single attribute of a record; they are composed of one or more characters. Records are groups of fields that go together for some logical reason. Files are groups of related records.

- When you use a data file in a program, you must declare the file and open it; opening a file associates an internal program identifier with the name of a physical file on a storage device. A sequential file is a file in which records are stored one after another in some order. When you read from a file, the data is copied into memory. When you write to a file, the data is copied from memory to a storage device. When you are done with a file, you close it.
- A control break program is one that reads a sorted, sequential file and performs special processing based on a change in one or more fields in each record in the file.
- Merging files involves combining two or more files while maintaining the sequential order of the records.
- Some related sequential files are primary files that hold relatively permanent data and transaction files that hold more temporary data. Commonly, you gather transactions for a period, store them in a file, and then use them one by one to update matching records in a primary file.
- Real-time, interactive applications require random access files in which records can be located and retrieved in any order. Files in which records must be accessed immediately are also called *instant access files* and *direct access files*.

Key Terms

ascending order
backup file
batch processing
binary file
byte
characters
child file
closing a file
computer file
control break
control break field
control break program
control break report
data hierarchy
database
default input and output devices
delimiter
descending order
direct access files
directories
fields
file's path
filename
filename extension
files
folders
gigabytes
instant access files
interactive program
kilobytes
megabytes
merging files
opening a file
parent file
permanent storage device
primary file
random access files
reading from a file
real-time applications
records
sequential files
single-level control break
sorting
text file
transaction file
update a primary file
writing to a file

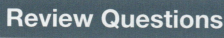

Review Questions

1. Random access memory is ______________. (7.1)
   a. volatile
   b. permanent
   c. persistent
   d. continual
2. Text files usually contain ______________. (7.1)
   a. data that can be read in a text editor
   b. images
   c. music
   d. both images and music

3. Every file on a storage device _______________. (7.1)
   a. has two names
   b. has a size
   c. has been backed up
   d. is a primary data file

4. Which of the following is true regarding the data hierarchy? (7.2)
   a. Fields contain records.
   b. Characters contain fields.
   c. Fields contain files.
   d. Files contain records.

5. The process of _______________ a file locates it on a storage device and associates a variable name within your program with the file. (7.3)
   a. declaring
   b. closing
   c. opening
   d. defining

6. When you write to a file, you _______________. (7.3)
   a. move data from a storage device to memory
   b. copy data from a storage device to memory
   c. move data from memory to a storage device
   d. copy data from memory to a storage device

7. Unlike when you print a report or display information on a screen, when a program's output is a data file, you do not _______________. (7.3)
   a. include explanations or formatting such as dollar signs
   b. open the file
   c. output all of the input fields
   d. close the file

8. When you close a file, it _______________. (7.3)
   a. becomes associated with an internal identifier
   b. cannot be reopened
   c. is no longer available to the program
   d. ceases to exist

9. A file in which records are stored one after another in order based on the contents of a field is a(n) _______________ file. (7.3)
   a. temporal
   b. alphabetical
   c. random
   d. sequential

10. When you combine two or more sorted files while maintaining their sequential order based on a field, you are _______________ the files. (7.5)
    a. tracking
    b. collating
    c. merging
    d. absorbing

11. A control break occurs when a program _______________. (7.4)
    a. pauses to perform special processing based on the value of a field
    b. ends prematurely, before all records have been processed
    c. takes one of two alternate courses of action for every record
    d. passes logical control to a module contained within another program

12. Which of the following is an example of a control break report? (7.4)
    a. a list of all customers of a business in zip code order, with a count of the number of customers who reside in each zip code
    b. a list of all students in a school, arranged in alphabetical order, with a total count at the end of the report
    c. a list of all employees in a company, with a *Retain* or *Dismiss* message following each employee record
    d. a list of medical clinic patients who have not seen a doctor for at least two years

13. A control break field ________________. (7.4)

    a. always is output prior to any group of records on a control break report
    b. always is output after any group of records on a control break report
    c. never is output on a report
    d. causes special processing to occur

14. Whenever a control break occurs during record processing in any control break program, you must ________________. (7.4)

    a. declare a control break field
    b. set the control break field to 0
    c. update the value in the control break field
    d. output the control break field

15. Assume that you are writing a program to merge two files named *FallStudents* and *SpringStudents*. Each file contains a list of students enrolled in a programming logic course during the semester indicated, and each file is sorted in student ID number order. After the program compares two records and subsequently writes a *FallStudents* record to output, the next step is to ________________. (7.5)

    a. read a *SpringStudents* record
    b. read a *FallStudents* record
    c. write a *SpringStudents* record
    d. write another *FallStudents* record

16. When you merge records from two or more sequential files, the usual case is that the records in the files ________________. (7.5)

    a. contain the same data
    b. have the same format
    c. are identical in number
    d. are sorted on different fields

17. A file that holds more permanent data than a transaction file is a(n) ________________ file. (7.6)

    a. perpetual
    b. primary
    c. key
    d. irreversible

18. A transaction file is often used to ________________ another file. (7.6)

    a. augment
    b. remove
    c. verify
    d. update

19. The saved version of a file that does not contain the most recently applied transactions is known as a ________________ file. (7.6)

    a. reflective
    b. child
    c. parent
    d. relative

20. Random access files are used most frequently in all of the following except ________________. (7.7)

    a. interactive programs
    b. batch processing
    c. real-time applications
    d. programs requiring direct access

Programming Exercises

Your downloadable files for Chapter 7 include one or more comma-delimited sample data files for each exercise in this section. You might want to use these files in any of several ways:

- You can look at the file contents to better understand the types of data each program uses.
- You can use the file contents as sample data when you desk-check the logic of your flowcharts or pseudocode.

- You can use the files as input files if you implement the solutions in a programming language and write programs that accept file input.
- You can use the data as guides for entering appropriate values if you implement the solutions in a programming language and write interactive programs.

1. Page Turner Publishing edits multivolume manuscripts for many authors. For each volume, they want a label that contains the author's name, the title of the work, and a volume number in the form *Volume 9 of 9*. For example, a set of three volumes requires three labels: *Volume 1 of 3*, *Volume 2 of 3*, and *Volume 3 of 3*. Design an application that reads records that contain an author's name, the title of the work, and the number of volumes. The application must read the records until `eof` is encountered and produce enough labels for each work. (7.3)

2. Geraldine's Landscaping Service and Gerard's Landscaping Service are merging their businesses and want to merge their customer files. Each file contains a customer number, last name, address, and property area in square feet, and each file is in customer number order. Design the logic for a program that merges the two files into one file containing all customers in customer number order. Assume there are no identical customer numbers. (7.5)

3. Laramie Park District has files of participants in its summer and winter programs this year. Each file is in participant ID number order and contains additional fields for first name, last name, age, and class taken (for example, *Beginning Swimming*).

   a. Design the logic for a program that merges the files for summer and winter programs to create a list of the first and last names of all participants for the year in ID number order.

   b. Modify the program so that if a participant has more than one record, the participant's ID number and name are output only once.

   c. Modify the program so that if a participant has more than one record, the ID number and name are output only once along with a count of the total number of classes the participant has taken. (7.5)

4. The Apgar Medical group keeps a patient file for each doctor in the office. Each record contains the patient's first and last name, home address, and birth year. The records are sorted in ascending birth year order. Two doctors, Dr. Best and Dr. Sosa, have formed a partnership.

   a. Design the logic that produces a merged list of patients' names in ascending order by birth year.

   b. Modify the program so that it does not display patients' names, but only produces a count of the number of patients born each year. (7.5)

5. Gimme Shelter Roofers maintains a file of past customers, including a customer number, name, address, date of job, and price of job. It also maintains a file of estimates given for jobs not yet performed; this file contains a customer number, name, address, proposed date of job, and proposed price. Each file is in customer number order. Design the logic that merges the two files to produce one combined file of all customers, whether past or proposed, with no duplicates; when a customer who has been given an estimate is also a past customer, use the proposed data. (7.5)

6. The Curl Up and Dye Beauty Salon maintains a primary file that contains a record for each of its clients. Fields in the primary file include the client's ID number, first name, last name, and total amount spent this year. Every week, a transaction file is produced. It contains a customer's ID number, the service received (for example, *Manicure*), and the price paid. Each file is sorted in ID number order.

   a. Design the logic for a program that matches the primary and transaction file records and updates the total paid for each client by adding the current week's price paid to the cumulative total. Not all clients purchase services each week. The output is the updated primary file and an error report that lists any transaction records for which no primary record exists.

b. Modify the program to output a coupon for a free haircut each time a client exceeds $1,000 in services. The coupon, which contains the client's name and an appropriate congratulatory message, is output during the execution of the update program when a client total surpasses $1,000. Make sure that only one coupon is printed per client, even if the client has purchased multiple services to pass the $1,000 cutoff value. (7.6)

7. The Timely Talent Temporary Help Agency maintains an employee primary file that contains an employee ID number, last name, first name, address, and hourly rate for each temporary worker. The file has been sorted in employee ID number order. Each week, a transaction file is created with a job number, job address, customer name, employee ID, and hours worked for every job filled by Timely Talent workers. The transaction file is also sorted in employee ID order.

   a. Design the logic for a program that matches the current week's transaction file records to the primary file and outputs one line for each transaction, indicating job number, employee ID number, hours worked, hourly rate, and gross pay. Assume that each temporary worker works at most one job per week. Output one line for each worker, even if the worker has completed no jobs during the current week.

   b. Modify the help agency program to output lines only for workers who have completed at least one job during the current week.

   c. Modify the help agency program so that any temporary worker can work any number of separate jobs during the week. Output one line for each job that week.

   d. Modify the help agency program so that it accumulates the worker's total pay for all jobs in a week and outputs one line per worker. (7.6)

Performing Maintenance

1. A file named *MAINTENANCE07-01.txt* is included in the Chapter07 folder of your downloadable student files. Assume that this program is a working program in your organization and that it needs modifications as described in the comments (lines that begin with two slashes) at the beginning of the file. Your job is to alter the program to meet the new specifications. (7.5)

Debugging Exercises

1. Your downloadable files for Chapter 7 include *DEBUG07-01.txt*, *DEBUG07-02.txt*, *DEBUG07-03.txt*, and *DEBUG07-04.jpg*. Each file starts with some comments that describe the problem. Comments are lines that begin with two slashes (//). Each file contains pseudocode or a flowchart that has mistakes. Find and correct all the bugs.

Game Zone

1. The International Rock Paper Scissors Society holds regional and national championships. Each region holds a semifinal competition in which contestants play 500 games of Rock Paper Scissors. The top 20 competitors in each region are invited to the national finals. Assume that you are provided with files for the East, Midwest, and Western regions. Each file contains the following fields for the top 20 competitors: last name, first name, and number of games won. The records in each file are sorted in alphabetical order by last name. Merge the three files to create a file of the top 60 competitors who will compete in the national championship. (7.5)

2. Design a guessing game that prompts the player for a player name. The application then generates a random number between 1 and 100, and the player tries to guess it. After each guess, display a message indicating whether the player's guess was correct, too high, or too low. When the player eventually guesses the correct number, display a score that represents a count of the number of required guesses. After a player plays the game exactly five times, save the best (lowest) score from the five games to a file. If the player's name already exists in the file, update the record with the new lowest score. If the player's name does not already exist in the file, create a new record for the player. After the file is updated, display all the best scores stored in the file. (7.3)

Chapter 8

Advanced Data Handling Concepts

Learning Objectives

When you complete this chapter, you will be able to:

8.1 Explain the need for sorting data

8.2 Describe the bubble sort algorithm

8.3 Sort records on multiple field values

8.4 Describe other sorting algorithms

8.5 Use multidimensional arrays

8.6 Describe indexed files and linked lists

8.1 Understanding the Need for Sorting Data

Stored data records exist in some type of order; that is, one record is first, another second, and so on. When records are in **sequential order**, they are arranged one after another on the basis of the value in one or more fields. Examples include employee records stored:

- In numeric order by Social Security number
- In numeric order by department number
- In alphabetical order by last name
- In numeric order by date hired within alphabetical order by department name

Even if the records do not seem to be stored in any particular order—for example, if they are in the order in which a clerk felt like entering them—they still exist one after the other, although probably not in the order desired for processing or viewing. Data records that are stored randomly, or that are not in the order needed for an application, need to be sorted.

Sorting records is the process of placing them in order based on the contents of one or more fields. You can sort data either in ascending order, arranging records from lowest to highest value within a field, or in descending order, arranging records from highest to lowest value.

> **Note** The sorting process usually is reserved for a relatively small number of data items. If thousands of customer records are stored, and they frequently need to be accessed in order based on different fields (alphabetical order by customer name one day, zip code order the next), the records would probably not be sorted at all, but would be indexed or linked. You learn about indexing and linking later in this chapter.

Examples of occasions when you would need to sort records might include:

- A college stores student records in ascending order by student ID number, but the registrar wants to view the data in descending order by credit hours earned so students who are close to graduation can be identified.
- A department store maintains customer records in ascending order by customer number, but at the end of a billing period, the credit manager wants to contact customers whose balances are 90 or more days overdue. The manager wants to list these overdue customers in descending order by the amount owed so the customers with the largest debt can be contacted first.
- A sales manager keeps records for salespeople in alphabetical order by last name, but the manager needs to list the annual sales figure for each salesperson so the median annual sale amount can be calculated.

> **Note** The **median** value in a list is the value of the middle item when the values are listed in order. (If the list contains an even number of values, the median is halfway between the two middle values.) The median is not the same as the arithmetic average, or **mean**. The median is often used as a statistic because it represents a more typical case—half the values are below it and half are above it. Unlike the median, the mean is skewed by a few very high or low values. For example, if five quiz scores are 2, 3, 3, 4, and 10, then the median value is 3, which is a typical score. However, the mean is 4.4, which is higher than the typical score because it is skewed by the 10.

- A store manager wants to create a control break report in which individual sales are listed in order in groups by their department. When you create a control break report, the records must have been sorted in order by the control break field.

When computers sort data, they always use numeric values to make comparisons between values. This is clear when you sort records by fields such as a numeric customer ID or balance due. However, even alphabetic sorts are numeric, because computer data items are stored as numbers using a series of 0s and 1s. Ordinary computer users seldom think about the numeric codes behind the letters, numbers, and punctuation marks they enter from their keyboards or see on a monitor. However, they see the consequence of the values behind letters when they see data sorted in alphabetical order. In every popular computer coding scheme, *B* is numerically one greater than *A*, and *y* is numerically one less than *z*. Because *A* is always less than *B*, *B* is always less than *C*, and so on, alphabetic sorts are ascending sorts. Unfortunately, your system dictates whether an uppercase *A* is represented by a number that is greater or smaller than the number representing a lowercase *a*. Therefore, if data items are not input using consistent capitalization, then the programmer must make conversions before sorting them.

> **Note** The most popular coding schemes include ASCII, Unicode, and EBCDIC. In each code, a number represents a specific computer character. Appendix A contains additional information about these codes.

As a professional programmer, you might never have to write a program that sorts data for one or more of the following reasons:

- Programmers in your organization might already have created a sorting module you can use.
- Your organization might have purchased a generic, "canned" sorting program.
- You might be using a language for which the compiler includes built-in modules that can sort data for you.

However, even if you never have to create code that sorts data, it is beneficial to understand the sorting process so that you can write a special-purpose sort when needed. Understanding the sorting process also improves your array-manipulating skills.

Two Truths & a Lie | Understanding the Need for Sorting Data

1. When you sort data in ascending order, you arrange records from lowest to highest based on the value in a specific field.
2. Normal alphabetical order, in which *A* precedes *B*, is descending order.
3. When computers sort data, they use numeric values to make comparisons, even when string values are compared.

The false statement is #2. Normal alphabetical order is ascending.

8.2 Using the Bubble Sort Algorithm

When you learn a method such as sorting, programmers say you are learning an algorithm—a set of instructions that accomplish a task. In this section, you will learn about the bubble sort algorithm for sorting a list of simple values; later in this chapter, you will learn more about how to sort records on multiple fields.

One of the simplest sorting techniques to understand is a **bubble sort**, in which items in a list are compared with each other in pairs. You can use a bubble sort to arrange data items in either ascending or descending order. A bubble sort examines items in a list, and when an item is out of order, it trades places, or is swapped, with the item below it. With an ascending bubble sort, after each adjacent pair of items in a list has been compared once, the largest item in the list will have "sunk" to the bottom. After many passes through the list, the smallest items rise to the top like bubbles in a carbonated drink. A bubble sort is sometimes called a *sinking sort*. To understand the bubble sort algorithm, you first must learn about swapping values.

Understanding Swapping Values

A concept central to many sorting algorithms, including the bubble sort, is the idea of swapping values. When you **swap values** stored in two variables, you exchange their values; you set the first variable equal to the value of the second, and the second variable equal to the value of the first. However, there is a trick to swapping any two values. Assume that you have declared two variables as follows:

```
num score1 = 90
num score2 = 85
```

You want to swap the values so that `score1` is 85 and `score2` is 90. If you first assign `score1` to `score2` using a statement such as `score2 = score1`, both `score1` and `score2` hold 90, and the value 85 is lost. Similarly, if you first assign `score2` to `score1` using a statement such as `score1 = score2`, both variables hold 85, and the value 90 is lost.

To correctly swap two values, you create a temporary variable to hold a copy of one of the scores so it doesn't get lost. Then, you can accomplish the swap, as shown in **Figure 8-1**. First, the value in `score2`, 85, is assigned to a temporary holding variable named `temp`. Then, the `score1` value, 90, is assigned to `score2`. At this point, both `score1` and `score2` hold 90. Then, the 85 in `temp` is assigned to `score1`. Therefore, after the swap process, `score1` holds 85 and `score2` holds 90.

Figure 8-1 Program segment that swaps two values

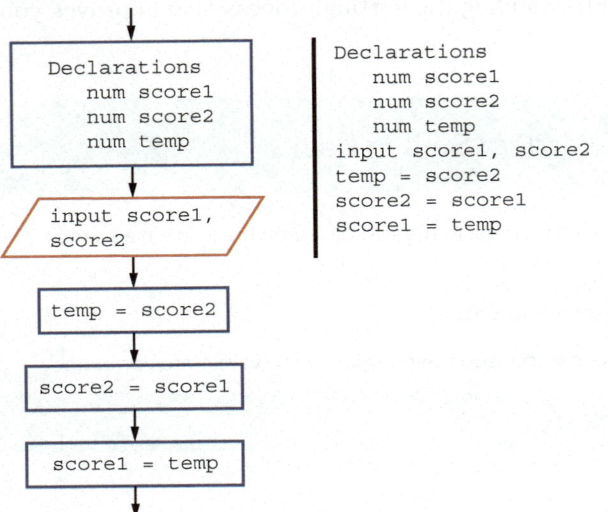

```
Declarations
   num score1
   num score2
   num temp
input score1, score2
temp = score2
score2 = score1
score1 = temp
```

In Figure 8-1, you could accomplish identical results by assigning `score1` to `temp`, assigning `score2` to `score1`, and finally assigning `temp` to `score2`.

Understanding the Bubble Sort

Assume that you want to sort five student test scores in ascending order. **Figure 8-2** shows a program in which a constant is declared to hold an array's size, and then the array is declared to hold five scores. (The other variables and constants will be discussed in the next paragraphs when they are used.) The program calls three main procedures—one to input the five scores, one to sort them, and the final one to display the sorted result.

Figure 8-2 Mainline logic for program that accepts, sorts, and displays scores

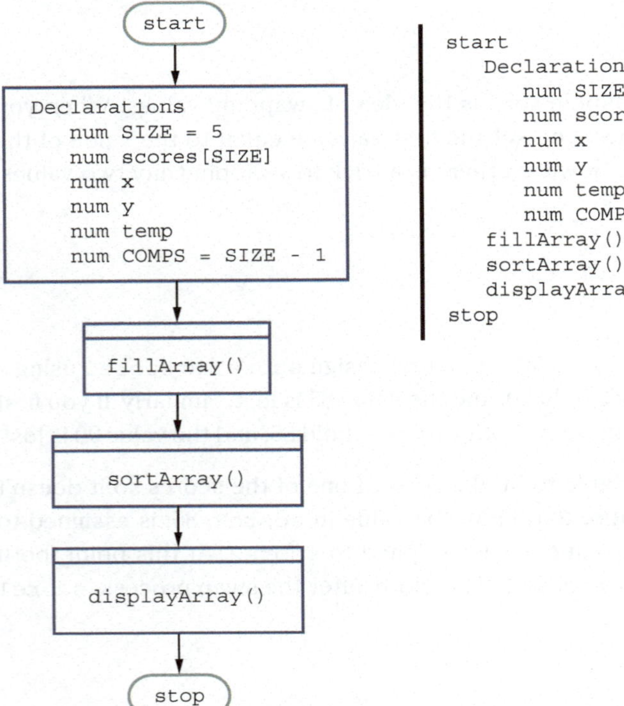

```
start
   Declarations
      num SIZE = 5
      num scores[SIZE]
      num x
      num y
      num temp
      num COMPS = SIZE - 1
   fillArray()
   sortArray()
   displayArray()
stop
```

Note Many modern languages allow you to use a built-in value as an array size, which relieves you of the requirement to declare a constant for the size. Because the name of the built-in value varies among programming languages, the examples in this chapter use a declared, named constant.

Figure 8-3 shows the `fillArray()` module. Within the module, a subscript, `x`, is initialized to 0 and each array element is filled in turn. After a user enters five scores, control returns to the main program.

Figure 8-3 The `fillArray()` module

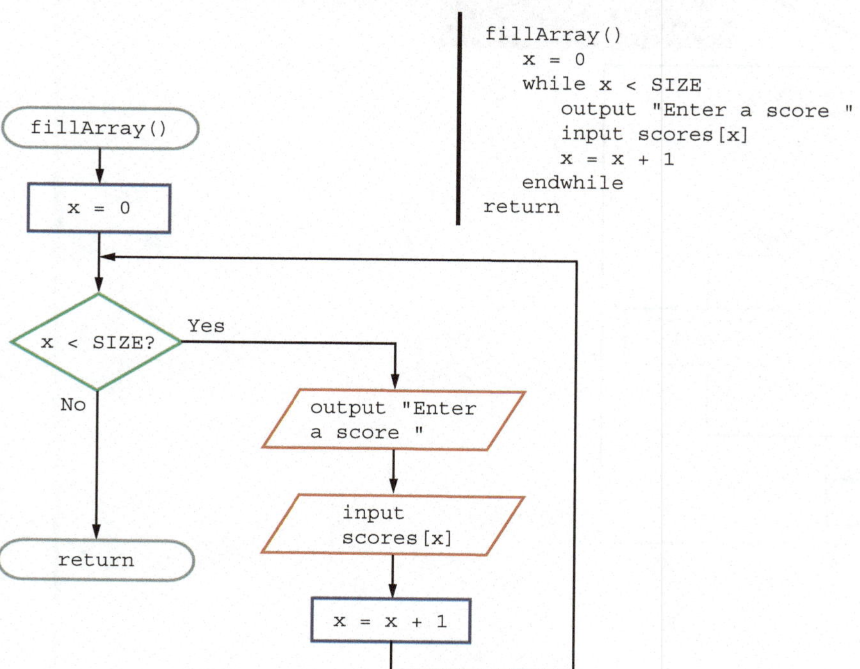
fillArray()
x = 0
while x < SIZE
output "Enter a score "
input scores[x]
x = x + 1
endwhile
return
fillArray()
x = 0
x < SIZE?
Yes
No
output "Enter a score "
input scores[x]
x = x + 1
return

The `sortArray()` module in **Figure 8-4** sorts the array elements by making a series of comparisons of adjacent element values and swapping them if they are out of order. To begin sorting this list of scores, you compare the first two scores, `scores[0]` and `scores[1]`. If they are out of order—that is, if `scores[0]` is larger than `scores[1]`—you want to reverse their positions, or swap their values.

For example, assume that the five entered scores are:

```
scores[0] = 90
scores[1] = 85
scores[2] = 65
scores[3] = 95
scores[4] = 75
```

In this list, `scores[0]` is 90 and `scores[1]` is 85; you want to exchange the values of the two elements so that the smaller value ends up earlier in the array. You call the `swap()` module, which places the scores in slightly better order than they were originally. **Figure 8-5** shows the `swap()` module. This module switches any two adjacent elements in the `scores` array.

Figure 8-4 The incomplete `sortArray()` module

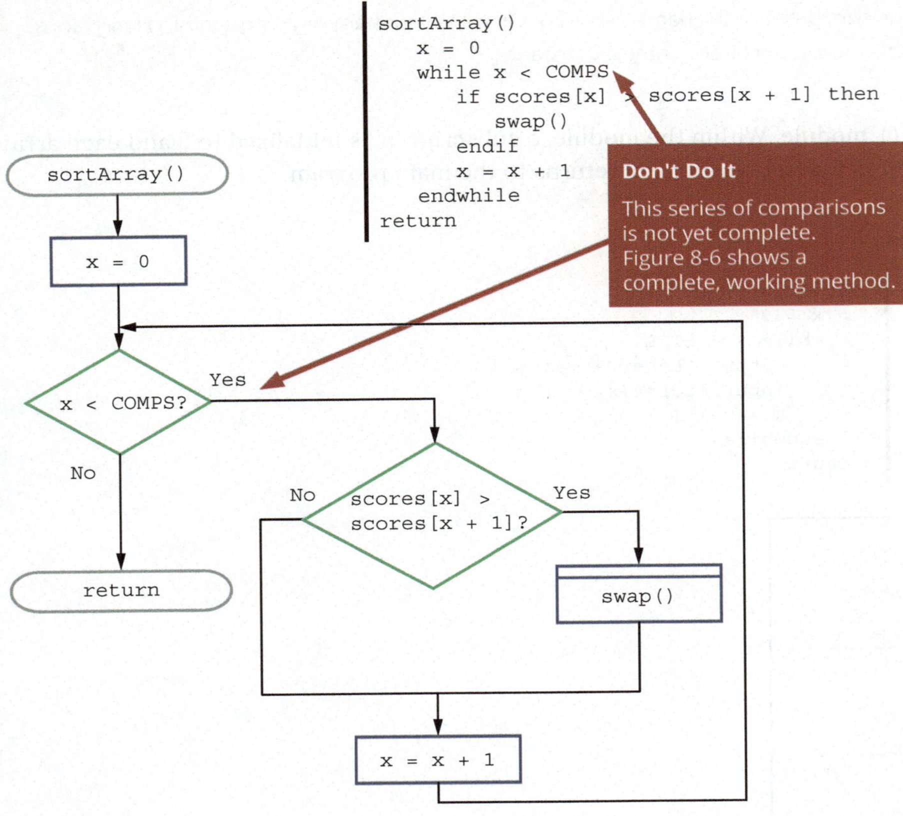
sortArray()
x = 0
x < COMPS?
Yes
No
scores[x] > scores[x + 1]?
No
Yes
swap()
return
x = x + 1
sortArray()
x = 0
while x < COMPS
if scores[x] > scores[x + 1] then
swap()
endif
x = x + 1
endwhile
return
Don't Do It
This series of comparisons is not yet complete. Figure 8-6 shows a complete, working method.

Figure 8-5 The `swap()` module

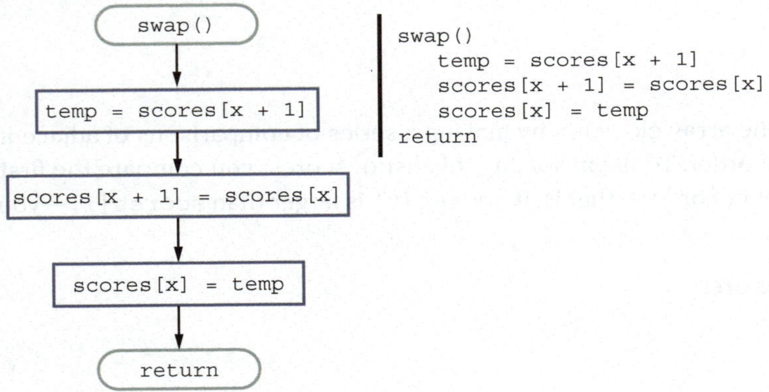
swap()
temp = scores[x + 1]
scores[x + 1] = scores[x]
scores[x] = temp
return
swap()
temp = scores[x + 1]
scores[x + 1] = scores[x]
scores[x] = temp
return

In Figure 8-4, the number of comparisons made is based on the value of the constant named `COMPS`, which was initialized to the value of `SIZE - 1`. That is, for an array of size 5, the `COMPS` constant will be 4. Therefore, the following comparisons are made:

```
scores[0] > scores[1]
scores[1] > scores[2]
scores[2] > scores[3]
scores[3] > scores[4]
```

Each element in the array is compared to the element that follows it. When `x` becomes `COMPS`, the `while` loop ends. If the loop continued when `x` became equal to `COMPS`, then the next comparison would use `scores[4]` and `scores[5]`. This would cause an error because the highest allowed subscript in a five-element array is 4. You must evaluate the expression `scores[x] > scores[x + 1]` four times—when `x` is 0, 1, 2, and 3.

For an ascending sort, you need to perform the `swap()` module whenever any given element of the `scores` array has a value greater than the next element. For any `x`, if the *x*th element is not greater than the element at position `x + 1`, the swap should not take place. For example, when `scores[x]` is 90 and `scores[x + 1]` is 85, a swap should occur. On the other hand, when `scores[x]` is 65 and `scores[x + 1]` is 95, then no swap should occur.

For a descending sort in which you want to end up with the highest value first, you would write the decision so that you perform the switch when `scores[x]` is *less than* `scores[x + 1]`.

As a complete example of how this application works using an ascending sort, suppose that you have these original scores:

```
scores[0] = 90
scores[1] = 85
scores[2] = 65
scores[3] = 95
scores[4] = 75
```

The logic of the `sortArray()` module proceeds like this:

1. Set `x` to 0.
2. The value of `x` is less than 4 (`COMPS`), so enter the loop.
3. Compare `scores[x]`, 90, to `scores[x + 1]`, 85. The two scores are out of order, so they are swapped.

   The list is now:

   ```
   scores[0] = 85
   scores[1] = 90
   scores[2] = 65
   scores[3] = 95
   scores[4] = 75
   ```

4. After the swap, add 1 to `x`, so `x` is 1.
5. Return to the top of the loop. The value of `x` is less than 4, so enter the loop a second time.
6. Compare `scores[x]`, 90, to `scores[x + 1]`, 65. These two values are out of order, so swap them.

   Now the result is:

   ```
   scores[0] = 85
   scores[1] = 65
   scores[2] = 90
   scores[3] = 95
   scores[4] = 75
   ```

7. Add 1 to `x`, so `x` is now 2.
8. Return to the top of the loop. The value of `x` is less than 4, so enter the loop.
9. Compare `scores[x]`, 90, to `scores[x + 1]`, 95. These values are in order, so no swap is necessary.

10. Add 1 to x, making it 3.
11. Return to the top of the loop. The value of x is less than 4, so enter the loop.
12. Compare `scores[x]`, 95, to `scores[x + 1]`, 75. These two values are out of order, so swap them.

    Now the list is as follows:

    ```
    scores[0] = 85
    scores[1] = 65
    scores[2] = 90
    scores[3] = 75
    scores[4] = 95
    ```

13. Add 1 to x, making it 4.
14. Return to the top of the loop. The value of x is 4, so do not enter the loop again.

When x reaches 4, every element in the list has been compared with the one adjacent to it. The highest score, 95, has "sunk" to the bottom of the list. However, the scores still are not in order. They are in slightly better ascending order than they were when the process began, because the largest value is at the bottom of the list, but they are still out of order. You need to repeat the entire procedure so that 85 and 65 (the current `scores[0]` and `scores[1]` values) can switch places, and 90 and 75 (the current `scores[2]` and `scores[3]` values) can switch places. Then, the scores will be 65, 85, 75, 90, and 95. You will have to go through the list yet again to swap 85 and 75.

As a matter of fact, if the scores had started in the worst possible order (95, 90, 85, 75, 65), the comparison process would have to take place four times. In other words, you would have to pass through the list of values four times, making appropriate swaps, before the numbers would appear in perfect ascending order. You need to place the loop in Figure 8-4 within another loop that executes four times.

Figure 8-6 shows the complete logic for the `sortArray()` module. The module uses a loop control variable named y to cycle through the list of scores four times. With an array of five elements, it takes four comparisons to work through the array once, comparing each pair, and it takes four sets of those comparisons to ensure that every element in the entire array is in sorted order. In the `sortArray()` module in Figure 8-6, x must be reset to 0 for each new value of y so that the comparisons always start at the top of the list.

When you sort the elements in an array this way, you use nested loops—an inner loop that swaps out-of-order pairs, and an outer loop that goes through the list multiple times. The general rules for making comparisons with the bubble sort are:

- The greatest number of pair comparisons you need to make during each loop is *one less* than the number of elements in the array. You use an inner loop to make the pair comparisons.
- The number of times you need to process the list of values is *one less* than the number of elements in the array. You use an outer loop to control the number of times you walk through the list.

As an example, if you want to sort a 10-element array, you make nine pair comparisons on each of nine iterations through the loop, executing a total of 81 score comparison statements.

The last module called by the score-sorting program in Figure 8-2 is the one that displays the sorted array contents. **Figure 8-7** shows this module.

Figure 8-6 The completed `sortArray()` module

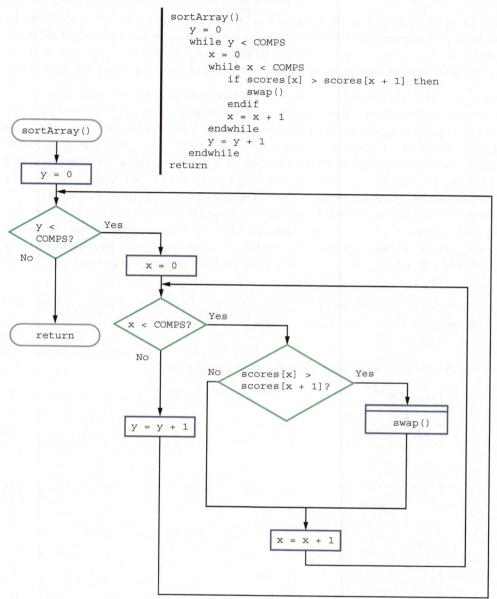

```
sortArray()
   y = 0
   while y < COMPS
      x = 0
      while x < COMPS
         if scores[x] > scores[x + 1] then
            swap()
         endif
         x = x + 1
      endwhile
      y = y + 1
   endwhile
return
```

Figure 8-7 The `displayArray()` module

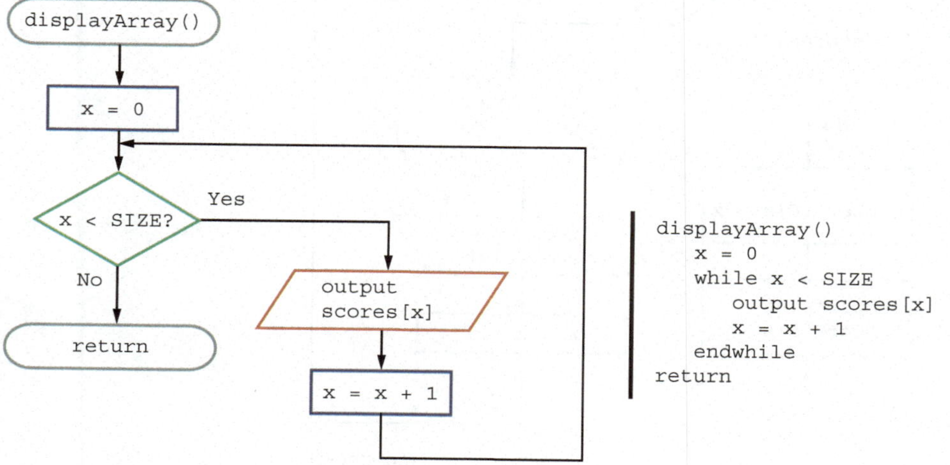


```
displayArray()
   x = 0
   while x < SIZE
      output scores[x]
      x = x + 1
   endwhile
return
```

Sorting a List of Variable Size

In the score-sorting program in the previous section, a `SIZE` constant was initialized to the number of elements to be sorted at the start of the program. At times, however, you don't want to create such a value because you might not know how many array elements will hold valid values. For example, on one program run you might want to sort only three or four scores, and on another run you might want to sort 20. In other words, the size of the list to be sorted might vary.

To keep track of the number of elements stored in an array, you can count the data items and create an application like the one shown in **Figure 8-8** that can sort up to 100 items. As in the original version of the program, you call the `fillArray()` module, and when you input each score, you increase `x` by 1 to place each new score into a successive element of the `scores` array. After you input one value and place it in the first element of the `scores` array, `x` is 1. After a second score is input and placed in `scores[1]`, `x` is 2, and so on. After you reach the end of input, `x` holds the number of scores that have been placed in the array, so you can store `x` in `numberOfEls`, and compute `comparisons` as `numberOfEls - 1`. With this approach, it doesn't matter if there are not enough values to fill the `scores` array. The `sortArray()` and `displayArray()` modules use `comparisons` and `numberOfEls` instead of `COMPS` and `SIZE` to process the array. For example, if 35 scores are input, `numberOfEls` will be set to 35 in the `fillArray()` module, and when the program sorts, it will use 34 as a cutoff point for the number of pair comparisons to make. The sorting program will never make pair comparisons on array elements 36 through 100—those elements will just "sit there," never being involved in a comparison or swap.

> **Note** | In the `fillArray()` module in Figure 8-8, notice that a priming read has been added. If the user enters the `QUIT` value at the first input, then the number of elements to be sorted will be 0.

Figure 8-8 Score-sorting application in which the number of elements to sort can vary

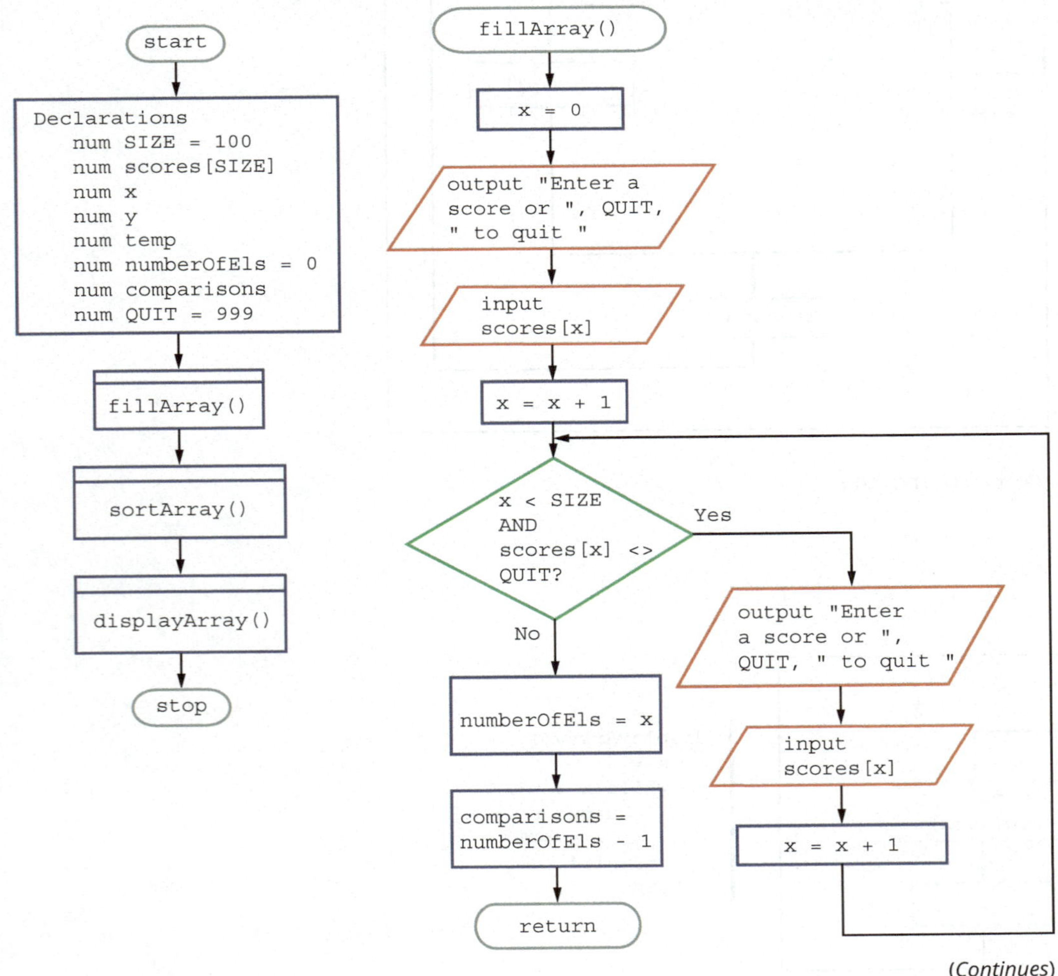

(*Continues*)

Figure 8-8 (*Continued*)

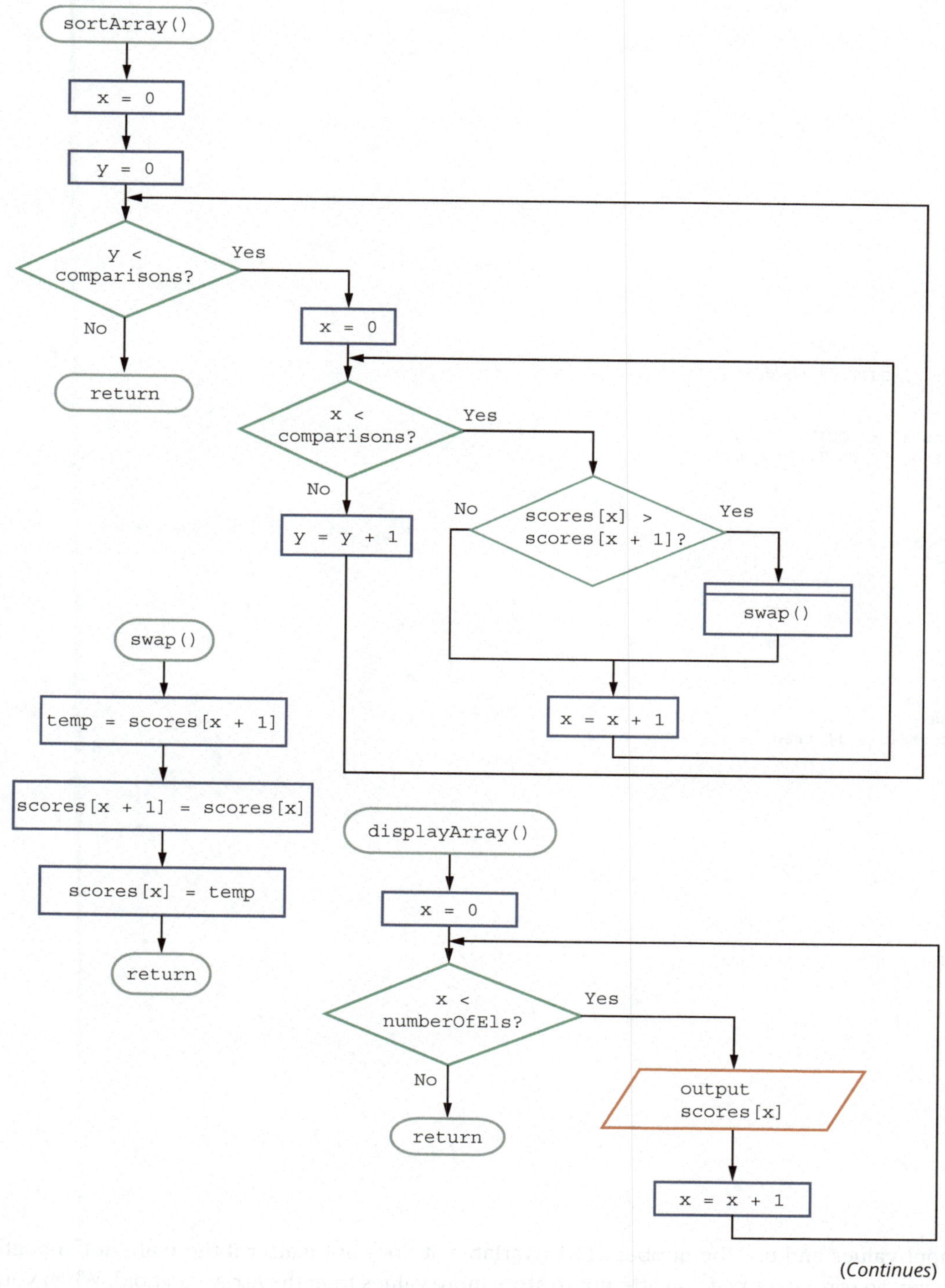

(*Continues*)

Figure 8-8 (*Continued*)

```
start
   Declarations
      num SIZE = 100
      num scores[SIZE]
      num x
      num y
      num temp
      num numberOfEls = 0
      num comparisons
      num QUIT = 999
   fillArray()
   sortArray()
   displayArray()
stop

fillArray()
   x = 0
   output "Enter a score or ", QUIT, " to quit "
   input scores[x]
   x = x + 1
   while x < SIZE AND scores[x] <> QUIT
      output "Enter a score or ", QUIT, " to quit "
      input scores[x]
      x = x + 1
   endwhile
   numberOfEls = x
   comparisons = numberOfEls - 1
return

sortArray()
   x = 0
   y = 0
   while y < comparisons
      x = 0
      while x < comparisons
         if scores[x] > scores[x + 1] then
            swap()
         endif
         x = x + 1
      endwhile
      y = y + 1
   endwhile
return

swap()
   temp = scores[x + 1]
   scores[x + 1] = scores[x]
   scores[x] = temp
return

displayArray()
   x = 0
   while x < numberOfEls
      output scores[x]
      x = x + 1
   endwhile
return
```

When you count the input values and use the `numberOfEls` variable, it does not matter if there are not enough scores to fill the array. However, an error occurs if you attempt to store more values than the array can hold. When you don't know how many elements will be stored in an array, you must overestimate the number of elements you declare.

Refining the Bubble Sort to Reduce Unnecessary Comparisons

You can make some improvements to the bubble sort created in the previous sections. As illustrated in Figure 8-8, when you perform the sorting module for a bubble sort, you pass through a list, making comparisons and swapping values if two adjacent values are out of order. If you are performing an ascending sort and you have made one pass through the list, the largest value is guaranteed to be in its correct final position at the bottom of the list. Similarly, the second-largest element is guaranteed to be in its correct second-to-last position after the second pass through the list, and so on. If you continue to compare every element pair on every pass through the list, you are comparing elements that are already guaranteed to be in their final correct position. In other words, after the first pass through the list, you no longer need to check the bottom element; after the second pass, you don't need to check the two bottom elements.

On each pass through the array, you can afford to stop your pair comparisons one element sooner. You can avoid comparing the values that are already in place by creating a new variable, `pairsToCompare`, and setting its initial value to `numberOfEls - 1`. On the first pass through the list, every pair of elements is compared, so `pairsToCompare` *should* equal `numberOfEls - 1`. In other words, with five array elements to sort, four pairs are compared, and with 50 elements to sort, 49 pairs are compared. On each subsequent pass through the list, `pairsToCompare` should be reduced by 1; for example, after the first pass is completed, it is not necessary to check the bottom element. See **Figure 8-9** to examine the use of the `pairsToCompare` variable.

Figure 8-9 Flowchart and pseudocode for `sortArray()` module using `pairsToCompare` variable

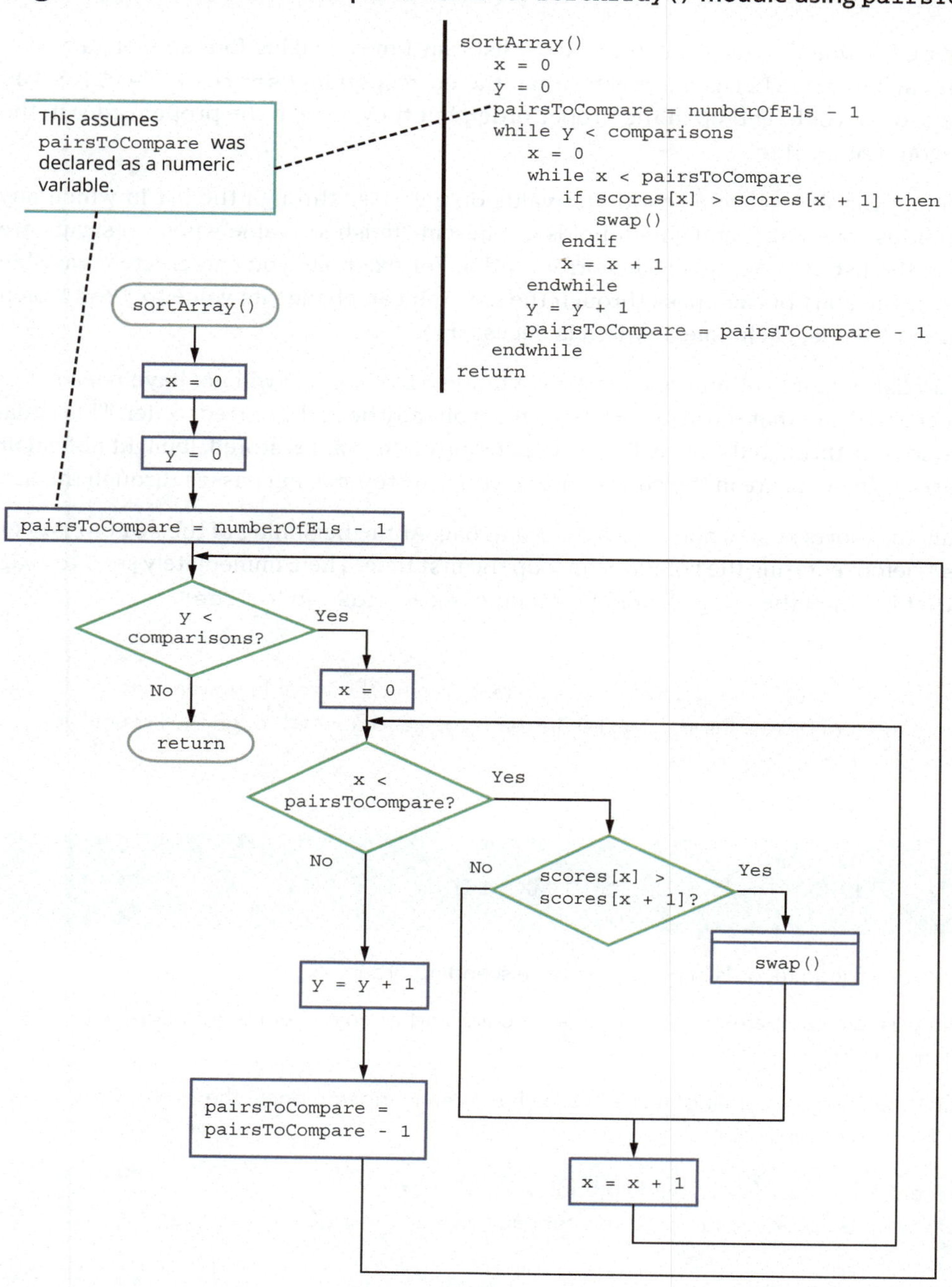


```
sortArray()
   x = 0
   y = 0
   pairsToCompare = numberOfEls - 1
   while y < comparisons
      x = 0
      while x < pairsToCompare
         if scores[x] > scores[x + 1] then
            swap()
         endif
         x = x + 1
      endwhile
      y = y + 1
      pairsToCompare = pairsToCompare - 1
   endwhile
return
```

Refining the Bubble Sort to Eliminate Unnecessary Passes

You could also improve the bubble sort module in Figure 8-9 by reducing the number of passes through the array when possible. If array elements are badly out of order, many passes through the list are required to place it in order; it takes one fewer pass than the value in `numberOfEls` to complete all the comparisons and swaps needed to sort the list. However, when the array elements are in order or nearly in order to start, all the elements might be correctly arranged after only a few passes through the list. All subsequent passes result in no swaps. For example, assume that the original scores are as follows:

```
scores[0] = 65
scores[1] = 75
scores[2] = 85
scores[3] = 90
scores[4] = 95
```

The bubble sort module in Figure 8-9 would pass through the array list four times, making four sets of pair comparisons. It would always find that each `scores[x]` is *not* greater than the corresponding `scores[x + 1]`, so no switches would ever be made. The scores would end up in the proper order, but they *were* in the proper order in the first place; therefore, a lot of time would be wasted.

A possible remedy is to add a flag variable set to a "continue" value on any pass through the list in which any pair of elements is swapped (even if just one pair), and which holds a different "finished" value when no swaps are made—that is, when all elements in the list are already in the correct order. For example, you can create a variable named `didSwap` and set it to `"No"` at the start of each pass through the list. You can change its value to `"Yes"` each time the `swap()` module is performed (that is, each time a switch is necessary).

If you make it through the entire list of pairs without making a switch, the `didSwap` flag will *not* have been set to `"Yes"`, meaning that no swap has occurred and that the array elements must already be in the correct order. This situation might occur on the first or second pass through the array list, or, depending on the values stored, it might not occur until a much later pass. Once the array elements are in the correct order, you can stop making passes through the list.

Figure 8-10 illustrates a module that sorts scores and uses a `didSwap` flag. At the beginning of the `sortArray()` module, initialize `didSwap` to `"Yes"` before entering the comparison loop the first time. Then, immediately set `didSwap` to `"No"`. When a switch occurs—that is, when the `swap()` module executes—set `didSwap` to `"Yes"`.

Note With the addition of the flag variable in Figure 8-10, you no longer need the variable `y`, which was keeping track of the number of passes through the list. Instead, you keep going through the list until you can make a complete pass without any swaps.

Two Truths & a Lie | Using the Bubble Sort Algorithm

1. You can use a bubble sort to arrange records in ascending or descending order.
2. In a bubble sort, items in a list are compared with each other in pairs, and when an item is out of order, it swaps values with the item below it.
3. With any bubble sort, after each adjacent pair of items in a list has been compared once, the largest item in the list will have "sunk" to the bottom.

The false statement is #3. Statement #3 is true of an ascending bubble sort. However, with a descending bubble sort, the smallest item in the list will have "sunk" to the bottom after each adjacent pair of items has been compared once.

Figure 8-10 Flowchart and pseudocode for `sortArray()` module using `didSwap` variable

This assumes `didSwap` was declared as a string variable.

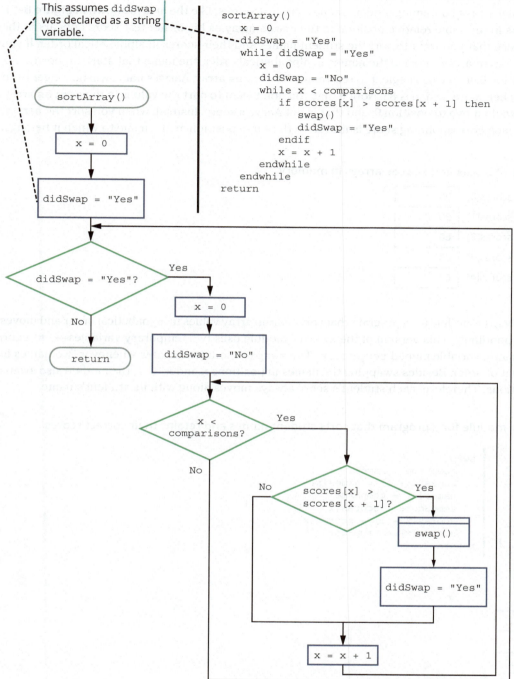

```
sortArray()
   x = 0
   didSwap = "Yes"
   while didSwap = "Yes"
      x = 0
      didSwap = "No"
      while x < comparisons
         if scores[x] > scores[x + 1] then
            swap()
            didSwap = "Yes"
         endif
         x = x + 1
      endwhile
   endwhile
return
```

8.3 Sorting Records on Multiple Fields

The bubble sort algorithm is useful for sorting a list of values, such as a list of test scores in ascending order or a list of names in alphabetical order. Records, however, are most frequently composed of multiple fields. When you want to sort records, you need to make sure data that belongs together stays together. When you sort records, two approaches you can take are to place related data items in parallel arrays and to sort records as a whole.

Sorting Data Stored in Parallel Arrays

Suppose that you have parallel arrays containing student names and test scores, like the arrays shown in **Figure 8-11**. Each student's name appears in the same relative position in the `names` array as his or her test score appears in the `scores` array. Further suppose that you want to sort the student names and their scores in alphabetical order. If you use a sort algorithm on the `names` array to place the names in alphabetical order, the name that starts in position 3, *Aarya*, should end up in position 0. If you also neglect to rearrange the `scores` array, Aarya's name will no longer be in the same relative position as her score, which is 85. Notice that you don't want to sort the values in the `scores` array. If you did, `scores[2]`, 60, would move to position 0, and that is not Aarya's score. Instead, when you sort the names, you want to make sure that each corresponding score is moved to the same position as the name to which it belongs.

Figure 8-11 Appearance of **`names`** and **`scores`** arrays in memory

names[0]	Cody	scores[0]	95
names[1]	Emma	scores[1]	90
names[2]	Brad	scores[2]	60
names[3]	Aarya	scores[3]	85
names[4]	Diego	scores[4]	67

Figure 8-12 shows the `swap()` module for a program that sorts `names` array values in alphabetical order and moves `scores` array values correspondingly. This version of the `swap()` module uses two temporary variables—a `string` named `tempName` and a numeric variable named `tempScore`. The `swap()` module executes whenever two names in positions `x` and `x + 1` are out of order. Besides swapping the names in positions `x` and `x + 1`, the module also swaps the scores in the same positions. Therefore, each student's score always moves along with its student's name.

Figure 8-12 The **`swap()`** module for a program that sorts student names and retains their correct scores

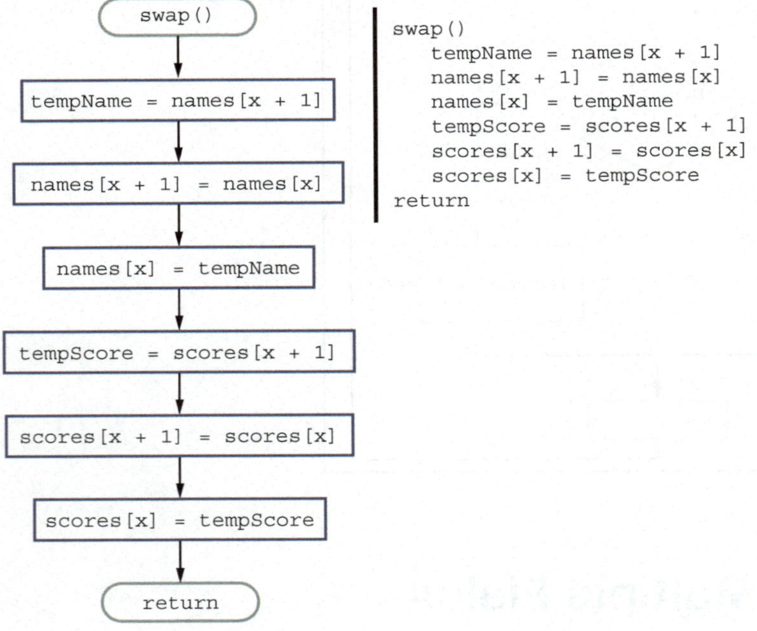


```
swap()
   tempName = names[x + 1]
   names[x + 1] = names[x]
   names[x] = tempName
   tempScore = scores[x + 1]
   scores[x + 1] = scores[x]
   scores[x] = tempScore
return
```

Sorting Records as a Whole

In most modern programming languages, you can create group items that can be manipulated more easily than single data items. Creating a group name for a set of related data fields is beneficial when you want to move related data items together, as when you sort records with multiple fields. These group items are sometimes called *structures*, but more frequently are created as *classes*. Later in this course, you will learn more about creating classes, but for now, understand that you can create a group item with syntax similar to the following:

```
class StudentRecord
    string name
    num score
endClass
```

To sort student records using the group name, you could do the following:

- Define a class named `StudentRecord`, as shown in the preceding code.
- Define what *greater than* means for a `StudentRecord`. For example, to sort records by student name, you would define *greater than* to compare `names` values, not `scores` values. The process for creating this definition varies among programming languages.
- Use a sort algorithm that swaps `StudentRecord` items, including both `names` and `scores`, whenever two `StudentRecords` are out of order.

Two Truths & a Lie | Sorting Records on Multiple Fields

1. To sort related parallel arrays, you must sort each in the same order—either ascending or descending.
2. When you sort related parallel arrays and swap values in one array, you must make sure that all associated arrays make the same relative swap.
3. Most modern programming languages allow you to create a group name for associated fields in a record.

The false statement is #1. To sort related parallel arrays successfully, you must make sure all items in each array are swapped in a synchronized manner. You do not want to sort the arrays separately.

8.4 Other Sorting Algorithms

The bubble sort works well and is relatively easy to understand and manipulate, but many other sorting algorithms have been developed.

When you use an **insertion sort**, you look at each list element one at a time. If an element is out of order relative to any of the items earlier in the list, you move each earlier item down one position and then insert the tested element. The insertion sort is similar to the technique you would most likely use to sort a group of objects manually. **Figure 8-13** shows how an ascending insertion sort would work for a list that starts out containing the values 4, 3, 1, 5, and 2.

Figure 8-13 The insertion sort algorithm

4	3	1	5	2

Start with the second element. Compare 3 and 4. They are out of order, so swap them.

Compare 1 and 3. They are out of order. So save 1 in a temporary variable, move 4 and 3 down, and insert 1 where 3 was.

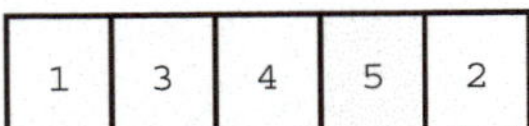

Compare 5 and 1. They are in order, so do nothing. Compare 5 and 3. They are in order, so do nothing. Compare 5 and 4. They are in order, so do nothing.

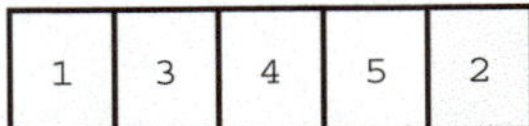

Compare 2 and 1. They are in order, so do nothing. Compare 2 and 3. They are out of order, so save 2 in a temporary variable, move 3, 4, and 5 down, and insert 2 where 3 used to be.

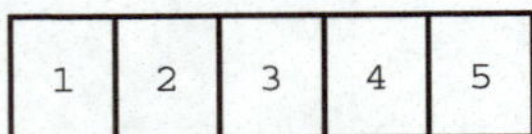

The sort is complete.

When you use a **selection sort**, you picture an array of values divided into two sublists—values already sorted and values not yet sorted. To start, the already-sorted list has zero elements. For an ascending sort, you find the smallest value in the unsorted sublist and swap its position with the leftmost value in the unsorted list. Then you move the rightmost boundary of the sorted sublist one element to the right. **Figure 8-14** shows how an ascending selection sort would work for a list that starts out containing the values 4, 3, 1, 5, and 2.

Note | You might want to investigate the logic used by other sorting algorithms such as the merge sort, heap sort, cocktail sort, gnome sort, and quick sort.

Two Truths & a Lie | Other Sorting Algorithms

1. The insertion sort algorithm moves list elements down when a tested item should be inserted before them.
2. Insertion sorts are used for ascending sorts and selection sorts are used for descending ones.
3. The selection sort algorithm uses two sublists.

The false statement is #2. Both insertion and selection sorts can be used for ascending and descending orders.

Figure 8-14 The selection sort algorithm

Sorted (0) Unsorted (5)

4 3 1 5 2

At first, the sorted sublist has zero elements and the unsorted sublist has five elements.

Find the smallest value in the unsorted list and swap it with the leftmost value in the unsorted list.

Sorted (0) Unsorted (5)

1 3 4 5 2

Then move the right edge of the sublist one element to the right.

Sorted (1) Unsorted (4)

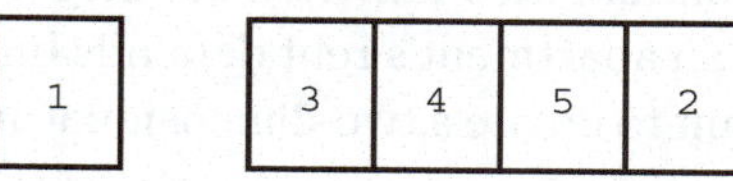

Now the sorted sublist has one element and the unsorted sublist has four.

Find the smallest value in the unsorted list and swap it with the leftmost value in the unsorted list.

Sorted (1) Unsorted (4)

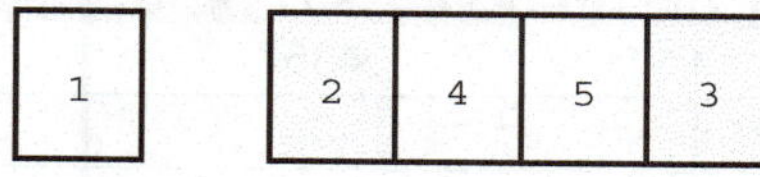

Then move the right edge of the sorted sublist one element to the right.

Sorted (2) Unsorted (3)

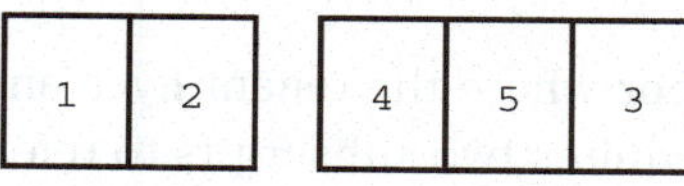

Now the sorted sublist has two elements and the unsorted sublist has three.

Find the smallest value in the unsorted list and swap it with the leftmost value in the unsorted list.

Sorted (2) Unsorted (3)

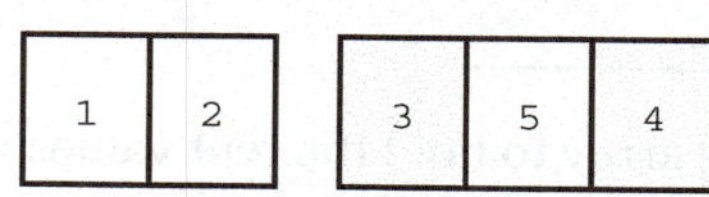

Then move the right edge of the sorted sublist one element to the right.

Sorted (3) Unsorted (2)

1 2 3 5 4

Now the sorted sublist has three elements and the unsorted sublist has two.

Find the smallest value in the unsorted list and swap it with the leftmost value in the unsorted list.

Sorted (3) Unsorted (2)

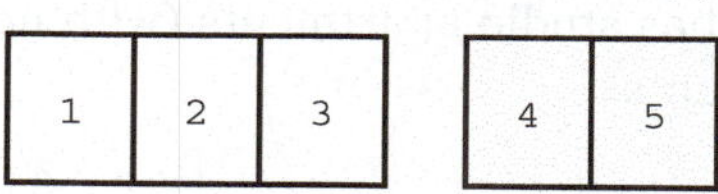

Then move the right edge of the sorted sublist one element to the right.

Sorted (4) Unsorted (1)

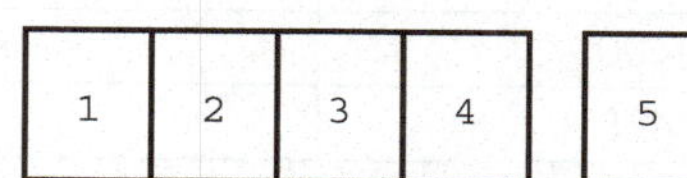

When the unsorted list has only one element, the sort is complete.

8.5 Using Multidimensional Arrays

You have learned that an array is a series or list of values in computer memory, all of which have the same name and data type but are differentiated with subscripts. Usually, all the values in an array have something in common; for example, they might represent a list of employee ID numbers or a list of prices for items sold in a store. A subscript, also called an index, is a number that indicates the position of a particular item within an array.

An array whose elements you can access using a single subscript is a one-dimensional array or single-dimensional array. The array has only one dimension because its data can be stored in a table that has just one dimension—height. If you know the vertical position of a one-dimensional array's element, you can find its value.

For example, suppose that you own an apartment building and charge five different rent amounts for apartments on different floors (including floor 0, the basement), as shown in **Figure 8-15**.

Figure 8-15 Rent schedule based on floor

Floor	Rent ($)
0	350
1	400
2	475
3	600
4	1000

You could declare the following array to hold the rent values shown in Figure 8-15:

```
num RENTS_BY_FLR[5] = 350, 400, 475, 600, 1000
```

The location of any rent value in Figure 8-15 depends on only a single variable—the floor of the building. So, when you create a single-dimensional array to hold rent values, you need just one subscript to identify the row.

Sometimes, however, locating a value in an array depends on more than one variable. An array that requires more than one subscript to access an element is a **multidimensional array**.

For example, if you must represent values in a table or grid that contains rows and columns instead of a single list, then you might want to use a **two-dimensional array**. A two-dimensional array contains two dimensions: height and width. That is, the location of any element depends on two factors. For example, if an apartment's rent depends on two variables—both the floor of the building and the number of bedrooms—then you want to create a two-dimensional array.

As an example of how useful two-dimensional arrays can be, assume that you own an apartment building with five floors, and that each of the floors has studio apartments (with no bedroom) and one- and two-bedroom apartments. **Figure 8-16** shows the rental amounts.

Figure 8-16 Rent schedule based on floor and number of bedrooms

Floor	Studio apartment	1-bedroom apartment	2-bedroom apartment
0	350	390	435
1	400	440	480
2	475	530	575
3	600	650	700
4	1000	1075	1150

To determine a tenant's rent, you need to know two pieces of information: the floor where the tenant lives and the number of bedrooms in the apartment. Each element in a two-dimensional array requires two subscripts to reference it—one subscript to determine the row and a second to determine the column. Thus, the 15 rent values for a two-dimensional array based on Figure 8-16 would be arranged in five rows and three columns and defined as follows:

```
num RENTS_BY_FLR_AND_BDRMS[5][3]= {350, 390, 435},
                                  {400, 440, 480},
                                  {475, 530, 575},
                                  {600, 650, 700},
                                  {1000, 1075, 1150}
```

Figure 8-17 shows how the one- and two-dimensional rent arrays might appear in computer memory.

Figure 8-17 One- and two-dimensional arrays in memory

A Single-Dimensional Array

```
num RENTS_BY_FLR[5] =
    350, 400, 475, 600, 1000
```

350
400
475
600
1000

A Two-Dimensional Array

```
num RENTS_BY_FLR_AND_BDRMS[5][3] =
    {350, 390, 435},
    {400, 440, 480},
    {475, 530, 575},
    {600, 650, 700},
    {1000, 1075, 1150}
```

350	390	435
400	440	480
475	530	575
600	650	700
1000	1075	1150

When a one-dimensional array has been declared in this course, a set of square brackets follows the array type and name. To declare a two-dimensional array, many languages require you to use two sets of brackets after the array type and name. For each element in the array, the first set of square brackets holds the number of rows and the second set holds the number of columns. In other words, the two dimensions represent the array's height and its width.

> **Note** Instead of two sets of brackets to indicate a position in a two-dimensional array, some languages use a single set of brackets but separate the subscripts with commas. Therefore, the elements in row 1, column 2 would be `RENTS_BY_FLR_AND_BDRMS[1, 2]`.

In the `RENTS_BY_FLR_AND_BDRMS` array declaration, the values that are assigned to each row are enclosed in curly braces to help you picture the placement of each number in the array. The first row of the array holds the three rent values 350, 390, and 435 for floor 0; the second row holds 400, 440, and 480 for floor 1; and so on.

You access a two-dimensional array value using two subscripts, in which the first subscript represents the row and the second one represents the column. The legal values for each of the dimensions include 0 through one less than the size of the array.

For example, some of the values in the two-dimensional rents array are as follows:

- `RENTS_BY_FLR_AND_BDRMS[0][0]` is 350
- `RENTS_BY_FLR_AND_BDRMS[0][1]` is 390
- `RENTS_BY_FLR_AND_BDRMS[0][2]` is 435
- `RENTS_BY_FLR_AND_BDRMS[4][0]` is 1000
- `RENTS_BY_FLR_AND_BDRMS[4][1]` is 1075
- `RENTS_BY_FLR_AND_BDRMS[4][2]` is 1150

If you declare two variables to hold the floor number and bedroom count as `num floor` and `num bedrooms`, any tenant's rent is `RENTS_BY_FLR_AND_BDRMS[floor][bedrooms]`.

> **Note** When mathematicians use a two-dimensional array, they often call it a **matrix** or a **table**. You may have used a spreadsheet, which is a two-dimensional array in which you need to know a row number and a column letter to access a specific cell.

Figure 8-18 shows a program that continually displays rents for apartments based on renter requests for floor location and number of bedrooms. Notice that although significant setup is required to provide all the values for the rents, the basic program is extremely brief and easy to follow. (You could improve the program in Figure 8-18 by making sure the values for `floor` and `bedrooms` are within range before using them as array subscripts.)

Figure 8-18 A program that determines rents

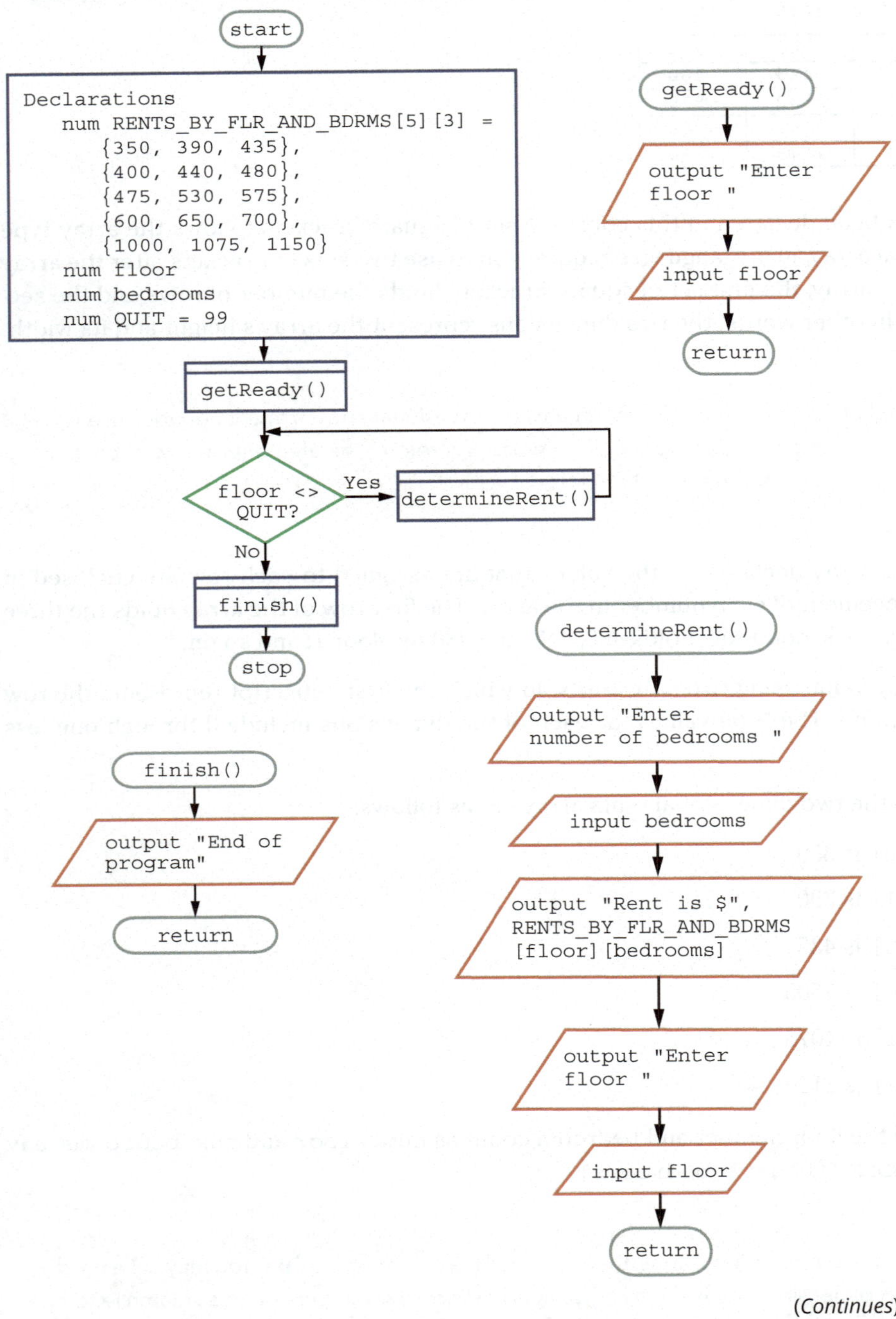

(Continues)

Figure 8-18 *(Continued)*

```
start
   Declarations
      num RENTS_BY_FLR_AND_BDRMS[5][3] = {350, 390, 435},
                                         {400, 440, 480},
                                         {475, 530, 575},
                                         {600, 650, 700},
                                         {1000, 1075, 1150}
      num floor
      num bedrooms
      num QUIT = 99
   getReady()
   while floor <> QUIT
      determineRent()
   endwhile
   finish()
stop

getReady()
   output "Enter floor "
   input floor
return

determineRent()
   output "Enter number of bedrooms "
   input bedrooms
   output "Rent is $", RENTS_BY_FLR_AND_BDRMS[floor][bedrooms]
   output "Enter floor "
   input floor
return

finish()
   output "End of program"
return
```

Two-dimensional arrays are never actually *required* in order to achieve a useful program. The same 15 categories of rent information in Figure 8-18 could be stored in three separate single-dimensional arrays of five elements each, and you could use a decision to determine which array to access. Of course, don't forget that even one-dimensional arrays are never required to solve a problem. You could also declare 15 separate rent variables and make 15 separate decisions to determine the rent.

Besides being able to use a one- or two-dimensional array, many programming languages also support using a **three-dimensional array**. For example, if you own a multistory apartment building with different numbers of bedrooms available in apartments on each floor, you can use a two-dimensional array to store the rental fees, but if you own several apartment buildings, you might want to employ a third dimension to store the building number. For example, if a three-dimensional array is stored on paper, you might need to know an element's row, column, and page to access it, as shown in **Figure 8-19**.

If you declare a three-dimensional array named `RENTS_BY_3_FACTORS`, then you can use an expression such as `RENTS_BY_3_FACTORS[floor][bedrooms][building]`, which refers to a specific rent value for an apartment whose floor and bedroom numbers are stored in the `floor` and `bedrooms` variables, and whose `building` number is stored in the `building` variable. Specifically, `RENTS_BY_3_FACTORS[0][1][2]` refers to a basement (floor 0) one-bedroom apartment in building 2 (which is the third building).

> **Note** Both two- and three-dimensional arrays are examples of multidimensional arrays. Some languages allow many more dimensions. For example, in C# and Visual Basic, an array can have 32 dimensions. However, it's usually hard for people to keep track of more than three dimensions.

Figure 8-19 Picturing a three-dimensional array

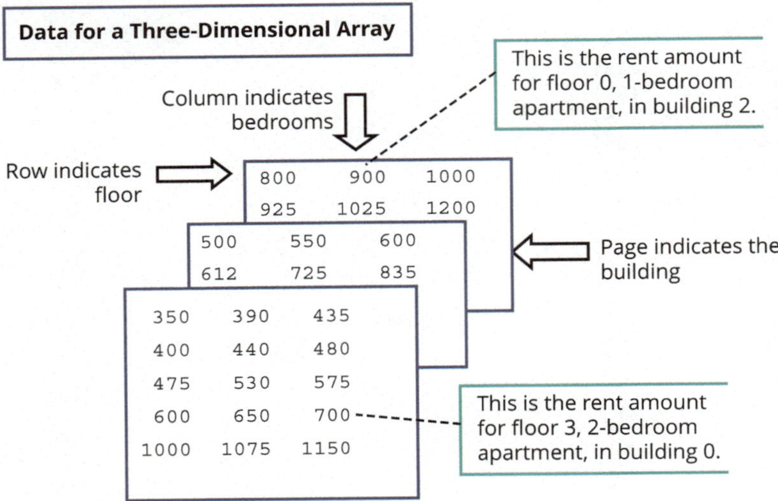

Two Truths & a Lie | Using Multidimensional Arrays

1. In every multidimensional array, the location of any element depends on two factors.
2. For each element in a two-dimensional array, the first subscript represents the row number and the second one represents the column.
3. Multidimensional arrays are never actually required in order to achieve a useful program.

The false statement is #1. In a two-dimensional array, the location of any element depends on two factors, but multidimensional arrays include those that depend on any number of factors.

8.6 Using Indexed Files and Linked Lists

Sorting a list of five or even 100 values does not require significant computer resources. However, many data files contain thousands of records, and each record might contain dozens of data fields. Sorting large numbers of data records requires considerable time and computer memory.

When a large data file needs to be processed in ascending or descending order based on a particular field, the most efficient approach is usually to access records based on their logical order rather than sorting and accessing them in their physical order. **Physical order** refers to a "real" order for storage; an example would be writing the names of 10 friends, each one on a separate index card. You can arrange the cards alphabetically by the friends' last names, chronologically by length of the friendship, or randomly by throwing the cards in the air and picking them up as you find them. Whichever way you do it, the records still follow each other in *some* order.

In addition to their current physical order, you can think of the cards as having a **logical order**; that is, a virtual order, based on any criterion you choose—from the tallest friend to the shortest, from the one who lives farthest away to the closest, and so on. Sorting the cards in a new physical order can take a lot of time; using the cards in their logical order without physically rearranging them is often more efficient.

Using Indexed Files

A common method of accessing records in logical order requires using an index. Using an index involves identifying a key field for each record. A record's **key field** is the field whose contents make the record unique among all records in a file. For example, multiple employees can have the same last name, first name, salary, or street address, but each employee possesses a unique employee identification number, so an ID number field might make a good key field for a personnel file. Similarly, a product number makes a good key field in an inventory file.

As pages in a book have numbers, computer memory and storage locations have **addresses**. Every variable has a numeric address in computer memory; likewise, every data record on a disk has a numeric address where it is stored. You can store records in any physical order on the disk, but when you **index records**, you store a list of key fields paired with the storage address for the corresponding data record. Then you can use the index to find the records in order based on their addresses.

When you use an index, you can store records on a **random-access storage device**, such as a disk, from which records can be accessed in any order. Each record can be placed in any physical location on the disk, and you can use the index as you would use an index in the back of a book. If you pick up a 600-page American history book because you need some facts about Betsy Ross, you do not want to start on page 1 and work your way through the book. Instead, you turn to the index, discover that Betsy Ross is mentioned on page 418, and go directly to that page. As a programmer, you do not need to determine a record's exact physical address in order to use it. A computer's operating system takes care of locating available storage for your records.

You can picture an index based on ID numbers by looking at the index in **Figure 8-20**. The index is stored on a portion of the disk. The address in the index refers to other scattered locations on the disk.

Figure 8-20 An index on a disk that associates ID numbers with disk addresses

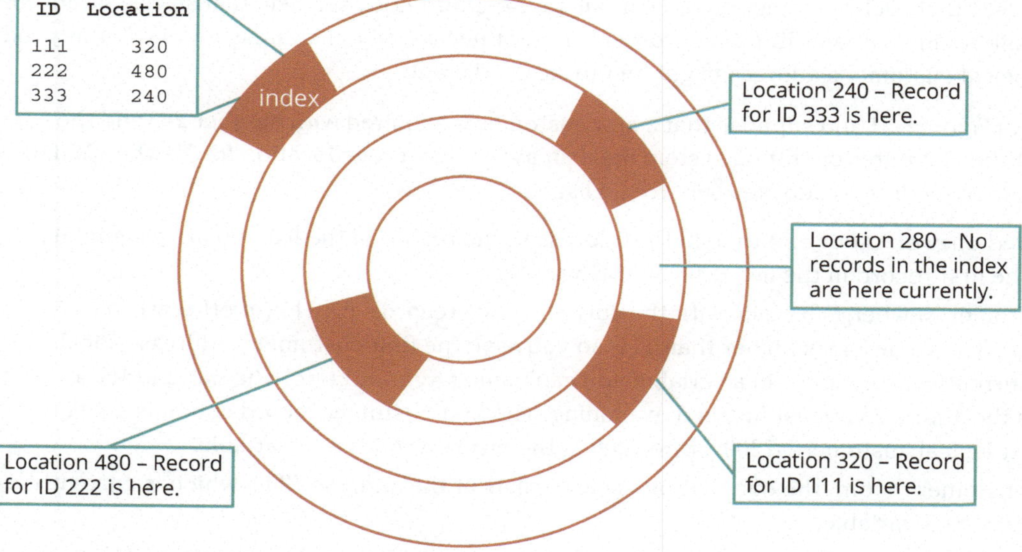

When you want to access the data for employee 333, you tell your computer to look through the ID numbers in the index, find a match, and then proceed to the memory location specified. Similarly, when you want to process records in order based on ID number, you tell your system to retrieve records at the locations in the index in sequence. Thus, employee 111 might have been hired last and the record might be stored at the highest physical address on the disk, but if the employee record has the lowest ID number, it will be accessed first during any ordered processing.

When a record is removed from an indexed file, it does not have to be physically removed. Its reference can simply be deleted from the index, and then it will not be part of any further processing.

Using Linked Lists

Another way to access records in a desired order, even though they might not be physically stored in that order, is to create a linked list. In its simplest form, creating a **linked list** involves creating one extra field in every record of stored data. This extra field holds the physical address of the next logical record. For example, a record that holds a customer's ID, name, and phone number might contain the following fields:

```
idNum
name
phoneNum
nextCustAddress
```

Every time you use a record, you access the next record based on the address held in the `nextCustAddress` field.

Every time you add a new record to a linked list, you search through the list for the correct logical location of the new record. For example, assume that customer records are stored at the addresses shown in **Figure 8-21** and that they are linked in customer ID order. Notice that the addresses of the records are not shown in sequential order. The records are shown in their logical order by `idNum`.

Figure 8-21 Sample linked customer list

Address	idNum	name	phoneNum	nextCustAddress
0000	111	Baker	234-5676	7200
7200	222	Vincent	456-2345	4400
4400	333	Mendoza	543-0912	6000
6000	444	Donovan	328-8744	eof

You can see from Figure 8-21 that each customer record contains a `nextCustAddress` field that stores the address of the next customer who follows in customer ID number order (and not necessarily in address order). For any individual customer, the next logical customer's address might be physically distant.

Examine the file shown in Figure 8-21 and suppose that a new customer is acquired with number *245* and the name *Newberg*. Also suppose that the computer operating system finds an available storage location for Newberg's data at address 8400. In this case, the procedure to add Newberg to the list is:

1. Create a variable named `currentAddress` to hold the address of the record in the list you are examining. Store the address of the first record in the list, 0000, in this variable.
2. Compare the new customer Newberg's ID, 245, with the current (first) record's ID, 111 (in other words, the ID at address 0000). The value 245 is higher than 111, so you save the first customer's address—0000, the address you are currently examining—in a variable you can name `saveAddress`. The `saveAddress` variable always holds the address you just finished examining. The first customer record contains a link to the address of the next logical customer—7200. Store 7200 in the `currentAddress` variable.
3. Examine the second customer record, the one that physically exists at the address 7200, which is currently held in the `currentAddress` variable.
4. Compare Newberg's ID, 245, with the ID stored in the record at `currentAddress`, 222. The value 245 is higher, so save the current address, 7200, in `saveAddress` and store its `nextCustAddress` address field, 4400, in the `currentAddress` variable.
5. Compare Newberg's ID, 245, with 333, which is the ID at `currentAddress` (4400). Up to this point, 245 had been higher than each ID tested, but this time the value 245 is lower, so customer 245 should logically precede customer 333. Set the `nextCustAddress` field in Newberg's record (customer 245) to 4400, which is the address of customer 333 and the address stored in `currentAddress`. This means that in any future processing, Newberg's record will logically be followed by the record containing 333. Also set the `nextCustAddress` field of the record located at `saveAddress` (7200, customer 222, Vincent, who logically preceded Newberg) to the new customer Newberg's address, 8400. The updated list appears in **Figure 8-22**.

Figure 8-22 Updated customer list

Address	idNum	name	phoneNum	nextCustAddress
0000	111	Baker	234-5676	7200
7200	222	Vincent	456-2345	8400
8400	245	Newberg	222-9876	4400
4400	333	Mendoza	543-0912	6000
6000	444	Donovan	328-8744	eof

As with indexing, when removing records from a linked list, the records do not need to be physically deleted from the medium on which they are stored. If you need to remove customer 333 from the preceding list, all you need to do is change Newberg's `nextCustAddress` field to the value in Mendoza's `nextCustAddress` field, which is Donovan's address: 6000. In other words, the value of 6000 is obtained not by knowing to which record Newberg should point, but by knowing to which record Mendoza previously pointed. When Newberg's record points to Donovan, Mendoza's record is then bypassed during any further processing that uses the links to travel from one record to the next.

More sophisticated linked lists are doubly linked—they store *two* additional fields with each record. One field stores the address of the next record, and the other field stores the address of the *previous* record so that the list can be accessed either forward or backward.

Two Truths & a Lie | Using Indexed Files and Linked Lists

1. When a large data file needs to be processed in order based on a particular field, the most efficient approach is usually to sort the records.
2. A record's key field contains a value that makes the record unique among all records in a file.
3. Creating a linked list requires you to create one extra field for every record; this extra field holds the physical address of the next logical record.

The false statement is #1. The most efficient approach is usually to store and access records based on their logical order rather than sorting and accessing them in their physical order.

Summary

- Frequently, data items need to be sorted. When you sort data, you can sort either in ascending order, arranging records from lowest to highest value, or in descending order, arranging records from highest to lowest value.
- In a bubble sort, items in a list are compared with each other in pairs, and appropriate swaps are made. With an ascending bubble sort, after each adjacent pair of items in a list has been compared once, the largest item in the list will have "sunk" to the bottom; after many passes through the list, the smallest items rise to the top. The bubble sort algorithm can be improved to sort varying numbers of values and to eliminate unnecessary comparisons.
- When you sort records, two possible approaches are to place related data items in parallel arrays and to sort records as a whole.

- When you use an insertion sort, you look at each list element, and when an element is out of order relative to any of the items earlier in the list, you move each earlier item down one position and then insert the tested element. When you use a selection sort, you use two sublists—values already sorted and values not yet sorted. You repeatedly look for the smallest value in the unsorted sublist, swap it with the item at the beginning of the unsorted list, and then add that element to the end of the sorted sublist.
- Two-dimensional arrays have both rows and columns of values. You must use two subscripts when you access an element in a two-dimensional array. Many languages support arrays with even more dimensions.
- You can use an index or linked list to access data records in a logical order that differs from their physical order. Using an index involves identifying a physical address and key field for each record. Creating a linked list involves creating an extra field within every record to hold the physical address of the next logical record.

Key Terms

addresses
bubble sort
index records
insertion sort
key field
linked list
logical order
matrix
mean
median
multidimensional array
one-dimensional array
physical order
random-access storage device
selection sort
sequential order
single-dimensional array
swap values
table
three-dimensional array
two-dimensional array

Review Questions

1. Employee records stored in order from highest-paid to lowest-paid have been sorted in _______________ order. (8.1)
   - **a.** descending
   - **b.** ascending
   - **c.** staggered
   - **d.** recursive
2. Student records stored in alphabetical order by last name have been sorted in _______________ order. (8.1)
   - **a.** descending
   - **b.** ascending
   - **c.** staggered
   - **d.** recursive
3. When computers sort data, they always _______________. (8.1)
   - **a.** place items in ascending order
   - **b.** use a bubble sort
   - **c.** use numeric values when making comparisons
   - **d.** begin the process by locating the position of the lowest value
4. Which of the following code segments correctly swaps the values of variables named x and y? (8.2)

a.
```
x = y
y = temp
x = temp
```
b.
```
temp = x
x = y
y = temp
```
c.
```
x = y
temp = x
y = temp
```
d.
```
temp = x
y = x
x = temp
```

5. Which type of sort compares list items in pairs, swapping any two adjacent values that are out of order? (8.2)
   a. insertion sort
   b. indexed sort
   c. bubble sort
   d. selection sort
6. To sort a list of 15 values using a bubble sort, the greatest number of times you would have to pass through the list making comparisons is ______________. (8.2, 8.3)
   a. 15
   b. 14
   c. 13
   d. 12
7. To completely sort a list of 10 values using a bubble sort, the greatest possible number of required pair comparisons is ______________. (8.2, 8.3)
   a. 9
   b. 10
   c. 81
   d. 100
8. When you do not know how many items need to be sorted in a program, you can create an array that has ______________. (8.2)
   a. variably sized elements
   b. at least as many elements as the number you predict you will need
   c. at least one element less than the number you predict you will need
   d. You cannot sort items if you do not know the number of items when you write the program.
9. In a bubble sort, on each pass through the list that must be sorted, you can stop making pair comparisons ______________. (8.2)
   a. one comparison sooner
   b. two comparisons sooner
   c. one comparison later
   d. two comparisons later
10. When performing a bubble sort on a list of 10 values, you can stop making passes through the list of values as soon as ______________ on a single pass through the list. (8.2, 8.3)
    a. no swaps are made
    b. exactly one swap is made
    c. no more than nine swaps are made
    d. no more than 10 swaps are made
11. The bubble sort is ______________. (8.2, 8.3)
    a. the most efficient sort
    b. a relatively fast sort compared to others
    c. a relatively easy sort to understand
    d. never used in object-oriented languages
12. Data stored in a table that can be accessed using row and column numbers is stored as a ______________ array. (8.5)
    a. single-dimensional
    b. two-dimensional
    c. three-dimensional
    d. nondimensional
13. A two-dimensional array declared as `num myArray[6][7]` has ______________ columns. (8.5)
    a. 5
    b. 6
    c. 7
    d. 8
14. In a two-dimensional array declared as `num myArray[6][7]`, the highest row number is ______________. (8.5)
    a. 5
    b. 6
    c. 7
    d. 8
15. If you access a two-dimensional array with the expression `output myArray[2][5]`, the output value will be ______________. (8.5)
    a. 0
    b. 2
    c. 5
    d. impossible to tell from the information given

16. Three-dimensional arrays ________________. (8.5)

a. are supported in many modern programming languages
b. always contain at least nine elements
c. are used only in object-oriented languages
d. are accessed using a single subscript

17. Student records are stored in ID number order but accessed by grade-point average for a report. In this example, grade-point average order is a(n) ________________ order. (8.6)

a. imaginary
b. physical
c. logical
d. illogical

18. When you store a list of key fields paired with the storage address for the corresponding data record, you are creating ________________. (8.6)

a. a directory
b. a three-dimensional array
c. a linked list
d. an index

19. When a record in an indexed file is not needed for further processing, ________________. (8.6)

a. its first character must be replaced with a special character, indicating it is a deleted record
b. its position must be retained, but its fields must be replaced with blanks
c. it must be physically removed from the file
d. the record can stay in place physically, but its reference is removed from the index

20. With a linked list, every record ________________. (8.6)

a. is stored in sequential order
b. contains a field that holds the address of another record
c. contains a code that indicates the record's position in an imaginary list
d. is stored in a physical location that corresponds to a key field

Programming Exercises

Several of the programming exercises in this section ask you to find the mean and median value in a list. Recall that the mean is the arithmetic average and that the median is the middle value in an ordered list. When a list contains an odd number of values, the median is the value in the middle position. When a list contains an even number of values, the median is the mean of the values in the two middle positions. Many languages support a remainder operator (often the percent sign) that you can use to determine whether a number is even or odd. When a number is divided by 2, the remainder is 0 if the number is even.

1. Design an application that accepts 10 numbers and displays them in descending order. (8.1, 8.2)

2. Design an application that accepts 15 words and displays them in alphabetical order. (8.1, 8.2)

3. **a.** Professor Zak allows students to drop the four lowest scores on the ten 100-point quizzes given during the semester. Design an application that accepts a student name and 10 quiz scores. Output the student's name and total points for the student's six highest-scoring quizzes.

b. Modify the application in Exercise 3a so that the student's mean and median scores on the six best quizzes are displayed. (8.1, 8.2)

4. Girl Scout Troop 815 has 18 members. Write a program in which the troop leader can enter the number of boxes of cookies sold by each scout and output the total number of boxes sold along with the mean and median values. (8.1, 8.2)

5. The village of Marengo conducted a census and collected records that contain household data, including the number of occupants in each household. The exact number of household records has not yet been determined, but you know that Marengo has fewer than 500 households. Develop the logic for a program that allows a user to enter each household size and determine the mean and median household size in Marengo. (8.1, 8.2)

6. a. Three Strikes Bowling Lanes hosts an annual tournament for 12 teams. Design a program that accepts each team's name and total score for the tournament and stores them in parallel arrays. Display the names of the top three teams.

   b. Modify the bowling tournament program so that, instead of the team's total score, the program accepts the score of each of the four team members. Display the names of the five top scorers in the tournament as well as their team names. (8.1, 8.2, 8.3)

7. a. *The Daily Trumpet* newspaper accepts classified advertisements in 15 categories such as *Apartments for Rent* and *Pets for Sale*. Develop the logic for a program that accepts classified advertising data, including a category code (an integer 1 through 15) and the number of words in the ad. Store these values in parallel arrays. Then sort the arrays so that records are sorted in ascending order by category. The output lists each category number, the number of ads in the category, and the total number of words in the ads in the category.

   b. Modify the newspaper advertising program in Exercise 7a to display a descriptive string with each category. For example, Category 1 might be *Apartments for Rent*. (8.1, 8.2, 8.3)

8. Le Chef Heureux Restaurant has 20 tables that can be reserved at 5 p.m., 7 p.m., or 9 p.m. Design a program that accepts reservations for specific tables at specific times; the user enters the number of customers, the table number, and the time. Do not allow more than four guests per table or invalid table numbers or times. If an attempt is made to reserve a table already taken, reprompt the user. Continue to accept reservations until the user enters a sentinel value or all slots are filled. Then display all empty tables in each time slot. (8.5)

9. Building Block Day Care Center charges varying weekly rates depending on the age of the child and the number of days per week the child attends, as shown in **Figure 8-23**. Develop the logic for a program that continually accepts child care data and displays the appropriate weekly rate. (8.5)

Figure 8-23 Day care rates

	Days per week				
Age in years	**1**	**2**	**3**	**4**	**5**
0	30.00	60.00	88.00	115.00	140.00
1	26.00	52.00	70.00	96.00	120.00
2	24.00	46.00	67.00	89.00	110.00
3	22.00	40.00	60.00	75.00	88.00
4 or more	20.00	35.00	50.00	66.00	84.00

10. Happy Paws Dog School holds a dog agility competition once a year. The competition evaluates a dog's speed through an agility course and the number of errors the dog makes while traversing the course. Develop the logic for a program that produces a summary table of the competition's results. Each row represents the number of dogs whose course speed falls within the following ranges in seconds: 0–60, 61–90, 91–120, and 121 or more. Each column represents the number of dogs who made different numbers of errors in the course—0 through 2 or more than 2. (8.3)

11. HappyTunes is an application for downloading music files. Each time a file is purchased, a transaction record is created that includes the music genre and price paid. The available genres are *Classical*, *Easy Listening*, *Jazz*, *Pop*, *Rock*, and *Other*. Develop the pseudocode for an application that accepts input data for each transaction and displays a report that lists each of the music genres, along with a count of the number of downloads in each of the following price categories:

- Over $10.00
- $6.00 through $9.99
- $3.00 through $5.99
- Under $3.00 (8.3, 8.5)

Performing Maintenance

1. A file named *MAINTENANCE08-01.txt* is included in the Chapter08 folder of your downloadable student files. Assume that this program is a working program in your organization and that it needs modifications as described in the comments (lines that begin with two slashes) at the beginning of the file. Your job is to alter the program to meet the new specifications. (8.1, 8.2, 8.3)

Debugging Exercises

1. Your downloadable files for Chapter 8 include *DEBUG08-01.txt*, *DEBUG08-02.txt*, *DEBUG08-03.txt*, and *DEBUG08-04.jpg*. Each file starts with some comments that describe the problem. Comments are lines that begin with two slashes (//). Each file contains pseudocode or a flowchart that has mistakes. Find and correct all the bugs.

Game Zone

1. Create the pseudocode for a guessing game that generates a random number between 1 and 100 and let a player try to guess it. After each guess, display a message indicating whether the player's guess was correct, too high, or too low. When the player eventually guesses the correct number, display a score that represents the number of guesses that were required. Allow a player to replay the game as many times as the player wants, up to 20 times. When the player is done, display the scores from highest to lowest, and display the mean and median scores. (8.1, 8.2)

2. a. Create a TicTacToe game. In this game, two players (one player is the computer) alternate placing *X*s and *O*s into a grid until one player has three matching symbols in a row, either horizontally, vertically, or diagonally. Create a game that displays a three-by-three grid containing the digits 1 through 9, similar to the first part of **Figure 8-24**. When the user chooses a position by typing a number, place an *X* in the appropriate spot. For example, after the user chooses 3, the screen looks like the second part of Figure 8-24. The *X* is in location 3, the program announces that the computer will play, and an *O* is placed in the grid in a position that is generated randomly. Do not allow the player or the computer to place a symbol where one has already been placed. When either the player or computer has three symbols in a row, declare a winner. If all positions have been used and no one has three symbols in a row, declare a tie.

Figure 8-24 A TicTacToe game

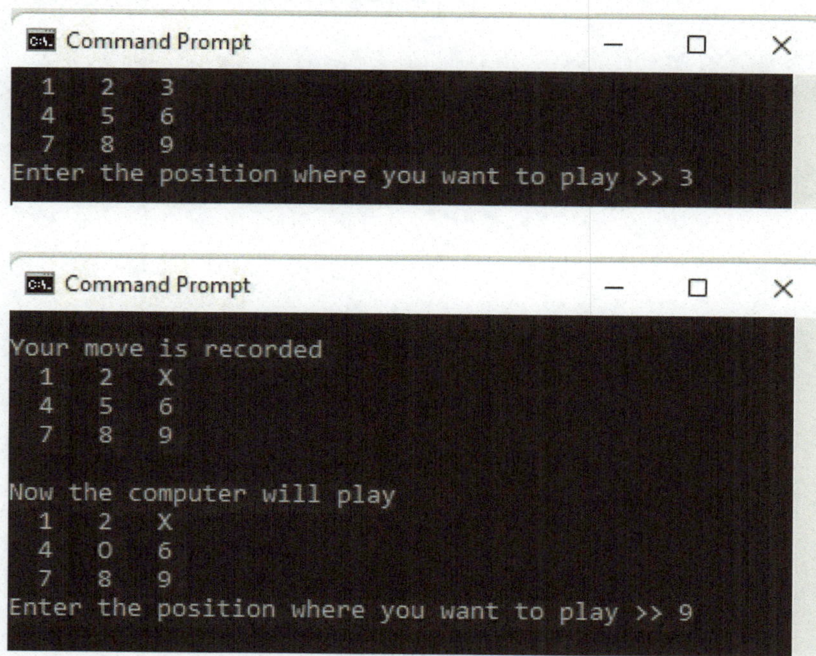

b. In the TicTacToe game in Game Zone Exercise 2a, the computer's selection is chosen randomly. Improve the game so that when the computer has two *O*s in any row, column, or diagonal, it selects the winning position for its next move rather than selecting a position randomly. (8.5)

Chapter 9

Advanced Modularization Techniques

Learning Objectives

When you complete this chapter, you will be able to:

- **9.1** Name the parts of a method
- **9.2** Design methods with no parameters
- **9.3** Design methods that require parameters
- **9.4** Design methods that return a value
- **9.5** Pass arrays to methods
- **9.6** Overload methods
- **9.7** Use predefined methods
- **9.8** Describe method design issues, including implementation hiding, cohesion, and coupling
- **9.9** Describe recursion

9.1 The Parts of a Method

In object-oriented programming languages such as Java and C#, modules are most often called *methods*. You might hear people use the terms *method* and *module* interchangeably, but there are some differences. Many features that you have learned about modules throughout this course are also true for object-oriented methods. For example:

- A method is a program module that contains a series of statements that carry out a task; you can invoke or call a method from another program or method. The calling program or method is the called method's **client**.
- As with the modules you have studied, any program can contain an unlimited number of methods, and each method can be called an unlimited number of times.
- The rules for naming methods are different in every programming language, but they often are similar to the language's rules for variable names. In this text, method names are followed by a set of parentheses.

- A method must include a **method header** (sometimes also called the *method declaration*), which contains identifying information about the method.
- A method includes a **method body**. The body contains the method's **implementation**—the statements that carry out the method's tasks.
- A **method `return` statement** returns control to the calling method after a method executes. Although methods with multiple `return` statements are allowed in many programming languages, that practice is not recommended. Structured programming requires that a method must contain a single entry point and a single exit point. Therefore, a method should have only one `return` statement, and it should be the last statement. In many programming languages, control is returned to the calling method even if the `return` statement is omitted, but for clarity, this course will include a `return` statement at the end of each method.
- As with the modules you have studied, variables and constants can be declared within a method. A data item declared in a method is *local* to that method, meaning it is in scope, or recognized only within that method. You will employ local variables and constants with object-oriented methods more than you have done with modules so far in this course.
- When a data item is known to all of a program's methods or modules, it is a *global* data item. Although you have seen global variables used frequently in this course, you will see local variables exclusively going forward. In general, programmers prefer local data items because when data is contained within the method that uses it, the method is more portable and less prone to error. (You have learned that when a method is described as *portable*, it can easily be moved to another application and used there.)

Methods differ from the modules you have been using because data values are passed into and out of methods. Methods differ from the modules you have studied in the following significant ways:

- Methods can have parameter lists that provide details about data passed into methods.
- Methods have return types that provide information about data the method returns. In some languages, like C++, a default return type is implied if no return type is listed.

Figure 9-1 shows important parts of a method. You learn more about these parts in the rest of this chapter.

Figure 9-1 The parts of a method

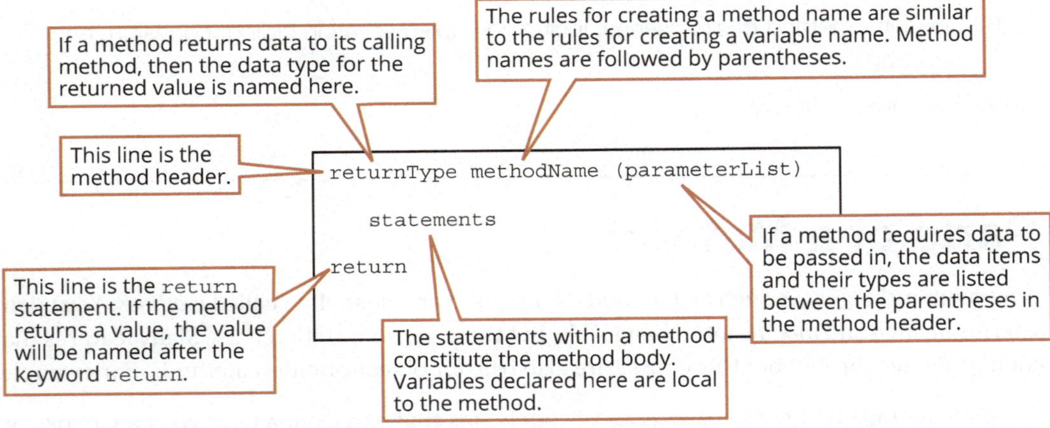

If a method returns data to its calling method, then the data type for the returned value is named here.
The rules for creating a method name are similar to the rules for creating a variable name. Method names are followed by parentheses.
This line is the method header.
returnType methodName (parameterList)
statements
return
If a method requires data to be passed in, the data items and their types are listed between the parentheses in the method header.
This line is the return statement. If the method returns a value, the value will be named after the keyword return.
The statements within a method constitute the method body. Variables declared here are local to the method.

Two Truths & a Lie | The Parts of a Method

1. A program can contain an unlimited number of methods, but each method can be called only once.
2. A method includes a header and a body.
3. Variables and constants are in scope within, or local to, only the method in which they are declared.

The false statement is #1. Each method can be called an unlimited number of times.

9.2 Using Methods with No Parameters

Figure 9-2 shows a program that allows a user to enter a preferred language (English or Spanish) and then, using the chosen language, asks the user to enter his or her weight. The program then calculates the user's weight on the moon as 16.6 percent of the user's weight on Earth. The main program contains declarations for two variables and a constant. The program calls the `displayInstructions()` method, which contains its own local variable and constants that are invisible (and therefore not available) to the main program. The method prompts the user for a language indicator and displays a prompt in the selected language. **Figure 9-3** shows a typical program execution in a command-line environment.

Figure 9-2 A program that calculates the user's weight on the moon

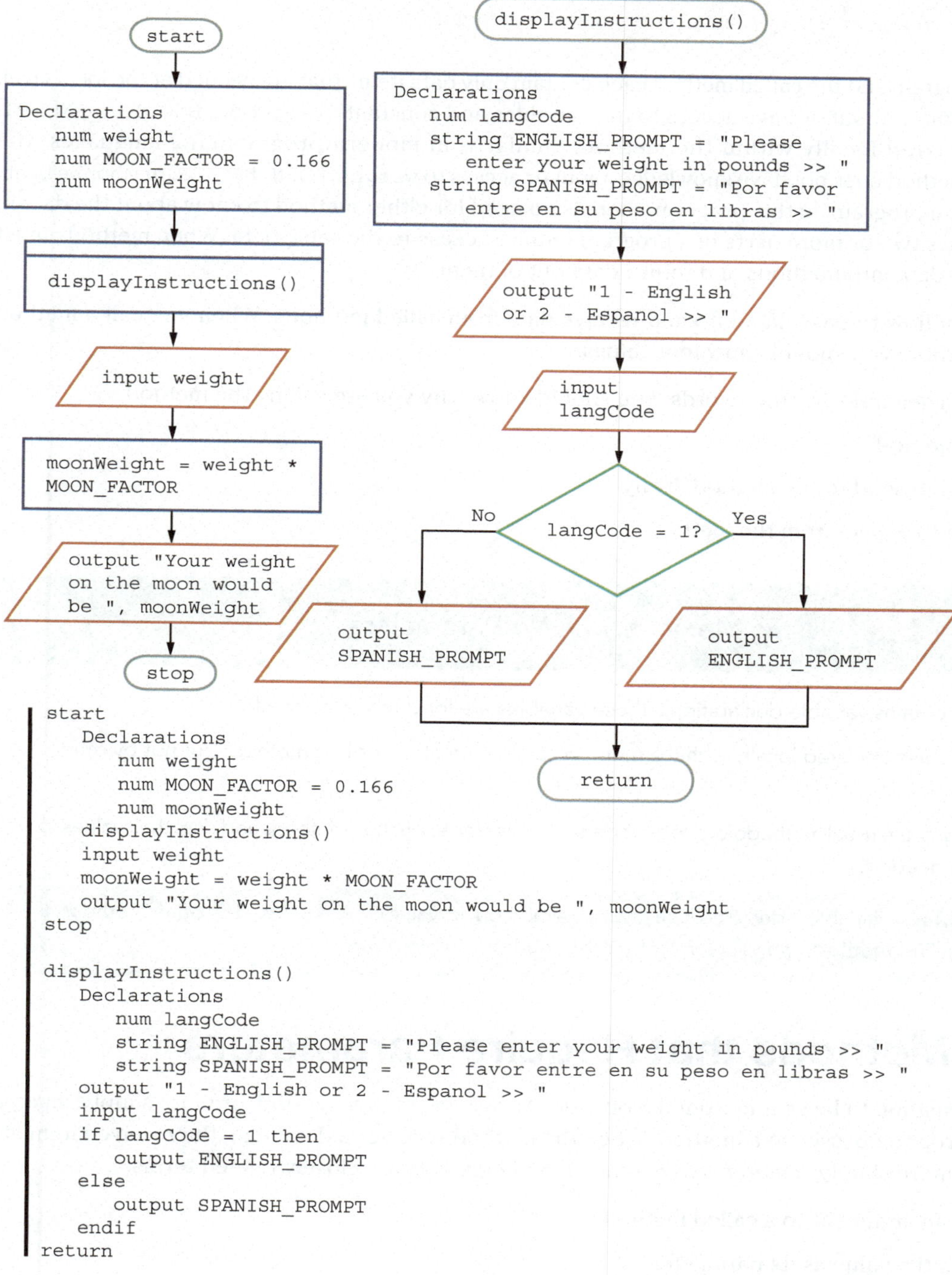


```
start
   Declarations
      num weight
      num MOON_FACTOR = 0.166
      num moonWeight
   displayInstructions()
   input weight
   moonWeight = weight * MOON_FACTOR
   output "Your weight on the moon would be ", moonWeight
stop

displayInstructions()
   Declarations
      num langCode
      string ENGLISH_PROMPT = "Please enter your weight in pounds >> "
      string SPANISH_PROMPT = "Por favor entre en su peso en libras >> "
   output "1 - English or 2 - Espanol >> "
   input langCode
   if langCode = 1 then
      output ENGLISH_PROMPT
   else
      output SPANISH_PROMPT
   endif
return
```

Figure 9-3 Execution of the moon weight calculator program in Figure 9-2

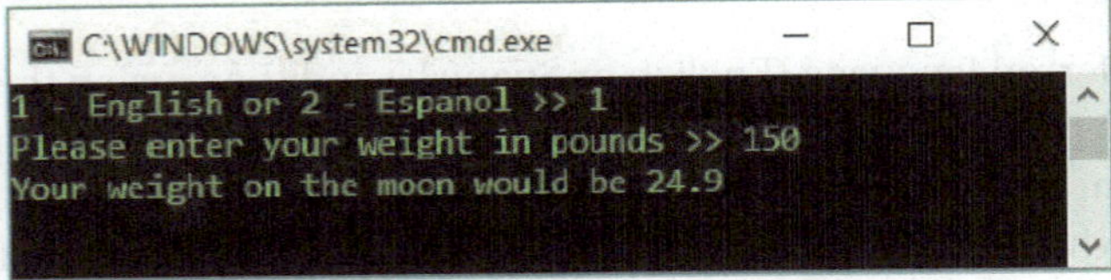

Note To represent a method call in a flowchart, some programmers prefer to use a rectangle with a horizontal stripe across the top. Other programmers prefer to use a rectangle with a vertical stripe on each side. You should use the convention your organization prefers. This course uses the shape with the horizontal stripe to depict a call to a method within the same program and reserves the shape with two vertical stripes to represent a method from a library that is external to the program.

In Figure 9-2, the main program and the called method each contain only data items that are needed at the local level. The main program does not know about or have access to the variables and constants `langCode`, `ENGLISH_PROMPT`, and `SPANISH_PROMPT` declared locally within the method. Similarly, in modern programming languages, the `displayInstructions()` method does not have knowledge about or access to `weight`, `MOON_FACTOR`, or `moonWeight`, which are declared in the main program. In this program, there is no need for either method to know about the data in the other. However, sometimes two or more parts of a program require access to the same data. When methods must share data, you can pass the data into methods and return data out of them.

In this chapter, you learn how to pass data into and receive data from called methods. When you call a method from a program or other method, you should know four things:

- What the method does in general—in other words, you should know why you are calling the method
- The name of the called method
- What type of information to send to the method, if any
- What type of return data to expect from the method, if any

Two Truths & a Lie | Using Methods with No Parameters

1. When a method contains variable declarations, those variables are local to the method.
2. The values of variables declared locally within a method can be used by a calling method, but not by other methods.
3. In modern languages, the usual methodology is to declare variables locally in their methods and pass their values to other methods as needed.

The false statement is #2. When a variable is declared locally within a method, its value cannot be used by other methods. If its value is needed by a calling method, the value must be returned from the method.

9.3 Creating Methods that Require Parameters

Some methods require information to be sent in from the outside. An **argument to a method**, or more simply, an *argument*, is a data item that a program passes to a method. When the method receives a data item, the received item is a **parameter to a method**, or more simply, a *parameter*. *Parameter* and *argument* are closely related terms.

- A calling method sends an argument to a called method.
- A called method accepts the value as its parameter.

If a method could not receive parameters, you would have to use global variables or write an infinite number of methods to cover every possible situation. As a real-life example, when you make a restaurant reservation, you do not need to employ a different method for every date of the year at every possible time of day. Rather, you can supply the date and time as information to the person who carries out the method. The method that records the reservation is carried out in the same manner, no matter what date and time are supplied.

As a programming example, if you design a `square()` method that multiplies a numeric value by itself, you should supply the method with a parameter that represents the value to be squared, rather than developing a `square1()` method that squares the value 1, a `square2()` method that squares the value 2, and so on. To call a `square()` method that accepts a parameter, you might write a statement that uses a constant, like `square(17)` or `square(86)`, or one that uses a variable, like `square(inputValue)`. This method uses the value of whatever argument you send.

When you write the declaration for a method that can receive a parameter, you must provide a **parameter list** that includes the following items for the parameter within the method declaration's parentheses:

- The type of the parameter
- A local name for the parameter

Later in this chapter, you learn to create parameter lists with more than one parameter. A method's name and parameter list constitute the method's **signature**.

For example, suppose that you decide to improve the moon weight program in Figure 9-2 by making the final output more user-friendly and adding the explanatory text in the chosen language. It makes sense that if the user can request a prompt in a specific language, the user would want to see the output explanation in the same language. However, in Figure 9-2, the `langCode` variable is local to the `displayInstructions()` method and therefore cannot be used in the main program. You could rewrite the program by taking several approaches:

- You could rewrite the program without including any methods. That way, you could prompt the user for a language preference and display the prompt and the result in the appropriate language. This approach works, but you would not be taking advantage of the benefits provided by modularization. Those benefits include making the main program more streamlined and abstract, and making the `displayInstructions()` method a self-contained unit that can easily be transported to other programs—for example, applications that might determine a user's weight on Saturn or Mars.
- You could retain the `displayInstructions()` method but make at least the `langCode` variable global by declaring it outside of any methods. If you took this approach, you would lose some of the portability of the `displayInstructions()` method because everything it used would no longer be contained within the method.
- You could retain the `displayInstructions()` method as is with its own local declarations, but add a section to the main program that also asks the user for a preferred language to display the result. The disadvantage to this approach is that the user must answer the same question twice during one execution of the program.
- You could store the variable that holds the language code in the main program so that it could be used to determine the result language. You could also retain the `displayInstructions()` method but pass the language code to it so the prompt would appear in the appropriate language. This is the best choice because it employs modularity, which keeps the main program simpler and creates a portable method. A program that uses the method is shown in **Figure 9-4**, and a typical execution appears in **Figure 9-5**.

In the main program in Figure 9-4, a numeric variable named `code` is declared and the user is prompted for a value. The value then is passed to the `displayInstructions()` method. The value of the language code is stored in two places in memory:

- The main method stores the code in the variable `code` and passes it to `displayInstructions()` as an argument.
- The `displayInstructions()` method accepts the value of the argument `code` as the value of the parameter `langCode`. In other words, within the method, `langCode` takes on the value that `code` had in the main program.

Figure 9-4 Moon weight program that passes an argument to a method

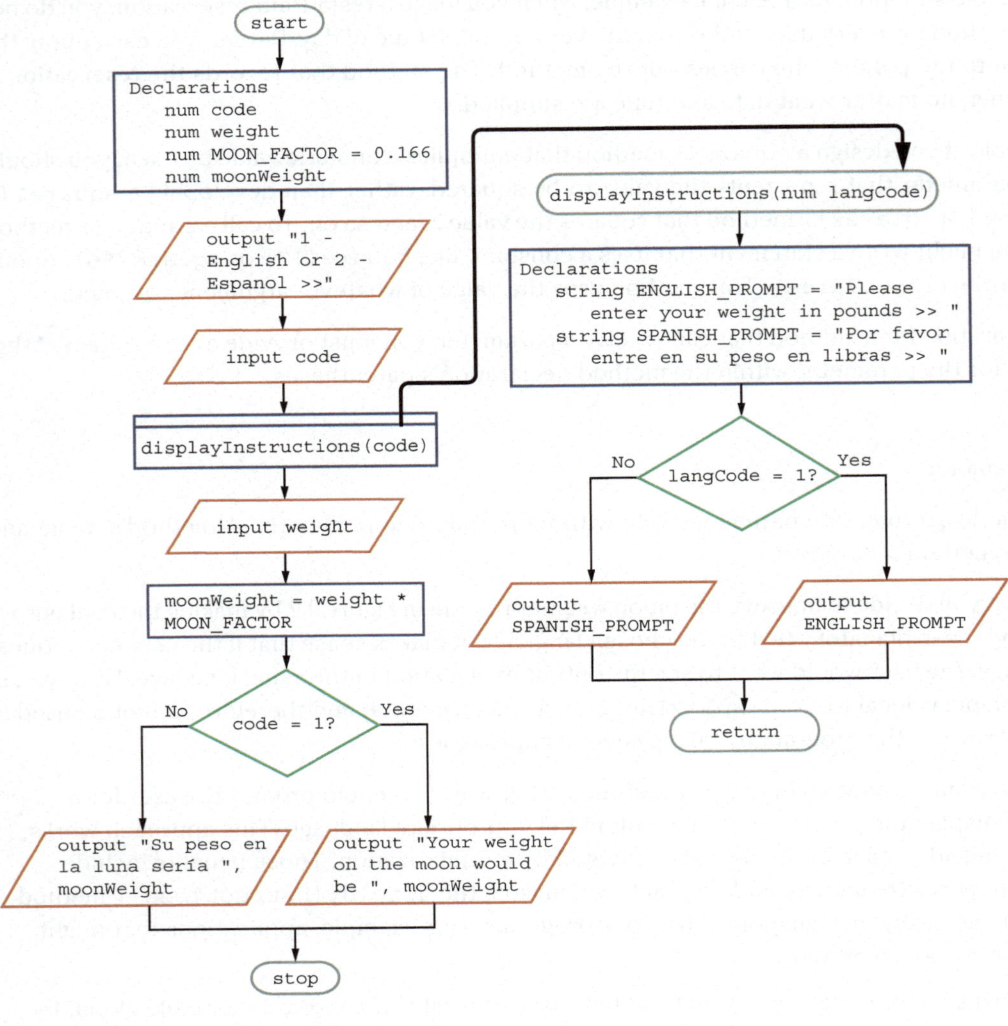


```
start
   Declarations
      num code
      num weight
      num MOON_FACTOR = 0.166
      num moonWeight
   output "1 - English or 2 - Espanol >>"
   input code
   displayInstructions(code)
   input weight
   moonWeight = weight * MOON_FACTOR
   if code = 1 then
      output "Your weight on the moon would be ", moonWeight
   else
      output "Su peso en la luna sería ", moonWeight
   endif
stop

displayInstructions(num langCode)
   Declarations
      string ENGLISH_PROMPT = "Please enter your weight in pounds >> "
      string SPANISH_PROMPT = "Por favor entre en su peso en libras >> "
   if langCode = 1 then
      output ENGLISH_PROMPT
   else
      output SPANISH_PROMPT
   endif
return
```

Figure 9-5 Typical execution of moon weight program in Figure 9-4

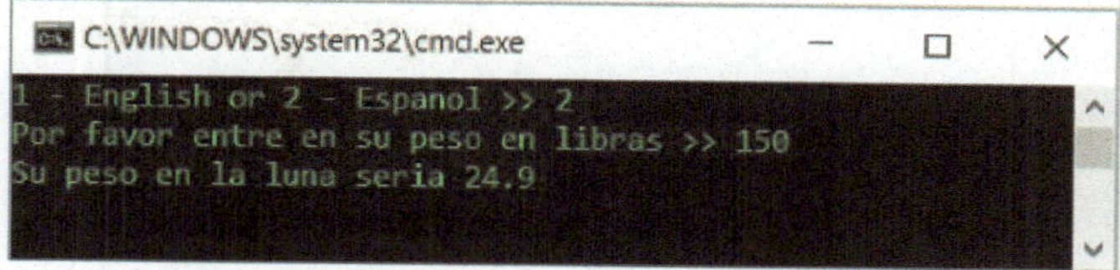

You can think of the parentheses in a method declaration as a funnel into the method; parameters listed there hold values that are "dropped in" to the method. A variable passed into a method is **passed by value**; that is, a copy of its value is sent to the method and stored in a new memory location accessible to the method. The `displayInstructions()` method could be called using any numeric value as an argument, whether it is a variable, a named constant, a literal constant, or even an arithmetic expression. In other words, suppose that the main program contains the following declarations:

```
num x = 2
num langCode = 2
num SPANISH = 2
```

Then any of the following statements would work to call the `displayInstructions()` method:

- `displayInstructions(x)`, using a variable
- `displayInstructions(langCode)`, using a different variable
- `displayInstructions(SPANISH)`, using a named constant
- `displayInstructions(2)`, using a literal constant

If the value used as an argument in the method call is a variable or named constant, it might possess the same identifier as the parameter declared in the method header, or it might possess a different identifier. Within a method, the passed variable or named constant is simply a temporary placeholder; it makes no difference what name the variable or constant "goes by" in the calling program.

Each time a method executes, any parameters listed in the method header are redeclared—that is, new memory locations are reserved and named. When the method ends at the `return` statement, the locally declared parameter variables cease to exist. For example, **Figure 9-6** shows a program that declares a variable, assigns a value to it, displays it, and sends it to a method. Within the method, the parameter is displayed, altered, and displayed again. When control returns to the main program, the original variable is displayed one last time. As the execution in **Figure 9-7** shows, even though the variable in the method was altered, the original variable in the main program retains its starting value because it never was altered; it occupies a different memory address from the variable in the method.

Creating Methods that Require Multiple Parameters

You create and use a method with multiple parameters by doing the following:

- You list the arguments within the method call, separated by commas.
- You list a data type and local identifier for each parameter within the method header's parentheses, separating each declaration with a comma. Even if multiple parameters are the same data type, the type must be repeated with each parameter.

Figure 9-6 A program that calls a method in which the argument and the parameter have the same identifier

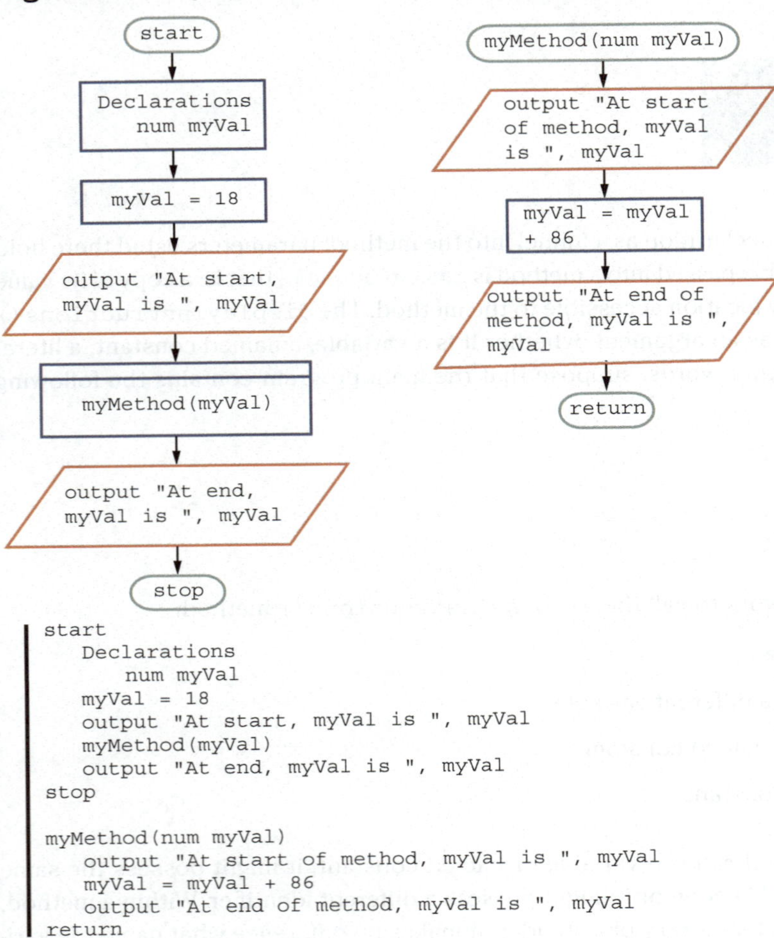


```
start
   Declarations
      num myVal
   myVal = 18
   output "At start, myVal is ", myVal
   myMethod(myVal)
   output "At end, myVal is ", myVal
stop

myMethod(num myVal)
   output "At start of method, myVal is ", myVal
   myVal = myVal + 86
   output "At end of method, myVal is ", myVal
return
```

Figure 9-7 Execution of the program in Figure 9-6

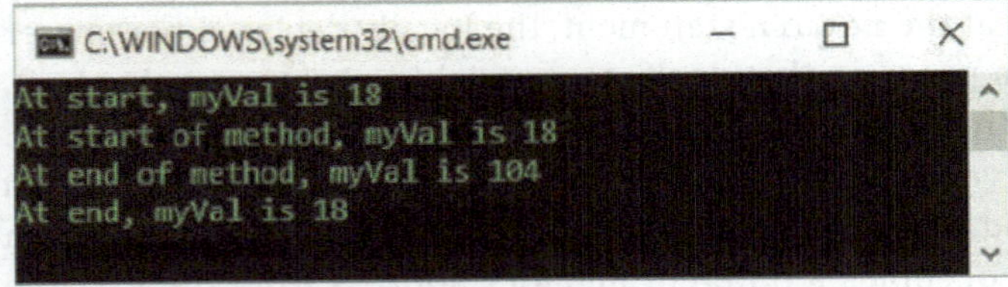

Note The arguments sent to a method in a method call are also called its *actual parameters*. The variables in the method declaration that accept the values from the actual parameters are *formal parameters*.

For example, suppose that you want to create a `computeTax()` method that calculates a tax on any value passed into it. You can create a method to which you pass two values—the amount to be taxed as well as a rate by which to tax it. **Figure 9-8** shows a method that accepts two such parameters.

Note In Figure 9-8, notice that one of the arguments to the method has the same name as the corresponding method parameter, and the other has a different name from its corresponding parameter. Each could have the same identifier as its counterpart, or all could be different. Each identifier is local to its own method.

Figure 9-8 A program that calls a `computeTax()` method that requires two parameters

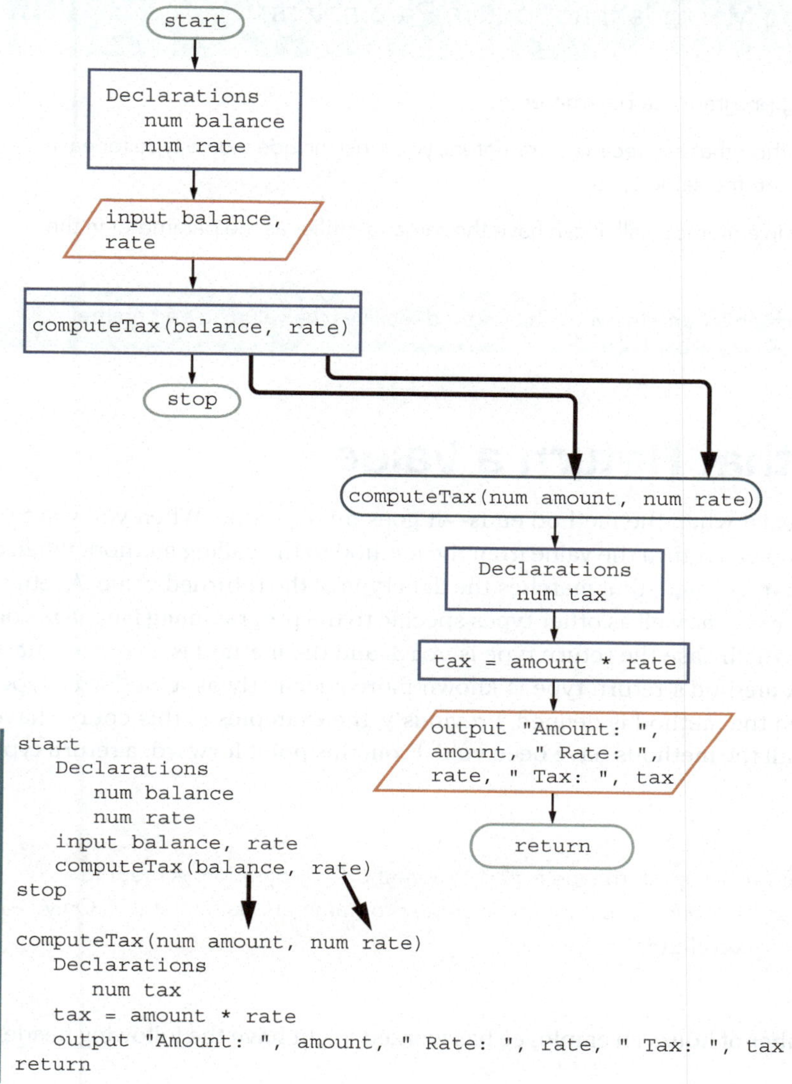


```
start
   Declarations
      num balance
      num rate
   input balance, rate
   computeTax(balance, rate)
stop

computeTax(num amount, num rate)
   Declarations
      num tax
   tax = amount * rate
   output "Amount: ", amount, " Rate: ", rate, " Tax: ", tax
return
```

In Figure 9-8, two parameters (`num amount` and `num rate`) appear within the parentheses in the method header. A comma separates each parameter, and each requires its own declared data type (in this case, both are numeric) as well as its own identifier. When multiple values are passed to a method, they are accepted into the parameters in the order in which they are passed. You can write a method so that it takes any number of parameters in any order. However, when you call a method, the arguments you send to the method must match in order—both in number and in type—the parameters listed in the method declaration. A call of `computeTax(rate, balance)` instead of `computeTax(balance, rate)` would result in incorrect values being displayed in the output statement. If method arguments are the same type—for example, two numeric arguments—passing them to a method in the wrong order results in a logical error. The program will compile and execute but will produce incorrect results in most cases. If a method expects arguments of diverse types—for example, a number and a string—then passing arguments in the wrong order is a syntax error, and the program will not compile.

Two Truths & a Lie | Creating Methods that Require Parameters

1. A value sent to a method from a calling program is a parameter.
2. When you write the declaration for a method that can receive parameters, you must include a data type for each parameter even if multiple parameters are the same type.
3. When a variable is used as an argument in a method call, it can have the same identifier as the parameter in the method header.

The false statement is #1. A calling method sends an argument; when the method receives the value, it is a parameter.

9.4 Creating Methods that Return a Value

A variable declared within a method ceases to exist when the method ends—it goes out of scope. When you want to retain a value that exists when a method ends, you can return the value from the method to the calling method. When a method returns a value, the method must have a **return type** that matches the data type of the returned value. A return type can be any type, which includes `num` and `string`, as well as other types specific to the programming language you are using. A method can also return nothing, in which case the return type is `void`, and the method is a **void method**. (The term *void* means "nothing" or "empty.") A method's return type is known more succinctly as a **method's type**, and it is listed in front of the method name when the method is defined. Previously, the examples in this course have not included return types for methods because all the methods have been void. From this point forward, a return type is included with every method header.

> **Note** | Along with an identifier and parameter list, a return type is part of a method's declaration. A method's return type is not part of its signature, although you might hear some programmers claim that it is. Only the method name and parameter list constitute the signature.

For example, a method that returns the number of hours an employee has worked might have the following header:

```
num getHoursWorked()
```

This method returns a numeric value, so its type is `num`.

When a method returns a value, you usually want to use the returned value in the calling method, although this is not required. For example, **Figure 9-9** shows how a program might use the value returned by the `getHoursWorked()` method.

- A variable named `hours` is declared in the main program.
- The `getHoursWorked()` method call is part of an assignment statement.
- When the method is called, logical control is transferred to the `getHoursWorked()` method, which contains a variable named `workHours`.
- A value is obtained for `workHours`, and the value is returned to the main program where it is assigned to `hours`.

Figure 9-9 A payroll program that calls a method that returns a value

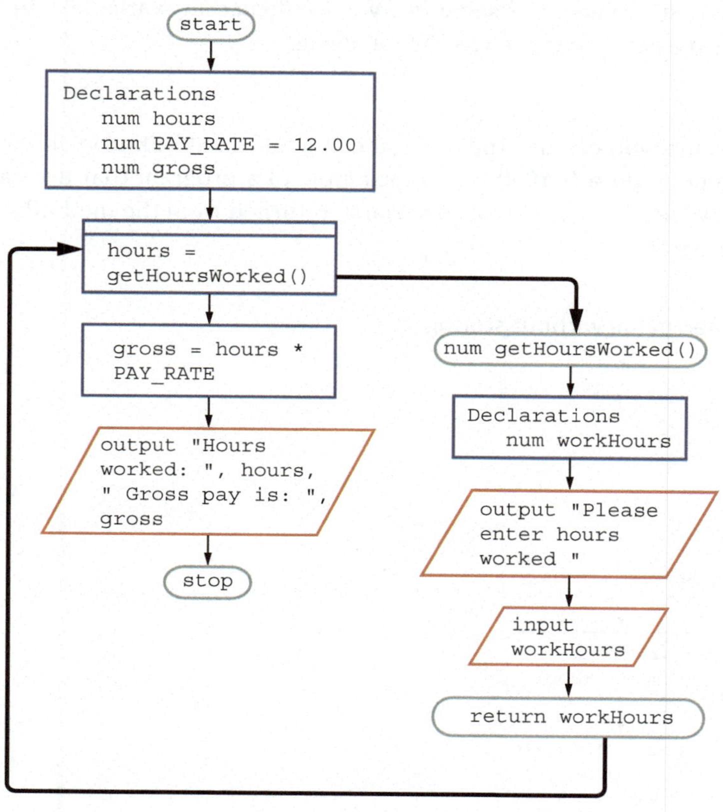

After logical control returns to the main program from the `getHoursWorked()` method, the method's local variable `workHours` no longer exists. However, its value has been stored in the main program where, as `hours`, it can be displayed and used in a calculation.

> **Note** As an example of when you might call a method but not use its returned value, consider a method that gets a character from the keyboard and returns its value to the calling program. In some applications, you would want to use the value of the returned characters. However, in other applications, you might want to tell the user to press any key. Then, you could call the method to accept the character from the keyboard, but you would not care which key was pressed or which key value was returned.

In Figure 9-9, notice the return type `num` that precedes the method name in the `getHoursWorked()` method header. A method's declared return type must match the type of the value used in the `return` statement; if it does not, the program will not compile. In Figure 9-9, a numeric value is correctly included in the `return` statement—the last statement in the `getHoursWorked()` method. When you place a value in a `return` statement, the value is sent from the called method back to the calling method.

A method's `return` statement can return one value at most. The returned value can be a variable or a constant. The value can be a simple or complex data type. Later in this course you will learn to create objects, which are complex data types.

You are not required to assign a method's return value to a variable to use the value. Instead, you can use a method's returned value directly, without storing it. You use a method's value in the same way you would use any variable of the same type. For example, you can output a return value in a statement such as the following:

```
output "Hours worked is ", getHoursWorked()
```

Because `getHoursWorked()` returns a numeric value, you can use the method call `getHoursWorked()` in the same way that you would use any simple numeric value. **Figure 9-10** shows an example of a program that uses a method's return value directly without storing it. The value of the `workHours` variable returned from the method is used directly in the calculation of `gross` in the main program.

Figure 9-10 A program that uses a method's returned value without storing it

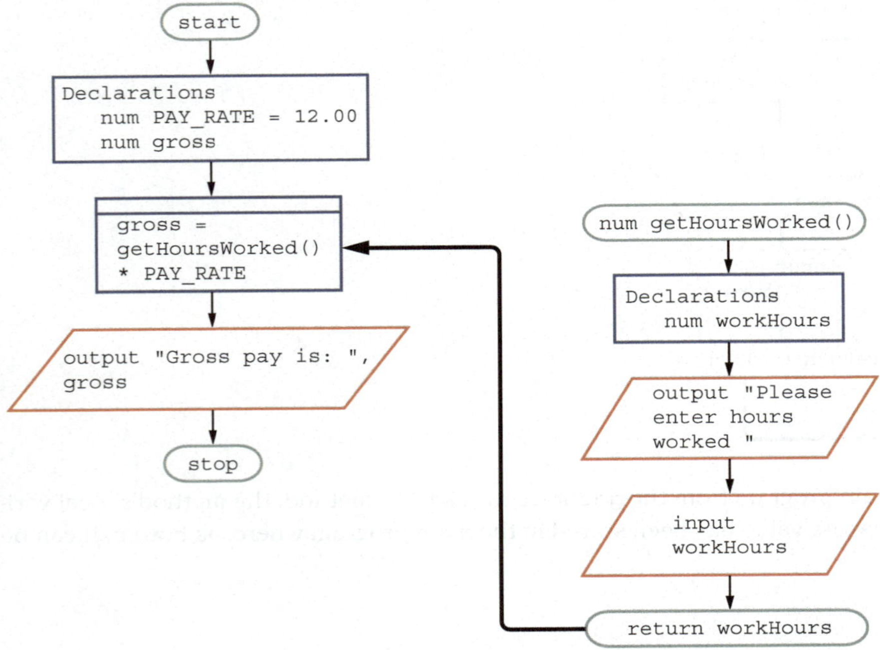

Note When a program needs to use a method's returned value in more than one place, it makes sense to store the returned value in a variable instead of calling the method multiple times. A program statement that calls a method requires more computer time and resources than a statement that does not call any outside methods. You have already learned that programmers use the term *overhead* to describe any extra time and resources required by an operation.

As mentioned earlier, in most programming languages you technically are allowed to include multiple `return` statements in a method, but this course does not recommend the practice for most business programs. For example, consider the `findLargest()` method in **Figure 9-11**. The method accepts three parameters and returns the largest of the values. Although this method works correctly and you might see this technique used, its style is awkward and not structured. Recall that structured logic requires each structure to contain one entry point and one exit point. The `return` statements in Figure 9-11 violate this convention by leaving decision structures before they are complete.

Figure 9-11 Unstructured approach to returning one of several values from a method

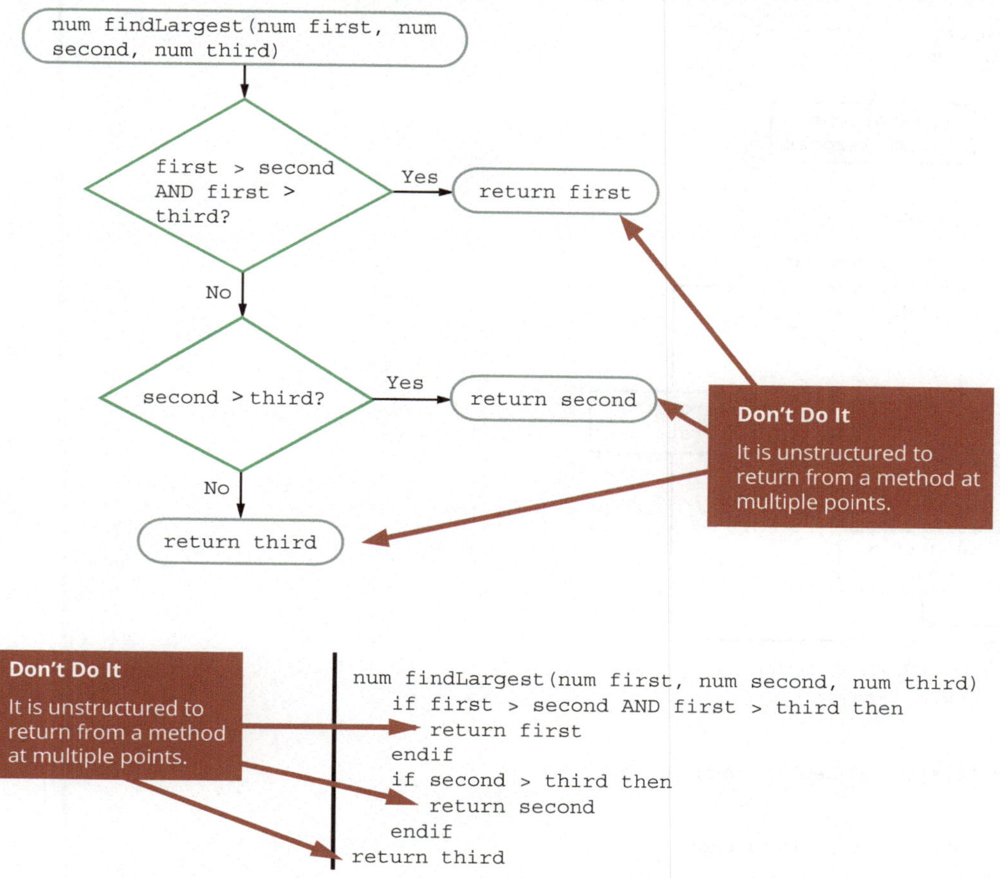
num findLargest(num first, num second, num third)
first > second AND first > third?
Yes
return first
No
second > third?
Yes
return second
No
return third
Don't Do It
It is unstructured to return from a method at multiple points.
Don't Do It
It is unstructured to return from a method at multiple points.
num findLargest(num first, num second, num third)
if first > second AND first > third then
return first
endif
if second > third then
return second
endif
return third

Figure 9-12 shows the superior and recommended way to handle the problem. In Figure 9-12, the largest value is stored in a variable. Then, when the nested decision structure is complete, the stored value is returned in the last method statement.

Using an IPO Chart

When designing methods to use within larger programs, some programmers find it helpful to use an **IPO chart**, a tool that identifies and categorizes each item needed within the method as pertaining to input, processing, or output. For example, consider a method that finds the smallest of three numeric values. When you think about designing this method, you can start by placing each of its components in one of the three processing categories, as shown in **Figure 9-13**.

The IPO chart in Figure 9-13 provides an overview of the processing steps involved in the method. Like a flowchart or pseudocode, an IPO chart is just another tool to help you plan the logic of your programs. Many programmers create an IPO chart only for specific methods in their programs and as an alternative to flowcharting or writing pseudocode. IPO charts provide an overview of input to the method, the processing steps that must occur, and the resulting output. This course emphasizes creating flowcharts and pseudocode, but you can find many more examples of IPO charts on the Web.

Figure 9-12 Recommended, structured approach to returning one of several values from a method

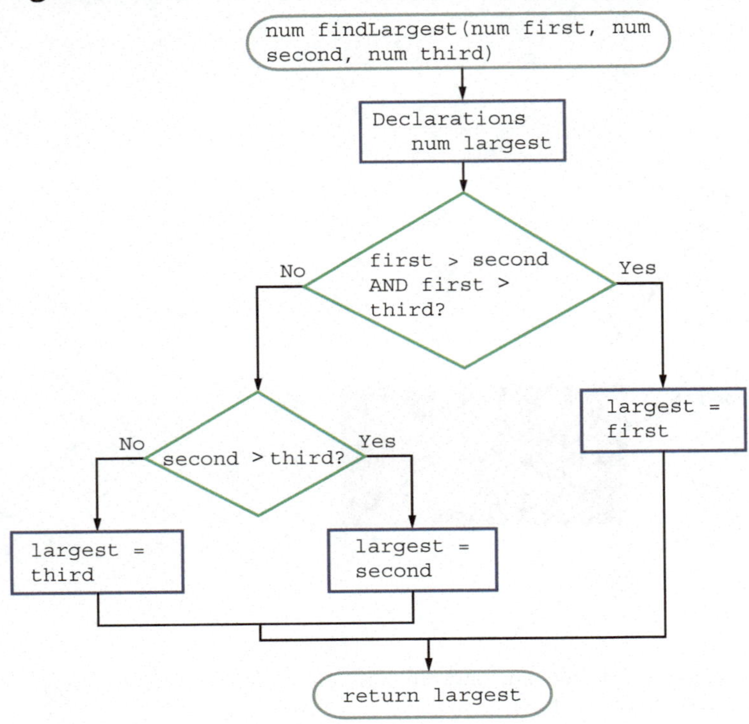


```
num findLargest(num first, num second, num third)
   Declarations
      num largest
   if first > second AND first > third then
      largest = first
   else
      if second > third then
         largest = second
      else
         largest = third
      endif
   endif
return largest
```

Figure 9-13 IPO chart for the method that finds the smallest of three numeric values

Input	Processing	Output
First value Second value Third value	If the first value is smaller than each of the other two, save it as the smallest value; otherwise, if the second value is smaller than the third, save it as the smallest value; otherwise, save the third value as the smallest value	Smallest value

Two Truths & a Lie | Creating Methods that Return a Value

1. The return type for a method can be any type, which includes numeric, character, and string, as well as other more specific types that exist in the programming language you are using.
2. A method's return type must be the same type as one of the method's parameters.
3. You are not required to use a method's returned value.

The false statement is #2. The return type of a method can be any type. The return type must match the type of value in the method's `return` statement. A method's return type is not required to match any of the method's parameters.

9.5 Passing an Array to a Method

You have learned that you can declare an array to create a list of elements, and that you can use any individual array element in the same manner you would use any single variable of the same type. For example, suppose that you declare a numeric array as follows:

```
num someNums[12]
```

You can subsequently output `someNums[0]` or perform arithmetic with `someNums[11]`, just as you would for any simple variable that is not part of an array. Similarly, you can pass a single array element to a method in exactly the same manner you would pass a variable or constant.

Consider the program shown in **Figure 9-14**. This program creates an array of four numeric values and then outputs them. Next, the program calls a method named `tripleTheValue()` four times, passing each of the array elements in turn. The method outputs the passed value, multiplies it by 3, and outputs it again. Finally, back in the calling program, the four numbers are output again. **Figure 9-15** shows an execution of this program in a command-line environment.

As you can see in Figure 9-15, the program displays the four original values, then passes each value to the `tripleTheValue()` method, where it is displayed, multiplied by 3, and displayed again. After the method executes four times, the logic returns to the main program where the four values are displayed again, showing that they are unchanged by the statements within `tripleTheValue()`. The `oneVal` variable is local to the `tripleTheValue()` method; therefore, any changes to it are not permanent and are not reflected in the array declared in the main program. The `oneVal` variable in the `tripleTheValue()` method holds only a copy of each array element passed into the method, and although `oneVal` is altered in the method, each newly assigned, larger value exists only while the `tripleTheValue()` method is executing. In all respects, a single array element acts just like any single variable of the same type would.

Instead of passing a single array element to a method, you can pass an entire array as an argument. You can indicate that a method parameter must be an array by using the convention of placing square brackets after the data type in the method's parameter list. Arrays, unlike simple built-in types, are **passed by reference**; the method receives the actual memory address of the array and has access to the actual values in the array elements. The name of an array represents a memory address, and the subscript used with an array name represents an offset from that address. Therefore, when you pass an array to a method, changes you make to array elements within the method are reflected in the original array that was sent to the method.

Figure 9-14 The `PassArrayElement` program

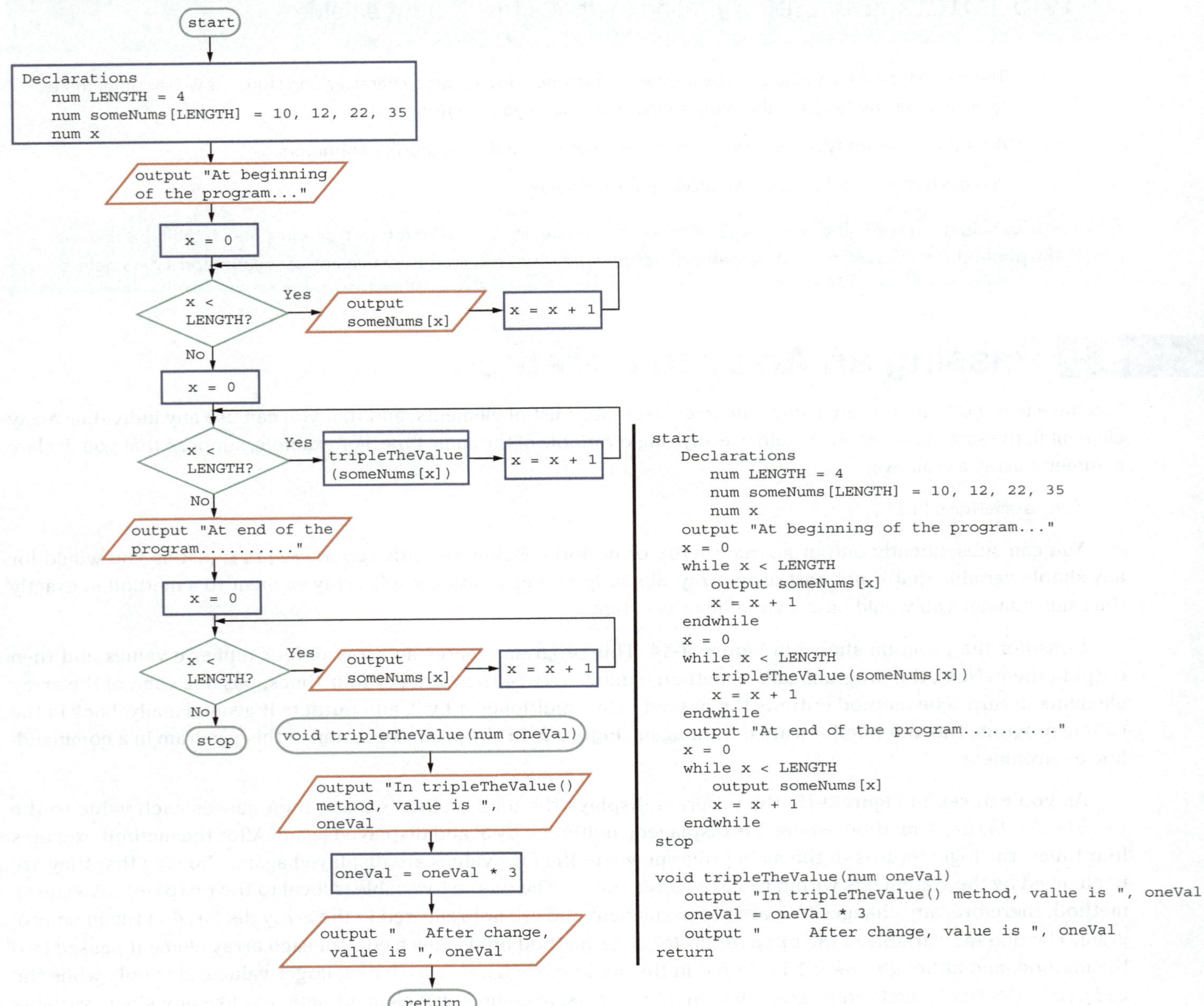

```
start
   Declarations
      num LENGTH = 4
      num someNums[LENGTH] = 10, 12, 22, 35
      num x
   output "At beginning of the program..."
   x = 0
   while x < LENGTH
      output someNums[x]
      x = x + 1
   endwhile
   x = 0
   while x < LENGTH
      tripleTheValue(someNums[x])
      x = x + 1
   endwhile
   output "At end of the program........."
   x = 0
   while x < LENGTH
      output someNums[x]
      x = x + 1
   endwhile
stop

void tripleTheValue(num oneVal)
   output "In tripleTheValue() method, value is ", oneVal
   oneVal = oneVal * 3
   output "      After change, value is ", oneVal
return
```

Figure 9-15 Execution of the `PassArrayElement` program

```
C:\WINDOWS\system32\cmd.exe
At beginning of the program...    10    12    22    35
In tripleTheValue() method, value is 10
      After change, value is 30
In tripleTheValue() method, value is 12
      After change, value is 36
In tripleTheValue() method, value is 22
      After change, value is 66
In tripleTheValue() method, value is 35
      After change, value is 105
At end of the program.........    10    12    22    35
```

Note Some languages, such as Visual Basic, use parentheses after an identifier to indicate an array as a parameter to a method. Many other languages, including Java, C++, and C#, use square brackets after the data type. Because this course uses parentheses following method names, it uses brackets to indicate arrays.

The program shown in **Figure 9-16** creates an array of four numeric values. After the numbers are output, the entire array is passed to a method named `quadrupleTheValues()`. Within the method header, the parameter is declared as an array by using square brackets after the parameter type. Within the method, the numbers are output, which shows that they retain their values from the main program upon entering the method. Then the array values are multiplied by 4. Even though `quadrupleTheValues()` returns nothing to the calling program, when the program displays the array for the last time within the mainline logic, all of the values have been changed to their new quadrupled values.

Figure 9-16 `PassEntireArray` program

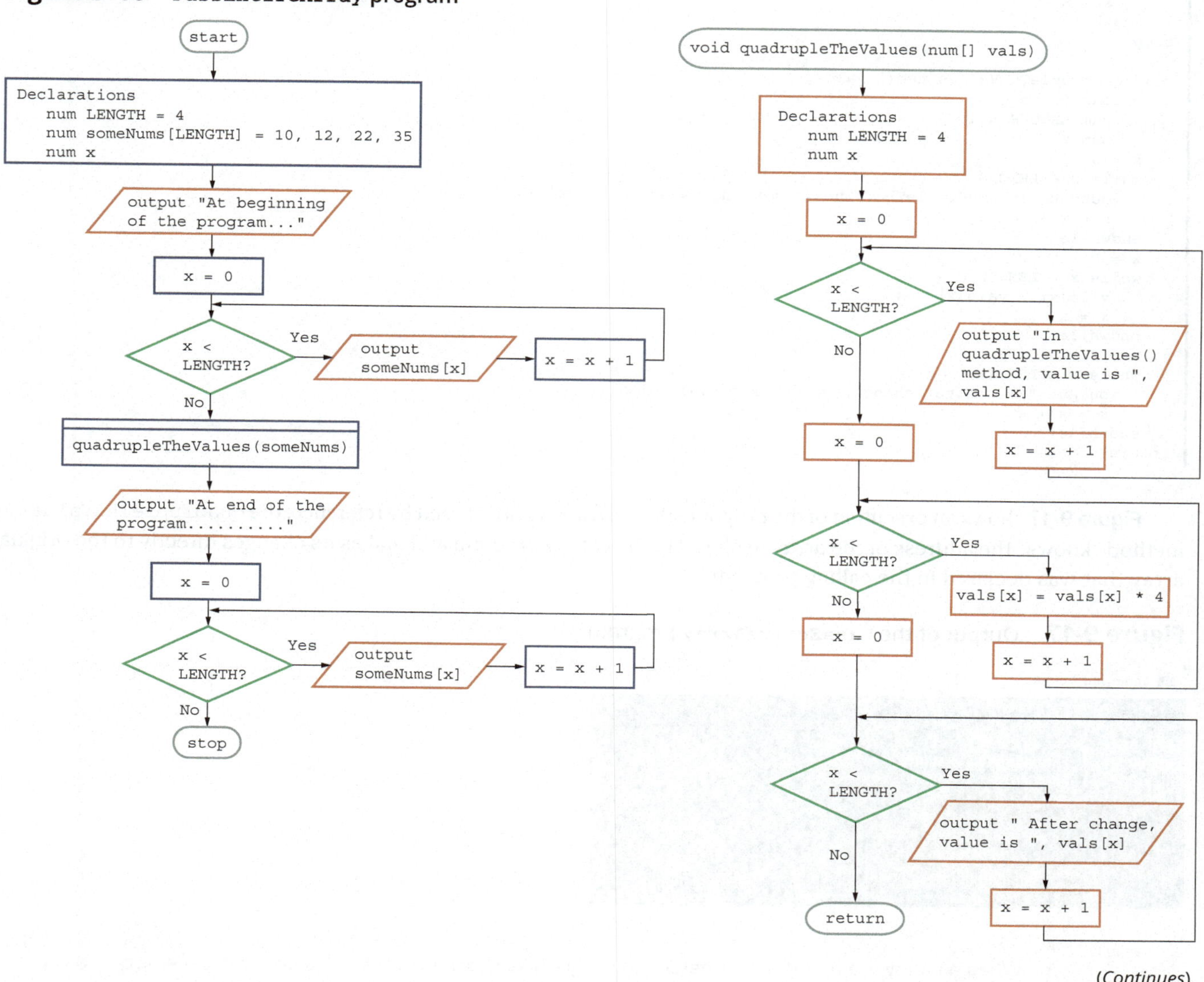

(Continues)

Figure 9-16 *(Continued)*

```
start
   Declarations
      num LENGTH = 4
      num someNums[LENGTH] = 10, 12, 22, 35
      num x
   output "At beginning of the program..."
   x = 0
   while x < LENGTH
      output someNums[x]
      x = x + 1
   endwhile
   quadrupleTheValues(someNums)
   output "At end of the program........."
   x = 0
   while x < LENGTH
      output someNums[x]
      x = x + 1
   endwhile
stop

void quadrupleTheValues(num[] vals)
   Declarations
      num LENGTH = 4
      num x
   x = 0
   while x < LENGTH
      output "In quadrupleTheValues() method, value is ", vals[x]
      x = x + 1
   endwhile
   x = 0
   while x < LENGTH
      vals[x] = vals[x] * 4
      x = x + 1
   endwhile
   x = 0
   while x < LENGTH
      output "     After change, value is ", vals[x]
      x = x + 1
   endwhile
return
```

Figure 9-17 shows an execution of the program. Because arrays are passed by reference, the `quadrupleTheValues()` method "knows" the address of the array declared in the calling program and makes its changes directly to the original array that was declared in the calling program.

Figure 9-17 Output of the `PassEntireArray` program

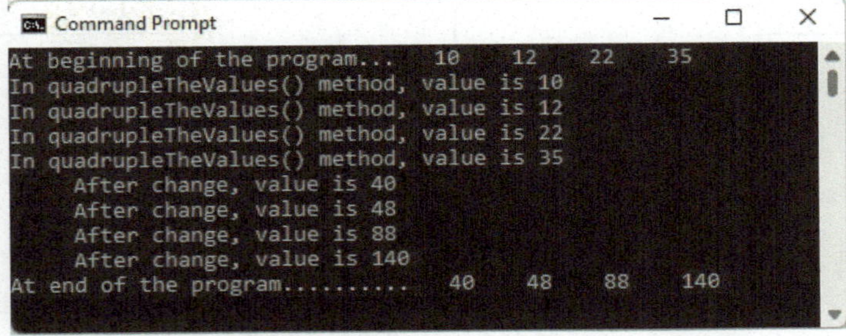

Note When an array is a method parameter, the square brackets in the method header remain empty and do not hold a size. The array name that is passed is a memory address that indicates the start of the array. Depending on the language you are working in, you can control the values you use for a subscript to the array in different ways. In some languages, you might also want to pass a constant that indicates the array size to the method. In other languages, you can access the automatically created length field for the array. Either way, the array size itself is never implied when you use the array name. The array name indicates only the starting point from which subscripts will be used.

Two Truths & a Lie | Passing an Array to a Method

1. You can pass an entire array as a method's argument.
2. You can indicate that a method parameter must be an array by placing square brackets after the data type in the method's parameter list.
3. Arrays, unlike simple built-in types, are passed by value; the method receives a copy of the original array.

The false statement is #3. Arrays, unlike simple built-in types, are passed by reference; the method receives the actual memory address of the array and has access to the actual values in the array elements.

9.6 Overloading Methods

In programming, **overloading** involves supplying diverse meanings for a single identifier. When you use the English language, you frequently overload words. When you say *break a window*, *break bread*, *break the bank*, and *take a break*, you describe four very different actions that use different methods and produce different results. However, anyone who speaks English well comprehends your meaning because *break* is understood in the context of the discussion.

Note In most programming languages, some operators are overloaded. For example, a + between two values indicates addition, but a single + to the left of a value means the value is positive. The + sign has different meanings based on the arguments used with it.

Note Overloading a method is an example of **polymorphism**—the ability of a method to act appropriately according to the context. Literally, *polymorphism* means "many forms."

When you **overload a method**, you write multiple methods with a shared name but different parameter lists. When you call an overloaded method, the language translator understands which version of the method to use based on the arguments used.

For example, suppose that you create a method to output a message and the amount due on a customer bill, as shown in **Figure 9-18**. The method receives a numeric parameter that represents the customer's balance and produces two lines of output. Assume that you also need a method that is similar to `printBill()`, except the new method applies a discount to the customer bill. One solution to this problem would be to write a new method with a different name—for example, `printBillWithDiscount()`. A downside to this approach is that a programmer who uses your methods must remember the names of each slightly different version. It is more natural for your methods' clients to use a single well-designed method name for the task of printing bills, but to be able to provide different arguments as appropriate. In this case, you can overload the `printBill()` method so that, in addition to the version that takes a single numeric argument, you can create a version that takes two numeric arguments—one that represents the balance and one that represents the discount rate. Figure 9-18 shows the two versions of the `printBill()` method.

If both versions of `printBill()` are included in a program and you call the method using a single numeric argument, as in `printBill(custBalance)`, the first version of the method in Figure 9-18 executes. If you use two numeric arguments in the call, as in `printBill(custBalance, rate)`, the second version of the method executes.

Figure 9-18 Two overloaded versions of the `printBill()` method

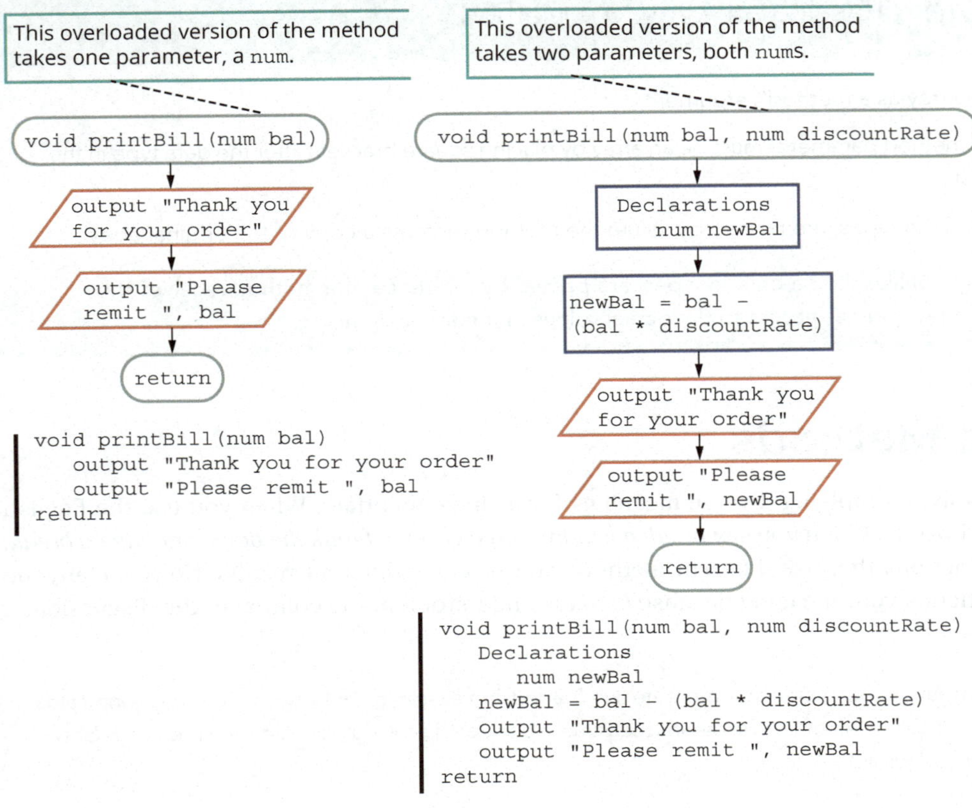


```
void printBill(num bal)
   output "Thank you for your order"
   output "Please remit ", bal
return
```

```
void printBill(num bal, num discountRate)
   Declarations
      num newBal
   newBal = bal - (bal * discountRate)
   output "Thank you for your order"
   output "Please remit ", newBal
return
```

If it suited your needs, you could provide more versions of the `printBill()` method, as shown in **Figure 9-19**. The first version accepts a numeric parameter that holds the customer's balance and a string parameter that holds an additional message that can be customized for the bill recipient and displayed on the bill. For example, if a program makes a method call such as the following, the first version of `printBill()` in the figure will execute:

```
printBill(custBal, "Due in 10 days")
```

The second version of the method in Figure 9-19 accepts three parameters, providing a balance, discount rate, and customized message. For example, the following method call would use this second version of the method in the figure:

```
printBill(balanceDue, discountRate, specialMessage)
```

Overloading methods is never required in a program. Instead, you could create multiple methods with unique identifiers such as `printBill()` and `printBillWithDiscountAndMessage()`. Overloading methods does not reduce your work when creating a program; you need to write each method individually. The advantage is provided to your method's clients; those who use your methods need to remember just one appropriate name for all related tasks.

> **Note** In many programming languages, the `output` statement is actually an overloaded method that you call. Using a single name such as `output`, whether you want to output a number, a `string`, or any combination of the two, is convenient.

Even if you write two or more overloaded versions of a method, many program clients will use just one version. For example, suppose that you develop a bill-creating program that contains all four versions of the `printBill()` method just discussed, and then sell it to different companies. An organization that adopts your program and its methods might want to use only one or two versions of the method. You probably own many devices for which only some of the features are meaningful to you; for example, some people who own microwave ovens use only the *Popcorn* button or never use *Defrost*.

Figure 9-19 Two additional overloaded versions of the `printBill()` method

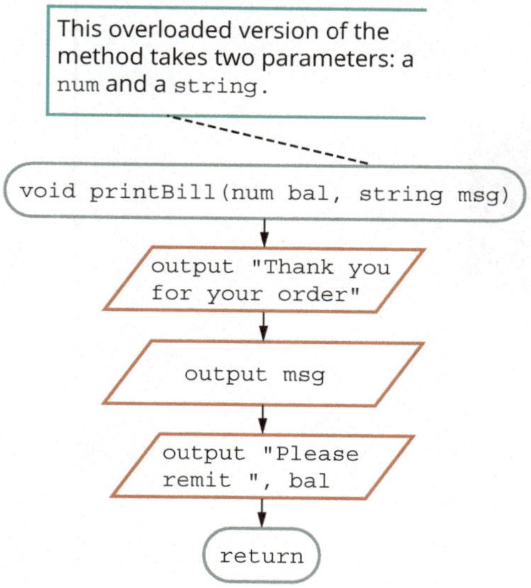

```
void printBill(num bal, string msg)
   output "Thank you for your order"
   output msg
   output "Please remit ", bal
return
```

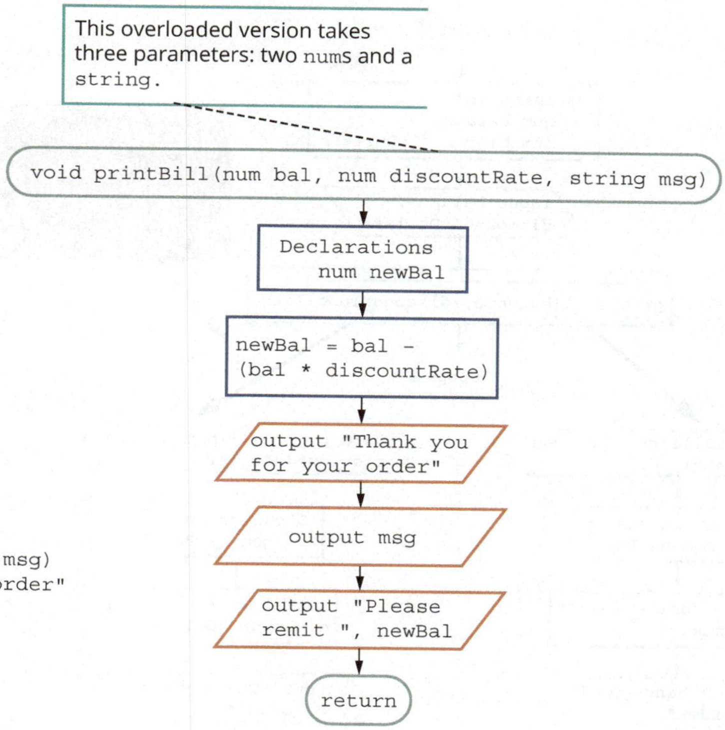

```
void printBill(num bal, num discountRate, string msg)
   Declarations
      num newBal
   newBal = bal - (bal * discountRate)
   output "Thank you for your order"
   output msg
   output "Please remit ", newBal
return
```

Avoiding Ambiguous Methods

When you overload a method, you run the risk of creating **ambiguous methods**—a situation in which the compiler cannot determine which method to use. Every time you call a method, the compiler decides whether a suitable method exists; if so, the method executes, and if not, you receive an error message.

For example, suppose that you write two versions of a `printBill()` method, as shown in the program in **Figure 9-20**. One version of the method is intended to accept a customer balance and a discount rate, and the other is intended to accept a customer balance and a discount amount expressed in dollars.

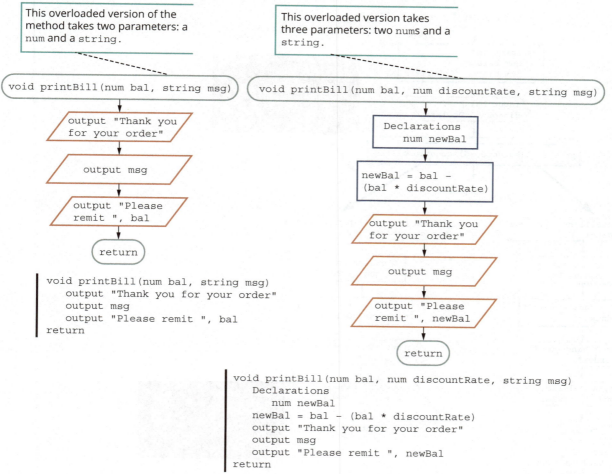

Each of the two versions of `printBill()` in Figure 9-20 is a valid method on its own. However, when the two versions exist in the same program, a problem arises. When the main program calls `printBill()` using two numeric arguments, the compiler cannot determine which version to call. You might think that the version of the method with a parameter named `discountInDollars` would execute, because the method call uses the identifier `discountInDollars`. However, the compiler determines which version of a method to call based on argument data types only, not their identifiers. Because both versions of the `printBill()` method could accept two numeric parameters, the compiler cannot determine which version to execute, so an error occurs and program compilation stops.

Note An overloaded method is not ambiguous on its own—it becomes ambiguous only if you make a method call that matches multiple method signatures. In many languages, a program with potentially ambiguous methods will run without problems if you don't make any method calls that match more than one method.

Figure 9-20 Program that contains ambiguous method call

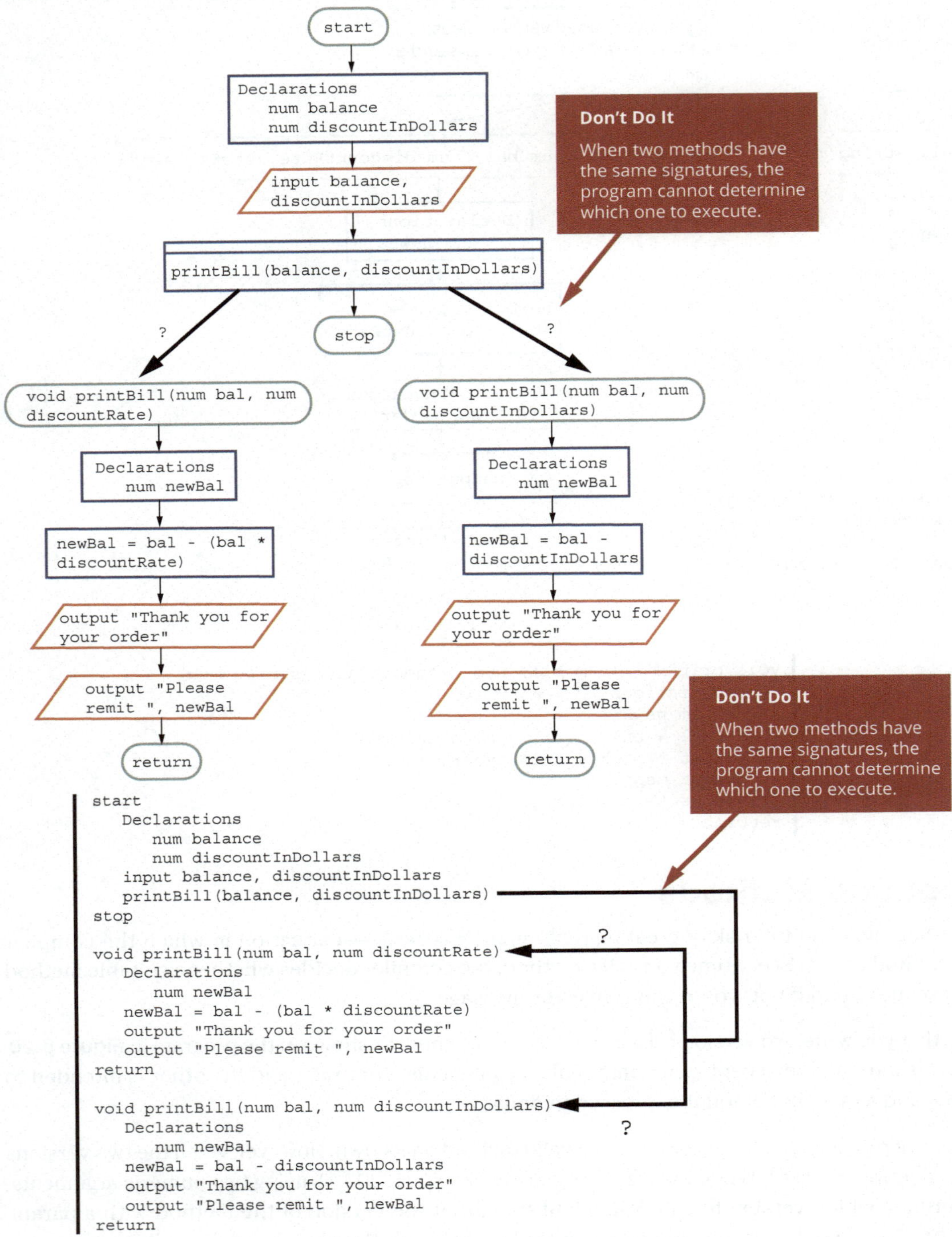

Methods can be overloaded correctly by providing different parameter lists for methods with the same name. Methods with identical names that have identical parameter lists but different return types are not overloaded—they are ambiguous. For example, the following two method headers create ambiguity:

```
string aMethod(num x)
num aMethod(num y)
```

The compiler determines which version of a method to call based on parameter lists, not return types. When the method call `aMethod(17)` is made, the compiler will not know which of the two methods to execute because both possible choices take a numeric argument.

Note All the popular object-oriented programming languages support multiple numeric data types. For example, Java, C#, C++, and Visual Basic all support integer (whole number) data types that are different from floating-point (decimal place) data types. Many languages have even more specialized numeric types, such as signed and unsigned. Methods that accept different specific types are correctly overloaded.

Two Truths & a Lie | Overloading Methods

1. In programming, overloading involves supplying diverse meanings for a single identifier.
2. When you overload a method, you write multiple methods with different names but identical parameter lists.
3. Methods can be overloaded correctly by providing different parameter lists for methods with the same name.

The false statement is #2. When you overload a method, you write methods with a shared name but different parameter lists.

9.7 Using Predefined Methods

All modern programming languages allow you to use many methods that have already been written for programmers. Predefined methods might originate from several sources:

- Some prewritten methods are built into a language. For example, methods that perform input and output are usually predefined.
- When you work on a program in a team, each programmer might be assigned specific methods to create, and your methods will interact with methods written by others.
- If you work for a company, many standard methods might already have been written and you will be required to use them. For example, the company might have a standard method that displays its logo.

Predefined methods save you time and effort. For example, in most languages, displaying a message on the screen involves using a built-in method. When you want to display *Hello* on the command prompt screen in C#, you write the following:

```
Console.WriteLine("Hello");
```

In Java, you write:

```
System.out.println("Hello");
```

In these statements, you can recognize `WriteLine()` and `println()` as method names because they are followed by parentheses; the parentheses hold an argument that represents the message to display. If these methods were not prewritten, you would have to know the low-level details of how to manipulate pixels on a screen to display the characters. Instead, by using the prewritten methods, you can concentrate on the higher-level task of displaying a useful and appropriate message.

Note In C#, the convention is to begin method names with an uppercase letter. In Java, method names conventionally begin with a lowercase letter. The `WriteLine()` and `println()` methods follow their respective language's convention. The `WriteLine()` and `println()` methods are both overloaded in their respective languages. For example, if you pass a string to either method, the version of the method that accepts a string parameter executes, but if you pass a number, another version that accepts a numeric parameter executes.

Most programming languages also contain a variety of mathematical methods, such as those that compute the square root or absolute value of a number. Other methods retrieve the current date and time from the operating system or select a random number to use in a game application. These methods were written as a convenience for you—computing a square root and generating random numbers are complicated tasks, so it is convenient to have methods already written, tested, and available when you need them. The names of the methods that perform these functions differ among programming languages, so you need to research the language's documentation to use them. For example, many of a language's methods are described in introductory programming language textbooks, and you can also find language documentation online.

Whether you want to use a predefined method or any other method, you should know the following four details:

- What the method does in general—for example, compute a square root.
- The method's name—for example, it might be `sqrt()`.
- The method's required parameters—for example, a square root method might require a single numeric parameter. There might be multiple overloaded versions of the method from which you can choose. For example, most languages support different data types for integers and floating-point numbers, so one square root method version might accept an integer and another version might accept a floating-point number.
- The method's return type—for example, a square root method most likely returns a numeric value that is the square root of the argument passed to the method.

You do not need to know how the method is implemented—that is, how the instruction statements are written within it. Like all methods, you can use built-in methods without worrying about their low-level implementation details.

Two Truths & a Lie | Using Predefined Methods

1. The name of a method that performs a specific function (such as generating a random number) is likely to be the same in various programming languages.
2. When you want to use a predefined method, you should know what the method does in general, along with its name, required parameters, and return type.
3. When you want to use a predefined method, you do not need to know how the method works internally to be able to use the method effectively.

The false statement is #1. Methods that perform standard functions are likely to have different names in various languages.

9.8 Method Design Issues: Implementation Hiding, Cohesion, and Coupling

To design effective methods, you should consider several program qualities:

- You should employ implementation hiding.
- You should strive to increase cohesion.
- You should strive to reduce coupling.

Understanding Implementation Hiding

An important principle of modularization is the notion of **implementation hiding**, the encapsulation of method details. That is, when a program makes a request to a method, it doesn't know the details of how the method is executed. For example, when you make a restaurant reservation, you do not need to know how the reservation is actually recorded at the restaurant—perhaps it is written in a book, marked on a large chalkboard, or entered into a computerized database. The implementation details don't concern you as a patron, and if the restaurant changes its methods from one year to the next, the change does not affect your use of the reservation method—you still call and provide your name, a date, and a time. With well-written methods, using implementation hiding means that a method that calls another must know only the following:

- The name of the called method
- What type of information to send to the method
- What type of return data to expect from the method

The **interface to a method**—its name and the data types passed in and out—is the only part of a method with which the method's client (or method's caller) interacts. The program does *not* need to know how the method works internally. Additionally, if you substitute a new, improved method implementation but the interface to the method does not change, you won't need to make changes in any methods that call the altered method. Programmers refer to hidden implementation details as existing in a **black box**—you can examine what goes in and what comes out, but not the details of how the method works inside.

Increasing Cohesion

When you begin to design computer programs, it is difficult to decide how much to put into a method. For example, a process that requires 40 instructions can be contained in a single 40-instruction method, two 20-instruction methods, five 8-instruction methods, or many other combinations. In most programming languages, any of these combinations is allowed; you can write a program that executes and produces correct results no matter how you divide the individual steps into methods. However, placing too many or too few instructions in a single method makes a program harder to follow and reduces flexibility.

To help determine the appropriate division of tasks among methods, you want to analyze each method's **cohesion**, which refers to how the internal statements of a method serve to accomplish the method's purpose. In highly cohesive methods, all the operations are related, or "go together." As you learned earlier in this course, such methods demonstrate *functional cohesion*—all their operations contribute to the performance of a single task. Functionally cohesive methods usually are more reliable than those that have low cohesion; they are considered stronger, and they make programs easier to write, read, and maintain.

For example, consider a method that calculates gross pay. The method receives parameters that define a worker's pay rate and number of hours worked. The method computes gross pay and displays it. The cohesion of this method is high because each of its instructions contributes to one task—computing gross pay. If you can write a sentence describing what a method does using only two words—for example, *Compute gross*, *Cube value*, or *Display record*—the method is probably functionally cohesive.

You might work in a programming environment that has a rule such as *No method will be longer than can be printed on one page* or *No method will have more than 30 lines of code*. The rule maker is trying to achieve more cohesion, but such rules are arbitrary. A two-line method could have low cohesion and a 40-line method might have high cohesion. Because good, functionally cohesive methods perform only one task, they tend to be short. However, the issue is not size. If it takes 20 statements to perform one task within a method, the method is still cohesive.

Most programmers do not consciously make decisions about cohesiveness for each method they write. Rather, they develop a "feel" for what types of tasks belong together, and for which subsets of tasks should be diverted to their own methods.

Reducing Coupling

Coupling is a measure of the strength of the connection between two program methods; it expresses the extent to which information is exchanged by methods. Coupling is either tight or loose, depending on how much one method relies on information from another. **Tight coupling**, which occurs when methods depend on each other excessively, makes programs more prone to errors. With tight coupling, you have many data paths to keep track of, many chances for bad data to pass from one method to another, and many chances for one method to alter information needed by another method. **Loose coupling** occurs when methods do not depend on others. In general, you want to reduce coupling as much as possible because connections between methods make them more difficult to write, maintain, and reuse.

Imagine four cooks wandering in and out of a kitchen while preparing a stew. If each is allowed to add seasonings at will without the knowledge of the other cooks, you could end up with a culinary disaster. Similarly, if four payroll program methods can alter your gross pay without the "knowledge" of the other methods, you could end up with a financial disaster. A program in which several methods have access to your gross pay figure has methods that are tightly coupled. A superior program would control access to the payroll value by passing it only to methods that need it.

You can evaluate whether coupling between methods is loose or tight by examining how methods share data.

- Tight coupling occurs when methods have access to the same globally defined variables. When one method changes the value stored in a variable, other methods are affected. You should avoid tight coupling, but be aware that you might see it in programs written by others.
- Loose coupling occurs when a copy of data that must be shared is passed from one method to another. That way, the sharing of data is always purposeful—variables must be explicitly passed to and from methods that use them. The loosest (best) methods pass a single argument, if possible, rather than many variables or entire records.

Additionally, there is a time and a place for shortcuts. If a memo must go out in five minutes, you don't have time to change fonts or add clip art with your word processor. Similarly, if you need a quick programming result, you might very well use cryptic variable names, tight coupling, and minimal cohesion. When you create a professional application, however, you should keep professional guidelines in mind.

Two Truths & a Lie | Method Design Issues: Implementation Hiding, Cohesion, and Coupling

1. A calling method must know the interface to any method it calls.
2. You should try to avoid loose coupling, which occurs when methods do not depend on others.
3. Functional cohesion occurs when all operations in a method contribute to the performance of only one task.

The false statement is #2. You should aim for loose coupling so that methods are independent.

9.9 Understanding Recursion

Recursion occurs when a method is defined in terms of itself. A method that calls itself is a **recursive method**. Some programming languages do not allow a method to call itself, but those that do can be used to create recursive methods that produce interesting effects. **Figure 9-21** shows a simple example of recursion. The program calls an `infinity()` method, which displays *Help!* and calls itself. The second call to `infinity()` displays *Help!* and generates a third call. The result is a large number of repetitions of the `infinity()` method. The output is shown in **Figure 9-22**.

Every time you call a method, the address to which the program should return at the completion of the method is stored in a memory location called the *stack*. When a method ends, the address is retrieved from the stack and the program returns to the location where the method call was made, then proceeds to the next instruction. For example, suppose that a program calls `methodA()` and that `methodA()` calls `methodB()`. When the program calls `methodA()`, a return address is stored in the stack, and then `methodA()` begins execution. When `methodA()` calls `methodB()`, a return address in `methodA()` is stored in the stack and `methodB()` begins execution. When `methodB()` ends, the last

Figure 9-21 A program that calls a recursive method

```
start
   infinity()
stop

infinity()
   output "Help! "
   infinity()
return
```

Figure 9-22 Output of the program in Figure 9-21

```
C:\WINDOWS\system32\cmd.exe
lp! Help! Help! Help! Help! Help! Help! Help! Help! Help! Help! Help! Help! Help! Help! Help! Hel
p! Help! Help! Help! Help! Help! Help! Help! Help! Help! Help! Help! Help! Help! Help! Help! Help
! Help! Help! Help! Help! Help! Help! Help! Help! Help! Help! Help! Help! Help! Help! Help! Help!
 Help! Help! Help! Help! Help! Help! Help! Help! Help! Help! Help! Help! Help! Help! Help! Help!
Help! Help! Help! Help! Help! Help! Help! Help! Help! Help! Help! Help! Help! Help! Help! Help! H
elp! Help! Help! Help! Help! Help! Help! Help! Help! Help! Help! Help! Help! Help! Help! Help! He
lp! Help! Help! Help! Help! Help! Help! Help! Help! Help! Help! Help! Help! Help! Help! Help! Hel
p! Help! Help! Help! Help! Help! Help! Help! Help! Help! Help! Help! Help! Help! Help! Help! Help
! Help! Help! Help! Help! Help! Help! Help! Help! Help! Help! Help! Help! Help! Help! Help! Help!
 Help! Help! Help! Help! Help! Help! Help! Help! Help! Help! Help! Help! Help! Help! Help! Help!
Help! Help! Help! Help! Help! Help! Help! Help! Help! Help! Help! Help! Help! Help! Help! Help! H
elp! Help! Help! Help! Help! Help! Help! Help! Help! Help! Help! Help! Help! Help! Help! Help! He
lp! Help! Help! Help! Help! Help! Help! Help! Help! Help! Help! Help! Help! Help! Help! Help! Hel
p! Help! Help! Help! Help! Help! Help! Help! Help! Help! Help! Help! Help! Help! Help! Help! Help
! Help! Help! Help! Help! Help! Help! Help! Help! Help! Help! Help! Help! Help! Help! Help! Help!
 Help! Help! Help! Help! Help! Help! Help! Help! Help! Help! Help! Help! Help! Help! Help! Help!
```

entered address is retrieved from the stack and program control returns to complete `methodA()`. When `methodA()` ends, the remaining address is retrieved from the stack and program control returns to the main program method to continue execution.

Like all computer memory, the stack has a finite size. When the program in Figure 9-21 calls the `infinity()` method, the stack receives so many return addresses that it eventually overflows. The recursive calls will end after an excessive number of repetitions and the program issues an error message.

Of course, there is no practical use for an infinitely recursive program. Just as you must be careful not to create endless loops, when you write useful recursive methods you must provide a way for the recursion to stop eventually. The input values that cause a method to recur are called the **recursive cases**, and the input value that makes the recursion stop is called the **base case** or **terminating case**.

Figure 9-23 shows an application that uses recursion productively. The program calls a recursive method that computes the sum of every integer from 1 up to and including the method's argument value. For example, the sum of every integer up to and including 3 is 1+2+3, or 6, and the sum of every integer up to and including 4 is 1+2+3+4, or 10.

Figure 9-23 Program that uses `cumulativeSum()` method

```
start
   Declarations
      num LIMIT = 10
      num number
   number = 1
   while number <= LIMIT
      output "When number is ", number,
         " then cumulativeSum(number) is ",
         cumulativeSum(number)
      number = number + 1
   endwhile
return

num cumulativeSum(num number)
   Declarations
      num returnVal
   if number = 1 then
      returnVal = number
   else
      returnVal = number + cumulativeSum(number - 1)
   endif
return returnVal
```

When thinking about cumulative summing relationships, remember that the sum of all the integers up to and including any number is that number plus the sum of the integers for the next lower number. In other words, consider the following:

- The sum of the digits from 1, up to and including 1, is simply 1.
- The sum of the digits from 1 through 2 is the previous sum, plus 2.
- The sum of the digits from 1 through 3 is the previous sum, plus 3.
- The sum of the digits from 1 through 4 is the previous sum, plus 4.
- And so on.

The recursive `cumulativeSum()` method in Figure 9-23 uses this knowledge. For each `number`, its cumulative sum consists of the value of the number itself plus the cumulative sum of all the previous lesser numbers. The program in Figure 9-23 calls the `cumulativeSum()` method 10 times in a loop to show the cumulative sum of every integer from 1 through 10. **Figure 9-24** shows the output.

Figure 9-24 Output of the program in Figure 9-23

```
C:\WINDOWS\system32\cmd.exe
When number is 1 then cumulativeSum(number) is 1
When number is 2 then cumulativeSum(number) is 3
When number is 3 then cumulativeSum(number) is 6
When number is 4 then cumulativeSum(number) is 10
When number is 5 then cumulativeSum(number) is 15
When number is 6 then cumulativeSum(number) is 21
When number is 7 then cumulativeSum(number) is 28
When number is 8 then cumulativeSum(number) is 36
When number is 9 then cumulativeSum(number) is 45
When number is 10 then cumulativeSum(number) is 55
```

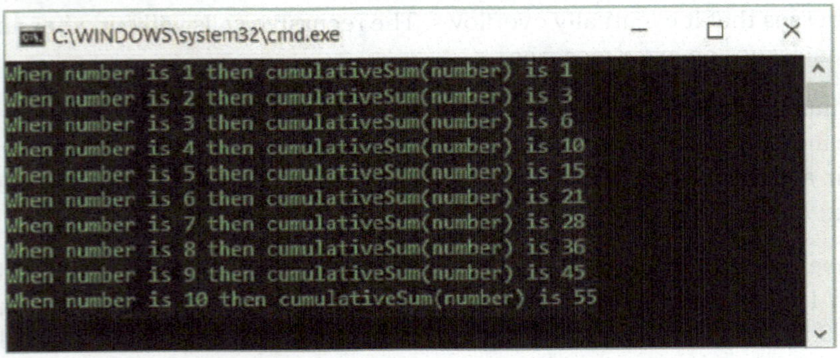

If you examine Figures 9-23 and 9-24 together, you can see the following:

- When 1 is passed to the `cumulativeSum()` method, the `if` statement within the method determines that the argument is equal to 1, `returnVal` becomes 1, and 1 is returned for output. (The input value 1 is the base case or terminating case.)
- On the next pass through the loop, 2 is passed to the `cumulativeSum()` method. When the method receives 2 as an argument, the `if` statement within the method is false, and `returnVal` is set to 2 plus the value of `cumulativeSum(1)`. (The input value 2 is a recursive case.) This second call to `cumulativeSum()` using 1 as an argument returns a 1, so when the method ends, it returns 2+1, or 3.
- On the third pass through the loop within the calling program, 3 is passed to the `cumulativeSum()` method. When the method receives 3 as an argument, the `if` statement within the method is false and the method returns 3 plus the value of `cumulativeSum(2)`. (The input value 3, like 2, is a recursive case.) The value of this call is 2 plus `cumulativeSum(1)`. The value of `cumulativeSum(1)` is 1. Ultimately, `cumulativeSum(3)` is 3+2+1.

Many sophisticated programs that operate on lists of items use recursive processing. However, following the logic of a recursive method can be difficult, and programs that use recursion are sometimes error-prone and hard to debug. Because such programs also can be hard for others to maintain, some business organizations forbid their programmers from using recursive logic in company programs. Many of the problems solved by recursive methods can be solved using loops. For example, examine the program in **Figure 9-25**. This program produces the same result as the previous recursive program, but in a more straightforward fashion.

Figure 9-25 Nonrecursive program that computes cumulative sums

```
start
   Declarations
      num number
      num total
      num LIMIT = 10
   total = 0
   number = 1
   while number <= LIMIT
      total = total + number
      output "When number is ", number,
         " then the cumulative sum of 1 through",
         number, " is ", total
      number = number + 1
   endwhile
stop
```

Note An everyday example of recursion is printed on shampoo bottles: *Lather, rinse, repeat.* If you search *recursion* in Google, the question appears: *Did you mean recursion?* A humorous dictionary entry is "Recursion: See Recursion." These examples contain an element of truth, but useful recursive algorithms always have a point at which the infinite loop is exited. In other words, when recursion is implemented correctly, the base case or terminating case is always reached at some point.

Two Truths & a Lie | Understanding Recursion

1. A method that calls itself is a recursive method.
2. Every time you call a method, the address to which the program should return at the completion of the method is stored in a memory location called the stack.
3. Following the logic of a recursive method is usually much easier than following the logic of an ordinary program, so recursion makes debugging easier.

The false statement is #3. Following the logic of a recursive method is difficult, and programs that use recursion are sometimes error-prone and hard to debug.

Summary

- A method is a program module. Any program can contain an unlimited number of methods, and each method can be called an unlimited number of times. A method must include a header, a body, and a `return` statement that marks the end of the method.
- Variables and constants are in scope within, or local to, only the method within which they are declared.
- When you pass a data item into a method, it is an argument to the method. When the method receives the data item, it is called a parameter. When you write the declaration for a method that can receive parameters, you must include the data type and a local name for each parameter within the method declaration's parentheses. You can pass multiple arguments to a called method by listing the arguments within the method call and separating them with commas. When you call a method, the arguments you send to the method must match in order—both in number and in type—the parameters listed in the method declaration.

- A method's return type indicates the data type of the value that the method will send back to the location where the method call was made. The return type also is known as a method's type and is placed in front of the method name when the method is defined. When a method returns a value, you usually want to use the returned value in the calling method, although this is not required.
- You can pass a single array element to a method in exactly the same manner you would pass a variable or constant. You can indicate that a method parameter is an array by placing square brackets after the data type in the method's parameter list. When you pass an array to a method, it is passed by reference; that is, the method receives the actual memory address of the array and has access to the actual values in the array elements.
- When you overload a method, you write multiple methods with a shared name but different parameter lists. The compiler understands your meaning based on the arguments you use when calling the method. Overloading a method introduces the risk of creating ambiguous methods—a situation in which the compiler cannot determine which version of a method to use.
- All modern programming languages contain many built-in, prewritten methods to save you time and effort.
- With well-written methods, the implementation is hidden, cohesion is high, and coupling is loose.
- Recursion occurs when a method is defined in terms of itself. Following the logic of a recursive method can be difficult, and programs that use recursion are sometimes error-prone and hard to debug.

Key Terms

ambiguous methods
argument to a method
base case
black box
client
cohesion
coupling
implementation
implementation hiding
interface to a method
IPO chart
loose coupling
method body
method header
method `return` statement
method's type
overload a method
overloading
parameter list
parameter to a method
passed by reference
passed by value
polymorphism
recursion
recursive cases
recursive method
return type
signature
terminating case
tight coupling
void method

Review Questions

1. Which of the following is true? (9.1)
   - **a.** A program can call one method at most.
   - **b.** A method can contain other methods.
   - **c.** A program can contain a method that calls another method.
   - **d.** A method can be used only once in a program.

2. Which of the following must every method have? (9.1–9.3)
   - **a.** a parameter list
   - **b.** a header
   - **c.** a return value
   - **d.** an empty parameter list

3. Which of the following is most closely related to the concept of *local*? (9.1)
   a. in scope
   b. object-oriented
   c. program level
   d. abstract

4. Although the terms *parameter* and *argument* are closely related, the difference is that *argument* refers to ________________. (9.3)
   a. a value in a method call
   b. a passed constant
   c. a formal parameter
   d. a variable that is local to a method

5. A method's interface includes its ________________. (9.3, 9.8)
   a. parameter list
   b. parameter list and return type
   c. identifier and parameter list
   d. return type, identifier, and parameter list

6. When you write the declaration for a method that can receive a parameter, which of the following must be included in the method declaration? (9.3)
   a. the name of the argument that will be used to call the method
   b. a local name for the parameter
   c. a return type that is the same as the parameter type
   d. the name of the method that will call the method

7. When you use a variable name in a method call, it ________________ as the variable in the method header. (9.3)
   a. can have the same name
   b. cannot have the same name
   c. must have the same name
   d. cannot have the same data type

8. Assume that you have written a method with the header `void myMethod(num a, string b)`. Which of the following is a correct method call? (9.3)
   a. `myMethod(12)`
   b. `myMethod("Goodbye")`
   c. `myMethod(12, "Hello")`
   d. `myMethod("Hola", 12)`

9. Assume that you have written a method with the header `num yourMethod(string name, num code)`. The method's type is ________________. (9.4)
   a. `num`
   b. `string`
   c. `num` and `string`
   d. `void`

10. Assume that you have written a method with the header `string myMethod(num score, string grade)`. Also assume that you have declared a numeric variable named `test`. Which of the following is a correct method call? (9.3)
    a. `myMethod()`
    b. `myMethod(test)`
    c. `myMethod(test, test)`
    d. `myMethod(test, "A")`

11. The value used in a method's `return` statement must ________________. (9.4)
    a. be numeric
    b. be a variable
    c. match the data type used before the method name in the header
    d. match the data type of at least one of the parameters

12. When a method receives a copy of the value stored in an argument used in the method call, it means the variable was ________________. (9.3)
    a. unnamed
    b. passed by value
    c. passed by reference
    d. assigned its original value when it was declared

13. A void method ________________. (9.4)
    a. contains no statements
    b. requires no parameters
    c. returns nothing
    d. has no name

14. When an array is passed to a method, it is ________________. (9.5)
    a. passed by reference
    b. passed by value
    c. unnamed in the method
    d. unalterable in the method

15. When you overload a method, you write multiple methods with the same ________________. (9.6)
    a. name
    b. parameter list
    c. number of parameters
    d. return type

16. A program contains a method with the header `num calculateTaxes(num amount, string name)`. Which of the following methods can coexist in the same program with no possible ambiguity? (9.6)
    a. `num calculateTaxes(string name, num amount)`
    b. `string calculateTaxes(num money, string taxpayer)`
    c. `num calculateTaxes(num annualPay, string taxpayerId)`
    d. `void calculateTaxes(num gross, string ssn)`

17. Methods in the same program with identical names and identical parameter lists are ________________. (9.6)
    a. overloaded
    b. overworked
    c. overwhelmed
    d. ambiguous

18. Methods in different programs with identical names and identical parameter lists are ________________. (9.6)
    a. overloaded
    b. illegal
    c. overloaded and illegal
    d. neither overloaded nor illegal

19. The notion of ________________ most closely describes the way a calling method is not aware of the statements within a called method. (9.8)
    a. abstraction
    b. object-oriented
    c. implementation hiding
    d. encapsulation

20. Programmers should strive to ________________. (9.8)
    a. increase coupling
    b. increase cohesion
    c. increase both coupling and cohesion
    d. decrease both coupling and cohesion

Programming Exercises

1. Create an IPO chart for each of the following methods:
    a. The method that calculates the amount owed on a restaurant check, including tip
    b. The method that calculates the cost to drive your car a mile
    c. The method that calculates your annual medical expenses after the insurance company has made its payments (9.4)

2. a. Create the logic for a program that calculates and displays the amount of money you would have if you invested $5000 at 2 percent simple interest for one year. Create a separate method to do the calculation and return the result to be displayed.

b. Modify the program in Exercise 2a so that the main program prompts the user for the amount of money and passes it to the interest-calculating method.

c. Modify the program in Exercise 2b so that the main program also prompts the user for the interest rate and passes both the amount of money and the interest rate to the interest-calculating method. (9.3)

3. Create the logic for a program that accepts a user's birth month and year and passes them to a method that calculates the user's age in the current month and returns the value to the main program to be displayed. (9.3, 9.4)

4. a. Create the logic for a program that performs arithmetic functions. Design the program to contain two numeric variables, and prompt the user for values for the variables. Pass both variables to methods named `sum()` and `difference()`. Create the logic for the methods `sum()` and `difference()`; they compute the sum of and difference between the values of two arguments, respectively. Each method should perform the appropriate computation and display the results.

   b. Modify the program in Exercise 4a so that the two entered values are passed to a method named `getChoice()`. The `getChoice()` method asks the user whether addition or subtraction should be performed and then passes the two values to the appropriate method, where the result is displayed. (9.3, 9.4)

5. Create the logic for a program that continually prompts a user for a numeric value until the user enters 0. The application passes the value in turn to the following methods:

   - A method that displays all whole numbers from 1 up to and including the entered number
   - A method that computes the sum of all the whole numbers from 1 up to and including the entered number
   - A method that computes the product of all the whole numbers from 1 up to and including the entered number (9.4)

6. Create the logic for a program that calls a method that computes and returns a homeowner's profit from a home's sale. Arguments passed to the method include the sale price and the following, which must be deducted from the sale price: mortgage payoff, realtor's commission, title insurance fee, and transfer tax amount. (9.3, 9.4)

7. Create the logic for a program that continually prompts the user for three numeric values that represent the length, width, and depth in inches of a proposed patio. Include two overloaded methods that compute the cost of construction. One method accepts all three parameters and calculates the cost at $0.12 per cubic inch. The other takes two numeric parameters that represent length and width and uses a default depth of 4 inches. Accept input and respond as follows:

   - When the user enters zero for the length value, end the program.
   - If the user enters a negative number for any value, continue to reprompt the user until the value is not negative.
   - If all numbers entered are greater than zero, call the method version that accepts three.
   - If the depth value is zero, call the version of the method that uses the default depth. (9.3)

8. a. Plan the logic for an insurance company program to determine policy premiums. The program continually prompts the user for an insurance policy number. When the user enters an appropriate sentinel value, end the program. Call a method that prompts each user for the type of policy needed—health or auto. While the user's response does not indicate health or auto, continue to prompt the user. When the value is valid, return it from the method. Pass the user's response to a new method where the premium is set and returned—$550 for a health policy or $225 for an auto policy. Display the results for each policy.

b. Modify Exercise 8a so that the premium-setting method calls one of two additional methods—one that determines the health premium or one that determines the auto premium. The health insurance method asks users whether they smoke; the premium is $550 for smokers and $345 for nonsmokers. The auto insurance method asks users to enter the number of traffic tickets they have received in the last three years. The premium is $225 for drivers with three or more tickets, $190 for those with one or two tickets, and $110 for those with no tickets. Each of these two methods returns the premium amount to the calling method, which returns the amount to be displayed. (9.4)

9. Create the logic for a program that prompts the user for numeric values for a month, day, and year. Then pass the three variables to the following methods:

- A method that displays the date with dashes in month-day-year order, as it is often represented in the United States—for example, *6-24-2025*
- A method that displays the date with dashes in day-month-year order, as it is often represented in the United Kingdom—for example, *24-6-2025*
- A method that displays the date with dashes in year-month-day order, as it is represented in the International Standard—for example, *2025-6-24*
- A method that prompts the user for the desired format ("US", "UK", or "IS") and then passes the three values to one of the methods just described (9.3, 9.4)

10. Create the logic for a program that computes hotel guest rates at Cornwall's Country Inn. Include two overloaded methods named `computeRate()`. One version accepts a number of days and calculates the rate at $99.99 per day. The other accepts a number of days and a code for a meal plan. If the code is *A*, three meals per day are included, and the price is $169.00 per day. If the code is *C*, breakfast is included, and the price is $112.00 per day. All other codes are invalid. Each method returns the rate to the calling program where it is displayed. The main program asks the user for the number of days in a stay and whether meals should be included; then, based on the user's response, the program either calls the first method or prompts for a meal plan code and calls the second method. (9.3, 9.4, 9.6)

11. Create the logic for a program that prompts a user for 12 numbers and stores them in an array. Pass the array to a method that reverses the order of the numbers. Display the reversed numbers in the main program. (9.3–9.5)

12. Create the logic for a program that prompts a user for 20 numbers and stores them in an array. Pass the array to a method that calculates the arithmetic average of the numbers and returns the value to the calling program. Display each number and how far it is from the arithmetic average. Continue to prompt the user for additional sets of 20 numbers until the user wants to quit. (9.3–9.5)

13. Each of the programs in **Figure 9-26** uses a recursive method. Try to determine the output in each case. (9.9)

Figure 9-26 Problems for Exercise 13

a.

```
start
   output recursiveA(0)
stop
num recursiveA(num x)
   num result
   if x = 0 then
      result = x
   else
      result = x *
         (recursiveA(x - 1))
   endif
return result
```

b.

```
start
   output recursiveB(2)
stop
num recursiveB(num x)
   num result
   if x = 0 then
      result = x
   else
      result = x *
         (recursiveB(x - 1))
   endif
return result
```

c.

```
start
   output recursiveC(2)
stop
num recursiveC(num x)
   num result
   if x = 1 then
      result = x
   else
      result = x *
         (recursiveC(x - 1))
   endif
return result
```

Performing Maintenance

1. A file named *MAINTENANCE09-01.txt* is included in the Chapter09 folder of your downloadable student files. Assume that this program is a working program in your organization and that it needs modifications as described in the comments (lines that begin with two slashes) at the beginning of the file. Your job is to alter the program to meet the new specifications. (9.3, 9.4)

Debugging Exercises

1. Your downloadable files for Chapter 9 include *DEBUG09-01.txt*, *DEBUG09-02.txt*, *DEBUG09-03.txt*, and *DEBUG09-04.jpg*. Each file starts with some comments that describe the problem. Comments are lines that begin with two slashes (//). Each file contains pseudocode or a flowchart that has mistakes. Find and correct all the bugs.

Game Zone

1. Design the logic for a quiz that contains an array of five multiple-choice questions related to the topic of your choice. Each question contains four answer choices. Also, create a parallel array that holds the correct answer to each question—*A*, *B*, *C*, or *D*. In turn, pass each question to a method that displays the question and accepts the player's answer. If the player does not enter a valid answer choice, force the player to reenter the choice. Return the user's valid (but not necessarily correct) answer to the main program. After the user's answer is returned to the main program, pass it and the correct answer to a method that determines whether the values are equal and displays an appropriate message. After the user answers all five questions, display the number of correct and incorrect answers that the user chose. (9.3–9.5)

2. Design the logic for the game Hangman, in which the user guesses letters in a hidden word. Store an array of 10 words. One at a time, pass each word to a method that allows the user to guess letters continually until the game is solved. The method returns the number of guesses it took to complete the word. Store the number in an array before returning to the method for the next word. After all 10 words have been guessed, display a summary of the number of guesses required for each word, as well as the average number of guesses per word. (9.3–9.5)

Chapter 10

Object-Oriented Programming

Learning Objectives

When you complete this chapter, you will be able to:

10.1 Describe the principles of object-oriented programming

10.2 Create classes and class diagrams

10.3 Use public and private access

10.4 Organize classes

10.5 Use instance methods

10.6 Use static methods

10.7 Use objects

10.1 Principles of Object-Oriented Programming

Object-oriented programming (OOP) is a programming model that focuses on an application's components and the data and methods the components use. With OOP, you consider the items that a program will manipulate—for example, a customer invoice, a loan application, a button that a user clicks, or a menu from which a user selects an option. These items are called *objects*, and when you program, you define their characteristics, functions, and capabilities.

OOP uses all of the familiar concepts of modular, procedural programming, such as variables, methods, and passing arguments. Methods in object-oriented programs continue to use sequence, selection, and looping structures and make use of arrays. However, OOP adds several new concepts to programming and requires that you learn new vocabulary to describe those concepts.

Five important features of object-oriented languages are:

- Classes
- Objects
- Polymorphism
- Inheritance
- Encapsulation

Classes and Objects

In object-oriented terminology, a **class** describes a group or collection of objects with common attributes. An **object** is one **instance** (or one **instantiation**) of a class. To create an object is to **instantiate** the object.

For example, a `Car` class might describe all the general features of an automobile. My `redChevroletAutomobileWithTheDent` is an instance of the class, as is your `brandNewBlackPorsche`. As another example, **Figure 10-1** depicts a `Dog` class and two instances of it.

Figure 10-1 A `Dog` class and two instances

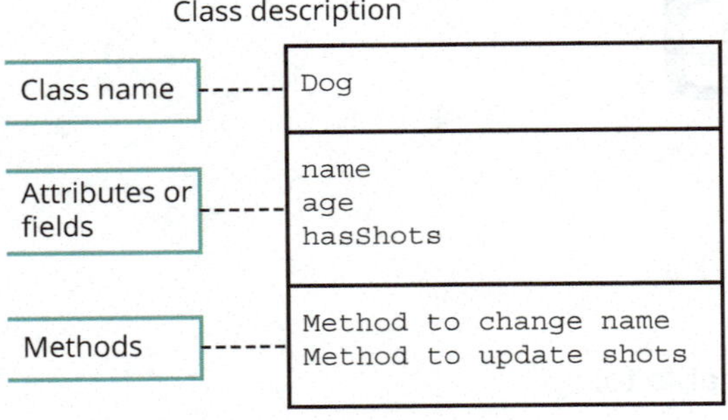

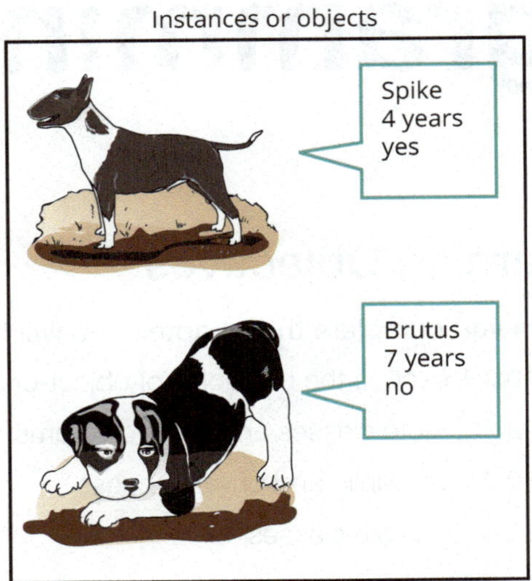

Objects both in the real world and in object-oriented programming can contain attributes and methods. An **attribute** is a characteristic of an object. For example, some of a `Car`'s attributes are its make, model, year, and purchase price. These attributes don't change during each object's life. Examples of attributes that might change frequently include whether the automobile is currently running, its gear, its speed, and whether it is dirty. All `Car` objects possess the same attributes, but not the same values for those attributes. Similarly, your `Dog` has attributes that include its breed, name, age, and whether its shots are current.

Methods are the actions that can be taken on an object; often they alter, use, or retrieve the attributes. For example, a `Car` has methods for changing and viewing its speed, and a `Dog` has methods for changing and viewing its shot status.

Thinking of items as instances of a class allows you to apply your general knowledge of the class to the individual objects created from it. You know what attributes an object has when you know what class defines it. For example, if your friend purchases a `Car`, you know it has a model name, and if your friend gets a `Dog`, you know the dog has a breed. You might not know the current status of your friend's `Car`, such as its current speed, or the status of your friend's `Dog`'s shots, but you do know what attributes exist for objects of the `Car` and `Dog` classes, which allows you to imagine these objects reasonably well before you see them. You know enough to ask the `Car`'s model and not its breed; you know enough to ask the `Dog`'s name and not its engine size. As another example, when you use a new application on your computer, you expect each component to have specific, consistent attributes, such as a button being clickable or a window being closable. Each component gains these attributes as an instance of the general class of GUI (graphical user interface) components.

> **Note** Most programmers employ a naming convention in which class names begin with an uppercase letter and multiple-word identifiers are run together, such as `SavingsAccount` or `TemporaryWorker`. Each new word within the identifier starts with an uppercase letter. Recall that this convention is known as Pascal casing.

Much of your understanding of the world comes from your ability to categorize objects and events into classes. As a young child, you learned the concept of *animal* long before you knew the word. Your first encounter with an animal might have been with the family dog, a neighbor's cat, or a goat at a petting zoo. As you developed speech, you might have used the same term for all of these creatures, gleefully shouting "Doggie!" as your parents pointed out cows, horses, and sheep in picture books or along the roadside on drives in the country. As you grew more sophisticated, you learned to distinguish dogs from cows; still later, you learned to distinguish breeds. Your understanding of the class `Animal` helps you see the similarities between dogs and cows, and your understanding of the class `Dog` helps you see the differences between a `Dog` and other `Animal`s as well as the similarities between a `GreatDane` and a `Chihuahua`. Understanding classes gives you a framework for categorizing new experiences. You might not know the term *okapi*, but when you learn it's an `Animal`, you begin to develop a concept of what an okapi might be like.

When you think in an object-oriented manner, everything is an object. You can think of any inanimate physical item as an object—your desk, your computer, and your house are all called *objects* in everyday conversation. You can think of living things as objects, too—your houseplant, your pet goldfish, and your sister are objects. Events also are objects—the stock purchase you made, the mortgage closing you attended, and your graduation party are all objects.

Everything is an object, and every object is an instance of a more general class. Your desk is an instance of the class that includes all desks, and your pet goldfish is an instance of the class that contains all fish. Each of these statements represents an **is-a relationship** because you can say, "My oak desk with the scratch on top *is a* `Desk` and my goldfish named Moby *is a* `Fish`." Your goldfish, my guppy, and the zoo's shark each constitute one instance of the `Fish` class.

Note | Object-oriented programmers also use the term *is-a* when describing inheritance. You will learn more about inheritance later in this chapter and in the next one.

The concept of a class is useful because of its reusability. For example, if you invite me to a graduation party, I automatically know many things about the party object. I assume that there will be attributes such as a starting time, a number of guests, some quantity of food, and gifts. I understand parties because of my previous knowledge of the `Party` class, of which all parties are tangible examples or instances. I might not know the number of guests or the date or time of this particular party, but I understand that because all parties have a date and time, then this one must as well. Similarly, even though every stock purchase is unique, each must have a dollar amount and a number of shares. All objects have predictable attributes because they are instantiated from specific classes.

The data components of a class that belong to every instantiated object are the class's **instance variables**. Instance variables often are called *fields* to help distinguish them from other variables you might use. The set of all the values or contents of an object's instance variables is known as its **state**. For example, the current state of a particular party might be *8 p.m.* and *Friday*; the state of a particular stock purchase might be *$10* and *five shares*.

In addition to their attributes, classes have methods associated with them, and every object instantiated from a given class possesses the same methods. For example, at some point you might want to issue invitations for a party. You might name the method `issueInvitations()`, and it might display some text as well as the values of the party's date and time fields. Your graduation party, then, might be named `myGraduationParty`. As an object of the `Party` class, it would have data members for the date and time, like all parties, and it would have a method to issue invitations. When you use the method, you might want to be able to send an argument to `issueInvitations()` that indicates how many copies to create. When you think about an object and its methods, it's as though you can send a message to the object to direct it to accomplish a particular task—you can tell the party object named `myGraduationParty` to create the number of invitations you request. Even though `yourAnniversaryParty` also is an instance of the `Party` class, and even though it also has access to the `issueInvitations()` method, you will send a different argument value to `yourAnniversaryParty`'s `issueInvitations()` method than I send to `myGraduationParty`'s corresponding method. Within an object-oriented program, you continually make requests to an object's methods, often including arguments as part of those requests.

Note | In grammar, a noun is equivalent to an object and the values of a class's attributes are adjectives—they describe the characteristics of the objects. An object also can have methods, which are equivalent to verbs.

When you program in object-oriented languages, you frequently create classes from which objects will be instantiated. You also write applications to use the objects, along with their data and methods. Often, you will write programs that use classes created by others; at other times, you might create a class that other programmers will use to instantiate objects within their own programs. A program or class that instantiates objects of another prewritten class is a **class client** or **class user**.

For example, your organization might already have a class named `Customer` that contains attributes such as `name`, `address`, and `phoneNumber`, and you might create clients that include arrays of thousands of `Customers`. Similarly, in a GUI operating environment, you might write applications that include prewritten components from classes with names like `Window` and `Button`.

Polymorphism

The real world is full of objects. Consider a door. A door is an object that needs to be opened and closed. You open a door with an easy-to-use interface known as a doorknob. Object-oriented programmers would say you are *passing a message* to the door when you tell it to open by turning its knob. The same message (turning a knob) has a different result when applied to your radio than when applied to a door. As depicted in **Figure 10-2**, the procedure you use to open something—call it the "open" procedure—works differently on a door than it does on a desk drawer, a bank account, a computer file, or your eyes. However, even though these procedures operate differently using the various objects, you can call each of these procedures "open." This concept is called *polymorphism*.

Figure 10-2 Examples of polymorphism

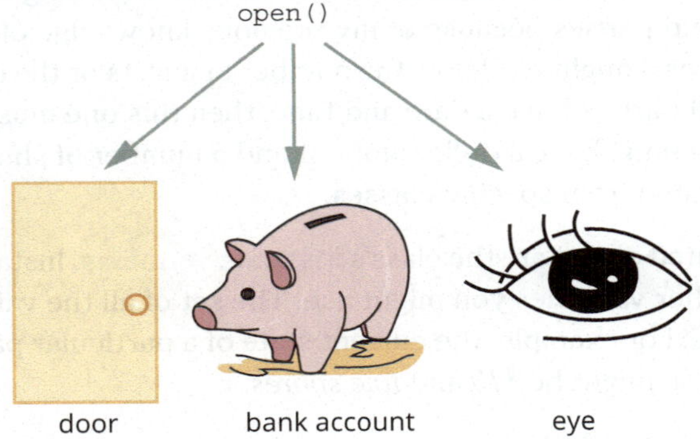
Polymorphism occurs when the same method name works appropriately for different object types.
open()
door
bank account
eye

Within classes in object-oriented programs, you can create multiple methods with the same name, which will act differently and appropriately when used with different types of objects. For example, you might use a method named `print()` to print a customer invoice, loan application, or envelope. Because you use the same method name to describe the different actions needed to print these diverse objects, you can write statements in object-oriented programming languages that are more like English; you can use the same method name to describe the same type of action, no matter what type of object is being acted upon. Using the method name `print()` is easier than remembering `printInvoice()`, `printLoanApplication()`, and so on. Object-oriented languages understand verbs in context, just as people do.

As another example of the advantages to using one name for a variety of objects, consider a screen you might design for a user to enter data into an application you are writing. Suppose that the screen contains a variety of objects—some forms, buttons, scroll bars, dialog boxes, and so on. Suppose also that you decide to make all the objects blue. Instead of having to memorize the method names that these objects use to change color—perhaps `changeFormColor()`, `changeButtonColor()`, and so on—your job would be easier if the creators of all those objects had developed a `changeColor()` method that works appropriately with each type of object.

> **Note** Purists find a subtle difference between overloading (which you have learned about when studying methods) and polymorphism. Although there are subtle differences, both terms refer to the ability to use a single name to communicate multiple meanings.

Inheritance

Inheritance is the process of acquiring the traits of one's predecessors. In the real world, a new door with a stained glass window inherits most of its traits from a standard door. It has the same purpose, it opens and closes in the same way, and it has the same knob and hinges. As **Figure 10-3** shows, the door with the stained glass window simply has one additional trait—its window. Even if you have never seen a door with a stained glass window, you know what it is and how to use it because you understand the characteristics of all doors. Inheritance is an important concept in object-oriented programming because once you create a class, you can develop new classes whose objects possess all the traits of objects of the original class plus any new traits the new class needs.

Figure 10-3 An example of inheritance

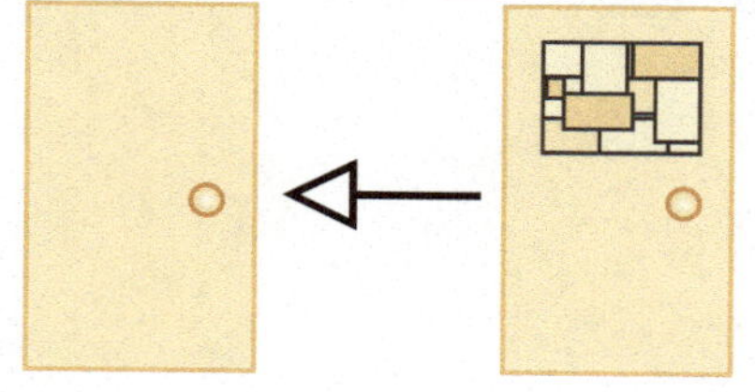
An example of inheritance: A door with a stained glass window inherits all the attributes and methods of a door.

For example, if you develop a `CustomerBill` class of objects, there is no need to develop an `OverdueCustomerBill` class from scratch. You can create the new class to contain all the characteristics of the already developed one, and simply add necessary new characteristics. This not only reduces the work involved in creating new classes, it also makes them easier to understand because they possess most of the characteristics of already-developed classes.

Encapsulation

Real-world objects often employ encapsulation and information hiding.

- Encapsulation is the process of combining all of an object's attributes and methods into a single package; the package includes data items that are frequently hidden from outside classes as well as methods that often are available to outside classes to access and alter the data.
- **Information hiding** is the concept that other classes should not alter an object's attributes—only the methods of an object's own class should have that privilege. (The concept is also called **data hiding**.) Outside classes should only be allowed to make a request that an attribute be altered; then it is up to the class's methods to determine whether the request is appropriate.

For example, when you use a door, you usually are unconcerned with the latch or hinge construction, and you don't have access to the interior workings of the knob. Those features are hidden, and the casual user cannot change them. You care only about the functionality and the interface to the door—the user-friendly boundary between the user and the internal mechanisms. When you turn a door's knob, you are interacting appropriately with the interface. Banging on the knob or speaking to it would be an inappropriate interaction because the door would not respond. Similarly, the detailed workings of objects you create within object-oriented programs can be hidden from outside programs and modules if necessary, and the methods you write can control how the objects operate. When the details are hidden, programmers can focus on the functionality and the interface, as people do with real-life objects.

In summary, understanding object-oriented programming means that you must consider five of its integral components: classes, objects, polymorphism, inheritance, and encapsulation. **Figure 10-4** illustrates these components.

Figure 10-4 Components of object-oriented programming

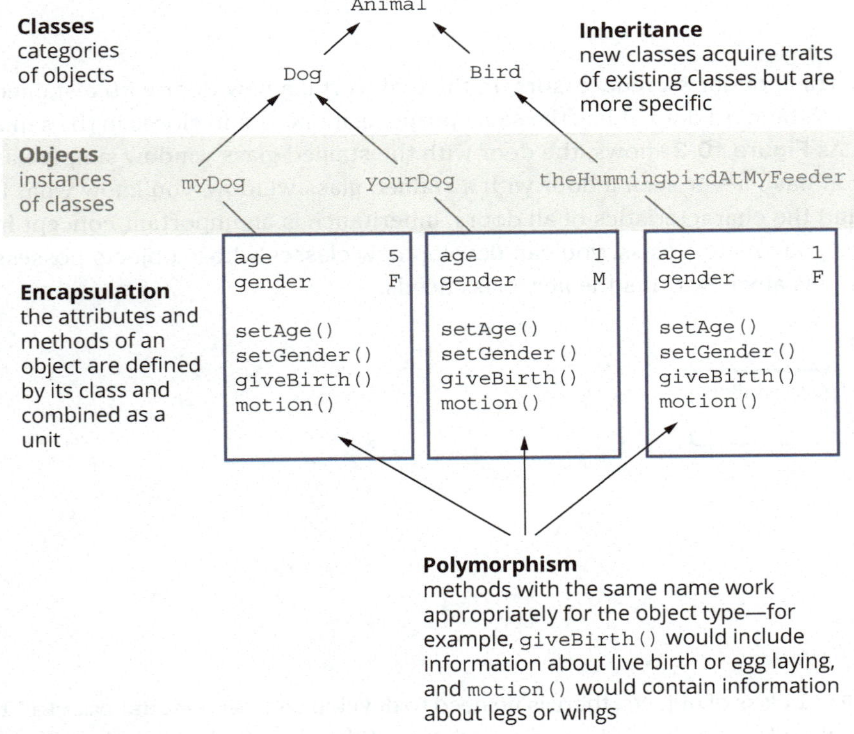
Animal
Classes
categories of objects
Dog
Bird
Inheritance
new classes acquire traits of existing classes but are more specific
Objects
instances of classes
myDog
yourDog
theHummingbirdAtMyFeeder
age 5
gender F
setAge()
setGender()
giveBirth()
motion()
age 1
gender M
setAge()
setGender()
giveBirth()
motion()
age 1
gender F
setAge()
setGender()
giveBirth()
motion()
Encapsulation
the attributes and methods of an object are defined by its class and combined as a unit
Polymorphism
methods with the same name work appropriately for the object type—for example, giveBirth() would include information about live birth or egg laying, and motion() would contain information about legs or wings

Two Truths & a Lie | Principles of Object-Oriented Programming

1. Learning about object-oriented programming is difficult because it does not use the concepts you already know, such as declaring variables and using modules.
2. In object-oriented terminology, a class describes a group or collection of objects with common attributes; an instance of a class is an existing object of a class.
3. A program or class that instantiates objects of another prewritten class is a class client or class user.

The false statement is #1. Object-oriented programming uses many features of procedural programming, including declaring variables and using modules.

10.2 Creating Classes and Class Diagrams

A class is a category of things; an object is a specific instance of a class. A **class definition** is a set of program statements that lists the characteristics of each object and the methods each object can use.

A class definition can contain three parts:

- Every class has a name.
- Most classes contain data, although this is not required.
- Most classes contain methods, although this is not required.

For example, you can create a class named `Employee`. Each `Employee` object will represent one employee who works for an organization. Data fields, or attributes of the `Employee` class, include fields such as `lastName`, `hourlyWage`, and `weeklyPay`.

The methods of a class include all the actions you want to perform with the class. Appropriate methods for an `Employee` class might include `setHourlyWage()`, `getHourlyWage()`, and `calculateWeeklyPay()`. The job of `setHourlyWage()` is to provide values for an `Employee`'s wage data field, the purpose of `getHourlyWage()` is to retrieve the wage value so it can, for example, be displayed or used in a calculation, and the purpose of `calculateWeeklyPay()` is to multiply the `Employee`'s `hourlyWage` by the number of hours in a workweek to calculate a weekly salary. With object-oriented languages, you think of the class name, data, and methods as a single encapsulated unit.

Declaring a class does not create actual objects. A class is just an abstract description of what an object will be if any objects are actually instantiated. Just as you might understand all the characteristics of an item you intend to manufacture before the first item rolls off the assembly line, you can create a class with fields and methods long before you instantiate objects from it.

When you declare a simple variable that is a built-in data type, you write a statement such as one of the following:

```
num money
string name
```

When you write a program that declares an object that is a class data type, you write a statement such as the following:

```
Employee myAssistant
```

This statement creates, or instantiates, one object named `myAssistant`.

Note In some object-oriented programming languages, you need to add more to the declaration statement to actually create an `Employee` object. For example, in Java you would write:

```
Employee myAssistant = new Employee();
```

You will understand more about the format of this statement when you learn about constructors later in this course.

When you declare the `myAssistant` object, it contains all the data fields within its class and has access to all the methods. In other words, a larger section of memory is set aside than when you declare a simple variable, because an `Employee` contains several fields. You can use any of an `Employee`'s methods with the `myAssistant` object. The usual syntax is to provide an object name, a dot (period), and a method name with parentheses and a possible argument list. For example, you can write a program that contains statements such as those shown in **Figure 10-5**.

Figure 10-5 Application that declares and uses an `Employee` object

```
start
   Declarations
      Employee myAssistant
   myAssistant.setLastName("Reynolds")
   myAssistant.setHourlyWage(26.75)
   output "My assistant makes ",
      myAssistant.getHourlyWage(), " per hour"
stop
```

Note The program segment in Figure 10-5 is very short. In a more useful real-life program, you might read employee data from a data file before assigning it to the object's fields, each `Employee` might contain dozens of fields, and your application might create hundreds or thousands of objects.

> **Note**
> Besides referring to `Employee` as a class, many programmers would refer to it as a **user-defined type**, but a more accurate term is **programmer-defined type**. A class from which objects are instantiated is the data type of its objects. Object-oriented programmers typically refer to a class like `Employee` as an **abstract data type (ADT)**; this term implies that the type's data is private and can be accessed only through methods. You will learn about private data later in this chapter.

When you write a statement such as `myAssistant.setHourlyWage(26.75)`, you are making a call to a method that is contained within the `Employee` class. Because `myAssistant` is an `Employee` object, it is allowed to use the `setHourlyWage()` method that is part of its class. You can tell from the method call that `setHourlyWage()` must have been written to accept a numeric parameter.

When you write the application in Figure 10-5, you do not need to know what statements are written within the methods in the `Employee` class, although you could make an educated guess based on the method names. Before you could execute the application in Figure 10-5, someone would have to write appropriate statements within the methods contained in the `Employee` class. If you wrote the methods, of course you would know their contents, but if another programmer has already written the methods, you could use the application without knowing the details contained in the methods. To use the methods, you need only to know their names, parameter lists, and return types.

The ability to use methods as a "black box" without knowing their contents is a feature of encapsulation. The real world is full of many black-box devices. For example, you can use your television and microwave oven without knowing how they work internally—all you need to understand is the interface. Similarly, with well-written methods that belong to classes you use, you need not understand how they work internally to be able to use them; you need only understand the ultimate result when you use them.

In the client program segment in Figure 10-5, the focus is on the object—the `Employee` named `myAssistant`—and the methods you can use with that object. This is the essence of object-oriented programming.

> **Note**
> In older object-oriented programming languages, simple numbers and characters are said to be **primitive data types**; this distinguishes them from objects that are class types. In the newest programming languages, every item you name, even one that is a numeric or string type, is an object created from a class that defines both data and methods.

> **Note**
> When you instantiate objects, their data fields are stored at separate memory locations. However, all objects of the same class share one copy of the class's methods. You will learn more about this concept later in this chapter.

Creating Class Diagrams

A **class diagram** consists of a rectangle divided into three sections, as shown in **Figure 10-6**. The top section contains the name of the class, the middle section contains the names and data types of the attributes, and the bottom section contains the methods. This generic class diagram shows two attributes and three methods, but a given class might have any number of attributes or methods, including none. Programmers often use a class diagram to plan or illustrate class features. Class diagrams also are useful for describing a class to nonprogrammers.

Figure 10-6 Generic class diagram

```
ClassName
-----------------------
Attribute1 : dataType
Attribute2 : dataType
-----------------------
Method1() : dataType
Method2() : dataType
Method3() : dataType
```

Note A class diagram is one part of the Unified Modeling Language (UML), which is a general-purpose development tool used in software design.

Figure 10-7 shows the class diagram for the `Employee` class. By convention, a class diagram lists the names of the data items first; each name is followed by a colon and the data type. Method names are listed next, and each is followed by its data type (return type). Listing the names first and the data types last emphasizes the purposes of the fields and methods.

Figure 10-7 `Employee` **class diagram**

```
Employee
---------------------------------------------
lastName: string
hourlyWage: num
weeklyPay: num
---------------------------------------------
setLastName(name : string) : void
setHourlyWage(wage : num) : void
getLastName() : string
getHourlyWage() : num
getWeeklyPay() : num
calculateWeeklyPay() : void
```

Note Some developers prefer to insert the word `void` within the parentheses of methods listed in class diagrams when the methods do not have parameter lists. For example, `void` could be inserted between the parentheses in `getLastName()` in the class diagram in Figure 10-7. Inserting `void` instead of writing nothing shows that a parameter list was not inadvertently omitted. You should follow the conventions of your organization.

Figures 10-6 and 10-7 both show that a class diagram is intended to be only an overview of class attributes and methods. A class diagram shows *what* data items and methods the class will use, not the details of the methods nor *when* they will be used. It is a design tool that helps you see the big picture in terms of class requirements. Figure 10-7 shows the `Employee` class containing three data fields that represent an employee's name, hourly pay rate, and weekly pay amount. Every `Employee` object created in a program that uses this class will contain these three data fields. In other words, when you declare an `Employee` object, the single declaration statement allocates enough memory to hold all three fields.

Figure 10-7 also shows that the `Employee` class contains six methods. For example, the first method is defined as follows:

```
setLastName(name : string) : void
```

This notation means that the method name is `setLastName()`, that it takes a single `string` parameter named `name`, and that it returns nothing.

Note Various books, websites, and organizations use class diagrams that describe methods in different ways. For example, some developers use the method name only, and others omit parameter lists. This course takes the approach of being as complete as possible, so the class diagrams you see here will contain each method's identifier, parameter list with types, and return type.

The `Employee` class diagram shows that two of the six methods—`setLastName()` and `setHourlyWage()`—take parameters. The diagram also shows the return type for each method—three void methods, two numeric methods, and one string method. The class diagram does not indicate what takes place inside the methods, although you might be able to make an educated guess. Later, when you write the code that creates the actual `Employee` class, you include method implementation details. For example, **Figure 10-8** shows some pseudocode you can use to list the details for the methods in the `Employee` class.

Figure 10-8 Pseudocode for `Employee` class described in class diagram in Figure 10-7

```
class Employee
   Declarations
      string lastName
      num hourlyWage
      num weeklyPay

   void setLastName(string name)
      lastName = name
   return

   void setHourlyWage(num wage)
      hourlyWage = wage
      calculateWeeklyPay()
   return

   string getLastName()
   return lastName

   num getHourlyWage()
   return hourlyWage

   num getWeeklyPay()
   return weeklyPay

   void calculateWeeklyPay()
      Declarations
         num WORK_WEEK_HOURS = 40
      weeklyPay = hourlyWage * WORK_WEEK_HOURS
   return
endClass
```

In Figure 10-8, the `Employee` class attributes are identified with a data type and a field name. In addition to listing the required data fields, the figure shows the complete methods for the `Employee` class. The purposes of the methods can be divided into three categories:

- Two of the methods accept values from a client and assign them to data fields; these methods, by convention, have the prefix *set*.
- Three of the methods send data to a client; these methods, by convention, have the prefix *get*.
- One method performs work within the class; this method is named `calculateWeeklyPay()`. This method does not communicate with any client; its purpose is to multiply `hourlyWage` by the number of hours in a week.

The Set Methods

In Figure 10-8, two methods begin with the word *set*; they are `setLastName()` and `setHourlyWage()`. The purpose of a **set method**, or **mutator method**, is to set or change the values of data fields defined within the class. There is no requirement that such method names start with *set*; the prefix is merely conventional and clarifies the intention of the methods. In the `setLastName()` method, a string `name` is passed in as a parameter and assigned to the field `lastName`. Because `lastName` is contained in the same class as this method, the method has access to the field and can alter it.

Similarly, the method `setHourlyWage()` accepts a numeric parameter named `wage` and assigns it to the class field `hourlyWage`. This method also calls the `calculateWeeklyPay()` method, which sets `weeklyPay` based on `hourlyWage`. By writing the `setHourlyWage()` method to call the `calculateWeeklyPay()` method automatically, you guarantee that the `weeklyPay` field is updated any time `hourlyWage` changes.

When you create an `Employee` object with a statement such as `Employee myAssistant`, you can use statements such as the following:

```
myAssistant.setLastName("Johnson")
myAssistant.setHourlyWage(20.00)
```

Instead of literal constants, you could pass variables or named constants to the methods as long as they were the correct data type. For example, if you write a program in which you make the following declaration, then the assignment in the next statement is valid.

```
Declarations
   num PAY_RATE_TO_START = 25.00
   myAssistant.setHourlyWage(PAY_RATE_TO_START)
```

Note In some languages—for example, Visual Basic and C#—you can create a **property** instead of creating a set method. Using a property provides a way to set a field value using a simpler syntax. By convention, if a class field is `hourlyWage`, its property would be `HourlyWage`, and in a program you could make a statement similar to `myAssistant.HourlyWage = PAY_RATE_TO_START`. The implementation of the property `HourlyWage` (with an uppercase initial letter) would be written in a format very similar to that of the `setHourlyWage()` method.

Like other methods, the methods that manipulate fields within a class can contain any statements you need. For example, a more complicated version of the `setHourlyWage()` method that validates input might be written as shown in **Figure 10-9**. In this version, the wage passed to the method is tested against minimum and maximum values and is assigned to the class field `hourlyWage` only if it falls within the prescribed limits. If the wage is too low, the `MINWAGE` value is substituted, and if the wage is too high, the `MAXWAGE` value is substituted.

Figure 10-9 A version of the `setHourlyWage()` method including validation

```
void setHourlyWage(num wage)
   Declarations
      num MINWAGE = 20.00
      num MAXWAGE = 70.00
   if wage < MINWAGE then
      hourlyWage = MINWAGE
   else
      if wage > MAXWAGE then
         hourlyWage = MAXWAGE
      else
         hourlyWage = wage
      endif
   endif
   calculateWeeklyPay()
return
```

Similarly, if the set methods in a class required them, the methods could contain output statements, loops, array declarations, or any other legal programming statements. However, if the main purpose of a method is *not* to set a field value, then for clarity the method should not be named with the *set* prefix.

The Get Methods

The purpose of a **get method**, or **accessor method**, is to return a value from the class to a client. In the `Employee` class in Figure 10-8, the three get methods have the prefix *get*: `getLastName()`, `getHourlyWage()`, and `getWeeklyPay()`. As with set methods, the prefix *get* is not required for a get method, but it is conventional and clarifies the method's purpose. Each of the get methods in the `Employee` class in Figure 10-8 contains only a `return` statement that simply returns the value in the field associated with the method name. Like set methods, any of these get methods could also contain more complex statements as needed. For example, in a more complicated class, you might return the hourly wage of an employee only if the user had also passed an appropriate security access code to the method, or you might return the weekly pay value as a string with a dollar sign and appropriate commas inserted instead of as a numeric value. When you declare an `Employee` object such as `Employee myAssistant`, you can then make statements in a program similar to the following:

```
Declarations
   string employeeName
employeeName = myAssistant.getLastName()
output "Wage is ", myAssistant.getHourlyWage()
output "Pay for half a week is ", myAssistant.getWeeklyPay() * 0.5
```

In other words, the value returned from a get method can be used as any other variable of its type would be used. You can assign the value to another variable, display it, perform arithmetic with it if it is numeric, or make any other statement that works correctly with the returned data type.

Work Methods

The `Employee` class in Figure 10-8 contains one method that is neither a get nor a set method. This method, `calculateWeeklyPay()`, is a **work method** within the class. A work method is also known as a **help method** or **facilitator**. The `calculateWeeklyPay()` method contains a locally named constant that represents the hours in a standard workweek, and it computes the `weeklyPay` field value by multiplying `hourlyWage` by the named constant.

From the implementation of the `calculateWeeklyPay()` method shown in Figure 10-8, you can see that no values need to be passed into this method, and no value is returned from it. The `calculateWeeklyPay()` method does not communicate with any client of the `Employee` class. Instead, this method is called only from another method in the same class (the `setHourlyWage()` method), and that method is called from a client. Each time a program uses the `setHourlyWage()` method to alter an `Employee`'s `hourlyWage` field, `calculateWeeklyPay()` is called to recalculate the `weeklyPay` field. No `setWeeklyPay()` method is included in this `Employee` class to directly assign a value to the `weeklyPay` field because the intention is that `weeklyPay` is set only inside the `calculateWeeklyPay()` method each time the `setHourlyWage()` method calls it. If you wanted programs to be able to set the `weeklyPay` field directly, you would have to write a method to allow it.

> **Note** Programmers who are new to class creation often want to pass the `hourlyWage` value into the `calculateWeeklyPay()` method so that it can use the value in its calculation. Although this technique would work, it is not required. The `calculateWeeklyPay()` method has direct access to the `hourlyWage` field by virtue of being a member of the same class.

For example, **Figure 10-10** shows a program that declares an `Employee` object and sets the hourly wage value. The program displays the `weeklyPay` value. Then a new value is assigned to `hourlyWage`, and `weeklyPay` is displayed again. As you can see from the output in **Figure 10-11**, the `weeklyPay` value has been recalculated even though it was never set directly by the client program.

Figure 10-10 Program that sets and displays `Employee` data two times

```
start
   Declarations
      num LOW = 20.00
      num HIGH = 30.00
      Employee myGardener
   myGardener.setLastName("Greene")
   myGardener.setHourlyWage(LOW)
   output "My gardener makes ",
      myGardener.getWeeklyPay(), " per week"
   myGardener.setHourlyWage(HIGH)
   output "My gardener makes ",
      myGardener.getWeeklyPay(), " per week"
stop
```

Figure 10-11 Execution of program in Figure 10-10

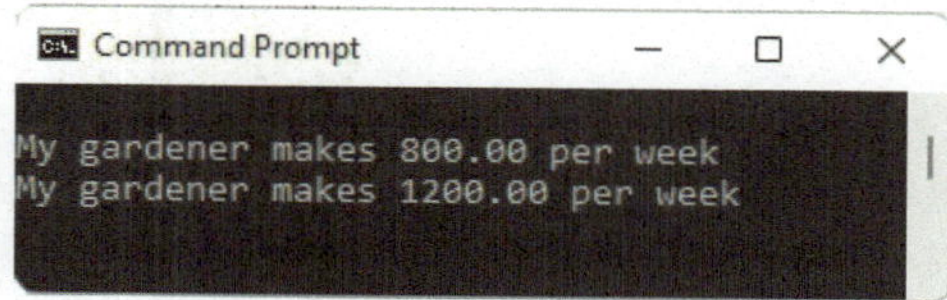
Command Prompt
My gardener makes 800.00 per week
My gardener makes 1200.00 per week

Two Truths & a Lie | Creating Classes and Class Diagrams

1. Every class has a name, data, and methods.
2. After an object has been instantiated, its methods can be accessed using the object's identifier, a dot, and a method call.
3. A class diagram consists of a rectangle divided into three sections; the top section contains the name of the class, the middle section contains the names and data types of the attributes, and the bottom section contains the methods.

The false statement is #1. Most classes contain data and methods, although neither is required.

10.3 Using Public and Private Access

When you buy a new product, one of the usual conditions of its warranty is that the manufacturer must perform all repair work. For example, if your computer has a warranty and something goes wrong with its operation, you cannot open the system unit yourself, remove and replace parts, and then expect to get your money back for a device that does not work properly. Instead, when something goes wrong, you must take the computer to an approved technician. The manufacturer guarantees that your machine will work properly only if the manufacturer can control how the computer's internal mechanisms are modified.

Similarly, in object-oriented design, you do not want outside programs or methods to alter your class's data fields unless you have control over the process. For example, you might design a class that performs complicated statistical analysis on some data, and you would not want others to be able to alter your carefully crafted result. Or, you might design a graphic and not want anyone to alter the dimensions of your artistic design. To prevent outsiders from changing your data fields in ways you do not endorse, you force other programs and methods to alter data by using a method that is part of your class. (Earlier in this chapter, you learned that the principle of keeping data private and inaccessible to outside classes is called *information hiding* or *data hiding*.)

To prevent unauthorized field modifications, object-oriented programmers usually specify that their data fields will have **private access**—the data cannot be accessed by any method that is not part of the class. The methods themselves, like `setHourlyWage()` in the `Employee` class, support public access. When methods have **public access**, other programs and methods can use the methods, often to get access to the private data.

Figure 10-12 shows a complete `Employee` class to which access specifiers have been added to describe each attribute and method. An **access specifier** is the adjective that defines the type of access (public or private) outside classes will have to the attribute or method.

Figure 10-12 `Employee` **class including public and private access specifiers**

```
class Employee
   Declarations
      private string lastName
      private num hourlyWage
      private num weeklyPay

   public void setLastName(string name)
      lastName = name
   return

   public void setHourlyWage(num wage)
      hourlyWage = wage
      calculateWeeklyPay()
   return

   public string getLastName()
   return lastName

   public num getHourlyWage()
   return hourlyWage

   public num getWeeklyPay()
   return weeklyPay

   private void calculateWeeklyPay()
      Declarations
         num WORK_WEEK_HOURS = 40
      weeklyPay = hourlyWage * WORK_WEEK_HOURS
   return
endClass
```

Note In many object-oriented programming languages, if you do not declare an access specifier for a data field or method, then it is private by default. For clarity, this course follows the convention of explicitly specifying access for every class member.

In Figure 10-12, each of the data fields is private, which means each field is inaccessible to an object declared in a client program. In other words, if a program declares an `Employee` object, such as `Employee myAssistant`, then the following statement is illegal:

```
myAssistant.hourlyWage = 25.00
```

Don't Do It
You cannot directly assign a value to a private data field from outside its class.

Instead, `hourlyWage` can be assigned only through a public method as follows:

```
myAssistant.setHourlyWage(25.00)
```

If you made hourlyWage public instead of private, then a direct assignment statement would work, but you would violate the important OOP principle of data hiding using encapsulation. Data fields should usually be private, and a client application should be able to access them only through the public interfaces—in other words, through the class's public methods. That way, if you have restrictions on the value of hourlyWage, those restrictions will be enforced by the public method that acts as an interface to the private data field. Similarly, a public get method might control how a private value is retrieved. Perhaps you do not want clients to have access to an Employee's hourlyWage if it is more than a specific value, or maybe you want to return the wage to the client as a string with a dollar sign attached. Even when a field has no data value requirements or restrictions, making data private and providing public set and get methods establishes a framework that makes such modifications easier in the future.

In the Employee class in Figure 10-12, all of the methods are public except one—the calculateWeeklyPay() method is private. That means if you write a program and declare an Employee object such as Employee myAssistant, then the following statement is not permitted:

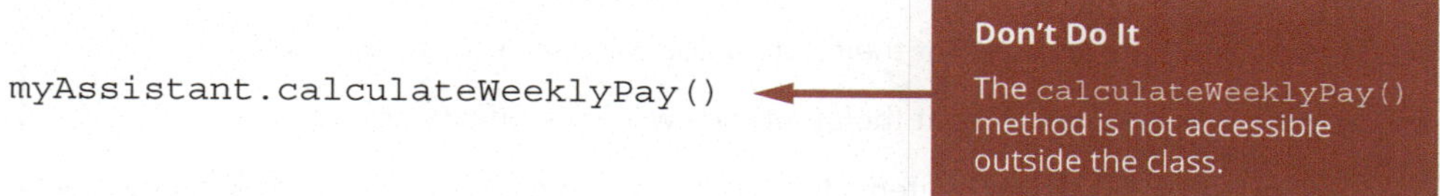

myAssistant.calculateWeeklyPay()
Don't Do It
The calculateWeeklyPay() method is not accessible outside the class.

Because it is private, the only way to call the calculateWeeklyPay() method is from another method that already belongs to the class. In this example, it is called from the setHourlyWage() method. This prevents a client program from setting hourlyWage to one value while setting weeklyPay to an incompatible value. By making the calculateWeeklyPay() method private, you ensure that the class retains full control over when and how it is used.

Classes usually contain private data and public methods, but as you have just seen, they can contain private methods. Classes can contain public data items as well. For example, an Employee class might contain a public constant data field named MINIMUM_WAGE; outside programs then would be able to access that value without using a method. Public data fields are not required to be named constants, but they frequently are.

Note In some object-oriented programming languages, such as C++, you can label a set of data fields or methods as public or private using the access specifier name just once, then follow it with a list of the items in that category. In other languages, such as Java, you use the specifier public or private with each field or method. For clarity, this course labels each field and method as public or private.

Many programmers like to specify in class diagrams whether each component in a class is public or private. **Figure 10-13** shows the conventions that are typically used. A minus sign (–) precedes the items that are private (less accessible); a plus sign (+) precedes those that are public (more accessible).

Figure 10-13 Employee class diagram with public and private access specifiers

```
Employee
-------------------------------------
-lastName : string
-hourlyWage : num
-weeklyPay : num
-------------------------------------
+setLastName(name : string) : void
+setHourlyWage(wage : num) : void
+getLastName() : string
+getHourlyWage() : num
+getWeeklyPay() : num
-calculateWeeklyPay() : void
```

Note When you learn more about inheritance, you will learn about an additional access specifier—the protected access specifier. In a class diagram, you use an octothorpe, also called a pound sign or number sign (#), to indicate protected access.

Note In object-oriented programming languages, the main program is most often written as a method named `main()` or `Main()`, and that method is virtually always defined as public.

Two Truths & a Lie | Using Public and Private Access

1. Object-oriented programmers usually specify that their data fields will have private access.
2. Object-oriented programmers usually specify that their methods will have private access.
3. In a class diagram, a minus sign (–) precedes the items that are private; a plus sign (+) precedes those that are public.

The false statement is #2. Object-oriented programmers usually specify that their methods will have public access.

10.4 Organizing Classes

The `Employee` class in Figure 10-13 contains just three data fields and six methods; most classes you create for professional applications will have many more. For example, in addition to a last name and pay information, real employees require an employee number, a first name, address, phone number, hire date, and so on, as well as methods to set and get those fields. As classes grow in complexity, deciding how to organize them becomes increasingly important.

Although it is not required, most programmers place data fields in some logical order at the beginning of a class. For example, an ID number is most likely used as a unique identifier for each employee, so it makes sense to list the employee ID number first in the class. An employee's last name and first name "go together," so it makes sense to store the two components adjacently. Despite these common-sense rules, in most languages you have considerable flexibility when positioning your data fields within a class. For example, depending on the class, you might choose to store the data fields alphabetically, or you might group together all the fields that are the same data type. Alternatively, you might choose to store all public data items first, followed by private ones, or vice versa.

In some languages, you can organize data fields and methods in any order within a class. For example, you could place all the methods first, followed by all the data fields, or you could organize the class so that data fields are followed by methods that use them. This course follows the convention of placing all data fields first so that you can see their names and data types before reading the methods that use them. This format also echoes the way data and methods appear in standard class diagrams.

For ease in locating a class's methods, some programmers store them in alphabetical order. Other programmers arrange them in pairs of get and set methods, in the same order as the data fields are defined. Another option is to list all accessor (get) methods together and all mutator (set) methods together. Depending on the class, you might decide to create other logically functional groupings. Of course, if your company distributes guidelines for organizing class components, you must follow those rules.

Two Truths & a Lie | Organizing Classes

1. As classes grow in complexity, deciding how to organize them becomes increasingly important.
2. You have a considerable amount of flexibility in how you organize data fields within a class.
3. In a class, methods must be stored in the order in which they are used.

The false statement is #3. Methods can be stored in alphabetical order, in pairs of get and set methods, in the same order as the data fields are defined, or in any other logically functional groupings.

10.5 Using Instance Methods

Classes contain data and methods, and every instance of a class possesses the same data and has access to the same methods. For example, **Figure 10-14** shows a class diagram for a simple `Student` class that contains just one private data field for a student's grade point average. The class also contains get and set methods for the field. **Figure 10-15** shows the pseudocode for the `Student` class. This class becomes the model for a new data type named `Student`; when `Student` objects are created eventually, each will have its own `gradePointAverage` field and have access to methods to get and set it.

Figure 10-14 Class diagram for `Student` class

Student
-gradePointAverage : num
+setGradePointAverage(gpa: num) : void +getGradePointAverage() : num

Figure 10-15 Pseudocode for the `Student` class

```
class Student
   Declarations
      private num gradePointAverage

   public void setGradePointAverage(num gpa)
      gradePointAverage = gpa
   return

   public num getGradePointAverage()
   return gradePointAverage
endClass
```

If you create multiple `Student` objects using the class in Figure 10-15, you need a separate storage location in computer memory to store each `Student`'s unique grade point average. For example, **Figure 10-16** shows a client program that creates three `Student` objects and assigns values to their `gradePointAverage` fields. It also shows how the `Student` objects look in memory after the values have been assigned.

Figure 10-16 Program that creates three `Student` objects and picture of how they look in memory

```
start
   Declarations
      Student oneSophomore
      Student oneJunior
      Student oneSenior
   oneSophomore.setGradePointAverage(2.6)
   oneJunior.setGradePointAverage(3.8)
   oneSenior.setGradePointAverage(3.4)
stop
```

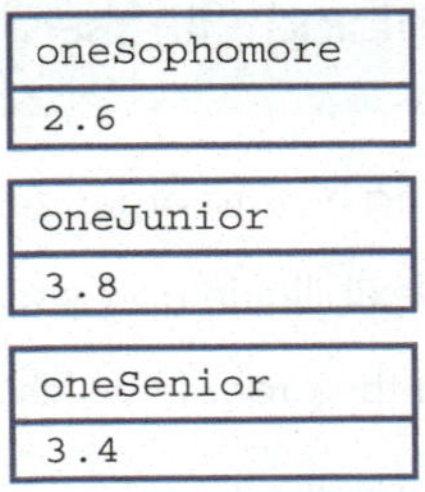

oneSophomore
2.6

oneJunior
3.8

oneSenior
3.4

It makes sense for each `Student` object in Figure 10-16 to have its own `gradePointAverage` field, but it does not make sense for each `Student` to have its own copy of the methods that get and set `gradePointAverage`. Creating identical copies of a method for each instance would be inefficient. Instead, even though every `Student` has its own `gradePointAverage` field, only one copy of each of the methods `getGradePointAverage()` and `setGradePointAverage()` is stored in memory. Each instantiated object of the class can use the single method copy. A method that works appropriately with different objects is an **instance method**.

Because only one copy of each instance method is stored no matter how many `Student` objects are created, the program needs a way to determine which `gradePointAverage` is being set or retrieved when one of the methods is called. The mechanism that handles this problem is illustrated in **Figure 10-17**. When a method call such as `oneSophomore.setGradePointAverage(2.6)` is made, the true method call, which is invisible and automatically constructed, includes the memory address of the `oneSophomore` object. (These method calls are represented by the three narrow boxes in the center of Figure 10-17.)

Within the `setGradePointAverage()` method in the `Student` class, an invisible and automatically created parameter is added to the list. (For illustration purposes, this parameter is named `aStudentAddress` in the `Student` class definition in Figure 10-17. In fact, no parameter is created with that name.) This parameter accepts the address of a `Student` object because the instance method belongs to the `Student` class; if this method belonged to another class—`Employee`, for example—then the method would accept an address for that type of object. The addresses are not written as code in any program—they are "secretly" sent and received behind the scenes. The address variable in Figure 10-17 is called a `this` reference. A **`this` reference** is an automatically created variable that holds the address of an object that is passed to an instance method whenever the method is called. It is called a `this` reference because it refers to "this particular object" that is using the method at the moment. In other words, an instance method receives a `this` reference to a specific class instance.

In the application in Figure 10-17, when `oneSophomore` uses the `setGradePointAverage()` method, the address of the `oneSophomore` object is contained in the `this` reference. Later in the program, when the `oneJunior` object uses the `setGradePointAverage()` method, the `this` reference will hold the address of that `Student` object.

Figure 10-17 shows each place the `this` reference is used in the `Student` class. It is implicitly passed as a parameter to each instance method. You never explicitly refer to the `this` reference when you write the method header for an instance method; Figure 10-17 just shows where it implicitly exists. Within each instance method, the `this` reference is implied any time you refer to one of the class data fields. For example, when you call `setGradePointAverage()` using a `oneSophomore` object, the `gradePointAverage` assigned within the method is the *this* `gradePointAverage`, or the one that belongs to the `oneSophomore` object. The phrase "this `gradePointAverage`" usually is written as `this`, followed by a dot, followed by the field name—`this.gradePointAverage`.

The `this` reference exists throughout every instance method. You can explicitly use the `this` reference with data fields, but it is not required. **Figure 10-18** shows two locations where the `this` reference can be used implicitly, or where you can (but do not have to) use it explicitly. Within an instance method, the following two identifiers mean exactly the same thing:

- Any field name defined in the class
- `this`, followed by a dot, followed by the same field name

Figure 10-17 How `Student` object memory addresses are passed from an application to an instance method of the `Student` class

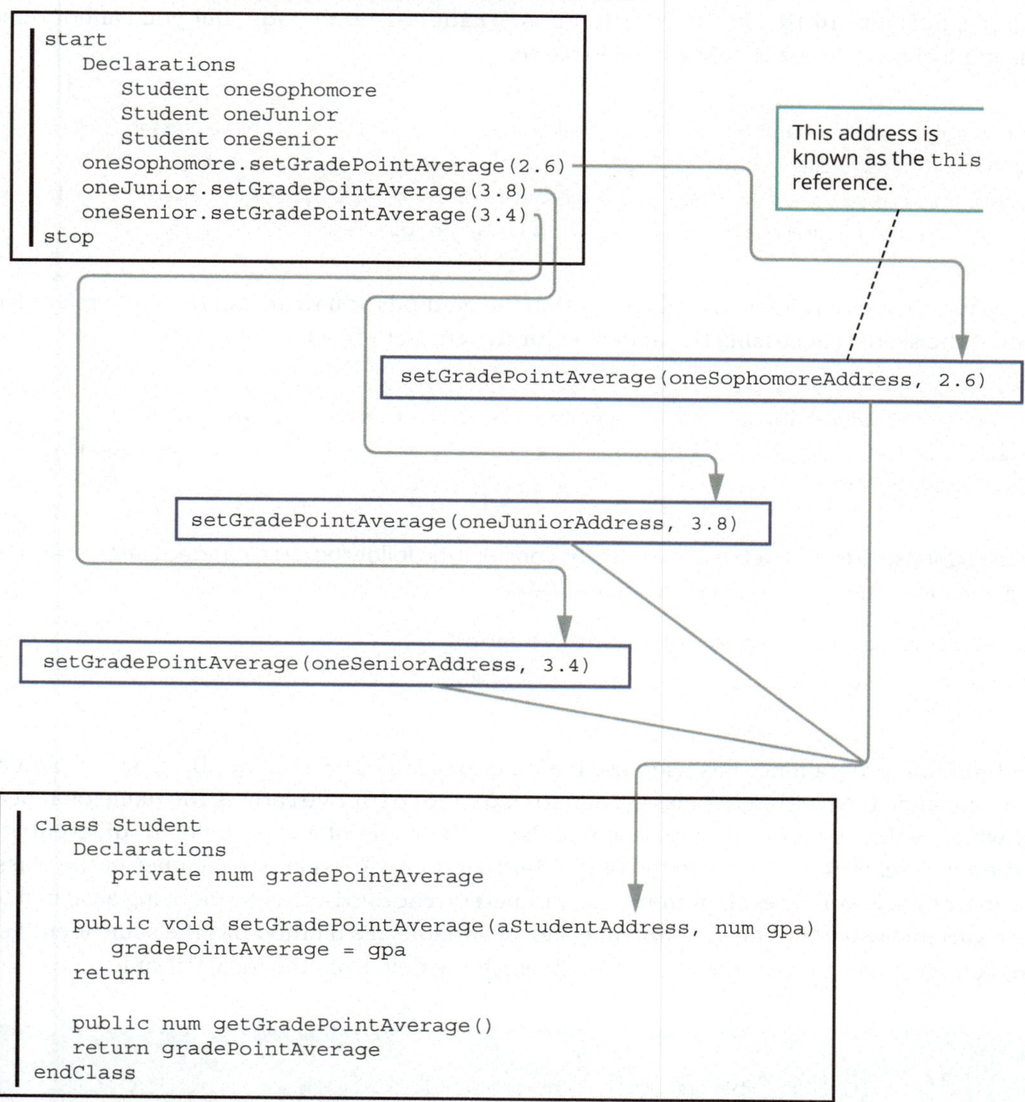
start
Declarations
Student oneSophomore
Student oneJunior
Student oneSenior
oneSophomore.setGradePointAverage(2.6)
oneJunior.setGradePointAverage(3.8)
oneSenior.setGradePointAverage(3.4)
stop
This address is known as the this reference.
setGradePointAverage(oneSophomoreAddress, 2.6)
setGradePointAverage(oneJuniorAddress, 3.8)
setGradePointAverage(oneSeniorAddress, 3.4)
class Student
Declarations
private num gradePointAverage
public void setGradePointAverage(aStudentAddress, num gpa)
gradePointAverage = gpa
return
public num getGradePointAverage()
return gradePointAverage
endClass

Figure 10-18 Explicitly using `this` in the `Student` class

```
class Student
   Declarations
      private num gradePointAverage

   public void setGradePointAverage(num gpa)
      this.gradePointAverage = gpa
   return

   public num getGradePointAverage()
   return this.gradePointAverage
endClass
```

You can write `this` as a reference in these locations.

For example, within the `setGradePointAverage()` method of the `Student` class, `gradePointAverage` and `this.gradePointAverage` refer to exactly the same memory location.

The this reference can be used only with identifiers that are part of the class definition—that is, field names or instance methods. You cannot use it with local variables that are parameters to instance methods or declared within the method bodies. For example, in Figure 10-18 you can refer to this.gradePointAverage, but you cannot refer to this.gpa because gpa is not a class field—it is only a local variable.

> **Note** The syntax for using this differs among programming languages. For example, within a class in C++, you can refer to the Student class gradePointAverage value as this->gradePointAverage or (*this).gradePointAverage, but in Java you refer to it as this.gradePointAverage. In Visual Basic, the this reference is named Me, so the variable would be Me.gradePointAverage.

Usually, you do not need to use the this reference explicitly within the methods you write, but the this reference is always there, working behind the scenes, accessing the data field for the correct object.

> **Note** Your organization might prefer that you explicitly use the this reference for clarity even though it is not required to create a workable program. It is the programmer's responsibility to follow the conventions established at work or by clients.

As an example of when you might use the this reference explicitly, consider the following setGradePointAverage() method and compare it to the version in the Student class in Figure 10-18.

```
public void setGradePointAverage(num gradePointAverage)
   this.gradePointAverage = gradePointAverage
return
```

In this version of the method, the programmer has used the identifier gradePointAverage both as the parameter to the method and as the instance field within the class. Therefore, gradePointAverage is the name of a local variable within the method whose value is received by passing; it also is the name of a class field. To differentiate the two, you explicitly use the this reference with the copy of gradePointAverage that is a member of the class. Omitting the this reference in this case would result in the local parameter gradePointAverage being assigned to itself, and the class's instance variable would not be set. Any time a local variable in a method has the same identifier as a field, the field is hidden; you must use a this reference to distinguish the field from the local variable.

Two Truths & a Lie | Using Instance Methods

1. An instance method operates correctly yet differently for each separate instance of a class.
2. A this reference is a variable you must explicitly declare with each class you create.
3. When you write an instance method in a class, the following two identifiers within the method always mean exactly the same thing: any field name or this followed by a dot, followed by the same field name.

The false statement is #2. A this reference is an automatically created variable that holds the address of an object and passes it to an instance method whenever the method is called. You do not declare it explicitly.

10.6 Using Static Methods

Some methods do not require a this reference because it makes no sense for them either implicitly or explicitly. For example, the displayStudentMotto() method in **Figure 10-19** could be added to the Student class. Its purpose is to display a motto that all Student objects use in the same way. The method does not use any data fields from the Student class, so it does not matter which Student object calls it. If you write a program in which you declare 100 Student objects, the displayStudentMotto() method executes in exactly the same way for each of them; it does not need to know whose motto is displayed and it does not need to access any specific object addresses. As a matter of fact, you might want to display the Student motto without instantiating *any* Student objects. Therefore, the displayStudentMotto() method can be written as a static method instead of an instance method.

Figure 10-19 Student **class** displayStudentMotto() **method**

```
public static void displayStudentMotto()
   output "Every student is an individual"
   output "in the pursuit of knowledge."
   output "Every student strives to be"
   output "a literate, responsible citizen."
return
```

When you write a class, you can indicate two types of methods:

- **Static methods**, also called **class methods**, are those for which no object needs to exist, like the displayStudentMotto() method in Figure 10-19. Static methods do not receive a this reference as an implicit parameter. Typically, static methods include the word static in the method header. (Java, C#, and C++ use the keyword static. In Visual Basic, the keyword Shared is used in place of static.)
- **Nonstatic methods** are methods that exist to be used with an object. These instance methods receive a this reference to a specific object. In most programming languages, you use the word static when you want to declare a static class member, but you do not use a special word when you want a class member to be nonstatic. In other words, methods in a class are nonstatic instance methods by default.

Note In everyday language, the word *static* means "stationary"; it is the opposite of dynamic, which means "changing." In other words, static methods are always the same for every instance of a class, whereas nonstatic methods act differently depending on the object used to call them.

In most programming languages, you use a static method with the class name (but not an object name), as in the following:

```
Student.displayStudentMotto()
```

In other words, no object is necessary with a static method.

Note In some languages, notably C++, besides using a static method with the class name, you also can use a static method with any object of the class, as in oneSophomore.displayStudentMotto().

Two Truths & a Lie | Using Static Methods

1. Class methods do not receive a this reference.
2. Static methods do not receive a this reference.
3. Nonstatic methods do not receive a this reference.

The false statement is #3. Nonstatic methods receive a this reference automatically.

10.7 Using Objects

A class is a complex data type defined by a programmer, but in many ways, you can use its instances as you use items of simpler data types. For example:

- You can pass an object to a method.
- You can return an object from a method.
- You can use an array of objects.

Consider the `InventoryItem` class in **Figure 10-20**. The class represents items that a company manufactures and holds in inventory. Each item has a number, description, and price. The class contains a get and set method for each of the three fields. You can treat each `InventoryItem` in many of the same ways you use simpler data.

Figure 10-20 `InventoryItem` class

```
class InventoryItem
   Declarations
      private string inventoryNumber
      private string description
      private num price

   public void setInventoryNumber(string number)
      inventoryNumber = number
   return

   public void setDescription(string description)
      this.description = description
   return

   public void setPrice(num price)
      if(price < 0)
         this.price = 0
      else
         this.price = price
      endif
   return

   public string getInventoryNumber()
   return inventoryNumber

   public string getDescription()
   return description

   public num getPrice()
   return price

endClass
```

Notice the uses of the `this` reference to differentiate between the method parameter and the class field.

Passing an Object to a Method

You can pass an object to a method in the same way you can pass a simple numeric or string variable. For example, **Figure 10-21** shows a program that declares an `InventoryItem` object and passes it to a method for display. The `InventoryItem` is declared in the main program and assigned values. Then the completed item is passed to a method, where it is displayed. **Figure 10-22** shows the execution of the program.

The `InventoryItem` declared in the main program in Figure 10-21 is passed to the `displayItem()` method in much the same way a numeric or string variable would be. The method receives a copy of the `InventoryItem` that is known locally by the identifier `item`. Within the method, the field values of the local item can be retrieved, displayed, and used in arithmetic statements in the same way they could have been in the main program where the `InventoryItem` was originally declared.

Figure 10-21 Application that declares and uses an `InventoryItem` object

```
start
   Declarations
      InventoryItem oneItem
   oneItem.setInventoryNumber("1276")
   oneItem.setDescription("Mahogany chest")
   oneItem.setPrice(450.00)
   displayItem(oneItem)
stop

public static void displayItem(InventoryItem item)
   Declarations
      num TAX_RATE = 0.06
      num tax
      num pr
      num total
   output "Item #", item.getInventoryNumber()
   output item.getDescription()
   pr = item.getPrice()
   tax = pr * TAX_RATE
   total = pr + tax
   output "Price is $", pr, " plus $", tax, " tax"
   output "Total is $", total
return
```

Figure 10-22 Output of the program in Figure 10-21

```
Command Prompt
Item #1276
Mahogany chest
Price is $450.00 plus $27.00 tax
Total is $477.00
```

Returning an Object from a Method

Figure 10-23 shows a more realistic application that uses `InventoryItem` objects. In the main program, an `InventoryItem` is declared, and the user is prompted for a number. As long as the user does not enter the `QUIT` value, a loop is executed in which the entered inventory item number is passed to the `getItemValues()` method. Within that method, a local `InventoryItem` object is declared. This local object gathers and holds the user's input values. The user is prompted for a description and price, and then the passed item number and newly obtained description and price are assigned to the local `InventoryItem` object via its set methods. The completed object is returned to the program, where it is assigned to the `InventoryItem` object that is then passed to the `displayItem()` method. As in the previous example, the method calculates tax and displays results. **Figure 10-24** shows a typical execution.

In Figure 10-23, notice that the return type for the `getItemValues()` method is `InventoryItem`. A method can return only a single value. Therefore, it is convenient that the `getItemValues()` method can encapsulate two strings and a number in a single `InventoryItem` object that it returns to the main program.

Using Arrays of Objects

When you declare an array of simple data items like numbers or strings, you use the data type, an identifier, and a size contained in brackets. For example, the following statements declare `num` and `string` arrays, respectively:

```
num scores[10]
string names[5]
```

You can use similar syntax to declare object arrays: a data type (class), an identifier, and a size in brackets. For example, you could declare an array of seven `InventoryItem` objects as follows:

```
InventoryItem items[7]
```

Any individual `items` array element could be used in the same way as any single object of the `InventoryItem` type. For example, the third element in the array could be passed to the `displayItem()` method in Figure 10-23 using the following statement:

```
displayItem(items[2])
```

Figure 10-23 Application that uses `InventoryItem` objects

```
start
   Declarations
      InventoryItem oneItem
      string itemNum
      string QUIT = "0"
   output "Enter item number or ", QUIT, " to quit... "
   input itemNum
   while itemNum <> QUIT
      oneItem = getItemValues(itemNum)
      displayItem(oneItem)
      output "Enter next item number or ", QUIT, " to quit... "
      input itemNum
   endwhile
stop

public static InventoryItem getItemValues(string number)
   Declarations
      InventoryItem inItem
      string desc
      num price
   output "Enter description... "
   input desc
   output "Enter price... "
   input price
   inItem.setInventoryNumber(number)
   inItem.setDescription(desc)
   inItem.setPrice(price)
return inItem

public static void displayItem(InventoryItem item)
   Declarations
      num TAX_RATE = 0.06
      num tax
      num pr
      num total
   output "Item #", item.getInventoryNumber()
   output item.getDescription()
   pr = item.getPrice()
   tax = pr * TAX_RATE
   total = pr + tax
   output "Price is $", pr, " plus $", tax, " tax"
   output "Total is $", total
return
```

Figure 10-24 Typical execution of program in Figure 10-23

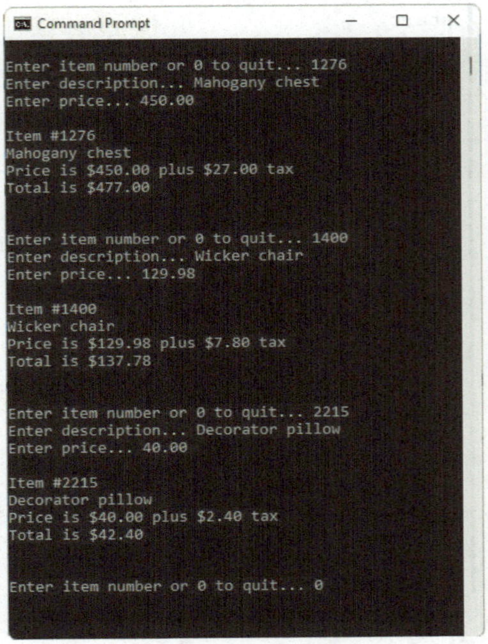

```
Command Prompt

Enter item number or 0 to quit... 1276
Enter description... Mahogany chest
Enter price... 450.00

Item #1276
Mahogany chest
Price is $450.00 plus $27.00 tax
Total is $477.00

Enter item number or 0 to quit... 1400
Enter description... Wicker chair
Enter price... 129.98

Item #1400
Wicker chair
Price is $129.98 plus $7.80 tax
Total is $137.78

Enter item number or 0 to quit... 2215
Enter description... Decorator pillow
Enter price... 40.00

Item #2215
Decorator pillow
Price is $40.00 plus $2.40 tax
Total is $42.40

Enter item number or 0 to quit... 0
```

The entire array can be passed to a method that defines an array of the correct type as a parameter. For example, the statement `displayArray(items)` can be used to call a method with the following header:

```
public static void displayArray(InventoryItem[] list)
```

Within this method, the array would be known as `list`.

Any public member of the `InventoryItem` class can be used with any object in the array by using a subscript to identify the element. For example, the *x*th element in the `items` array can use the public `setInventoryNumber()` method of the `InventoryItem` class by using the following statement:

```
items[x].setInventoryNumber(34);
```

Figure 10-25 shows a complete program that declares seven `InventoryItem` objects, sets their values, and displays them.

Figure 10-25 Application that uses an array of `InventoryItem` objects

```
start
   Declarations
      num SIZE = 7
      InventoryItem items[SIZE]
      num sub
   sub = 0
   while sub < SIZE
      items[sub] = getItemValues()
      sub = sub + 1
   endwhile
   displayItems(items, SIZE)
stop

public static InventoryItem getItemValues()
   Declarations
      InventoryItem item
      num itemNum
      string desc
      num price
   output "Enter item number... "
   input itemNum
   output "Enter description... "
   input desc
   output "Enter price... "
   input price
   item.setInventoryNumber(number)
   item.setDescription(desc)
   item.setPrice(price)
return item

public static void displayItems(InventoryItem[] items, num SIZE)
   Declarations
      num TAX_RATE = 0.06
      num tax
      num pr
      num total
      int x
   x = 0
   while x < SIZE
      output "Item number #", items[x].getInventoryNumber()
      output items[x].getDescription()
      pr = items[x].getPrice()
      tax = pr * TAX_RATE
      total = pr + tax
      output "Price is $", pr, " plus $", tax, " tax"
      output "Total is $", total
      x = x + 1
   endwhile
return
```

In the program in Figure 10-25, a constant is declared for the size of the array, and then the array is declared. The program uses a `while` loop to call a method named `getItemValues()` seven times. The method accepts no parameters. It declares an `InventoryItem` object, and then it prompts the user for an item number, description, and price. Those values are assigned to the `InventoryItem` object using its public methods. The completed object is then returned to the main program, which passes the array and its size to a method named `displayItems()` that displays data for all the items.

The program in Figure 10-25 could have been written using different techniques:

- The program calls the method to get values seven times. Instead, it could have been written to call the method just once but pass the entire array. Then a loop could have been used within the method.
- The program in Figure 10-25 sends the entire array to the display method. Instead, it could have been written so that the display method accepts only one `InventoryItem`, and then it would have been necessary to call the method seven times in a loop.

As you have learned throughout this course, there are often multiple ways to accomplish the same goal. One method in the program in Figure 10-25 was used to get values, and a different one was used to display values to demonstrate how both approaches work.

Two Truths & a Lie | Using Objects

1. You can pass an object to a method.
2. Because only one value can be returned from a method, you cannot return an object that holds more than one field.
3. You can declare an object locally within a method.

The false statement is #2. An object with any number of fields can be returned from a method.

Summary

- Classes are the basic building blocks of object-oriented programming. A class describes a collection of objects; each object is an instance of a class. A class's fields, or instance variables, hold its data, and every object that is an instance of a class has access to the same methods. A program or class that instantiates objects of another prewritten class is a class client or class user. In addition to classes and objects, three important features of object-oriented languages are polymorphism, inheritance, and encapsulation.
- A class definition is a set of program statements that lists the fields and methods each object can use. A class definition can contain a name, data, and methods. Programmers often use a class diagram to illustrate class features. Many methods contained in a class can be divided into three categories: set methods, get methods, and work methods.
- Object-oriented programmers usually specify that their data fields will have private access—that is, the data cannot be accessed by any method that is not part of the class. The methods frequently support public access, which means that other programs and methods can use the methods that control access to the private data. In a class diagram, a minus sign (–) precedes each item that is private; a plus sign (+) precedes each item that is public.
- As classes grow in complexity, deciding how to organize them becomes increasingly important. Depending on the class, you might choose to store the data fields by listing a key field first. You also might list fields alphabetically, by data type, or by accessibility. Methods might be stored in alphabetical order or in pairs of get and set methods.
- An instance method operates correctly yet differently for every object instantiated from a class. When an instance method is called, a `this` reference that holds the object's memory address is automatically and implicitly passed to the method.
- A class can contain two types of methods: static methods, which are also known as class methods and do not receive a `this` reference as an implicit parameter; and nonstatic methods, which are instance methods and receive a `this` reference implicitly.
- You can use objects in many of the same ways you use items of simpler data types, such as passing them to and from methods and storing them in arrays.

Key Terms

abstract data type (ADT)
access specifier
accessor method
attribute
class
class client
class definition
class diagram
class methods
class user
data hiding
facilitator
get method
help method
information hiding
inheritance
instance
instance method
instance variables
instantiate
instantiation
is-a relationship
mutator method
nonstatic methods
object
primitive data types
private access
programmer-defined type
property
public access
set method
state
static methods
`this` reference
user-defined type
work method

Review Questions

1. Which of the following means the same as *object*? (10.1)

a. instance
b. class
c. field
d. category

2. Which of the following means the same as *instance variable*? (10.1)

a. class
b. field
c. category
d. record

3. A program that instantiates objects of another prewritten class is a(n) ________________. (10.1)

a. instance
b. object
c. client
d. GUI

4. The relationship between an instance and a class is a(n) ________________ relationship. (10.1)

a. has-a
b. hostile
c. polymorphic
d. is-a

5. Which of these does not belong with the others? (10.1)

a. instance variable
b. attribute
c. object
d. field

6. The process of acquiring the traits of one's predecessors is ________________. (10.1)

a. polymorphism
b. encapsulation
c. inheritance
d. orientation

7. When discussing classes and objects, *encapsulation* means that ________________. (10.1)

a. all the fields belong to the same object
b. all the fields are private
c. all the fields and methods are grouped together
d. all the methods are public

8. Every class definition must contain ______________. (10.2)

   a. a name
   b. data
   c. methods
   d. a name, data, and methods

9. Assume that a working program contains the following statement:

   ```
   myDog.setName("Bowser")
   ```

   Which of the following do you know? (10.2)

   a. `setName()` is a public method.
   b. `setName()` accepts a string parameter.
   c. `setName()` is public and accepts a string parameter.
   d. `setName()` is a private method.

10. Assume that a working program contains the following statement:

    ```
    name = myDog.getName()
    ```

    Which of the following do you know? (10.2)

    a. `getName()` returns a string.
    b. `getName()` returns a value that is the same data type as `name`.
    c. `getName()` does not return anything.
    d. `getName()` returns a number.

11. A class diagram ______________. (10.2)

    a. provides an overview of a class's data and methods
    b. provides method implementation details
    c. is never used by nonprogrammers because it is too technical
    d. contains the standard flowchart symbols

12. Which of the following is the most likely scenario for a class? (10.3)

    a. Its data is private and its methods are public.
    b. Its data is public and its methods are private.
    c. Its data and methods are both public.
    d. Its data and methods are both private.

13. An instance method ______________. (10.5, 10.6)

    a. is static
    b. receives a `this` reference
    c. is static and receives a `this` reference
    d. is nonstatic and does not receive a `this` reference

14. Assume that you have created a class named `Dog` that contains a data field named `weight` and an instance method named `setWeight()`. Further assume that the `setWeight()` method accepts a numeric parameter named `weight`. Which of the following statements correctly sets a `Dog`'s weight within the `setWeight()` method? (10.5, 10.6)

    a. `weight = weight`
    b. `this.weight = this.weight`
    c. `weight = this.weight`
    d. `this.weight = weight`

15. A static method is also known as a(n) ______________ method. (10.6)

    a. instance
    b. class
    c. private
    d. public

16. By default, methods contained in a class are ______________ methods. (10.6)

    a. static
    b. nonstatic
    c. class
    d. public

17. Assume that you have created a class named `MyClass`, and that a working program contains the following statement:

```
output MyClass.numberOfStudents
```

Which of the following do you know? (10.6)

a. `numberOfStudents` is a numeric field.
b. `numberOfStudents` is a static field.
c. `numberOfStudents` is an instance variable.
d. `numberOfStudents` is an instance variable and static.

18. Assume that you have created an object named `myObject` and that a working program contains the following statement:

```
output myObject.getSize()
```

Which of the following do you know? (10.6)

a. `getSize()` is a static method.
b. `getSize()` returns a number.
c. `getSize()` receives a `this` reference.
d. `getSize()` is static and returns a number.

19. Assume that you have created a class that contains a private field named `myField` and a nonstatic public method named `myMethod()`. Which of the following is true? (10.6)

a. `myMethod()` has access to `myField` and can use it.
b. `myMethod()` does not have access to `myField` and cannot use it.
c. `myMethod()` can use `myField` but cannot pass it to other methods.
d. `myMethod()` can use `myField` only if it is passed to `myMethod()` as a parameter.

20. An object can be ________________. (10.7)

a. stored in an array but not passed to a method
b. passed to a method but not returned from a method
c. passed to and returned from a method, but not stored in an array
d. stored in an array, passed to a method, and returned from a method

Programming Exercises

1. Identify three objects that might belong to each of the following classes:

a. `Author`
b. `RaceHorse`
c. `Country`
d. `RetailPurchase` (10.1)

2. Identify three different classes that might contain each of these objects:

a. `myBlueDenimShirt`
b. `presidentOfTheUnitedStates`
c. `myPetCat`
d. `myCousinLindsey` (10.1)

3. Design a class named `TermPaper` that holds an author's name, the subject of the paper, and an assigned letter grade. Include methods to set the values for each data field and display the values for each data field. Create the class diagram and write the pseudocode that defines the class. (10.2)

4. Design a class named `Computer` that holds the make, model, and amount of memory of a computer. Include methods to set the values for each data field, and include a method that displays all the values for each field. Create the class diagram and write the pseudocode that defines the class. (10.2, 10.7)

5. Complete the following tasks:

   a. Design a class named `AutomobileLoan` that holds a loan number, make and model of automobile, and balance. Include methods to set values for each data field and a method that displays all the loan information. Create the class diagram and write the pseudocode that defines the class.

   b. Design an application that declares two `AutomobileLoan` objects and sets and displays their values.

   c. Design an application that declares an array of 20 `AutomobileLoan` objects. Prompt the user for data for each object, and then display all the values.

   d. Design an application that declares an array of 20 `AutomobileLoan` objects. Prompt the user for data for each object, and then pass the array to a method that determines the sum of the balances. (10.2, 10.7)

6. Complete the following tasks:

   a. Design a class named `StockTransaction` that holds a stock symbol (typically one to four characters), stock name, and price per share. Include methods to set and get the values for each data field. Create the class diagram and write the pseudocode that defines the class.

   b. Design an application that declares two `StockTransaction` objects and sets and displays their values.

   c. Design an application that declares an array of 15 `StockTransaction` objects. Prompt the user for data for each object, and then display all the values.

   d. Design an application that declares an array of 15 `StockTransaction` objects. Prompt the user for data for each object, and then pass the array to a method that determines and displays the two stocks with the highest and lowest price per share. (10.2, 10.7)

7. Complete the following tasks:

   a. Design a class named `Cake`. Data fields include two string fields for cake flavor and icing flavor and numeric fields for diameter in inches and price. Include methods to get and set values for each of these fields. Create the class diagram and write the pseudocode that defines the class.

   b. Design an application that declares two `Cake` objects and sets and displays their values.

   c. Design an application that declares an array of 250 `Cake` objects. Prompt the user for data for each `Cake`, then display all the values.

   d. Design an application that declares an array of 25 `Cake` objects. Prompt the user for a flavor, topping, and diameter for each `Cake`, and pass each object to a method that computes the price and returns the complete `Cake` object to the main program. Then display all the `Cake` values. An 8-inch cake is $19.99, a 9-inch cake is $22.99, and a 10-inch cake is $25.99. Any other entered size is invalid and should cause the price to be set to 0. (10.2, 10.7)

8. Complete the following tasks:

   a. Design a class named `BaseballGame` that has fields for two team names and a final score for each team. Include methods to set and get the values for each data field. Create the class diagram and write the pseudocode that defines the class.

   b. Design an application that declares three `BaseballGame` objects and sets and displays their values.

   c. Design an application that declares an array of 12 `BaseballGame` objects. Prompt the user for data for each object, and display all the values. Then pass each object to a method that displays the name of the winning team or *Tie* if the score is a tie. (10.2, 10.7)

Performing Maintenance

1. A file named *MAINTENANCE10-01.txt* is included in the Chapter10 folder of your downloadable student files. Assume that this program is a working program in your organization and that it needs modifications as described in the comments (lines that begin with two slashes) at the beginning of the file. Your job is to alter the program to meet the new specifications. (10.2, 10.7)

Debugging Exercises

1. Your downloadable files for Chapter 10 include *DEBUG10-01.txt*, *DEBUG10-02.txt*, *DEBUG10-03.txt*, and *DEBUG10-04.jpg*. Each file starts with some comments that describe the problem. Comments are lines that begin with two slashes (//). Each file contains pseudocode or a flowchart that has mistakes. Find and correct all the bugs.

Game Zone

1. a. Playing cards are used in many computer games, including versions of such classics as Solitaire, Hearts, and Poker. Design a `Card` class that contains a string data field to hold a suit (spades, hearts, diamonds, or clubs) and a numeric data field for a value from 1 to 13. Include get and set methods for each field. In each of the set methods, add a test to ensure that the accepted parameter is in range; if it is not, use a default value for the field.

   b. Write an application that randomly selects two playing cards and displays their values.

   c. Using two `Card` objects, design an application that plays a simple version of the card game War. Deal two `Cards`—one for the computer and one for the player. Determine the higher card, then display a message indicating whether the cards are equal, the computer won, or the player won. (Playing cards are considered equal when they have the same value, no matter what their suit is.) For this game, assume that the Ace (value 1) is low. Make sure that the two `Cards` dealt are not the same `Card`. For example, a deck cannot contain more than one Queen of Spades. (10.2)

Chapter 11

More Object-Oriented Programming Concepts

Learning Objectives

When you complete this chapter, you will be able to:

11.1 Create constructors

11.2 Create destructors

11.3 Describe composition

11.4 Describe inheritance

11.5 Describe how predefined classes are used to create GUI objects

11.6 Describe exception handling

11.7 List the advantages of object-oriented programming

11.1 Creating Constructors

You have learned that you can create classes to encapsulate data and methods, and that you can instantiate objects from the classes you define. For example, you can create an `Employee` class that contains fields such as `lastName`, `hourlyWage`, and `weeklyPay`, and methods that set and return values for those fields. When you instantiate an object with a statement that uses the class type and an object identifier, such as `Employee chauffeur`, you are actually calling a method named `Employee()`. A method that has the same name as a class and that establishes an object is a constructor method, or more simply, a **constructor**. A constructor is a special type of method that gets an object ready for use by establishing a location for it in memory and often by setting initial values for the object's fields. In some programming languages, such as Visual Basic and C++, you do not need to use the constructor's name when declaring an object, but the constructor is called nevertheless. In other languages, such as Java and C#, you include the keyword `new` and the constructor's name in the object declaration. The keyword new indicates that a new object is being created. For example, an `Employee` declaration often looks like the following:

```
Employee chauffeur = new Employee()
```

Constructors fall into two broad categories:

- A **default constructor** is one that requires no arguments.
- A **nondefault constructor** or a **parameterized constructor** requires arguments.

All nondefault constructors are written by a programmer, but there are two categories of default constructors:

- An automatically created default constructor exists in a class in which the programmer has not explicitly written any constructors.
- A programmer-written default constructor can reside in any class and replaces the automatically created one.

In object-oriented programming languages, you can write both default and nondefault constructors for a class; if so, the constructors are overloaded. (Recall that you have learned you can overload methods by writing multiple versions of a method with the same name. Also recall that being able to use one name to implement multiple actions is called *polymorphism*.)

A constructor for a class named `Employee` instantiates one `Employee` object. If the class contains no programmer-written constructors, then it contains an automatically supplied default constructor. Depending on the programming language, the automatically supplied constructor might provide initial values for the object's data fields; for example, in many languages, all numeric fields are set to zero by default. If you do not want an object's fields to hold default values, or if you want to perform additional tasks when you create an instance of a class, you can write your own constructor.

Any constructor you write:

- Must have the same name as the class in which it is defined.
- Does not have a return type.

Normally, you declare constructors to be public so that other classes can instantiate objects that belong to the class. You can create constructors for a class with or without parameters. Once you write a constructor, regardless of whether you include parameters, the automatically supplied default constructor no longer exists. When you write a constructor that does not include parameters, your constructor becomes the default constructor for the class. In other words, a class can have three types of constructors:

- A class can contain a default (parameterless) constructor that is created automatically. When a class contains an automatically created default constructor, it means that no constructors have been explicitly written for the class.
- A class can contain a default (parameterless) constructor that you create explicitly. A class with an explicitly created default constructor no longer contains the automatically supplied version, but it can coexist with one or more nondefault constructors that you write.
- A class can contain a nondefault constructor (with one or more parameters), which must be explicitly created. A class with a nondefault constructor no longer contains the automatically supplied default version, but it can coexist with an explicitly created default constructor and with other nondefault constructors.

Default Constructors

As an example of a default constructor, suppose you create the `Employee` class that appears in **Figure 11-1** and that you want every `Employee` object to have a starting hourly wage of $20.00 as well as the correct weekly pay for that wage. Any `Employee` object instantiated will have an `hourlyWage` field equal to 20.00 and a `weeklyPay` field equal to 800.00. Because the `lastName` field is not assigned in the constructor, each object will hold the default value for strings in the programming language in which this class is implemented.

Figure 11-1 `Employee` class with a default constructor that sets `hourlyWage` and `weeklyPay`

```
class Employee
   Declarations
      private string lastName
      private num hourlyWage
      private num weeklyPay

   public Employee()
      hourlyWage = 20.00
      calculateWeeklyPay()
   return

   public void setLastName(string name)
      lastName = name
   return

   public void setHourlyWage(num wage)
      hourlyWage = wage
      calculateWeeklyPay()
   return

   public string getLastName()
   return lastName

   public num getHourlyWage()
   return hourlyWage

   public num getWeeklyPay()
   return weeklyPay

   private void calculateWeeklyPay()
      Declarations
         num WORK_WEEK_HOURS = 40
      weeklyPay = hourlyWage * WORK_WEEK_HOURS
   return
endClass
```

Programmer-created default constructor

The `Employee` constructor in Figure 11-1 calls the `calculateWeeklyPay()` method. You can write any statement you want in a constructor, including calling other methods, accepting input, declaring local variables, and so on. You can place a constructor anywhere inside the class, outside of any other method. Often, programmers list constructors first among the methods, because a constructor is the first method called when an object is created.

Figure 11-2 shows a class diagram for the `Employee` class. Notice that the constructor is included in the bottom section of the class diagram along with the class's methods, and that the constructor shows no return type.

Figure 11-2 Class diagram for `Employee` class in Figure 11-1

```
Employee
--------------------------------
-lastName : string
-hourlyWage: num
-weeklyPay : num
--------------------------------
+Employee()
+setLastName(name : string) : void
+setHourlyWage(wage : num) : void
+getLastName() : string
+getHourlyWage : num
+getWeeklyPay : num
-calculateWeeklyPay() : void
```

Figure 11-3 shows a program in which two `Employee` objects are declared, their constructors are called, and their `hourlyWage` values are displayed. In the output in **Figure 11-4**, you can see that even though the `setHourlyWage()` method is never called directly in the program, the `Employee`s possess valid hourly wages as set by their constructors.

Figure 11-3 Program that declares `Employee` objects using class in Figure 11-1

```
start
   Declarations
      Employee myPersonalTrainer = new Employee()
      Employee myInteriorDecorator  = new Employee()
   output "Trainer's wage: ",
      myPersonalTrainer.getHourlyWage()
   output "Decorator's wage: ",
      myInteriorDecorator.getHourlyWage()
stop
```

Figure 11-4 Output of program in Figure 11-3

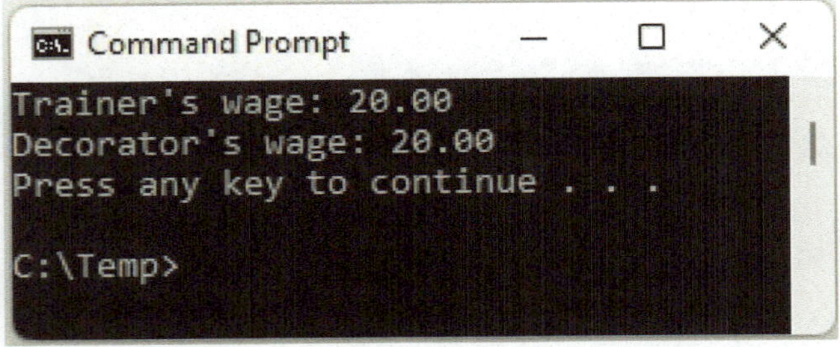

The `Employee` class in Figure 11-1 sets an `Employee`'s hourly wage to 20.00 at construction, but the class also contains a `setHourlyWage()` method that a client application could use later to change the initial `hourlyWage` value. A superior way to write the `Employee` class constructor is shown in **Figure 11-5**. In this version of the constructor, a named constant with the value 20.00 is passed to `setHourlyWage()`. Using this technique provides several advantages:

- The statement to call `calculateWeeklyPay()` is no longer required in the constructor because the constructor calls `setHourlyWage()`, which in turn calls `calculateWeeklyPay()`.
- In the future, if restrictions should be imposed on `hourlyWage`, the code will need to be altered in only one location. For example, if the `setHourlyWage()` method is modified to add decisions that disallow rates that are too high and too low, the code will change only in the `setHourlyWage()` method and will not also have to be modified in the constructor. This reduces the amount of work required and reduces the possibility for error.

Figure 11-5 Improved version of the `Employee` class constructor

```
public Employee()
   Declarations
      num DEFAULT_WAGE = 20.00
   setHourlyWage(DEFAULT_WAGE)
return
```

Of course, if different `hourlyWage` requirements are needed at initialization from those that are required when the value is set after construction, then different statements will be written in the constructor from those written in the `setHourlyWage()` method.

Nondefault Constructors

Nondefault constructors accept one or more parameters. A class does not need to contain a nondefault constructor, but it can contain one or more. When you create any constructor, whether it is default or nondefault, the automatically supplied default constructor is no longer accessible. You could explicitly create a default (parameterless) constructor in addition to any number of nondefault ones, in which case the constructors would be overloaded.

For example, instead of forcing every `Employee` to be constructed with the same initial values, you might choose to create `Employee` objects that each are initialized with a unique `hourlyWage` by passing a numeric value for the wage to the constructor. **Figure 11-6** shows an `Employee` constructor that receives an argument.

Figure 11-6 `Employee` constructor that accepts a parameter

```
public Employee(num rate)
   setHourlyWage(rate)
return
```

When you declare an object using the `Employee` class that contains the constructor in Figure 11-6, you pass an argument to the constructor using a declaration similar to one of the following:

- `Employee partTimeWorker = new Employee(18.81)`, using an unnamed literal constant
- `Employee partTimeWorker = new Employee(BASE_PAY)`, using a named constant
- `Employee partTimeWorker = new Employee(valueEnteredByUser)`, using a variable

In each of these cases, when the constructor executes, the numeric value within the constructor call is passed to `Employee()`, where the parameter `rate` takes on the value of the argument. The value is assigned to `hourlyWage` within the constructor.

If you create an `Employee` class with a constructor such as the one shown in Figure 11-6, and it is the only constructor in the class, then every `Employee` object you create must use a numeric argument in its declaration. In other words, with this new version of the class that contains a single nondefault constructor, the following declaration no longer works:

```
Employee partTimeWorker = new Employee()
```

However, if the class also contains a default constructor, then the constructors are overloaded, and you can use either version when an object is instantiated.

Overloading Instance Methods and Constructors

You have learned that you can overload methods by writing multiple versions of a method with the same name but different parameter lists. You can overload a class's instance methods and constructors in the same way. For example, **Figure 11-7** shows a version of the `Employee` class that contains two constructors.

Recall that a method's signature is its name and list of argument types. The constructors in Figure 11-7 have different signatures—one version requires no argument and the other requires a numeric argument. In other words, this version of the class contains both a default constructor and a nondefault constructor.

When you use the version of the class shown in Figure 11-7, then you can make statements such as the following:

- `Employee deliveryPerson = new Employee()`—When you declare an `Employee` using this statement, an `hourlyWage` of 20.00 is automatically set because the statement uses the parameterless version of the constructor.
- `Employee myButler = new Employee(25.85)`—When you declare an `Employee` using this statement, `hourlyWage` is set to the passed value.

Any method or constructor in a class can be overloaded, and you can provide as many versions as you want, provided that each version has a unique signature. (In the next section, you learn about destructors, which cannot be overloaded.)

Figure 11-7 `Employee` **class with overloaded constructors**

```
class Employee
   Declarations
      private string lastName
      private num hourlyWage
      private num weeklyPay

   public Employee()
      Declarations
         num DEFAULT_WAGE = 20.00      --------- Default constructor
      setHourlyWage(DEFAULT_WAGE)
   return

   public Employee(num rate)           --------- Nondefault constructor
      setHourlyWage(rate)
   return

   public void setLastName(string name)
      lastName = name
   return

   public void setHourlyWage(num wage)
      hourlyWage = wage
      calculateWeeklyPay()
   return

   public string getLastName()
   return lastName

   public num getHourlyWage()
   return hourlyWage

   public num getWeeklyPay()
   return weeklyPay

   private void calculateWeeklyPay()
      Declarations
         num WORK_WEEK_HOURS = 40
      weeklyPay = hourlyWage * WORK_WEEK_HOURS
   return
endClass
```

As an example, you could add a third constructor to the `Employee` class. **Figure 11-8** shows a version that can coexist with the other two constructors because the parameter list is different from either existing version. With this version you can specify the hourly rate for the `Employee` as well as a name. If an application makes a statement similar to the following, then this two-parameter version would execute:

```
Employee myHousekeeper = new Employee(22.50, "Parker")
```

Figure 11-8 A third possible `Employee` class constructor

```
public Employee(num rate, string name)
   lastName = name
   setHourlyWage(rate)
return
```

You might create an `Employee` class with several constructor versions to provide flexibility for client programs. For example, a particular client program might use only one version, a different client might use another, and a third client might use them all.

Two Truths & a Lie | Creating Constructors

1. A constructor is a method that establishes an object.
2. A default constructor is defined as one that is created automatically.
3. Depending on the programming language, a default constructor might provide initial values for the object's data fields.

The false statement is #2. A default constructor is one that takes no arguments. Although the automatically created constructor for a class is a default constructor, not all default constructors are created automatically.

11.2 Understanding Destructors

A **destructor** contains the actions you require when an instance of a class is destroyed. Most often, an instance of a class is destroyed when the object goes out of scope. For example, when an object is declared within a method, the object goes out of scope when the method ends. As with constructors, if you do not explicitly create a destructor for a class, one is provided automatically.

The most common way to declare a destructor explicitly is to use an identifier that consists of a tilde (~) followed by the class name. You cannot provide parameters to a destructor; it must have an empty parameter list. As a consequence, destructors cannot be overloaded; a class can have only one destructor. Like a constructor, a destructor has no return type.

Note | The rules for creating and naming destructors vary among programming languages. For example, in Visual Basic classes, the destructor for a class is called `Finalize`.

Figure 11-9 shows an `Employee` class that contains only one field (`idNumber`), a constructor, and a destructor. Although it is unusual for a constructor or destructor to output anything, the ones in Figure 11-9 display messages so you can see when the objects are created and destroyed. When you execute the client program in **Figure 11-10**, you instantiate two `Employee` objects, each with its own `idNumber` value. When the program ends, the two `Employee` objects go out of scope, and the destructor for each object is called automatically. **Figure 11-11** shows the output.

Figure 11-9 `Employee` class with destructor

```
class Employee
   Declarations
      private string idNumber
   public Employee(string empID)
      idNumber = empId
      output "Employee ", idNumber, " is created"
   return
   public ~Employee()
      output "Employee ", idNumber, " is destroyed"
   return
endClass
```

Figure 11-10 Program that declares two `Employee` objects using the class version with the explicitly coded destructor

```
start
   Declarations
      Employee aWorker = new Employee("101")
      Employee anotherWorker = new Employee("202")
stop
```

Figure 11-11 Output of program in Figure 11-10

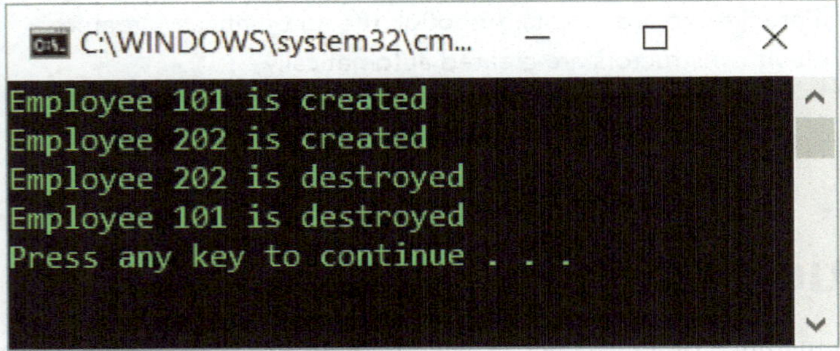
C:\WINDOWS\system32\cm...
Employee 101 is created
Employee 202 is created
Employee 202 is destroyed
Employee 101 is destroyed
Press any key to continue . . .

The program in Figure 11-10 never explicitly calls the `Employee` class destructor, yet you can see from the output that the destructor executes twice. Destructors are invoked automatically; you usually do not explicitly call one, although in some languages you can. Interestingly, you can see from the output in Figure 11-11 that the last object created is the first object destroyed; the same relationship would hold true no matter how many objects the program instantiated if the objects went out of scope at the same time.

> **Note** An instance of a class becomes eligible for destruction when it is no longer possible for any code to use it—that is, when it goes out of scope. In many languages, the actual execution of an object's destructor might occur at any time after the object becomes eligible for destruction.

For now, you have little reason to create a destructor except to demonstrate how it is called automatically. Later, when you write more sophisticated programs that work with files, databases, or large quantities of computer memory, you might want to perform specific cleanup or close-down tasks when an object goes out of scope. If you develop a game in which the player attempts to eliminate monsters or pop bubbles, you might want to perform an action such as adding points to the player's score when an object in the game is destroyed. In these examples, you could place appropriate instructions within a destructor.

Two Truths & a Lie | Understanding Destructors

1. Unlike constructors, you must explicitly create a destructor if you want one for a class.
2. A destructor must have an empty parameter list.
3. Destructors cannot be overloaded; a class can have only one destructor.

The false statement is #1. As with constructors, if you do not explicitly create a destructor for a class, one is provided automatically.

11.3 Understanding Composition

A class can contain simple variables as data fields, and it can contain objects of another class as data fields. For example, you might create a class named `Date` that contains a month, day, and year, and add two `Date` fields to an `Employee` class to hold the `Employee`'s birth date and hire date. Then you might create a class named `Department` that represents every department in a company, and modify the class to contain a supervisor, who is an `Employee`. **Figure 11-12** contains a diagram of these relationships. When a class contains objects of another class, the relationship is called a **whole-part relationship** or **composition**. The relationship created is also called a **has-a relationship** because one class "has an" instance of another—for example, a `Department` has an `Employee` and an `Employee` has a hire `Date`.

Figure 11-12 Diagram of typical composition relationships

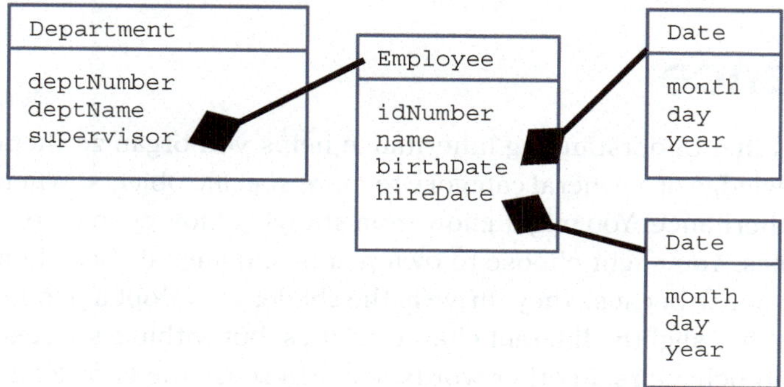

> **Note**
>
> Placing one or more objects within another object is often known as *composition* when the parts cease to exist if the whole ceases to exist, and as *aggregation* when the parts can exist without the whole. For example, the relationship of a `Business` to its `Departments` is composition because if the `Business` ceases to exist, so do its `Departments`. However, the relationship of a `Department` to its `Employees` might be called aggregation because the `Employees` continue to exist even if their `Department` does not.

When your classes contain objects that are members of other classes, your programming task becomes increasingly complex. For example, you sometimes must refer to a method by a very long name. Suppose you create a `Department` class that contains an array of `Employee` objects (those who work in the department), and a method named `getHighestPaidEmployee()` that returns a single `Employee` object. The `Employee` class contains a method named `getHireDate()` that returns a `Date` object—an `Employee`'s hire date. Further suppose the `Date` class contains a method that returns the year portion of the `Date`, and that you create a `Department` object named `sales`. An application might contain a statement such as the following, which outputs the year that the highest-paid employee in the Sales department was hired:

```
output sales.getHighestPaidEmployee().getHireDate().getYear()
```

> **Note**
>
> The syntax to create an array of objects can differ among programming languages. For this course, you can assume that if you have a class named `Employee` that contains a default constructor, you can create an array of ten `Employee` objects with a statement like the following:
>
> ```
> Employee employees[10] = new Employee()[10]
> ```

Additionally, when classes contain objects that are members of other classes, all the corresponding constructors and destructors execute in a specific order. As you work with object-oriented programming languages, you will learn to manage these complex issues.

Two Truths & a Lie | Understanding Composition

1. A class can contain objects of another class as data fields.
2. Composition occurs when you use an object as a field within another class.
3. Composition is called an is-a relationship because one class "is an" instance of another.

The false statement is #3. Composition is called a has-a relationship because one class "has an" instance of another.

11.4 Understanding Inheritance

Understanding classes helps you organize objects in real life. Understanding inheritance helps you organize them more precisely. Inheritance enables you to apply your knowledge of a general category to more specific objects. When you use the term *inheritance*, you might think of genetic inheritance. You might know from studying biology that your blood type and eye color are determined by inherited genes. You might choose to own plants and animals based on their inherited attributes. You plant impatiens next to your house because they thrive in the shade; you adopt a poodle because you know poodles don't shed. Every plant and pet has slightly different characteristics, but within a species, you can count on many consistent inherited attributes and behaviors. In other words, you can reuse the knowledge you gain about general categories and apply it to more specific categories.

Similarly, the classes you create in object-oriented programming languages can inherit data and methods from existing classes. When you create a class by making it inherit from another class, the new class contains fields and methods automatically, allowing you to reuse fields and methods that are already written and tested.

You already know how to create classes and how to instantiate objects that are members of those classes.

For example, consider the `Employee` class in **Figure 11-13**. The class contains two data fields, `empNum` and `weeklySalary`, as well as methods that get and set each field.

Figure 11-13 An `Employee` class

```
class Employee
   Declarations
      private string empNum
      private num weeklySalary

   public void setEmpNum(string number)
      empNum = number
   return

   public string getEmpNum()
   return empNum

   public void setWeeklySalary(num salary)
      weeklySalary = salary
   return

   public num getWeeklySalary()
   return weeklySalary
endClass
```

Suppose that you hire a new type of `Employee` who earns a commission as well as a weekly salary. You could create a class with a name such as `CommissionEmployee` and provide this class with three fields (`empNum`, `weeklySalary`, and `commissionRate`) and six methods (to get and set each of the three fields). However, this would duplicate much of the work that you already have done when creating the `Employee` class. The wise and efficient alternative is to create the `CommissionEmployee` class so it inherits all the attributes and methods of `Employee`. Then, you can add just the single field and two methods (the get and set methods for the new field) that are needed to complete the new class. **Figure 11-14** depicts these relationships. The complete `CommissionEmployee` class is shown in **Figure 11-15**.

Figure 11-14 `CommissionEmployee` inherits from `Employee`

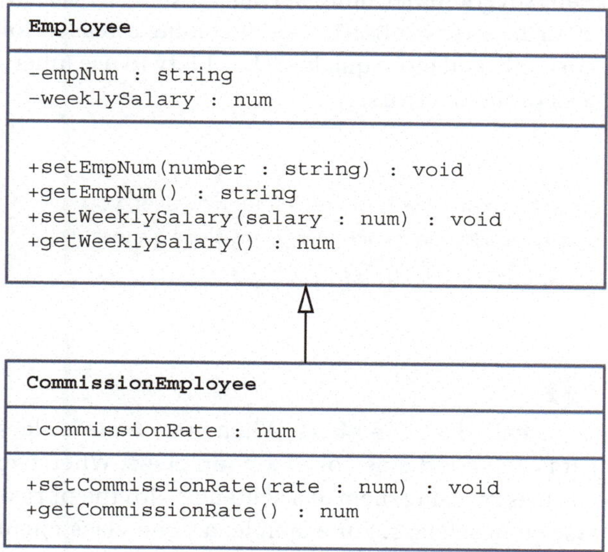

Figure 11-15 `CommissionEmployee` class

```
class CommissionEmployee inheritsFrom Employee
   Declarations
      private num commissionRate

   public void setCommissionRate(num rate)
      commissionRate = rate
   return

   public num getCommissionRate()
   return commissionRate
endClass
```

> **Note** The class in Figure 11-15 uses the phrase `inheritsFrom Employee` to indicate inheritance. Each programming language uses its own syntax. For example, in Java you would write `extends`, in Visual Basic you would write `Inherits`, and in C++ and C# you would use a colon between the new class name and the one from which it inherits.

When you use inheritance to create the `CommissionEmployee` class, you acquire the following benefits:

- You save time because you need not re-create the `Employee` fields and methods.
- You reduce the chance of errors because the `Employee` methods have already been written and tested.
- You make it easier for anyone who has used the `Employee` class to understand the `CommissionEmployee` class because these users can concentrate on the new features only.

- You reduce the chance for errors and inconsistencies in shared fields. For example, if your company decides to change employee ID numbers from four digits to five, and you have code in the `Employee` class constructor that ensures valid ID numbers, then you can simply change the code in the `Employee` class; every `CommissionEmployee` object will automatically acquire the change. Without inheritance, not only would you have to make the change in multiple places, but the likelihood would increase that you would forget to make the change in one of the classes or introduce an inconsistency when making a change in one of the classes.

Imagine that besides `CommissionEmployee`, you want to create several other more specific `Employee` classes (perhaps `PartTimeEmployee`, including a field for hours worked, or `DismissedEmployee`, including a reason for dismissal). By using inheritance, you can develop each new class correctly and more quickly. The ability to use inheritance makes programs easier to write, easier to understand, and less prone to errors.

Note In part, the concept of class inheritance is useful because it makes class code reusable. However, you do not use inheritance simply to save work. When properly used, inheritance always involves general-to-specific relationships that make logical sense.

Understanding Inheritance Terminology

A class that is used as a basis for inheritance, such as `Employee`, is called a **base class**. When you create a class that inherits from a base class (such as `CommissionEmployee`), it is a **derived class** or **extended class**. When two classes have a base-derived relationship, you can distinguish the classes by using them in a sentence with the phrase *is a*. A derived class always "is a" case or instance of the more general base class. For example, a `Tree` class might be a base class to an `Evergreen` class. Every `Evergreen` *is a* `Tree`; however, it is not true that every `Tree` is an `Evergreen`. Thus, `Tree` is the base class and `Evergreen` is the derived class. Similarly, a `CommissionEmployee` *is an* `Employee`—not always the other way around—so `Employee` is the base class and `CommissionEmployee` is derived.

You can use the terms **superclass** and **subclass** as synonyms for *base class* and *derived class*. Thus, `Evergreen` can be called a subclass of the `Tree` superclass. You also can use the terms **parent class** and **child class**. A `CommissionEmployee` is a child to the `Employee` parent.

As an alternative way to discover which of two classes is the base class and which is the derived class, you can try saying the two class names together, although this technique might not work with every base–subclass pair. When people say their names in the English language, they state the more specific name before the all-encompassing family name, such as *Mary Johnson*. Similarly, with classes, the order that "makes more sense" is the child–parent order. Thus, because "Evergreen Tree" makes more sense than "Tree Evergreen," you can deduce that `Evergreen` is the child class. It also is convenient to think of a derived class as building upon its base class by providing the "adjectives" or additional descriptive terms for the "noun." Frequently, the names of derived classes are formed in this way, as in `CommissionEmployee` or `EvergreenTree`.

Finally, you usually can distinguish base classes from their derived classes by size. Although it is not required, a derived class is generally larger than its base class, in the sense that it usually has additional fields and methods. A subclass description might look small, but any subclass contains all of its base class's fields and methods as well as its own more specific fields and methods.

Do not think of a subclass as a subset of another class—in other words, as possessing only parts of its base class. In fact, a derived class usually contains more than its parent.

A derived class can be further extended. In other words, a subclass can have a child of its own. For example, after you create a `Tree` class and derive `Evergreen`, you might derive a `Spruce` class from `Evergreen`. Similarly, a `Poodle` class might derive from `Dog`, `Dog` from `DomesticPet`, and `DomesticPet` from `Animal`. The entire list of parent classes from which a child class is derived constitutes the **ancestors** of the subclass.

> **Note** After you create the `Spruce` class, you might be ready to create `Spruce` objects. For example, you might create `theTreeInMyBackYard`, or you might create an array of 1000 `Spruce` objects for a tree farm. On the other hand, before you are ready to create objects, you might first want to create even more specific child classes such as `ColoradoSpruce` and `NorwaySpruce`.

A child inherits all the data fields and methods of all its ancestors. For example, when you declare a `Spruce` object, it contains all the attributes and methods of both an `Evergreen` and a `Tree`, and a `CommissionEmployee` contains all the attributes and methods of an `Employee`. In other words, the components of `Employee` and `CommissionEmployee` are as follows:

- `Employee` contains two fields and four methods, as shown in Figure 11-13.
- `CommissionEmployee` contains three fields and six methods, even though you do not see all of them in Figure 11-15. Two of its fields and four of its methods are defined in its parent's class.

Although a child class contains all the data fields and methods of its parent, a parent class does not gain any child class data or methods. Therefore, when `Employee` and `CommissionEmployee` classes are defined as in Figures 11-13 and 11-15, the statements in **Figure 11-16** are all valid in an application. The `salesperson` object can use all the methods of its parent, and it can use its own `setCommissionRate()` and `getCommissionRate()` methods. **Figure 11-17** shows the output of the program as it would appear in a command-line environment.

Figure 11-16 Program that declares an `Employee` and a `CommissionEmployee`

```
start
   Declarations
      Employee manager
      CommissionEmployee salesperson
   manager.setEmpNum("111")
   manager.setWeeklySalary(700.00)
   salesperson.setEmpNum("222")
   salesperson.setWeeklySalary(300.00)
   salesperson.setCommissionRate(0.12)
   output "Manager ", manager.getEmpNum(), manager.getWeeklySalary()
   output "Salesperson ", salesperson.getEmpNum(),
      salesperson.getWeeklySalary(), salesperson.getCommissionRate()
stop
```

Figure 11-17 Output of the program in Figure 11-16

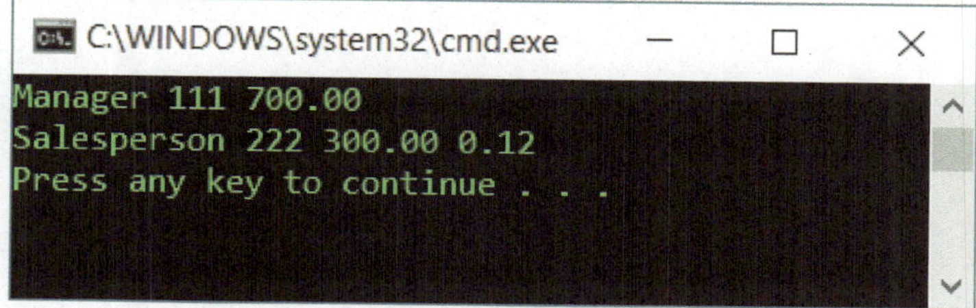

The following statements would not be allowed in the application in Figure 11-16 because `manager`, as an `Employee` object, does not have access to the methods of the `CommissionEmployee` child class:

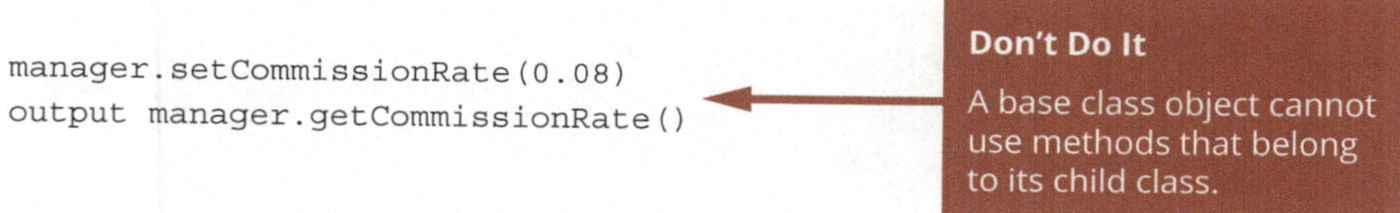

manager.setCommissionRate(0.08)
output manager.getCommissionRate()
Don't Do It
A base class object cannot use methods that belong to its child class.

> **Note** When you create your own inheritance chains, you want to place fields and methods at their most general level. In other words, a method named `grow()` rightfully belongs in a `Tree` class, whereas it would be appropriate to place a `leavesTurnColor()` method in a `DeciduousTree` class rather than separately within `Oak` or `Maple` child classes.

It makes sense that a parent class object does not have access to its child's data and methods. When you create the parent class, you do not know how many future child classes might be created, or what their data or methods might look like. In addition, derived classes are more specific, so parent class objects cannot use them. For example, a `Cardiologist` class and an `Obstetrician` class are children of a `Doctor` class. You do not expect all members of the general parent class `Doctor` to have the `Cardiologist`'s `repairHeartValve()` method or the `Obstetrician`'s `performCaesarianSection()` method. However, `Cardiologist` and `Obstetrician` objects have access to the more general `Doctor` methods `takeBloodPressure()` and `billPatients()`. As with specialization of doctors, it is convenient to think of derived classes as *specialists*. That is, their fields and methods are more specialized than those of the parent class.

> **Note** In some programming languages, such as C#, Visual Basic, and Java, every class you create is a child of one ultimate base class, often called the `Object` class. The `Object` class usually provides basic functionality that is inherited by all the classes you create—for example, the ability to show its name or an object's memory location.

Accessing Private Fields and Methods of a Parent Class

When you create classes, the most common scenario is for methods to be public but for data to be private. Making data private is an important concept in object-oriented programming. By making data fields private and allowing access to them only through a class's methods, you control the ways in which data items can be altered and used.

When a data field within a class is private, no outside class can use it—including a child class. The principle of data hiding would be lost if you could access a class's private data merely by creating a child class. However, it can be inconvenient when the methods of a child class cannot directly access the data fields it inherits.

For example, suppose that some employees do not earn a weekly salary as defined in the `Employee` class, but are paid by the hour. You might create an `HourlyEmployee` class that descends from `Employee`, as shown in **Figure 11-18**. The class contains two new fields, `hoursWorked` and `hourlyRate`, and a get and set method for each.

Figure 11-18 Class diagram for **`HourlyEmployee`** class inheriting from **`Employee`**

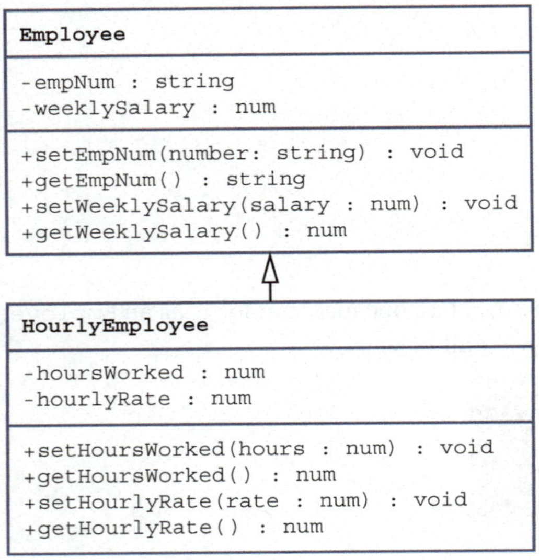

```
Employee
-----------------------------------------------
-empNum : string
-weeklySalary : num
-----------------------------------------------
+setEmpNum(number: string) : void
+getEmpNum() : string
+setWeeklySalary(salary : num) : void
+getWeeklySalary() : num

                 ▲
                 |

HourlyEmployee
-----------------------------------------------
-hoursWorked : num
-hourlyRate : num
-----------------------------------------------
+setHoursWorked(hours : num) : void
+getHoursWorked() : num
+setHourlyRate(rate : num) : void
+getHourlyRate() : num
```

You can implement the child class shown in **Figure 11-19**. Whenever you set either `hoursWorked` or `hourlyRate`, you want to recalculate `weeklySalary` using the newly modified values for the hours and rate. The logic makes sense, but when you write the code in a programming language, it does not compile. The `HourlyEmployee` class is attempting to modify the `weeklySalary` field. Although every `HourlyEmployee` *has* a `weeklySalary` field by virtue of being a child of `Employee`, the `HourlyEmployee` class methods do not have access to the `weeklySalary` field, because `weeklySalary` is private within the `Employee` class. The private `weeklySalary` field is **inaccessible** to any class other than the one in which it is defined.

Figure 11-19 Implementation of `HourlyEmployee` class that attempts to access `weeklySalary`

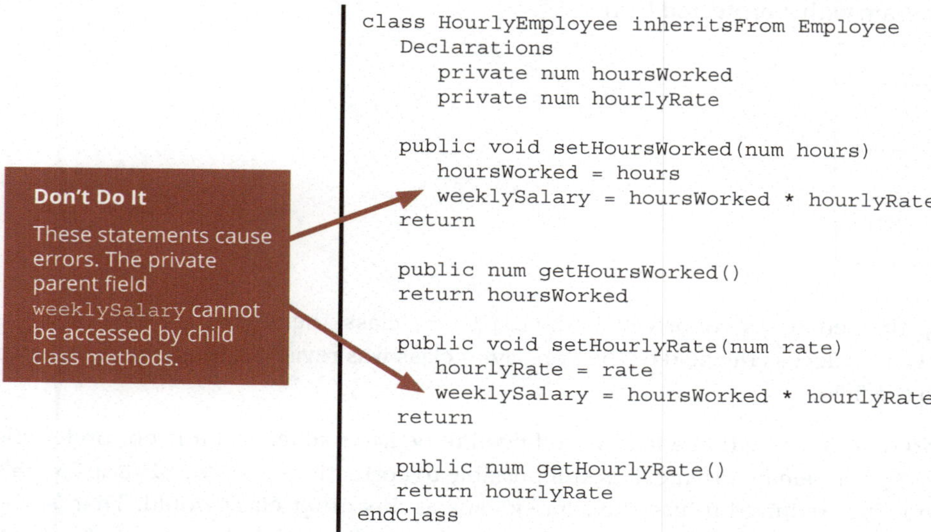

Don't Do It
These statements cause errors. The private parent field weeklySalary cannot be accessed by child class methods.


```
class HourlyEmployee inheritsFrom Employee
   Declarations
      private num hoursWorked
      private num hourlyRate

   public void setHoursWorked(num hours)
      hoursWorked = hours
      weeklySalary = hoursWorked * hourlyRate
   return

   public num getHoursWorked()
   return hoursWorked

   public void setHourlyRate(num rate)
      hourlyRate = rate
      weeklySalary = hoursWorked * hourlyRate
   return

   public num getHourlyRate()
   return hourlyRate
endClass
```

One solution to this problem would be to make `weeklySalary` public in the parent `Employee` class. Then the child class could use it. However, that action would violate the important object-oriented principle of data hiding. Good object-oriented style dictates that your data should be altered only by the methods you choose and only in ways that you can control. If outside classes could alter an `Employee`'s private fields, then the fields could be assigned values that the `Employee` class could not control. In such a case, the principle of data hiding would be destroyed, causing the behavior of the object to be unpredictable.

Therefore, OOP languages allow a medium-security access specifier that is more restrictive than public but less restrictive than private. The **`protected` access specifier** is used when you want no outside classes to be able to use a data field except classes that are children of the original class. **Figure 11-20** shows a rewritten `Employee` class that uses the `protected` access specifier on its `weeklySalary` data field.

Figure 11-20 `Employee` class with a protected field

```
class Employee
   Declarations
      private string empNum
      protected num weeklySalary

   public void setEmpNum(string number)
      empNum = number
   return

   public string getEmpNum()
   return empNum

   public void setWeeklySalary(num salary)
      weeklySalary = salary
   return

   public num getWeeklySalary()
   return weeklySalary
endClass
```

When this modified `Employee` class is used as a base class for another class, such as `HourlyEmployee`, the child class's methods will be able to access the protected item originally defined in the parent class. When the `Employee` class is defined with a protected `weeklySalary` field, as shown in Figure 11-20, the code in the `HourlyEmployee` class in Figure 11-19 works correctly.

Figure 11-21 contains the class diagram for the version of the `Employee` class shown in Figure 11-20. Notice that the `weeklySalary` field is preceded with an octothorpe (#)—the character that conventionally is used in class diagrams to indicate protected class members.

Figure 11-21 `Employee` **class diagram with a protected field**

Employee
-empNum : string #weeklySalary : num
+setEmpNum(number: string) : void +getEmpNum() : string +setWeeklySalary(salary : num) : void +getWeeklySalary() : num

If `weeklySalary` is defined as protected instead of private in the `Employee` class, then either the creator of the class knew that a child class would want to access the field or the `Employee` class was revised after it became known the child class would need access to the field.

If the `Employee` class's creator did not foresee that a field would need to be accessible, or if it is not preferable to revise the class, then `weeklySalary` will remain private. It is still possible to correctly set an `HourlyEmployee`'s weekly pay—the `HourlyEmployee` is just required to use the same means as any other class would. That is, the `HourlyEmployee` class can use the public method `setWeeklySalary()` that already exists in the parent class. Any class, including a child, can use a public field or method of the base class. So, assuming that `weeklySalary` remains private in `Employee`, **Figure 11-22** shows how `HourlyEmployee` could be written to correctly set `weeklySalary`.

Figure 11-22 The `HourlyEmployee` **class when** `weeklySalary` **remains private**

```
class HourlyEmployee inheritsFrom Employee
   Declarations
      private num hoursWorked
      private num hourlyRate
   public void setHoursWorked(num hours)
      hoursWorked = hours
      setWeeklySalary(hoursWorked * hourlyRate)
   return

   public num getHoursWorked()
   return hoursWorked

   public void setHourlyRate(num rate)
      hourlyRate = rate
      setWeeklySalary(hoursWorked * hourlyRate)
   return

   public num getHourlyRate()
   return hourlyRate
endClass
```

In the version of `HourlyEmployee` in Figure 11-22, the statements within `setHoursWorked()` and `setHourlyRate()` assign a value to the corresponding child class field (`hoursWorked` or `hourlyRate`, respectively). Each method then calls the public parent class method `setWeeklySalary()`. In this example, no `protected` access specifiers are needed for any fields in the parent class, and the creators of the parent class did not have to foresee that a child class would eventually need to access any of its fields. Instead, any child classes of `Employee` simply follow the same access rules as any other outside class would. As an added benefit, if the parent class method `setWeeklySalary()` contained additional code (for example, to require a minimum base weekly pay for all employees), then that code would be enforced even for `HourlyEmployees`.

So, in summary, when you create a child class that must access a private field of its parent's class, you can take one of several approaches:

- If you are the developer of the parent class, you can modify the parent class to make the field public. Usually, this is not advised because it violates the principle of data hiding.
- If you are the developer of the parent class, you can modify the parent class to make the field protected so that child classes have access to it, but other outside classes do not. This approach is necessary if you do not want public methods to be able to access the parent class field. Be aware that some programmers oppose making any data fields nonprivate. They feel that public methods should always control data access, even by a class's children.
- The child class can use a public method within the parent class that modifies the field, just as any other outside class would. This is frequently, but not always, the best option.

Using the `protected` access specifier for a field can be convenient, and it improves program performance a little by using a field directly instead of "going through" another method. Also, using the `protected` access specifier is occasionally necessary when no existing public method accesses a field in a way required by the child class. However, protected data members should be used sparingly. Whenever possible, the principle of data hiding should be observed, and even child classes should have to go through methods to "get to" their parent's private data.

The likelihood of future errors increases when child classes are allowed direct access to a parent's fields. For example, if the company decides to add a bonus to every `Employee`'s weekly salary, you might make a change in the `setWeeklySalary()` method. If a child class is allowed direct access to the `Employee` field `weeklySalary` without using the `setWeeklySalary()` method, then any child class objects will not receive the bonus. Classes that depend on field names from parent classes are said to be **fragile** because they are prone to errors—that is, they are easy to "break."

Note Some OOP languages, such as C++, allow a subclass to inherit from more than one parent class. For example, you might create an `InsuredItem` class that contains data fields such as value and purchase date for each insured possession, and an `Automobile` class with appropriate data fields (for example, vehicle identification number, make, model, and year). When you create an `InsuredAutomobile` class for a car rental agency, you might want to include information and methods for `Automobiles` and `InsuredItems`, so you might want to inherit from both. The capability to inherit from more than one class is called **multiple inheritance**.

Sometimes, a parent class is so general that you never intend to create any specific instances of the class. For example, you might never create an object that is "just" an `Employee`; each `Employee` is more specifically a `SalariedEmployee`, `HourlyEmployee`, or `ContractEmployee`. A class such as `Employee` that you create only to extend from, but not to instantiate objects from, is an abstract class. An **abstract class** is one from which you cannot create any concrete objects, but from which you can inherit.

Note The syntax to create an abstract class differs among programming languages. For example, Java and C# use the keyword `abstract` when defining an abstract class, but Visual Basic uses `MustInherit`.

Overriding Parent Class Methods in a Child Class

Overriding is the mechanism by which a child class method is used by default when a parent class contains a method with the same signature. That is, by default, the child class version of the method is used with any child class object.

For example, suppose that an `Employee` class contains a `setEmpNum()` method that accepts a string parameter and assigns it to a private data field named `empNum`. If you create a `CommissionEmployee` class that is a child of `Employee`, and if the `CommissionEmployee` class does not contain its own `setEmpNum()` method that accepts a string parameter, the parent class method executes when you use the method name with a child class object.

However, suppose that `CommissionEmployee` is a child of `Employee` and that it also contains a `setEmpNum()` method that accepts a string parameter, but concatenates a *C* to the value before assigning it to `empNum`. When you declare an `Employee` object and use the method name with it, the parent class version of the method executes. When you declare a `CommissionEmployee` object and use the method name with it, the child class version of the method overrides the parent class version and executes appropriately.

Using Inheritance to Achieve Good Software Design

When an automobile company designs a new car model, it does not build every component of the new car from scratch. The company might design a new feature; for example, at some point a carmaker designed the first air bag. However, many of a new car's features are simply modifications of existing features. The manufacturer might create a larger gas tank or more comfortable seats, but even these new features still possess many properties of their predecessors in the older models. Many features of new car models are not even modified; instead, existing components such as air filters and windshield wipers often are included on the new model without any changes.

Similarly, you can create powerful computer programs more easily if many of their components are used either "as is" or with slight modifications. Inheritance makes your job easier because you don't have to create every part of a new class from scratch. Professional programmers constantly create new class libraries for use with OOP languages. Having classes in these libraries that are available to use and extend makes programming large systems more manageable. When you create a useful, extendable superclass, you and other future programmers gain several advantages:

- Subclass creators save development time because much of the code needed for the class has already been written.
- Subclass creators save testing time because the superclass code has already been tested and probably used in a variety of situations. In other words, the superclass code is reliable.
- Programmers who create or use new subclasses already understand how the superclass works, so the time it takes to learn the new class features is reduced.
- When you create a new subclass, neither the superclass source code nor the translated superclass code is changed. The superclass maintains its integrity.

When you consider classes, you must think about their commonalities, and then you can create superclasses from which to inherit. You might be rewarded professionally when you see your own superclasses extended by others in the future.

Two Truths & a Lie | Understanding Inheritance

1. When you create a class by making it inherit from another class, you save time because you need not re-create the base class fields and methods.
2. A class that is used as a basis for inheritance is called a base class, derived class, or extended class.
3. When a data field within a class is private, no outside class can use it—including a child class.

The false statement is #2. A class that is used as a basis for inheritance is called a base class, superclass, or parent class. A derived class is a subclass, extended class, or child class.

11.5 An Example of Using Predefined Classes: Creating GUI Objects

When you purchase or download a compiler for an object-oriented programming language, it comes packaged with many predefined, built-in classes. The classes are stored in **libraries** or **packages**—collections of classes that serve related purposes. Some of the most helpful are the classes you can use to create graphical user interface (GUI) objects such as frames, buttons, labels, and text boxes. You place these GUI components within interactive programs so that users can manipulate them by typing on a keyboard, clicking a mouse, or touching or swiping a screen. For example, if you want to place a clickable button on the screen using a language that supports GUI applications, you instantiate an object that belongs to an existing class with a name similar to `Button`. You then create objects with names such as `yesButton` or `buyProductNowButton`. The `Button` class contains private data fields such as `text` and `height` and public methods such as `setText()` and `setHeight()` that allow you to alter the objects' fields. For example, you might write a statement such as the following to change the text on a `Button` object:

```
buyProductNowButton.setText("Click here to buy now")
```

If no predefined GUI object classes existed, you could create your own. However, this would present several disadvantages:

- It would be a lot of work. Creating graphical objects requires a substantial amount of code and at least a modicum of artistic talent.
- It would be repetitious work. Almost all GUI programs require standard components such as buttons and labels. If each programmer created the classes for these components from scratch, much of this work would be repeated unnecessarily.
- The components would look different in various applications. If programmers created their own component classes, objects such as buttons would look different and operate in slightly different ways. Users prefer standardization in their components—title bars on windows that are a uniform height, buttons that appear to be pressed when clicked, frames and windows that contain maximize and minimize buttons in predictable locations, and so on. By using standard component classes, programmers are assured that the GUI components in their programs have the same look and feel as those in other programs.

Programming languages that supply existing GUI classes often provide a **visual development environment** in which you can create programs by dragging components such as buttons and labels onto a screen and arranging them visually. (In several languages, the visual development environment is known by the acronym **IDE**, which stands for *integrated development environment*.) Then you write programming statements to control the actions that take place when a user manipulates the controls—by clicking them using a mouse, for example. Many programmers never create classes of their own from which they will instantiate objects, but only write application classes that use built-in GUI component classes. Some languages—for example, Visual Basic and C#—lend themselves very well to this type of programming.

Two Truths & a Lie | An Example of Using Predefined Classes: Creating GUI Objects

1. Collections of classes that serve related purposes are called annals.
2. GUI components are placed within interactive programs so that users can manipulate them using input devices.
3. By using standard component classes, programmers are assured that the GUI components in their programs have the same look and feel as those in other programs.

The false statement is #1. Collections of classes that serve related purposes are stored in libraries or packages.

11.6 Understanding Exception Handling

A great deal of the effort that goes into writing programs involves checking data items to make sure they are valid and reasonable. Professional data-entry operators who create the files used in business applications spend their entire working day entering facts and figures, so operators can and do make typing errors. When programs depend on data entered by average users who are not trained typists, the likelihood of errors is even greater.

> **Note** Earlier in this course, you learned that programmers use the acronym *GIGO* to describe what happens when worthless or invalid input causes inaccurate or unrealistic results. GIGO is an acronym for "garbage in, garbage out."

In procedural programs, programmers handled errors in various ways that were effective, but the techniques had some drawbacks. The introduction of object-oriented programming has led to a new model called exception handling.

Drawbacks to Traditional Error-Handling Techniques

In traditional programming, probably the most common error-handling outcome was to terminate the program, or at least to terminate the method in which the offending statement executed. For example, suppose that a program prompts a user to enter an insurance premium type from the keyboard, and that the entered value should be *A* or *H* for *Auto* or *Health*. **Figure 11-23** shows a segment of pseudocode that causes the `determinePremium()` method to end if `policyType` is invalid; in the `if` statement, the method ends abruptly when `policyType` is not *A* or *H*. This method of handling an error is not only unforgiving, it isn't even structured. Recall that a structured method should have exactly one entry point and exactly one exit point. The method in Figure 11-23 contains two exit points at the two `return` statements.

Figure 11-23 A method that handles an error in an unstructured manner

```
public void determinePremium()
   Declarations
      string policyType
      string AUTO = "A"
      string HEALTH = "H"
   output "Please enter policy type "
   input policyType
   if policyType <> AUTO AND policyType <> HEALTH then
      return
   else
      // Calculations for auto and health premiums go here
   endif
return
```

Don't Do It
A structured method should not have multiple `return` statements.

In the example shown in Figure 11-23, if `policyType` contains an invalid value, the method in which the code appears is terminated. The client program might continue with an invalid value or it might stop working. If the program that contains this method is part of a business program or a game, the user might be annoyed. However, an early termination in a program that monitors a hospital patient's vital signs or navigates an airplane might have far more serious consequences.

Rather than ending a method prematurely just because it encounters a piece of invalid data, a more elegant solution involves repeating data entry in a loop until the data item becomes valid, as shown in **Figure 11-24**. As long as the value of `policyType` is invalid, the user is prompted continually to enter a new value. Only when `policyType` is *A* or *H* does the method continue.

Figure 11-24 A method that handles an error using a loop

```
public void determinePremium()
   Declarations
      string policyType
      string AUTO = "A"
      string HEALTH = "H"
   output "Please enter policy type "
   input policyType
   while policyType <> AUTO AND policyType <> HEALTH
      output "You must enter ", AUTO, " or ", HEALTH
      input policyType
   endwhile
   // Calculations for auto and health premiums go here
return
```

The error-handling logic shown in Figure 11-24 has at least two shortcomings:

- The method is not as reusable as it could be.
- The method is not as flexible as it might be.

One of the principles of modular and object-oriented programming is reusability. The method in Figure 11-24 is reusable only under limited conditions. The `determinePremium()` method allows the user to reenter policy data any number of times, but other programs in the insurance system might need to limit the number of chances the user gets to enter correct data, or might allow no second chance at all. A more flexible `determinePremium()` method would be able to detect an error and then notify the calling program or method that an error has occurred. Each client that uses the `determinePremium()` method then could handle the mistake appropriately for the current application.

The other drawback to forcing the user to reenter data is that the technique works only with interactive programs. A more flexible program accepts any kind of input, including data stored in a file. Program errors can occur as a result of many factors—for example, a disk drive might not be ready, a file might not exist in the specified location, or stored data items might be invalid. You cannot continue to reprompt a storage device for valid data the way you can reprompt a user in an interactive program; if stored data values are invalid, they remain invalid.

In the next section, you will learn object-oriented exception-handling techniques that overcome the limitations of traditional error handling.

The Object-Oriented Exception-Handling Model

Object-oriented programs employ a group of techniques for handling errors called **exception handling**. The generic name used for errors in object-oriented languages is **exceptions** because errors are not usual occurrences; they are the "exceptions to the rule."

In object-oriented terminology, when you foresee that an exception might occur and you want to be able to fix the problem, you **try some code statements** that might **throw an exception**. If an exception is thrown, it is passed to a block of code that can **catch an exception**, which means to receive it in a way similar to how a parameter is received by a method. In some languages, the exception object that is thrown can be any data type—a number, a string, or a programmer-created object. However, even when a language permits any data type to be thrown, most programmers throw an object of the built-in class `Exception`, or they use inheritance techniques to derive a class from a built-in `Exception` class.

For example, **Figure 11-25** shows a `determinePremium()` method that throws an exception only if `policyType` is neither *H* nor *A*. If `policyType` is invalid, an object of type `Exception` named `mistake` is instantiated and thrown from the method by a `throw` statement. A **throw statement** is one that sends an `Exception` object out of the current code block or method so it can be handled elsewhere. If `policyType` is *H* or *A*, the method continues, the premium is calculated, and the method ends normally.

Figure 11-25 A method that creates and throws an `Exception` object

```
public void determinePremium()
   Declarations
      string policyType
      string AUTO = "A"
      string HEALTH = "H"
   output "Please enter policy type "
   input policyType
   if policyType <> AUTO AND policyType <> HEALTH then
      Declarations
         Exception mistake = new Exception()
      throw mistake
   else
      // Calculations for auto and health premiums go here
   endif
return
```

> **Note** | In Figure 11-25, the `mistake` object is declared in the same way other objects are—by calling its constructor. In many programming languages, the constructor will require an argument.

When you create a segment of code in which something might go wrong, you place the code in a **`try` block**, which is a block of code you attempt to execute while acknowledging that an exception might occur. A `try` block consists of the keyword `try` followed by any number of statements, including some that might cause an exception to be thrown. If a statement in the block causes an exception, the remaining statements in the `try` block do not execute and the `try` block is abandoned. For pseudocode purposes, you can end a `try` block with a sentinel keyword such as `endtry`.

You often code at least one `catch` block immediately following a `try` block. A **`catch` block** is a segment of code written to handle an exception that might be thrown by the `try` block that precedes it. Each `catch` block "catches" one type of exception that it handles—in many languages the caught object must be of type `Exception` or one of its child classes. You create a `catch` block using the following pseudocode elements:

- The keyword `catch`, followed by parentheses that contain an `Exception` type and an identifier
- Statements that take action to handle the error condition
- An `endcatch` keyword to indicate the end of the `catch` block in the pseudocode

Figure 11-26 shows a client program that calls the `determinePremium()` method that throws the `mistake` `Exception`. Because `determinePremium()` has the potential to throw an exception, the call to the method is contained in a `try` block. If `determinePremium()` throws an exception, the `catch` block in the program executes and a message is output. If all goes well and `determinePremium()` does not throw an exception, the `catch` block is bypassed and the program continues with any statements that follow the `endcatch` statement.

Figure 11-26 A program that contains a `try...catch` pair

```
start
   try
      determinePremium()
   endtry
   catch(Exception mistake)
      output "A mistake occurred"
   endcatch
   // Other statements that would execute whether
   // or not the exception was thrown could go here
stop
```

A `catch` block looks like a method named `catch()`, which takes an argument that is some type of `Exception`. However, it is not a method; it has no `return` type, and you can't call it directly.

In the program in Figure 11-26, a message (*A mistake occurred*) is displayed when an exception is thrown. Another application might take different actions. For example, you might write an application in which the `catch` block forces the `policyType` to *H* or to *A*, or reprompts the user for a valid value. Various programs can use the `determinePremium()` method and handle an error in the way that is considered most appropriate for that application.

Note In the method in Figure 11-26, the variable `mistake` in the `catch` block is an object of type `Exception`. The object is not used within the `catch` block, but it could be. For example, depending on the language, the `Exception` class might contain a method named `getMessage()` that returns a string explaining the cause of the error. In that case, you could place a statement such as `output mistake.getMessage()` in the `catch` block.

Note Even when a program uses a method that throws an exception, the exceptions are created and thrown only occasionally, when something goes wrong. Programmers sometimes refer to the more common situation in which nothing goes wrong as the **sunny day case**.

The general principle of exception handling in object-oriented programming is that a method that uses data should be able to detect errors but not be required to handle them. The handling should be left to the application that uses the object so that each application can use each method appropriately.

Using Built-in Exceptions and Creating Your Own Exceptions

Many OOP languages provide built-in types that are subclasses of the language's basic `Exception` type. For example, Java, Visual Basic, and C# each provide dozens of categories of automatically created exception types with names like `ArrayOutOfBoundsException`, which is thrown when you attempt to use an invalid subscript with an array, and `DivideByZeroException`, which is thrown when a program attempts to divide a number by zero.

Figure 11-27 shows a method that might automatically throw a `DivideByZeroException` in some languages. The method accepts a parameter called `miles`. It then prompts the user for a value for `gallons` so it can divide `miles` by `gallons` and return `mpg`. If the user enters any numeric value other than 0, the division will go smoothly, and the method will return a valid numeric value. However, there is a small chance that the user will enter 0 for `gallons`, and the method will automatically throw a `DivideByZeroException`. If the method that calls `computeMpg()` does not handle the thrown exception, then the program will crash.

Figure 11-27 A method that might throw a `DivideByZero` exception

```
public num computeMpg(num miles)
   Declarations
      num gallons
      num mpg
   output "Enter gallons used "
   input gallons
   mpg = miles / gallons
return mpg
```

Figure 11-28 shows how you might choose to write a method that calls `computeMpg()`. In this example, the user enters a value for `miles`, and then a call to `computeMpg()` is placed in a `try` block. If `computeMpg()` does not throw an exception, then the value of `mpg` is valid, and the `catch` block is bypassed. If `computeMpg()` does throw an exception, then `mpg` is forced to 0. After the `catch` block ends, either a computed `mpg` or 0 is displayed. A different program that uses the `computeMpg()` method might handle the error differently. For example, it might display an error message, set `mpg` to a different value, or allow the user additional attempts at correct data entry.

Figure 11-28 A method that places a call to `getData()` in a `try` block and handles the exception that might be thrown

```
public void getData()
   Declarations
      num miles
      num mpg
   output "Enter miles "
   input miles
   try
      mpg = computeMpg(miles)
   endtry
   catch(Exception mistake)
      mpg = 0
   endcatch
   output "Mpg is ", mpg
return
```

Although some actions, such as dividing by zero, are errors in all programming situations, the built-in `Exceptions` in a programming language cannot cover *every* condition that might be an `Exception` in your applications. For example, you might want to declare an `Exception` when your bank balance is negative or when an outside party attempts to access your email account. Most organizations have specific rules for exceptional data; for example, an employee number must not exceed three digits or an hourly salary must not be less than the legal minimum wage. You can check for each of these potential error situations with `if` statements and create and throw `Exceptions` if needed. Then, the methods that catch your `Exceptions` can react appropriately for their application.

For example, if you want to throw an exception when a value is negative, you can write a statement such as the following:

```
if value < 0 then
   Exception mistake = new Exception()
   throw mistake
endif
```

In this statement, if `value` is less than 0, then an `Exception` object named `mistake` is created by calling the `Exception` class constructor using the `new` operator.

To create your own throwable `Exception`, you can extend a built-in `Exception` class. For example, you might create a class named `NegativeBankBalanceException` or `EmployeeNumberTooLargeException`. (When you create a class that derives from `Exception`, it is conventional, but not required, to use `Exception` in the name.) By inheriting from the `Exception` class, you gain access to methods contained in the parent class, such as those that display a default message describing the `Exception`. Depending on the language you are using, you might be able to extend from other throwable classes as well as `Exception`.

When you use built-in `Exception` types, they derive from the general `Exception` class. When you create specialized `Exception` types of your own, you also frequently derive them from the general `Exception` class. Either way, all the types can be caught by a `catch` block that is written to catch the general `Exception` type. In most object-oriented programming languages, a method can throw any number of exceptions. Either a general or more specific `catch` block must be available for each type of exception that is thrown; otherwise, the program terminates and issues an error message.

Two Truths & a Lie | Understanding Exception Handling

1. In object-oriented terminology, you try some code that might throw an exception, and the exception can then be caught and handled.
2. A `catch` block is a segment of code that can handle an exception that might be thrown by the `try` block preceding it.
3. The general principle of exception handling in object-oriented programming is that a method that uses data should be able both to detect and to handle most common errors.

The false statement is #3. The general principle of exception handling in object-oriented programming is that a method that uses data should be able to detect errors but not be required to handle them.

11.7 Reviewing the Advantages of Object-Oriented Programming

You have been exposed to many concepts and features of object-oriented programming, which provide extensive benefits as you develop programs. Whether you instantiate objects from classes you have created or from those created by others, you save development time because each object automatically includes appropriate, reliable methods and attributes. When using inheritance, you can develop new classes more quickly by extending classes that already exist and work; you need to concentrate only on new features added by the new class. When using existing classes, you need to concentrate only on the interface to those classes, not on the internal instructions that make them work. By overloading methods, you can use reasonable, easy-to-remember names for methods and concentrate on their purpose rather than on memorizing different method names. Using exception handling techniques allows you to make your programs more flexible.

Two Truths & a Lie | Reviewing the Advantages of Object-Oriented Programming

1. When you instantiate objects in programs, you save development time because each object automatically includes appropriate, reliable methods and attributes.
2. When using inheritance, you can develop new classes more quickly by extending existing classes that already work.
3. By overloading methods, you can avoid the strict rules of procedural programming and take advantage of more flexible object-oriented methods.

The false statement is #3. By overloading methods, you can use reasonable, easy-to-remember names for methods and concentrate on their purpose rather than on memorizing different method names.

Summary

- A constructor is a method that instantiates an object. A default constructor is one that requires no arguments; in OOP languages, a default constructor is created automatically by the compiler for every class you write. If you want to perform specific tasks when you create an instance of a class, then you can write your own constructor. In most programming languages, a constructor has the same name as its class, and cannot have a return type. Once you write a constructor for a class, you no longer receive the automatically written default constructor.
- A destructor contains the actions you require when an instance of a class is destroyed—most often when the object goes out of scope. As with constructors, if you do not explicitly create a destructor for a class, one is automatically provided. The most common way to declare a destructor explicitly is to use an identifier that consists of a tilde (~) followed by the class name. You cannot provide parameters to a destructor; as a consequence, destructors cannot be overloaded. Like a constructor, a destructor has no return type.
- A class can contain objects of another class as data fields. Creating whole-part relationships is known as composition or aggregation (a has-a relationship).
- When you create a class by making it inherit from another class, you are provided with prewritten and tested data fields and methods automatically. Using inheritance helps you save time, reduces the chance of errors and inconsistencies, and makes it easier for readers to understand your classes. A class that is used as a basis for inheritance is called a base class. A class that inherits from a base class is a derived class or extended class. The terms *superclass* and *parent class* are synonyms for *base class*. The terms *subclass* and *child class* are synonyms for *derived class*.
- Some of the most useful classes packaged in language libraries are used to create graphical user interface (GUI) objects such as frames, buttons, labels, and text boxes. Programming languages that supply existing GUI classes often provide a visual development environment in which you can create programs by dragging components such as buttons and labels onto a screen and arranging them visually.
- Exception-handling techniques are used to handle errors in object-oriented programs. When you try a block of code, you attempt to use it, and if an exception occurs, it is thrown. A `catch` block of the correct type can receive the thrown exception and handle it. Many OOP languages provide built-in `Exception` types, and you can create your own types by extending the `Exception` class.
- When you use object-oriented programming techniques, you save development time because each object automatically includes appropriate, reliable methods and attributes. Efficiency is achieved through both inheritance and overloading.

Key Terms

abstract class
ancestors
base class
catch an exception
`catch` block
child class
composition
constructor
default constructor
derived class
destructor
exception handling
exceptions
extended class
fragile
has-a relationship
IDE
inaccessible
libraries
multiple inheritance
`new`
nondefault constructor
overriding
packages
parameterized constructor
parent class
`protected` access specifier
subclass
sunny day case
superclass
throw an exception
`throw` statement
`try` block
try some code statements
visual development environment
whole-part relationship

Review Questions

1. When you instantiate an object, the automatically created method that is called is a(n) ________________. (11.1)
   a. creator
   b. initiator
   c. constructor
   d. architect

2. Every class has ________________. (11.1)
   a. exactly one constructor
   b. at least one constructor
   c. at least two constructors
   d. a default constructor and a programmer-written constructor

3. Which of the following can be overloaded? (11.1)
   a. constructors, but not instance methods
   b. instance methods, but not constructors
   c. both constructors and instance methods
   d. neither constructors nor instance methods

4. Every default constructor ________________. (11.1)
   a. requires no parameter
   b. sets a default value for every field in a class
   c. is created automatically
   d. is the only constructor that is explicitly written in a class

5. When you write a constructor that receives a parameter, ________________. (11.1)
   a. the automatically created default constructor no longer exists
   b. the parameter must be used to set a data field
   c. it becomes the default constructor
   d. the constructor body must be empty

6. When you write a constructor that receives no parameters, ________________. (11.1)
   a. the automatically created constructor no longer exists
   b. it becomes known as the nondefault constructor
   c. the automatically created constructor is overloaded
   d. you get an error message in most programming languages

7. Most often, a destructor is called when ________________. (11.2)
   a. an explicit call is made to it
   b. an object is instantiated
   c. an object goes out of scope
   d. a value is returned from a class method

8. Which of the following is *not* a similarity between constructors and destructors? (11.1, 11.2)
   a. Both can be called automatically.
   b. Both can be overloaded.
   c. Both have the same name as their class.
   d. Both have no return type.

9. Which of the following is *not* an advantage of creating a class that inherits from another class? (11.4)
   a. You make it easier for anyone who has used the original class to understand the new class.
   b. You save time because you need not re-create the fields and methods in the original class.
   c. You reduce the chance of errors because the original class's methods have already been used and tested.
   d. You save time because subclasses are created automatically from those that come built in as part of a programming language.

10. Employing inheritance reduces errors because ________________. (11.4)

- **a.** the new classes have access to fewer data fields
- **b.** the new classes have access to fewer methods
- **c.** you can copy and paste methods that you already created
- **d.** many of the methods you need have already been used and tested

11. A class that is used as a basis for inheritance is called a ________________. (11.4)

- **a.** derived class
- **b.** subclass
- **c.** base class
- **d.** child class

12. Which of the following is another name for a derived class? (11.4)

- **a.** base class
- **b.** child class
- **c.** superclass
- **d.** parent class

13. Which of the following is *not* another name for a derived class? (11.4)

- **a.** extended class
- **b.** subclass
- **c.** child class
- **d.** superclass

14. Which of the following is true? (11.4)

- **a.** A base class usually has more fields than its descendant.
- **b.** A child class can also be a parent class.
- **c.** A class's ancestors consist of its entire list of children.
- **d.** To be considered object oriented, a class must have a child.

15. A derived class inherits ________________ data and methods of its ancestors. (11.4)

- **a.** all
- **b.** only the public
- **c.** only the private
- **d.** no

16. Which of the following is true? (11.4)

- **a.** A class's methods usually are public; its data fields usually are private.
- **b.** A class's data fields usually are public; its methods usually are private.
- **c.** A class's methods and data fields are usually both public.
- **d.** A class's methods and data fields are usually both private.

17. A ________________ is a collection of predefined, built-in classes that you can use when writing programs. (11.5)

- **a.** vault
- **b.** black box
- **c.** library
- **d.** store

18. An environment in which you can develop GUI programs by dragging components to their desired positions is a(n) ________________. (11.5)

- **a.** visual development environment
- **b.** integrated compiler
- **c.** text-based editor
- **d.** GUI formatter

19. In object-oriented programs, errors are known as ________________. (11.6)

- **a.** faults
- **b.** gaffes
- **c.** exceptions
- **d.** omissions

20. The general principle of exception handling in object-oriented programming is that a method that uses data should ________________. (11.6)

- **a.** be able to detect errors but not be required to handle them
- **b.** be able to handle errors but not detect them
- **c.** be able to handle and detect errors
- **d.** not be able to detect or handle errors

Programming Exercises

1. Complete the following tasks:

   a. Design a class named `Circle` with fields named `radius`, `area`, and `diameter`. Include a constructor that sets the radius to 1. Include get methods for each field but include a set method only for the radius. When the radius is set, do not allow it to be zero or a negative number. When the radius is set, calculate the diameter (twice the radius) and the area (the radius squared times pi, which is approximately 3.14). Create the class diagram and write the pseudocode that defines the class.

   b. Design an application that declares two `Circles`. Set the radius of one circle manually but allow the other to use the default value supplied by the constructor. Then, display each `Circle`'s values. (11.1)

2. Complete the following tasks:

   a. Design a class named `PhoneCall` with four fields: two string fields that hold the 10-digit phone numbers that originated and received the call, and two numeric fields that hold the length of the call in minutes and the cost of the call. Include a constructor that sets the phone numbers to *X*s and the numeric fields to 0. Include get and set methods for the phone number and call detail fields, but do not include a set method for the cost field. When the call length is set, calculate the cost of the call at three cents per minute for the first 10 minutes and two cents per subsequent minute. Create the class diagram and write the pseudocode that defines the class.

   b. Design an application that declares three `PhoneCalls`. Set the length of one `PhoneCall` to 10 minutes, another to 11 minutes, and allow the third object to use the default value supplied by the constructor. Then, display each `PhoneCall`'s values.

   c. Create a child class named `InternationalPhoneCall` that inherits from `PhoneCall`. Override the parent class method that sets the call length to calculate the cost of the call at 40 cents per minute. Create a class diagram and show the pseudocode for `InternationalPhoneCall`.

   d. Create the logic for an application that instantiates a `PhoneCall` object and an `InternationalPhoneCall` object and displays the costs for each. (11.1, 11.4)

3. Complete the following tasks:

   a. Design a class named `ItemForSale` that holds data about items placed for sale on Carlos's List, a classified advertising website. Fields include an ad number, item description, asking price, and phone number. Include get and set methods for each field. Include a static method that displays the website's motto ("Sell Stuff Locally!"). Include two overloaded constructors as follows:

      - A default constructor that sets the ad number to 101, the asking price to $1, and the item description and phone number both to *XXX*
      - A constructor that allows you to pass values for all four fields

      Create the class diagram and write the pseudocode that defines the class.

   b. Design an application that declares two `ItemForSale` objects using a different constructor version with each object. Display each `ItemForSale`'s values and then display the motto. (11.1)

4. Complete the following tasks:

   a. Create a class named `Meal` that includes a string variable for the meal's description (for example, `"Dinner"`), an array of strings that holds up to five of the `Meal`'s components (for example, `"roasted chicken"`, `"mashed potatoes"`, and `"green beans"`), and a numeric variable that holds the calorie count. Include a constructor that prompts the user for a value for each field. Also create two overloaded methods named `display()`. The first method takes no parameters and displays the `Meal` details. The second takes a numeric parameter that indicates how many of the `Meal`'s components to display, or an error message if the parameter value is less than 0 or more than 5.

   b. Create an application that declares two `Meal` objects, sets their values, and demonstrates how both method versions can be called. (11.1)

5. Complete the following tasks:

a. Create a class named `Apartment` that includes an apartment number, number of bedrooms, number of baths, and monthly rent. Include two overloaded constructors. The default constructor sets each field to 0. The nondefault constructor accepts four parameters—one for each field. Include two overloaded `display()` methods. The parameterless version displays all the `Apartment` details. The second version accepts a value that represents a maximum rent and displays the `Apartment` details only if the `Apartment`'s rent is no greater than the parameter.

b. Create an application that instantiates several `Apartment` objects and demonstrates all the methods. (11.1)

6. Complete the following tasks:

a. Design a class named `Book` that holds a stock number, author, title, price, and number of pages. Include methods to set and get the values for each data field. Also include a `displayInfo()` method that displays each of the `Book`'s data fields with explanations.

b. Design a class named `TextBook` that is a child class of `Book`. Include a new data field for the grade level of the book. Override the `Book` class `displayInfo()` method to accommodate the new grade-level field. Include both the class diagram and the pseudocode.

c. Design an application that instantiates an object of each type and demonstrates all the methods. (11.4)

7. Complete the following tasks:

a. Design the class diagram and the pseudocode for a class named `Player` that holds a player number and name for a sports team participant. Include methods to set and get the values for each data field and to output the values for each data field.

b. Design two classes named `BaseballPlayer` and `BasketballPlayer` that are child classes of `Player`. Include a new data field in each class for the player's position. Include an additional field in the `BaseballPlayer` class for batting average. Include a new field in the `BasketballPlayer` class for free-throw percentage. Override the `Player` class methods that set and output the data so that you accommodate the new fields.

c. Design an application that instantiates an object of each type and demonstrates all the methods. (11.4)

8. Complete the following tasks:

a. Create a class for a cell phone service named `Message` that includes a field for the price of the message. Create get and set methods for the field.

b. Derive three subclasses—`VoiceMessage`, `TextMessage`, and `PictureMessage`. The `VoiceMessage` class includes a numeric field to hold the length of the message in minutes and a get and set method for the field. When a `VoiceMessage`'s length value is set, the price is calculated at 4 cents per minute. The `TextMessage` class includes a numeric field to hold the length of the message in words and a get and set method for the field. When a `TextMessage`'s length value is set, the price is calculated at 2 cents per word. The `PictureMessage` class includes a numeric field that holds the size of the picture in kilobytes and get and set methods for the field. When a `PictureMessage`'s length value is set, the price is calculated at 1 cent per kilobyte.

c. Design a program that instantiates one object of each of the three classes, and demonstrate using all the methods defined for each class. (11.4)

9. Complete the following tasks:

a. Create a class named `Order` that performs order processing of a single item. The class has four fields: customer name, customer number, quantity ordered, and unit price. Include set and get methods for each field. The set methods prompt the user for values for each field. This class also needs a `computePrice()` method to compute the total price (quantity multiplied by unit price) and a method to display the field values.

b. Create a subclass named `ShippedOrder` that overrides `computePrice()` by adding a shipping and handling charge of $9.00.

c. Create the logic for an application that instantiates an object of each of these two classes. Prompt the user for data for the `Order` object and display the results; then prompt the user for data for the `ShippedOrder` object and display the results.

d. Create the logic for an application that continually prompts for order information until the user enters *ZZZ* for the customer name or 10 orders have been taken, whichever comes first. Ask the user whether each order will be shipped, and create an `Order` or a `ShippedOrder` accordingly. Store each order in an array element. When the user finishes entering data, display all the order information taken as well as the total price that was computed for each order. (11.4)

10. Complete the following tasks:

a. Design a method that calculates the cost of boarding a horse at Delmar Stables. The method accepts a code for the type of boarding: *S* for *self-care*, which provides just shelter and costs $400 per month, or *F* for *full service*, which provides all care, including feeding and grooming, and costs $1200 per month. The method should throw an exception if the boarding code is invalid.

b. Write a method that calls the method designed in Exercise 10a. If the method throws an exception, force the price of boarding to 0.

c. Write a method that calls the method designed in Exercise 10a. If the method throws an exception, require the user to reenter the code.

d. Write a method that calls the method designed in Exercise 10a. If the method throws an exception, force the code to *F* and the price to $1200. (11.6)

11. Design a method that calculates the monthly cost to rent a roadside billboard. Variables include the size of the billboard (*S*, *M*, or *L* for small, medium, or large) and its location (*H*, *M*, or *L* for high-, medium-, or low-traffic areas). The method should throw an exception if the size or location code is invalid. The monthly rental cost is shown in **Figure 11-29**. (11.6)

Figure 11-29 Monthly billboard rental rates

	High traffic	Medium traffic	Low traffic
Small size	900	500	200
Medium size	1600	1200	600
Large size	2000	1500	800

Performing Maintenance

1. A file named *MAINTENANCE11-01.txt* is included in the Chapter11 folder of your downloadable student files. Assume that this program is a working program in your organization and that it needs modifications as described in the comments (lines that begin with two slashes) at the beginning of the file. Your job is to alter the program to meet the new specifications. (11.1)

Debugging Exercises

1. Your downloadable files for Chapter 11 include *DEBUG11-01.txt*, *DEBUG11-02.txt*, *DEBUG11-03.txt*, and *DEBUG11-04.jpg*. Each file starts with some comments that describe the problem. Comments are lines that begin with two slashes (//). Each file contains pseudocode or a flowchart that has mistakes. Find and correct all the bugs.

Game Zone

1. a. Computer games often contain different characters or creatures. For example, you might design a game in which alien beings possess specific characteristics such as color, number of eyes, or number of lives. Create the class diagram and pseudocode for an `Alien` class. Include at least three data fields of your choice. Include a constructor that requires a value for each data field and a method named `toString()` that returns a string containing a complete description of the `Alien`.

   b. Create two classes—`Martian` and `Jupiterian`—that descend from `Alien`. Supply each with a constructor that sets the `Alien` data fields with values you choose. For example, you can decide that a `Martian` has four eyes but a `Jupiterian` has only two.

   c. Create an application that instantiates one `Martian` and one `Jupiterian`. Call the `toString()` method with each object and display the results. (11.1, 11.4)

2. You have learned that in many programming languages you can generate a random number between 1 and a limiting value named `LIMIT` by using a statement similar to `randomNumber = random(LIMIT)`. Create the logic for a guessing game in which the application generates a random number and the player tries to guess it by entering a number. If the player enters a letter or other nonnumeric character, the method that gets the guess throws an automatically generated exception. (In other words, you do not need to create an exception object; one will be thrown from the method whenever the entered data is not numeric.) Handle any exception by informing the user about the error and allow the user to enter data again. If the user enters a numeric value, tell the user whether the guess was correct, too high, or too low. After the user guesses correctly, display a count of the number of attempts that were required. (11.6)

3. a. Develop a `Card` class that contains a string data field to hold a suit and a numeric data field for a value from 1 to 13. Extend the class to create a class called `BlackjackCard`. In the game of Blackjack, each card has a point value as well as a face value. These two values match for cards with values of 2 through 10, and the point value is 10 for jacks, queens, and kings (face values 11 through 13). For a simplified version of the game, assume that the value of the ace is 11. (In the official version of Blackjack, the player chooses whether each ace is worth 1 or 11 points.)

   b. Randomly assign values to 10 `BlackjackCard` objects, then design an application that plays a modified version of Blackjack. The objective is to accumulate cards whose total value equals 21 or whose value is closer to 21 than the opponent's total value without exceeding 21. Deal five `BlackjackCard`s each to the player and the computer. Make sure that each `BlackjackCard` is unique. For example, a deck cannot contain more than one queen of spades.

   Determine the winner as follows:

   - If the player's first two, first three, first four, or all five cards have a total value of exactly 21, the player wins, even if the computer also achieves a total of 21.
   - If the player's first two cards do not total exactly 21, sum as many as needed to achieve the highest possible total that does not exceed 21. For example, suppose that the player's five cards are valued as follows: 10, 4, 5, 9, 2. In that case, the player's total for the first three cards is 19; counting the fourth card would cause the total to exceed 21.
   - After you have determined the player's total, sum the computer's cards in sequence. For example, suppose that the computer's cards are 10, 10, 5, 6, 7. The first two cards total 20; you would not use the third card because it would cause the total to exceed 21.
   - The winner has the highest total among the cards used. For example, if the player's total using the first three cards is 19 and the computer's total using the first two cards is 20, the computer wins. If the player's total and the computer's total are the same, the player wins.

   Display a message that indicates who won. (11.4)

Chapter 12

Event-Driven GUI Programming, Multithreading, and Animation

Learning Objectives

When you complete this chapter, you will be able to:

12.1 Describe the principles of event-driven programming

12.2 Describe user-initiated actions and GUI components

12.3 List design issues in graphical user interfaces

12.4 Develop an event-driven application

12.5 Describe threads and multithreading

12.6 Explain how to create animation

12.1 Principles of Event-Driven Programming

From the 1950s, when businesses began to use computers, through the 1980s, almost all interactive dialogues between people and computers took place at the command prompt. (Programmers also call the command prompt the *command line*, and users of the Disk Operating System often call the command line the **DOS prompt**.) The command line is used to type entries to communicate with the computer's operating system—the software that runs a computer and manages its resources. In the early days of computing, interacting with an operating system was difficult because users had to know the exact syntax to use when typing commands, and they had to spell and type those commands accurately. **Figure 12-1** shows the command prompt in the Windows operating system.

Figure 12-1 Command prompt screen

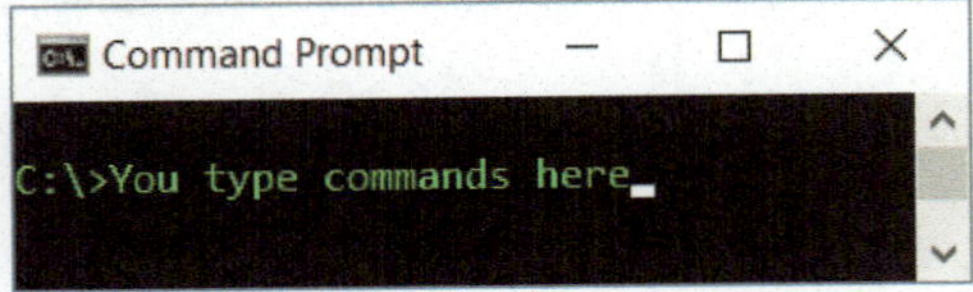

> **Note** You can access the command prompt in a variety of ways, depending on the operating system you are using. In most systems, you can use a menu option or icon to get to the command prompt. In Windows, there are at least 10 ways to access the command prompt. You can search the Web for instructions that apply to your operating system.

Fortunately for today's computer users, operating system software allows them to use their fingers, a mouse, or another pointing device to select screen controls, such as buttons and scroll bars or pictures (also called **icons**). This type of environment is a graphical user interface, or GUI. Computer users can expect to see a standard interface in GUI programs. Rather than memorizing difficult commands that must be typed at a command line, GUI users can select options from menus and click buttons to make their preferences known to a program. The icons used on buttons and other components are best understood when they follow convention—for example, an *X* button is expected to mean *Close*. Sometimes, users can select icons that look like their real-world counterparts and get the expected results. For example, users can select an icon that looks like a pencil when they want to write a memo, or they can drag an icon shaped like a folder to a recycling bin icon to delete the folder and its contents. **Figure 12-2** shows a Windows program named Paint in which icons representing paintbrushes and other objects appear on clickable buttons.

Figure 12-2 A GUI application that contains buttons and icons

Performing an operation on a control or using an icon (for example, clicking or dragging it) causes an **event**—an occurrence that generates a message sent to an object. GUI programs frequently are called **event-driven programs** or **event-based programs** because actions occur in response to user-initiated events such as tapping a screen or clicking a mouse button. When you program with event-driven languages, the emphasis is on objects that users can manipulate, such as text boxes, buttons, and menus, and on events that users can initiate with those objects, such as typing, pointing, clicking, or double-clicking. The programmer writes instructions within modules that execute in response to each type of event that a user can initiate during the program's execution.

Throughout this course, the program logic you have developed has been procedural, and not event-driven; each step occurs in the order the programmer determines. In a procedural application, if you write statements that display a prompt and accept a user's response, the processing stops after the prompt is displayed, and the program goes no further until input is received. When you write a procedural program, you have complete control over the order in which all the statements will execute. If you call `moduleA()` before calling `moduleB()`, `moduleB()` does not execute until `moduleA()` is finished.

In contrast, with most event-driven programs, the user might initiate any number of events in any order. For example, when you use an event-driven word-processing program, you have dozens of choices at your disposal at any moment. You can type words, select text with the mouse, click a button to change the text style to bold or italics, choose a menu item such as *Save* or *Print*, and so on. With each word-processing document you create, the program must be ready to respond to any event you initiate. The programmers who created the word processor are not guaranteed that you will select *Bold* before you select *Italics*, or that you will select *Save* before you select *Quit*, so they must write programs that are more flexible than their procedural counterparts.

Within an event-driven program, a component from which an event is generated is the **source of an event**. A button that users can click to cause an action is an example of a source; a text box in which users enter typed characters is another source. An object that is "interested in" an event to which you want it to respond is a **listener**. It "listens for" events so it knows when to respond. Not all objects can receive all events—you probably have used programs in which clicking many areas of the screen has no effect. If you want an object such as a button to be a listener for an event such as a mouse click, you must write two types of appropriate program statements:

- You write the statements that define the object as a listener.
- You write the statements that constitute the event.

Although event-driven programming is newer than procedural programming, the instructions that programmers write to respond to events are still simply sequences, selections, and loops. Event-driven programs still have methods that declare variables, use arrays, and contain all the attributes of their procedural-program ancestors. The user's screen in an event-driven program might contain buttons or check boxes with labels such as *Sort Records*, *Merge Files*, or *Total Transactions*, but each of these processes represents a method that uses the same logic you have learned throughout this course for programs that did not have a graphical interface.

In object-oriented languages, a procedural module that depends on user-initiated events is often called a **script**. Writing event-driven programs involves thinking of possible events, writing scripts to execute actions, and writing the statements that link user-initiated events to the scripts.

Two Truths & a Lie | Principles of Event-Driven Programming

1. GUI programs are called event-driven or event-based because actions occur in response to user-initiated events such as clicking a mouse button.
2. With event-driven programs, the user might initiate any number of events in any order.
3. Within an event-driven program, a component from which an event is generated, such as a button, is a listener. An object that is "interested in" an event is the source of the event.

The false statement is #3. Within an event-driven program, a component from which an event is generated is the source of the event, and an object that is "interested in" an event to which you want it to respond is a listener.

12.2 User-Initiated Actions and GUI Components

To understand GUI programming, you need to have a picture of the possible events a user can initiate. A partial list is shown in **Table 12-1**. Most languages allow you to distinguish between many additional events. For example, you might be able to initiate three different events when a mouse key is pressed, during the time it is held down, and when it is released.

Table 12-1 Common user-initiated events

Event	Description of user's action
Tap	Tapping on the screen
Swipe	Quickly dragging a finger across the screen
Zoom	Dragging across the screen with two fingers slightly apart to zoom out, or closer together to zoom in
Key press	Pressing a key on the keyboard
Mouse point or mouse over	Placing the mouse pointer over an area on the screen
Mouse click or left mouse click	Pressing the left mouse button
Right mouse click	Pressing the right mouse button
Mouse double-click	Pressing the left mouse button twice in rapid sequence
Mouse drag	Holding down the left mouse button while moving the mouse over the desk surface

You also need to be able to picture common GUI components. **Table 12-2** describes some common GUI components, and **Figure 12-3** shows how they look on a screen.

Table 12-2 Common GUI components

Component	Description
Label	A rectangular area that displays text
Text box	A rectangular area into which the user can type text
Check box	A label placed beside a small square; you can click the square to display or remove a check mark, which selects or deselects an option
Option buttons	A group of controls that are similar to check boxes. When the controls are square, users typically can select any number of them; they are called a *check box group*. When the controls are round, they are often mutually exclusive and are called *radio buttons*.
List box	When the user clicks a list box, a menu of items appears. Depending on the options the programmer sets, you might be able to make only one selection, or you might be able to make multiple selections.
Button	A rectangular control you can click; when you do, its appearance usually changes to look pressed

Figure 12-3 Common GUI components

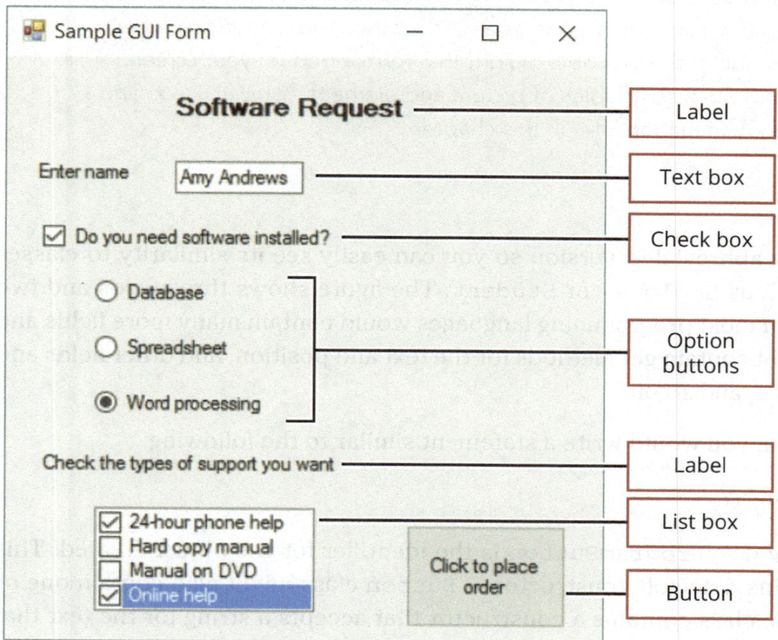

When you write a program that uses GUI components, you do not create them from scratch. Instead, you call prewritten methods that draw the GUI components on the screen for you. The components themselves are created using existing classes complete with names, attributes, and methods. In some programming languages, you can work in a text environment and write statements that instantiate GUI objects. In other languages, you can work in a graphical environment, drag GUI objects onto your screen from a toolbox, and arrange them appropriately for your application. Some languages offer both options. Either way, you do not think about the details of creating the components. Instead, you concentrate on the actions that should occur when a user initiates an event from one of the components. Thus, GUI components are excellent examples of the best principles of object-oriented programming—they represent objects with attributes and methods that operate like black boxes, making them easy for you to use.

When you use existing GUI components, you instantiate objects, each of which belongs to a prewritten class. For example, you might use a `Button` object when you want the user to click a button to make a selection. Depending on the programming language, the `Button` class might contain attributes or properties such as the text on the `Button` and its position on the screen. The class might also contain methods such as `setText()` and `setPosition()`. For example, **Figure 12-4** shows how a built-in `Button` class might be written.

Figure 12-4 `Button` class

```
class Button
   Declarations
      private string text
      private num x_position
      private num y_position

   public void setText(string messageOnButton)
      text = messageOnButton
   return

   public void setPosition(num x, num y)
      x_position = x
      y_position = y
   return
endClass
```

Note The `x_position` and `y_position` of the `Button` object in Figure 12-4 refer to horizontal and vertical coordinates where the `Button` appears on an object, such as a window that appears on the screen during program execution. A **pixel** is one of the tiny dots of light that form a grid on your screen. The term *pixel* derives from combining the first syllables of *picture* and *element*. You will use x- and y-positions again when you learn about animation later in this chapter.

The `Button` class shown in Figure 12-4 is an abbreviated version so you can easily see its similarity to classes you have worked with earlier in this course, such as `Employee` or `Student`. The figure shows three fields and two set methods. A complete, working `Button` class in most programming languages would contain many more fields and methods. For example, a full-blown class also might contain get methods for the text and position, and other fields and methods to manipulate a `Button`'s font, color, size, and so on.

To create a `Button` object in a client program, you would write a statement similar to the following:

```
Button myProgramButton = new Button()
```

In this statement, `Button` is the data type and `myProgramButton` is the identifier for the object created. This statement assumes that the `Button` class contains a default constructor. A `Button` class might also contain one or more nondefault constructors. For example, if the class contains a constructor that accepts a string for the text that appears on the `Button`, then instantiating a `Button` object might look like the following:

```
Button myProgramButton = new Button("Press here")
```

To use a `Button`'s methods, you might write statements such as the following:

```
myProgramButton.setText("Click here")
myProgramButton.setPosition(10, 30)
```

Different GUI classes support different attributes and methods. For example, a `CheckBox` class might contain a method named `getCheckedStatus()` that returns true or false, indicating whether the `CheckBox` object has been checked. A `Button`, however, would have no need for such a method.

Note Throughout this course you have used `num` and `string` type variables. Most modern languages also support a Boolean data type. A method like `getCheckedStatus()` that returns true or false has a Boolean return type. This makes a method call usable in expressions like `if getCheckedStatus()` or `while getCheckedStatus()`.

Note An important advantage of using GUI data-entry objects for user entries is that you often can limit users' options. When you provide a finite set of buttons to click or a limited number of menu items from which to choose, the user cannot make unexpected, illegal, or bizarre choices. For example, if you provide only two buttons so the user must click *Yes* or *No*, you can eliminate writing code to handle invalid typed entries like *Don't Know* or *Maybe*.

Two Truths & a Lie | User-Initiated Actions and GUI Components

1. In a GUI program, a key press is a common user-initiated event, and a check box is a typical GUI component.
2. When you program in a language that supports event-driven logic, you call prewritten methods that draw GUI components on the screen for you.
3. An advantage of using GUI objects is that each class you use to create the objects supports identical methods and attributes.

The false statement is #3. Different GUI classes support different attributes and methods.

12.3 Designing Graphical User Interfaces

A user's experience with a graphical interface is important. If a website or application isn't pleasing to users, they might abandon it. You should consider several general design principles when creating a program that will use a GUI:

- The interface should be natural and predictable.
- The interface should be attractive, easy to read, and nondistracting.
- To some extent, it's helpful if the user can customize your applications.
- The program should be forgiving.
- The GUI is only a means to an end.

The Interface Should Be Natural and Predictable

The GUI program interface should represent objects like their real-world counterparts. In other words, it makes sense to use an icon that looks like a recycling bin to let a user drag files or other components to the bin and delete them. Using a recycling bin icon is "natural" in that people use one in real life when they want to discard actual items. Using a trash can or recycling bin for discarded items is also predictable, because users are already familiar with the icon in other programs. Some icons might be natural, but if they are not predictable as well, then they are not as effective. An icon that depicts a recycling truck might seem just as natural as one that depicts a bin, but because other programs do not use such imagery, it is not as predictable.

GUIs should also be predictable in their layout. For example, when a user must enter personal information in text boxes, the street address is expected to come before the city and state. If you arrange an input screen so that the user enters the city and state first, users will generate a lot of errors. Also, a menu bar appears at the top of the screen in most GUI programs, and the first menu item in many applications is *File*. If you design a program interface in which the menu runs vertically down the right side of the screen, or in which *File* is the last menu option instead of the first, you will confuse users. Either they will make mistakes when using your program or they might give up using it entirely. It doesn't matter if you can prove that your layout plan is more efficient than the standard one—if you do not use a predictable layout, your program likely will be rejected in the marketplace.

Note Many studies have proven that the Dvorak keyboard layout is more efficient for typists than the QWERTY keyboard layout that most of us use. The QWERTY keyboard layout gets its name from the first six letter keys in the top row. With the Dvorak layout, which is named for its inventor, the most frequently used keys are in the home row, allowing typists to complete many more keystrokes per minute. However, the Dvorak keyboard has not caught on because it is not predictable to users who know the QWERTY keyboard.

> **Note** Stovetops often have an unnatural interface, making unfamiliar stoves more difficult for you to use. Most stovetops have four burners arranged in two rows, but the knobs that control the burners frequently are placed in a single horizontal row. Because there is not a natural correlation between the placement of a burner and its control, you are likely to select the wrong knob when adjusting the burner's flame or heating element.

The Interface Should Be Attractive, Easy to Read, and Nondistracting

If your interface is attractive, people are more likely to use it. If it is easy to read, users are less likely to make mistakes. When it comes to GUI design, fancy fonts and weird color combinations are the signs of amateur designers. In addition, you should make sure that unavailable screen options are either dimmed (also called *grayed*) or removed so the user does not waste time clicking components that aren't functional. An excellent way to learn about good GUI design is to pay attention to the design features used in popular applications and in websites you visit. Notice that the designs you like to use feel more "natural."

Screen designs should not be distracting. When a screen has too many components, users can't find what they're looking for. When a component is no longer needed, it should be removed from the interface. GUI programmers sometimes refer to screen space as *real estate*. Just as a plot of land becomes unattractive when it supports no open space, your screen becomes unattractive when you fill the limited space with too many components.

You also want to avoid distracting users with overly creative design elements. When users click a button to open a file, they might be amused the first time a filename dances across the screen or the speakers play a tune. However, after one or two experiences with your creative additions, users find that intruding design elements hamper the actual work of the program. Also, creative embellishments might consume extensive memory and CPU time, slowing an application's performance.

To Some Extent, It's Helpful If the User Can Customize Your Applications

All users work in their own way. If you are designing an application that will use numerous menus and toolbars, it's helpful if users can position components in the order that's easiest for them. Users appreciate being able to change features like color schemes. Allowing a user to change the background color in your application might seem frivolous to you, but to users who are color blind or visually impaired, it might make the difference in whether they use your application at all. Making programs easier to use for people with physical limitations is known as enhancing **accessibility**. When designing applications, you might consider adding captions to videos for users with impaired hearing, providing text alternatives to pictures for users with impaired vision, and allowing multiple options for data entry, such as mouse, keyboard, and touch, for users who have trouble with one technique.

Don't forget that many programs are used internationally. If you can allow the user to work with a choice of languages, you might be able to market your program more successfully in other countries. If you can allow the user to convert prices to multiple currencies, you might be able to make sales in more markets.

The Program Should Be Forgiving

Perhaps you have had the inconvenience of accessing a voice mail system in which you selected several sequential options, only to find yourself at a dead end with no recourse but to hang up and redial the number. Good program design avoids similar problems. You should always provide an escape route to accommodate users who make bad choices or change their minds. By providing a Back button or a working Escape key, you provide more functionality to your users.

It also can be helpful to include an option for the user to revert to the default settings after making changes. Some users might be afraid to alter an application's features if they are not sure they can easily return to the original settings.

Users also appreciate being able to perform tasks in a variety of ways. For example, you might allow a user to select a word on a screen by highlighting it using a mouse, by touching it on the screen, or by holding down the Ctrl and Shift keys while pressing the right arrow key. A particular technique might be easier for people with disabilities, and it might be the only one available after the mouse batteries fail or the user accidentally disables the keyboard by spilling coffee on it.

The GUI Is Only a Means to an End

The most important principle of GUI design is to remember that a GUI is only an interface. Using a mouse to click items and drag them around is not the point of any business programs except those that train people how to use a mouse. Instead, the point of a graphical interface is to help people be more productive. To that end, the design should help the user see what options are available, allow the use of components in the ordinary way, and not force the user to concentrate on how to interact with your application. The real work of a GUI program—making decisions, performing calculations, sorting records, and so on—is done after the user clicks a button or makes a list box selection.

Two Truths & a Lie | Designing Graphical User Interfaces

1. To keep the user's attention, a well-designed GUI interface should contain unique and creative controls.
2. To be most useful, a GUI interface should be attractive, easy to read, and nondistracting.
3. To avoid frustrating users, a well-designed program should be forgiving.

The false statement is #1. A GUI interface should be natural and predictable.

12.4 Developing an Event-Driven Application

Earlier in this course, you learned the steps to developing a procedural computer program:

1. Understanding the problem
2. Planning the logic
3. Coding the program
4. Translating the program into machine language
5. Testing the program
6. Putting the program into production
7. Maintaining the program

When you develop an event-driven application, you expand on Step 2 (planning the logic) and you might include four new substeps as follows:

- **2a.** Creating wireframes
- **2b.** Creating storyboards
- **2c.** Defining the objects
- **2d.** Defining the connections between the screens the user will see

For example, suppose that you want to create a simple, interactive program that determines semiannual premiums for prospective insurance customers. A graphical interface will allow users to select a policy type—health or auto. Next, users answer pertinent questions about their age, driving record, and whether they smoke. Although most insurance premiums would be based on more characteristics than these, assume that policy rates are determined using the factors shown in **Figure 12-5**. The final output of the program is a second screen that shows the semiannual premium amount for the chosen policy.

Figure 12-5 Insurance premiums based on customer characteristics

Health policy premiums	Auto policy premiums
Base rate: $500	Base rate: $750
Add $100 if over age 50	Add $400 if more than 2 tickets
Add $250 if smoker	Subtract $200 if over age 50

Creating Wireframes

A **wireframe** is a picture or sketch of a screen the user will see when running a program. A wireframe, also called a **page schematic** or **screen blueprint**, is a visual guide that helps developers and their user clients decide on the basic features of an interactive program or website. Wireframes can be pencil sketches or they can be produced by software applications. Typically, they do not contain graphics or show the final font styles that will be used; instead, they focus on the functionality of an application. **Figure 12-6** shows two wireframes for the program that determines insurance premiums. They represent the introductory screen, at which the user selects a premium type and answers questions, and the final screen, which displays the semiannual premium.

Figure 12-6 Storyboard for the insurance program, which is composed of two wireframes

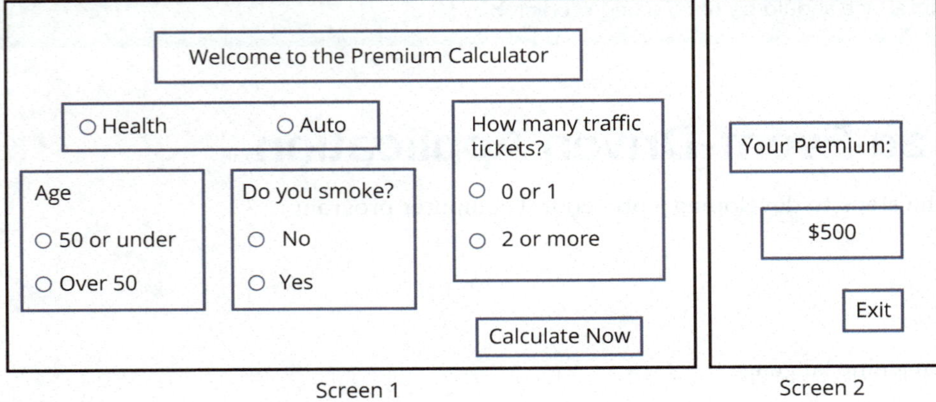

Creating Storyboards

A **storyboard** contains a series of wireframes that represent a user's experience with proposed software. Filmmakers have long used storyboards to illustrate key moments in the plots they are developing; similarly, GUI storyboards represent "snapshot" views of the screens the user will encounter during the run of a program. If the user could view up to 10 screens during the insurance premium program, then you would draw 10 storyboard cells, or wireframes. Sometimes, developers will enhance wireframes with color and graphics when incorporating them into a storyboard. The two wireframes shown in Figure 12-6 represent the insurance application's storyboard.

Defining the Storyboard Objects in an Object Dictionary

An event-driven program can contain dozens or even hundreds of objects. To keep track of them, programmers often use an object dictionary. An **object dictionary** is a list of the objects used in a program, the screens where the objects are used, and any associated code (script).

Figure 12-7 shows an object dictionary for the insurance premium program. The type and name of each object to be placed on a screen are listed in the columns on the left. The third column shows the screen number on which the object appears. The fourth column names any variables that are affected by an action on the object. The last column indicates whether any code or script is associated with the object. For example, the label named `welcomeLabel` appears on the first screen. It has no associated actions—nothing a user does to it executes any methods or changes any variables; it is just a label. When a user clicks the `calcButton`, however, a method named `calcRoutine()` is called. This method calculates the semiannual premium amount and stores it in the `premiumAmount` variable. Depending on the programming language, you might need to name `calcRoutine()` something similar to `calcButton.click()`. In languages that use this format, a standard method named `click()` holds the statements that execute when the user clicks the `calcButton`.

Figure 12-7 Object dictionary for insurance premium program

Object type	Name	Screen number	Variables affected	Script?
Label	welcomeLabel	1	none	none
RadioButton	healthRadioButton	1	premiumAmount	none
RadioButton	autoRadioButton	1	premiumAmount	none
Label	ageLabel	1	none	none
RadioButton	lowAgeRadioButton	1	premiumAmount	none
RadioButton	highAgeRadioButton	1	premiumAmount	none
Label	smokeLabel	1	none	none
RadioButton	smokeNoRadioButton	1	premiumAmount	none
RadioButton	smokeYesRadioButton	1	premiumAmount	none
Label	ticketsLabel	1	none	none
RadioButton	lowTicketsRadioButton	1	premiumAmount	none
RadioButton	highTicketsRadioButton	1	premiumAmount	none
Button	calcButton	1	premiumAmount	calcRoutine()
Label	premiumLabel	2	none	none
Label	premAmtLabel	2	none	none
Button	exitButton	2	none	exitRoutine()

Defining Connections Between the User Screens

The insurance premium program is small, but with larger programs you might need to draw connections between the screens to show how they interact. **Figure 12-8** shows an interactivity diagram for the screens used in the insurance premium program. An **interactivity diagram** shows the relationship between screens in an interactive GUI program. Figure 12-8 shows that the first screen calls the second screen, and the program ends.

Figure 12-8 Interactivity diagram for insurance premium program

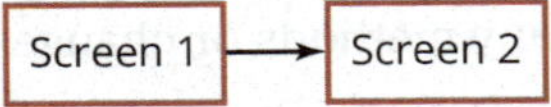

Figure 12-9 shows how a diagram might look for a more complicated program in which the user has several options available at Screens 1, 2, and 3. Notice how each of these screens can lead to different screens, depending on the options the user selects.

Figure 12-9 Interactivity diagram for a complicated program

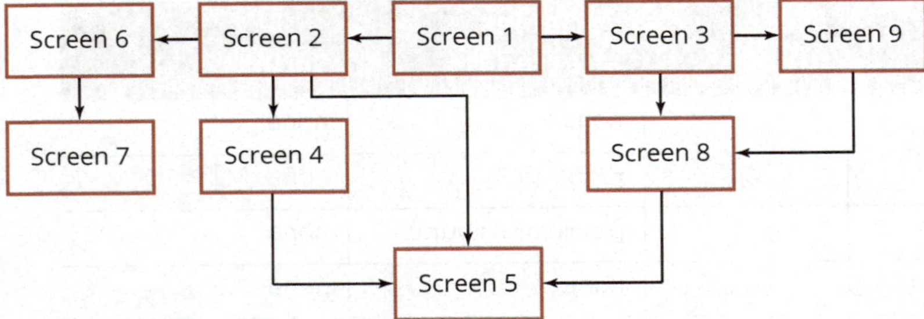

Planning the Logic

In an event-driven program, you design the screens, define the objects, and define how the screens will connect. Then you can start to plan the client program. For example, following the storyboard plan for the insurance program based on the criteria shown in Figure 12-5, you need to create the first screen, which contains four labels, four sets of radio buttons, and a button. **Figure 12-10** shows the pseudocode that creates these components.

When you use an integrated development environment to create applications, you can drag components like the `RadioButtons`, `Labels`, and `Button` in Figure 12-10 onto a screen without explicitly writing all the statements shown in the pseudocode. In that case, the coding statements will be generated for you. It's beneficial to understand these statements so that you can more easily modify and debug your programs.

In Figure 12-10, the following statement specifies that the method `calcRoutine()` executes when a user clicks the `calcButton`:

```
calcButton.registerListener(calcRoutine())
```

With most object-oriented programming (OOP) languages, you must **register components**, or sign them up so that they can react to events initiated by other components. The details of the syntax vary among languages, but the basic process is to write a statement that links the appropriate method (such as the `calcRoutine()` or `exitRoutine()` method) with an event such as a user's button click. In many development environments, the statement that registers a component to react to a user-initiated event is written for you automatically when you click components while designing your screen.

Figure 12-10 Component definitions for first screen of insurance program

```
Declarations
   Label welcomeLabel = new Label()
   RadioButton healthRadioButton = new RadioButton()
   RadioButton autoRadioButton = new RadioButton()
   Label ageLabel = new Label()
   RadioButton lowAgeRadioButton = new RadioButton()
   RadioButton highAgeRadioButton = new RadioButton()
   Label smokeLabel = new Label()
   RadioButton smokeNoRadioButton = new RadioButton()
   RadioButton smokeYesRadioButton = new RadioButton()
   Label ticketsLabel = new Label()
   RadioButton lowTicketsRadioButton = new RadioButton()
   RadioButton highTicketsRadioButton = new RadioButton()
   Button calcButton = new Button()

welcomeLabel.setText("Welcome to the Premium Calculator")
welcomeLabel.setPosition(30, 10)

healthRadioButton.setText("Health")
healthRadioButton.setPosition(15, 40)

autoRadioButton.setText("Auto")
autoRadioButton.setPosition(50, 40)

ageLabel.setText("Age")
ageLabel.setPosition(5, 60)

lowAgeRadioButton.setText("50 or under")
lowAgeRadioButton.setPosition(5, 70)

highAgeRadioButton.setText("Over 50")
highAgeRadioButton.setPosition(5, 80)

smokeLabel.setText("Do you smoke?")
smokeLabel.setPosition(40, 60)

smokeNoRadioButton.setText("No")
smokeNoRadioButton.setPosition(40, 70)

smokeYesRadioButton.setText("Yes")
smokeYesRadioButton.setPosition(40, 80)

ticketsLabel.setText("How many traffic tickets?")
ticketsLabel.setPosition(60, 50)

lowTicketsRadioButton.setText("0 or 1")
lowTicketsRadioButton.setPosition(60, 70)

highTicketsRadioButton.setText("2 or more")
highTicketsRadioButton.setPosition(60, 90)

calcButton.setText("Calculate Now")
calcButton.setPosition(60, 100)
calcButton.registerListener(calcRoutine())
```

Note

In reality, you might generate more code than what is shown in Figure 12-10 when you create the insurance program components. For example, each component might require a color and font. You also might want to initialize some components with default values to indicate they are selected. For example, you might want one radio button in a group to be selected already, which requires the user to click a different option only if the user does not want the default selection.

You also need to create the component that holds all the GUI elements in Figure 12-10. Depending on the programming language, you might use a class with a name such as `Screen`, `Form`, or `Window`. Each of these is a **container**, or a class of objects whose main purpose is to hold other elements. The container class contains methods that allow you to set physical properties such as height and width, as well as methods that allow you to add the appropriate components to a container. **Figure 12-11** shows how you would define a `Screen` object, set its size, and add the necessary components.

Figure 12-11 Statements that create `screen1`

```
Declarations
   Screen screen1 = new Screen()
screen1.setSize(150, 150)
screen1.add(welcomeLabel)
screen1.add(healthRadioButton)
screen1.add(autoRadioButton)
screen1.add(ageLabel)
screen1.add(lowAgeRadioButton)
screen1.add(highAgeRadioButton)
screen1.add(smokeLabel)
screen1.add(smokeNoRadioButton)
screen1.add(smokeYesRadioButton)
screen1.add(ticketsLabel)
screen1.add(lowTicketsRadioButton)
screen1.add(highTicketsRadioButton)
screen1.add(calcButton)
```

Similarly, **Figure 12-12** shows how you can create and define the components for the second screen in the insurance program and how to add the components to the container. Notice the label that holds the user's insurance premium is not filled with text because the amount is not known until the user makes all the selections on the first screen.

Figure 12-12 Statements that define and create `screen2` and its components

```
Declarations
   Screen screen2 = new Screen()
   Label premiumLabel = new Label()
   Label premAmtLabel = new Label()
   Button exitButton = new Button()

screen2.setSize(100, 100)

premiumLabel.setText("Your Premium:")
premiumLabel.setPosition(5, 30)

premAmtLabel.setPosition(20, 50)

exitButton.setText("Exit")
exitButton.setPosition(60, 80)
exitButton.registerListener(exitRoutine())

screen2.add(premiumLabel)
screen2.add(premAmtLabel)
screen2.add(exitButton)
```

After the GUI components are designed and arranged, you can plan the logic for each of the methods or scripts that the program will use. For example, given the program requirements shown earlier in Figure 12-5, you can write the pseudocode for the `calcRoutine()` method of the insurance premium program, as shown in **Figure 12-13**. The `calcRoutine()` method does not execute until the user clicks the `calcButton`. At that point, the user's choices are sent to the method and used to calculate the premium amount.

The pseudocode in Figure 12-13 should look very familiar to you—it declares numeric constants and a variable and uses decision-making logic you have used since the early chapters of this course. After the premium is calculated based on the user's choices, it is placed in the label that appears on the second screen. The basic control structures of sequence, selection, and loop will continue to serve you well, whether you are programming in a procedural or event-driven environment.

Figure 12-13 Pseudocode for `calcRoutine()` method of insurance premium program

```
public void calcRoutine()
   Declarations
      num HEALTH_AMT = 500
      num HIGH_AGE = 100
      num SMOKER = 250
      num AUTO_AMT = 750
      num HIGH_TICKETS = 400
      num HIGH_AGE_DRIVER_DISCOUNT = 200
      num premiumAmount
   if healthRadioButton.getCheckedStatus() then
      premiumAmount = HEALTH_AMT
      if highAgeRadioButton.getCheckedStatus() then
         premiumAmount = premiumAmount + HIGH_AGE
      endif
      if smokeYesRadioButton.getCheckedStatus() then
         premiumAmount = premiumAmount + SMOKER
      endif
   else
      premiumAmount = AUTO_AMT
      if highTicketsRadioButton.getCheckedStatus() then
         premiumAmount = premiumAmount + HIGH_TICKETS
      endif
      if highAgeRadioButton.getCheckedStatus() then
         premiumAmount = premiumAmount - HIGH_AGE_DRIVER_DISCOUNT
      endif
   endif
   premAmtLabel.setText(premiumAmount)
   screen1.remove()
   screen2.display()
return
```

The last two statements in the `calcRoutine()` method indicate that after the insurance premium is calculated and placed in its label, the first screen is removed and the second screen is displayed. Screen removal and display are accomplished differently in different languages; this example assumes that the appropriate methods are named `remove()` and `display()`.

Two more program segments are needed to complete the insurance premium program. These segments include the main program that executes when the program starts and the last method that executes when the program ends. In many GUI languages, the process is slightly more complicated, but the general logic appears in **Figure 12-14**. The final method in the program is associated with the `exitButton` object on `screen2`. In Figure 12-14, this method is called `exitRoutine()`. In this example, the main program sets up the first screen and the last method removes the last screen.

Figure 12-14 The main program and `exitRoutine()` method for the insurance program

```
start
   screen1.display()
stop

public void exitRoutine()
   screen2.remove()
return
```

Two Truths & a Lie | Developing an Event-Driven Application

1. A storyboard represents a diagram of the logic used in an interactive program.
2. An object dictionary is a list of the objects used in a program, the screens where the objects are used, and any associated code.
3. An interactivity diagram shows the relationship between screens in an interactive GUI program.

The false statement is #1. A storyboard represents a picture or sketch of the series of screens the user will see when running a program.

12.5 Understanding Threads and Multithreading

A **thread** is the flow of execution of one set of program statements. When you execute a program statement by statement, from beginning to end, you are following a thread. Many applications follow a single thread; this means that the application executes only a single program statement at a time. For example, **Figure 12-15** shows how three tasks might execute in a single thread in a computer with a single CPU. Each task must end before the next task starts.

Figure 12-15 Executing multiple tasks as single threads in a single-processor system

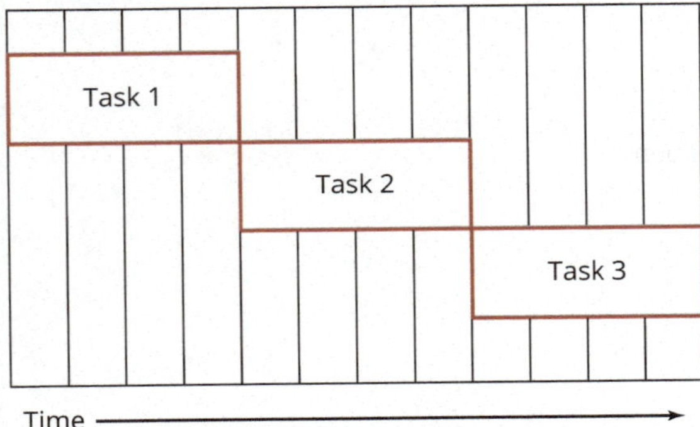

Even if the computer has only one CPU, all major OOP languages allow you to launch, or start, multiple threads of execution by using a technique known as **multithreading**. With multithreading, threads share the CPU's time, as shown in **Figure 12-16**. The CPU devotes a small amount of time to one task, and then devotes a small amount of time to another. The CPU never actually performs two tasks at the same instant. Instead, it performs a piece of one task and then part of another. The CPU performs so quickly that each task seems to execute without interruption.

Figure 12-16 Executing multiple threads in a single-processor system

Part of Task 1
Part of Task 2
Part of Task 3
Part of Task 1
Part of Task 2
Part of Task 3
Time

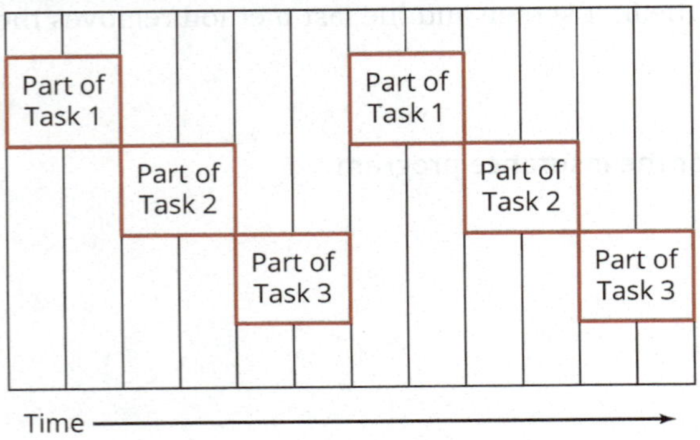

Perhaps you have seen an expert chess player participate in games with several opponents at once. The expert makes a move on the first chess board, and then moves to a second board against a second opponent while the first opponent analyzes the next move. The expert can go to a third board, make a move, and return to the first board before the first opponent is even ready to respond. To the first opponent, it might seem as though the expert is only playing the first game. Because the expert is so fast, the expert can play other opponents while the first opponent contemplates the next move. Executing multiple threads on a single CPU is a similar process. The CPU transfers its attention from thread to thread so quickly that the tasks don't even "miss" the CPU's attention.

You use multithreading to improve the performance of your programs. Multithreaded programs often run faster, but more importantly, they are more user-friendly. With a multithreaded program, a user can continue to make choices by clicking buttons while the program is reading a data file. An animated figure can appear on one part of the screen while the user makes menu selections elsewhere on the screen. Multithreading is important in online games in which multiple players can interact with characters concurrently rather than taking turns, as in traditional games like chess.

Multithreading is also important if you are working on a website that sells a product or service or relies on advertising income that is based on the number and duration of user visits. For example, users can begin to read a long text file, watch a video, or listen to an audio file while the file is still downloading. Web users are likely to abandon a site if they cannot use it before a lengthy downloading process completes. When a website employs multithreading to perform concurrent tasks, visitors are less likely to abandon the website. Some applications, like online stores, would be basically impossible if multithreading did not exist. When you are browsing a product description at an online store or adding the product to your shopping cart, it would be highly impractical for you to wait until other shoppers were finished looking at the same product.

Note Programmers sometimes describe thread execution as a *lightweight process* because it is not a full-blown program. Rather, a thread must run within the context of a full, heavyweight program.

Note If a computer has more than one central processing unit (CPU), then each can execute a thread at the same time. However, if a computer has a single CPU and the system only supports single threading, then tasks must occur one at a time.

Writing good code to execute multithreading requires skill. Without careful coding, problems such as deadlock and starvation can arise. **Deadlock** occurs when two or more threads wait for each other to execute, and **starvation** occurs when a thread is abandoned because other threads occupy all the computer's resources.

When threads share an object, special care is needed to avoid unwanted results. For example, consider a customer order program in which two clerks are allowed to fill orders concurrently. Imagine the following scenario:

- The first clerk accesses an inventory file and tells a customer that only one item is available.
- A second clerk accesses the file and tells a different customer that only one item (the same item) is available.
- The first customer places an order, and inventory is reduced to 0.
- The second customer places an order, and inventory is reduced to −1.

Two items have been ordered, but only one exists, and the inventory file is now incorrect. There will be confusion in the warehouse, problems in the Accounting department, and one unsatisfied customer. Similar problems can occur in programs that reserve airline seats or concert tickets. OOP languages provide sophisticated techniques, known as **thread synchronization**, that help avoid these potential problems.

Object-oriented languages often contain a built-in `Thread` class that contains methods to help handle and synchronize multiple threads. For example, a `sleep()` method is sometimes used to pause program execution for a specified amount of time, perhaps a few seconds. Computer processing speed is so rapid that sometimes you have to slow down processing for human consumption. The next section describes one application that frequently requires using a `sleep()` method—computer animation.

Two Truths & a Lie | Understanding Threads and Multithreading

1. In the last 10 years, few programs that follow a single thread have been written.
2. Single-thread programs contain statements that execute in very rapid sequence, but only one statement executes at a time.
3. When you use a computer with multiple CPUs, the computer can execute multiple instructions simultaneously.

The false statement is #1. Many applications follow a single thread; this means that at any one time the application executes only a single program statement.

12.6 Creating Animation

Animation is the rapid display of still images, each slightly different from the previous one, that produces the illusion of movement. Cartoonists create animated films by drawing a sequence of frames or cells. These individual drawings are shown to the audience in rapid succession to create the sense of natural movement. You create computer animation using the same techniques. If you display computer images as fast as your CPU can process them, you might not be able to see anything. Most computer animation employs a `Thread` class `sleep()` method to pause for short intervals between the display of animation cells so the human brain has time to absorb each image's content.

Many object-oriented languages offer built-in classes that contain methods you can use to draw geometric figures. The methods typically have names like `drawLine()`, `drawCircle()`, `drawRectangle()`, and so on. You place figures on the screen based on a graphing coordinate system. Each component has a horizontal, or **x-axis**, position as well as a vertical, or **y-axis**, position on the screen. The upper-left corner of a display is position 0, 0. The first, or **x-coordinate**, value increases as you travel from left to right across the window. The second, or **y-coordinate**, value increases as you travel from top to bottom. **Figure 12-17** shows four screen coordinate positions.

Figure 12-17 Selected screen coordinate positions

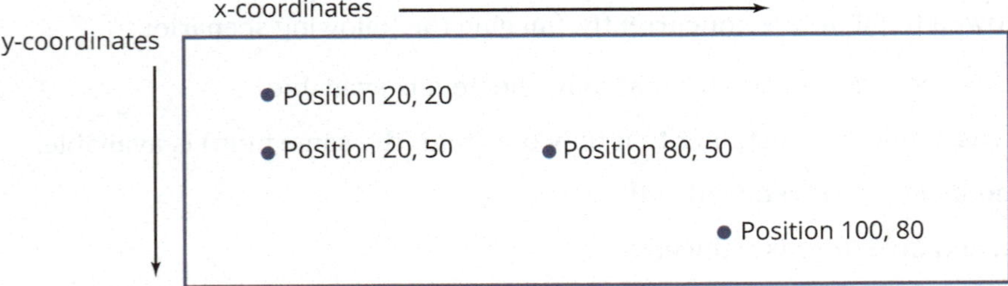

Artists often spend a great deal of time creating the exact images they want to use in an animation sequence. As a simple example, **Figure 12-18** shows pseudocode for a `MovingCircle` class. As its name implies, the class moves a circle across the screen. The class contains data fields to hold x- and y-coordinates that identify the location at which a circle appears. The constants `SIZE` and `INCREASE` define the size of the first circle drawn and the relative increase in size and position of each subsequent circle. The `MovingCircle` class assumes that you are working with a language that provides a `drawCircle()` method, which creates a circle when given parameters for horizontal and vertical positions and a radius. Assuming you are working with a language that provides a `sleep()` method to accept a pause time in milliseconds, the `SLEEP_TIME` constant provides a 100-millisecond gap before the production of each new circle. For simplicity, the class also assumes that you are working with a language in which no error occurs when the circles eventually move off the screen. You might want to provide statements to stop the drawing when the circle size and position exceed predetermined limits.

Figure 12-18 The `MovingCircle` class

```
public class MovingCircle
   Declarations
      private num x = 20
      private num y = 20
      private num SIZE = 40
      private num INCREASE = SIZE / 10
      private num SLEEP_TIME = 100

   public void main()
      while true
         repaintScreen()
      endwhile
   return

   public void repaintScreen()
      drawCircle(x, y, SIZE)
      x = x + INCREASE
      y = y + INCREASE
      SIZE = SIZE + INCREASE
      Thread.sleep(SLEEP_TIME)
   return
endClass
```

In most object-oriented languages, a method named `main()` executes automatically when a class object is created. The `main()` method in the `MovingCircle` class executes a continuous loop. A similar technique is used in many languages that support GUI interfaces. Program execution will cease only when the user quits the application—by clicking a window's Close button, for example. In the `repaintScreen()` method of the `MovingCircle` class, a circle is drawn at the `x, y` position, and then `x`, `y`, and the circle size are increased. The application sleeps for one-tenth of a second (the `SLEEP_TIME` value), and then the `repaintScreen()` method draws a new circle more to the right, further down, and a little larger. The effect is a moving circle that leaves a trail of smaller circles behind as it moves diagonally across the screen. **Figure 12-19** shows the output as a Java version of the application executes and after execution is complete.

Figure 12-19 Output of the `MovingCircle` application at two points in time

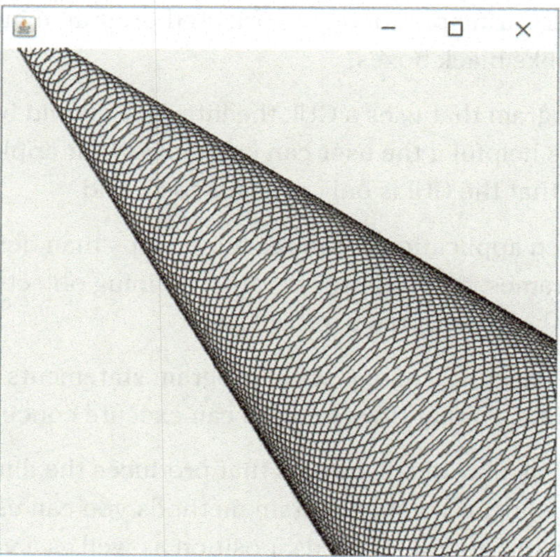

Although an object-oriented language might make it easy to draw geometric shapes, you also can substitute a variety of more sophisticated, predrawn animated images to achieve the graphic effects you want within your programs. An image is loaded in a separate thread of execution, which allows program execution to continue while the image loads. This is a significant advantage because loading a large image can be time-consuming.

> **Note** | Many animated images are available on the Web for you to use freely. Use your search engine and keywords such as *gif files*, *jpeg files*, and *animation* to find sources for free files.

Two Truths & a Lie | Creating Animation

1. Each component you place on a screen has a horizontal, or x-axis, position as well as a vertical, or y-axis, position.
2. The x-coordinate value increases as you travel from left to right across a window.
3. You almost always want to display animation cells as fast as your processor can handle them.

The false statement is #3. If you display computer images as fast as your CPU can process them, you might not be able to see anything. Most computer animation employs a method to pause for short periods of time between animation cells.

Summary

- Interacting with a computer operating system from the command line is difficult; it is easier to use an event-driven graphical user interface (GUI), in which users manipulate objects such as buttons and menus. Within an event-driven program, a component from which an event is generated is the source of the event, and an object that is "interested in" an event listens for it.
- A user can initiate many events, such as tapping a screen or clicking a mouse. Common GUI components include labels, text boxes, buttons, check boxes, check box groups, option buttons, and list boxes. GUI components are examples of the best principles of object-oriented programming; they represent objects with attributes and methods that operate like black boxes.
- When you create a program that uses a GUI, the interface should be natural, predictable, attractive, easy to read, and nondistracting. It's helpful if the user can customize your applications. The program should be forgiving, and you should not forget that the GUI is only a means to an end.
- Developing event-driven applications requires more steps than developing procedural programs. The steps include creating wireframes, creating storyboards, defining objects and dictionaries for them, and defining the connections between the screens the user will see.
- A thread is the flow of execution of one set of program statements. Many applications follow a single thread; others use multithreading so that diverse tasks can execute concurrently.
- Animation is the rapid display of still images that produces the illusion of movement. Many object-oriented languages contain built-in classes that contain methods you can use to draw geometric figures on the screen. Each component has a horizontal, or x-axis, position as well as a vertical, or y-axis, position on the screen.

Key Terms

accessibility
animation
container
deadlock
DOS prompt
event
event-based programs
event-driven programs
icons
interactivity diagram
listener
multithreading
object dictionary
page schematic
pixel
register components
screen blueprint
script
source of an event
starvation
storyboard
thread
thread synchronization
wireframe
x-axis
x-coordinate
y-axis
y-coordinate

Review Questions

1. Compared to using a command line, an advantage to using an operating system that employs a GUI is ________. (12.1)
   a. you can interact directly with the operating system
   b. you do not have to deal with confusing icons
   c. you do not have to memorize complicated commands
   d. the icons used vary significantly between applications, preventing boredom
2. When users can initiate actions by clicking the mouse on an icon, the program is ________-driven. (12.1)
   a. command
   b. event
   c. prompt
   d. incident
3. A component from which an event is generated is the ________ of the event. (12.1)
   a. base
   b. icon
   c. identifier
   d. source
4. An object that responds to an event is a ________. (12.1)
   a. listener
   b. snooper
   c. transponder
   d. source
5. All of the following are user-initiated events except a ________. (12.1, 12.2)
   a. key press
   b. key drag
   c. right mouse click
   d. mouse drag
6. All of the following are typical GUI components except a ________. (12.2)
   a. button
   b. text box
   c. list box
   d. handle

7. GUI components operate most like ________________. (12.2)

   a. looping structures
   b. procedural functions
   c. black boxes
   d. command lines

8. Which of the following is *not* a principle of good GUI design? (12.3)

   a. The interface should be predictable.
   b. The fancier the screen design, the better.
   c. The program should be forgiving.
   d. The user should be able to customize applications.

9. Which of the following aspects of a GUI layout is most predictable and natural for the user? (12.3)

   a. A menu bar runs down the right side of the screen.
   b. *Help* is the first option on a menu.
   c. A dollar sign icon represents saving a file.
   d. Pressing *Esc* allows the user to cancel a selection.

10. In most GUI programming environments, which of the following attributes of components can programmers not change? (12.3)

    a. color
    b. screen location
    c. size
    d. class

11. Depending on the programming language, you might do any of the following to change a screen component's attribute *except* ________________. (12.3)

    a. use an assignment statement
    b. call a module
    c. enter a value into a list of properties
    d. assign the component to a different class

12. When you create an event-driven application, which of the following must be done before defining objects? (12.4)

    a. Translate the program.
    b. Create wireframes and storyboards.
    c. Test the program.
    d. Code the program.

13. A ________________ is a sketch of a screen the user will see when running a program. (12.4)

    a. flowchart
    b. hierarchy chart
    c. storyboard
    d. tale timber

14. An object ________________ is a list of objects used in a program. (12.4)

    a. thesaurus
    b. dictionary
    c. index
    d. glossary

15. A(n) ________________ diagram shows the connections between the various screens a user might see during a program's execution. (12.4)

    a. interactivity
    b. help
    c. cooperation
    d. communication

16. The flow of execution of one set of program statements is a ________________. (12.5)

    a. thread
    b. string
    c. path
    d. route

17. When a computer contains a single CPU, it can execute ________________ computer instruction(s) at a time. (12.5)

    a. one
    b. several
    c. an unlimited number of
    d. from several to thousands of

18. Multithreaded programs usually ________ than their procedural counterparts. (12.5)

- **a.** run faster
- **b.** are harder to use
- **c.** are older
- **d.** produce more errors

19. An object's horizontal position on the computer screen is its ________. (12.6)

- **a.** a-coordinate
- **b.** h-coordinate
- **c.** x-coordinate
- **d.** y-coordinate

20. You create computer animation by ________. (12.6)

- **a.** drawing an image and setting its animation property to true
- **b.** drawing a single image and executing it on a multiprocessor system
- **c.** drawing a sequence of frames that are shown in rapid succession
- **d.** drawing multiple frames that execute in random sequence

Programming Exercises

1. Take a critical look at three GUI applications you have used—for example, a spreadsheet, a word-processing program, and a game. Describe how well each conforms to the GUI design guidelines listed in this chapter. (12.3)

2. Select one element of poor GUI design in a program you have used. Describe how you would improve the design. (12.3)

3. Select a GUI program that you have never used before. Describe how well it conforms to the GUI design guidelines listed in this chapter. (12.3)

4. Design the wireframes and storyboard, interactivity diagram, object dictionary, and any necessary scripts for an interactive program for customers of Sanderson's Ice Cream Sundaes.

Allow customers the option of choosing a three-scoop, two-scoop, or one-scoop creation at a base price of $4.00, $3.00, or $2.20, respectively. Let the customer choose chocolate, strawberry, or vanilla as the primary flavor. If the customer adds nuts, whipped cream, or cherries to the order, add $0.50 for each to the base price. After the customer clicks an *Order Now* button, display the price of the order. (12.4)

5. Design the wireframes and storyboard, interactivity diagram, object dictionary, and any necessary scripts for an interactive program for customers of Fortune's Vacation Resort.

Allow customers the option of choosing a studio, one-bedroom, or two-bedroom cabin, each of which costs a different weekly rental amount. Also allow the option of a lake view, which increases the rental fee. The total fee is displayed when the user clicks a *Reserve Cabin* button. (12.4)

6. Design the wireframes and storyboard, interactivity diagram, object dictionary, and any necessary scripts for an interactive program for customers of the Natural Munches Sandwich Shop.

Allow customers the option of choosing one of three types of bread and any number of six filler items for a sandwich. Create a price for each option. After the customer clicks an *Order Now* button, display the price of the sandwich. (12.4)

7. Design the wireframes and storyboard, interactivity diagram, object dictionary, and any necessary scripts for an interactive program for customers of the Friar Farm Market.

Allow customers the option of choosing tomatoes ($3.00 per pound), peppers ($2.50 per pound), or onions ($2.25 per pound). The customer enters a weight in pounds in a text box. After the customer clicks a *Select* button, display the price of the order. (12.4)

8. Design the wireframes and storyboard, interactivity diagram, object dictionary, and any necessary scripts for an interactive program for clients of Larry's Lawn Service.

   Allow clients to choose the size of their yard so they can be charged accordingly. For example, a lot that covers less than one-third of an acre costs $50 per service call; a lot that covers one-third to two-thirds of an acre costs $72.50 per service call; and a lot that covers more than two-thirds of an acre costs $84 per service call. Also, allow clients to choose a schedule of weekly or semiweekly lawn maintenance. After the customer clicks a *Select* button, display the price of the service per week. Note that semiweekly service comes with a 10 percent discount. (12.4)

Performing Maintenance

1. A file named *MAINTENANCE12-01.txt* is included in the Chapter12 folder of your downloadable student files. Assume that this program is a working program in your organization and that it needs modifications as described in the comments (lines that begin with two slashes) at the beginning of the file. Your job is to alter the program to meet the new specifications. (12.1, 12.2, 12.4)

Debugging Exercises

1. Your downloadable files for Chapter 12 include *DEBUG12-01.txt*, *DEBUG12-02.txt*, *DEBUG12-03.txt*, and *DEBUG12-04.jpg*. Each file starts with some comments that describe the problem. Comments are lines that begin with two slashes (//). Each file contains pseudocode or a flowchart that has mistakes. Find and correct all the bugs.

Game Zone

1. Design the wireframes and storyboard, interactivity diagram, object dictionary, and any necessary scripts for an interactive program that allows a user to play a card game named Lucky Seven. In real life, the game can be played with seven cards, each containing a number from 1 through 7, that are shuffled and dealt number-side down. To start the game, a player turns over any card. The exposed number on the card determines the position (reading from left to right) of the next card that must be turned over. For example, if the player turns over the first card and its number is 7, the next card turned must be the seventh card (counting from left to right). If the player turns over a card whose number denotes a position that was already turned, the player loses the game. If the player succeeds in turning over all seven cards, the player wins.

   Instead of cards, you will use seven buttons labeled 1 through 7 from left to right. Randomly associate one of the seven values 1 through 7 with each button. (In other words, the associated value might or might not be equivalent to the button's labeled value.) When the player clicks a button, reveal the associated hidden value. If the value represents the position of a button already clicked, the player loses. If the revealed number represents an available button, force the user to click it—that is, do not take any action until the user clicks the correct button. After a player clicks a button, remove the button from play.

For example, a player might click `Button 7`, revealing a 4. Then the player clicks `Button 4`, revealing a 2. Then the player clicks `Button 2`, revealing a 7. The player loses because `Button 7` is already "used." (12.2, 12.4)

2. Design the wireframes and storyboard, interactivity diagram, object dictionary, and any necessary scripts for a version of the game Hangman, in which the user clicks lettered buttons to fill in a secret word. Draw a "hanged" person piece by piece with each missed letter. For example, when the user chooses a correct letter, place it in the appropriate position or positions in the word, but the first time the user chooses a letter that is not in the target word, draw a head for the "hanged" man. The second time the user makes an incorrect guess, add a torso. Continue with arms and legs. If the complete body is drawn before the user has guessed all the letters in the word, display a message indicating that the player has lost the game. If the user completes the word before all the body parts are drawn, display a message that the player has won. Assume that you can use built-in methods named `drawCircle()` and `drawLine()`. The `drawCircle()` method requires three parameters—the x- and y-coordinates of the center, and a radius size. The `drawLine()` method requires four parameters—the x- and y-coordinates of the start of the line, and the x- and y-coordinates of the end of the line. (12.2, 12.4)

Appendix A

Understanding Numbering Systems and Computer Codes

Learning Objectives

When you complete this appendix, you will be able to:

- **A.1** Work with the binary numbering system
- **A.2** Describe computer codes
- **A.3** Work with the hexadecimal system
- **A.4** Measure computer storage

A.1 The Binary Numbering System

The numbering system you know best is the **decimal numbering system**: the system based on 10 digits, 0 through 9. Mathematicians call decimal-system numbers **base 10** numbers. When you use the decimal system, only the value symbols 0 through 9 are available; if you want to express a value larger than 9, you must use multiple digits from the same pool of 10, placing them in columns.

When you use the decimal system, you analyze a multicolumn number by mentally assigning place values to each column. The value of the far right column is 1, the value of the next column to the left is 10, the next column is 100, and so on; the column values are multiplied by 10 as you move to the left. There is no limit to the number of columns you can use; you simply keep adding columns to the left as you need to express higher values. For example, **Figure A-1** shows how the value 305 is represented in the decimal system. You simply multiply each digit by the value of its column and then sum the results.

Figure A-1 Representing 305 in the decimal system

```
Column value
100  10   1
| 3 | 0 | 5 |

3 * 100 = 300
0 * 10  =   0
5 * 1   =   5
          ---
          305
```

The **binary numbering system** works in the same way as the decimal numbering system, except that it uses only two digits, 0 and 1. When you use the binary system, you must use multiple columns if you want to express a value greater than 1 because no single symbol is available that represents any value other than 0 or 1. Instead of each new column to the left being 10 times greater than the previous column, each new column in the binary system is only two times the value of the previous column.

For example, **Figure A-2** shows how the numbers 9 and 305 are represented in the binary system. Notice that in both the binary system and the decimal system, it is perfectly acceptable, and often necessary, to create numbers with 0 in one or more columns. Mathematicians call numbers expressed in binary **base 2** numbers. As with the decimal system, there is no limit to the number of columns used in a binary number; you can use as many as it takes to express a value.

Figure A-2 Representing decimal values 9 and 305 in the binary system

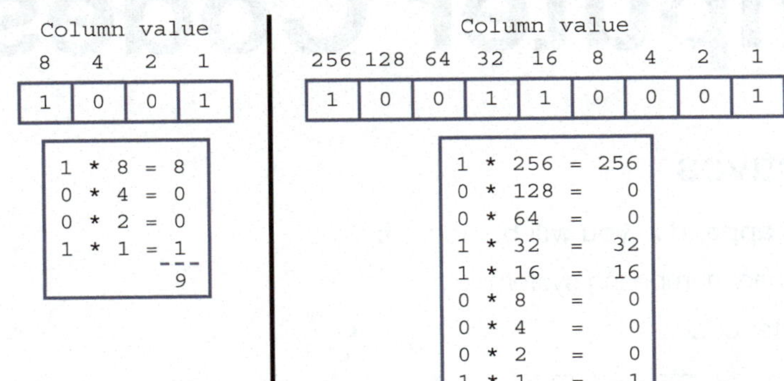

A.2 Understanding Computer Codes

A computer stores every piece of data it uses as a set of 0s and 1s. Each 0 or 1 is known as a **bit**, which is short for *binary digit*. Every computer uses 0s and 1s because all values in a computer are stored as electronic signals that are either on or off. This two-state system is most easily represented using just two digits.

Computers use a set of binary digits to represent stored characters. The size of the set is most often 8 or 16.

- If computers used only one binary digit to represent characters, then only two different characters could be represented because the single bit could be only 0 or 1.
- If computers used only two digits to represent characters, then only four characters could be represented—the four codes 00, 01, 10, and 11, which in decimal values are 0, 1, 2, and 3, respectively.
- Many computers use sets of eight binary digits to represent each character they store, because using eight binary digits provides 256 different combinations.

A set of eight bits is a byte. One byte's combination of bits can represent an *A*, another a *B*, still others *a* and *b*, and so on. Two hundred fifty-six combinations are enough so that each capital letter, lowercase letter, digit, and punctuation mark used in English has its own code; even a space has a code. For example, in the system named the **American Standard Code for Information Interchange (ASCII)**, 0100 0001 represents the character *A*. The binary number 0100 0001 has a decimal value of 65, but this numeric value is not important to ordinary computer users; it is simply a code that stands for *A*.

Note | Because a long series of 0s and 1s is difficult to read, many people insert a space after each group of four digits. Four bits, or a half byte, is a **nibble**.

The ASCII code is not the only computer code, but it is typical, and is the one used in most personal computers. The **Extended Binary Coded Decimal Interchange Code (EBCDIC)** is an eight-bit code that is used in IBM mainframe and midrange computers. In these computers, the principle is the same—every character is stored in a byte as a series of binary digits. However, the actual values used are different. For example, in EBCDIC, an *A* is 1100 0001, or 193. Another code used by languages such as Java and C# is **Unicode**; with this code, 16 bits are used to represent each character. The character *A* in Unicode has the same decimal value as the ASCII *A*, 65, but it is stored as 0000 0000 0100 0001.

Using two bytes (16 bits) provides many more possible combinations than using only eight bits. With Unicode, enough codes are available to represent all English letters and digits, as well as characters from many international alphabets and game symbols such as playing cards and domino tiles.

Ordinary computer users seldom think about the numeric codes behind the letters, numbers, and punctuation marks they enter from their keyboards or see displayed on a monitor. However, they see the consequence of the values behind letters when they see data sorted in alphabetical order. When you sort a list of names, *Asmee* comes before *Brian* and *Caroline* comes after *Brian* because the numeric code for *A* is lower than the code for *B*, and the numeric code for *C* is higher than the code for *B*, no matter whether you use ASCII, EBCDIC, or Unicode.

Table A-1 shows the decimal and binary values behind the most commonly used characters in the ASCII character set—the letters, numbers, and punctuation marks you can enter from your keyboard using a single key press. Other values not shown in Table A-1 also have specific purposes. For example, when you display the character that holds the decimal value 7, nothing appears on the screen, but a bell sounds. Programmers often use this character when they want to alert a user to an error or some other unusual condition.

Table A-1 Decimal and binary values for common ASCII characters

Decimal number	Binary number	ASCII character
32	0010 0000	Space
33	0010 0001	! Exclamation point
34	0010 0010	“ Quotation mark, or double quote
35	0010 0011	# Number or pound sign
36	0010 0100	$ Dollar sign
37	0010 0101	% Percent
38	0010 0110	& Ampersand
39	0010 0111	’ Apostrophe, single quote
40	0010 1000	(Left parenthesis
41	0010 1001	) Right parenthesis
42	0010 1010	* Asterisk
43	0010 1011	+ Plus sign
44	0010 1100	, Comma
45	0010 1101	- Hyphen or minus sign
46	0010 1110	. Period or decimal point
47	0010 1111	/ Slash or front
48	0011 0000	0
49	0011 0001	1
50	0011 0010	2
51	0011 0011	3
52	0011 0100	4
53	0011 0101	5
54	0011 0110	6
55	0011 0111	7
56	0011 1000	8
57	0011 1001	9
58	0011 1010	: Colon
59	0011 1011	; Semicolon
60	0011 1100	< Less-than sign
61	0011 1101	= Equal sign
62	0011 1110	> Greater-than sign
63	0011 1111	? Question mark
64	0100 0000	@ At sign
65	0100 0001	A
66	0100 0010	B
67	0100 0011	C
68	0100 0100	D
69	0100 0101	E
70	0100 0110	F
71	0100 0111	G
72	0100 1000	H
73	0100 1001	I
74	0100 1010	J

(continues)

Table A-1 *(continued)*

Decimal number	Binary number	ASCII character
75	0100 1011	K
76	0100 1100	L
77	0100 1101	M
78	0100 1110	N
79	0100 1111	O
80	0101 0000	P
81	0101 0001	Q
82	0101 0010	R
83	0101 0011	S
84	0101 0100	T
85	0101 0101	U
86	0101 0110	V
87	0101 0111	W
88	0101 1000	X
89	0101 1001	Y
90	0101 1010	Z
91	0101 1011	[Opening or left bracket
92	0101 1100	\ Backslash
93	0101 1101	] Closing or right bracket
94	0101 1110	^ Caret
95	0101 1111	_ Underline or underscore
96	0110 0000	` Grave accent
97	0110 0001	a
98	0110 0010	b
99	0110 0011	c
100	0110 0100	d
101	0110 0101	e
102	0110 0110	f
103	0110 0111	g
104	0110 1000	h
105	0110 1001	i
106	0110 1010	j
107	0110 1011	k
108	0110 1100	l
109	0110 1101	m
110	0110 1110	n
111	0110 1111	o
112	0111 0000	p
113	0111 0001	q
114	0111 0010	r
115	0111 0011	s
116	0111 0100	t
117	0111 0101	u
118	0111 0110	v
119	0111 0111	w
120	0111 1000	x
121	0111 1001	y
122	0111 1010	z
123	0111 1011	{ Opening or left brace
124	0111 1100	| Vertical line or pipe
125	0111 1101	} Closing or right brace
126	0111 1110	~ Tilde

A.3 The Hexadecimal System

The **hexadecimal numbering system** is the **base 16** system; it uses 16 digits. As shown in **Table A-2**, the digits are 0 through 9 and A through F. Computer professionals often use the hexadecimal system to express addresses and instructions as they are stored in computer memory because hexadecimal provides convenient shorthand expressions for groups of binary values. In Table A-2, each hexadecimal value represents one of the 16 possible combinations of 4-digit binary values. Therefore, instead of referencing memory contents as a 16-digit binary value, for example, programmers can use a 4-digit hexadecimal value.

Table A-2 Values in the decimal and hexadecimal systems

Decimal value	Hexadecimal value	Binary value (shown using four digits)
0	0	0000
1	1	0001
2	2	0010
3	3	0011
4	4	0100
5	5	0101

(continues)

Table A-2 *(continued)*

Decimal value	Hexadecimal value	Binary value (shown using four digits)
6	6	0110
7	7	0111
8	8	1000
9	9	1001
10	A	1010
11	B	1011
12	C	1100
13	D	1101
14	E	1110
15	F	1111

In the hexadecimal system, each column is 16 times the value of the column to its right. Therefore, column values from right to left are 1, 16, 256, 4096, and so on. **Figure A-3** shows how 78, 171, and 305 are expressed in hexadecimal.

Figure A-3 Representing decimal values 78, 171, and 305 in the hexadecimal system

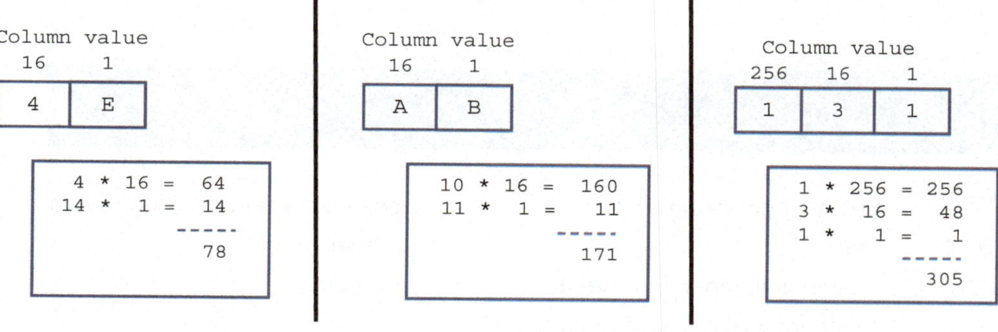

A.4 Measuring Storage

In computer systems, both internal memory and external storage are measured in bits and bytes. Eight bits make a byte, and a byte frequently holds a single character (in ASCII or EBCDIC) or half a character (in Unicode). Because a byte is such a small unit of storage, the size of memory and files is often expressed in thousands or millions of bytes. **Table A-3** describes some commonly used terms for storage measurement.

Table A-3 Commonly used terms for computer storage

Term	Abbreviation	Number of bytes using binary system	Number of bytes using decimal system
Kilobyte	KB or kB	1,024	one thousand
Megabyte	MB	1,048,576 (1,024 × 1,024 kilobytes)	one million
Gigabyte	GB	1,073,741,824 (1,024 megabytes)	one billion
Terabyte	TB	1,024 gigabytes	one trillion
Petabyte	PB	1,024 terabytes	one quadrillion
Exabyte	EB	1,024 petabytes	one quintillion
Zettabyte	ZB	1,024 exabytes	one sextillion
Yottabyte	YB	1,024 zettabytes	one septillion (a 1 followed by 24 zeros)

Note

In the metric system, the prefix *kilo* means 1,000. However, in Table A-3, notice that a kilobyte is 1,024 bytes. The discrepancy occurs because everything stored in a computer is based on the binary system, so multiples of two are used in most measurements. If you multiply 2 by itself 10 times, the result is 1,024, which is a little over 1000. Similarly, a gigabyte is 1,073,741,824 bytes, which is more than a billion.

Confusion arises because many hard-drive manufacturers use the decimal system instead of the binary system to describe storage. For example, if you buy a hard drive that holds one petabyte, it holds exactly 1,000,000,000,000 bytes. (This number is also known as one thousand billion or one quadrillion.) However, in the binary system, if you continually multiply 2 by itself, you will find that one terabyte is 1,099,511,627,776 bytes, which is almost 10 percent more.

Note

Conventionally, an uppercase *B* is used for byte and a lowercase *b* is used for bit. So, if you see *Kb*, the writer probably is referring to kilo*bits*, but KB probably refers to kilo*bytes*. Bits are commonly used to express data transmission rates, but bytes are more commonly used to express storage capacities.

Key Terms

American Standard Code for Information Interchange (ASCII)
base 2
base 10
base 16
binary numbering system
bit
decimal numbering system
Extended Binary Coded Decimal Interchange Code (EBCDIC)
hexadecimal numbering system
nibble
Unicode

Appendix B

Solving Difficult Structuring Problems

Learning Objectives

When you complete this appendix, you will be able to:

B.1 Solve a difficult structuring problem

B.1 Solving Difficult Structuring Problems

You have learned that you can solve any logical problem using only the three standard structures—sequence, selection, and loop. Modifying an unstructured program to make it adhere to structured rules is often a simple matter. Sometimes, however, structuring a more complicated program can be challenging. Still, no matter how complicated, large, or poorly structured a problem is, the same tasks can *always* be accomplished in a structured manner.

Consider the flowchart segment in **Figure B-1**. Is it structured?

Figure B-1 Unstructured flowchart segment

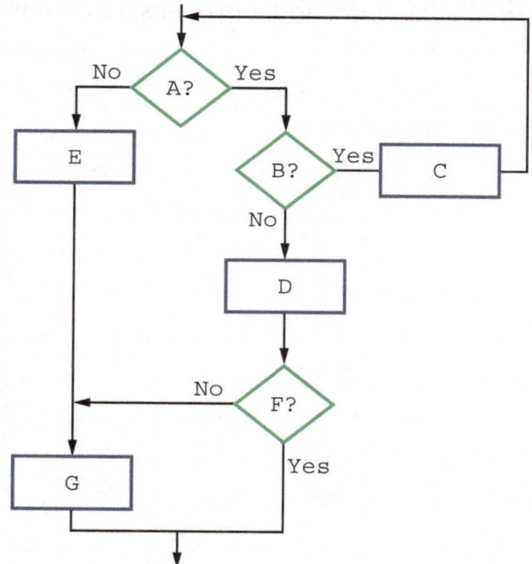

No, it is not structured. To straighten out the flowchart segment, thereby making it structured, you can use the "spaghetti" method. Untangle each path of the flowchart as if you were attempting to untangle strands of spaghetti in a bowl. The objective is to create a new flowchart segment that performs exactly the same tasks as the first, but using only the three structures—sequence, selection, and loop.

To begin to untangle the unstructured flowchart segment, you start at the beginning with the evaluation labeled `A`, shown in **Figure B-2**. This step must represent the beginning of either a selection or a loop, because a sequence would not contain any possibility of branching.

Figure B-2 Structuring, Step 1

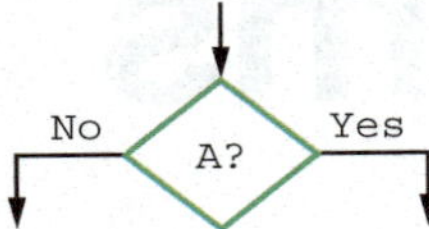

If you follow the logic on the *No* side, or the left side, of the question in the original flowchart, you can imagine pulling up on the left branch of the evaluation. You encounter process `E`, followed by `G`, followed by the end, as shown in **Figure B-3**. Compare the *No* actions after the evaluation of `A` in the first flowchart (Figure B-1) with the actions after `A` in Figure B-3; they are identical.

Figure B-3 Structuring, Step 2

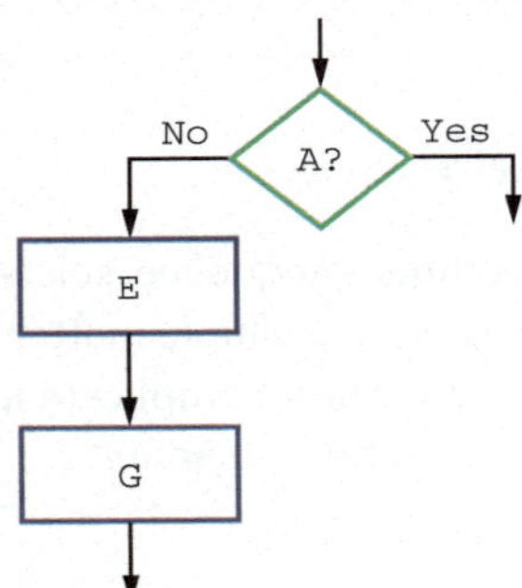

Now continue to work on the right side, or the *Yes* side, of the `A` evaluation in Figure B-1. When you follow the flowline, you encounter a decision symbol labeled `B`. Imagine pulling on `B`'s left side, and a process, `D`, comes up next. See **Figure B-4**.

Figure B-4 Structuring, Step 3

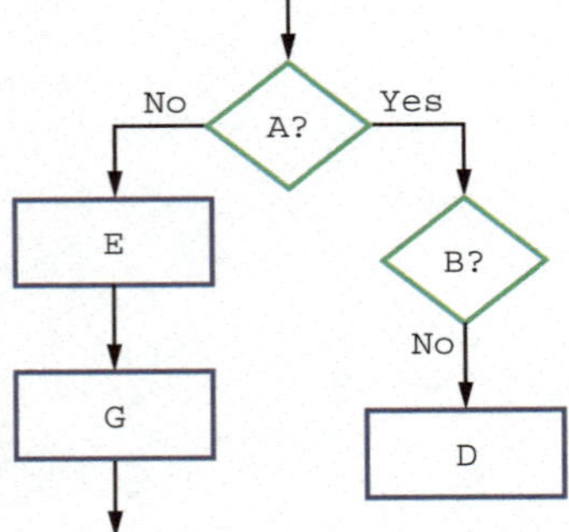

After Step `D` in the original diagram, an evaluation labeled `F` comes up. Pull on its left, or *No*, side and you get a process, `G`, and then the end. When you pull on `F`'s right side, or *Yes* side, in the original flowchart, you simply reach the end, as shown in **Figure B-5**. Notice in Figure B-5 that the `G` process now appears in two locations. When you improve unstructured flowcharts so that they become structured, you often must repeat steps to eliminate crossed lines and spaghetti logic, which is difficult to follow.

Figure B-5 Structuring, Step 4

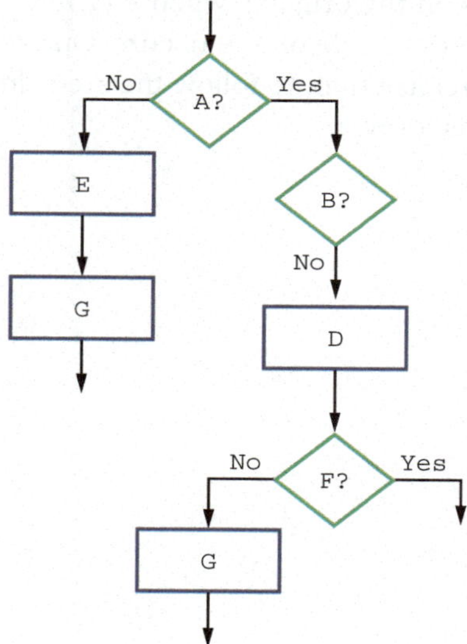

The biggest problem in structuring the original flowchart segment from Figure B-1 follows the right, or *Yes*, side of the `B` evaluation. When the evaluation of `B` is *Yes*, you encounter process `C`, as shown in Figures B-1 and **B-6**.

Figure B-6 Structuring, Step 5

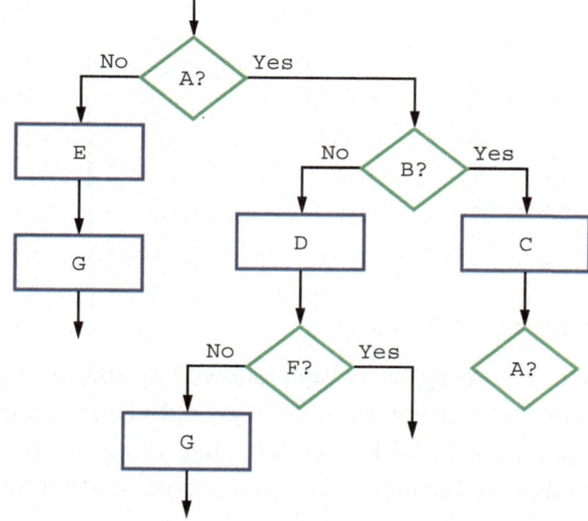

The structure that begins with the evaluation of `C` looks like a loop because it doubles back, up to `A`. However, a structured loop must have the appearance shown in **Figure B-7**: a question followed by a structure, returning right back to the question. In Figure B-1, if the path coming from `C` returned directly to `B`, there would be no problem; it would be a simple, structured loop. However, as it is, Question `A` must be repeated. The spaghetti technique requires that if lines of logic are tangled up, you must start repeating the steps in question. So, you repeat an `A` evaluation after `C`, as Figure B-6 shows.

Figure B-7 A structured loop

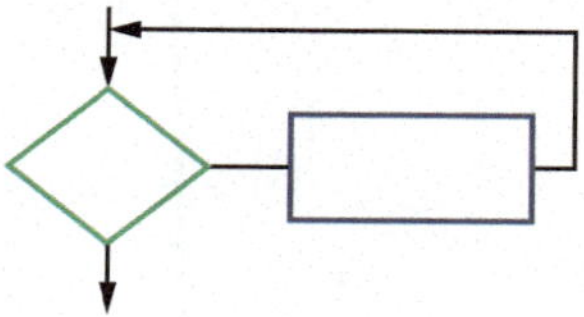

In the original flowchart segment in Figure B-1, when `A` is *Yes*, Question `B` always follows. So, in **Figure B-8**, after `A` is *Yes* and `B` is *Yes*, Step `C` executes, and `A` is asked again; when `A` is *Yes*, `B` repeats. In the original, when `B` is *Yes*, `C` executes, so in Figure B-8, on the right side of `B`, `C` repeats. After `C`, `A` occurs. On the right side of `A`, `B` occurs. On the right side of `B`, `C` occurs. After `C`, `A` should occur again, and so on. Soon you should realize that, to follow the steps in the same order as in the original flowchart segment, you will repeat these same steps forever.

Figure B-8 Structuring, Step 6

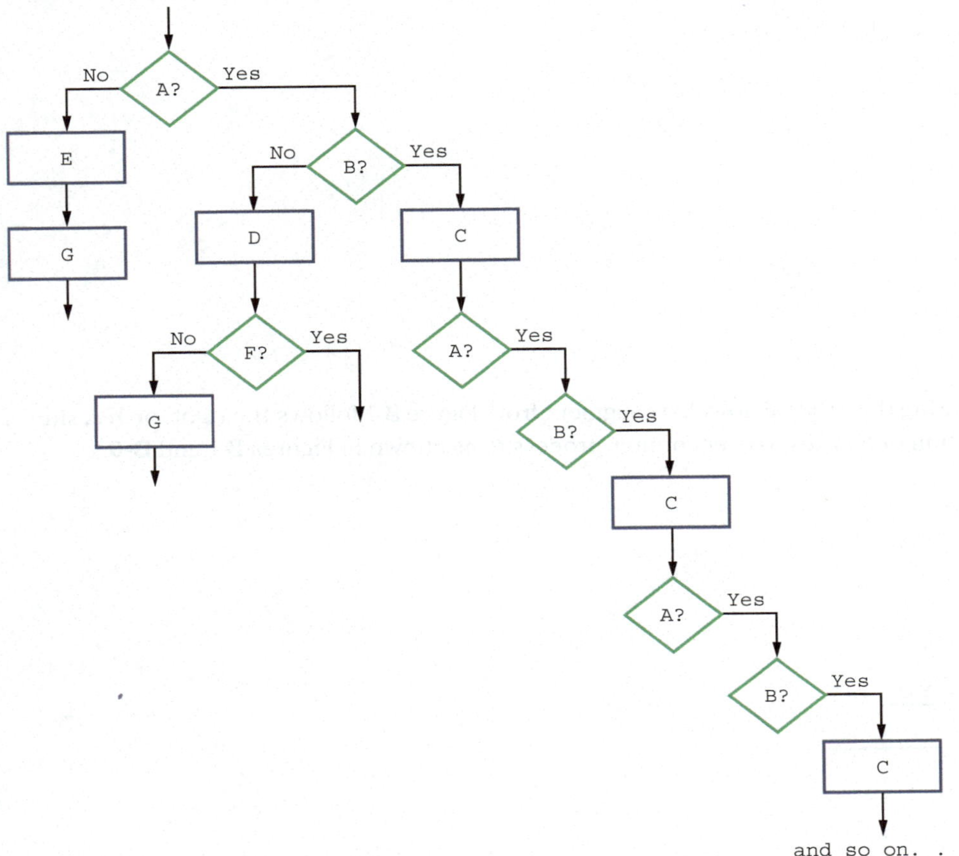

If you continue with Figure B-8, you will never be able to finish the flowchart; every `C` is always followed by another `A`, `B`, and `C`. Sometimes, to make a program segment structured, you have to add an extra flag variable to get out of an infinite mess. A flag is a variable that you set to indicate a true or false state. Typically, a variable is called a flag when its only purpose is to tell you whether some event has occurred. You can create a flag variable named `shouldRepeat` and set its value to *Yes* or *No*, depending on whether it is appropriate to repeat the evaluation of `A`. When `A` is *No*, the `shouldRepeat` flag should be set to *No* because, in this situation, you never want to repeat Question `A` again. See **Figure B-9**.

Figure B-9 Adding a flag to the flowchart

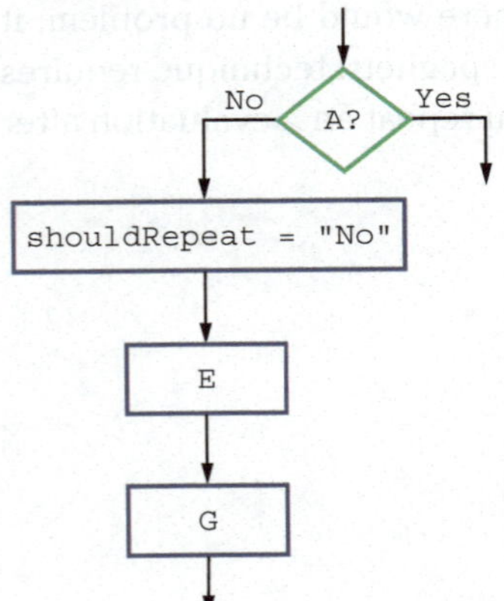

Similarly, after A is *Yes*, but when B is *No*, you never want to repeat Question A again. **Figure B-10** shows that you set shouldRepeat to "No" when the B decision is false. Then you continue with D and the F evaluation that determines whether G should execute.

Figure B-10 Adding a flag to a second path in the flowchart

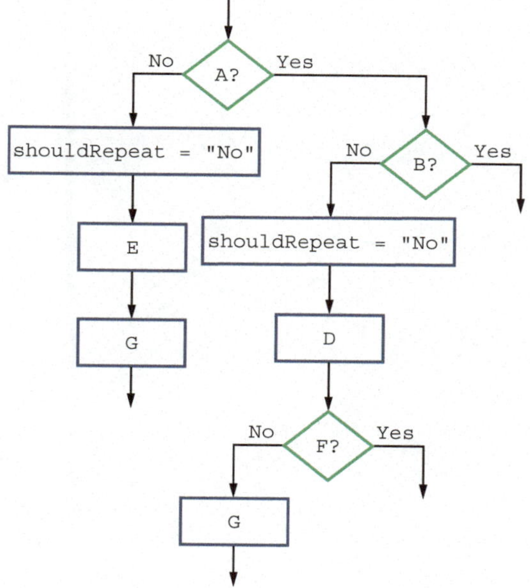

However, in the original flowchart segment in Figure B-1, when the B evaluation result is *Yes*, you *do* want to repeat A. So, when B is *Yes*, perform the process for C and set the shouldRepeat flag equal to *Yes*, as shown in **Figure B-11**.

Figure B-11 Adding a flag to a third path in the flowchart

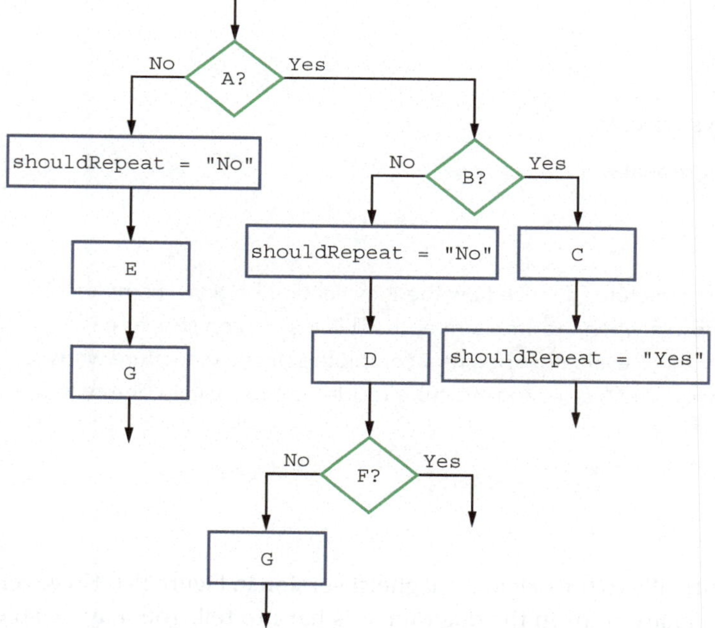

Now all paths of the flowchart can join together at the bottom with one final question: Is shouldRepeat equal to "Yes"? If it isn't, exit; but if it is, extend the flowline to go back to repeat Question A. See **Figure B-12**. Take a moment to verify that the steps that would execute following Figure B-12 are the same steps that would execute following Figure B-1.

Figure B-12 Tying up the loose ends

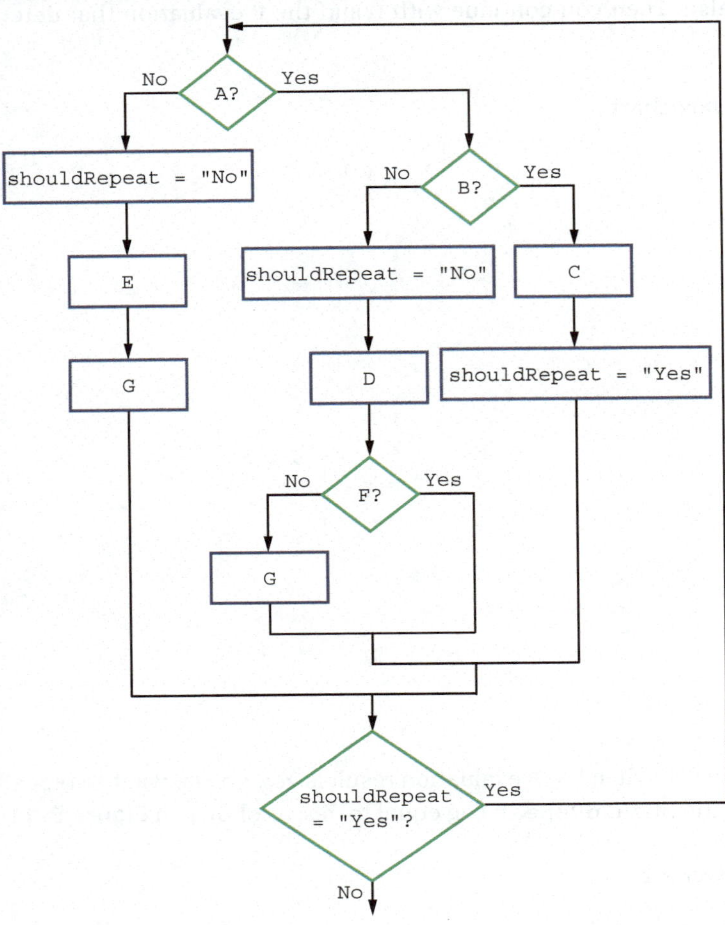

- When A is *No*, E and G always execute.
- When A is *Yes* and B is *No*, D and evaluation F always execute.
- When A is *Yes* and B is *Yes*, C always executes and A repeats.

Note Figure B-12 contains three nested selection structures. Notice how the F evaluation begins a complete selection structure whose Yes and No paths join when the structure ends. This F selection structure is within one path of the B decision structure; the B evaluation begins a complete selection structure whose Yes and No paths join at the bottom. Likewise, the B selection structure resides entirely within one path of the A selection structure.

The flowchart segment in Figure B-12 performs identically to the original spaghetti version in Figure B-1. However, is this new flowchart segment structured? There are so many steps in the diagram, it is hard to tell. You may be able to see the structure more clearly if you create a module named aThroughG(). If you create the module shown in **Figure B-13**, then the original flowchart segment can be drawn as in **Figure B-14**.

Figure B-13 The `aThroughG()` module

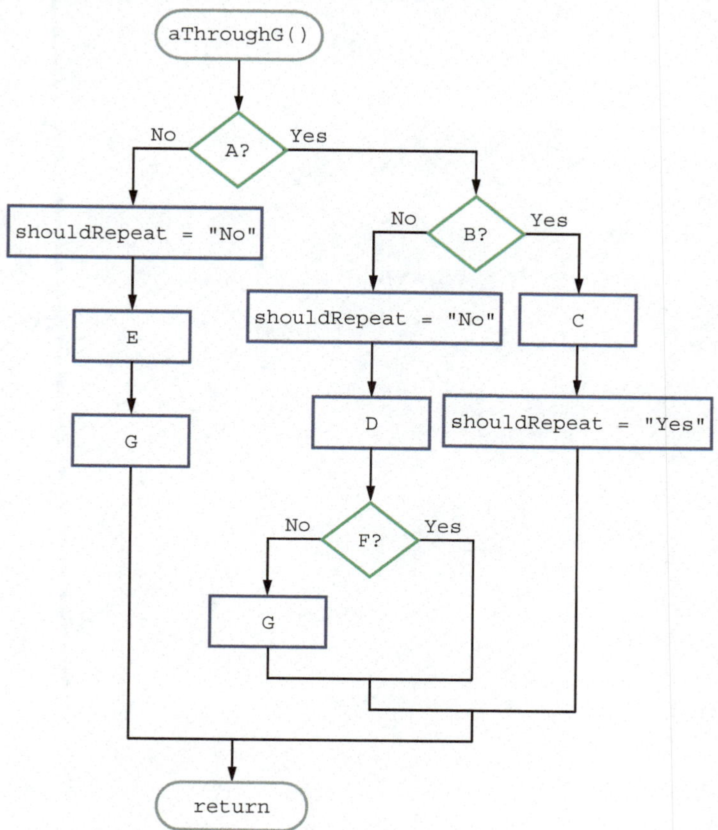

Figure B-14 Logic in Figure B-12, substituting a module for steps A through G

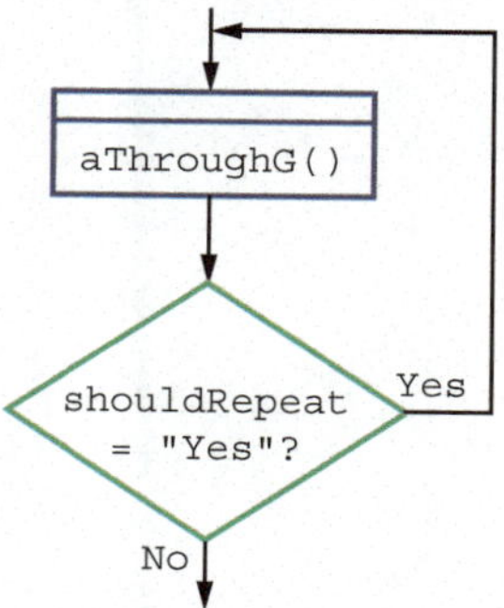

Now you can see that the completed flowchart segment in Figure B-14 is a `do-until` loop. If you prefer to use a `while` loop, you can redraw Figure B-14 to perform a sequence followed by a `while` loop, as shown in **Figure B-15**.

Figure B-15 Logic in Figure B-14, substituting a sequence and `while` loop for the `do-until` loop

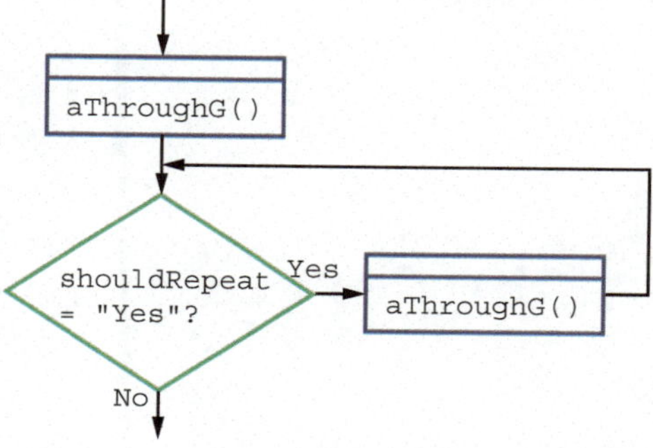

It has taken some extra effort, including repeating some steps and using some flag variables, but every logical problem can be solved and made to conform to structured rules by using the three structures: sequence, selection, and loop.

Glossary

A

abstract class a class from which concrete objects cannot be instantiated, but which can serve as a basis for inheritance.

abstract data type (ADT) a programmer-defined type, such as a class, as opposed to a built-in data type.

abstraction the process of paying attention to important properties while ignoring nonessential details.

access specifier the adjective that defines the type of access outside classes will have to an attribute or method.

accessibility describes screen design issues that make programs easier to use for people with physical limitations.

accessor method an instance method that returns a value from a field defined in a class. See also *get method.*

accumulator a variable used to gather or accumulate values.

addresses numbers that identify computer memory and storage locations.

algorithm the sequence of steps necessary to solve any problem.

alphanumeric values the set of values that includes alphabetic characters, numbers, and punctuation.

ambiguous methods methods between which the compiler cannot distinguish because they have the same name and parameter types.

American Standard Code for Information Interchange (ASCII) an eight-bit character-coding scheme used on many personal computers.

ancestors in inheritance, the entire list of parent classes from which a class is derived.

AND decision a decision in which two conditions must both be true for an action to take place.

AND operator a binary operator that combines two Boolean expressions; both must be true for the combined expression to be true.

animation the rapid display of still images, each slightly different from the previous one, that produces the illusion of movement.

annotation symbol a flowchart symbol used to hold comments; it is most often represented by a three-sided box connected with a dashed line to the step it explains.

app a piece of application software.

application software the programs that help users with tasks (e.g., accounting or word processing). Contrast with *system software.*

argument to a method a value passed to a method in the method call.

array a series or list of variables or constants in contiguous computer memory locations, all of which have the same name but are differentiated with subscripts.

ascending order describes the arrangement of data items from lowest value to highest.

assignment operator (=) the operator that assigns a value to a memory location on its left side; the equal sign.

assignment statement a statement that stores a value on its right side to the named location on its left side.

attribute one field in or characteristic of an object; an instance variable.

B

backup file a copy of a file that is kept in case altered values need to be restored to their original state.

base 2 describes numbers created using the binary numbering system.

base 10 describes numbers created using the decimal numbering system.

base 16 describes numbers created using the hexadecimal numbering system.

base case describes the input that halts a recursive method; also called *terminating case.*

base class a class that is used as a basis for inheritance. See also *parent class* and *superclass*.

batch processing a data handling technique that performs the same tasks with many records in sequence.

binary file a file that contains data that has not been encoded as text. Contrast with *text file*.

binary language a computer language represented using a series of 0s and 1s.

binary numbering system the numbering system that uses two digits, 0 and 1, and in which column values are multiples of 2.

binary operator an operator that requires two operands—one on each side.

binary search a search that compares a target value to an element in the middle of a sorted list, and then determines whether it should continue higher or lower to find the target.

bit a binary digit; a unit of storage equal to one-eighth of a byte.

black box the analogy that programmers use to refer to the details of hidden methods.

block a group of statements that execute as a single unit.

Boolean expression an expression that evaluates to one of two states, usually expressed as true or false.

bubble sort a sorting algorithm in which list elements are arranged in ascending or descending order by comparing items in pairs and swapping them when they are out of order.

byte a storage measurement equal to eight bits.

C

call a module to use a module's name to invoke it, causing it to execute.

camel casing a naming convention in which the initial letter is lowercase, multiple-word names are run together, and each new word within the name begins with an uppercase letter. See also *lower camel casing*.

cascading `if` statement a series of nested `if` statements.

case structure a structure that tests a single variable against multiple values, providing separate actions for each logical path.

catch an exception to receive an exception from a throw so it can be handled.

`catch` block a segment of code written to handle an exception that might be thrown by the `try` block that precedes it.

central processing unit (CPU) the computer hardware component that processes data.

characters letters, numbers, or special symbols such as *A*, *7*, or *$*.

child class a derived class. See also *derived class*, *extended class*, and *subclass*.

child file a copy of a file after revision. Contrast with *parent file*.

class a group or collection of objects with common attributes.

class client a program or class that instantiates objects of another prewritten class. See also *class user*.

class definition a set of program statements that define the fields and methods of a class.

class diagram a tool for describing a class that consists of a rectangle divided into three sections that show the name, data, and methods of a class.

class methods static methods; a class method is not an instance method, and it does not receive a `this` reference.

class user a program or class that instantiates objects of another prewritten class. See also *class client*.

client a program or other method that uses a method.

closing a file an action that makes a file no longer available to an application.

cloud remote computers accessed through the Internet.

coding the program the act of writing the statements of a program in a programming language.

cohesion a measure of how a method's internal statements are focused to accomplish the method's purpose.

command line the location on a computer screen where entries are typed to communicate with the computer's operating system.

compiler software that translates all the statements in a high-level programming language at once into machine language and identifies syntax errors. Contrast with *interpreter*.

composition the technique of placing an object within an object of another class. See also *whole-part relationship*.

compound condition an evaluation with multiple parts.

computer file a collection of data stored on a nonvolatile device in a computer system.

computer memory the temporary, internal storage within a computer.

computer system a combination of all the components required to process and store data using a computer.

conditional AND operator a symbol used to combine decisions so that two or more conditions must be true for an action to occur. Also called an *AND operator*.

conditional OR operator a symbol used to combine decisions when any one condition can be true for an action to occur. Also called an *OR operator*.

constructor an automatically called method that instantiates an object.

container one of a class of objects whose main purpose is to hold other elements—for example, a window.

control break a temporary detour in the logic of a program for special group processing.

control break field a variable that holds the value that signals a special processing break in a program.

control break program a program in which a change in the value of a variable initiates special actions or processing.

control break report a report that lists items in groups. Frequently, each group is followed by a subtotal.

conversion the set of actions an organization must take in order to switch over to using a new program or system.

counted loop a loop whose repetitions are managed by a counter. See also *counter-controlled loop*.

counter a numeric variable used to count the number of times an event has occurred.

counter-controlled loop a loop whose repetitions are managed by a counter. See also *counted loop*.

coupling a measure of the strength of the connection between two program methods.

D

data dictionary a list of every variable name used in a program, along with its type, size, and description.

data hiding the concept that other classes should not alter an object's attributes—only the methods of an object's own class should have that privilege. See also *information hiding*.

data hierarchy represents the relationship between databases, files, records, fields, and characters.

data items the text, numbers, and other information processed by a computer.

data type the characteristic of a program value; a variable or constant's data type describes the kind of values it can hold and the types of operations that can be performed with it.

database a logical container that holds related data that can easily be retrieved to serve the information needs of an organization.

dead path a logical path that can never be traveled. See also *unreachable path*.

deadlock a flaw in multithreaded programs in which two or more threads wait for each other to execute.

debugging the process of finding and correcting program errors.

decimal numbering system the numbering system based on 10 digits (0 through 9) in which column values are multiples of 10.

decision structure a program structure in which a condition is tested, and, depending on the result, one of two courses of action is taken; then, no matter which path is followed, the paths join and the next task executes.

decision symbol a diamond-shaped symbol that represents a decision in a flowchart.

declaration a statement that names a variable and its data type.

decrement to change a variable's value by decreasing it by a constant value, frequently 1.

default constructor a constructor that requires no arguments. Contrast with *nondefault constructor*.

default input and output devices hardware devices that do not require opening; usually they are the keyboard and monitor, respectively.

defensive programming a technique in which programmers try to prepare for all possible errors before they occur.

definite loop a loop for which the number of repetitions is a predetermined value.

delimiter a character, such as a comma, used to separate fields in a data file.

derived class an extended class. See also *child class* and *subclass*.

descending order describes the arrangement of data items from highest value to lowest.

desk-checking the process of walking through a program solution on paper.

destructor an automatically called method that contains the actions required when an instance of a class is destroyed.

detail loop tasks the steps that are repeated for each set of input data.

direct access files random access files.

directories organization units on storage devices that can contain multiple files as well as additional directories; also called *folders*.

`do-until` loop a posttest loop that iterates until its controlling condition is false.

`do-while` loop a posttest loop that iterates until its controlling condition is false.

documentation all of the supporting material that goes with a program.

DOS prompt the command line in the DOS operating system.

dual-alternative `if` a selection structure that defines one action to be taken when the tested condition is true, and another action to be taken when it is false. Also called *dual-alternative selection*. See also *`if-then-else`*.

dual-alternative selection a selection structure that defines one action to be taken when the tested condition is true, and another action to be taken when it is false. Also called *dual-alternative `if`*. See also *`if-then-else`*.

dummy value a preselected value that stops the execution of a program.

E

echoing input the act of repeating input back to a user either in a subsequent prompt or in output.

element one item in an array.

`else` clause the part of a selection structure that holds the action or actions that execute only when the tested Boolean expression is false.

encapsulation the technique of containing program elements within a module.

end users people who work with, and benefit from, computer programs; see also *users*.

end-of-job tasks the steps at the end of a program to finish an application.

end-structure statement a statement that designates the end of a pseudocode structure.

`eof` end-of-data file marker, short for end of file.

event an occurrence that generates a message sent to an object; for example, a mouse click.

event-based programs programs and actions that occur in response to user-initiated events such as clicking a mouse button. See also *event-driven programs*.

event-driven programs programs and actions that occur in response to user-initiated events such as clicking a mouse button. See also *event-based programs*.

exception handling the object-oriented techniques for managing errors.

exceptions the generic term used for errors in object-oriented languages.

execute to have a computer use a written and compiled program; also called *run*.

Extended Binary Coded Decimal Interchange Code (EBCDIC) an eight-bit character-coding scheme used on many larger computers.

extended class a class that is extended from a base class. See also *child class*, *derived class*, and *subclass*.

external documentation all of the external material that programmers develop to support a program. Contrast with *internal documentation* and *program comments*.

F

facilitator a method that performs tasks within a class. See also *help method* and *work method*.

fields single data items that represent a single attribute of a record or class, such as `lastName`, `streetAddress`, or `annualSalary`.

file's path the combination of the disk drive plus the complete hierarchy of directories in which a file resides.

filename an identifying name given to a computer file that frequently describes the contents.

filename extension a group of characters added to the end of a filename that indicates the file type.

files groups of records that go together for some logical reason.

flag a variable whose value indicates whether some event has occurred.

floating-point values numeric values that contain decimal points.

flowchart a pictorial representation of the logical steps it takes to solve a problem.

flowlines arrows that connect the steps in a flowchart.

folders organization units on storage devices that can contain multiple files as well as additional folders; also called *directories*.

`for` loop a statement that can be used to code definite loops and that contains a loop control variable that it automatically initializes, evaluates, and alters. See also *`for` statement*.

`for` statement a statement that can be used to code definite loops and that contains a loop control variable that it automatically initializes, evaluates, and alters. See also *`for` loop*.

forcing data overriding a variable's value by setting it to a specific, default value.

fragile describes classes that depend on field names from parent classes and are prone to errors.

function a program unit that contains a series of statements that carry out a task. See also *method*, *module*, *procedure*, and *subroutine*.

functional cohesion the extent to which all operations in a method contribute to the performance of only one task.

functional decomposition the act of reducing a large program into more manageable modules.

G

garbage describes the unknown value stored in an unassigned variable.

get method an instance method that returns a value from a field defined in a class. See also *accessor method*.

gigabytes a measurement of storage; billions of bytes.

GIGO acronym for *garbage in*, *garbage out*; it means that if input is incorrect, output is worthless.

global describes variables that are known to an entire program.

goto-less programming describes structured programming because structured programmers do not use a "go to" statement.

graphical user interface (GUI) a program interface that allows users to interact with a program in a graphical environment.

H

hardware the equipment of a computer system.

has-a relationship a whole-part relationship; the type of relationship that exists when using composition.

help method a method that performs tasks within a class. See also *facilitator* and *work method*.

hexadecimal numbering system the numbering system based on 16 digits (0 through 9 and A through F) in which column values are multiples of 16.

high-level programming language a programming language that is English-like. Contrast with *low-level programming language*.

housekeeping tasks tasks that must be performed at the beginning of a program to prepare for the rest of the program.

Hungarian notation a naming convention that stores a data type or other information as part of a name.

I

I/O symbol an input/output symbol.

icons small pictures on a screen that help a user navigate a system.

IDE the acronym for Integrated Development Environment, which is the visual development environment in some programming languages.

identifier a program component's name.

`if-then` a selection structure that contains a tested Boolean expression and takes action only when the expression is true. See also *single-alternative `if`* and *single-alternative selection*.

`if-then-else` a selection structure that defines one action to be taken when the tested condition is true, and another action to be taken when it is false. Also called *dual-alternative `if`* and *dual-alternative* selection.

`if-then` clause the part of a selection structure that holds the action or actions that execute only when the tested Boolean expression is true.

implementation the statements that carry out a method's tasks.

implementation hiding a programming principle that describes the encapsulation of method details.

in bounds describes a subscript that is within the range of acceptable subscripts for its array.

in scope the characteristic of variables and constants that describes the extent to which they are available for use.

inaccessible describes any field or method that cannot be reached.

increment to change a variable by adding a constant value to it, frequently 1.

indefinite loop a loop for which the number of executions cannot be predicted when the program is written.

index a term sometimes used as a synonym for *subscript*.

index records describe storage in which a list of key fields is paired with the storage address for the corresponding data record.

indirect relationship the relationship between parallel arrays in which an element in the first array does not directly access its corresponding value in the second array.

infinite loop a repeating flow of logic without an ending.

information processed data.

information hiding the concept that other classes should not alter an object's attributes—only the methods of an object's own class should have that privilege. See also *data hiding*.

inheritance the process of acquiring the traits of one's predecessors.

initialization list a series of values assigned to an array when it is declared.

initializing a variable the act of assigning the first value to a variable, often at the same time that the variable is created.

inner loop the loop that is contained within the other loop when loops are nested. Contrast with *outer loop*.

input describes the entry of data items into computer memory using hardware devices such as keyboards and mice.

input symbol a parallelogram-shaped symbol used in flowcharts to indicate input operations.

input/output symbol a parallelogram used within flowcharts to indicate input or output operations; also called an *I/O symbol*.

insertion sort a sorting algorithm in which each list element is examined one at a time; if an element is out of order relative to any of the items earlier in the list, each earlier item is moved down one position and then the tested element is inserted.

instance an existing object or tangible example of a class.

instance method a method that operates correctly yet differently for each class object; an instance method is nonstatic and receives a `this` reference.

instance variables the data components that belong to every instantiated object.

instant access files random access files in which records can be accessed immediately.

instantiate to create an object.

instantiation an instance of a class; an object.

integer values numeric whole number values without decimal points.

integrated development environment (IDE) a software package that provides an editor, compiler, and other programming tools.

interactive program a program in which a user makes direct requests or provides input while a program executes.

interactivity diagram a diagram that shows the relationship between screens in an interactive GUI program.

interface to a method a method's return type, name, and arguments; the part of a method that a client sees and uses.

internal documentation documentation within a program. See also *program comments*. Contrast with *external documentation*.

interpreter software that translates the statements in a high-level programming language one at a time into machine language and identifies syntax errors. Contrast with *compiler*.

IPO chart a program development tool that delineates input, processing, and output tasks.

is-a relationship the relationship between an object and each of the classes in its ancestry.

iteration repetition; looping.

K

kebob case a term sometimes used to describe the naming convention in which dashes separate parts of a name.

key field the field whose contents make a record unique among all records in a file.

keywords the limited word set that is reserved in a language.

kilobytes a measurement of storage; thousands of bytes.

L

left-to-right associativity describes operators that evaluate the expression to the left first. Contrast with *right-to-left associativity*.

libraries stored collections of classes that serve related purposes. See also *packages*.

linear search a search through a list from one end to the other.

linked list a list that contains an extra field in every record that holds the physical address of the next logical record.

listener in object-oriented programming, an object that is interested in an event and responds to it.

literal numeric constant a number without an identifier. See also *numeric constant*.

literal string constant a group of characters enclosed within quotation marks. See also *string constant*.

local describes variables that are declared within the method that uses them.

logic the complete sequence of instructions that lead to a problem solution.

logical errors errors that occur when incorrect instructions are performed, or when instructions are performed in the wrong order.

logical order the order in which a list is used, even though it is not necessarily stored in that physical order.

loop a structure that repeats a series of steps that continue to execute while a condition continues to be met.

loop body the set of actions or statements within a loop.

loop control variable a variable that determines whether loop execution will continue.

loop structure a structure that repeats actions while a test condition remains true. Contrast with *selection structure* and *sequence structure*.

loose coupling a relationship that occurs when methods do not depend on others.

low-level programming language a programming language not far removed from machine language. Contrast with *high-level programming language*.

lower camel casing a naming convention in which the initial letter is lowercase, multiple-word names are run together, and each new word within the name begins with an uppercase letter. See also *camel casing*.

lvalue the memory address identifier to the left of an assignment operator.

M

machine language a computer's on/off circuitry language; the low-level language made up of 1s and 0s that the computer understands.

magic number an unnamed numeric constant whose purpose is not immediately apparent.

main program a program that runs from start to stop and often calls other modules.

mainline logic the overall logic in a program's main module.

maintenance all the improvements and corrections made to a program after it is in production.

matrix a term sometimes used by mathematicians to describe a two-dimensional array.

mean the arithmetic average.

median the value in the middle position of a list when the values are sorted.

megabytes a measurement of storage; millions of bytes.

merging files the act of combining two or more sequentially ordered files while maintaining the order.

method a program unit that contains a series of statements that carry out a task. See also *function*, *module*, *procedure*, and *subroutine*.

method body the set of all the statements in a method.

method header a program component that precedes a method body; the header includes the method identifier and, possibly, other necessary information, such as a return type and parameter list.

method return statement a statement that marks the end of the method and identifies the point at which control returns to the calling method.

method's type the data type of a method's return value.

mixed case with underscores a naming convention similar to snake casing, in which words are separated with underscores, but new words start with an uppercase letter.

modularization the process of breaking down a program into modules.

module a program unit that contains a series of statements that carry out a task. See also *function*, *method*, *procedure*, and *subroutine*.

module body the part of a module that contains all of its statements. Contrast with *module header* and *module return statement*.

module header the part of a module that includes the module identifier and, possibly, other necessary identifying information. Contrast with *module body* and *module return statement*.

module `return` statement the part of a module that marks its end and identifies the point at which control returns to the program or module that called the module. Contrast with *module header* and *module body*.

multidimensional array lists with more than one dimension; more than one subscript is required to access an element.

multiple inheritance the ability to inherit from more than one class that is allowed in some programming languages.

multithreading using multiple threads of execution.

mutator method an instance method that sets or changes the values of a data field within a class object. See also *set method*.

N

named constant a named memory location whose value never changes after assignment; conventionally, constants are named using all capital letters.

nested decision a decision within the `if-then` or `else` clause of another decision; also called a nested `if`.

nested `if` a decision within the `if-then` or `else` clause of another decision; also called a nested decision.

nested loops loop structures that contain another loop structure.

nesting structures placing a structure within another structure.

`new` a keyword in some object-oriented programming languages that creates a new instance of a class.

nibble half a byte or four bits.

nondefault constructor a constructor that requires at least one argument. See also *parameterized constructor.* Contrast with *default constructor.*

nonstatic methods methods that exist to be used with an object; instance methods that receive a `this` reference. Contrast with *static methods*.

nonvolatile describes storage that retains its contents when power is lost.

`NOT` operator a symbol that reverses the meaning of a Boolean expression.

null case the branch of a decision structure in which no action is taken.

numeric describes data that consists of numbers and with which numeric operations can be performed.

numeric constant a number without an identifier. See also *literal numeric constant*.

numeric variable a variable that holds numeric values.

O

object one tangible example of a class; an instance of a class.

object code program statements that have been translated into machine language.

object dictionary a list of the objects used in a program, including which screens they are used on and whether any code, or script, is associated with them.

object-oriented programming (OOP) a programming model that focuses on components and data items (objects) and describes their attributes and behaviors. Contrast with *procedural programming*.

one-dimensional array a list accessed using a single subscript. See also *single-dimensional array*.

opening a file the process of locating a file on a storage device, physically preparing it for reading, and associating it with an identifier inside a program.

operand a value used by an operator.

operating system the software that supports a computer's basic functions including controlling devices such as keyboards and mice and scheduling tasks.

`OR` decision a decision that contains two or more conditions; if at least one condition is met, then the resulting action takes place.

`OR` operator a binary operator that combines two Boolean expressions; one or both must be true for the combined expression to be true.

order of operations rules that dictate the order in which operations in the same statement are carried out. See also *rules of precedence*.

out of bounds describes an array subscript that is not within the range of acceptable subscripts.

outer loop a loop that contains another loop nested within it. Contrast with *inner loop*.

output describes the operation of retrieving information from memory and sending it to a device, such as a monitor or printer, so that people can view, interpret, and work with the results.

output symbol a parallelogram-shaped symbol used in flowcharts to indicate output operations.

overhead all the resources and time required by an operation.

overload a method to create multiple methods with the same name but different parameter lists.

overloading supplying diverse meanings for a single identifier.

overriding the mechanism by which a child class method is used by default when a parent class contains a method with the same signature.

P

packages stored collections of classes that serve related purposes. See also *libraries*.

page schematic a wireframe.

parallel arrays two or more arrays in which each element in one array is associated with the element in the same relative position in the other array or arrays.

parameter list all the data types and parameter names that appear in a method header.

parameter to a method a data item defined in a method header that accepts data passed into the method from the outside.

parameterized constructor a constructor that requires at least one argument. See also *nondefault constructor*. Contrast with *default constructor*.

parent class a base class. See also *superclass*.

parent file a copy of a file before revision. Contrast with *child file*.

Pascal casing a naming convention in which the initial letter is uppercase, multiple-word names are run together, and each new word within the name begins with an uppercase letter.

passed by reference describes a method parameter that represents the item's memory address.

passed by value describes a variable that has a copy of its value sent to a method and stored in a new memory location accessible to the method.

permanent storage device a hardware device that holds nonvolatile data; examples include hard disks, DVDs, Zip disks, USB drives, and reels of magnetic tape.

physical order the order in which a list is stored even though it might be accessed in a different logical order.

pixel a picture element; one of the tiny dots of light that form a grid on a monitor.

polymorphism the ability of a method to act appropriately depending on the context.

populating the array to assign values to array elements.

portable describes a module that can easily be reused in multiple programs.

posttest loop a loop that tests its controlling condition after each iteration, guaranteeing that the loop body executes at least one time. Contrast with *pretest loop*.

pretest loop a loop that tests its controlling condition before each iteration, meaning that the loop body might never execute. Contrast with *posttest loop*.

primary file a file that holds relatively permanent data. Contrast with *transaction file*.

priming input the statement that reads the first input data record. See also *priming read*.

priming read the statement that reads the first input data record. See also *priming input*.

primitive data types simple number and character types that are not class types.

private access a privilege of class members in which data or methods cannot be used by any method that is not part of the same class.

procedural programming a programming technique that focuses on procedures or actions. Contrast with *object-oriented programming*.

procedure a program unit that contains a series of statements that carry out a task. See also *function*, *method*, *module*, and *subroutine*.

processing working with data items, such as organizing them, checking them for accuracy, or performing mathematical operations on them.

processing symbol a rectangular symbol used in flowcharts to represent working with data.

program a set of instructions for a computer written by a programmer.

program code a set of instructions written in a programming language.

program comments nonexecuting statements placed within code to explain program statements in English. See also *internal documentation*.

program development cycle the steps that occur during a program's lifetime, including planning, coding, translating, testing, producing, and maintaining the program.

program hierarchy chart a diagram that illustrates program modules' relationships to each other.

programmer-defined type a data type that is not built into a language but is created by an application's programmer. See also *user-defined type*.

programming the act of developing and writing programs.

programming language a language, such as Visual Basic, C#, C++, Java, or COBOL, used to write programs.

prompt a message that is displayed on a screen, asking the user for a response.

property a method that gets and sets a field value using simple syntax.

`protected` access specifier a specifier used when outside classes should not be able to use a data field unless they are children of the original class.

pseudocode an English-like representation of the logical steps it takes to solve a problem.

public access a privilege of class members in which other programs and methods can use the specified data or methods within a class.

R

random access files files that contain records that can be accessed directly. Contrast with *sequential files*.

random access memory (RAM) temporary, internal computer storage.

random-access storage device a storage device, such as a disk, from which records can be accessed in any order.

range check the comparison of a variable to a series of values that mark the limiting ends of ranges.

reading from a file the act of copying data from a file on a storage device into computer memory. Contrast with *writing to a file*.

real numbers floating-point numbers; numbers that contain a decimal point.

real-time applications describe applications that require a record to be accessed immediately while a client is waiting.

records groups of data fields that go together for some logical reason.

recursion a programming event that occurs when a method is defined in terms of itself.

recursive cases the input values that cause a recursive method to execute again.

recursive method a method that calls itself.

register components to sign up components so they can react to events initiated by other components.

relational comparison operators symbols that express Boolean comparisons such as =, >, <, >=, <=, and <>.

reliability the feature of a program or module that ensures that it has been tested and proven to function correctly.

remainder operator an arithmetic operator that provides the remainder after values are divided.

repetition a loop.

return type the data type for any value a method returns.

reusability the feature of a module that allows it to be used in a variety of applications.

right-associativity describes operators that evaluate the expression to the right first. Also called *right-to-left associativity*. Contrast with *left-to-right associativity*.

right-to-left associativity describes operators that evaluate the expression to the right first. Contrast with *left-to-right associativity*.

rules of precedence rules that dictate the order in which operations in the same statement are carried out. See also *order of operations*.

run to have a computer use a written and compiled program; also called *execute*.

S

screen blueprint a wireframe.

script a procedural module that depends on user-initiated events in object-oriented programs.

scripting language a language, such as Python, Lua, Perl, or PHP, used to write programs that are typed directly from a keyboard and are stored as text, rather than as binary executable files; also called *script language* or *scripting programming language*.

selection sort a sorting algorithm in which list values are divided into sorted and unsorted sublists; the unsorted sublist is repeatedly examined for its smallest value, which is then moved to the end of the sorted sublist.

selection structure a program structure that defines one action to be taken when the tested condition is true, and another action to be taken when it is false. See also *dual-alternative `if`* and *dual-alternative selection*. Contrast with *loop structure* and *sequence structure*.

self-documenting describes programs that contain meaningful and descriptive identifiers.

sentinel value a data value that represents an entry or exit point.

sequence structure a program structure that contains steps that execute in order with no chance to branch off and skip any of the tasks. Contrast with *loop structure* and *selection structure*.

sequential files files in which records are stored one after another in some order and whose records must be accessed in sequence. Contrast with *random access files*.

sequential order the arrangement of records when they are stored one after another on the basis of the value in a field or fields.

set method an instance method that sets or changes the values of a data field within a class object. See also *mutator method*.

short-circuit evaluation a logical feature in which each part of a larger expression is evaluated only as far as necessary to determine the final outcome.

signature a method's name and parameter list.

single-alternative `if` a selection structure that contains a tested Boolean expression and takes action only when the expression is true. See also `if-then` and *single-alternative selection*. Contrast with `dual-alternative if` and `if-then-else`.

single-alternative selection a selection structure that contains a tested Boolean expression and takes action only when the expression is true. See also `if-then` and *single-alternative* `if`. Contrast with `dual-alternative selection` and `if-then-else`.

single-dimensional array a list accessed using a single subscript. See also *one-dimensional array*.

single-level control break a break in the logic of a program based on the value of a single variable.

size of the array the number of elements held in an array.

snake casing a naming convention in which parts of a name are separated by underscores.

software programs; computer instructions.

sorting the process of placing records in order by the value in a specific field or fields.

source code the readable statements of a program, written in a programming language; they are later translated into object code.

source of an event the component (e.g., a button) from which an event (such as a click) is generated.

spaghetti code unstructured program logic. See also *unstructured programs*.

stack a memory location that holds the memory addresses to which a program's logic should return after a method executes.

stacking structures attaching program structures end to end.

starvation a flaw in multithreaded programs in which a thread is abandoned because other threads occupy all the computer's resources.

state the set of all the values or contents of a class's instance variables.

static methods methods for which no object needs to exist; static methods are not instance methods, and they do not receive a `this` reference. Contrast with *nonstatic methods*.

step value a number used to alter a loop control variable on each pass through a loop.

storage device a hardware apparatus that holds data or information for later retrieval.

storyboard a picture or sketch of screens the user will see when running a program.

string describes data that is nonnumeric.

string constant a group of characters enclosed within quotation marks. See also *literal string constant*.

string variable a variable that can hold text that includes letters, digits, and special characters, such as punctuation marks.

structure a basic unit of programming logic; each structure is a sequence, selection, or loop.

structured programs programs that follow the rules of structured logic.

subclass a derived class. See also *child class* and *extended class*.

subroutine a program unit that contains a series of statements that carry out a task. See also *function*, *method*, *module*, and *procedure*.

subscript a number that indicates the position of an element within an array; also called an *index*.

summary report a report that lists only totals, without individual detail records.

sunny day case a program execution in which no errors occur and nothing goes wrong.

superclass a base class. See also *parent class*.

swap values to exchange the values of two variables.

syntax the rules of a language.

syntax errors errors in a language's usage, including spelling and grammar.

system software the programs that manage a computer. Contrast with *application software*.

T

table a term sometimes used by mathematicians to describe a two-dimensional array.

temporary variable a variable that holds intermediate results during a program's execution; see also *work variable*.

terminal symbols lozenge-shaped symbols used at the beginning and end of a flowchart; also called *start/stop symbols*.

terminating case the input that halts a recursive method; also called *base case*.

text editor a program used to create simple text files; similar to a word processor, but without as many features.

text file a file that contains data that can be read in a text editor. Contrast with *binary file*.

`this` reference an automatically created variable that holds the address of an object and passes it to an instance method whenever the method is called.

thread the flow of execution of one set of program statements.

thread synchronization a set of techniques that coordinates threads of execution to help avoid potential multithreading problems.

three-dimensional array an array in which each element is accessed using three subscripts.

throw an exception to pass an exception out of a block where it occurs, usually to a block that can handle it.

`throw` statement an object-oriented programming statement that sends an exception object out of a method or code block to be caught and handled elsewhere.

tight coupling a problem that occurs when methods depend excessively on each other; it makes programs more prone to errors.

transaction file a file that holds temporary data used to update a primary file.

trivial expression an expression that always evaluates to the same value.

truth table a diagram used in mathematics and logic to help describe the truth of an entire expression based on the truth of its parts.

`try` block a block of code that attempts to execute while acknowledging that an exception might occur.

try some code statements to execute some code that might throw an exception that you want to handle.

two-dimensional array an array that has rows and columns of values and in which each element is accessed using two subscripts.

type-safety the feature of programming languages that prevent assigning values of an incorrect data type.

U

unary operator an operator that uses only one operand.

Unicode a 16-bit character-coding scheme.

unnamed constant a literal value.

unnamed numeric constant a literal numeric value.

unnamed string constant a literal string value.

unreachable path a logical path that can never be traveled. See also *dead path*.

unstructured programs programs that do not follow the rules of structured logic. See also *spaghetti code*.

update a primary file apply transactions to a primary file making it current.

upper camel casing another name for the Pascal casing naming convention.

user-defined type a data type that is not built into a language but is created by an application's programmer. See also *programmer-defined type*.

users people who work with, and benefit from, computer programs; see also *end users*.

V

validate data the process of ensuring that data items are meaningful and useful, are correct data types, fall within an acceptable range, or are reasonable.

variable a named memory location whose contents can vary or differ over time.

visible a characteristic of data items that means they "can be seen" only within the method in which they are declared.

visual development environment a programming environment in which programs are created by dragging components such as buttons and labels onto a screen and arranging them visually.

void method a method that returns no value.

volatile a characteristic of internal memory in which its contents are lost every time the computer loses power.

W

`while` loop a loop in which a condition is tested and executes statements while the condition continues to be true. See also *`while`...do loop*.

`while`...do loop a loop in which a condition is tested and executes statements while the condition continues to be true. See also *`while` loop*.

whole-part relationship a relationship in which an object of one class is contained within an object of another class. See also *composition*.

wireframe a picture or sketch of a screen the user will see when running a program.

work method a method that performs tasks within a class. See also *facilitator* and *help method*.

work variable a variable that holds intermediate results during a program's execution; see also *temporary variable*.

writing to a file the act of copying data from computer memory into persistent storage. Contrast with *reading from a file*.

x-axis an imaginary line that represents horizontal positions in a screen window.

x-coordinate a position value that increases from left to right across a screen window.

y-axis an imaginary line that represents vertical positions in a screen window.

y-coordinate a position value that increases from top to bottom across a screen window.

Index

Note: Page numbers in **boldface** type indicate where key terms are defined.

Special Characters
* (asterisk), 36, 38
{} (curly braces), 153
= (equal sign), **33**, 38
! (exclamation point), 117
> (greater-than operator), 97
>= (greater-than-or-equal-to operator), 97, 98
< (less-than operator), 97
<= (less-than-or-equal-to operator), 97
- (minus sign), 36, 38, 323
<> (not-equal-to operator), 97
% (percent sign), 38
+ (plus sign), 36, 38, 323
; (semicolon), 153
/ (slash), 36, 38
~ (tilde), 347

A

abbreviations, caution about use, 52
abstract classes, **357**
abstract data types (ADTs), **316**
abstraction, **39**, 39–40
accessibility, **380**
accessor methods, **320**
access specifiers, **322**
  private and public, 321–324, **322**
  protected, **355**, 355–357
accumulators, **157**, 159
actions, user-initiated, 376
addition operator (+), 36, 38
addresses, **263**
ADTs. *See* abstract data types (ADTs)
algorithms, **8**, 241
alphanumeric values, **30**
ambiguous methods, **293**, 293–295
American Standard Code for Information Interchange (ASCII), **400**, 401
ancestors, **352**
AND decisions, **100**, 100–102
  avoiding common errors, 106–108
  nested, 101, 103–104
AND operator, **104**, 104–106
  combining with OR operator, precedence, 122–124
  conditional, **104**
animation, **390**, 390–392
annotation symbol, **51**
application software (app), **2**
arguments (argument to a method), **276**
arithmetic operations, 36–39
arrays, **173**, 173–197
  bounds, remaining within, 193–196
  constants with, 181–182
  objects, 331–334
  parallel, **185**, 185–191
  passing to method, 287–291
  populating, **174**
  processing using `for` loops, 196–197
  replacing nested decisions, 176–181
  searching for exact matches, 183–185
  searching for range matches, 190–193
  storing data in, 173–175
ascending order, **211**–212
assignment operators, **33**, 36–38
assignment statements, **33**
asterisk (*), multiplication operator, 36, 38
attributes, **310**

B

backup files, **213**
  generations, 226
base 2 numbers, **400**
base 10 numbers, **399**
base 16, 6, **402**
base 16 system, **402**
base case, **299**
base classes, **352**
batch processing, **231**
binary files, **206**
binary language, **3**
binary numbering system, 399–400, **400**
binary operators, **34**
binary searches, **190**
bits, **400**
black box, **297**
blocks, **71**
body, modules, **41**
Boolean expressions, **67**, 68, 93. *See also* AND decisions; OR decisions
  completeness, 107, 112
  inadvertently trivial, avoiding, 107–108
bounds, subscripts, 194–196
bubble sort algorithm, **241**, 242–247
  mainline logic, 242
  procedures, 242
  reducing unnecessary comparisons, 250–251
  refining, to eliminate unnecessary passes, 252–253
  sorting, variable size list, 248–250
  swapping values, 241–242
built-in exceptions, 363–365
`Button` class, 377–378
button, GUIs, 376, 377
bytes, **206**

C

calling a module, **39**
camel casing, **32**, 53
cascading `if` statements, **101**
`case` structure, 84, **125**, 125–126
catch an exception, **361**
`catch` blocks, **362**
central processing unit (CPU), **2**
  multithreading, 388–390
characters, **207**
check boxes, GUIs, 376
child classes, **352**, 353, 354
  overriding parent class methods in, 357–358
child files, **213**, 226
clarity
  statements, 54
  structure use, 80
class(es), **310**, 310–312
  abstract, **357**
  base, **352**
  `Button`, 377–378
  clients (class users), **312**
  definitions, **314**, 314–316
  derived (extended), **352**, 354
  diagrams, **316**, 316–318
  fragile, **357**
  instances, **310**
  methods, **329**
  organization, 324–325
  predefined, 359
  subclasses, **352**
  superclasses, **352**
client, **273**
closing files, **212**
cloud, **2**
code
  object, **3**
  program, **2**
  pseudocode, 12–13
  reliable, 358
  source, **3**
  spaghetti, **65**, 65–67
  statements, **361**
coding the program, **2**, 8–9
cohesion, **297**
  functional, **44**
command line, **20**, 373
comments, 50–52
compilers, **3**
composition, **349**, 349–350
compound conditions, **100**
computer codes, 400–402
computer files, 205–207, **206**
  backup, **213**, 226
  binary, **206**

computer files (continued)
  child, **213**, 231
  closing, **212**
  data hierarchy, 207–209
  declaring file identifiers, 209
  direct access, 231–**232**
  grandparent, 226
  instant access, **231**
  merging, 218–225
  opening, 209–210
  organizing, 206–207
  parent, **213**, 226
  primary, **225**, 225–231
  program performing file operations, 213–214
  random access, **231**, 231–232
  reading and processing data from, 210–212
  sequential, **211**, 218–225
  size, 206
  text, **206**
  transaction, **225**, 225–231
  writing data, 212
computer memory, **3**, 6
  RAM, **3**
  temporary, 210
computer systems, **1**, 1–4
conditional operators
  logical operators *vs.*, 106
  AND operator, **104**
  OR operator, **110**
consistency of data, validating, 163–164
constants
  as array element values, 182
  as array subscripts, 182
  declaring within modules, 44–46
  global, 45
  local, 45
  naming, 53
  numeric (literal numeric), **30**
  as size of array, 181–182
  string (literal string), **30**
  unnamed, **30**, 181, 182
constructors, **341**, 341–347
  default, **342**, 342–344
  nondefault (parameterized), **342**, 344–345
  overloading, 345–347
containers, **386**
control break(s), **214**, 214–218
  fields, **216**
  programs, **214**
  reports, **215**
  single-level, **216**
conversion, **11**
counted loops, **137**
counter(s), **138**
counter-controlled loop, **137**
coupling, **297**, 297–298
curly braces({}), statements, 153

D

databases, **208**
data dictionaries, **53**
data handling
  bubble sort algorithm, 241–253
  indexed files and linked lists, 262–265
  insertion sort, **255**, 255–256
  multidimensional arrays, 257–262
  multifield records sorting, 253–255
  selection sort, **256**, 256–257
  sorting data, 239–241
data hiding, **313**, 321
data hierarchy, **207**, 207–209
data items, **2**
  visible (in scope), 45
data types, **29**, 29–30, 31
  abstract, **316**
  integers, 38–39
  primitive, **316**
  validating, 163
  variables, 31
deadlock, **389**
dead paths, **119**
debugging, **10**
decimal numbering system, **399**
decision making process, 176–179
decision structure, **67**, 67–69, 103. *See also* selection structure
decision symbol, **16**
declarations, **31**
decrement, **138**
default constructors, **342**, 342–344
default input and output devices, **212**
defensive programming, **160**, 164
definite loops, **137**, 137–138
delimiter, **210**
derived classes, **352**, 354
descending order, **212**
desk-checking, **8**, 50
destructors, **347**, 347–348
detail loop tasks, **46**
dimmed screen options, 380
direct access files, 231–**232**
directories, **206**, 207
display, definition, 214
division operator (/), 36, 38
documentation, **7**
  external, **51**
  internal, **51**
`do` loop, 84
DOS prompt, **373**
doubly linked list, 265
`do-until` loop, **156**
`do-while` loop, **154**
drawing
  flowcharts, 13–15
  symbols, 12–16, 51, 154
dual-alternative `if`, **68**
dual-alternative selections, **68**
dummy values, **17**

E

echoing input, **56**, 57
efficiency
  AND decisions, 103–104
  OR decisions, 108–110
  searching arrays, 189–190
  structure use, 80
elements
  of array, **174**
  constants as values, 182
`else` clause, **96**
encapsulation, **42**, 313–314
end-of-job tasks, **46**
end-structure statement, **68**
end users, **7**
`eof`, **17**
equal sign (=)
  assignment operator, **33**, 38
  equivalency operator, 97
event(s), **374**
  source of, **375**
event-based programs, **374**
event-driven application, 381–388
  defining connections between user screens, 384
  planning logic, 384–388
  storyboards, **382**
  wireframes (page schematics; screen blueprints), **382**
event-driven programming, 373–375, **374**
exception(s), **361**
  built-in, 363–365
  catching, **361**
  throwing, **361**
  user-created, 363–365
exception handling, 360–365, **361**
  built-in and user-created exceptions, 363–365
  drawbacks to traditional techniques, 360–361
  object-oriented model, 361–363
exclamation point (!), NOT operator, 117
executing a program, **4**
Extended Binary Coded Decimal Interchange Code (EBCDIC), **401**
extended classes, **352**, 354
external documentation, **51**

F

facilitators, **320**
fields, **208**, 311, 315
  inaccessible, **355**
  private, parent classes, accessing, 354–357
filename, **206**
filename extension, **206**
files, **208**. *See also* computer files
file's path, **206**, 207
flags, **183**
floating-point values, **30**
flowcharts, **12**
flowlines, **14**
folders, **206**, 207
forcing data, **162**
`for` loops, **152**, 152–154
  processing arrays, 196–197
`for` statement, 152
fragile classes, **357**
function, **39**
functional cohesion, **44**, 297
functional decomposition, **39**

G

garbage, **34**
garbage in, garbage out (GIGO), **160**, 360
generations, backup files, 226
get methods, **320**
gigabytes, **206**

GIGO. *See* garbage in, garbage out (GIGO)
global data item, 274
global variables and constants, **45**
goto-less programming, **80**
grandparent files, 226
graphical user interfaces (GUIs), **20**, 20–21
  accessibility, **380**
  attractiveness, readability, and nondistracting nature, 380
  components, 376–379
  design, 379–381
  forgiving nature, 380–381
  naturalness and predictability, 379–380
  objects, creating, 359
  principle of, 381
grayed screen options, 380
greater-than operator (>), 97
greater-than-or-equal-to operator (>=), 97, 98
GUIs. *See* graphical user interfaces (GUIs)

H

hardware, **1**
has-a relationships, **349**
headers, modules, **41**
help methods, **320**, 320–321
hexadecimal numbering system, **402**, 402–403
hierarchy charts, 48–50
high-level programming languages, **9**
housekeeping tasks, **46**
Hungarian notation, **32**

I

icons, **374**
identifiers, **31**, 52–53
  variables, 31–33
`if-then`, **69**
`if-then` clause, **96**
`if-then-else`, **68**
implementation, **274**
implementation hiding, **296**, 296–297
inaccessible fields, **355**
in bounds, **194**
increment, **138**
indefinite loops, **139**, 139–140
index, **174**
indexed files, 263
index records, **263**
indirect relationships, **188**
infinite loops, **15**
information, **2**
information hiding, **313**, 321
inheritance, **313**, 350–358
  accessing private fields and methods of parent classes, 354–357
  multiple, **357**
  overriding parent class methods in child classes, 357–358
  terminology, 352–354
  using to achieve good software design, 358
initialization list, **175**
initializing the variable, **34**
  loop control variables, 145
inner loop, **140**
input(s), **2**
  echoing, **56**
  priming, 74–79
input devices, default, **212**
input/output (I/O) symbol, **13**
input symbol, **13**
in-scope data items, **45**
insertion sort, **255**, 256
instance methods, 325–328, **326**
instance(s), classes, **310**
instance variables, **311**
instant access files, **231**
instantiation, **310**
instructions, repeating, 15–16
integer(s)
  data types, 38–39
  values, **30**
integrated development environments (IDE), **19**, 19–20, **359**
interactive programs, **231**, 232
interactivity diagrams, **384**
interface, to method, **297**
internal documentation, **51**
interpreters, **3**
IPO chart, **285**, 285–287
is-a relationships, **311**
iteration, **69**

K

kebob case, **32**
key field, **263**
key press event, 376
keywords, **32**
kilobytes, **206**

L

labels, GUIs, 376
left mouse click event, 376
left-to-right associativity, **37**
less-than operator (<), 97
less-than-or-equal-to operator (<=), 97
libraries, **359**
linear searches, **183**
line breaks, confusing, avoiding, 54
linked lists, **264**, 264–265
list boxes, GUIs, 376
listeners, **375**
literal numeric constants, **30**
literal string constants, **30**
local data item, 274
local variables and constants, **45**
logic, 4–6
  event-driven programs, planning, 384–388
  mainline, **41**, 140
  planning, 8
  understanding loops in, 140
  unstructured, structuring and modularizing, 83–86
logical errors, **4**
logical operators
  conditional operators *vs.*, 106
  NOT operator, **115**, 115–117
logical order, **262**
loop(s), **15**, 75, 76, 135–166
  accumulating totals, 157–160
  avoiding common mistakes, 145–151
  counted, **137**
  counter-controlled, **137**
  creating, 135–137
  definite, **137**, 137–138
  `do`, 84
  `do-until`, **156**
  `do-while`, **154**
  `for`, **152**, 152–154, 196–197
  including statements in loop body that belong outside loop, 148–151
  indefinite, **139**, 139–140
  infinite, **15**
  inner, **140**
  loop control variables, 137–140
  mainline logic, 140
  nested, **140**, 140–145
  outer, **140**
  posttest, **154**, 154–155
  pretest, **153**
  reprompting, limiting, 160–163
  selections compared, 164–166
  structured, 156–157
  unstructured, 156
  validating data types, 163
  validating data using, 160–164
  validating reasonableness and consistency of data, 163–164
  `while`, **69**, 84
loop body, **69**
loop control variables, **137**, 137–140
  decrement, 138
  definite loops with counters, 137–138
  failing to initialize, 145
  increment, 138
  indefinite loops with sentinel values, 139–140
  neglecting to alter, 145–147
  program's mainline logic, 140
  using wrong type of comparison when testing, 147–148
loop structure, **69**, 69–70
loose coupling, **298**
Lovelace, Ada Byron, 21
lower camel casing, **32**
low-level programming languages, **9**
lvalues, **34**

M

machine language, **3**
  translating programs into, 9–10
magic numbers, **35**, 181
mainline logic, **41**
main program, **41**
maintenance, 11, **11**
  structure use, 80
making decision, 22
matrix, **259**
mean, **240**
median, **240**
megabytes, **206**
merging files, **218**, 218–225
methods, **39**, 273
  ambiguous, **293**, 293–295
  body, **274**
  client, **273**

methods (continued)
  cohesion, **297**
  coupling reduction, **297**, 297–298
  design issues, 296–298
  get (accessor), **320**
  header, **274**
  implementation, **274**
  implementation hiding, **296**, 296–297
  instance, 325–328, **326**
  nonstatic, **329**
  with no parameters, 275–276
  overloading, **291**, 291–295
  parent classes, accessing, 354–357
  parts of, 273–274
  passing array to, 287–291
  passing objects to, 330–331
  predefined, 295–296
  recursion, **298**, 298–301
  require multiple parameters, 279–282
  requiring parameters, 276–282
  returning objects from, 331, 332
  `return` statement, **274**
  return value, 282–287
  set (mutator), **318**, 318–319
  `sleep()`, 390, 391
  static (class), 328–329, **329**
  type, **282**
  work (help), **320**, 320–321
Microsoft Visual Studio IDE, 19
minus sign (-)
  private access specifier, 323
  subtraction operator, 36, 38
mixed case with underscores, **32**
modularization, **39**, 39–50
  abstraction, **39**, 39–40
  declaring variables and constants within modules, 44–46
  mainline logic, 46–48
  methods (*See* methods)
  multiple programmers, 40
  programs, 41–50
  recursion, **298**, 298–301
  reusing work, 40–41
  unstructured logic, 83–86
module(s), **39**
  abstraction, **39**, 39–40
  calling, **39**
  declaring variables and constants within, 44–46
  hierarchy charts, 48–50
  naming, 41
  reuse, 43
  structure use, 80
module body, **41**
module header, **41**
module `return` statement, **41**
modulo (modulus) operator (%), 38
mouse click event, 376
mouse double-click event, 376
mouse drag event, 376
mouse over event, 376
mouse point event, 376
multidimensional arrays, **258**
  one-dimensional/single-dimensional array, **257**, 259
  three-dimensional arrays, **261**, 262
  two-dimensional array, **258**, 259, 261
multiple fields, record sorting
  sorting data, parallel arrays, 254
  sorting records as a whole, 255
multiple inheritance, **357**
multiplication operator (*), 36, 38
multithreading, **388**, 388–390
mutator methods, **318**, 318–319

N

named constants, **35**
  declaring, 35–36
name(s), self-documenting, **52**
naming
  constants, 53
  modules, 41
  variables, 52
nested decisions, **101**, 103–104
  replacing with arrays, 176–181
nested `if`, **101**, 106
nested loops, **140**, 140–145
nesting structures, **71**, 71–72
`new` keyword, **341**, 342
nibble, **400**
nondefault constructors, **342**, 344–345
nonstatic methods, **329**
nonvolatile storage, **3**
`not eof?` question, 76
not-equal-to operator (<>), 97
NOT operator, **115**, 115–116
  avoiding common error in, 116–117
null case (null branch), **69**
numeric constants, **30**
  unnamed, **30**
numeric data, **30**
numeric variables, 34

O

object(s), **310**, 310–312, 330–334
  arrays, 331–334
  attributes, **310**
  passing to methods, 330–331
  returning from methods, 331, 332
object code, **3**
object dictionary, **383**
object-oriented programming (OOP), **21**, 309–334, 341–365
  advantages, 365
  class definition, **314**, 314–316
  class diagram, **316**, 316–318
  classes, **310**, 310–312
  composition, **349**, 349–350
  constructors, **341**, 341–347
  destructors, **347**, 347–348
  encapsulation, 313–314
  exception handling, 360–365, **361**
  get method, 319
  inheritance, **313**, 350–358
  instance methods, 325–328
  objects, **310**, 310–312
  organizing classes, 324–325
  polymorphism, 312–313
  predefined classes, 359
  principles, 309–314
  public and private access, 321–324
  set methods, 318–319
  static methods, 328–329
  thread, 390
  using objects, 330–334
  work method, 319–320
one-dimensional array, **257**, 259
opening files, **209**, 209–210
operands, **34**
operating systems, **2**, 373, 374
option buttons, GUIs, 376
`OR` decisions, **108**
  avoiding common errors, 112–115
  efficiency, 108–110
order of operations, **36**, 37
`OR` operator, **110**, 110–111
  combining with `AND` operator, precedence, 122–124
  conditional, **110**
outer loop, **140**
out of bounds, **194**
output, **2**
output devices, default, **212**
output symbol, **13**
overhead, **35**, 43, 284
overloading, **291**
  constructors, 345–347
  methods, **291**, 291–295, 345–347
overriding, **357**, 357–358

P

packages, **359**
page schematics, **382**
parallel arrays, **185**, 185–191
  sorting data stored in, 254
parameterized constructors, **342**, 344–345
parameter list, **277**
parameter to a method, **277**
parent classes, **352**, 354
  accessing private fields and methods, 354–357
  overriding parent class methods in child classes, 357–358
parent files, **213**, 226
parentheses, variable names within, 42
Pascal casing, **32**
passed by reference, **287**
passed by value, **279**
passing array, to method, 287–291
passing objects to methods, 330–331
paths, dead (unreachable), 119
percent sign (%), remainder (modulo, modulus) operator, 38
permanent storage devices, **205**, 206
physical order, **262**
pixels, **378**
planning, logic, 8
plus sign (+)
  addition operator, 36, 38
  public access specifier, 323
polymorphism, **291**, 312–313
populating the array, **174**
portable modules, **45**
posttest loops, **154**, 154–155
precedence, combining `AND` and `OR` operators, 122–124
predefined classes, 359
predefined methods, 295–296
pretest loop, **153**

primary files, **225**, 225–231
priming inputs (priming reads), 74–79, **77**
primitive data types, **316**
print, definition, 214
private access, 321–324, **322**
procedural programming, **21**
procedure, **39**
processing, **2**
  symbol, **13**
production, putting programs into, 11
professionalism, structure use, 80
program(s), **2**
  coding, **2**, 8–9
  ending with sentinel values, 16–18
  executing (running), **4**
  good design features, 50–57
  interactive, **231**, 232
  main, **41**
  modularizing, 41–50
  structured, **65**
  translating into machine language, 9–10
  unstructured, **65**, 65–67
program code, **2**
program comments, **50**, 50–52
program development cycle, **6**, 6–11
  coding step, 8–9
  maintenance step, 11
  planning logic step, 8
  production step, 11
  testing step, 10–11
  translating program into machine language, 9–10
  understanding problem step, 7–8
program-ending test, 79
program hierarchy chart, **49**
program logic, 4–6
programmer-defined types, **316**
programming, **2**
  defensive, **160**, 164
  environments, 18–20
  event-driven, 373–375
  good habits, 57
  multiple programmers, 40
  object-oriented, 21
  procedural, 21
  reusing work, 40–41
programming language, **2**
programming models, evolution, 21–22
prompts, **55**, 55–56
  clear, 55–56
properties, **319**
`protected` access specifier, **355**, 355–357
pseudocode, **12**, 12–13
  writing, 12–13
public access, 321–324, **322**

R

random access files, **231**, 231–232
random access memory (RAM), **3**
random-access storage device, **263**
range checks, **117**
  avoiding common errors, 119–122
reading from files, **210**, 210–212
read(s), priming, 74–79, **77**
real estate screen space, 380
real numbers, **30**
real-time applications, **231**
reasonableness of data, validating, 163–164
records, **208**
recursion, **298**, 298–301
recursive cases, **299**
recursive method, **298**
refining bubble sort, to eliminate unnecessary passes, 252–253
register components, **384**
relational comparison operators, **97**, 97–100
reliability, **41**
reliable code, 358
remainder operator, **38**
repetition, **69**
reports
  control break, **215**
  summary, **160**
returning value, creating methods, 282–287
`return` statement, 283
  modules, **41**
return type, **282**
reusability, **41**
right-associativity, **34**
right mouse click event, 376
right-to-left associativity, **34**
rules of precedence, 36, **36**, 37
running a program, **4**

S

score-sorting application, 248–250
screen blueprints, **382**
script(s), **375**
scripting language, **4**
searches
  binary, **190**
  linear, **183**
searching arrays
  exact matches, 183–185
  improving efficiency, 189–190
  range matches, 190–193
selection(s)
  loops compared, 164–166
  within ranges, 117–122
selection sort, **256**, 257
selection structure, **67**, 67–69, 76, 93–97
self-documenting names, **52**
semicolon (;), separating actions, 153
sentinel symbols, flowcharts, 42
sentinel values, **17**
  ending programs, 16–18
sequence structure, **67**
sequential files, **211**
  merging, 218–225
sequential order, **239**
set methods, **318**, 318–319
short-circuit evaluation, **105**
signature, **277**
single-alternative `if` (single-alternative selections), **69**
single-dimensional array, **257**
single-level control breaks, **216**
size of the array, **174**
  constant as, 181–182
slash (/), division operator, 36
`sleep()` method, 390, 391
snake casing, **32**
software, **2**
  design, advantages of inheritance, 358
  translating programs into machine language, 9–10
solving difficult structuring problems, 405–411
sorting, data, **211**, 239–241
  numeric values, 240
  sequential order, **239**
source code, **3**
source of an event, **375**
spaghetti code, **65**, 65–67
stack, **43**, 298
stacking structures, **70**, 71
starvation, **389**
state, **311**
statements
  clarity, 54
  long, temporary variables to clarify, 54
  throw, **361**
static methods, 328–329, **329**
step values, **152**
storage
  devices, **2**
  measurement, 403–404
  temporary and permanent, 205
storyboards, **382**
  object dictionary, **383**
string constants, **30**
  unnamed, **30**
string data, **30**
string variables, **31**
strongly-typed languages, 31
structure(s), 65–86, **67**
  combining, 70–74
  priming input to structure programs, 74–79
  reasons for, 79–80
  recognizing, 80–82
  selection, 67–69, 112
  sequence, **67**
  spaghetti code, 65–67
  structuring and modularizing unstructured logic, 83–86
structure charts, 49
structured loops, 156–157
structured programs, **65**
structuring problems, solving, 405–411
subclasses, **352**
  ancestors, **352**
subprocedures, 39
subroutines, **39.** *See also* module(s)
subscripts, **174**
  bounds, 194–196
  constants, 182
subtraction operator (-), 36, 38
summary reports, **160**
sunny day case, **363**
superclasses, **352**
swap values, **241**, 241–242
swipe event, 376
symbols, flowcharts, 12–16, 51, 154
syntax, **2**, 8
syntax errors, **2**, 3, 9
system software, **2**

T

tables, 208, **259**
tap event, 376
temporary storage, 205, 207
temporary variables, **54**
  clarifying long statements, 54
terminal symbols, **14**
terminating cases, **299**
testing
  loop control variables, 147–148
  programs, 10–11
text boxes, GUIs, 376
text editors, **19**
text files, **206**
`this` references, **326**, 326–328
thread(s), **388**, 388–390
`Thread` class, 390
thread synchronization, **389**
three-dimensional arrays, **261**, 262
throw an exception, **361**
`throw` statements, **361**
tight coupling, **298**
tilde (~), destructors, 347
totals, accumulating using loops, 157–160
transaction files, **225**, 225–231
translating programs into machine language, 9–10
trivial expressions, **98**
truncation, 38
truth tables, **105**
`try` blocks, **362**
trying code statements, **361**
Turing, Alan, 21
two-dimensional array, **258**, 259, 261
type-safety, **31**

U

unary operators, **116**
Unicode, **401**
uninitialized variables, 159
unnamed constants, **30**
unnamed numeric constants, **30**
unnamed string constants, **30**
unreachable paths, **119**
unstructured loops, 156
unstructured programs, **65**, 65–67
updating a primary file, **225**, 225–231
upper camel casing, **32**
user(s), **7**
  class, **312**
user-created exceptions, 363–365
user-defined types, **316**
user environments, 20–21
user-initiated actions, 376
user screens, defining connections between, 384

V

validating data, **160**, 160–164
  data types, 163
  reasonableness and consistency of data, 163–164
values, assigning to variables, 33–35
variables, **5**, 30–31
  assigning values to, 33–35
  data dictionaries, **53**
  data types, 31
  declaring within modules, 44–46
  decrement, 138
  global, **45**
  identifier, 31–33
  increment, 138
  initializing, 34
  instance, **311**
  local, **45**
  naming, 52
  numeric, **31**, 34
  parentheses around names, 42
  string, **31**
  uninitialized, 159
variable `workhours`, 283
visible, data items, **45**
visual development environments, **359**
void method, **282**
volatile storage, **3**

W

`while...do` loop, **69**, 69–70
`while` loops, **69**, 152–154
whole-part relationships, **349**
wireframes, **382**
work methods, **320**, 320–321
work variables, **54**
writing to files, **212**

X

x-axis, **390**
x-coordinate, **390**

Y

y-axis, **390**
y-coordinate, **390**

Z

zero, uninitialized variables, 159
zoom event, 376